CCNP Security
FIREWALL 642-618
Official Cert Guide

David Hucaby
Dave Garneau
Anthony Sequeira

Cisco Press

800 East 96th Street

Indianapolis, IN 46240

CCNP Security FIREWALL 642-618 Official Cert Guide

David Hucaby
Dave Garneau
Anthony Sequeira

Published by:
Cisco Press
800 East 96th Street
Indianapolis, IN 46240 USA

Printed in the United States of America

Second Printing: June 2013

The Library of Congress Cataloging-in-Publication Data is on file.

ISBN-13: 978-1-58714-271-0

ISBN-10: 1-58714-271-6

Warning and Disclaimer

This book is designed to provide information for the Cisco CCNP Security 642-618 FIREWALL exam. Every effort has been made to make this book as complete and as accurate as possible, but no warranty or fitness is implied.

The information is provided on an "as is" basis. The authors, Cisco Press, and Cisco Systems, Inc. shall have neither liability nor responsibility to any person or entity with respect to any loss or damages arising from the information contained in this book or from the use of the discs or programs that may accompany it.

The opinions expressed in this book belong to the authors and are not necessarily those of Cisco Systems, Inc.

Trademark Acknowledgments

All terms mentioned in this book that are known to be trademarks or service marks have been appropriately capitalized. Cisco Press or Cisco Systems, Inc., cannot attest to the accuracy of this information. Use of a term in this book should not be regarded as affecting the validity of any trademark or service mark.

Corporate and Government Sales

The publisher offers excellent discounts on this book when ordered in quantity for bulk purchases or special sales, which may include electronic versions and/or custom covers and content particular to your business, training goals, marketing focus, and branding interests. For more information, please contact: **U.S. Corporate and Government Sales**   1-800-382-3419   corpsales@pearsontechgroup.com

For sales outside the United States, please contact: **International Sales**   international@pearsoned.com

Feedback Information

At Cisco Press, our goal is to create in-depth technical books of the highest quality and value. Each book is crafted with care and precision, undergoing rigorous development that involves the unique expertise of members from the professional technical community.

Readers' feedback is a natural continuation of this process. If you have any comments regarding how we could improve the quality of this book, or otherwise alter it to better suit your needs, you can contact us through e-mail at feedback@ciscopress.com. Please make sure to include the book title and ISBN in your message.

We greatly appreciate your assistance.

Publisher: Paul Boger	**Cisco Press Program Manager:** Anand Sundaram
Associate Publisher: Dave Dusthimer	**Cisco Representative:** Erik Ullanderson
Executive Editor: Brett Bartow	**Senior Development Editor:** Christopher Cleveland
Managing Editor: Sandra Schroeder	**Project Editor:** Mandie Frank
Copy Editor: Sheri Cain	**Technical Editors:** Kenny Hackworth, Doug McKillip
Editorial Assistant: Vanessa Evans	**Designer:** Gary Adair
Composition: Mark Shirar	**Indexer:** Brad Herriman
Proofreader: Apostrophe Editing Services	

CISCO

Americas Headquarters	Asia Pacific Headquarters	Europe Headquarters
Cisco Systems, Inc.	Cisco Systems (USA) Pte. Ltd.	Cisco Systems International BV
San Jose, CA	Singapore	Amsterdam, The Netherlands

Cisco has more than 200 offices worldwide. Addresses, phone numbers, and fax numbers are listed on the Cisco Website at **www.cisco.com/go/offices.**

CCDE, CCENT, Cisco Eos, Cisco HealthPresence, the Cisco logo, Cisco Lumin, Cisco Nexus, Cisco StadiumVision, Cisco TelePresence, Cisco WebEx, DCE, and Welcome to the Human Network are trademarks; Changing the Way We Work, Live, Play, and Learn and Cisco Store are service marks; and Access Registrar, Aironet, AsyncOS, Bringing the Meeting To You, Catalyst, CCDA, CCDP, CCIE, CCIP, CCNA, CCNP, CCSP, CCVP, Cisco, the Cisco Certified Internetwork Expert logo, Cisco IOS, Cisco Press, Cisco Systems, Cisco Systems Capital, the Cisco Systems logo, Cisco Unity, Collaboration Without Limitation, EtherFast, EtherSwitch, Event Center, Fast Step, Follow Me Browsing, FormShare, GigaDrive, HomeLink, Internet Quotient, IOS, iPhone, iQuick Study, IronPort, the IronPort logo, LightStream, Linksys, MediaTone, MeetingPlace, MeetingPlace Chime Sound, MGX, Networkers, Networking Academy, Network Registrar, PCNow, PIX, PowerPanels, ProConnect, ScriptShare, SenderBase, SMARTnet, Spectrum Expert, StackWise, The Fastest Way to Increase Your Internet Quotient, TransPath, WebEx, and the WebEx logo are registered trademarks of Cisco Systems, Inc. and/or its affiliates in the United States and certain other countries.

All other trademarks mentioned in this document or website are the property of their respective owners. The use of the word partner does not imply a partnership relationship between Cisco and any other company. (0812R)

About the Authors

David Hucaby, CCIE No. 4594, is a network architect for the University of Kentucky, where he works with healthcare networks based on the Cisco Catalyst, ASA, FWSM, and Unified Wireless product lines. David has a bachelor of science degree and master of science degree in electrical engineering from the University of Kentucky. He is the author of several Cisco Press titles, including *Cisco ASA, PIX, and FWSM Firewall Handbook*, Second Edition; *Cisco Firewall Video Mentor*; *Cisco LAN Switching Video Mentor*; and *CCNP SWITCH Exam Certification Guide*.

David lives in Kentucky with his wife, Marci, and two daughters.

Dave Garneau is a senior member of the Network Security team at Rackspace Hosting, Inc. Before that, he was the principal consultant and senior technical instructor at The Radix Group, Ltd. In that role, Dave trained more than 3,000 students in nine countries on Cisco technologies, mostly focusing on the Cisco security products line, and worked closely with Cisco in establishing the new Cisco Certified Network Professional Security (CCNP Security) curriculum. Dave has a bachelor of science degree in mathematics from Metropolitan State College of Denver. Dave lives in San Antonio, Texas, with his wife, Vicki, and their two brand new baby girls, Elise and Lauren.

Anthony Sequeira, CCIE No. 15626, is a Cisco Certified Systems Instructor (CCSI) and author regarding all levels and tracks of Cisco Certification. Anthony formally began his career in the information technology industry in 1994 with IBM in Tampa, Florida. He quickly formed his own computer consultancy, Computer Solutions, and then discovered his true passion—teaching and writing about Microsoft and Cisco technologies. Anthony joined Mastering Computers in 1996 and lectured to massive audiences around the world about the latest in computer technologies. Mastering Computers became the revolutionary online training company, KnowledgeNet, and Anthony trained there for many years. Anthony is currently pursuing his second CCIE in the area of Security and is a full-time instructor for the next-generation of KnowledgeNet, StormWind Live. Anthony is also a VMware Certified Professional.

About the Technical Reviewers

Doug McKillip, P.E., CCIE No. 1851, is an independent consultant specializing in Cisco Certified Training in association with Global Knowledge, a training partner of Cisco. He has more than 20 years of experience in computer networking and security. McKillip provided both instructional and technical assistance during the initial deployment of MCNS Version 1.0, the first Cisco Security training class, which debuted in early 1998, and has been a lead instructor for the security curriculum ever since. Doug has supplemented his instruction by authoring numerous security troubleshooting white papers and security blogs for Global Knowledge. He holds bachelors and master's degrees in chemical engineering from MIT and a master's degree in computer and information sciences from the University of Delaware. He resides in Wilmington, Delaware.

Kenny Hackworth is a senior network automation engineer at Rackspace Hosting, the service leader in cloud computing. His current expertise includes supporting content switching (Cisco CSS and F5 LTMs) and security appliances (Cisco and Juniper firewalls). His primary focus is currently on automation, particularly configuration changes as well as equipment deployments. Prior to Rackspace, Kenny supported the NSA while working for the Air Intelligence Agency, performing Digital Network Exploitation analysis and Cryptanalysis.

Dedications

From David Hucaby:

As always, this book is dedicated to the most important people in my life: my wife, Marci, and my two daughters, Lauren and Kara. Their love, encouragement, and support carry me along. I'm so grateful to God, who gives endurance and encouragement (Romans 15:5), and who has allowed me to work on projects like this.

From Dave Garneau:

I am also dedicating this book to the most important people in my life: my wife, Vicki, our daughters, Elise and Lauren, and my stepson, Ben. Without their love and support, I doubt I would succeed in any major endeavor, much less one of this magnitude. Additionally, I want to dedicate this book to my mother, Marian, who almost 40 years ago, believed a very young version of myself when he declared he would one day grow up and write a book. I am glad I was finally able to live up to that promise.

From Anthony Sequeira:

This book is dedicated to the many, many students I have had the privilege of teaching over the past several decades. I hope that my passion for technology and learning has conveyed itself and helped motivate—and perhaps even inspire.

Acknowledgments

It has been my great pleasure to work on another Cisco Press project. I enjoy the networking field very much—and technical writing even more. And more than that, I'm thankful for the joy and inner peace that Jesus Christ gives, making everything more abundant and worthwhile.

I've now been writing Cisco Press titles continuously for more than 10 years. I always find it to be quite fun, but other demands seem to be making writing more difficult and time-consuming. That's why I am so grateful that Dave Garneau and Anthony Sequeira came along to help tote the load. It's also been a great pleasure to work with Brett Bartow and Chris Cleveland. I'm glad they put up with me yet again, especially considering how much I let the schedule slip.

I am grateful for the insight, suggestions, and helpful comments that the technical editors contributed. Each one offered a different perspective, which helped make this a more well-rounded book—and me a more educated author.

—*David Hucaby*

The creation of this book has certainly been a maelstrom of activity. I was originally slated to be one of the technical reviewers, but became a coauthor at David Hucaby's request.

Right after accepting that challenge, I started a new job, moved to a new city, and built a new house. Throughout all the resulting chaos, Brett Bartow and Christopher Cleveland demonstrated the patience of Job, while somehow keeping this project on track. Hopefully, their patience was not exhausted, and I look forward to working with them again on future projects.

I am also thankful to our technical reviewers for their meticulous attention to detail. The input of Doug McKillip and Kenny Hackworth, both of whom I count as a close friends, was invaluable. The extremely thorough reviews provided by Doug and Kenny definitely improved the quality of the material for the end readers.

—*Dave Garneau*

Brett Bartow is a great friend, and I am so incredibly thankful to him for the awesome opportunities he has helped me to achieve with the most respected line of IT texts in the world, Cisco Press. I am also really thankful that he continues to permit me to participate in his fantasy baseball league.

It was such an honor to help on this text with the incredible David Hucaby and Dave Garneau. While they sought out a third author named David, it was so kind of them to make a concession for an Anthony.

I cannot thank David Hucaby enough for the assistance he provided me in accessing the latest and greatest Cisco ASAs for the lab work and experimentation that was required for my chapters of this text.

Finally, thanks to my family, Joette and Annabella and the dog Sweetie, for understanding all the hours I spent hunched over a keyboard. That reminds me, thanks also to my chiropractor, Dr. Paton.

—*Anthony Sequeira*

Contents at a Glance

Contents

Icons Used in This Book

Cisco ASA

IPS

Content Services
Module

AAA Server

CA

SSL VPN
Gateway

IPsec VPN
Gateway

Router

Layer 3
Switch

Layer 2
Switch

PC

IP Phone

Server

Network Cloud

Access Point

Wireless Connection

Ethernet Connection

Introduction

This book helps you prepare for the Cisco FIREWALL 642-618 certification exam. The FIREWALL exam is one in a series of exams required for the Cisco Certified Network Professional Security (CCNP Security) certification. This exam focuses on the application of security principles with regard to the Cisco Adaptive Security Appliance (ASA) device.

Who Should Read This Book

Network security is a complex business. It is important that you have extensive experience in and an in-depth understanding of computer networking before you can begin to apply security principles. The Cisco FIREWALL program was developed to introduce the ASA security products, explain how each product is applied, and explain how it can be leveraged to increase the security of your network. The FIREWALL program is for network administrators, network security administrators, network architects, and experienced networking professionals who are interested in applying security principles to their networks.

How to Use This Book

This book consists of 17 chapters. Each chapter tends to build upon the chapter that precedes it. Each chapter includes case studies or practice configurations that can be implemented using both the command-line interface (CLI) and Cisco Adaptive Security Device Manager (ASDM).

The chapters of this book cover the following topics:

- **Chapter 1, "Cisco ASA Adaptive Security Appliance Overview":** This chapter discusses basic network security and traffic filtering strategies. It also provides an overview of ASA operation, including the ASA feature set, product licensing, and how various ASA models should be matched with the environments they will protect.

- **Chapter 2, "Working with a Cisco ASA":** This chapter reviews the basic methods used to interact with an ASA and to control its basic operation. Both the CLI and ASDM are discussed.

- **Chapter 3, "Configuring ASA Interfaces":** This chapter explains how to configure ASA interfaces with the parameters they need to operate on a network.

- **Chapter 4, "Configuring IP Connectivity":** This chapter covers the ASA features related to providing IP addressing through DHCP and to exchanging IP routing information through several different dynamic routing protocols.

- **Chapter 5, "Managing a Cisco ASA":** This chapter reviews the configuration commands and tools that can be used to manage and control an ASA, both locally and remotely.

- **Chapter 6, "Recording ASA Activity":** This chapter describes how to configure an ASA to generate logging information that can be collected and analyzed. The logging information can be used to provide an audit trail of network and security activity.

- **Chapter 7, "Using Address Translation":** This chapter describes how IP addresses can be altered or translated as packets move through an ASA. The various types of Network Address Translation (NAT) and Port Address Translation (PAT) are covered. This chapter covers address translation methods for OS versions both before and after 8.3, where translation configuration was completely transformed.

- **Chapter 8, "Controlling Access Through the ASA":** This chapter reviews access control lists and host shunning, and how these features can be configured to control traffic movement through an ASA.

- **Chapter 9, "Inspecting Traffic":** This chapter covers the Modular Policy Framework, a method used to define and implement many types of traffic inspection policies. It also covers ICMP, UDP, TCP, and application protocol inspection engines, as well as more advanced inspection tools, such as Botnet Traffic Filtering and threat detection.

- **Chapter 10, "Using Proxy Services to Control Access":** This chapter discusses the features that can be leveraged to control the authentication, authorization, and accounting (AAA) of users as they pass through an ASA.

- **Chapter 11, "Handling Traffic":** This chapter covers the methods and features that can be used to handle fragmented traffic, to prioritize traffic for QoS, to police traffic rates, and to shape traffic bandwidth.

- **Chapter 12, "Using Transparent Firewall Mode":** This chapter reviews transparent firewall mode and how it can be used to make an ASA more stealthy when introduced into a network. The ASA can act as a transparent bridge, forwarding traffic at Layer 2.

- **Chapter 13, "Creating Virtual Firewalls on the ASA":** This chapter discusses the multiple context mode that can be used to allow a single physical ASA device to provide multiple virtual firewalls or security contexts.

- **Chapter 14, "Deploying High Availability Features":** This chapter covers two strategies that can be used to implement high availability between a pair of ASAs.

- **Chapter 15, "Integrating ASA Service Modules":** This chapter explains the basic steps needed to configure an ASA to work with the AIP and CSC Security Services Modules (SSM), which can be used to offload in-depth intrusion protection and content handling.

- **Chapter 16, "Traffic Analysis Tools":** This chapter discusses two troubleshooting tools that you can use to test and confirm packet movement through an ASA.

- **Chapter 17, "Final Preparation":** This short chapter lists the exam preparation tools useful at this point in the study process and provides a suggested study plan now that you have completed all the earlier chapters in this book.

- **Appendix A, "Answers to the 'Do I Know This Already?' Quizzes":** This appendix provides the answers to the "Do I Know This Already?" quizzes that you will find at the beginning of each chapter.

- **Appendix B, "CCNP Security 642-618 FIREWALL Exam Updates: Version 1.0":** This appendix provides you with updated information if Cisco makes minor modifications to the exam upon which this book is based. When Cisco releases an entirely new exam, the changes are usually too extensive to provide in a simple update appendix. In those cases, you need to consult the new edition of the book for the updated content. This additional content about the exam will be posted as a PDF document on this book's companion website (www.ciscopress.com/title/9781587142796).

- **Glossary of Key Terms:** This glossary defines the key terms that appear at the end of each chapter, for which you should be able to provide definitions on your own in preparation for the exam.

Each chapter follows the same format and incorporates the following tools to assist you by assessing your current knowledge and emphasizing specific areas of interest within the chapter:

- **"Do I Know This Already?" Quiz:** Each chapter begins with a quiz to help you assess your current knowledge of the subject. The quiz is divided into specific areas of emphasis that enable you to best determine where to focus your efforts when working through the chapter.

- **Foundation Topics:** The foundation topics are the core sections of each chapter. They focus on the specific protocols, concepts, or skills that you must master to successfully prepare for the examination.

- **Exam Preparation:** Near the end of each chapter, the Exam Preparation section highlights the key topics from the chapter and the pages where you can find them for quick review. This section also provides a list of key terms that you should be able to define in preparation for the exam. It is unlikely that you will be able to successfully complete the certification exam by just studying the key topics and key terms, although they are a good tool for last-minute preparation just before taking the exam.

- **Command References:** Each chapter ends with a series of tables containing the commands that were covered. The tables provide a convenient place to review the commands, their syntax, and the sequence in which they should be used to configure a feature.

- **CD-ROM-based practice exam:** This book includes a CD-ROM containing several interactive practice exams. It is recommended that you continue to test your knowledge and test-taking skills by using these exams. You will find that your test-taking skills will improve by continued exposure to the test format. Remember that the potential range of exam questions is limitless. Therefore, your goal should not be to "know" every possible answer but to have a sufficient understanding of the subject matter so that you can figure out the correct answer with the information provided.

Certification Exam and This Preparation Guide

The questions for each certification exam are a closely guarded secret. The truth is that if you had the questions and could only pass the exam, you would be in for quite an embarrassment as soon as you arrived at your first job that required these skills. The point is to know the material, not just to successfully pass the exam.

We do know which topics you must know to successfully complete this exam because Cisco publishes them as "642-618 Deploying Cisco ASA Firewall Solutions Exam Topics (Blueprint)" on the Cisco Learning Network. Table I-1 lists each FIREWALL v2.0 exam topic listed in the blueprint along with a reference to the chapter that covers the topic. These are the same topics you should be proficient in when configuring the Cisco ASA in the real world.

Table I-1   *FIREWALL v2.0 Exam Topics and Chapter References*

Exam Topic	Chapter Where Topic Is Covered
ASA Basic Configurations	
Identify the ASA product family	Chapters 1, 15
Implement ASA licensing	Chapter 1
Manage the ASA boot process	Chapter 2
Implement ASA interface settings	Chapters 3, 8
Implement ASA management features	Chapters 2, 4, 5, 6, 16
Implement ASA access control features	Chapters 8, 10
Implement NAT on the ASA	Chapter 7
Implement ASDM public server feature	Chapter 2
Implement ASA QoS settings	Chapter 11
Implement ASA transparent firewall	Chapter 12
ASA Routing Features	
Implement ASA static routing	Chapter 4
Implement ASA dynamic routing	Chapter 4
ASA Inspection Policy	
Implement ASA inspections features	Chapter 9
ASA Advanced Network Protections	
Implement ASA botnet traffic filter	Chapter 9
ASA High Availability	
Implement ASA interface redundancy and load sharing features	Chapter 3
Implement ASA virtualization feature	Chapter 13
Implement ASA stateful failover	Chapter 14

Notice that not all the chapters map to a specific exam topic. Each version of the exam can have topics that emphasize different functions or features, while some topics can be rather broad and generalized. The goal of this book is to provide the most comprehensive coverage to ensure that you are well prepared for the exam. In order to do this, all possible topics that have been addressed in different versions of this exam (past and present) are covered. Many of the chapters that do not specifically address exam topics provide a foundation that is necessary for a clear understanding of network security. Your short-term goal might be to pass this exam, but your long-term goal should be to become a qualified network security professional.

It is also important to understand that this book is a "static" reference, whereas the exam topics are dynamic. Cisco can and does change the topics covered on certification exams often.

This exam guide should not be your only reference when preparing for the certification exam. You can find a wealth of information available at Cisco.com that covers each topic in great detail. The goal of this book is to prepare you as well as possible for the FIRE-WALL exam. Some of this is completed by breaking a 600-page (average) implementation guide into a 30-page chapter that is easier to digest. If you think that you need more detailed information on a specific topic, you should read the Cisco documentation that focuses on that topic.

Note that because security vulnerabilities and preventive measures continue to develop, Cisco reserves the right to change the exam topics without notice. Although you can refer to the list of exam topics listed in Table I-1, always check Cisco.com to verify the actual list of topics to ensure that you are prepared before taking the exam. You can view the current exam topics on any current Cisco certification exam by visiting the Cisco.com website, hovering over Training & Events, and selecting from the Certifications list. Note also that, if needed, Cisco Press might post additional preparatory content on the web page associated with this book at www.ciscopress.com/title/9781587142710. It's a good idea to check the website a few weeks before taking your exam to be sure that you have up-to-date content.

Overview of the Cisco Certification Process

The network security market is currently in a position where the demand for qualified engineers vastly surpasses the supply. For this reason, many engineers consider migrating from routing/networking over to network security. Remember that "network security" is just "security" applied to "networks." This sounds like an obvious concept, but it is actually an important one if you are pursuing your CCNP Security certification. You must be familiar with networking before you can begin to apply the security concepts. For example, the skills required to complete the CCNA or CCNP will give you a solid foundation that you can expand into the network security field.

Taking the FIREWALL Certification Exam

As with any Cisco certification exam, you should strive to be thoroughly prepared before taking the exam. There is no way to determine exactly what questions are on the exam, so the best way to prepare is to have a good working knowledge of all subjects covered on the exam. Schedule yourself for the exam and be sure to be rested and ready to focus when taking the exam.

The best place to find out the latest available Cisco training and certifications is under the Training & Events section at Cisco.com.

Tracking Cisco Certification Status

You can track your certification progress by checking www.cisco.com/go/certifications/login. You must create an account the first time you log in to the site.

How to Prepare for an Exam

The best way to prepare for any certification exam is to use a combination of the preparation resources, labs, and practice tests. This guide has integrated some practice questions and example scenarios to help you better prepare. If possible, you should get some hands-on experience with the Cisco ASA. There is no substitute for real-world experience; it is much easier to understand the commands and concepts when you can actually work with a live ASA device.

Cisco.com provides a wealth of information about the ASA and its software and features. No single source can adequately prepare you for the FIREWALL exam unless you already have extensive experience with Cisco products and a background in networking or network security. At a minimum, you will want to use this book combined with the Support and Downloads site resources (www.cisco.com/cisco/web/support/index.html) to prepare for the exam.

Assessing Exam Readiness

Exam candidates never know if they are adequately prepared for the exam until they have completed about 30 percent of the questions. At that point, if you are not prepared, it is too late. The best way to determine your readiness is to work through the "Do I Know This Already?" quizzes at the beginning of each chapter, review the foundation and key topics presented in each chapter, and review the command reference tables at the end of each chapter. It is best to work your way through the entire book unless you can complete each subject without having to do any research or look up any answers.

Cisco Security Specialist in the Real World

Cisco has one of the most recognized names on the Internet. Cisco Certified Security Specialists can bring quite a bit of knowledge to the table because of their deep understanding of the relationship between networking and network security. This is why the Cisco certification carries such high respect in the marketplace. Cisco certifications demonstrate to potential employers and contract holders a certain professionalism, expertise, and dedication required to complete a difficult goal. If Cisco certifications were easy to obtain, everyone would have them.

Exam Registration

The FIREWALL exam is a computer-based exam, with around 60 to 70 multiple choice, fill-in-the-blank, list-in-order, and simulation-based questions. You can take the exam at any Pearson VUE (www.pearsonvue.com) testing center. According to Cisco, the exam should last about 90 minutes. Be aware that when you register for the exam, you might be told to allow a certain amount of time to take the exam that is longer than the testing time indicated by the testing software when you begin. This discrepancy is because the testing center will want you to allow for some time to get settled and take the tutorial about the test engine.

Book Content Updates

Because Cisco occasionally updates exam topics without notice, Cisco Press might post additional preparatory content on the web page associated with this book at http://www.ciscopress.com/title/9781587142710. It is a good idea to check the website a few weeks before taking your exam to review any updated content that might be posted online. We also recommend that you periodically check back to this page on the Cisco Press website to view any errata or supporting book files that may be available.

Premium Edition eBook and Practice Test

This Cert Guide contains a special offer for a 70% discount off the companion CCNP Security FIREWALL 642-618 Official Cert Guide Premium Edition eBook and Practice Test. The Premium Edition combines an eBook version of the text with an enhanced Pearson IT Certification Practice Test. By purchasing the Premium Edition, you get access to two eBook versions of the text: a PDF version and an EPUB version for reading on your tablet, eReader, or mobile device. You also get an enhanced practice test that contains an additional two full practice tests of unique questions. In addition, all the practice test questions are linked to the PDF eBook, allowing you to get more detailed feedback on each question instantly. To take advantage of this offer, you will need the coupon code included on the paper in the CD sleeve. Just follow the purchasing instructions that accompany the code to download and start using your Premium Edition today!

This chapter covers the following topics:

- **Firewall Overview:** This section provides an overview of protecting networks by establishing security domains and positioning firewalls to protect them.

- **Firewall Techniques:** This section describes various firewall and network security methods.

- **Cisco ASA Features:** This section covers the long list of security features that a Cisco ASA can provide.

- **Selecting a Cisco ASA Model:** This section presents an overview and specifications of each ASA model so that the appropriate device can be selected.

- **Selecting ASA Licenses:** Once an ASA model is selected to secure a network, it must be licensed to perform everything that is required. This section explains the variety of feature licenses and how to select them, based on the ASA model.

CHAPTER 1

Cisco ASA Adaptive Security Appliance Overview

The Cisco Adaptive Security Appliance (ASA) is a versatile device that is used to secure a network. This chapter explains the concepts behind firewalls and other security tools, as they apply to the Cisco ASA. In addition, this chapter covers how to select an ASA model, the appropriate ASA features, and the correct ASA licenses based on high-level design requirements.

"Do I Know This Already?" Quiz

The "Do I Know This Already?" quiz allows you to assess whether you should read this entire chapter thoroughly or jump to the "Exam Preparation Tasks" section. If you are in doubt about your answers to these questions or your own assessment of your knowledge of the topics, read the entire chapter. Table 1-1 lists the major headings in this chapter and their corresponding "Do I Know This Already?" quiz questions. You can find the answers in Appendix A, "Answers to the 'Do I Know This Already?' Quizzes."

Table 1-1 *"Do I Know This Already?" Section-to-Question Mapping*

Foundation Topics Section	Questions
Firewall Overview	1–2
Firewall Techniques	3–5
Cisco ASA Features	6–8
Selecting a Cisco ASA Model	9–11
Selecting ASA Licenses	12

Caution: The goal of self-assessment is to gauge your mastery of the topics in this chapter. If you do not know the answer to a question or are only partially sure of the answer, you should mark that question wrong for purposes of the self-assessment. Giving yourself credit for an answer you correctly guess skews your self-assessment results and might provide you with a false sense of security.

1. Which of the following are recommended tasks for making a security domain secure? (Choose all that apply.)

    a. Place a router at the boundary of trusted and untrusted areas of the network, and then place a firewall inside the trusted area.

    b. Place a firewall at the boundary of trusted and untrusted areas of the network.

    c. Make the firewall the only path into and out of the security domain.

    d. Make the firewall the only path into and out of the untrusted domain.

    e. Harden the firewall against attacks.

    f. Force protected traffic through the firewall and bypass other traffic around it.

2. Which one of the following is considered to be the most secure?

    a. Logically separating a network with a firewall.

    b. Physically separating a network with a firewall.

    c. Putting the trusted and untrusted areas on different VLANs that are connected to a firewall over a trunk link.

    d. None of these answers are correct.

3. Consider the following list of rules, and then choose the answer that best describes it.

```
10        Permit all HTTP traffic
20        Permit all SMTP traffic to host 10.10.1.10
30        Permit all DNS queries
40        Deny everything
```

    a. Reactive access control

    b. Permissive access control

    c. Restrictive access control

    d. Protective access control

4. Which one of the following techniques would be the best choice for filtering HTTP (TCP port 80) sessions?

    a. Stateless packet filtering

    b. Stateful packet filtering

    c. Stateful packet filtering with application inspection and control

    d. Network intrusion protection system

    e. Network behavior analysis

5. Which of the following is not typically used for a restrictive approach to traffic filtering?

    a. Stateless packet filtering

    b. Stateful packet filtering

    c. Stateful packet filtering with AIC

    d. Network IPS

    e. Network behavior analysis

6. A company wants to join its network with another business partner, but wants to place a firewall between the two. Users within the company's home network should appear to use the business partner's IP address space when they access the partner's servers. Which of the following Cisco ASA features should be used to meet this requirement?

   a. Stateful packet filtering

   b. NAT

   c. IPS

   d. AIC

   e. NBA

7. A business has been the target of several attacks recently, where its network was scanned or probed to find unsuspecting victims. Which Cisco ASA feature should you leverage to detect and prevent further attacks?

   a. Remote Access VPNs

   b. Virtualization

   c. Traffic policing

   d. Botnet Traffic Filtering

   e. Threat detection

8. A company wants to begin using a firewall to protect its network, but it doesn't want to disrupt its operations with any IP address reconfiguration. In fact, it doesn't want to change the IP addresses on any of its existing network devices when the firewall is installed. Which Cisco ASA feature could you use to meet this requirement?

   a. NAT

   b. Virtualization

   c. IP routing

   d. Transparent firewall mode

   e. AIC

9. A medium-sized business would like to implement a firewall where it borders the public Internet. The business also plans to add intrusion prevention at the border. Assuming the business's Internet bandwidth will not exceed 350 Mbps, which of the following ASA models in combination with an integrated IPS module should you select?

   a. ASA 5505 with an AIP-SSC-5

   b. ASA 5510 with an AIP-SSM-10

   c. ASA 5520 with an AIP-SSM-20

   d. ASA 5550 with an AIP-SSM-40

   e. Any of the combinations in these answers will work.

10. Which one of the following represents a typical environment or application for an ASA 5550?

    a. A remote office

    b. A teleworker's home

    c. A data center requiring 10-Gbps throughput

    d. A large enterprise requiring 5-Gbps throughput

    e. A large enterprise requiring 1-Gbps throughput

11. Assuming the correct license has been purchased and activated, which of the following ASA models can support 50 virtual firewalls or security contexts? (Choose all that apply.)

    a. ASA 5510

    b. ASA 5520

    c. ASA 5540

    d. ASA 5550

    e. ASA 5580

    f. ASA 5585-X

12. Which one of the following functions requires the purchase of an additional feature license for a Cisco ASA 5520?

    a. Strong encryption

    b. Botnet Traffic Filtering

    c. DHCP server

    d. Threat protection

    e. Stateful packet filtering with AIC

Foundation Topics

To preserve the integrity and stability of resources on a network, they must be protected from things that can't always be trusted or controlled. Rather than begin with a list of possible network attacks, exploits, and vulnerabilities, this chapter presents an overview of a firewall, its features, and how it fits into various scenarios to protect a network. Individual security threats are described throughout this book as the appropriate firewall features to protect against those threats are introduced.

Firewall Overview

Network security engineers must protect valuable resources within a network. For example, corporate data might be confidential or critical to the operation of a business or to offering patient care, in which case it must be kept from prying eyes and protected from tampering. Similarly, the computers in a network might need to be protected from outside interference so that they are kept stable and in good working order.

To protect these resources, the network must somehow be divided into *trusted* and *untrusted* parts. The trusted portions of the network are known as *security domains*; everything inside the security domain is protected from everything outside the domain. As a simple example, a small company decides to protect itself from the public Internet. The security domain forms where the company's network meets the Internet, and everything inside the company network resides within a secure boundary. Figure 1-1 illustrates this scenario.

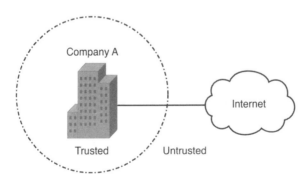

Figure 1-1   *A Simple Security Domain*

The most common and effective way to implement a security domain is to place a firewall at the boundary between the trusted and untrusted parts of a network. By definition, a *firewall* is a device that enforces an access control policy between two or more security domains. Firewalls have interfaces that connect into the network. In order for a firewall to do its job, all traffic that crosses a security domain boundary must pass through the firewall. In effect, a firewall becomes the only pathway or "chokepoint" to get in or out of the security domain.

For the simple network shown in Figure 1-1, a firewall would sit on the trust boundary and become the only path between Company A's internal trusted network and the untrusted public Internet, as shown in Figure 1-2. Although Figure 1-2 shows the addition of the firewall, several things must happen before the firewall can make the security domain truly secure:

■   The firewall must be the only path into and out of the secured network. No other paths around the firewall or "backdoors" into the network behind the firewall can exist. The firewall can enforce security policies on only the traffic that passes *through* it, not around or behind it.

■   The firewall itself must be hardened or made resistant to attack or compromise. Otherwise, malicious users on the untrusted side might take control of the firewall and alter its security policies.

Sometimes, a single security domain with a single firewall isn't enough. Suppose Company A wants to secure itself from the public Internet, but it also has a data center that needs to be even more secure. Company A trusts its employees to perform their job functions, but it can't risk letting anyone access its mission critical resources in an improper way or disrupt any services in its data center. Therefore, Company A decides to make a second security domain around the data center, as shown in Figure 1-3.

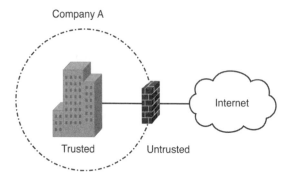

Figure 1-2   *Implementing a Security Domain with a Firewall*

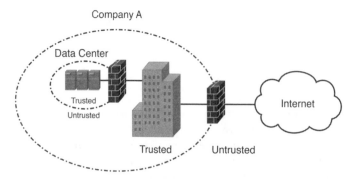

Figure 1-3   *Multiple Security Domains and Firewalls*

Each security domain is implemented with a firewall at its border. On the inside of the security domain or firewall, trusted resources exist; on the outside are untrusted things. This trust relationship is only locally significant, however. Consider the data center boundary firewall in Figure 1-3. The users just outside the data center are untrusted (at least from the perspective of that firewall), but they are still trusted from the perspective of the Internet boundary firewall. Each firewall has its own set of security policies and its own concept of a trust boundary.

Now consider a different scenario. Company A is surrounded by a security domain at the Internet boundary. It wants to allow its internal, trusted users to connect to resources out on the public Internet through the Internet firewall. Company A also has some web servers that it wants to have face the public so that untrusted Internet users can interact with the business.

If the web servers are located somewhere inside the security domain, then untrusted users would be granted access into the trusted environment. That isn't necessarily bad, except that malicious users might be able to attack or compromise one of the web servers. Because the web server is already a trusted resource, the malicious users might then use that server to attack other trusted resources.

A better solution is to put the web servers into a security domain of their own, somewhere between the trusted internal network and the untrusted Internet. This is commonly called a *demilitarized zone (DMZ)*. Figure 1-4 shows one solution that leverages the Internet firewall. With the addition of a third interface, the firewall can act as the boundary between a trusted domain, an untrusted public network, and a new "somewhat trusted" domain full of web servers.

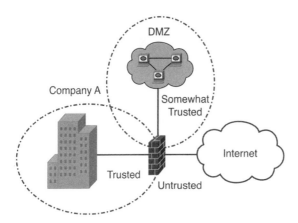

Figure 1-4   *Using a Single Firewall to Form Multiple Security Domains*

Whenever a firewall is used to form a security domain boundary, it must somehow separate the network into distinct parts. This can be done in one of two ways: physical separation or logical separation.

Physical separation requires that each physical firewall interface must be connected into a distinct network infrastructure. This usually requires additional hardware and additional cost. For example, Figure 1-5 shows how a firewall physically separates a network into two distinct pieces, with each firewall interface connecting into a different switch. Physical separation provides the utmost security because traffic cannot pass between security domains without some sort of physical intervention—the firewall would have to be disconnected, cables rerouted, and so on.

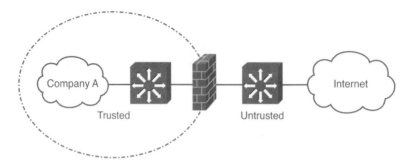

Figure 1-5   *Physical Separation of Security Domains*

A firewall can also be positioned to offer logical separation. In this case, the security domains exist on the same physical network infrastructure, but are separated logically into different *virtual local area networks (VLAN)*, *virtual storage area networks (VSAN)*, or *Multiprotocol Label Switching Virtual Private Networks (MPLS VPN)*. In Figure 1-6, a firewall forms a boundary between two security domains that are carried over two separate VLANs.

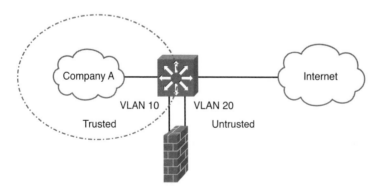

Figure 1-6   *Logical Separation of Security Domains*

While the firewall could use two physical interfaces to connect to the two VLANs, the VLANs could just as easily be carried over a single trunk link or one physical firewall interface. Logical networks are cost effective and can be flexible and complex. This makes logical separation less secure than physical separation, simply because a firewall might be bypassed or breached through a misconfiguration or failure of a logical network component or through an exploit of the logical separation itself.

Firewall Techniques

In its most basic form, a firewall strives to isolate its interfaces from each other and to carefully control how packets are forwarded from one interface to another. A firewall can enforce access control across a security boundary based on layers in the Open Systems Interconnection (OSI) model.

For example, a firewall performing *network layer access control* can make decisions based on Layers 2 through 4, or the data link, network, and transport layers. Such a firewall might control whether IP traffic can pass through, whether hosts on one side can open UDP or TCP connections to resources on the other side, and so on.

Firewalls that perform *application layer access control* enforce security policies at Layers 5 through 7, or the session, presentation, and application layers. Such a firewall can control what users do within applications that pass data from one side to another. For example, an application layer firewall might verify that a user's web browsing sessions are conforming to the industry standard protocols, or that a user's email or file transfers do not contain viruses or confidential material.

A firewall can take one of the following approaches to its access control:

Key Topic

- **Permissive access control:** All traffic is allowed to pass through unless it is explicitly blocked.

- **Restrictive access control:** No traffic is allowed to pass through unless it is explicitly allowed.

Permissive access control is also known as a *reactive* approach because it can react or block traffic only after potentially threatening things are identified and rules are put in place. Otherwise, everything else is allowed to pass through. Permissive rules are usually added to a firewall by intrusion prevention systems (IPS) and antivirus systems, which are tools that react to things that are detected on the network in real time.

Restrictive access control is also known as a *proactive* approach. Every acceptable type of traffic is identified ahead of time and entered into the firewall rules so that it may pass without further intervention. Any other traffic, whether it is malicious, undesirable, or just unidentified, is blocked by default. This is the same approach that is used by Cisco IOS access lists—traffic rules are processed in sequential order but always end with an implicit "deny all" rule.

A firewall can use its access control approach to evaluate and filter traffic based on the methods and techniques described in the following sections.

Stateless Packet Filtering

Some firewalls examine traffic based solely on values found in a packet's header at the network or transport layer. Decisions to forward or block a packet are made on each packet independently. Therefore, the firewall has no concept of a connection state; it knows only whether each packet conforms to the security policies.

Stateless packet filtering is performed by using a statically configured set of firewall rules. Even if a connection involves dynamic negotiation of further sessions and protocol port numbers, the stateless firewall is unaware. Stateless packet filters can be characterized by the attributes listed in Table 1-2.

Table 1-2 *Characteristics of a Stateless Packet Filter*

Feature	Limitation
Statically configured rules, usually for a restrictive approach	Effective filtering is limited by human rule configuration
Effective for Layer 3 address, protocol, or Layer 4 port number filtering	No tracking of dynamically negotiated sessions or changing port numbers
Efficient and cost-effective	Relatively easy to exploit

Stateful Packet Filtering

Stateful packet filtering (SPF) requires that a firewall keep track of individual connections or sessions as packets are encountered. The firewall must maintain a state table for each active connection that is permitted, to verify that the pair of hosts is following an expected behavior as they communicate. As well, the firewall must inspect traffic at Layer 4 so that any new sessions that are negotiated as part of an existing connection can be validated and tracked. Tracking the negotiated sessions requires some limited inspection of the application layer protocol.

Stateful packet filters can be characterized by the attributes listed in Table 1-3.

Table 1-3 *Characteristics of a Stateful Packet Filter*

Feature	Limitation
Reliable filtering of traffic at Layers 3 and 4; typically used for a restrictive approach	No visibility into Layers 5 through 7
Simple configuration; less reliance on human knowledge of protocols	—
High performance	No protocol verification

Stateful Packet Filtering with Application Inspection and Control

To move beyond stateful packet filtering, firewalls must add additional analysis at the application layer. Inspection engines in the firewall reassemble UDP and TCP sessions and look inside the application layer protocols that are passing through. *Application inspection and control (AIC) filtering*, also known as *deep packet inspection (DPI)*, can be performed based on the application protocol header and its contents, allowing greater visibility into a user's activity.

AIC comes at a price, as a firewall needs more processing power and more memory to be able to inspect and validate application sessions and they unfold.

SPF with AIC can be characterized by the attributes listed in Table 1-4.

Table 1-4   *Characteristics of Stateful Packet Filtering with Application Inspection and Control*

Feature	Limitation
Reliable filtering of Layers 3 through 7; typically used for a restrictive approach	Limited buffering for thorough application analysis
Simple configuration; less reliance on human knowledge of protocols	—
Medium performance	AIC requires greater processing power

Network Intrusion Prevention System

A *network intrusion prevention system (NIPS)* examines and analyzes network traffic and compares it to a database of known malicious activity. The database contains a large number of signatures or patterns that describe specific known attacks or exploits. As new attacks are discovered, new signatures are added to the database.

In some cases, NIPS devices can detect malicious activity from single packets or atomic attacks. In other cases, groups or streams of packets must be collected, reassembled, and examined. A NIPS can also detect malicious activity based on packet and session rates, such as a denial-of-service TCP SYN flood, that differ significantly from normal activity on the network.

A network IPS usually operates with a permissive approach, where traffic is allowed to cross security domains unless something suspicious is detected. Once that occurs, the NIPS can generate firewall rules dynamically to block or reset malicious packets or connections.

A NIPS can be characterized by the attributes listed in Table 1-5.

Table 1-5   *Characteristics of a Network Intrusion Prevention System*

Feature	Limitation
A rich signature database of attack patterns, covering Layers 3 through 7	Limited buffering for thorough application analysis
Usually used in a permissive approach	Requires inline operation or partnership with a firewall to react to detected threats; cannot usually detect attacks that are new or not previously known
Medium performance	Requires periodic tuning to manage false positive and false negative threat detection

Network Behavior Analysis

Network behavior analysis (NBA) systems examine network traffic over time to build statistical models of normal, baseline activity. This isn't a simple bandwidth or utilization average; rather, the models consider things like traffic volume, traffic rates, connection rates, and types of application protocols that are normally used. An NBA system continually examines traffic and refines its models automatically, although human intervention is needed to tune the results.

Once the models are built, an NBA system can trigger on any activity that it considers to be an anomaly or that falls outside the normal conditions. In fact, NBA systems are often called anomaly-based network IPSs. Even when malicious activity involves a previously unknown scheme, an NBA system can often detect it if it involves traffic patterns or volumes that fall outside the norm. An NBA system can be characterized by the attributes listed in Table 1-6.

Table 1-6 *Characteristics of a Network Behavior Analysis System*

Feature	Limitation
Examines inline network traffic or offline traffic data to build profiles or models of normal network activity	Human intervention is required for model tuning.
Can detect previously unknown attacks	Generates false positives if legitimate traffic appears to be an anomaly.
Uses a restrictive approach, detecting or blocking everything that is not known good activity	—

Application Layer Gateway (Proxy)

An application layer gateway (ALG) or proxy is a device that acts as a gateway or intermediary between clients and servers. A client must send its application layer requests to the proxy, in place of any destination servers. The proxy masquerades as the client and relays the client's requests on to the actual servers. Once the servers answer the requests, the proxy evaluates the content and decides what to do with them.

Because a proxy operates on application requests, it can filter traffic based on the IP addresses involved, the type of application request, and the content of any data that is returned from the server.

Proxies can perform detailed and thorough analysis of client-server connections. Traffic can be validated against protocol standards at Layers 3 through 7, and the results can be normalized or made to conform to the standards, as needed. An ALG or proxy can be characterized by the attributes listed in Table 1-7.

Table 1-7 *Characteristics of an Application Layer Gateway (Proxy)*

Feature	Limitation
Protocol analysis and normalization	Not available for all protocols or applications.
Deep and thorough content analysis	Analysis might take too long for real-time traffic.
Access control over Layers 3 through 7	—
Can be permissive or restrictive	Can require configuration on the clients.

Cisco ASA Features

The Cisco ASA is the focus of the FIREWALL exam. Is the ASA a firewall? Yes. Is it more than a firewall? Yes! The Cisco ASA platform has the capability to perform any of the firewall techniques described in the previous sections.

Even further, the ASA has many features that go beyond the basic firewall techniques, giving it great versatility. A summary of the ASA features is presented in the following sections. You should become familiar with these features, as you will need to be able to select the appropriate ASA features and technologies on the exam, given some high-level design criteria:

Key Topic

■ **Stateful packet filtering engine:** The SPF engine tracks connections and their states, performing TCP normalization and conformity checks, as well as dynamic session negotiation. Chapter 9, "Inspecting Traffic," covers the SPF engine in more detail.

■ **Application inspection and control:** The AIC function analyzes application layer protocols to track their state and to make sure they conform to protocol standards. Chapter 9 covers the AIC functionality in more detail.

■ **User-based access control:** The ASA can perform inline user authentication followed by Cut-through Proxy, which controls the access that specific users are allowed to have. Once a user is authenticated, Cut-through Proxy also accelerates inspection of a user's traffic flows. Chapter 10, "Using Proxy Services to Control Access," covers these functions in more detail.

■ **Session auditing:** Accounting records can be generated for user-based sessions, as well as for application layer connections and sessions. Chapter 6, "Recording ASA Activity," covers session auditing in more detail. Session auditing can be used to generate audit trails, traffic accounting, and incident investigation.

■ **Security Services Modules:** The ASA platform supports several Security Services Modules (SSM) that contain specialized hardware to offload processor-intensive security functions. An ASA can contain one SSM, offloading either IPS or content security services. Chapter 15, "Integrating ASA Service Modules," covers SSMs in more detail.

■ **Reputation-based Botnet Traffic Filtering:** An ASA can detect and filter traffic involved with botnet activity on infected hosts. The Botnet Traffic Filter database used to detect botnet threats is periodically updated by Cisco. Chapter 9 covers Botnet Traffic Filtering in more detail.

- **Category-based URL filtering:** An ASA can leverage an external URL filtering server to enforce acceptable use policies and control user access to various types of web services.

- **Cryptographic Unified Communications (UC) proxy:** When Cisco Unified Communications traffic must pass through an ASA, the ASA can be configured as an authorized UC proxy. The ASA can then terminate and relay cryptographically protected UC sessions between clients and servers.

- **Denial-of-service prevention:** An ASA can leverage traffic-control features like protocol normalization, traffic policing, and connection rate controls to minimize the effects of denial-of-service (DoS) attacks. Chapter 9 covers DoS prevention in more detail.

- **Traffic correlation:** The threat detection feature examines and correlates traffic from many different connections and sessions to detect and block anomalies stemming from network attacks and reconnaissance activity. Chapter 9 covers threat detection in more detail.

- **Remote access VPNs:** An ASA can support secure VPN connections from trusted users located somewhere on an untrusted network. Clientless SSL VPNs can be used to offer a secure web portal for limited remote access to users, without requiring VPN client software. For complete secure network access, full tunneling of all user traffic is supported with either SSL VPNs or IPsec VPNs, which require VPN client software. Remote access VPNs are covered in the *CCNP Security VPN 642-648 Official Cert Guide*.

- **Site-to-site VPNs:** An ASA can support IPsec VPN connections between sites or enterprises. Site-to-site or LAN-to-LAN VPN connections are usually built between firewalls or routers at each location. Site-to-site VPNs are covered in the *CCNP Security VPN 642-648 Official Cert Guide*.

- **High availability failover clustering:** Two identical ASA devices can be configured to operate as a failover pair, making the ASA security functions redundant in case of a hardware failure. Chapter 14, "Deploying High Availability Features," covers failover clustering in more detail.

- **Redundant interfaces:** To increase availability within a single ASA, interfaces can be configured as redundant pairs so that one is always active, while the other takes over after an interface hardware failure. Redundant interfaces are covered in Chapter 3, "Configuring ASA Interfaces," and can be used in conjunction with failover clustering.

- **EtherChannel:** Multiple ASA interfaces can be aggregated or bundled together as a single logical interface. By connecting an EtherChannel between an ASA and a switch, you can scale the bandwidth and offer additional redundancy. EtherChannels are covered in Chapter 3.

- **Traffic and policy virtualization:** An ASA can be configured to operate multiple virtual instances or security contexts, each acting as an independent firewall. Each virtual context has its own set of logical interfaces, security policies, and administrative control. Chapter 13, "Creating Virtual Firewalls on the ASA," covers virtual security contexts in more detail.

- **Rich IP routing functionality:** An ASA can forward traffic onto the local networks connected to each of its interfaces without any additional IP routing information. It can also be configured to use static routes or a dynamic routing protocol such as RIPv1, RIPv2, EIGRP, and OSPF to make more complex routing decisions. Chapter 4, "Configuring IP Connectivity," covers IP routing in more detail.

- **Powerful Network Address Translation (NAT):** As an ASA inspects and forwards packets, it can apply a rich set of NAT functions to alter source and destination addresses. Chapter 7, "Using Address Translation," covers NAT in more detail.

- **Transparent (bridged) operation:** An ASA can be configured to operate as a transparent firewall, effectively becoming a secure bridge between its interfaces. Transparent firewall mode allows an ASA to be wedged into an existing network without requiring any readdressing of the network. Chapter 12, "Using Transparent Firewall Mode," covers transparent firewall mode in more detail.

- **Integrated DHCP, DDNS, and PPPoE:** An ASA can be configured to act as a DHCP client or a PPP over Ethernet (PPPoE) client to obtain a dynamic IP address for its interfaces from the network, and as a Dynamic DNS (DDNS) client to record information for hostname-to-address resolution. As well, an ASA can act as a DHCP server to offer IP addressing services to other hosts on the network. Chapter 4 covers most of these features.

- **IPv6 support:** An ASA can be configured to operate natively in an IPv6 network.

- **IP multicast support:** An ASA can leverage the Internet Group Management Protocol (IGMP) and the Protocol Independent Multicast (PIM) protocol to participate in handling IP multicast traffic.

- **Management control and protocols:** An ASA supports several different methods of management control, including a console port, Telnet, Secure Shell (SSH), Secure HTTP (HTTPS), and Simple Network Management Protocol (SNMP; Versions 1, 2c, and 3). A dedicated out-of-band management port is also available. An ASA can send event notifications using SNMP traps, NetFlow, and syslog. Chapter 5, "Managing a Cisco ASA," covers management control in more detail.

- **Simple software management:** An ASA supports a local file system and remote file transfers for software upgrades. Software upgrades can be performed manually, automatically, or in a zero-downtime fashion on a failover cluster of ASAs. Chapter 13 covers software management in more detail.

- **Configuration flexibility and scalability:** Security policies and rules can be configured using reusable objects. Through the Modular Policy Framework (MPF), security features can be configured and applied in a flexible and versatile manner.

Chapter 8, "Controlling Access Through the ASA," and Chapter 9 cover these features in more detail.

■ **Cisco Security Management Suite:** Multiple ASAs can be managed from the Cisco Security Management Suite for ease of administration.

Selecting a Cisco ASA Model

The Cisco ASA family consists of seven different models. In the FIREWALL exam, you will probably have to select an appropriate ASA model based on some high-level design criteria. How can you learn all of the specifications about every model? Fortunately, the model numbers can be used as a crude guide because they increase as the firewall capabilities or capacities increase.

The following sections briefly describe each of the ASA models, presented in order of increasing performance. The ASA features are consistent across the entire platform range, with some models limited only by feature licensing. Therefore, when you need to select an ASA model for a given scenario, your decision will most often hinge on the type of environment and the performance that is required.

ASA 5505

The ASA 5505 is the smallest model in the ASA lineup, in both physical size and performance. It is designed for small offices and home offices (SOHO). For a larger enterprise, the ASA 5505 is frequently used to support teleworkers in remote locations. Figure 1-7 shows front and rear views of the ASA 5505.

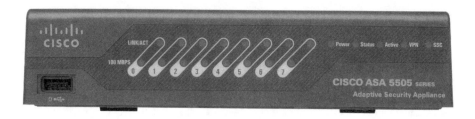

Figure 1-7 *ASA 5505 Front and Rear Views*

There are eight FastEthernet ports on the ASA 5505, all connected to an internal switch. Two of the ports are capable of offering Power over Ethernet (PoE) to attached devices. (The ASA itself cannot be powered by PoE.) By default, all eight ports are connected to the same VLAN in the switch, allowing connected devices to communicate with each other at Layer 2 directly.

The switch ports can be broken up into multiple VLANs to support different areas or functions within a small office. The ASA connects to each VLAN through individual logical interfaces. Any traffic crossing between VLANs must pass through the ASA and its security policies.

The ASA 5505 has one Security Services Card (SSC) slot that can accept an optional AIP-SSC-5 IPS module. With the module installed, the ASA can augment its security features with network IPS functions.

ASA 5510, 5520, and 5540

The ASA 5510, 5520, and 5540 models all use a common chassis and have identical front panel indicators and hardware connections. Figure 1-8 shows front and rear views of the common platform.

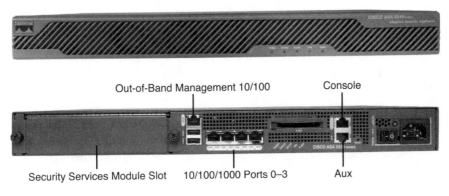

Figure 1-8 *ASA 5510, 5520, and 5540 Front and Rear Views*

The models differ in their security performance ratings, however. The ASA 5510 is designed for small to medium businesses (SMB) and remote offices for larger enterprises. The ASA 5520 is appropriate for medium-sized enterprises, while the ASA 5540 is more suited for medium- and large-sized enterprises and service provider networks.

The ASA 5520 and 5540 models has four 10/100/1000 Ethernet ports that can be used to connect into the network infrastructure. The four ports are dedicated firewall interfaces and are not connected to each other. An ASA 5510 can use all four Ethernet ports in FastEthernet (10/100) mode by default. If a Security Plus license is purchased and activated, two of the ports can operate as Gigabit Ethernet (10/100/1000) and two as FastEthernet. A fifth management Ethernet interface is also available.

The ASA 5510, 5520, and 5540 chassis have one SSM slot that can be populated with one of the following:

- **Four-port Gigabit Ethernet SSM:** This module adds four additional physical firewall interfaces, as either 10/100/1000 RJ45 or small form-factor pluggable (SFP)-based ports.

- **Advanced Inspection and Prevention (AIP) SSM:** This module adds inline network IPS capabilities to the ASA's security suite.

- **Content Security and Control (CSC) SSM:** This module adds comprehensive content control and antivirus services to the ASA's security suite.

Each of the SSMs is described in more detail in the section, "Security Services Modules."

The ASA 5510, 5520, and 5540 models have one AUX port that can be used for out-of-band management through an asynchronous serial connection or a modem. It also has one FastEthernet port that is designated for management traffic but can be reconfigured for normal data traffic if needed.

ASA 5550

The ASA 5550 is designed to support large enterprises and service provider networks. Figure 1-9 shows both front and rear views. Notice that the ASA 5550 looks identical to the ASA 5510, 5520, and 5540 models. The most noticeable difference is that the ASA 5550 has one fixed four-port Gigabit Ethernet (4GE-SSM) module in the SSM slot, which cannot be removed or changed.

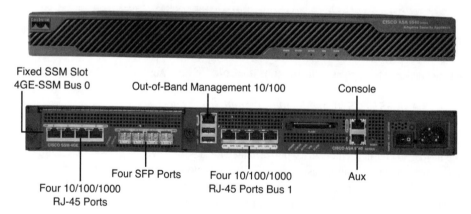

Figure 1-9   *ASA 5550 Front and Rear Views*

The ASA 5550 architecture features two groups of physical interfaces that connect to two separate internal buses. The interface groups are referred to as slot 0 and slot 1, corresponding to bus 0 and bus 1. Slot 0 consists of four built-in copper Gigabit Ethernet ports.

Slot 1 consists of four built-in copper and four built-in SFP Gigabit Ethernet ports, though only four of the eight ports can be used at any time.

The ASA 5550 offers high performance for demanding environments. To maximize the firewall throughput, the bulk of the traffic should go from the switch ports on bus 0 to the switch ports on bus 1. The ASA can forward traffic much more efficiently from bus to bus than it can if traffic stays within a single bus.

ASA 5580

The ASA 5580 is a high-performing model in the family and is designed for large enterprises, data centers, and large service providers. It can support up to 24 Gigabit Ethernet interfaces or up to 12 10Gigabit Ethernet interfaces. It is one of two models that has a chassis larger than one standard rack unit (RU).

Note: As of February 10, 2011, the ASA 5580 reached end-of-life status. In all likelihood, although it still exists as a product at press time, the FIREWALL course and exam will no longer cover the model.

The ASA 5580, shown in Figure 1-10, comes in two performance models: the ASA 5580-20 (5-Gbps throughput) and the ASA 5580-40 (10-Gbps throughput). The chassis includes two built-in 10/100/1000 Gigabit Ethernet ports, which are normally used for out-of-band management traffic. The system also uses dual redundant power supplies.

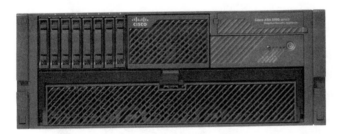

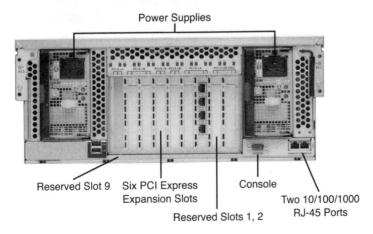

Figure 1-10 *ASA 5580 Front and Rear Views*

The ASA 5580 chassis has a total of nine PCI Express expansion slots. Slot 1 is reserved for a cryptographic accelerator module, to support high-performance VPN operations. Slots 2 and 9 are reserved for future use, leaving six slots available for the following network interface cards:

- 4-port 10/100/1000BASE-T copper Gigabit Ethernet interfaces

- 4-port 1000BASE-SX fiber-optic Gigabit Ethernet interfaces

- 2-port 10GBASE-SR 10Gigabit Ethernet fiber-optic interfaces

The ASA 5580 architecture has two I/O bridges that provide connectivity to the expansion slots, as shown in Figure 1-10. Unlike the ASA 5550, maximum throughput on the ASA 5580 is achieved when traffic flows stay *within* a single I/O bridge. The interfaces in slots 7 and 8 are all connected to I/O bridge 1, while the interfaces in slots 3, 4, 5, and 6 are connected to I/O bridge 2.

Any 10Gigabit Ethernet interfaces should be installed in slots 5, 7, or 8, which are high-capacity PCIe-x8 slots.

Security Services Modules

Many of the ASA models can accept one Security Services Module (SSM). The SSM contains dedicated hardware that can offload specialized or processor-intensive functions. Cisco offers the Advanced Inspection and Prevention (AIP) SSM, the Content Security and Control (CSC) SSM, and the 4-port Gigabit Ethernet (4GE) SSM, which are shown in Figure 1-11 and described in the following sections.

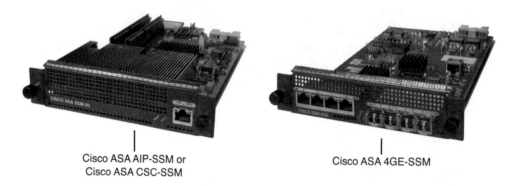

Cisco ASA AIP-SSM or
Cisco ASA CSC-SSM

Cisco ASA 4GE-SSM

Figure 1-11 *Cisco ASA AIP-SSM, CSC-SSM, and 4GE-SSM*

Note: The AIP-SSM and the CSC-SSM use identical hardware form factors, but run entirely different software.

Advanced Inspection and Prevention (AIP) SSM

The AIP-SSM runs the Cisco IPS Software image and performs network intrusion prevention functions in conjunction with the ASA. The ASA can put the AIP-SSM inline, where traffic is internally redirected to the module for inspection and handling before it is forwarded. Otherwise, the AIP-SSM can operate in promiscuous mode, where the ASA copies traffic to the module as it is being forwarded.

To be effective as a network IPS, the AIP-SSM must update its IPS signature database in a timely fashion. Signature updates are available only by subscribing to the Cisco Services for IPS service. The signature database is maintained and updated by Cisco Security Intelligence Operations (SIO) and contains well over 25,000 threat signatures. As new threats are discovered and identified, new signatures are added to the database, which must be downloaded into the AIP-SSM.

The AIP-SSM is available in several models, as listed in Table 1-8. The models are numbered sequentially, in order of increasing performance. Notice that not all models can work in every ASA platform. Higher-performing ASA models require higher-performing AIP-SSMs. Also notice that the ASA 5550 and 5580 models cannot accept an AIP-SSM at all.

Table 1-8   *AIP-SSM Models*

AIP SSM Model	ASA 5505	ASA 5510	ASA 5520	ASA 5540
AIP-SSC-5	75 Mbps			
AIP-SSM-10		150 Mbps	225 Mbps	
AIP-SSM-20		300 Mbps	375 Mbps	500 Mbps
AIP-SSM-40			450 Mbps	650 Mbps

Content Security and Control (CSC) SSM

The CSC-SSM performs comprehensive antivirus, antispyware, antispam, antiphishing, file blocking, URL blocking and filtering, and content filtering in conjunction with the ASA. The ASA internally redirects traffic through the CSC-SSM, which runs the Trend Micro InterScan for Cisco CSC-SSM software image. Because so many of the CSC-SSM's functions mitigate such a wide range of malware approaches, it is commonly referred to as the "Anti-X" module. HTTP, FTP, SMTP, and POP3 traffic are protected by the CSC-SSM.

For the CSC-SSM to be effective, it must stay updated with the latest content security information from Trend Micro. This is done automatically but requires a subscription service license from Cisco.

The CSC-SSM is available in two models, as listed in Table 1-9. The CSC-SSM-10 can support up to 50 users by default but can be expanded to 500 users through the purchase of additional licenses. The CSC-SSM-20 begins with 500 users and can be expanded to 1000 users with additional licenses.

Table 1-9   *CSC-SSM Models*

CSC-SSM Model	ASA 5505	ASA 5510	ASA 5520	ASA 5540
CSC-SSM-10		Up to 500 users	Up to 500 users	
CSC-SSM-20		Up to 1000 users	Up to 1000 users	Up to 1000 users

Both models come with a standard license that includes the antivirus, antispyware, and file-blocking features. If a Security Plus license is purchased, the CSC-SSM can also perform antispam, antiphishing, URL blocking/filtering, and content control.

4-port Gigabit Ethernet (4GE) SSM

The 4GE-SSM provides four additional Gigabit Ethernet ports to an ASA 5510, 5520, or 5540 model. Although the module has four copper 10/100/1000 RJ-45 ports and four SFP fiber-optic ports, only four ports of any type can be used at any time.

ASA 5585-X

The ASA 5585-X is the highest-performing model in the family and is designed for large enterprises and mission critical data centers. It has a 2-RU two-slot chassis and dual redundant power supplies, as shown in Figure 1-12. Each slot can accept a Security Services Processor (SSP).

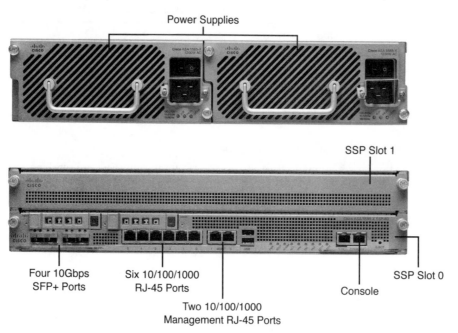

Figure 1-12 *ASA 5585-X Front and Rear Views*

The ASA 5585-X comes in four performance models, depending on which one of the following SSPs is installed with the firewall/VPN SSP: the SSP-10 (3-Gbps throughput), the SSP-20 (7-Gbps throughput), the SSP-40 (12-Gbps throughput), and the SSP-60 (20-Gbps throughput). Depending on the model, the firewall/VPN SSP can offer up to four 10-Gbps Ethernet, six 10/100/1000, and two 10/100/1000 management interfaces, as shown in Figure 1-12.

The ASA 5585-X can also provide high-performance IPS operation in four performance models, through the addition of one of the following IPS SSPs in the upper slot (slot 1):

■   IPS SSP-10 (2-Gbps throughput)

■   IPS SSP-20 (3-Gbps throughput)

■   IPS SSP-40 (5-Gbps throughput)

■   IPS SSP-60 (10-Gbps throughput)

Figure 1-13 shows an ASA 5585-X with a firewall/VPN SSP installed in slot 0 and an IPS SSP in slot 1. The firewall/VPN SSP is always in control of and passes traffic to and from the IPS SSP. Notice that the two SSPs look identical, although they perform totally different functions. When an IPS SSP is added to a chassis, it also brings up to four 10-Gbps Ethernet and six 10/100/1000 additional interfaces that are controlled by the firewall/VPN SSP.

Figure 1-13   *ASA5585-X Populated with a Firewall/VPN and IPS SSPs*

Note: The ASA 5585-X requires Cisco ASA software 8.2(3) or later. However, if an IPS SSP is installed, the ASA must run release 8.4(2) or later and Cisco IPS 7.1(1)E4 or later.

ASA Performance Breakdown

Sometimes, you will need to select an ASA model based on sheer performance ratings. For example, the exam might ask you to choose an appropriate ASA model based on the relative size of an organization or on the expected traffic or connection loads. You can use Table 1-10 and Table 1-11 to study how each ASA model relates to the type of environment or application it can typically support. The table also lists the throughput for bandwidth, connections, and packet handling.

Table 1-10   *Traffic Performance of ASA Models*

	5505	5510	5520	5540	5550	5580-20	5580-40
Typical application	Small office, home office, teleworker	Small to medium businesses, remote offices	Medium sized enterprise	Medium to large enterprises	Large enterprise, service provider	Large enterprise, data center, service provider	Large enterprise, data center, service provider
Firewall throughput	150 Mbps	300 Mbps	450 Mbps	500–650 Mbps	1–1.2 Gbps	5–10 Gbps	10–20 Gbps
Connections per second	4000	9000	12,000	25,000	36,000	90,000	150,000
Packets per second (64-byte)	85,000	190,000	320,000	500,000	600,000	2.5 M	4 M
Maximum connections	10,000/25,000[1]	50,000/130,000[1]	280,000	400,000	650,000	1 M	2 M

[1] ASA 5505, 5510: Base license/Security Plus license

Table 1-11   *Traffic Performance of ASA 5585-X Models*

	5585-X SSP-10	5585-X SSP-20	5585-X SSP-40	5585-X SSP-60
Typical application	Mission-critical data centers	Mission-critical data centers	Mission-critical data centers	Mission-critical data centers
Firewall throughput	3 Gbps	7 Gbps	12 Gbps	20 Gbps
Connections per second	65,000	140,000	240,000	350,000
Packets per second (64 byte)	1.5 M	3.2 M	6 M	10.5 M
Maximum connections	1 M	2 M	4 M	10 M

You should also be familiar with the number of interfaces that each ASA model can support. Table 1-12 and Table 1-13 list each ASA model along with the default number of physical interfaces that are installed, the maximum number of physical interfaces supported, and the number of VLANs or logical interfaces supported.

Table 1-12 *Interfaces Supported by ASA Models*   Key Topic

	5505	5510	5520	5540	5550	5580-20	5580-40
Default interfaces	8 FE switch (2 PoE)	5 FE or 2 GE + 3 FE	4 GE + 1 FE	4 GE + 1 FE	8 GE	2 GE	2 GE
Maximum interfaces	8 FE switch (2 PoE)	4 GE + 5 FE or 6 GE + 3 FE	8 GE + 1 FE	8 GE + 1 FE	8 GE + 1 FE	24 GE or 12 10 GE	24 GE or 12 10 GE
VLANs	3/20[1]	50/100[1]	150	200	250	250	250

[1] ASA 5505, 5510: Base license/Security Plus license

Table 1-13 *Interfaces Supported by ASA 5585-X Models*   Key Topic

	5585-X SSP-10	5585-X SSP-20	5585-X SSP-40	5585-X SSP-60
Default interfaces	8 GE + 2 10 GE	8 GE + 2 10 GE	6 GE + 4 10 GE	6 GE + 4 10 GE
Maximum interfaces	16 GE + 4 10 GE	16 GE + 4 10 GE	12 GE + 8 10 GE	12 GE + 8 10 GE
VLANs	1024	1024	1024	1024

Except for the ASA 5505, all other models can support virtual firewalls, also called security contexts. Each virtual firewall can operate independently, sharing processor, memory, and interface resources from the hardware platform. The number of supported virtual firewalls is listed in Table 1-14 and Table 1-15.

Table 1-14 *Virtual Firewalls and High Availability Supported by ASA Models*   Key Topic

	5505[1]	5510[1]	5520	5540	5550	5580-20	5580-40
Virtual firewalls (security contexts)[2]	0/0	0/5	20	50	50	50	50
High availability[3]	—/Stateless A/S	—/A/A and A/S	A/A and A/S	A/A and A/S	A/A and A/S	A/A and A/S	A/A and A/S

[1] ASA 5505, 5510: Base license/Security Plus license.

[2] All models include two security contexts by default, except the ASA 5505 and ASA 5510 Base, which include none.

[3] A/S = Active/Standby, A/A = Active/Active.

Table 1-15 *Virtual Firewalls and High Availability Supported by ASA 5585-X Models*

	5585-X SSP-10	5585-X SSP-20	5585-X SSP-40	5585-X SSP-60
Virtual firewalls (security contexts)[1]	100	250	250	250
High availability[2]	A/A and A/S	A/A and A/S	A/A and A/S	A/A and A/S

[1] All models include two security contexts by default, except the ASA 5505 and ASA 5510 Base, which include none.

[2] A/S = Active/Standby, A/A = Active/Active.

ASA devices can also be configured to offer high availability by operating as clusters or failover pairs. The high availability mode varies depending upon the model and the installed license. In Table 1-14 and Table 1-15, the mode is shown to be Active/Standby (A/S), where one ASA actively protects a network while the other ASA sits idle in standby mode, or Active/Active (A/A), where both ASAs in a pair can actively participate in network protection.

Although the FIREWALL course and exam do not cover VPN topics in detail, you should still be familiar with the VPN capabilities of the ASA product family. Table 1-16 and Table 1-17 list the VPN throughput and maximum session ratings for each ASA model. VPN performance becomes important when an ASA must also support secure access for remote users and remote sites. By selecting the appropriate ASA model, you can make sure that the number of VPN users and the bandwidth they require are supported.

Table 1-16 *VPN Performance by ASA Model*

	5505	5510	5520	5540	5550	5580-20	5580-40
Max VPN throughput	100 Mbps	170 Mbps	225 Mbps	325 Mbps	425 Mbps	1 Gbps	1 Gbps
Max IPsec VPN sessions	10/25[1]	250	750	5000	5000	10,000	10,000
Max SSL VPN sessions	25	250	750	5000	5000	10,000	10,000

[1] ASA 5505: Base license/Security Plus license.

Table 1-17 *VPN Performance by ASA 5585-X Model*

	5585-X SSP-10	5585-X SSP-20	5585-X SSP-40	5585-X SSP-60
Max VPN throughput	1 Gbps	2 Gbps	3 Gbps	5 Gbps
Max IPsec VPN sessions	5000	10,000	10,000	10,000
Max SSL VPN sessions	5000	10,000	10,000	10,000

Selecting ASA Licenses

The Cisco ASA has a long list of security features (some common and some not so common) such that no one size fits all. To tailor an ASA to a specific environment or application, features and capabilities are unlocked through an aggregated licensing scheme based on the ASA's serial number. Each ASA model comes with a Base license that opens up a basic set of features. If additional capabilities are required, additional licenses must be purchased and their license activation keys must be entered into the ASA's permanent memory. These licenses are considered to be permanent licenses because they are applied to the ASA on a permanent basis.

Suppose you want to try out an ASA feature or capability without a commitment to purchase the license just yet. Cisco also offers temporary time-based licenses so that you can evaluate a feature or upgrade a capability until a permanent license can be purchased. Most of the time-based licensees are valid for a time limit from 1 to 52 weeks. Once they are requested from Cisco, time-based license activation keys can be entered into the ASA.

For ASAs running Cisco ASA Software Release 8.0(4) or later, time-based licenses can be aggregated or used in conjunction with permanent licenses. Until a time-based license expires, the permanent and time-based licenses are combined. With features like Unified Communications Proxy and Multiple Security Contexts, the permanent and time-based licenses are added together. With most other features, the higher value of the two licenses is used. In contrast, Releases 8.0(3) or earlier consider time-based licenses to override any permanent licenses for a given feature. Beginning with Release 8.3, you can install multiple time-based license keys so that you can evaluate several features.

When two ASAs are configured as a failover pair for high availability, the licenses between the two units must be compatible. Prior to Cisco ASA Software Release 8.3(1), both ASAs must have identical licenses installed. Beginning with Release 8.3(1), the two units can have disparate licensing. For feature licenses that involve a numerical limit, the sum of license on the two failover units is used. For feature licenses that are either enabled or disabled, the feature is enabled if the license is found on either ASA. If a time-based license is installed on either unit, the duration found on each unit is combined for a total license duration.

ASA licenses are broken up into the following categories:

- **Base license:** The default set of features.

- **Platform-specific licenses:** The ASA 5505 and 5510 are unique because they offer a Base license that can be upgraded to a Security Plus license. On the ASA 5505, the Security Plus license increases the maximum number of connections, VPN sessions, and VLANs, and it unlocks stateless firewall high availability. On the ASA 5510, Security Plus increases the maximum number of connections, physical interfaces, VLANs, and virtual firewalls, and it unlocks VPN load balancing and full high availability support. The specific differences between the Base and Security Plus licenses are shown in Tables 1-10, 1-12, 1-14, and 1-16.

  The ASA 5505 also keeps track of the number of concurrent active hosts or IP addresses on its inside network interface. The ASA can be purchased with an initial license of 10, 50, or an unlimited number of internal users. The number of internal users can also be upgraded to a total of 10, 50, or an unlimited number at a later time.

- **Feature licenses:** The features listed in Table 1-18 can be licensed individually.

Table 1-18   *ASA Aggregated Feature Licenses*

Feature License	Description
Botnet Traffic Filter	Enables Botnet Traffic Filtering
Strong Encryption	Enables 3DES and AES encryption algorithms for VPN sessions (free license)
GTP/GPRS Inspection	Enables GPRS Tunneling Protocol inspection (ASA 5520 and higher)
Cisco IME	Enables the Intercompany Media Engine functionality
AnyConnect Essentials	Enables the maximum number of AnyConnect SSL VPN clients only
AnyConnect Premium	Enables the maximum number of AnyConnect SSL VPN clients, clientless SSL VPN, and Cisco Secure Desktop features
AnyConnect for Mobile	Enables AnyConnect client access for Windows Mobile touch screen devices (also requires AnyConnect Essentials or Premium license)
Advanced Endpoint Assessment	Enables enhanced host scanning with Cisco Secure Desktop and AnyConnect SSL VPN clients
VPN Shared Licensing	Enables a license with a large number of SSL VPN sessions to be shared among several ASAs
FIPS Validation License	Enables Cisco AnyConnect SSL VPN client version 2.4 users for federal agencies requiring Federal Information Processing Standard (FIPS) 140-2 compliance

■ **Virtualization licenses:** By default, every ASA (except the 5505 and 5510 Base licenses) comes with two virtual firewalls or security contexts. The number of contexts can be increased by purchasing either an initial feature license of 5, 10, 20, 50, or 100 contexts or a feature upgrade license to go from 5 to 10, 10 to 20, 20 to 50, or 100 to 250 contexts. The maximum number of contexts is limited by the ASA model.

■ **Per-user cryptographic UC proxy licenses:** An ASA can extend Unified Communications (UC) services to remote users on the outside of a network through the cryptographic UC proxy features. Each remote user can be supported by any or all of the following proxy functions: ASA Phone Proxy, ASA Mobility Proxy, ASA Presence Federation Proxy, and ASA TLS Proxy.

By default, each ASA model comes with two user UC proxy licenses. UC proxy functions can be increased by purchasing an initial license of 24, 50, 100, 250, 500, 750, 1000, 2000, 5000, or 10,000 users, depending on the ASA model being used. As well, the number of users can be increased by purchasing an upgrade license to go from the initial number of users to the next increment of users.

■ **Per-user Premium SSL VPN licenses:** An ASA can support remote access to users over SSL VPN connections. By default, every ASA comes with a license that allows two Cisco AnyConnect SSL VPN users to connect. Premium SSL VPN includes support for users who have the Cisco AnyConnect client software installed, clientless SSL VPN users, and the Cisco Secure Desktop protected environment.

The number of AnyConnect users can be increased by purchasing an initial license of 10, 25, 50, 100, 250, 500, 750, 1000, 2500, 5000, or 10,000 users, depending on the ASA model being used. The number of VPN users can also be increased by purchasing an upgrade license to go from the initial number of users to the next increment of users.

ASA Memory Requirements

All ASA models ship with a default amount of DRAM installed, which is based on the feature set and the newest code image that are available at that time. As more features and functions are added into the code image, the ASA needs more memory resources at its disposal.

Cisco ASA Software Release 8.3 added many new features over previous releases. As a result, Cisco increased the minimum amount of DRAM required to run the image, as shown in Table 1-19. ASAs shipped with Release 8.3 or newer have the appropriate amount of memory installed; however, many ASA models that were put into service before Release 8.3 do not have the minimum memory to run 8.3 or newer. Cisco offers memory upgrades to bring such models into alignment with the newer code images.

Table 1-19   *ASA Memory Requirements*

ASA Model	Minimum DRAM Required Prior to 8.3	Minimum DRAM Required 8.3 and Later
5505	256 MB	256 MB
5505 Unlimited User and Security Plus	256 MB	512 MB
5510	256 MB	1 GB
5520	512 MB	2 GB
5540	1 GB	2 GB
5550	4 GB	4GB
5580-20	8 GB	8 GB
5580-40	12 GB	12 GB
5585-X SSP-10	N/A	6 GB
5585-X SSP-20	N/A	12 GB
5585-X SSP-40	N/A	12 GB
5585-X SSP-60	N/A	24 GB

Exam Preparation Tasks

As mentioned in the section, "How to Use This Book," in the "Introduction," you have a couple of choices for exam preparation: the exercises here, Chapter 17, "Final Preparation," and the exam simulation questions on the CD-ROM.

Review All Key Topics

Review the most important topics in this chapter, noted with the Key Topic icon in the outer margin of the page. Table 1-20 lists a reference of these key topics and the page number on which each is found.

Table 1-20   *Key Topics for Chapter 1*

Key
Topic

Key Topic Element	Description	Page Number
Paragraph	Explains security domains	7
List	Lists the two approaches to firewall access control	11
Paragraph	Explains stateful packet filtering with application inspection and control	12
List	List of the major Cisco ASA features and technologies	15
Tables 1-10 and 1-11	List of ASA models and their performance characteristics	26
Tables 1-12 and 1-13	List of ASA models and the number of supported interfaces	27
Tables 1-14 and 1-15	List of ASA models and their virtual firewall and high availability support	27–28
List	Explains the types of Cisco ASA licenses	30

Define Key Terms

Define the following key terms from this chapter and check your answers in the glossary:

firewall, security domain, demilitarized zone (DMZ), network layer access control, application layer access control, permissive access control, restrictive access control, stateless packet filtering, stateful packet filtering (SPF), application inspection and control (AIC) filtering, deep packet inspection (DPI), network intrusion prevention system (NIPS), network behavior analysis (NBA) system, application layer gateway (ALG), security context

This chapter covers the following topics:

- **Using the CLI:** This section describes the Cisco ASA command-line interface (CLI) and how you can use it to configure and display information about an ASA device.

- **Using Cisco ASDM:** This section describes the Adaptive Security Device Manager (ASDM) and how you can enter an initial ASA configuration to use it.

- **Understanding the Factory Default Configuration:** Every Cisco ASA comes with a factory default or preinstalled initial configuration. This section explains the initial configuration and how it bootstraps an ASA so that you can connect and make configuration changes.

- **Working with Configuration Files:** This section describes the startup and running configurations that an ASA uses as it boots and runs.

- **Working with the ASA File System:** This section covers the nonvolatile flash file system that an ASA uses to store configuration files, image files, and other types of files.

- **Reloading an ASA:** This section describes the ASA bootup sequence, how you can make an ASA reload, and how you can upgrade the operating system image during a reload.

CHAPTER 2

Working with a Cisco ASA

A Cisco Adaptive Security Appliance (ASA), like any other networking device, offers several ways for an administrative user to connect to and interact with it. The command-line interface (CLI) is an important part of that process. As you work with an ASA, you also need to understand its configuration files, file systems, and how to reboot or reload it when necessary.

"Do I Know This Already?" Quiz

The "Do I Know This Already?" quiz allows you to assess whether you should read this entire chapter thoroughly or jump to the "Exam Preparation Tasks" section. If you are in doubt about your answers to these questions or your own assessment of your knowledge of the topics, read the entire chapter. Table 2-1 lists the major headings in this chapter and their corresponding "Do I Know This Already?" quiz questions. You can find the answers in Appendix A, "Answers to the 'Do I Know This Already?' Quizzes."

Table 2-1 *"Do I Know This Already?" Section-to-Question Mapping*

Foundation Topics Section	Questions
Using the CLI	1–3
Understanding the Factory Default Configuration	4–5
Working with Configuration Files	6–8
Working with the ASA File System	9–11
Reloading an ASA	12

Caution: The goal of self-assessment is to gauge your mastery of the topics in this chapter. If you do not know the answer to a question or are only partially sure of the answer, you should mark that question as wrong for purposes of the self-assessment. Giving yourself credit for an answer you correctly guess skews your self-assessment results and might provide you with a false sense of security.

1. Which of the following are modes that an ASA can offer through the CLI? (Choose all that apply.)

   a.   Configuration mode

   b.   Privileged EXEC mode

   c.   Service mode

   d.   User EXEC mode

   e.   Specific configuration mode

   f.   ROMMON mode

   g.   Routed mode

2. Which keyboard key can be used to autocomplete a command in the ASA CLI?

   a.   Space

   b.   ESC

   c.   ?

   d.   Tab

   e.   *

3. You want to display an ASA's running configuration to find any occurrence of the **deny** keyword, but the output is so large that it scrolls by too fast on your terminal emulator. Which one of the following commands can help you pinpoint the information?

   a.   **show running-config deny**

   b.   **show running-config | begin deny**

   c.   **show running-config | include deny**

   d.   **show running-config > grep deny**

   e.   **show running-config all**

4. An ASA is booted up with its initial factory default configuration. You connect a PC to the appropriate Ethernet interface on the ASA so that you can use a web browser to open an ASDM session. Which IP address should you use for the ASA in your web browser?

   a.   10.0.0.1

   b.   10.1.1.1

   c.   192.168.0.1

   d.   192.168.1.1

   e.   1.1.1.1

5. Which one of the following commands should you use to force an ASA to return to its initial factory default configuration?

   a.   **write erase**

   b.   **copy factory-config startup-config**

   c.   **configure factory-default**

   d.   **clear configure default**

   e.   **reload /default**

6. After making some configuration changes to an ASA, you would like to save the changes permanently. Which one of the following commands should you use?

- **a.** save all
- **b.** copy start run
- **c.** copy startup-config
- **d.** reload /save
- **e.** copy run start

7. Suppose you decide to use a new startup configuration file called new-startup.cfg on an ASA. Based on the following commands and console output, which startup configuration will the ASA use after it is reloaded?

```
ciscoasa# copy run disk0:/new-startup.cfg
ciscoasa# config term
ciscoasa(config)# boot config disk0:/new-startup.cfg
ciscoasa(config)# exit
ciscoasa#
ciscoasa# show bootvar
BOOT variable = disk0:/asa823-k8.bin
Current BOOT variable =
CONFIG_FILE variable =
Current CONFIG_FILE variable = disk0:/new-startup.cfg
ciscoasa# reload
```

- **a.** The initial factory default configuration.
- **b.** The original startup configuration.
- **c.** The new disk0:/new-startup.cfg file.
- **d.** The disk0:/asa823-k8.bin file.
- **e.** None; the ASA will boot into ROMMON mode.

The original startup-configuration will be used because the running configuration has not yet been saved. If the running configuration had been saved, "CONFIG_FILE variable" would be shown as "disk0:/new-startup.cfg."

8. Suppose you enter the **write erase** command on a functioning ASA. What should you do before the next time the ASA is reloaded?

- **a.** Enter **copy startup-config running-config**.
- **b.** Enter **copy running-config startup-config**.
- **c.** Do nothing, because the ASA will be just fine.
- **d.** Panic because the ASA just lost its running configuration.

9. Entering the command **dir flash:** will actually show the contents of which one of the following file systems?

    a. Running configuration

    b. /

    c. disk0:/

    d. disk1:/

    e. All of the answers are correct.

10. A new startup configuration file has been saved on an ASA as disk0:/mystartup.cfg. The **boot config disk0:/mystartup.cfg** command has already been entered. Which of the following commands can be used to view the contents of the new file? (Choose all that apply.)

    a. **show disk0:/mystartup.cfg**

    b. **show startup-config**

    c. **show running-config**

    d. **more disk0:/mystartup.cfg**

    e. **view disk0:/mystartup.cfg**

11. An ASA is currently in production in your network. Suppose that you want it to be running operating system release 8.4(8) to leverage some new features and bug fixes. The 8.4(8) image file is located on a TFTP server. The following output is obtained from the **show version**, **show boot**, and **dir flash:** commands:

```
ciscoasa# show version
Cisco Adaptive Security Appliance Software Version 8.4(2)
Device Manager Version 6.4(5)


Compiled on Fri 10-Jan-11 07:51 by builders
System image file is "disk0:/asa842-k8.bin"
Config file at boot was "startup-config"


ciscoasa up 2 days 6 hours

Hardware:   ASA5510-K8, 256 MB RAM, CPU Pentium 4 Celeron 1599 MHz
Internal ATA Compact Flash, 256MB
BIOS Flash M50FW080 @ 0xffe00000, 1024KB

Encryption hardware device : Cisco ASA-55x0 on-board accelerator (revision 0x0)
                            Boot microcode    : CN1000-MC-BOOT-2.00
                            SSL/IKE microcode: CNLite-MC-SSLm-PLUS-2.03
                            IPSec microcode   : CNlite-MC-IPSECm-MAIN-2.04
```

```
  0: Ext: Ethernet0/0          : address is 001a.a22d.1ddc, irq 9
  1: Ext: Ethernet0/1          : address is 001a.a22d.1ddd, irq 9
[output truncated for brevity]

ciscoasa# show boot

BOOT variable =
Current BOOT variable =
CONFIG_FILE variable =
Current CONFIG_FILE variable =
ciscoasa#
ciscoasa# dir flash:
Directory of disk0:/
93      -rwx   14503836     14:46:38 Sep 17 2010   asdm-645.bin
94      -rwx   15243264     14:44:02 Sep 17 2010   asa842-k8.bin
3       drwx   8192         14:04:34 Apr 27 2007   log
13      drwx   8192         14:05:02 Apr 27 2007   crypto_archive
255426560 bytes total (225050624 bytes free)
ciscoasa#
```

Which one of the following answers reflects the most logical next step you should take in the upgrade process?

   a.   Do nothing; the ASA is already running the upgraded image.

   b.   Enter the **reload** command.

   c.   Enter the **boot system disk0:/asa848-k8.bin** command.

   d.   Enter the **copy tftp: disk0:/asa848-k8.bin** command.

   e.   Enter the **copy running-config startup-config** command.

12. Which one of the following commands can be used to show the operating system version that is currently running on an ASA?

   a.   show image

   b.   show version

   c.   dir disk0:/

   d.   show system

   e.   show running-config | include image

Foundation Topics

To work with a Cisco ASA, you need to be able to interact with it and perform some basic maintenance procedures. This chapter covers the CLI, ASA configuration files, ASA file systems, and how to reload an ASA as part of the system maintenance or upgrade processes.

Using the CLI

Security professionals usually need to make changes to a firewall's security policies and its configuration. Other day-to-day tasks might include monitoring firewall activity and troubleshooting how a firewall is handling the traffic that is passing through it. An ASA offers the following ways for an administrative user to connect to and interact with it:

■   CLI by an asynchronous console connection

■   CLI by a Telnet session

■   CLI by Secure Shell (SSH) version 1.x or 2

■   Adaptive Security Device Manager (ASDM) through a web browser

In addition, before an ASA has fully booted up, it can provide a user interface to its ROM monitor bootstrap code when the normal operating system is not yet running.

Only the CLI itself is covered in this chapter. The mechanisms to reach it (Telnet, SSH, and ASDM) are covered in Chapter 5, "Managing a Cisco ASA."

The CLI-based user interface of a Cisco Firewall consists of several modes, each providing a different level of administrative capability and a different function:

■   **User EXEC mode:** By default, the initial access to an ASA places a user in user EXEC mode and offers a limited set of commands. When you connect to the firewall, a user EXEC level password is required. When you are in user EXEC mode, the ASA always gives a prompt of this form:
```
ciscoasa>
```

■   **Privileged EXEC mode:** The privileged EXEC level offers complete access to all firewall information, configuration editing, and debugging commands. Once you gain access to user EXEC mode, you can use the **enable** command to enter the privileged EXEC or "enable" mode. The ASA prompts for a password before granting access to the privileged EXEC mode. To leave privileged EXEC mode, use the **disable, quit,** or **exit** command. The syntax for entering privileged EXEC mode is as follows:
```
ciscoasa> enable
password: password
ciscoasa#
```

Notice that the ASA changes the command prompt to differentiate the privileged EXEC and user EXEC modes. For privileged EXEC mode, a pound, or number, sign (#) is added at the end of the prompt.

- **Global configuration mode:** From privileged EXEC mode, you can enter global configuration mode. From this mode, you can issue firewall commands to configure any feature that is available in the operating system. To leave configuration mode and return to EXEC mode, enter **exit** or press **Ctrl-Z**. You can also use the **exit** command to exit a submode and return to global configuration mode.

  The syntax for entering global configuration mode is as follows:
  ```
  ciscoasa# configure terminal
  ciscoasa(config)#
  ```

  Notice how the ASA added (config) to the prompt to indicate global configuration mode.

- **Specific configuration mode:** The ASA offers many specific configuration sub-modes, much like Cisco IOS Software. More specific submodes are indicated by adding a suffix after config in the command prompt. For example, interface configuration mode is indicated by ciscoasa(config-if)#.

- **ROMMON mode:** As an ASA is booting, it runs an initial firmware from its read-only memory (ROM) that provides a limited interface that you can use to monitor the ASA hardware (hence, the name ROM monitor [ROMMON]).

From the CLI, you can enter commands and get helpful information about entering commands. As well, you can filter the information that an ASA displays in a CLI session as a result of a command. These mechanisms are discussed in the following sections.

Entering Commands

You can enable a feature or parameter by entering the command and its options into a CLI session. To disable a command that is in effect, begin the command with the **no** keyword, followed by the command. Be sure to include enough options to identify the command uniquely as it exists in the ASA session or configuration. For example, the following configuration commands enable and then disable the embedded HTTP server:

```
ciscoasa(config)# http server enable
ciscoasa(config)# no http server enable
```

You can see the configuration commands that are currently in effect by using one of the following commands:

```
ciscoasa# write terminal
```

or

```
ciscoasa# show running-config [command]
```

Notice that an ASA allows you to specify a *command* keyword in the **show running-config** command. If it is included, only the related configuration commands are shown, rather than the entire configuration.

> **Note:** Some ASA configuration commands and their options are not shown if they use their default values. To see every configuration command that is enabled or active, even if it is a default, you can use the **show running-config all** [*command*] syntax.
> The running configuration is covered in more detail in the section, "Working with Configuration Files."

Commands and their options can be abbreviated with as few letters as possible without becoming ambiguous. For example, to enter configuration mode, the command **configure terminal** would normally be used. In Example 2-1, the command **configure** is shortened to **co** and the keyword **terminal** is shortened to just its first letter, **t**. Because there are other possible commands that begin with the letters "co," the command is flagged as ambiguous. Adding one more letter, **con**, successfully identifies the right command, and configuration mode is entered.

Example 2-1   *Abbreviating an ASA Command*

```
ciscoasa# co t
ERROR: % Ambiguous command:   "co t"
ciscoasa#
ciscoasa# con t
ciscoasa(config)#
```

The ASA also offers a keyword-completion function. If you enter a shortened or truncated keyword, you can press the **Tab** key to make the firewall complete the keyword for you. Keyword completion can be useful when you are entering keywords that are long or are hyphenated. For example, pressing the Tab key after entering **show ru** produces the completed command **show running-config**:

```
Firewall# show ru<Tab>
Firewall# show running-config
```

This works only if the truncated keyword is unambiguous; otherwise, the firewall can't decide which one of several similar keywords you want. If you press Tab and the keyword stays the same, you know you haven't entered enough characters to make it unambiguous.

You can edit a command line as you enter it by using the left and right arrow keys to move within the line. If you enter additional characters, the remainder of the line to the right is spaced over. You can use the Backspace and Delete keys to make corrections.

Sometimes, the firewall might display an informational or error message while you are entering a command. To see what you've entered so far, you can press **Ctrl-l** (lowercase *L*) to redisplay the line and continue editing.

For example, suppose you are trying to enter the **hostname** configuration command to change the ASA's hostname. Before you can enter the command, the ASA displays a logging message that interrupts the command line, as shown in Example 2-2. Pressing **Ctrl-l** displays the line again without all the clutter.

Example 2-2 *Redisplaying an Interrupted Command Line*

```
ciscoasa# config t

ciscoasa(config)# hostnJan 10 2012 09:21:08  %ASA-5-502103: User priv level
  changed:
Uname: enable_15 From: 1 To: 15<Ctrl-l>
ciscoasa(config)# hostn
```

Command Help

An ASA offers context-based help within the command line, much like Cisco IOS Software. Entering a question mark after a command keyword causes the ASA to list all the possible keywords or options that can be used. If you enter a question mark alone on a command line, the ASA will display *all* the available commands.

Suppose that you are interested in displaying the ASA's ARP table, but you can't remember the command syntax to use after the **show** command. Example 2-3 shows how the context-based help can be used as an aid. Entering **show ?** displays all the possible keywords that can go along with the **show** command. The **show arp** command appears to be the one that you want in this case. From there, you might use another question mark to find out what other possible parameters you can enter at the end of the **show arp** command. As shown in the example, **show arp** can be followed by the **statistics** keyword, a pipe symbol (|), or the Enter key (<cr>).

Example 2-3 *Using Context-Based Help*

```
ciscoasa# show ?
  aaa             Show information for AAA runtime data
  aaa-server      Show aaa-server configuration information
  access-list     Show hit counters for access policies
  activation-key  Show activation-key

  arp             Show ARP table or ARP statistics
  asdm            Show Device Manager history, sessions or log
  asp             Show the current contents of selected memory in the
                  Accelerated Security Path
  auto-update     Show Auto Update
  banner          Show login/session banners
  blocks          Show system buffer utilization
[output truncated for brevity]

ciscoasa# show arp ?
  statistics  Show ARP statistics
  |           Output modifiers
  <cr>
ciscoasa# show arp
```

You can also end a partially completed command keyword with a question mark if you don't know the exact spelling or form to use. The ASA will display all possible keywords that can be formed from the truncated word. For example, suppose you don't remember which commands can be used to configure access lists. In Example 2-4, entering **access?** in configuration mode reveals two possible commands: **access-group** and **access-list**. Notice that the truncated command keyword is displayed again, ready to be completed with more typing.

Example 2-4   *Using Context-Based Help to List Possible Commands*

```
ciscoasa(config)# access?
access-group  access-list
ciscoasa(config)# access
```

If you enter a command but use the wrong syntax, you see the following error:

```
Type help or '?' for a list of available commands
```

An ASA will also display a carat (^) symbol below the command-line location to point out the error. In Example 2-5, suppose you forget the correct command and enter the command **config type** rather than **config term**. The carat points to the keyword **type**, starting at the **y**, where the syntax error begins.

Example 2-5   *An ASA Pointing Out a Syntax Error*

```
Firewall# config type
             ^
ERROR: % Invalid input detected at '^' marker.
Firewall#
```

You can also use the **help** [*command*] command to display some concise information about how to use a command, a description of the command, and the command syntax. Example 2-6 shows the help output generated from entering **help passwd** from within configuration mode.

Example 2-6   *Help Output Generated from the* **help passwd** *Command*

```
ciscoasa(config)# help passwd
USAGE:
        [no] password|passwd <password> encrypted
        clear configure passwd
DESCRIPTION:
passwd          Change Telnet console access password
SYNTAX:
<password>      A password of up to 16 alphanumeric characters
                Factory-default password is cisco
```

```
encrypted         Indicate the <password> entered is encrypted
see also:         telnet
ciscoasa(config)#
```

Command History

An ASA keeps a history of the last 19 commands that were entered in each CLI session. You can see the entire history list for your current session with the **show history** command.

You can use the command history to recall a previous command that you want to use again. This can save you time in entering repetitive commands while allowing you to make edits or changes after you recall them.

Each press of the up arrow key (c) or Ctrl-p recalls the next older or previous command. Each press of the down arrow key (T) or Ctrl-n recalls the next most recent command. When you reach either end of the history cache, the firewall displays a blank command line.

When commands are recalled from the history, they can be edited as if you just entered them. You can use the left arrow key (d) or right arrow key (S) to move within the command line and begin typing to insert new characters. You can also use the Backspace or Delete key to delete characters.

Note: The arrow keys require the use of an American National Standards Institute (ANSI)-compatible terminal emulator, such as PuTTY. You can find PuTTY at www.chiark.greenend.org.uk/~sgtatham/putty/download.html.

Searching and Filtering Command Output

A **show** command can generate a long output listing. If the listing contains more lines than the terminal session can display (24 lines by default), the listing is displayed one screenful at a time, with the following prompt at the bottom:

```
<---More --->
```

To see the next screen, press the spacebar. To advance one line, press the **Enter** key one time. To exit to the command line, press the **q** key.

Sometimes, you might need to sift through a long output listing for some specific information. You can use a regular expression to match against lines of output. Regular expressions are made up of patterns—either simple text strings (such as **permit** or **route**) or more complex matching patterns. Typically, regular expressions are regular text words that offer a hint to a location in the output of a show command. You can use the following command structure to perform a regular-expression search:

Key Topic

```
Firewall# show command ...|{begin|include|exclude|grep [-v]}
   reg-expression
```

To search for a specific regular expression and start the output listing there, use the **begin** keyword. This can be useful if your firewall has a large configuration. Rather than using the spacebar to eventually find a certain configuration line, you can use **begin** to jump right to the desired line.

To display only the lines that include a regular expression, use the **include** (or **grep**) keyword. To display all lines that don't include a regular expression, use the **exclude** (or **grep-v**) keyword.

A more complex regular expression can be made up of patterns and operators. Table 2-2 lists and defines the characters that can be used as operators.

Table 2-2 *Regular Expression Operators*

Character	Description
.	Matches a single character.
*	Matches zero or more sequences of the preceding pattern.
+	Matches one or more sequences of the preceding pattern.
?	Matches zero or one occurrences of the preceding pattern.
^	Matches at the beginning of the string.
$	Matches at the end of the string.
_	Matches a comma, braces, parentheses, the beginning or end of a string, or a space.
[ ]	Defines a range of characters as a pattern.
( )	Groups characters as a pattern. If used around a pattern, the pattern can be re-called later in the expression using the backslash (\) and the pattern occurrence number.

Example 2-7 shows how the command **show log | include 302013** can be used to display all the logging messages with message ID 302013 currently stored in the logging buffer. Because message 302013 records TCP connections that are built in either the inbound or outbound direction, you might decide to rework the regular expression to find more specific information. To display only the inbound TCP connections recorded, the regular expression could be changed to include 302013, any number of other characters (.*), and the string "inbound," as shown at the bottom of the example.

Example 2-7 *Searching Through Command Output*

```
ciscoasa# show logging| include 302013
302013: Built outbound TCP connection 1788652405 for outside:69.25.38.107/80
  (69.25.38.107/80) to inside:10.1.198.156/1667 (207.246.96.46/52531)
302013: Built outbound TCP connection 1788652406 for outside:218.5.80.219/21
  (218.5.80.219/21) to inside:10.1.100.61/3528 (207.246.96.46/52532)
[output truncated]

ciscoasa# show log| include 302013.*inbound
```

```
302013: Built inbound TCP connection 1788639636 for outside:216.117.177.135/54780
  (216.117.177.135/54780) to inside:10.1.3.16/25 (207.246.96.46/25)
ciscoasa#
```

You might also use a regular expression to display command output that contains IP addresses within a range. For example, the following command filters the output to contain only IP addresses that begin with 10.10.5, 10.10.6, and 10.10.7:

```
ciscoasa# show log | include 10.10.[5-7].*
```

Terminal Screen Format

By default, all output from an ASA is displayed for a terminal session screen that is 80 characters wide by 24 lines long. To change the terminal screen width, use the following configuration command:

```
ciscoasa(config)# terminal width characters
```

Here, *characters* is a value from 40 to 511. You can also specify 0, meaning the full 511-character width.

To change the screen length, or the number of lines displayed when paging through a large amount of output, use the following configuration command:

```
ciscoasa(config)# pager [lines] number
```

Here, *number* can be any positive value starting at 1. The **lines** keyword is optional, where the number of lines given is the same either with or without it.

You can also disable screen paging completely by using **pager 0** or **no pager**. This action might be useful if you are capturing a large configuration or logging message output with a terminal emulator. With paging disabled, all of the output could scroll by and be captured into the emulator's capture buffer. Otherwise, you would have to use the spacebar to page through the output and then later remove all the <-- More --> prompts that were captured.

Using Cisco ASDM

Cisco ASDM provides a GUI that you can use to administer, configure, and monitor an ASA. Although ASDM does not use a regular web browser, it does use the HTTPS protocol to communicate with the ASA.

To access ASDM, you need a PC-based launcher utility. The launcher allows you to select an ASA and enter administrator credentials. The launcher will then connect to the ASA, download the ASDM application (if it has not already been installed on the PC), and automatically launch it on the PC.

Before you can use ASDM, you need to enter an initial "bootstrap" configuration in the
ASA using the following steps:

Step 1.   Copy an ASDM image file into ASA flash memory.

Use a file transfer method such as TFTP to copy an ASDM image file from
your PC to the ASA's flash memory. Be aware that a specific ASDM image release might work with only a specific release of the ASA operating system.
You can verify that the ASDM image is ready to use by using the **dir disk0:/**
command to display the flash file system contents, as shown here:

```
ciscoasa# dir disk0:/
Directory of disk0:/
132     -rwx   17232256      18:37:02 Nov 02 2011   asdm-645.bin
131     -rwx   25159680      18:36:08 Nov 02 2011   asa842-k8.bin
3       drwx   8192          14:04:34 Apr 27 2007   log
13      drwx   8192          14:05:02 Apr 27 2007   crypto_archive

255426560 bytes total (225050624 bytes free)
ciscoasa#
```

Step 2.   Specify the ASDM image file to use.

Use the **asdm image** configuration command to specify which ASDM image
file to use. For example, the following command tells the ASA to use ASDM
release 6.4(5), contained in file disk0:/asdm-645.bin:

```
ciscoasa(config)# asdm image disk0:/asdm-645.bin
```

Once the ASDM image file has been specified, you can use the **show asdm
image** command to display the file location and name.

Step 3.   Enable the HTTP server process.

Use the following command to enable the HTTP server on the ASA. Both
HTTP and HTTPS are supported, although ASDM uses only HTTPS.

```
ciscoasa(config)# http server enable
```

Step 4.   Specify IP addresses that are permitted to access ASDM.

Because ASDM uses the HTTP server process, you can enter the following
command to specify which IP addresses are permitted to access ASDM
through a specified interface:

```
ciscoasa(config)# http ip-address subnet-mask interface
```

For example, you can use the following commands to permit clients in the
192.168.100.0/24 subnet on the outside interface and 192.168.2.0/24 on the inside interface to access ASDM:

```
ciscoasa(config)# http 192.168.100.0 255.255.255.0 outside
ciscoasa(config)# http 192.168.2.0 255.255.255.0 inside
```

You can also use the **http 0.0.0.0 0.0.0.0 outside** command to permit ASDM
access to any host on the outside interface.

Next, you need to access ASDM for the first time. Open a web browser to the ASA interface that you have configured to permit HTTP connections. In Figure 2-1, the web
browser has been opened to https://192.168.100.10—the outside interface of an ASA.

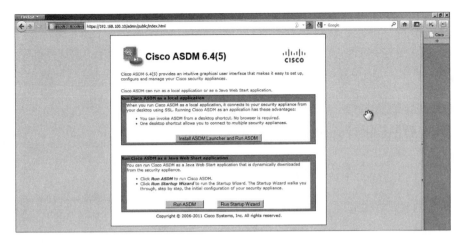

Figure 2-1 *Accessing ASDM*

The initial ASDM page gives you the following three options:

- **Install ASDM Launcher and Run ASDM:** The Launcher and ASDM will run as native applications on the PC, without the need for a web browser.

- **Run ASDM:** You can run ASDM from within the web browser as a Java application.

- **Run Startup Wizard:** ASDM will initiate a wizard to step you through the initial ASA configuration, if you have not already done so.

The first option is the most common choice and needs to be done only once. After the Launcher application is installed, you can run it directly to initiate an ASDM session. Click the **Install ASDM Launcher and Run ASDM** button. You will be prompted for an ASA username and password. The installer must authenticate with the ASA to download the Launcher file. ASDM always needs "enable" or the highest available user access in order to launch and run.

Next, the ASA prompts you to enter a location to store the downloaded Launcher installer, as shown in Figure 2-2. Click **Save File** and browse to the desired location. Once the installer file has been downloaded onto your PC, find the file and double-click it. The Launcher application will install and run automatically.

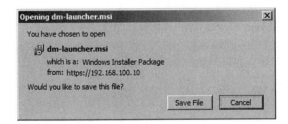

Figure 2-2 *Saving the ASDM Installer File*

Figure 2-3 shows the ASDM Launcher application. To connect to an ASA and begin an ASDM session, enter the ASA's IP address and administrator credentials. The IP address will be cached and added to a list of possible ASAs so that you can choose from a list the next time you run the Launcher.

Figure 2-3   *ASDM Launcher Application*

Once the Launcher successfully connects to the ASA, the full-blown ASDM application window appears. Figure 2-4 shows the initial ASDM Home view. By clicking the buttons in the upper-left portion of the window, you can navigate through the following functions:

■   **Home:** Displays information about the ASA platform, VPN sessions, CPU and memory resource usage, interface status, and traffic bandwidth.

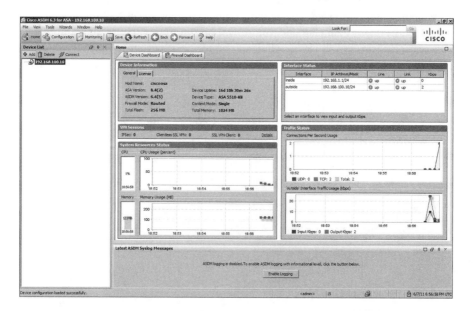

Figure 2-4   *ASDM Home View*

- **Configuration:** Provides a hierarchy of ASA features and parameters that you configure and verify.

- **Monitoring:** Offers categories and lists of specific ASA parameters that you can monitor or observe.

At any time, you can click the **Save** button to save the current running configuration to the startup configuration, or click the **Refresh** button to load the current running configuration into ASDM.

In Configuration view, which is shown in Figure 2-5, you can select any of the following different feature categories in the lower-left area of the window:

- **Device Setup:** Features such as interfaces, routing, device name, and system time that are necessary for the ASA to operate

- **Firewall:** Stateful inspection features needed to inspect traffic and secure a network

- **Remote Access VPN:** Virtual private networks (VPN) used for remote clients to securely connect to the ASA

- **Site-to-Site VPN:** VPNs used for remote sites to securely connect to the ASA

- **Device Management:** Features such as management access, feature licensing, high availability, logging, DNS, and DHCP services

After selecting a feature category, you can select a specific feature to configure from the list in the middle-left portion of the ASDM window. You can then configure individual parameters that are shown in the main part of the window.

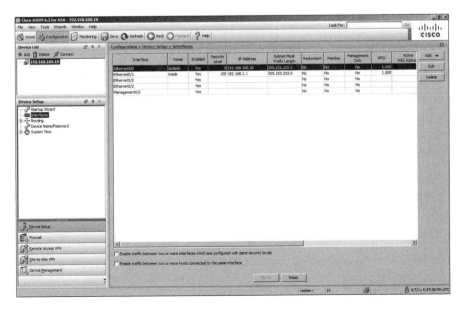

Figure 2-5 *ASDM Configuration View*

As you make configuration changes in ASDM, be aware that the changes are not made to the ASA dynamically. Instead, you must click the **Apply** button that is shown in Configuration view to actually apply the ASDM changes to the ASA's running configuration.

In Monitoring view, shown in Figure 2-6, you can select categories of ASA functions to monitor. For example, you can select interface operation, VPN status, routing activity, device properties, and logging.

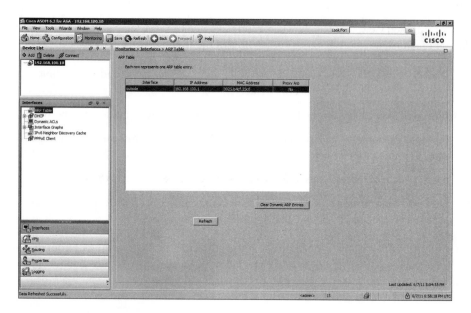

Figure 2-6   *ASDM Monitoring View*

Understanding the Factory Default Configuration

When an ASA boots for the first time, it comes up running a factory default or initial configuration. For the most part, the configuration is barebones, but provides enough functionality so that someone can connect a PC to the ASA and configure it further.

The initial configuration brings up the following basic functions:

■   One interface is set aside as a protected "management" network, where a PC will be connected.

■   A DHCP server is enabled on the management network, to automatically provide an IP address for the PC.

■   An HTTP server is enabled on the management network, to allow the PC to access secure web-based ASDM sessions with the ASA via HTTPS over TCP port 443.

In the initial configuration, the management interface is always configured to use IP address 192.168.1.1 and subnet mask 255.255.255.0. The DHCP server is configured to provide addresses from a range of 192.168.1.2 to 192.168.1.254. The HTTP server is configured to allow ASDM sessions from devices on the 192.168.1.0/24 management network.

On ASA 5510 and higher platforms, the initial configuration always uses the Management0/0 physical interface for the management network, as shown in the top portion of Figure 2-7. The ASA 5505, however, doesn't have a dedicated management interface. Instead, it uses VLAN 1 for the secure "inside" network, which is assigned to physical interfaces Ethernet0/1 through 0/7.

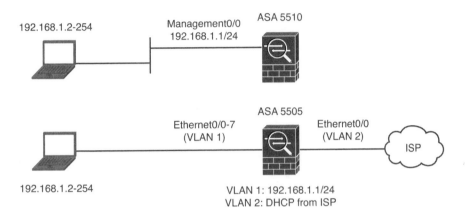

Figure 2-7   *Using the ASA Factory Default Configuration*

Because the ASA 5505 is usually installed in smaller environments, it often connects directly to an Internet service provider (ISP) through a broadband connection. The ASA 5505 default configuration provides basic connectivity from its inside network to the outside world, as shown in the bottom portion of Figure 2-7. The outside network must be connected to physical interface Ethernet0/0, which is mapped to VLAN 2. The ASA is configured to obtain an IP address for its outside interface automatically, through a DHCP request. Then, any device that is connected to the inside network will have its IP address translated as it passes through the ASA toward the outside world.

At any time in the future, you can force an ASA to return to its factory default configuration by entering the **configure factory-default** command in configuration mode. Be aware that this command immediately takes effect, with no further confirmation, as shown in Example 2-8. If you are connected to the ASA remotely, through Telnet, SSH, or ASDM, you will likely be cut off; instead, you should enter this command only while directly connected to the ASA console port.

Example 2-8   *Returning an ASA to the Factory Default Configuration*

```
ciscoasa(config)# configure factory-default
Based on the management IP address and mask, the DHCP address
pool size is reduced to 253 from the platform limit 256
```

```
WARNING: The boot system configuration will be cleared.
The first image found in disk0:/ will be used to boot the
system on the next reload.
Verify there is a valid image on disk0:/ or the system will
not boot.


Begin to apply factory-default configuration:
Clear all configuration
Executing command: interface management0/0
Executing command: nameif management
INFO: Security level for "management" set to 0 by default.
Executing command: ip address 192.168.1.1 255.255.255.0
Executing command: security-level 100
Executing command: no shutdown
Executing command: exit
Executing command: http server enable
Executing command: http 192.168.1.0 255.255.255.0 management
Executing command: dhcpd address 192.168.1.2-192.168.1.254 management
Executing command: dhcpd enable management
Executing command: logging asdm informational
Factory-default configuration is completed
ciscoasa(config)#
```

Working with Configuration Files

An ASA keeps a "startup" configuration file in flash memory. The configuration commands in the startup configuration are not lost after a reload or power failure. As soon as an ASA boots, the startup configuration commands are copied to the "running" configuration file in RAM (volatile) memory. Any command that is entered or copied into the running configuration is also executed at that time.

You can see the contents of the startup configuration by entering the **show startup-config** command, as demonstrated in Example 2-9. The first line denotes that the startup configuration has been saved at least once in the ASA's lifetime. The next line records a timestamp that shows the last date and time that the running configuration has been saved to the startup configuration. In addition, a user called enable_15 (someone in privileged EXEC or enable mode) saved the configuration.

Example 2-9 *Displaying the Startup Configuration Contents*

```
ciscoasa# show startup-config
: Saved

: Written by enable_15 at 13:47:39.249 UTC Wed Nov 9 2011
!
ASA Version 8.4(2)
!
```

```
hostname ciscoasa
enable password 8Ry2YjIyt7RRXU24 encrypted
passwd 2KFQnbNIdI.2KYOU encrypted
names
!
interface Ethernet0/0
 shutdown
 no nameif
[output truncated for clarity]
```

You can see the current contents of the running configuration by entering the **show running-config** command. If the configuration is lengthy, you can always use the CLI filtering tools to jump to a specific string or to pick out specific items. For example, if you want to start the display where the **access-list** commands are located, you could use the **show running-config | begin access-list** command. Rather than paging through large amounts of configuration output, you can instantly find what you're looking for.

From the CLI, you can start editing the running configuration by entering the **configure terminal** command. Any number of commands can then be entered. When you are finished editing, use the **quit** command or press **Ctrl-Z**.

After you enter new configuration commands, be aware that they are present only in the temporary running configuration. After you verify the operation of the new configuration commands, you should be sure to save the running configuration into flash memory. This preserves the configuration in case the firewall reloads later.

ASA platforms can maintain one or more startup configuration files in flash, provided that there is sufficient space to store them. Only one of these can be used at boot time. Having multiple startup configurations makes configuration rollback easy. For example, the startup configuration contents can be saved in one file during the time that the firewall configuration is stable. If major configuration changes need to be made, the new, updated running configuration can be saved to a new, different startup configuration file.

The next time the ASA is booted, it can use this new startup configuration file. Then, if you encounter problems with the new configuration, you can make one configuration change to force the firewall to roll back or use a previous version of the startup configuration, found in the original file in flash memory.

By default, an ASA stores its startup configuration in a hidden partition of flash memory. That file has no usable name and can be viewed only through the **show startup-configuration** command.

To force the ASA to use a different startup configuration filename, use the following command:

```
ciscoasa(config)# boot config url
```

Here, *url* represents the location of the startup configuration file. It can be **flash:***path*, **disk0:***path*, or **disk1:***path*, where *path* represents the directory path that points to the file. For example, if a new startup configuration is stored in a file called newconfig in the root directory of the disk0: flash file system, you would enter the **boot config disk0:/ newconfig** command.

The **boot config** *url* command effectively changes an environment variable used only by the running configuration. When you use this command, be sure to save the running configuration with the **copy running-config startup-config** command. At this point, the ASA uses the new *url* and saves the startup configuration in that file, not in the default hidden location. If the file doesn't exist, a new file is created; if it does exist, the running configuration is merged with that file's contents. The environment variable is also updated and is used during the next boot cycle to find the new startup configuration file automatically.

You can see the current startup configuration environment variable with the **show bootvar** command. In Example 2-10, an ASA begins with the default startup configuration location, signified by the empty Current CONFIG FILE variable value. When the **boot config** command is used, the current value is updated to show the new file location.

However, until the running configuration is saved to the new startup configuration location, the new file is not even present in the flash memory. As well, the startup configuration file used at boot time is still the default (shown by an empty CONFIG FILE variable line). The running configuration must be saved before the new file can be used during the next firewall boot.

Example 2-10   *Using a New Startup Configuration File*

```
ciscoasa# show bootvar
BOOT variable = disk0:/asa842-k8.bin
Current BOOT variable =
CONFIG_FILE variable =
Current CONFIG_FILE variable =
ciscoasa#


ciscoasa# config term
ciscoasa(config)# boot config disk0:/new-startup.cfg
ciscoasa(config)# exit
ciscoasa#
ciscoasa# show bootvar
BOOT variable = disk0:/asa842-k8.bin
Current BOOT variable =
CONFIG_FILE variable =
Current CONFIG_FILE variable = disk0:/new-startup.cfg
ciscoasa#


ciscoasa# copy running-config startup-config
Source filename [running-config]?
Cryptochecksum: afbf65d8 203b6346 b1251849 000dfa47


2981 bytes copied in 3.350 secs (993 bytes/sec)
ciscoasa#
```

```
ciscoasa# show bootvar
BOOT variable =
Current BOOT variable =
CONFIG_FILE variable = disk0:/new-startup.cfg
Current CONFIG_FILE variable = disk0:/new-startup.cfg
ciscoasa#
```

Notice that even though a new location and a new filename are used for the startup configuration, you don't have to specify those when you save the running configuration from that point on. The firewall continues to work with the **startup-config** keyword, but it uses the new URL to reference the actual file. In other words, **copy running-config startup-config** will automatically save the running configuration in the new file location in flash memory.

Clearing an ASA Configuration

Sometimes, you might need to clear a portion of the running configuration on an ASA if a function is no longer needed. On other occasions, you might need to clear the entire running configuration so that an existing ASA can be redeployed in a different scenario. You can use one of the following forms of the **clear configure** command in global configuration mode to erase all or certain parts of the running configuration:

- **clear configure all:** Clears the entire running configuration

- **clear configure primary:** Clears all commands related to connectivity, including the **ip address**, **mtu**, **monitor-interface**, **boot**, **route**, **failover**, **tftp-server**, and **shun** commands

- **clear configure secondary:** Clears all commands not related to ASA connectivity

- **clear configure** *command***:** Clears all commands that use the *command* keyword

Usually, you can disable or delete individual commands out of a running configuration by re-entering the command, but beginning with the **no** keyword. For example, if an interface has been configured with an IP address by using the **ip address 192.168.1.1 255.255.255.0** interface configuration command, you can clear the IP address by using the **no ip address 192.168.1.1 255.255.255.0** command. Some commands don't allow the use of the **no** keyword. In those cases, **clear configure** *command* can be used instead.

In Example 2-11, an ASA has an access list already added to its running configuration. A single access list entry can be deleted by beginning with the **no** keyword and repeating the access list entry command as it appears in the running configuration. However, the entire access list cannot be deleted by entering the **no access-list test** command. Instead, the **access-list test** command is cleared with the **clear configure access-list test** global configuration command.

Example 2-11   *Clearing Portions of an ASA Running Configuration*

```
ciscoasa# show running-config access-list test
access-list test extended permit ip any any
access-list test extended permit tcp any any
access-list test extended permit udp any any
access-list test extended permit icmp any any
ciscoasa#
ciscoasa# configure terminal
ciscoasa(config)# no access-list test extended permit ip any any
ciscoasa(config)#
ciscoasa(config)# no access-list test
ERROR: % Incomplete command
ciscoasa(config)#
ciscoasa(config)# clear configure access-list test
ciscoasa(config)# exit
ciscoasa# show running-config access-list test
ciscoasa#
```

Finally, you might have to clear the entire startup configuration if you need to take an ASA out of service or reboot it with an empty configuration. You could use the **clear configure all** configuration command to clear out the running configuration, followed by the **copy running-config startup-config** command to save the empty running configuration into the startup configuration.

A much easier approach is to use the **write erase** command, which erases everything in the startup configuration directly. This command does not disturb or erase the current running configuration. After the startup configuration is erased, you can reboot the ASA. Refer to the section, "Reloading an ASA," for more information.

Working with the ASA File System

A Cisco ASA has a built-in flash (nonvolatile) memory file system that contains files such as an operating system image, a management application image, and the firewall configuration.

When an ASA boots, it uncompresses and copies an executable operating system image from flash into RAM. The image is actually run from RAM. While an image is being run, a different image can be copied or written into flash memory. In fact, the running image can be safely overwritten in flash, because it is run from RAM. The new image is not run until the next time the ASA reloads.

The management application, ASDM, is run from a separate file in the flash file system. ASDM offers a GUI front end to manage the ASA, and is run only on demand. The operating system and ASDM images must be compatible before ASDM can be used.

An image file can be transferred into an ASA's flash memory by any of the following methods:

- TFTP at the monitor prompt, as the ASA begins its bootup procedure

- TFTP from an administrative session (ASA console, Telnet, or SSH)

- HTTP or HTTPS from a web server via ASDM

An ASA can also poll an Auto Update Server (AUS) device periodically to see if a new image is available for it. If so, the image is downloaded automatically using HTTPS.

After an ASDM image is downloaded into flash memory, it can be used immediately. After an operating system image is downloaded, however, the ASA must be manually rebooted so that it can run the new image.

Navigating an ASA Flash File System

ASA devices organize their flash file systems much like a traditional Cisco IOS file system, which must be formatted, and can contain a tree of directories, each containing arbitrary files. An ASA supports several different devices that can each contain a file system. For example, every ASA offers a disk0: and a flash: device. These both refer to the same internal flash memory file system. When you connect to an ASA, your session begins in the disk0:/ root directory. That directory can contain other files or subdirectories that also contain files and subdirectories, and so on. ASA models also support a disk1: device, which is a removable flash drive.

To view the contents of a flash directory, use the **dir** [*device*:][*path*] command. The device and pathname fields are each optional. If you omit the device name, the disk0: device is assumed. If you omit the pathname, the current directory is assumed. You can also use regular expressions or wildcard characters in the pathname to match specific patterns within filenames. Example 2-12 shows the contents of the flash file system in disk0:/.

Example 2-12 *Listing the Contents of an ASA Flash File System*

```
ciscoasa# dir disk0:/
Directory of disk0:/
131    -rwx  25159680     18:36:08 Nov 02 2011  asa842-k8.bin
132    -rwx  17232256     18:37:02 Nov 02 2011  asdm-645.bin
3      drwx  8192         13:52:08 Sep 09 2010  log
6      drwx  8192         13:52:08 Sep 09 2010  crypto_archive
255426560 bytes total (231604224 bytes free)
ciscoasa#
```

You can also add the **/all** keyword to list all the files in the directory, and add the **/recursive** keyword to recursively look in all nested directories and list the files that are found along the way.

You can use the **cd** [*device*:][*path*] command to change to a different directory. For example, the **cd disk:/log** command would move the CLI session into the log subdirectory. Because you can move around within the flash file system hierarchy, it's easy to forget where the current directory is pointed. You can use the **pwd** command to see the current directory location for your CLI session.

If you need to create a new directory to hold some files, you can use the **mkdir** [**/noconfirm**] [*device*:]*path* command. To remove a directory, you can use the **rmdir**

[/**noconfirm**] [*device*:]*path* command. A directory must be empty of all files and other directories before it can be removed.

By default, the ASA will ask you to confirm each item that is created or deleted. You can use the /**noconfirm** option to proceed without any confirmation.

Working with Files in an ASA File System

You can manipulate any files that are stored in an ASA's file system. For example, to view the contents of a file, use the following command:

```
more [/ascii|/binary|/ebcdic] [device:]path
```

The file found at *device:path* is displayed, one page at a time, in the current CLI session. By default, the file contents are shown as plain text. You can add the /**ascii** or /**binary** option to display both hex and ASCII representations of the file contents. Similarly, the /**ebcdic** option displays the contents in both EBCDIC and ASCII. In Example 2-13, the contents of the disk0:/mytest text file is displayed, first in plain text, then in hex and ASCII.

Example 2-13 *Displaying File Contents*

```
ciscoasa# more disk0:/mytest
hello this is a test
the end
ciscoasa#
ciscoasa#
ciscoasa# more /ascii disk0:/mytest
00000000:   68656c6c 6f207468 69732069 73206120    hell o th is i s a
00000010:   74657374 0d0a7468 6520656e 64XXXXXX    test ..th e en dXXX
ciscoasa#
```

Note: Be careful when you use the **more** command. If you attempt to view the contents of a large binary file, such as by using **more image.bin** to view the ASA image file, you could be stuck waiting a long time while every byte is shown as a literal (and often cryptic) character to your CLI session. If you want to look at the contents of a binary file, always use the **more /binary** or **more /ascii** forms of the command.

Key Topic

You can also copy files to and from an ASA file system. This becomes useful when you need to download a new image file into an ASA or upload a configuration or log file from an ASA. Use one of the following commands to copy a file from an ASA or to an ASA, respectively:

```
copy [/noconfirm] source destination
```

Here, the source and destination fields can be given in the form *device:path*, using the options listed in Table 2-3. You can also copy the running configuration or the startup configuration by using the **running-config** and **startup-config** keywords for either source or destination.

Table 2-3 *Source and Destination Designations for Copying Files*

Source or Destination	Description
disk0:*path*	
disk1:*path*	
flash:*path*	An ASA flash file system device
ftp:*url*	An FTP server, where the path is given as a URL
http:*url*	
https:*url*	A web server, where the path is given as a URL
smb:*url*	A UNIX file server, where the path is given as a URL
tftp:*url*	A TFTP server, where the path is given as a URL

You can also use source and destination device names alone, without specifying paths or filenames. In that case, the ASA will prompt for each of the missing fields before the file copy begins.

Example 2-14 demonstrates three different uses of the **copy** command. First, an ASA image file asa843-k8.bin is copied from a TFTP server to the ASA's disk0: file system. All the file copy parameters are given in the command line. Notice that the ASA still prompts for each parameter and offers the command-line parameters as a default for each. Second, an ASDM image file is copied from a TFTP server to flash, but the parameters have been omitted from the command line to force the ASA to prompt for them. Finally, the running configuration is copied from the ASA to a TFTP server.

Example 2-14 *Copying Files to an ASA File System*

```
ciscoasa# copy tftp://192.168.100.10/asa843-k8.bin disk0:/asa843-k8.bin
Address or name of remote host [192.168.100.10]?
Source filename [asa843-k8.bin]?
Destination filename [asa843-k8.bin]?

Accessing tftp://192.168.100.10/asa843-k8.bin...!!!!!!!!!!!!!!!!!!!!!!!!!!!!!
!!!!!!!!!!!!!!!!!!!!!!!!!!!!!!!!!!!!!!!!!!!!!!!!!!!!!!!!!!!!!!!!!!!!!!!!!!!!!!!
!!!!!!!!!!!!!!!!!!!!!!!!!!!!!!!!!!!!!!!!!!!!!!!!!!!!!!!!!!!!!
Writing file disk0:asa843-k8.bin...
!!!!!!!!!!!!!!!!!!!!!!!!!!!!!!!!!!!!!!!!!!!!!!!!!!!!!!!!!!!!!!!!!!!!!!!!!!!!!!!!
!!!!!!!!!!!!!!!!!!!!!!!!!!!!!!!!!!!!!!!!!!!!!!!!!!!!!!!!!!!!!!!!!!!!!!!!!!!!!!!!
!!!!!!!!!!!
14524416 bytes copied in 31.200 secs (465526 bytes/sec)
ciscoasa#

ciscoasa# copy tftp: disk0:
Address or name of remote host [192.168.100.10]?
```

```
Source filename [asdm-646.bin]?
Destination filename [asdm-646.bin]?


Accessing tftp://192.168.100.10/asdm-646.bin...!!!!!!!!!!!!!!!!!!!!!!!!!!!!
!!!!!!!!!!!!!!!!!!!!!!!!!!!!!!!!!!!!!!!!!!!!!!!!!!!!!!!!!!!!!!!!!!!!!!!!!!!!!
!!!!!!!!!!!!!!!!!!!!!!!!!!!!!!!!!!!!!!!!!!!!!!!!!!!!!!!!!!!!!!!!!!!!!!!!!
Writing file disk0:asdm-646.bin...
!!!!!!!!!!!!!!!!!!!!!!!!!!!!!!!!!!!!!!!!!!!!!!!!!!!!!!!!!!!!!!!!!!!!!!!!!!!!!!
!!!!!!!!!!!!!!!!!!!!!!!!!!!!!!!!!!!!!!!!!!!!!!!!!!!!!!!!!!!!!!!!!!!!!!!!!!!!!!
!!!!!!!!!!!
14503836 bytes copied in 42.700 secs (338668 bytes/sec)
ciscoasa#


ciscoasa# copy running-config tftp:
Source filename [running-config]?
Address or name of remote host []? 192.168.100.10
Destination filename [running-config]? ciscoasa-confg
Cryptochecksum: 3313140e 3161fb4a 30902dbb 8e519a27
!
1598 bytes copied in 2.10 secs (799 bytes/sec)
ciscoasa#
```

Note: If you are copying files to or from a server that requires user authentication or a specific port number, you can add the extra information in the following URL format: ftp://[username[:password]@]server[:port]/[path/]filename

To rename an existing file in a flash file system, you can use the following command:

```
ciscoasa# rename [/noconfirm] [device:]source-path [device:]destination-path
```

In Example 2-15, the file **backup-config** is renamed to **config-old**. Because the CLI session begins in the disk0:/ directory, the device names can be omitted from the command.

Example 2-15 *Renaming a File in an ASA File System*

```
ciscoasa# pwd
disk0:/
ciscoasa# rename backup-config config-old
Source filename [backup-config]?
Destination filename [config-old]?
ciscoasa#
```

Finally, you can delete files from an ASA file system with the following command:

```
ciscoasa# delete [/noconfirm] [/recursive] [device:]path
```

You can use the **/noconfirm** keyword to delete the file without being asked to confirm the action. Without this keyword, you must press the **Enter** key each time the ASA prompts you for confirmation. You can also delete an entire directory and all of its contents recursively by using the **/recursive** keyword.

In Example 2-16, suppose an old configuration file called **reallyold-config** exists in flash and needs to be deleted. First, a directory is shown to find the correct filename, and then the file is deleted.

Example 2-16 *Deleting a File in an ASA File System*

```
ciscoasa# dir disk0:/
Directory of disk0:/
131     -rwx   25159680      18:36:08 Nov 02 2011   asa842-k8.bin
132     -rwx   17232256      18:37:02 Nov 02 2011   asdm-645.bin
3       drwx   8192          13:52:08 Sep 09 2010   log
6       drwx   8192          13:52:08 Sep 09 2010   crypto_archive
83      -rwx   2946          16:36:04 Sep 09 2010   reallyold-config
255426412 bytes total (231604034 bytes free)
ciscoasa#
ciscoasa# delete reallyold-config
Delete filename [reallyold-config]?
Delete disk0:/reallyold-config? [confirm]
ciscoasa#
```

You can also destroy or erase an entire flash file system in special cases, where the entire contents of the flash memory (both accessible and hidden flash file systems) need to be erased. This might be desirable if an ASA is to be turned over or transferred to a different owner and the flash contents need to remain confidential. To do this, use the **erase** *device:* or **format** *device:* command, with **disk0:**, **disk1:**, or **flash:** as the device name.

Every file, including image files, configuration files, and licensing files, is overwritten with a 0xFF data pattern so that it is completely removed. A generic flash file system is then rebuilt, but no other files are created. Even after the flash file system is erased, the ASA can continue to operate because its image file and running configuration are already loaded into RAM. However, once the ASA is rebooted, its operation will be affected.

Reloading an ASA

An ASA allows one or more operating system images to be stored in flash memory, as long as there is sufficient space to store them. Naturally, only one of the image files can be running on the firewall at any time, so you must select one file for use. Use the following command to select the bootable image:

```
ciscoasa(config)# boot system device:path
```

The ASA searches for the specified file as soon as the command is entered, just to confirm that the image file exists. If the file can't be found in a flash file system, the command is accepted but a warning message is displayed.

The **boot system** command is stored in the running configuration after it is entered. It should also be written into the startup configuration so that the image can be identified during the next reload or bootup sequence. Once the startup configuration has been written, the ASA also stores the image file location in an environment variable called BOOT.

With a factory default configuration, the **boot system** command is not present and the BOOT environment variable is empty. Therefore, as it boots, the ASA will search for and run the first valid image file it can find in its flash file system.

You can use the **show version** command to find out information about the ASA hardware platform and which operating system image and release are currently running. In Example 2-17, the ASA 5510 is running image release 8.4(2) (found at disk0:/asa842-k8.bin) and ASDM 6.4(5).

Example 2-17 *Determining ASA Hardware Platform, OS Image, and Release Information*

```
ciscoasa# show version
Cisco Adaptive Security Appliance Software Version 8.4(2)
Device Manager Version 6.4(5)

Compiled on Wed 15-Jun-11 18:17 by builders
System image file is "disk0:/asa842-k8.bin"
Config file at boot was "startup-config"

ciscoasa up 16 days 14 hours

Hardware:   ASA5510-K8, 1024 MB RAM, CPU Pentium 4 Celeron 1600 MHz
Internal ATA Compact Flash, 256MB
BIOS Flash M50FW080 @ 0xfff00000, 1024KB

Encryption hardware device : Cisco ASA-55x0 on-board accelerator (revision 0x0)
                            Boot microcode    : CN1000-MC-BOOT-2.00
                            SSL/IKE microcode: CNLite-MC-SSLm-PLUS-2.03
                            IPSec microcode   : CNlite-MC-IPSECm-MAIN-2.06
 0: Ext: Ethernet0/0        : address is 001a.a22d.1ddc, irq 9
 1: Ext: Ethernet0/1        : address is 001a.a22d.1ddd, irq 9
 2: Ext: Ethernet0/2        : address is 001a.a22d.1dde, irq 9
 3: Ext: Ethernet0/3        : address is 001a.a22d.1ddf, irq 9
 4: Ext: Management0/0      : address is 001a.a22d.1ddb, irq 11
 5: Int: Internal-Data0/0   : address is 0000.0001.0002, irq 11
[output truncated for clarity]
```

Upgrading the ASA Software at the Next Reload

By configuring the bootable image location, you can toggle between two image files to upgrade to a different software release. The upgrade procedure is straightforward by following these steps:

Step 1. Copy a new operating system image file onto the flash file system.

Step 2. Use the **boot system** command to point to the new image file.

Step 3. Save the running configuration with the **copy running-config startup-config** command.

Step 4. Reload the ASA.

You can also enter the **boot system** command more than once to configure a list of image files that can be executed. The list of filenames is tried in sequence so that if one file is not found in flash memory, the next file is tried, and so on.

You can display the current boot image setting with the **show bootvar** command. In Example 2-18, an ASA has two operating system image files in the disk0: file system. The ASA is currently running the asa823-k8.bin image file. A new image file named asa842-k8.bin has been copied onto the disk0: file system.

Notice that the example begins with an empty BOOT variable. The asa823-k8.bin image was the only valid image found at bootup time. The **boot system disk0:/asa842-k8.bin** command is then entered so that the ASA will run an upgraded image after its next reload. Immediately afterward, the Current BOOT variable line indicates that the new image has been identified, but will not yet be used.

Finally, the running configuration is saved to the startup configuration. At that point, the BOOT variable = line shows that the new image file will be booted at the next ASA reload.

Example 2-18 *Preparing to Boot a Different Operating System Image File*

```
ciscoasa# show bootvar
BOOT variable =
Current BOOT variable =
CONFIG_FILE variable =
Current CONFIG_FILE variable =
ciscoasa#

ciscoasa# dir disk0:
Directory of disk0:/
86      -rwx  15243264    22:49:21 Sep  9 2010  asa823-k8.bin
131     -rwx  25159680    18:36:08 Nov 02 2011  asa842-k8.bin
132     -rwx  17232256    18:37:02 Nov 02 2011  asdm-645.bin
3       drwx  8192        13:56:28 Sep 30 2009  log
6       drwx  8192        13:56:28 Sep 30 2009  crypto_archive
255426560 bytes total (233480192 bytes free)
ciscoasa#
```

```
ciscoasa# configure terminal
ciscoasa(config)# boot system disk0:/asa842-k8.bin
ciscoasa(config)#
ciscoasa# show bootvar
BOOT variable =
Current BOOT variable = disk0:/asa842-k8.bin
CONFIG_FILE variable =
Current CONFIG_FILE variable =
ciscoasa#

ciscoasa# copy running-config startup-config
Source filename [running-config]?
Cryptochecksum: 8e6d767d 3b9988d9 4758e4a7 6511b017
2756 bytes copied in 3.780 secs (918 bytes/sec)
ciscoasa#
ciscoasa# show bootvar
BOOT variable = disk0:/asa842-k8.bin
Current BOOT variable = disk0:/asa842-k8.bin
CONFIG_FILE variable =
Current CONFIG_FILE variable =
ciscoasa#
```

Performing a Reload

You can force an ASA to reload immediately by issuing the **reload** command alone. The ASA will check to see if the running configuration has already been saved; if not, it will prompt to ask if the configuration should be saved before reloading. The ASA will then prompt to ask if you want to proceed with the reload. To confirm, you simply press the **Enter** key. Any other response will cancel the reload. Once the reload process begins, the ASA performs an orderly shutdown of all of its subsystems and processes. Example 2-19 demonstrates the reload procedure.

Example 2-19 *Manually Reloading an ASA*

```
ciscoasa# reload
System config has been modified. Save? [Y]es/[N]o: Y
Cryptochecksum: 7565471f dc99fab5 64b052ca 952ce15c
2299 bytes copied in 1.550 secs (2299 bytes/sec)
Proceed with reload? [confirm]
ciscoasa#
***
*** --- START GRACEFUL SHUTDOWN ---
Shutting down isakmp
Shutting down webvpn
Shutting down File system
```

```
***
*** --- SHUTDOWN NOW ---
Process shutdown finished
Rebooting.....
CISCO SYSTEMS
Embedded BIOS Version 1.0(12)6 08/21/06 17:26:53.43
Low Memory: 632 KB
High Memory: 251 MB
[output truncated for clarity]
```

You can also schedule a reload for a specific date and time by using the following command syntax:

```
ciscoasa# reload at hh:mm [day month | month day]
```

Here, *hh:mm* specifies the reload time of hours and minutes. If no date is specified, today is assumed.

To schedule a reload after a time interval, you can use the following command syntax:

```
ciscoasa# reload in {mm | hhh:mm}
```

Here, the time interval can be given in either minutes or hours and minutes from the time the **reload** command is entered.

Once you schedule a reload, you can check the schedule and status with the **show reload** command. You can cancel a scheduled reload at any time before it actually begins by entering the **reload cancel** command.

You can add any of the following keywords and options after any form of the **reload** command:

- **max-hold-time {*mm* | *hhh:mm*}:** The ASA will wait a maximum elapsed time for the subsystems and processes to be gracefully shut down, and then it will perform a quick reload without waiting any further.

- **noconfirm:** Performs the reload without asking for confirmation.

- **quick:** Performs the reload without waiting for processes to be shut down gracefully.

- **reason *string*:** Records a text string in the ASA logs to indicate why the reload was requested; the reason text will be displayed to active VPN sessions, SSH, Telnet, console, and ASDM session users so that they are aware of the impending reload.

- **save-config:** Saves the running configuration before the reload begins.

Manually Upgrading the ASA Software During a Reload

Sometimes, you might have to install or upgrade the operating system image file on an ASA before it fully boots. You can do this by downloading an image file from a TFTP server when the ASA has booted into its ROMMON mode. At this point, the firewall is not inspecting any traffic and has no running configuration.

Follow the steps listed in Table 2-4 to download a firewall operating system image via TFTP.

Table 2-4   *Steps for Upgrading an ASA Image File at Bootup*

Step	ROMMON Command
1. Interrupt the bootup sequence.	Press **Esc** or **Break** at the appropriate time
2. Identify an ASA interface where the TFTP server is located.	rommon> **interface** *physical-name*
3. Assign an IP address to the ASA interface.	rommon> **address** *ip-address*
4. Assign a default gateway.	rommon> **gateway** *ip-address*
5. Identify the TFTP server address.	rommon> **server** *ip-address*
6. Identify the image filename.	rommon> **file** *filename*
7. Test connectivity to the TFTP server.	rommon> **ping** *ip-address*
8. Initiate the TFTP file download.	rommon> **tftpdnld**

As an ASA is booting, it goes through a series of initial hardware and firmware checks, as shown in Example 2-20. At a certain point in the bootup sequence, the ASA announces that you can press the Esc or Break key to interrupt the remaining bootup process. Doing so leaves the ASA in the ROMMON mode, where the manual image-download commands can be entered.

Example 2-20   *An ASA Bootup Sequence*

```
Booting system, please wait...
CISCO SYSTEMS
Embedded BIOS Version 1.0(11)2 01/25/06 13:21:26.17
Low Memory: 631 KB
High Memory: 1024 MB
PCI Device Table.
Bus Dev Func VendID DevID Class              Irq
 00  00   00   8086   2578  Host Bridge
 00  01   00   8086   2579  PCI-to-PCI Bridge
 00  03   00   8086   257B  PCI-to-PCI Bridge
 00  1C   00   8086   25AE  PCI-to-PCI Bridge
 00  1D   00   8086   25A9  Serial Bus          11
 00  1D   01   8086   25AA  Serial Bus          10
 00  1D   04   8086   25AB  System
 00  1D   05   8086   25AC  IRQ Controller
 00  1D   07   8086   25AD  Serial Bus           9
 00  1E   00   8086   244E  PCI-to-PCI Bridge
 00  1F   00   8086   25A1  ISA Bridge
 00  1F   02   8086   25A3  IDE Controller      11
```

```
00  1F  03  8086  25A4  Serial Bus         5
00  1F  05  8086  25A6  Audio              5
02  01  00  8086  1075  Ethernet           11
03  01  00  177D  0003  Encrypt/Decrypt    9
03  02  00  8086  1079  Ethernet           9
03  02  01  8086  1079  Ethernet           9
03  03  00  8086  1079  Ethernet           9
03  03  01  8086  1079  Ethernet           9
04  02  00  8086  1209  Ethernet           11
04  03  00  8086  1209  Ethernet           5

Evaluating BIOS Options ...
Launch BIOS Extension to setup ROMMON
Cisco Systems ROMMON Version (1.0(11)2) #0: Thu Jan 26 10:43:08 PST 2006
Platform ASA5510-K8

Use BREAK or ESC to interrupt boot.
Use SPACE to begin boot immediately.
Boot interrupted.

Management0/0
Ethernet auto negotiation timed out.
Interface-4 Link Not Established (check cable).
Default Interface number-4 Not Up

Use ? for help.
rommon #0>
```

The parameters you enter are used only temporarily until the ASA can download and run the new image file. None of the commands are stored in a configuration; as soon as the ASA reboots, they are lost.

Example 2-21 shows a sample image download. ASA interface Ethernet0/0 is used because the TFTP server is connected there. The interface is given IP address 192.168.100.5. The default gateway is optional and is needed only if the TFTP server is not located on the interface's local subnet. The TFTP server is found at IP address 192.168.100.10 and the new image file is called asa842-k8.bin. As soon as the **tftpdnld** command is entered, the TFTP file transfer begins. Once the image file has been downloaded, the ASA automatically boots and runs the new image.

Note: Be aware that even though the image file is downloaded and executed by the ASA, it is not permanently stored anywhere. After the ASA finishes booting, copy the same image file onto a flash file system by using the **copy** command.

Example 2-21   *Manually Downloading an Image File in ROMMON Mode*

```
Link is UP
rommon #1> address 192.168.100.5
rommon #2> gateway 192.168.100.1
rommon #3> server 192.168.100.10
rommon #4> file asa842-k8.bin
rommon #6> ping 192.168.100.10
Sending 20, 100-byte ICMP Echoes to 192.168.100.10, timeout is 4 seconds:
?!!!!!!!!!!!!!!!!!!!!!
Success rate is 95 percent (19/20)
rommon #7>
rommon #7> tftpdnld
ROMMON Variable Settings:
  ADDRESS=192.168.100.5
  SERVER=192.168.100.10
  GATEWAY=192.168.100.1
  PORT=Ethernet0/0
  VLAN=untagged
  IMAGE=asa842-k8.bin
  CONFIG=
  LINKTIMEOUT=20
  PKTTIMEOUT=4
  RETRY=20

tftp asa842-k8.bin@192.168.100.10 via 192.168.100.1
!!!!!!!!!!!!!!!!!!!!!!!!!!!!!!!!!!!!!!!!!!!!!!!!!!!!!!!!!!!!!!!!!!!!!!!!!!!!!!!!!!!!!!!
!!!!!!!!!!!!!!!!!!!!!!!!!!!!!!!!!!!!!!!!!!!!!!!!!!!!!!!!!!!!!!!!!!!!!!!!!!!!!!!!!!!!!!!
!!!!!!!!!!!!!!!!!!!!!!!!!!!!!!!!!!!!!!!!!!!!!!!!!!!!!!!!!!!!!!!!!!!!!!!!!!!!!!!!!!!!!!!
[output truncated for clarity]
!!!!!!!!!!!!!!!!!!!!!!!!!!!!!!!!!!!!!!!!!!!!!!!!!!!!!!!!!!!!!!!!!!!!
Received 15243264 bytes

Launching TFTP Image...
Cisco Security Appliance admin loader (3.0) #0: Fri Aug  6 07:52:16 MDT 2010
Cisco Adaptive Security Appliance Software Version 8.4(2)
[output truncated for clarity]
Cryptochecksum (unchanged): 1f9718cc 8bfafb64 55268ff4 b8fe0c26
Type help or '?' for a list of available commands.
ciscoasa>
```

Exam Preparation Tasks

As mentioned in the section, "How to Use This Book," in the Introduction, you have a couple of choices for exam preparation: the exercises here, Chapter 17, "Final Preparation," and the exam simulation questions on the CD-ROM.

Review All Key Topics

Review the most important topics in this chapter, noted with the Key Topics icon in the outer margin of the page. Table 2-5 lists a reference of these key topics and the page numbers on which each is found.

Table 2-5 *Key Topics for Chapter 2*

Key Topic Element	Description	Page Number
List	Describes CLI modes	40
Paragraph	Explains how to show the running configuration	41
Paragraph	Describes filtering or searching through output from a **show** command	45
Paragraph	Explains how to show the startup configuration	54
Section	Explains how to clear all or a portion of the configuration	57
Paragraph	Describes how to copy files to and from an ASA flash file system	60
Paragraph	Explains how to configure an ASA to run a specific image file	63
Paragraph	Explains how to reload or reboot an ASA	66

Define Key Terms

Define the following key terms from this chapter and check your answers in the glossary:

user EXEC mode, privileged EXEC mode, global configuration mode, specific configuration modes, ROMMON (ROM monitor) mode, running configuration, startup configuration

Command Reference to Check Your Memory

This section includes the most important configuration and EXEC commands covered in this chapter. It might not be necessary to memorize the complete syntax of every command, but you should be able to remember the basic keywords that are needed.

To test your memory of the commands, cover the right side of Tables 2-6 through 2-9 with a piece of paper, read the description on the left side, and then see how much of the command you can remember.

The FIREWALL exam focuses on practical, hands-on skills that are used by a networking professional. Therefore, you should be able to identify the commands needed to configure and test an ASA feature.

Table 2-6   *ASA CLI Commands*

Task	Command Syntax
Enter privileged EXEC mode	ciscoasa# **enable**
Enter global configuration mode	ciscoasa# **configure terminal**
Display helpful information about a command	ciscoasa# **help** [*command*]
Display the CLI command history	ciscoasa# **show history**
Display and filter command output	ciscoasa# **show** *command* ...	{**begin**	**include**	**exclude**	**grep** [**-v**]} *reg-expression*
Set the CLI screen width	ciscoasa(config)# **terminal width** *characters*
Set the CLI screen height	ciscoasa(config)# **pager** [**lines**] *number*

Table 2-7   *ASA Configuration File Commands*

Task	Command Syntax
Display the running configuration	ciscoasa# **show running-config**
Display the startup configuration	ciscoasa# **show startup-config**
Force the ASA to return to its factory default configuration	ciscoasa(config)# **configure factory-default**
Identify the startup configuration file in flash	ciscoasa(config)# **boot config** *url*
Save the running configuration	ciscoasa# **copy running-config startup-config**
Clear or delete commands in the running configuration	ciscoasa# **clear configure** {**all**	**primary**	**secondary**	*command*}
Clear the entire startup configuration	ciscoasa# **write erase**

Table 2-8 *ASA Flash File System Commands*

Task	Command Syntax
List the contents of a flash file system	ciscoasa# **dir** [**/all**] [**/recursive**] [*device:*][*path*]
Change to a directory location in flash	ciscoasa# **cd** [*device:*][*path*]
Display the current working directory within the flash file system	ciscoasa# **pwd**
Make a new directory	ciscoasa# **mkdir** [**/noconfirm**] [*device:*]*path*
Remove a directory	ciscoasa# **rmdir** [**/noconfirm**] [*device:*]*path*
View the contents of a file	ciscoasa# **more** [**/ascii** | **/binary** | **/ebcdic**] [*device:*]*path*
Copy a file	ciscoasa# **copy** [**/noconfirm**] *source destination*
Rename a file	ciscoasa# **rename** [**/noconfirm**] [*device:*]*source-path* [*device:*]*destination-path*
Delete a file	ciscoasa# **delete** [**/noconfirm**] [**/recursive**] [*device:*]*path*

Table 2-9 *Commands Related to Reloading an ASA*

Task	Command Syntax
Identify the operating system image file to run after the next reload	ciscoasa(config)# **boot system** *device:path*
Display the current boot variables	ciscoasa# **show bootvar**
Schedule a reload at a certain date and time	ciscoasa# **reload at** *hh:mm* [*day month* | *month day*]
Schedule a reload after a time interval	ciscoasa# **reload in** {*mm* | *hhh:mm*}
Display the current reload schedule	ciscoasa# **show reload**
Cancel a scheduled reload	ciscoasa# **reload cancel**

This chapter covers the following topics:

- **Configuring Physical Interfaces:** This section discusses Cisco ASA interfaces that can be connected to a network through physical cabling, as well as the parameters that determine how the interfaces will operate.

- **Configuring VLAN Interfaces:** This section covers logical interfaces that can be used to connect an ASA to VLANs over a trunk link.

- **Configuring Interface Security Parameters:** This section explains the parameters you can set to assign a name, an IP address, and a security level to an ASA interface.

- **Configuring the Interface MTU:** This section discusses the maximum transmission unit size and how it can be adjusted to set the largest possible Ethernet frame that can be transmitted on an Ethernet-based ASA interface.

- **Verifying Interface Operation:** This section covers the commands you can use to display information about ASA interfaces and confirm whether they are operating as expected.

CHAPTER 3

Configuring ASA Interfaces

A Cisco Adaptive Security Appliance (ASA) must be configured with enough information to begin accepting and forwarding traffic before it can begin doing its job of securing networks. Each of its interfaces must be configured to interoperate with other network equipment and to participate in the IP protocol suite. This chapter discusses each of these topics in detail.

"Do I Know This Already?" Quiz

The "Do I Know This Already?" quiz allows you to assess whether you should read this entire chapter thoroughly or jump to the "Exam Preparation Tasks" section. If you are in doubt about your answers to these questions or your own assessment of your knowledge of the topics, read the entire chapter. Table 3-1 lists the major headings in this chapter and their corresponding "Do I Know This Already?" quiz questions. You can find the answers in Appendix A, "Answers to the 'Do I Know This Already?' Quizzes."

Table 3-1 *"Do I Know This Already?" Section-to-Question Mapping*

Foundation Topics Section	Questions
Configuring Physical Interfaces	1–4
Configuring VLAN Interfaces	5–7
Configuring Interface Security Parameters	8–10
Configuring the Interface MTU	11
Verifying Interface Operation	12

Caution: The goal of self-assessment is to gauge your mastery of the topics in this chapter. If you do not know the answer to a question or are only partially sure of the answer, you should mark this question wrong for purposes of the self-assessment. Giving yourself credit for an answer you correctly guess skews your self-assessment results and might provide you with a false sense of security.

1. Which of the following answers describe an attribute of a redundant interface? (Choose all that apply.)

   a. A redundant interface load balances traffic across member interfaces.

   b. A redundant interface is made up of two or more physical interfaces.

   c. An ASA can have up to eight redundant interface pairs.

   d. Each member interface of a redundant interface cannot have its own security level.

   e. IP addresses must be applied to the member physical interfaces of a redundant interface.

   f. The member interfaces swap the active role when one of them fails.

2. What must happen for a member interface to take over the active role as part of a redundant interface?

   a. Three hello messages must be missed.

   b. The link status of the current active interface goes down.

   c. A member interface, which was previously active before it went down, regains its link status.

   d. Its member priority is higher than other member interfaces.

   e. A timer must expire.

3. Which ASA command can be used to display a list of all physical interfaces?

   a. show interfaces physical

   b. show interface list

   c. show hardware

   d. show version

   e. show ports

   f. show

4. Suppose you want to double the bandwidth between an ASA's outside interface and a neighboring switch. A single GigabitEthernet link exists today; a second link would also add redundancy. Which one of the following describes the best approach to meet the requirements?

   a. Bring up a second GigabitEthernet interface on the same VLAN as the first one.

   b. Configure the two interfaces as a redundant interface.

   c. Configure the two interfaces as an EtherChannel.

   d. Dual links are not possible on an ASA.

5. You have been assigned the task of configuring a VLAN interface on an ASA 5510. The interface will use VLAN 50. Which one of the following sets of commands should be entered first to accomplish the task?

   a. `interface vlan 50`
          `no shutdown`

   b. `interface ethernet0/0`
          `no shutdown`

   c. `interface ethernet0/0.5`
          `vlan 50`
          `no shutdown`

   d. `interface ethernet0/0.50`
          `no shutdown`

6. Which of the following are correct attributes of an ASA interface that is configured to support VLAN interfaces? (Choose all that apply.)

   a. The physical interface operates as an ISL trunk.

   b. The physical interface operates as an 802.1Q trunk.

   c. The subinterface numbers of the physical interface must match the VLAN number.

   d. All packets sent from a subinterface are tagged for the trunk link.

   e. An ASA can negotiate a trunk link with a connected switch.

7. Which one of the following answers contains the commands that should be entered on an ASA 5505 to create an interface for VLAN 6?

   a. interface vlan 6

   b. vlan 6

   c. interface ethernet0/0.6

   d. interface ethernet0/0.6

8. Which of the following represent security attributes that must be assigned to an active ASA interface when the ASA is in routed firewall mode? (Choose three answers.)

   a. IP address

   b. Access list

   c. Interface name

   d. Security level

   e. Interface priority

   f. MAC address

9. Which one of the following interfaces should normally be assigned a security level value of 100?

   a.   outside

   b.   dmz

   c.   inside

   d.   None of these answers are correct.

10. An ASA has two active interfaces, one with security level 0 and one with security level 100. Which one of the following statements is true?

   a.   Traffic is permitted to be initiated from security level 0 toward security level 100.

   b.   Traffic is permitted to be initiated from security level 100 toward security level 0.

   c.   Traffic is not permitted in either direction.

   d.   The interfaces must have the same security level by default before traffic can flow.

11. Suppose you are asked to adjust the MTU on the "inside" ASA interface Ethernet0/1 to 1460 bytes. Which one of the following answers contains the correct command(s) to enter?

   a.   `ciscoasa(config)# `**`mtu 1460`**

   b.   `ciscoasa(config)# mtu inside 1460`

   c.   `ciscoasa(config)# `**`interface ethernet0/1`**
          `ciscoasa(config-if)# `**`mtu 1460`**

   d.   None of these answers are correct; the MTU must be greater than 1500.

12. From the following output, which of the following statements are true about ASA interface Ethernet0/2? (Choose all that apply.)

```
ciscoasa# show nameif
Interface                   Name                    Security
Ethernet0/0                 outside                    0
Ethernet0/1                 inside                   100
Management0/0               management               100
ciscoasa#
ciscoasa# show interface ethernet0/2
Interface Ethernet0/2 "", is administratively down, line protocol is down
   Hardware is i82546GB rev03, BW 100 Mbps, DLY 100 usec
        Auto-Duplex, Auto-Speed
        Input flow control is unsupported, output flow control is unsupported
        Available but not configured via nameif
        MAC address 001a.a22d.1dde, MTU not set
        IP address 10.1.1.1, subnet mask 255.255.255.0
        0 packets input, 0 bytes, 0 no buffer
        Received 0 broadcasts, 0 runts, 0 giants
        0 input errors, 0 CRC, 0 frame, 0 overrun, 0 ignored, 0 abort
        0 pause input, 0 resume input
        0 L2 decode drops
        0 packets output, 0 bytes, 0 underruns
        0 pause output, 0 resume output
        0 output errors, 0 collisions, 1 interface resets
        0 late collisions, 0 deferred
        0 input reset drops, 0 output reset drops, 0 tx hangs
        input queue (blocks free curr/low): hardware (255/255)
        output queue (blocks free curr/low): hardware (255/255)
ciscoasa#
```

a. The interface is configured and is live on the network.

b. The interface is not ready to use; the **no shutdown** command has not been issued.

c. The interface is not ready to use; it doesn't have an IP address configured.

d. The interface is not ready to use; it doesn't have a MAC address configured.

e. The interface is not ready to use; it doesn't have a security level configured.

f. The interface is not ready to use; it doesn't have an interface name configured.

Answer E might also be true, but you cannot confirm that a security level has
been configured from the command output given. Because an interface name
has not been configured with the **nameif** command, neither the interface name
nor the security level is shown in the output.

Foundation Topics

Every ASA has one or more interfaces that can be used to connect to some other part of the network so that traffic can be inspected and controlled. ASA interfaces can be *physical*, where actual network media cables connect, or *logical*, where the interfaces exist internally and are passed to the network over a physical link. In this chapter, you learn how to configure both types of interfaces for connectivity and IP addressing.

In addition, to pass and inspect traffic, each interface must be configured with the following three security attributes:

- Interface name
- IP address and subnet mask
- Security level

You learn how to configure the security parameters in the section, "Configuring Interface Security Parameters."

Configuring Physical Interfaces

An ASA supports multiple physical interfaces that can be connected into the network or to individual devices. From the Configuration tab in Cisco ASDM, you can view the list of interfaces by selecting **Device Setup > Interfaces**, as shown in Figure 3-1.

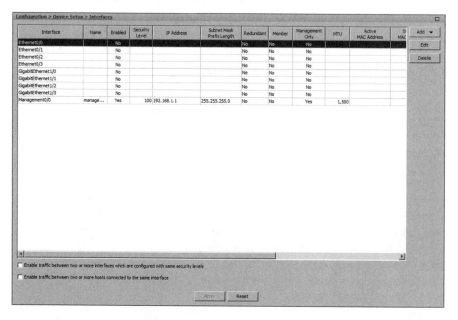

Figure 3-1   *Using ASDM to View a List of Interfaces*

From the CLI, you can see a list of the physical firewall interfaces that are available by using the following command:

```
ciscoasa# show version
```

Firewall interfaces are referenced by their hardware index and their physical interface names. Example 3-1 lists the physical interfaces in an ASA 5510. Ethernet0/0 through 0/3 and Management0/0 are built-in interfaces, while GigabitEthernet1/0 through 1/3 are installed as a 4GE-SSM module.

Example 3-1 *Listing Physical ASA Interfaces*

```
ciscoasa# show version

Cisco Adaptive Security Appliance Software Version 8.2(3)
Device Manager Version 6.3(4)

Compiled on Fri 06-Aug-10 07:51 by builders
System image file is "disk0:/asa823-k8.bin"
Config file at boot was "startup-config"

ciscoasa up 1 day 10 hours

Hardware:   ASA5510-K8, 256 MB RAM, CPU Pentium 4 Celeron 1600 MHz
Internal ATA Compact Flash, 256MB
BIOS Flash M50FW080 @ 0xffe00000, 1024KB

Encryption hardware device : Cisco ASA-55x0 on-board accelerator (revision 0x0)
                            Boot microcode   : CN1000-MC-BOOT-2.00
                            SSL/IKE microcode: CNLite-MC-SSLm-PLUS-2.03
                            IPSec microcode  : CNlite-MC-IPSECm-MAIN-2.04

 0: Ext: Ethernet0/0        : address is 001a.a22d.1ddc, irq 9
 1: Ext: Ethernet0/1        : address is 001a.a22d.1ddd, irq 9
 2: Ext: Ethernet0/2        : address is 001a.a22d.1dde, irq 9
 3: Ext: Ethernet0/3        : address is 001a.a22d.1ddf, irq 9
 4: Ext: Management0/0      : address is 001a.a22d.1ddb, irq 11
 5: Int: Internal-Data0/0   : address is 0000.0001.0002, irq 11
 6: Int: Not used           : irq 5
 7: Ext: GigabitEthernet1/0 : address is 001a.a22d.20f1, irq 255
 8: Ext: GigabitEthernet1/1 : address is 001a.a22d.20f2, irq 255
 9: Ext: GigabitEthernet1/2 : address is 001a.a22d.20f3, irq 255
10: Ext: GigabitEthernet1/3 : address is 001a.a22d.20f4, irq 255
11: Int: Internal-Data1/0   : address is 0000.0003.0002, irq 255

Licensed features for this platform:
Maximum Physical Interfaces     : Unlimited
```

```
Maximum VLANs              : 100
Inside Hosts               : Unlimited
Failover                   : Active/Active
VPN-DES                    : Enabled
[output truncated for clarity]
```

Before you begin configuring the ASA interfaces, you should first use the interface list to identify each of the interfaces you will use. At a minimum, you need one interface as the "inside" of the ASA and one as the "outside."

Default Interface Configuration

Some interfaces come predefined in the initial factory default configuration. You can view the interface mappings with the **show nameif** EXEC command. As shown in Example 3-2, an ASA 5510 or higher model defines only one interface, Management0/0, for use by default. The interface is named "management" and is set aside for out-of-band management access.

Example 3-2   *Default Interface Configuration on ASA 5510 and Higher Models*

```
ciscoasa# show nameif
Interface             Name              Security
Management0/0         management        100
ciscoasa#
```

An ASA 5505 takes a different approach with its default interfaces, as shown in Example 3-3. Rather than use physical interfaces, it defines an "inside" and an "outside" interface using two logical VLANs: VLAN 1 and VLAN 2.

Example 3-3   *Default Interface Configuration on the ASA 5505*

```
ciscoasa# show nameif
Interface             Name              Security
Vlan1                 inside            100
Vlan2                 outside             0
ciscoasa#
```

These two VLANs are then applied to the physical interfaces such that interface Ethernet0/0 is mapped to VLAN 2, while Ethernet0/1 through 0/7 are mapped to VLAN 1 (inside). This configuration gives one outside interface that can be connected to a service provider network for an Internet connection. The remaining seven inside interfaces can be connected to individual devices on the protected network.

You can display the ASA 5505 interface-to-VLAN mapping by entering the **show switch vlan** command, as shown in Example 3-4.

Example 3-4 *Displaying the ASA 5505 Interface-to-VLAN Mapping*

```
ciscoasa# show switch vlan
VLAN Name                                 Status    Ports
---- ----------------------------------   --------  ----------------------------
1    inside                               up        Et0/1, Et0/2, Et0/3, Et0/4
                                                    Et0/5, Et0/6, Et0/7
2    outside                              up        Et0/0
ciscoasa#
```

Configuring Physical Interface Parameters

For each physical interface, you can configure the speed, duplex, and the interface state. In ASDM, select **Configuration > Interfaces**, select an interface, and click the **Edit** button. In the General tab, click **Configure Hardware Properties**, as shown in Figure 3-2.

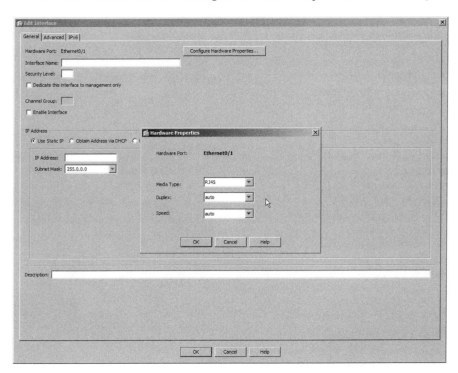

Figure 3-2 *Configuring Physical Interface Parameters in ASDM*

You can do the same task from the CLI by using the following commands:

```
ciscoasa(config)# interface hardware-id
ciscoasa(config-if)# speed {auto | 10 | 100 | 1000}
ciscoasa(config-if)# duplex {auto | full | half}
ciscoasa(config-if)# [no] shutdown
```

By default, an interface uses autodetected speed and autonegotiated duplex mode, as if the **speed auto** and **duplex auto** commands had been entered. As long as the ASA interface and the device connected to it are configured the same, the interface will automatically come up using the maximum speed and full-duplex mode. You can also statically configure the interface speed to **10, 100,** or **1000** Mbps, as well as **full** or **half** duplex mode.

By default, physical interfaces are administratively shut down. Use the **no shutdown** interface configuration command to enable each one individually. As well, you can shut an interface back down with the **shutdown** command.

> **Note:** Other parameters, such as the interface name, security level, and IP address, should be configured, too. These are discussed in the section, "Configuring Interface Security Parameters."

Mapping ASA 5505 Interfaces to VLANs

By default, an ASA 5505 maps interface Ethernet0/0 to VLAN 2 and interfaces Ethernet0/1 through 0/7 to VLAN 1. All eight interfaces are connected to an internal 8-port switch, with each interface configured as an access link mapped to a single VLAN.

Figure 3-3 shows how ASDM can be used to map a physical interface to a different VLAN number. First, a new interface is created and named vlan 10. At the top of the Add Interface dialog box, Ethernet0/3 is added to the list of interfaces that are mapped to VLAN 10.

You can use the following CLI command to accomplish the same task:

```
ciscoasa(config-if)# switchport access vlan vlan-id
```

The *vlan-id* parameter represents a VLAN interface that has already been created and configured. The section, "Configuring VLAN Interfaces," covers this in detail.

In Example 3-5, interface Ethernet0/3 is mapped to VLAN 10, while Ethernet0/4 is mapped to VLAN 20.

Example 3-5   *Mapping Interfaces to VLANs on an ASA 5505*

```
ciscoasa(config)# interface ethernet0/3
ciscoasa(config-if)# switchport access vlan 10
ciscoasa(config-if)# interface ethernet0/4
ciscoasa(config-if)# switchport access vlan 20
```

Configuring Interface Redundancy

By default, each physical ASA interface operates independently of any other interface. The interface can be in one of two operating states: up or down. When an interface is down for some reason, the ASA cannot send or receive any data through it. For example, the switch port where an ASA interface connects might fail, causing the ASA interface to go down, too.

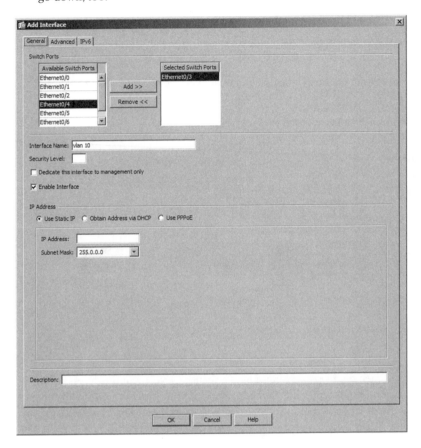

Figure 3-3 *Mapping an ASA 5505 Interface to a VLAN*

To keep an ASA interface up and active all the time, you can configure physical interfaces as redundant pairs. As a redundant pair, two interfaces are set aside for the same ASA function (inside, outside, and so on), and connect to the same network. Only one of the interfaces is active at any given time; the other interface stays in a standby state. As soon as the active interface loses its link status and goes down, the standby interface becomes active and takes over passing traffic.

Both physical interfaces in a redundant pair are configured as members of a single logical "redundant" interface. To join two interfaces as a redundant pair, the interfaces must be of the same type (10/100/1000BASE-TX, for example).

The redundant interface, rather than its physical member interfaces, is configured with a unique interface name, security level, and IP address—all the parameters used in ASA interface operations.

First, you must create the redundant interface by entering the following configuration command:

```
ciscoasa(config)# interface redundant number
```

You can define up to eight redundant interfaces on an ASA. Therefore, the interface *number* can be 1 through 8.

Next, use the following command to add a physical interface as a member of the redundant interface:

```
ciscoasa(config-int)# member-interface physical_interface
```

Here, *physical_interface* is the hardware name and number, like ethernet0/1 or gigabitethernet0/1, for example. In Figure 3-4, ASA interfaces Ethernet0/0 and Ethernet0/1 are member interfaces of a logical redundant interface called Redundant1, while Ethernet0/2 and Ethernet0/3 are members of interface Redundant2.

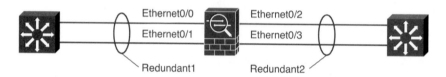

Figure 3-4   *Example Redundant Interfaces*

Be aware that the member interface cannot have a security level or an IP address configured. In fact, as soon as you enter the **member-interface** command, the ASA will automatically clear those parameters from the physical interface configuration. You should repeat this command to add a second physical interface to the redundant pair.

Keep in mind that the order in which you configure the interfaces is important. The first physical interface added to a logical redundant interface will become the active interface. That interface will stay active until it loses its link status, causing the second or standby interface to take over. The standby interface can also take over when the active interface is administratively shut down with the **shutdown** interface configuration command.

However, the active status will not revert to the failed interface, even when it comes back up. The two interfaces trade the active role back and forth only when one of them fails.

The redundant interface also takes on the MAC address of the first member interface that you configure. Regardless of which physical interface is active, that same MAC address will be used. You can override this behavior by manually configuring a unique MAC address on the redundant interface with the **mac-address** *mac_address* interface configuration command.

In Example 3-6, interfaces Ethernet0/0 and Ethernet0/1 are configured to be used as logical interface redundant 1.

Example 3-6 *Configuring a Redundant Interface Pair*

```
ciscoasa(config)# interface redundant 1
ciscoasa(config-if)# member-interface ethernet0/0
INFO: security-level and IP address are cleared on Ethernet0/0.
ciscoasa(config-if)# member-interface ethernet0/1
INFO: security-level and IP address are cleared on Ethernet0/1.
ciscoasa(config-if)# no shutdown
```

The redundant interface is now ready to be configured as a normal ASA interface. From this point on, you should not configure anything on the two physical interfaces other than the port speed and duplex.

Note: Make sure the logical redundant interface and the two physical interfaces are enabled with the **no shutdown** command. Even though they are all logically associated, they can be manually shut down or brought up independently.

To accomplish the same thing through ASDM, first select **Add > Redundant Interface** from the drop-down menu in the upper-right corner of the interface listing. A new Add Redundant Interface dialog box appears, as shown in Figure 3-5. Select the redundant interface number and the two physical interfaces that will operate as a redundant pair. To enable the new redundant interface for use, be sure to check the **Enable Interface** check box.

Note: Other parameters, such as the interface name, security level, and IP address, should be configured, too. These are discussed in the section, "Configuring Interface Security Parameters."

Configuring an EtherChannel

A single link between an ASA and a switch provides simple connectivity, but it is a single point of failure. If the link goes down, no data can travel across it. In the previous section, you learned that a redundant interface binds two physical interfaces into one logical interface. The possibility of a link failure is reduced, because one of the two interfaces will always be up and available; however, only one of the two links can pass data at any given time.

How can you maximize availability with more than one link, while leveraging the bandwidth of all of them at the same time? Beginning with ASA software release 8.4(1), you can use an EtherChannel to make that all possible. With an EtherChannel, two to eight active physical interfaces can be grouped or bundled together as a single logical port-channel interface. Each interface must be of the same type, speed, and duplex mode before an EtherChannel can be built.

Figure 3-6 shows an EtherChannel that is built out of multiple physical GigabitEthernet interfaces that connect an ASA to a Catalyst switch. On the ASA, the resulting logical interface is named interface port-channel 1. Notice that the individual links in the EtherChannel can have different interface names on each end. The interfaces can also be

connected and grouped in any arbitrary order. What matters is that the interfaces form
one common EtherChannel link between the two devices.

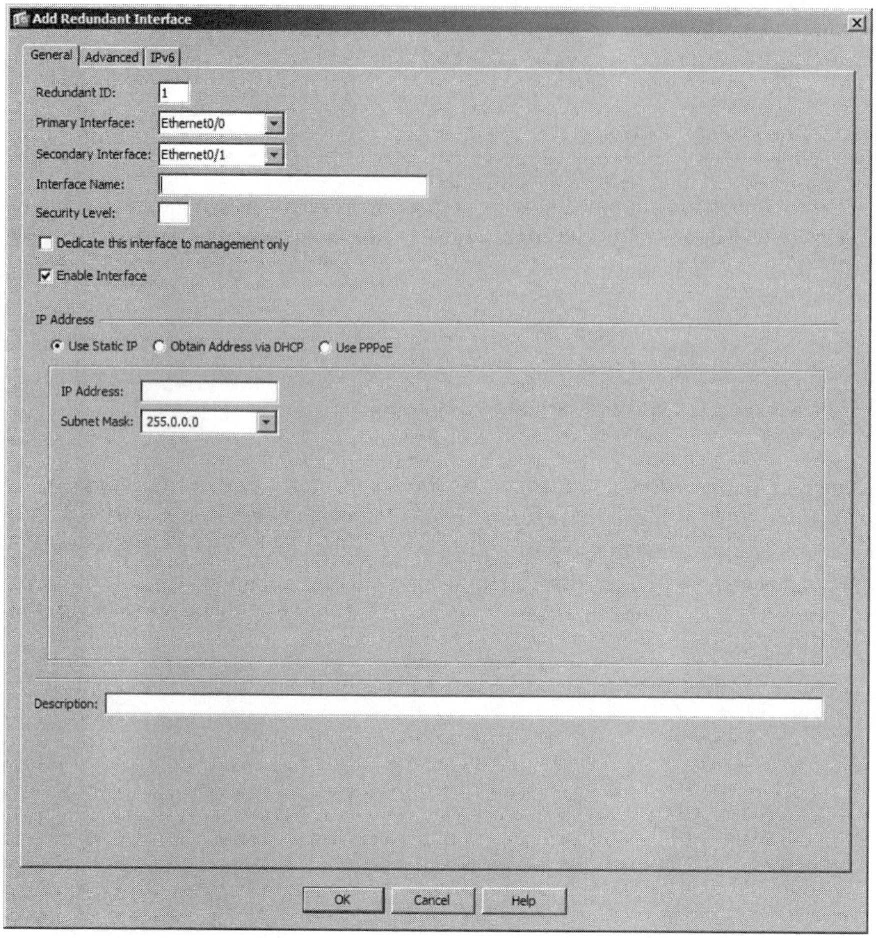

Add Redundant Interface

General | Advanced | IPv6 |

Redundant ID: 1

Primary Interface: Ethernet0/0

Secondary Interface: Ethernet0/1

Interface Name:

Security Level:

☐ Dedicate this interface to management only

☑ Enable Interface

IP Address

⦿ Use Static IP   ○ Obtain Address via DHCP   ○ Use PPPoE

    IP Address:

    Subnet Mask: 255.0.0.0

Description:

OK   Cancel   Help

Figure 3-5   *Adding a Redundant Interface in ASDM*

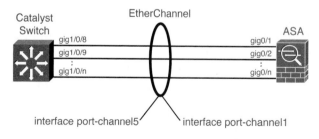

Figure 3-6   *Building an EtherChannel from Multiple Physical Links*

An ASA can support up to eight active interfaces in a single EtherChannel; however, you can configure up to 16 different interfaces per EtherChannel, although only eight of them can be active at any time. If one active interface fails, another one automatically takes its place. Although Figure 3-6 shows a single EtherChannel link, an ASA can support up to 48 different EtherChannels.

Because multiple interfaces are active in an EtherChannel, the available bandwidth can be scaled over that of a single interface. Traffic is load balanced by distributing the packets across the active interfaces. The ASA computes a hash value based on values found in the packet header, such as the source or destination MAC address, IP address, or the UDP or TCP port number. You can configure a preset combination of fields that are used. As long as the number of active interfaces is a multiple of two, the ASA can evenly distribute packets across them.

To build an EtherChannel, the ASA and the switch must both agree to do so. You can configure the ASA interfaces to statically participate, where the EtherChannel is "always on." In that case, the switch interfaces must also be configured for "always on" operation. Instead, you can configure the ASA and switch to negotiate an EtherChannel with each other.

Negotiation uses the Link Aggregation Control Protocol (LACP), which is a standards-based protocol. LACP packets are exchanged between the ASA and the switch over the interfaces that can become part of an EtherChannel. The ASA and the switch use a system priority (a 2-byte priority value followed by a 6-byte switch MAC address) to decide which one is allowed to make decisions about what interfaces are actively participating in the EtherChannel at a given time.

Interfaces are selected and become active according to their port priority value (a 2-byte priority followed by a 2-byte port number), where a low value indicates a higher priority. A set of up to 16 potential links can be defined for each EtherChannel. Through LACP, up to eight of these having the lowest port priorities can become active EtherChannel links at any given time. The other links are placed in a standby state and will be enabled in the EtherChannel if one of the active links goes down.

LACP can be configured in the active mode, in which the ASA actively asks a far-end switch to negotiate an EtherChannel, or in passive mode, in which the ASA negotiates an EtherChannel only if the far end initiates it. Table 3-2 summarizes the EtherChannel negotiation methods and characteristics.

Table 3-2   *EtherChannel Negotiation Methods*

Negotiation Mode	Negotiation Packets Sent?	Characteristics
On	No	All ports channeling all the time
Passive	Yes	Waits to channel until asked
Active	Yes	Actively asks to form a channel

To configure an EtherChannel in ASDM, begin by defining the port-channel interface. Select **Configuration > Device Setup > Interfaces**, click the **Add** button, and select

EtherChannel Interface. Under the General tab, enter an arbitrary Port Channel ID number (1 to 48) that will identify the port-channel interface.

Next, select an interface from the Available Physical Interface list and click the **Add>>** button to make it a member of the EtherChannel. You can repeat this process to add multiple interfaces. Make sure to select the Enable Interface check box to enable the port-channel interface for use. In Figure 3-7, interface port-channel1 has been created. Ethernet0/2 and Ethernet0/3 have been added as member interfaces.

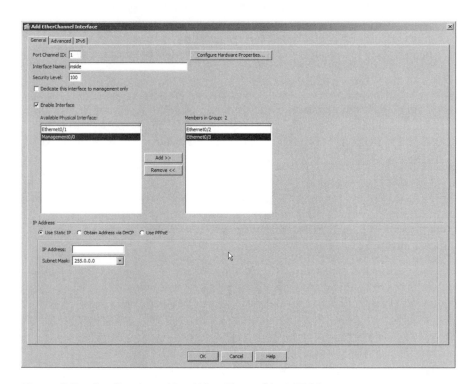

Figure 3-7 *Configuring a New EtherChannel in ASDM*

Note: Before an interface can be configured for an EtherChannel, it must not have a name configured. After the EtherChannel interfaces are configured, you can define a name and other security parameters on the port-channel interface.

Notice that Figure 3-7 also has fields for Interface Name, Security Level, and IP Address. These fields are not applied to the individual member interfaces; instead, they are applied to the port-channel interface. The fields are covered in the section, "Configuring Interface Security Parameters."

Next, configure the method that the ASA will use to distribute packets across the links within the EtherChannel. By default, a packet's source and destination IP addresses are used to compute a hash index that points to the link that will carry the packet. This is the appropriate choice in most cases, as long as the source and destination IP addresses are unique and diverse. The more varied the hash input values, the better the traffic will be distributed across the links in the EtherChannel.

In some scenarios, the majority of the traffic might travel between the same two IP addresses, causing most of the packets to travel over only one link of the EtherChannel. In that case, you can configure the EtherChannel load-balancing method to use additional information, such as a Layer 4 port number, MAC addresses, or a VLAN number, to provide more uniqueness so that the packets can be spread more evenly across the EtherChannel links. The possible load-balancing methods are as follows:

- Destination IP

- Destination IP and Layer 4 Port

- Destination MAC Address

- Destination Layer 4 Port

- Source and Destination IP Address

- Source and Destination MAC Address

- Source and Destination IP Address and Layer 4 Port

- Source and Destination Layer 4 Port

- Source IP Address

- Source IP Address and Layer 4 Port

- Source MAC Address

- Source Layer 4 Port

- VLAN Destination IP Address

- VLAN Destination IP and Layer 4 Port

- VLAN Only

- VLAN Source and Destination IP Address

- VLAN Source and Destination IP Address and Layer 4 Port

- VLAN Source IP Address

- VLAN Source IP Address and Layer 4 Port

To configure the load-balancing method, select the **Advanced** tab in the Add EtherChannel Interface screen and choose the method from the drop-down list at the bottom of the screen, as shown in Figure 3-8.

Next, you need to configure a negotiation method for the EtherChannel. ASDM uses a default method of "active" on each member interface, where the ASA will use LACP to actively ask the far-end switch to bring up the EtherChannel. To configure the method, select **Configuration > Device Setup > Interfaces**, select an interface that is a member of the EtherChannel, and click the **Edit** button. In Figure 3-9, interfaces Ethernet0/2 and 0/3 are shown to be members of the Port-channel1 group. Because their individual configurations are restricted, they are shown with a lock icon next to their names. Remember that the security parameters of an EtherChannel are configured on the Port-channel interface instead.

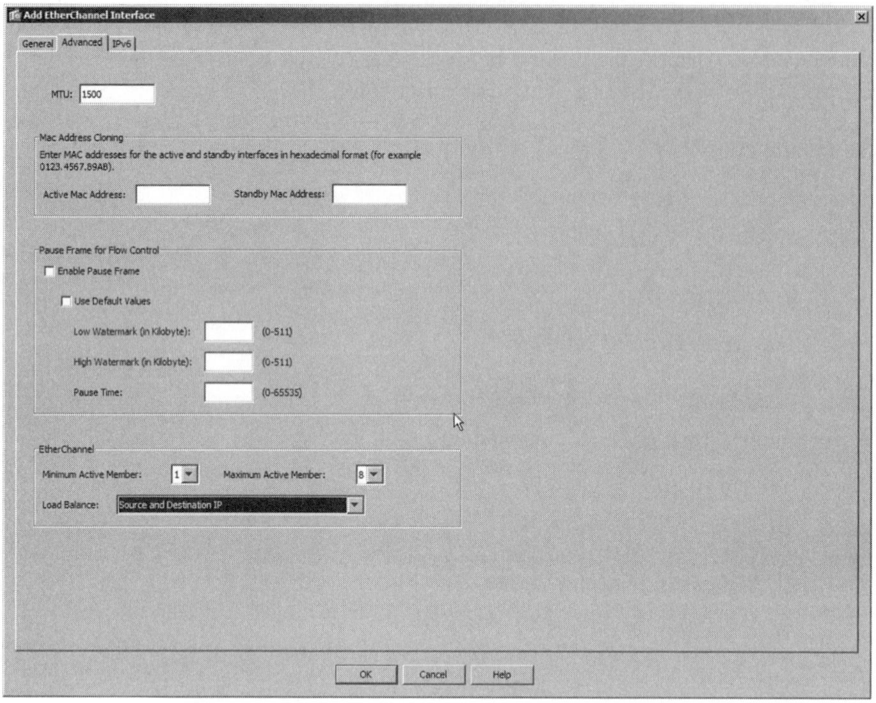

Figure 3-8   *Configuring the EtherChannel Load-Balancing Method*

Under the General tab of the Edit Interface screen, make sure that the **Enable Interface** check box under the Channel Group is selected. Select the **Advanced** tab and use the EtherChannel drop-down menu to set the negotiation mode, which can be either **Active**, **Passive**, or **On**, as shown in Figure 3-10.

You can configure more interfaces in the channel group *number* than are allowed to be active in the channel. This prepares extra standby interfaces to replace failed active ones. Set a lower LACP port priority (1 to 65,535; default 32,768) for any interfaces that must be active and a higher priority for interfaces that might be held in the standby state. Otherwise, just use the default scenario, in which all ports default to 32,768, and the lower port numbers (in interface number order) are used to select the active ports.

By default, an ASA uses LACP system priority of 32,768. If the ASA and the switch both use the same value, the one with the lower MAC address becomes the decision maker over the LACP negotiations. You can change the system priority by selecting **Configuration > Device Setup > EtherChannel**.

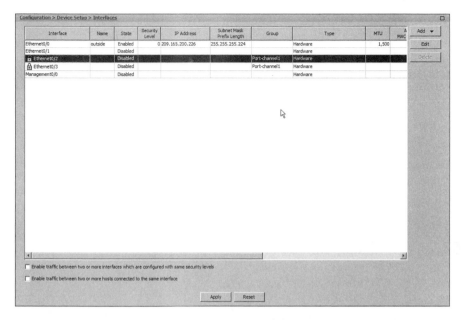

Figure 3-9   *Selecting an EtherChannel Interface for Configuration*

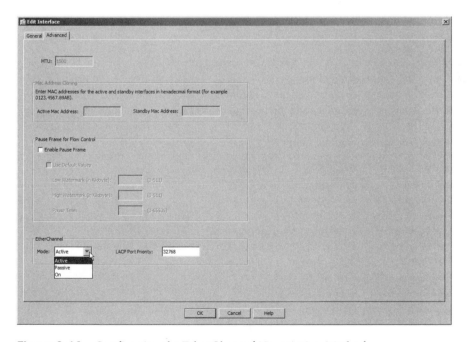

Figure 3-10   *Configuring the EtherChannel Negotiation Method*

You can also configure an EtherChannel by using the CLI. Select a physical interface that will be a member of the EtherChannel, and then identify the port-channel number where it will belong, along with the negotiation method that will be used:

```
ciscoasa(config)# lacp system-priority priority
ciscoasa(config)# interface type mod/num
ciscoasa(config-if)# channel-protocol lacp
ciscoasa(config-if)# channel-group number mode {on | passive | active}
ciscoasa(config-if)# lacp port-priority priority
```

As an example of LACP configuration, suppose that you want to configure an ASA to actively negotiate an EtherChannel using interfaces Ethernet0/2 and 0/3. You can use the commands listed in Example 3-7 to accomplish this.

Example 3-7 *Configuring an EtherChannel Using the CLI*

```
CISCOASA(config)# interface ethernet0/2
CISCOASA(config-if)# channel-protocol lacp
CISCOASA(config-if)# channel-group 1 mode active
CISCOASA(config-if)# exit
CISCOASA(config)# interface ethernet0/3
CISCOASA(config-if)# channel-protocol lacp
CISCOASA(config-if)# channel-group 1 mode active
CISCOASA(config-if)# exit
```

If you find that an EtherChannel is having problems, remember that the entire concept is based on consistent configurations on *both* ends of the channel. You can verify the Ether-Channel state with the **show port-channel summary** command. Each port in the channel is shown, along with flags indicating the port's state, as shown in Example 3-8.

Example 3-8 show port-channel summary *Command Output*

```
CISCOASA# show port-channel summary
Flags:  D - down        P - bundled in port-channel
        I - stand-alone s - suspended
        H - Hot-standby (LACP only)
        U - in use      N - not in use, no aggregation/nameif
        M - not in use, no aggregation due to minimum links not met
        w - waiting to be aggregated
Number of channel-groups in use: 1
Group  Port-channel  Protocol    Ports
------+-------------+-----------+---------------------------------------------
1      Po1(U)          LACP    Et0/2(P)   Et0/3(P)
CISCOASA#
```

The status of the port channel shows the EtherChannel logical interface as a whole. This should show U (in use) if the channel is operational. You also can examine the status of each interface within the channel. Notice that both of the channel interfaces have flags (P), which indicate that they are active in the port-channel.

Configuring VLAN Interfaces

A physical ASA interface can be configured to connect to multiple logical networks. To do this, the interface is configured to operate as a VLAN trunk link. On ASA 5510 and higher platforms, each VLAN that is carried over the trunk link terminates on a unique subinterface of a physical interface. On an ASA 5505, each VLAN is defined by a unique VLAN interface and can connect to physical interfaces and be carried over a VLAN trunk link.

VLAN Interfaces and Trunks on ASA 5510 and Higher Platforms

An ASA trunk link supports only the IEEE 802.1Q trunk encapsulation method. As each packet is sent over a trunk link, it is tagged with its source VLAN number. As packets are removed from the trunk, the tag is examined and removed so that the packets can be forwarded to their appropriate VLANs. Figure 3-11 shows how a trunk link between an ASA and a switch can encapsulate or carry frames from multiple VLANs.

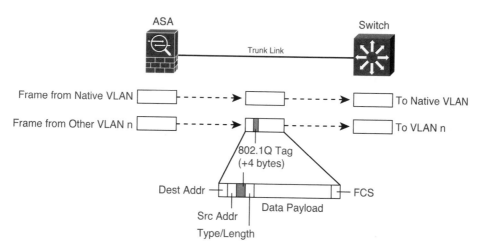

Figure 3-11 *IEEE 802.1Q Trunk Link Operation with an ASA*

IEEE 802.1Q trunk links support the concept of a native VLAN. Frames coming from the native VLAN are sent over the trunk link without a tag, while frames from other VLANs have a tag added while in the trunk. By default, only packets that are sent out the ASA's physical interface itself are not tagged, and they appear to use the trunk's native VLAN. Packets that are sent out a subinterface do receive a VLAN tag.

Note: Although a Cisco switch can be configured to negotiate the trunk status or encapsulation through the Dynamic Trunking Protocol (DTP), ASA platforms cannot. Therefore, an ASA trunk link is either on or off, according to the subinterface configuration. You should make sure that the switch port is configured to trunk unconditionally, too.

You can configure a trunk link by using the following configuration commands:

```
ciscoasa(config)# interface hardware_id.subinterface
ciscoasa(config-subif)# vlan vlan_id
```

First, use the **interface** command to identify the physical interface that will become a trunk link and the subinterface that will be associated with a VLAN number. The physical interface is given as *hardware_id*, such as Ethernet0/3, followed by a dot or period. A subinterface number is added to the physical interface name to create the logical VLAN interface. This is an arbitrary number that must be unique for each logical interface.

Use the **vlan** *vlan_id* subinterface configuration command to specify the VLAN number. The subinterface number does not have to match the VLAN number, although it can for convenience and readability.

As an example, Figure 3-12 shows a network diagram of a trunk link between an ASA and a switch. ASA physical interface Ethernet0/3 is used as the trunk link. VLAN 10 is carried over ASA subinterface Ethernet0/3.1, while VLAN 20 is carried over Ethernet0/3.2. The trunk link can be configured with the commands listed in Example 3-9.

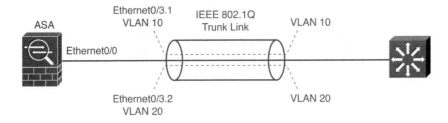

Figure 3-12   *Network Diagram for Example 3-9 Trunk Link Configuration*

Example 3-9   *Configuring a Trunk Link on an ASA*

```
ciscoasa(config)# interface ethernet0/3
ciscoasa(config-if)# no shutdown
ciscoasa(config-if)# interface ethernet0/3.1
ciscoasa(config-subif)# vlan 10
ciscoasa(config-subif)# no shutdown
ciscoasa(config-subif)# interface ethernet0/3.2
ciscoasa(config-subif)# vlan 20
ciscoasa(config-subif)# no shutdown
```

The same trunk link configuration can be accomplished with ASDM. Subinterfaces used in a trunk link must first be added or created. In the interface list view, select the **Add > Interface** function in the upper-right corner of the ASDM application. Select the hardware port or physical interface that will be used for the trunk link. In Figure 3-13, Ethernet0/3 is used. Because subinterface Ethernet0/3.1 is being created, the subinterface ID is set to 1. The VLAN ID is set to 10.

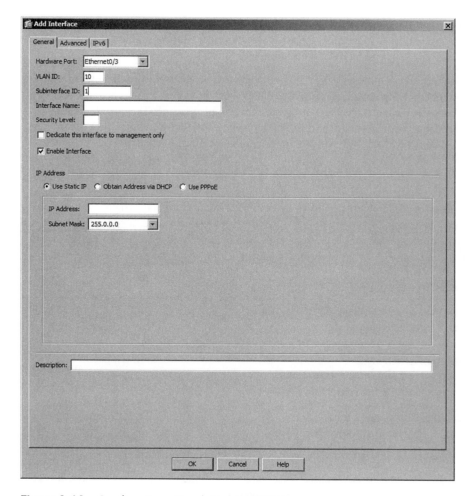

Figure 3-13   *Configuring a Trunk Link in ASDM*

Note: Other parameters, such as the interface name, security level, and IP address, should be configured, too. These are discussed in the section, "Configuring Interface Security Parameters."

VLAN Interfaces and Trunks on an ASA 5505

On an ASA 5505, VLANs are supported on the physical interfaces, but only if corresponding logical VLAN interfaces are configured. For example, if VLAN 1 is to be used, the **interface vlan 1** command must be entered to create the internal VLAN and the VLAN interface.

Key Topic

By default, the ASA 5505 platform includes the **interface vlan 1** and **interface vlan 2** commands in its configuration.

Other parameters, such as the interface name, security level, and IP address, should be configured on VLAN interfaces rather than on physical interfaces. These are discussed in the section, "Configuring Interface Security Parameters."

If you need to carry multiple VLANs over a link to a neighboring switch, you can configure an ASA 5505 physical interface as a VLAN trunk link. First, create the individual VLANs with the **interface vlan** *vlan-id* configuration command. Then, configure the physical interface to operate in IEEE 802.1Q trunk mode and allow specific VLANs to be carried over it with the following interface configuration commands:

```
ciscoasa(config-if)# switchport mode trunk
ciscoasa(config-if)# switchport trunk allowed vlan vlan-list
```

By default, no VLANs are permitted to be carried over a trunk link. You must identify which VLANs can be carried by entering *vlan-list*, which is a comma-separated list of VLAN numbers. In Example 3-10, an ASA 5505 is configured to support VLANs 10 and 20 and carry those VLANs over interface Ethernet0/5, which is configured as a trunk link.

Example 3-10 *ASA VLAN CLI Configuration*

```
ciscoasa(config)# interface vlan 10
ciscoasa(config-if)# exit
ciscoasa(config)# interface vlan 20
ciscoasa(config-if)# exit
ciscoasa(config)# interface ethernet0/5
ciscoasa(config-if)# switchport mode trunk
ciscoasa(config-if)# switchport trunk allowed vlan 10,20
```

Configuring Interface Security Parameters

Once you identify an ASA interface that will be connected to the network, you will need to apply the following three security parameters to it:

- Interface name

- IP address

- Security level

These parameters are explained in the following sections.

Naming the Interface

ASA interfaces are known by two different names:

- **Hardware name:** Specifies the interface type, hardware module, and port number. The hardware names of physical interfaces can include Ethernet0/0, Management0/0, and GigabitEthernet1/0. Hardware names of VLAN interfaces have a subinterface suffix, such as Ethernet0/0.1. Hardware names are predefined and cannot be changed.

- **Interface name:** Specifies the function of the interface, relative to its security posture. For example, an interface that faces the outside, untrusted world might be named "outside," whereas an interface that faces the inside, trusted network might be named "inside." Interface names are arbitrary. An ASA uses the interface name when security policies are applied.

To assign an interface name to an ASA interface, you must first enter the interface configuration mode. Then, you can define the interface hardware name with the following interface configuration command:

```
ciscoasa(config-if)# nameif if_name
```

In Example 3-11, interface Ethernet0/0 is configured with the interface name "outside."

Example 3-11 *Assigning an Interface Name*

```
ciscoasa(config)# interface ethernet0/0
ciscoasa(config-if)# nameif outside
```

You can set the interface name in ASDM by editing an existing interface or adding a new interface. The interface name is set by entering the name into the Interface Name field.

Assigning an IP Address

To communicate with other devices on a network, an ASA interface needs its own IP address. (The only exception is when the ASA is configured to operate in transparent mode. This mode is covered in Chapter 12, "Using Transparent Firewall Mode.")

You can use the following interface configuration command to assign a static IP address and subnet mask to an ASA interface, if one is known and available:

```
ciscoasa(config-if)# ip address ip-address [subnet-mask]
```

If you omit the *subnet-mask* parameter, the firewall assumes that a classful network (Class A, B, or C) is being used. For example, if the first octet of the IP address is 1 through 126 (1.0.0.0 through 126.255.255.255), a Class A subnet mask (255.0.0.0) is assumed.

If you use subnetting in your network, be sure to specify the correct subnet mask rather than the classful mask (255.0.0.0, 255.255.0.0, or 255.255.255.0) that the firewall derives from the IP address.

Continuing the process from Example 3-9, so that the outside interface is assigned IP address 192.168.254.2 with a subnet mask of 255.255.255.0, enter the following:

```
ciscoasa(config-if)# ip address 192.168.254.2 255.255.255.0
```

If the ASA is connected to a network that offers dynamic IP address assignment, you should not configure a static IP address on the interface. Instead, you can configure the ASA to request an IP address through DHCP or PPPoE. Only DHCP is covered in the FIREWALL course and exam.

You can use the following interface configuration command to force the interface to request its IP address from a DHCP server:

```
ciscoasa(config-if)# ip address dhcp [setroute]
```

Adding the **setroute** keyword causes the ASA to set its default route automatically, based on the default gateway parameter that is returned in the DHCP reply. This is handy because the default route should always correlate with the IP address that is given to the interface. If the **setroute** keyword is not entered, you will have to explicitly configure a default route.

Once the ASA obtains an IP address for the interface via DHCP, you can release and renew the DHCP lease by re-entering the **ip address dhcp** command.

You can set a static interface IP address in ASDM by editing an existing interface or adding a new one. First, select **Use Static IP** in the IP Address section, as shown previously in Figure 3-13, and then enter the IP address. For the subnet mask, you can type in a mask or select one from a drop-down menu.

If the interface requests an IP address through DHCP, select the **Obtain Address via DHCP** option. By default, the ASA will use the interface MAC address in the DHCP request. To get a default gateway automatically through DHCP, check the **Obtain Default Route Through DHCP** check box. You can click the **Renew DHCP Lease** button at any time to release and renew the DHCP lease.

Setting the Security Level

ASA platforms have some inherent security policies that are based on the relative trust or security level that has been assigned to each interface. Interfaces with a higher security level are considered to be more trusted than interfaces with a lower security level. The security levels can range from 0 (the least amount of trust) to 100 (the greatest amount of trust).

Usually, the "outside" interface that faces a public, untrusted network should receive security level 0. The "inside" interface that faces the community of trusted users should receive security level 100. Any other ASA interfaces that connect to other areas of the network should receive a security level between 1 and 99. Figure 3-14 shows a typical scenario with an ASA and three interfaces.

By default, interface security levels must be unique so that the ASA can apply security policies across security-level boundaries. This is because of the two following inherent policies that an ASA uses to forward traffic between its interfaces:

- Traffic is allowed to flow from a higher-security interface to a lower-security interface (inside to outside, for example), provided that any access list, stateful inspection, and address translation requirements are met.

- Traffic from a lower-security interface to a higher one cannot pass unless additional explicit inspection and filtering checks are passed.

This concept is shown in Figure 3-15, applied to an ASA with only two interfaces.

In addition, the same two security policies apply to any number of interfaces. Figure 3-16 shows an ASA with three different interfaces and how traffic is inherently permitted to flow from higher-security interfaces toward lower-security interfaces. For example, traffic coming from the inside network (security level 100) can flow toward the DMZ network (security level 50) because the security levels are decreasing. As well, DMZ traffic (security level 50) can flow toward the outside network (security level 0).

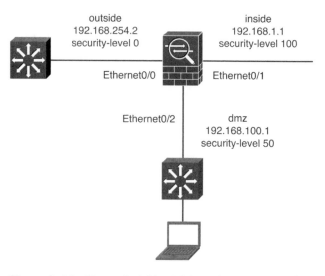

Figure 3-14   *Example ASA with Interface Names and Unique Security Levels*

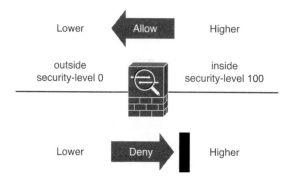

Figure 3-15   *Inherent Security Policies Between ASA Interfaces*

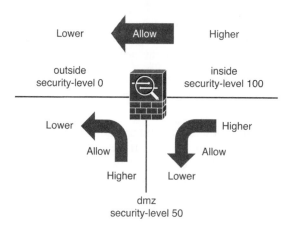

Figure 3-16   *Traffic Flows Are Permitted from Higher to Lower Security Levels*

Traffic that is initiated in the opposite direction, from a lower security level toward a higher one, cannot pass so easily. Figure 3-17 shows the same ASA with three interfaces and the possible traffic flow patterns.

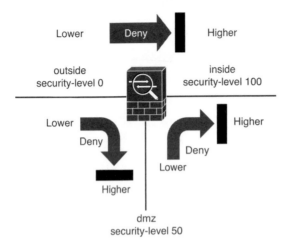

Figure 3-17   *Traffic Flows Are Blocked from Lower to Higher Security Levels*

You can assign a security level of 0 to 100 to an ASA interface with the following inter-face configuration command:

```
ciscoasa(config-if)# security-level level
```

From ASDM, you can set the security level when you edit an existing interface or add a new one.

Continuing from the configuration in the section, "Assigning an IP Address," you can as-sign the outside interface with a security level of 0 by entering the following:

```
ciscoasa(config-if)# security-level 0
```

By default, interface security levels do not have to be unique on an ASA. However, if two interfaces have the same security level, the default security policy will not permit any traf-fic to pass between the two interfaces at all. You can override this behavior with the **same-security-traffic permit inter-interface** command.

In addition, there are two cases in which it is not possible to assign unique security levels to each ASA interface:

■ **The number of ASA interfaces is greater than the number of unique security level values:** Because the security level can range from 0 to 100, there are 101 unique values. Some ASA platforms can support more than 101 VLAN interfaces, so it becomes impossible to give them all unique security levels. In this case, you can use the following command in global configuration mode so that you can reuse secu-rity level numbers and relax the security level constraint *between* interfaces, as shown in the left portion of Figure 3-18:

```
ciscoasa(config)# same-security-traffic permit inter-interface
```

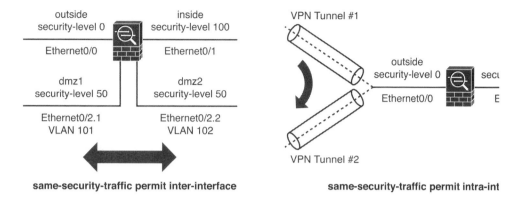

Figure 3-18 *Permitting Traffic to Flow Across the Same Security Levels*

- **Traffic must enter and exit through the same interface, traversing the same security level:** When an ASA is configured to support logical VPN connections, multiple connections might terminate on the same ASA interface. This VPN architecture looks much like the spokes of a wheel, where the ASA interface is at the hub or center. When traffic comes from one VPN spoke and enters another spoke, it essentially enters the ASA interface and comes out of one VPN connection, only to enter a different VPN connection and go back out the same interface. In effect, the VPN traffic follows a hairpin turn on a single interface.

  If an ASA is configured for VPN connections, you can use the following command in global configuration mode to relax the security level constraint *within* an interface, as shown in the right portion of Figure 3-18:

  ```
  ciscoasa(config)# same-security-traffic permit intra-interface
  ```

If you are using ASDM, you can accomplish the same tasks from the **Configuration > Device Setup > Interfaces** using the two check boxes at the bottom of the interface list, as illustrated in Figure 3-19.

Interface Security Parameters Example

The ASA in Figure 3-14 has three interfaces. Example 3-12 shows the commands that can be used to configure each of the interfaces with the necessary security parameters.

Example 3-12 *Configuring the ASA Interfaces from Figure 3-14*

```
ciscoasa(config)# interface ethernet0/0
ciscoasa(config-if)# nameif outside
ciscoasa(config-if)# ip address 192.168.254.2 255.255.255.0
ciscoasa(config-if)# security-level 0
ciscoasa(config-if)# interface ethernet0/1
ciscoasa(config-if)# nameif inside
ciscoasa(config-if)# ip address 192.168.1.1 255.255.255.0
ciscoasa(config-if)# security-level 100
ciscoasa(config-if)# interface ethernet0/2
ciscoasa(config-if)# nameif dmz
ciscoasa(config-if)# ip address 192.168.100.1 255.255.255.0
ciscoasa(config-if)# security-level 50
```

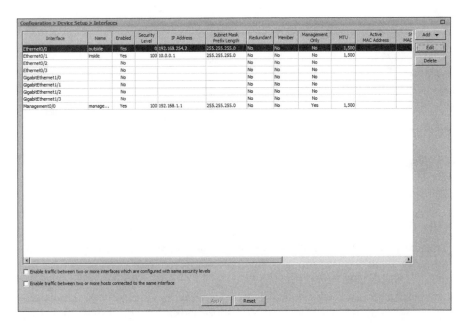

Figure 3-19   *Check Boxes to Permit Traffic to Traverse the Same Security Levels*

As a comparison, Figure 3-20 shows the same outside interface configuration done in ASDM.

Configuring the Interface MTU

By default, any Ethernet interface has its maximum transmission unit (MTU) size set to 1500 bytes, which is the maximum and expected value for Ethernet frames. If a packet is larger than the MTU, it must be fragmented before being transmitted. And before the packet can be presented at the destination, all of its fragments must be reassembled in their proper order.

The whole fragmentation and reassembly process takes time, memory, and CPU resources, so it should be avoided if possible. Normally, the default 1500-byte MTU is sufficient because Ethernet frames are limited to a standard maximum of 1500 bytes of payload data. Various IEEE standards use expanded frame sizes to carry additional information. As well, data centers often leverage Ethernet "giant" or "jumbo" frames, which are much larger than normal, to move large amounts of data efficiently.

If packets larger than 1500 bytes are commonplace in a network, you can increase the MTU size to prevent the packets from being fragmented at all. In some cases, you might need to reduce the MTU to avoid having to fragment encrypted packets where the encryption protocols add too much overhead to an already maximum-sized packet. Ideally, the MTU should be increased on every network device and interface along the entire data path.

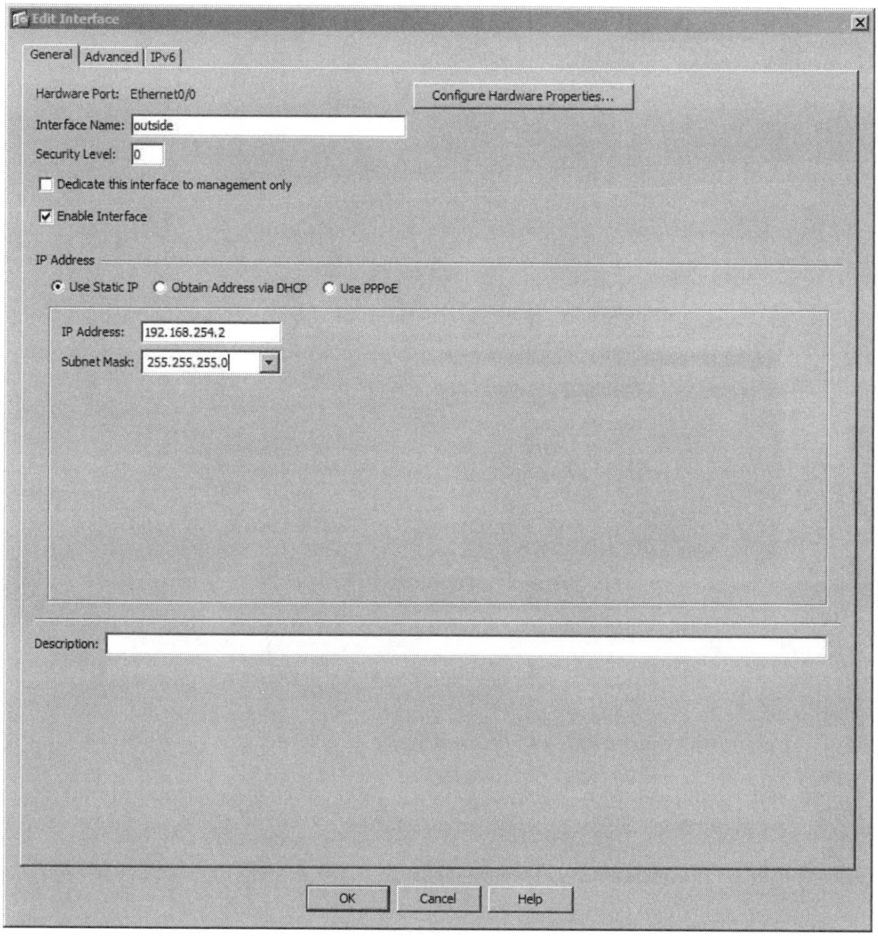

Figure 3-20 *Configuring the Outside ASA Interface*

To adjust the interface MTU from ASDM, first select **Configuration > Device Setup > Interfaces**, select an interface, and click the **Edit** button. Next, select the **Advanced** tab and enter the new MTU value, as shown in Figure 3-21. Although ASDM lets you type a new value, it won't permit the value to change if the interface has not been configured with a name.

To accomplish the same task from the CLI, you can use the following global configuration command to adjust the MTU on an ASA interface:

```
ciscoasa(config)# mtu if_name bytes
```

Identify the interface using its name, such as "inside" or "outside," rather than the hardware name. The transmitted MTU can be sized from 64 to 9216 bytes.

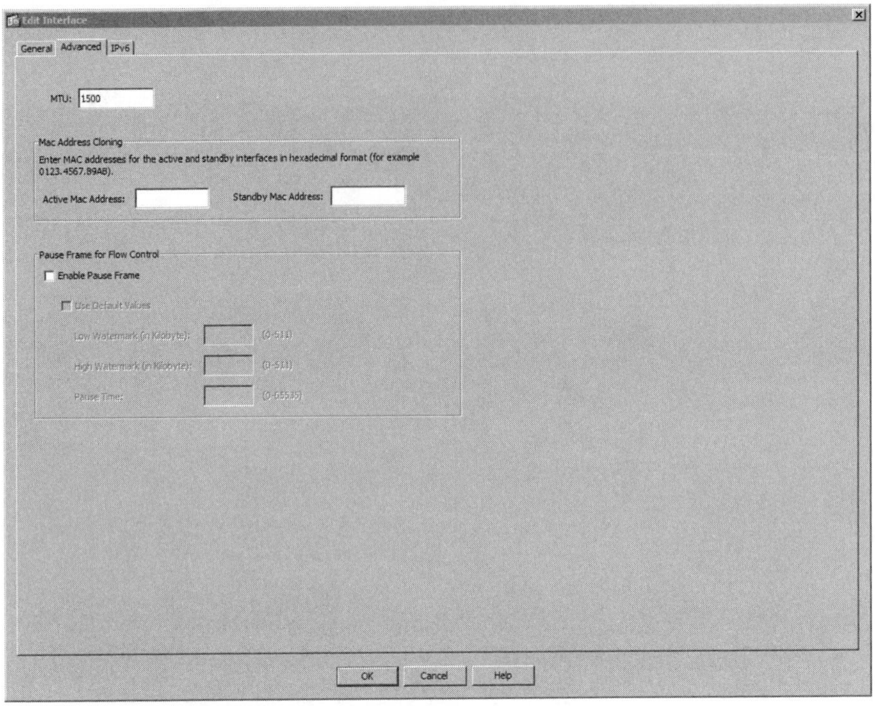

Figure 3-21 *Configuring an Interface MTU in ASDM*

You should also use the following interface configuration command to enable jumbo frame processing as frames are received on an interface:

```
ciscoasa(config-if)# jumbo-frame reservation
```

Although you can increase the MTU size on any ASA platform, be aware that the **jumbo-frame reservation** command is supported only on the ASA 5585-X.

You can display the current MTU configuration for all firewall interfaces by using the **show running-config mtu** command. Interface MTU settings are also displayed as a part of the **show interface** command output. Example 3-13 shows the output from each of the commands.

Example 3-13 *Displaying the Interface MTU*

```
ciscoasa# show running-config mtu
mtu outside 1500
mtu inside 1500
ciscoasa# show interface outside
Interface Ethernet0/0 "outside", is up, line protocol is up
  Hardware is i82546GB rev03, BW 1000 Mbps, DLY 10 usec
        Auto-Duplex(Full-duplex), Auto-Speed(100 Mbps)
        Input flow control is unsupported, output flow control is unsupported
        MAC address 001a.a22d.1ddc, MTU 1500
```

```
        IP address 192.168.100.10, subnet mask 255.255.255.0
        1996 packets input, 127860 bytes, 0 no buffer
        Received 533 broadcasts, 0 runts, 0 giants
```

Verifying Interface Operation

To verify that an ASA interface is operating correctly, you can use the following command:

```
ciscoasa# show interface if_name
```

Here, you can specify either a hardware name, such as ethernet0/0, or an interface name, such as outside. The **show interface** command displays the current status, current speed and duplex mode, MAC address, IP address, and many statistics about the data being moved into and out of the interface. The command also lists traffic statistics, such as packets and bytes in the input and output directions, and traffic rates. The rates are shown as 1-minute and 5-minute averages. Example 3-14 shows a sample of the output.

Example 3-14 *Sample Output from the* **show interface** *Command*

```
ciscoasa# show interface ethernet0/0
Interface Ethernet0/0 "outside", is up, line protocol is up
  Hardware is i82546GB rev03, BW 1000 Mbps, DLY 10 usec
        Auto-Duplex(Full-duplex), Auto-Speed(100 Mbps)
        Input flow control is unsupported, output flow control is unsupported
        MAC address 001a.a22d.1ddc, MTU 1500
        IP address 192.168.254.2, subnet mask 255.255.255.0
        26722691 packets input, 27145573880 bytes, 0 no buffer
        Received 62291 broadcasts, 0 runts, 0 giants
        0 input errors, 0 CRC, 0 frame, 0 overrun, 0 ignored, 0 abort
        0 pause input, 0 resume input
        0 L2 decode drops
        19039166 packets output, 5820422387 bytes, 0 underruns
        0 output errors, 0 collisions, 0 interface resets
        0 late collisions, 0 deferred
        0 input reset drops, 0 output reset drops
        0 rate limit drops
        input queue (blocks free curr/low): hardware (255/253)
        output queue (blocks free curr/low): hardware (255/255)
  Traffic Statistics for "outside":
        26722691 packets input, 27145573880 bytes
        19039166 packets output, 5820422387 bytes
        49550 packets dropped
      1 minute input rate 16 pkts/sec,  16110 bytes/sec
      1 minute output rate 17 pkts/sec,  16240 bytes/sec
      1 minute drop rate, 0 pkts/sec
      5 minute input rate 12 pkts/sec,  13867 bytes/sec
```

```
     5 minute output rate 15 pkts/sec,  15311 bytes/sec
     5 minute drop rate, 0 pkts/sec
ciscoasa#
```

You can verify the interface status in the second line of output. If the interface is shown as "up," the interface has been enabled. If the line protocol is shown as "up," there is an active link between the ASA interface and some other device.

To display a summary of all ASA interfaces and their IP addresses and current status, you can use the **show interface ip brief** command, as shown in Example 3-15.

Example 3-15 *Sample Output from the* **show interface ip brief** *Command*

```
ciscoasa# show interface ip brief
Interface              IP-Address      OK? Method Status                Protocol
Ethernet0/0            192.168.254.2   YES manual up                    up
Ethernet0/1            10.0.0.1        YES manual up                    up
Ethernet0/2            unassigned      YES unset  administratively down down
Ethernet0/3            unassigned      YES unset  administratively down down
Internal-Data0/0       unassigned      YES unset  administratively down up
Management0/0          192.168.1.1     YES manual up                    up
GigabitEthernet1/0     unassigned      YES unset  administratively down down
GigabitEthernet1/1     unassigned      YES unset  administratively down down
GigabitEthernet1/2     unassigned      YES unset  administratively down down
GigabitEthernet1/3     unassigned      YES unset  administratively down down
Internal-Data1/0       unassigned      YES unset  up                    up
ciscoasa#
```

You can monitor the redundant interface status with the following command:

```
ciscoasa# show interface redundant number
```

Example 3-16 shows the output for interface redundant 1. Notice that physical interface Ethernet0/0 is currently the active interface, while Ethernet0/1 is not. The output also reveals the date and time of the last switchover.

Example 3-16 *Verifying the Status of a Redundant Interface*

```
ciscoasa# show interface redundant 1
Interface Redundant1 "inside", is up, line protocol is up
  Hardware is i82546GB rev03, BW 100 Mbps, DLY 1000 usec
        Auto-Duplex(Full-duplex), Auto-Speed(100 Mbps)
        MAC address 0016.c789.c8a5, MTU 1500

[output omitted for clarity]
```

```
    Redundancy Information:
         Member Ethernet0/0(Active), Ethernet0/1
         Last switchover at 01:32:27 EDT Sep 24 2010
ciscoasa#
```

Exam Preparation Tasks

As mentioned in the section, "How to Use This Book," in the Introduction, you have a couple of choices for exam preparation: the exercises here, Chapter 17, "Final Preparation," and the exam simulation questions on the CD-ROM.

Review All Key Topics

Review the most important topics from inside the chapter, noted with the Key Topics icon in the outer margin of the page. Table 3-3 lists a reference of these key topics and the page numbers on which each is found.

Table 3-3 *Key Topics for Chapter 3*

Key Topic Element	Description	Page Number
Paragraph	Discusses physical interface configuration	83
Paragraph	Explains redundant interfaces	85
Paragraph	Describes EtherChannel negotiation with LACP	89
Paragraph	Explains how to configure a trunk link	95
Paragraph	Explains how to configure VLAN interfaces on an ASA 5505	97
List	Describes the three necessary interface security parameters	98
Paragraph	Describes how to display interface status information and statistics	107

Key Topic

Define Key Terms

Define the following key terms from this chapter and check your answers in the glossary:

hardware name, interface name, security level, physical interface, redundant interface, member interface, EtherChannel, LACP, VLAN interface, VLAN trunk link, MTU

Command Reference to Check Your Memory

This section includes the most important configuration and EXEC commands covered in this chapter. It might not be necessary to memorize the complete syntax of every command, but you should be able to remember the basic keywords that are needed.

To test your memory of the commands, cover the right side of Table 3-4 with a piece of paper, read the description on the left side, and then see how much of the command you can remember.

The FIREWALL exam focuses on practical, hands-on skills that are used by a networking professional. Therefore, you should be able to identify the commands needed to configure and test an ASA feature.

Table 3-4 *Commands Related to ASA Interface Configuration and Verification*

Task	Command Syntax
List physical interfaces	ciscoasa# **show version**
List interfaces that have a name and security level	ciscoasa# **show nameif**
List ASA 5505 interfaces and VLAN mapping	ciscoasa# **show switch vlan**
Configure the speed, duplex mode, and state of a physical interface	ciscoasa(config)# **interface** *hardware-id* ciscoasa(config-if)# **speed {auto | 10 | 100 | 1000}** ciscoasa(config-if)# **duplex {auto | full | half}** ciscoasa(config-if)# **[no] shutdown**
Map an ASA 5505 physical interface to a VLAN	ciscoasa(config-if)# **switchport access vlan** *vlan-id*
Define a redundant interface and its member interfaces	ciscoasa(config)# **interface redundant** *number* ciscoasa(config-int)# **member-interface** *physical_interface* ciscoasa(config-if)# **[no] shutdown**
Set the LACP system priority	ciscoasa(config)# **lacp system-priority-** *priority*
Configure a physical interface to become a member of an EtherChannel	ciscoasa(config)# **interface** *type mod/num* ciscoasa(config-if)# **channel-protocol lacp** ciscoasa(config-if)# **channel-group** *number* **mode {on | passive | active}** ciscoasa(config-if)# **lacp port-priority** *priority*
Define a physical subinterface that is mapped to a VLAN number	ciscoasa(config)# **interface** *hardware_id.subinterface* ciscoasa(config-subif)# **vlan** *vlan_id*
Configure an ASA 5505 VLAN interface	ciscoasa(config)# **interface vlan** *vlan-id*
Assign an interface name	ciscoasa(config-if)# **nameif** *if_name*

Table 3-4 *Commands Related to ASA Interface Configuration and Verification*

Task	Command Syntax
Assign an IP address to an interface	ciscoasa(config-if)# **ip address** *ip-address* [*subnet-mask*]
Configure an interface to request an IP address from a DHCP server	ciscoasa(config-if)# **ip address dhcp** [**setroute**]
Assign a security level to an interface	ciscoasa(config-if)# **security-level** *level*
Allow traffic to pass between interfaces with the same security level, either across two interfaces or across logical interfaces within a single physical interface, respectively	ciscoasa(config)# **same-security-traffic permit inter-interface** ciscoasa(config)# **same-security-traffic permit intra-interface**
Set the interface MTU size	ciscoasa(config)# **mtu** *if_name bytes*
Allow jumbo Ethernet frames on an ASA 5580	ciscoasa(config-if)# **jumbo-frame reservation**
Display interface details	ciscoasa# **show interface** *if_name*
Display the status of a redundant interface	ciscoasa# **show interface redundant** *number*
Display interfaces and their IP addresses and status	ciscoasa# **show interface ip brief**
Display a summary status of an Ether-Channel and its member interfaces	ciscoasa# **show port-channel summary**

This chapter covers the following topics:

- **Deploying DHCP Services:** This section covers how a Cisco ASA can operate as a DHCP server and a DHCP relay. These functions support dynamic addressing for protected hosts, either by the ASA or by an external dedicated DHCP server.

- **Using Routing Information:** This section presents an overview of the various sources of routing information and how an ASA can use them.

- **Configuring Static Routing:** This section covers manual configuration of static routes, as well as static route tracking, which can make static routes respond to changing conditions.

- **Routing with RIPv2:** This section covers the Routing Information Protocol (RIP) version 2 dynamic routing protocol.

- **Routing with EIGRP:** This section covers the Enhanced Interior Gateway Routing Protocol (EIGRP) and how it can provide an ASA with dynamic routing information.

- **Routing with OSPF:** This section covers the Open Shortest Path First (OSPF) dynamic routing protocol and how an ASA can interact with other OSPF routers.

- **Verifying the ASA Routing Table:** This section provides an overview of some tools you can use to verify the information in an ASA's routing table and the relationship with neighboring routers.

CHAPTER 4

Configuring IP Connectivity

This chapter covers two ways that a Cisco Adaptive Security Appliance (ASA) can help provide IP addressing information for hosts that it protects on a network—by operating as a DHCP server or as a DHCP relay.

Once you configure ASA interfaces with IP addresses, an ASA can inherently reach other devices that are connected to those interfaces and located on the respective IP subnets. But, before an ASA can reach other subnets and networks that are located outside its immediate surroundings, it must use either static routing information that you have configured manually or routing information exchanged dynamically with other Layer 3 routing devices.

This chapter discusses each of these topics in detail.

"Do I Know This Already?" Quiz

The "Do I Know This Already?" quiz allows you to assess whether you should read this entire chapter thoroughly or jump to the "Exam Preparation Tasks" section. If you are in doubt about your answers to these questions or your own assessment of your knowledge of the topics, read the entire chapter. Table 4-1 lists the major headings in this chapter and their corresponding "Do I Know This Already?" quiz questions. You can find the answers in Appendix A, "Answers to the 'Do I Know This Already?' Quizzes."

Table 4-1 *"Do I Know This Already?" Section-to-Question Mapping*

Foundation Topics Section	Questions
Deploying DHCP Services	1–2
Using Routing Information	3–5
Configuring Static Routing	6–7
Routing with RIPv2	8
Routing with EIGRP	9
Routing with OSPF	10–11
Verifying the ASA Routing Table	12

Caution: The goal of self-assessment is to gauge your mastery of the topics in this chapter. If you do not know the answer to a question or are only partially sure of the answer, you should mark that question as wrong for purposes of the self-assessment. Giving yourself credit for an answer you correctly guess skews your self-assessment results and might provide you with a false sense of security.

1. Which one of the following is a valid scenario for using the DHCP relay feature on an ASA?

   a. A group of users and a DHCP server are located on the same ASA interface.

   b. A group of users is located on one ASA interface; a DHCP server is located on another ASA interface.

   c. A group of users is located on an ASA interface, but no DHCP server exists.

   d. Malicious users attempt to exploit DHCP requests.

2. Which one of the following represents the complete command to enable the DHCP server feature on an ASA?

   a. dhcp server enable

   b. dhcpd

   c. dhcpd enable

   d. dhcpd enable inside

3. Which source of routing information is considered to be the most stable?

   a. Static routes

   b. Routes learned through RIPv2

   c. Routes learned through EIGRP

   d. Routes learned through OSPF

4. Which of the following are recommended practices when configuring routing on an ASA? (Choose all that apply.)

   a. Always use OSPF whenever possible.

   b. Always rely on static routing unless the size of the network is too large.

   c. Always authenticate all dynamic routing protocol peers.

   d. Use route filtering to choose one routing protocol over another.

5. If static routes are the most trusted, which one of the following sources of routing information is the next most trusted?

   a. EIGRP internal

   b. RIPv2

   c. OSPF

   d. Directly connected route

6. Which of the following represents a correct command syntax for configuring a default route on an ASA? (Choose all that apply.)

   a. route outside default 10.10.10.10

   b. route outside 0.0.0.0 0.0.0.0 10.10.10.10

   c. route outside 0 0 10.10.10.10

   d. ip route outside 0.0.0.0 0.0.0.0 10.10.10.10

7. Which ASA feature is used as the basis for tracking a static route based on the results of pinging a target address?

   a. ICMP tracking

   b. Reverse route injection

   c. SLA monitor

   d. Object grouping

8. Which of the following enables RIPv2 on an ASA?

   a. ripv2 enable

   b. router ripv2

   c. router rip
        `version 2`

   d. router rip

9. The following configuration commands are entered into an ASA. Which of the following answers are correct regarding the inside network? (Choose all that apply.)

```
router eigrp 100
    network 192.168.1.0
    passive-interface inside
```

   a. The inside interface subnet will be advertised.

   b. The inside interface subnet will not be advertised.

   c. The ASA will discover an EIGRP peer on its inside interface.

   d. The ASA will not discover an EIGRP peer on its inside interface.

10. If an ASA connects to OSPF area 0 on its inside interface and OSPF area 1 on its dmz interface, it is called which one of the following?

   a. ABR

   b. ASBR

   c. SPF

   d. Nothing; this is an invalid configuration.

11. Suppose you have configured OSPF on an ASA, but the **show ospf neighbor** command displays no active OSPF peers. Which one of the following could be the cause of the problem?

    a. The MD5 authentication key entered on the ASA doesn't match the key entered on any OSPF peer.

    b. The ASA has not been configured with any access list rules to permit OSPF traffic.

    c. You forgot to enter the **copy running-config startup-config** command.

    d. The ASA and any neighboring routers should not be configured with the same OSPF area.

12. Which one of the following commands can be used to display the routing table on an ASA?

    a. show routing-table

    b. show ip route

    c. show route

    d. show run route

Foundation Topics

To forward traffic between its interfaces, an ASA must know how to reach other subnets and networks located outside its immediate surroundings. You can configure an ASA to use static routing information or information exchanged dynamically with other routing devices.

You can also configure an ASA to provide various DHCP services so that hosts connected to its interfaces can get their IP addresses dynamically.

This chapter discusses each of these topics in detail.

Deploying DHCP Services

Client devices that are connected to a network need to use unique IP addresses so that they can communicate. Although a client can be configured with a static IP address, most often it relies on a DHCP server to provide an IP address that can be "checked out" or leased for a period of time.

When a network architecture includes an ASA, either the clients have no local DHCP server or the clients can become separated or isolated from a working DHCP server. You can configure an ASA to assist the clients in either of these cases, as described in the sections that follow.

Configuring a DHCP Relay

When a client needs an IP address for itself, it sends a DHCP request, hoping that a DHCP server can hear the request and answer. DHCP requests are normally sent as broadcasts, because the DHCP server address is not known ahead of time. Therefore, a DHCP server must be located within the same broadcast domain as a client.

When an ASA is introduced into a network, it might also introduce a new security domain boundary that separates clients from a DHCP server. For example, a group of clients might be connected to one ASA interface, and the DHCP server might be connected to a different interface. By default, an ASA will not forward DHCP requests from one of its interfaces to another.

You can configure an ASA to use the DHCP relay agent feature to relay DHCP requests (broadcasts) received on one interface to a DHCP server found on another interface. The ASA does this by converting the requests to UDP port 67 unicast packets. The ASA can also intercept the DHCP replies that are returned by the DHCP server so that the default router address can be changed to become the IP address of the ASA itself.

Note: Once you enable the DHCP relay agent, the ASA will handle the DHCP packets as they are sent and received. You do not have to configure any specific rules or security policies to permit the DHCP packets to pass through any of the ASA interfaces.

To enable the DHCP relay agent in ASDM, select **Configuration > Device Management > DHCP > DHCP Relay** and click the **Add** button. Define the IP address of a DHCP server and identify the ASA interface where the server can be found. In Figure 4-1, a DHCP server is at 192.168.50.11, located on the ASA's dmz interface.

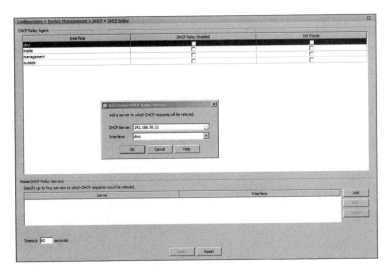

Figure 4-1 *Defining a DHCP Server for the DHCP Relay Agent in ASDM*

Next, look through the list of DHCP relay agent interfaces and find the one where the DHCP clients are located. Check the **DHCP Relay Enabled** check box to enable DHCP relay on that interface. You can check the **Set Route** check box to override the default gateway parameter in DHCP replies with the ASA interface address, as shown in Figure 4-2. The DHCP clients are located on the inside interface.

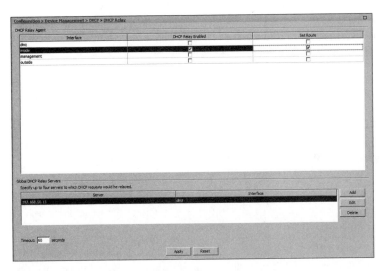

Figure 4-2 *Enabling the DHCP Relay Feature on an ASA Interface*

You can use the CLI to configure DHCP Relay with the following steps:

Step 1.   Identify the DHCP server and its location:

```
ciscoasa(config)# dhcprelay server ip-address interface
```

If you have more than one DHCP server, you can repeat this command to define up to four different servers. In this case, the DHCP requests are relayed to
each of the servers simultaneously.

Step 2.   Identify the DHCP client locations:

```
ciscoasa(config)# dhcprelay enable interface
```

Step 3.   Override the default router returned in the DHCP offers:

```
ciscoasa(config)# dhcprelay setroute interface
```

Example 4-1 shows the configuration commands that can be used to enable the DHCP relay agent for the clients located on the inside interface, where the server is located on the
dmz interface.

Example 4-1   *Configuring the DHCP Relay Agent Feature*

```
ciscoasa(config)# dhcprelay server 192.168.50.11 dmz
ciscoasa(config)# dhcpreley enable inside
ciscoasa(config)# dhcprelay setroute inside
```

Configuring a DHCP Server

In some cases, a network might not have a dedicated DHCP server. You can configure an
ASA to act as a DHCP server, assigning IP addresses dynamically to requesting clients.
The DHCP server can also generate dynamic DNS information, allowing DNS records to
be updated dynamically as hosts acquire an IP address.

An ASA will return its own interface address for the client to use as the default gateway.
The interface subnet mask is returned for the client to use as well. You can define and enable DHCP servers on more than one interface, if clients are located there.

Note: No provisions are available for configuring static address assignments. An ASA can
manage only dynamic address assignments from a pool of contiguous IP addresses.

As an example, suppose an ASA is configured as a DHCP server for clients on its inside interface. The inside interface has already been configured with IP address 192.168.10.1. The
clients are to be assigned an address from the pool 192.168.10.10 through 192.168.10.254.
The clients should also receive DNS addresses 192.168.1.20 and 192.168.1.21, WINS addresses 192.168.1.22 and 192.168.1.23, and a default domain name of
mynewnetwork.com.

Figure 4-3 shows how you can begin to configure the scenario through ASDM. Navigate
to **Configuration > Device Management > DHCP > DHCP Server**. Select the interface

that will face the DHCP clients and click the **Edit** button. Check the **Enable DHCP Server** check box to enable the service, and then specify the first and last IP address in the DHCP address pool. You can also enter DNS, WINS, and a domain name that are specific to this DHCP scope, if needed; otherwise, leave those fields blank and click the **OK** button.

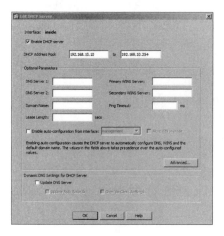

Figure 4-3   *Configuring the DHCP Server Feature with ASDM*

Next, in the **Configuration > Device Management > DHCP > DHCP Server** window, enter the values for global DNS and WINS, as well as a domain name. These parameters apply to all DHCP scopes on the ASA, as long as they are not overridden with specific values in a scope. In Figure 4-4, the global parameters for the example scenario are entered.

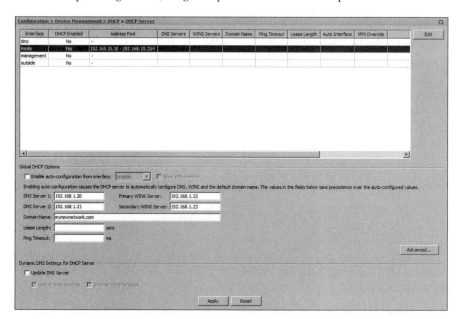

Figure 4-4   *Entering Global DHCP Server Parameters*

Alternatively, you can configure the DHCP server feature from the CLI by using the following steps:

Step 1. Enable the DHCP server on an ASA interface that faces the clients:

```
ciscoasa(config)# dhcpd enable interface
```

Step 2. Create an address pool for clients on an interface:

```
ciscoasa(config)# dhcpd address ip1[-ip2] interface
```

The DHCP scope of IP addresses begins with *ip1* and ends with *ip2*. These two addresses must be separated by a hyphen and must belong to the same subnet. In addition, the pool of addresses must reside in the same IP subnet assigned to the ASA interface.

Step 3. Configure DHCP options for clients.

You can use the **dhcp option** command to define any specific DHCP options that clients need to receive. With the following command syntax, you can configure an option code number with an ASCII string, an IP address, or a hex string:

```
ciscoasa(config)# dhcpd option code {ascii string | ip ip_address |
   hex hex_string}
```

As an example, you might want to hand out DHCP option 66 (TFTP server) or DHCP option 150 (multiple TFTP servers) to Cisco IP Phone clients. By default, an ASA hands out its own interface address as the client's default gateway, but you can override that value by configuring an IP address with DHCP option 3 (default router).

Step 4. Configure any global DHCP parameters.

Some parameters are global in nature and can be handed out in all DHCP replies. You can define the DNS and WINS server addresses and the default domain name with the following commands, respectively:

```
ciscoasa(config)# dhcpd dns dns1 [dns2]
ciscoasa(config)# dhcpd wins wins1 [wins2]
ciscoasa(config)# dhcpd domain domain_name
```

By default, each DHCP lease is sent with a lease time of 3600 seconds, or 1 hour. You can override that value globally with the following command, where the lease length is given in seconds:

```
ciscoasa(config)# dhcpd lease lease_length
```

Finally, when an ASA receives a DHCP request from a potential client, it looks up the next available IP address in the pool. Before a DHCP reply is returned, the ASA sends an ICMP echo (ping) as a test to make sure that the IP address is not already in use by some other host. By default, the ASA waits 750 ms for an ICMP reply; if no reply is received, it assumes that the IP address is indeed available and assigns it to the client. If an ICMP reply is received from that address, the firewall knows that the address is already taken, so the next address from the pool is tried.

You can override the ping test timer by issuing the following command with a timeout (100 to 10,000) in milliseconds:

```
ciscoasa(config)# dhcpd ping_timeout timeout
```

Example 4-2 shows the commands that you can use to configure the example scenario on the ASA.

Example 4-2   *Configuring the DHCP Server Feature*

```
ciscoasa(config)# dhcpd enable inside
ciscoasa(config)# dhcpd address 192.168.10.10-192.168.10.254 inside
ciscoasa(config)# dhcpd dns 192.168.1.20 192.168.1.21
ciscoasa(config)# dhcpd wins 192.168.1.22 192.168.1.23
ciscoasa(config)# dhcpd domain mynewnetwork.com
```

You can verify the DHCP server operation with the **show dhcpd state** EXEC command. As well, you can display the active DHCP leases with the **show dhcpd binding all** command.

Using Routing Information

Once you configure an IP address and a subnet mask on an ASA interface, the entire IP subnet used on that interface becomes reachable from the ASA. This is known as a directly connected subnet or route. Before the ASA can forward packets toward other subnets that are not directly connected, it needs additional routing information.

An ASA keeps a table of routes to all IP subnets that are known to it. At a minimum, each route contains an IP subnet, a subnet mask, and the IP address of the next-hop router that can reach the subnet. By default, the routing table is populated with every directly connected subnet, where the next hop is the ASA's own interface. An ASA can also import routing information into its routing table from the following sources:

■   **Static routes:** Routes that are manually configured and do not change.

■   **RIP version 2:** Routes learned dynamically from other routers running the Routing Information Protocol version 2 (RIPv2); RIPv1 is also supported, but is not covered on the FIREWALL exam.

■   **EIGRP:** Routes learned dynamically from other routers running the Enhanced Interior Gateway Routing Protocol (EIGRP).

■   **OSPF:** Routes learned dynamically from other routers running the Open Shortest Path First (OSPF) routing protocol.

An ASA can also advertise routes found in its own routing table to other routers running the RIPv2, EIGRP, and OSPF routing protocols. If multiple routing protocols are used, an ASA can even redistribute routing information from one protocol into another.

With so many choices for routing information exchange, how should you go about choosing and configuring an ASA? First, decide if there are other subnets in the network that are not directly connected to the ASA, but must be reachable from the ASA. Typically, these subnets are found on the trusted or secure interfaces. All subnets that are found on the outside, or untrusted, interface can be summarized by a default "catch all" route.

In a small network environment, you might find that there are no other subnets besides those that are directly connected. In that case, no other routing information is needed beyond a static default route leaving the outside interface.

If there are other subnets, begin considering how the ASA can learn about them. Use Table 4-2 as a general guide for choosing static routing or a dynamic routing protocol.

Table 4-2 *Considerations for Routing Information Sources*

Key
Topic

Source	Considerations
Static routes	Use in small networks having fewer than five routers or a hub-and-spoke topology, where dynamic routing protocols are not being used. If there are many static routes to update and maintain, a dynamic routing protocol might be a better choice.
RIPv2	Use in small networks where RIPv2 is in use.
EIGRP	Use in medium-sized or large networks where Cisco routers and EIGRP are in use. EIGRP offers a composite metric and advanced options.
OSPF	Use in large networks where OSPF is in use. OSPF is standards-based and works across equipment from multiple vendors. OSPF is more complex to configure and requires more hardware resources than other routing protocols.

If no other routers in the network are running dynamic routing protocols, it doesn't make sense to configure a routing protocol on the ASA. Configure a routing protocol on an ASA interface only if there is a neighboring router that can exchange routing information. You can configure different routing protocols on different ASA interfaces, if necessary.

If various sources of routing information are used, the same subnet or route could be learned by more than one method. For example, suppose the route 10.10.0.0/16 has been configured as a static route, but has also been learned via RIP and OSPF. Each of the routing sources might come up with different next-hop addresses for the route, so which one should the ASA trust?

To prevent any confusion, some sources are generally considered to be more trustworthy than others. The degree of trustworthiness is given by the administrative distance, an arbitrary value from 0 to 255. Routes with a distance of 0 are the most trusted, whereas those with a distance of 255 are the least trusted. Table 4-3 lists the administrative distances for every possible source of routing information. Notice that directly connected routes are the most trusted, followed by static routes that are manually configured.

Table 4-3   *Administrative Distance Values for Routing Information Sources*

Route Source	Administrative Distance
Directly connected route	0
Static route	1
EIGRP summary route	5
RIP	120
EIGRP	90 (internal)
	170 (external)
OSPF	110

Consider the following rules of thumb when you are planning to use dynamic routing protocols on an ASA:

■   Static routing is always preferred over dynamic routing protocols, because of the manual, trusted configuration and route stability. If static routing is impractical or cumbersome, consider dynamic routing protocols.

■   Always use peer authentication with a dynamic routing protocol. However, you should never use cleartext authentication; use MD5 instead.

■   Use route filtering to prevent internal, private subnets from being leaked or advertised to the unsecure side.

■   Use route filtering to prevent spoofed or bogus routing information from being learned. This is especially important when the ASA must peer with untrusted routers.

■   Use route summarization if possible, to reduce the complexity of routing information that is advertised from the ASA.

Although the following sections explain how to configure each source of routing information, this chapter is not meant to be a comprehensive source of information about each dynamic routing protocol. Instead, it explains the most common features that can be configured on an ASA, as included in the CCNP Security FIREWALL course and exam. You should already have a foundation in routing topics from the CCNA and CCNP ROUTE courses and exams.

Configuring Static Routing

Static routes are manually configured and are not learned or advertised by default. An IP subnet defined by an IP address and a subnet mask can be reached by forwarding packets out a specific ASA interface. The packets are forwarded to the next-hop gateway address By default, a static route receives an administrative distance of 1. You can override this behavior by specifying a distance value of 1 to 255.

As an example, suppose an ASA has its inside interface configured for the 192.168.10.0/24 subnet. The ASA will automatically define a directly connected route to 192.168.10.0 255.255.255.0 using its inside interface. In addition, the 192.168.200.0/24 subnet can be found through gateway 192.168.10.254 located on the inside interface. Because this subnet isn't directly connected, you can configure a static route to reach it

You can configure static routes in ASDM by navigating to **Configuration > Device Setup > Routing > Static Routes**. In Figure 4-5, a new static route for subnet 192.168.200.0/24 and gateway 192.168.100.254 is being added. Don't forget to click the **Apply** button to apply the newly configured route to the ASA running configuration.

Figure 4-5   *Adding a New Static Route with ASDM*

A default route is a special-case static route, where the IP address and subnet mask are written as 0.0.0.0 0.0.0.0 (or more simply as 0 0 to save typing) to represent any address. The ASA must assume that the next-hop router or gateway listed in the default route knows how to reach any destination that isn't found in the ASA's routing table.

You can configure up to three different default routes on an ASA. If more than one default route exists, the ASA will distribute outbound traffic across the default-route next-hop gateways to load balance the traffic. In Figure 4-6, the list of static routes has grown after a default route has been added for network 192.168.200.0/24, with a next-hop gateway of 192.168.10.254.

You can use the CLI to define a static route for an IP subnet by using the **route** configuration command, as follows:

```
ciscoasa(config)# route interface ip_address netmask gateway_ip [distance]
```

A static route for the example scenario can be configured by using the following command:

```
ciscoasa(config)# route inside 192.168.200.0 255.255.255.0 192.168.10.254
```

In the following command, a default route is created with a next-hop gateway at 192.168.100.254:

```
ciscoasa(config)# route outside 0.0.0.0 0.0.0.0 192.168.100.254
```

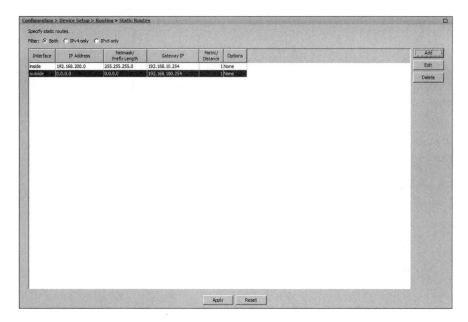

Figure 4-6 *IDS and IPS Operational Differences*

Tracking a Static Route

Normally, if a static route is configured, it stays active until it is manually removed with the **no route** configuration command. A static route is simply an unchanging definition of a next-hop destination, regardless of whether that destination is reachable. If a single Internet service provider (ISP) is the sole means of reaching the outside world, a static default route works nicely to point all outbound traffic to the ISP's gateway address.

Suppose that you had connections to two ISPs, so you configured one default route to each. One ISP might be favored over the other, but the ASA will treat the default routes to each ISP equally and will try to balance the outbound traffic across the two connections. Even if the connection to one ISP goes down, the firewall will still use the static default route that points to that ISP as if nothing had happened—effectively sending some outbound traffic into a black hole.

You can leverage the static route tracking feature to make a static route conditional, based on the reachability of some target address. If the target address is reachable, the tracked static route remains active; if the target is not reachable, the static route becomes inactive, allowing other similar routes to be preferred. This allows you to configure multiple static or default routes without worrying about whether or not one ISP connection is working.

To make a static route conditional, you configure a service-level agreement (SLA) monitor process that monitors an arbitrary target address. That process is associated with a static route so that the route tracks the reachability of the target.

Figure 4-7 shows an example scenario where the ASA has two paths to the outside world. Therefore, it could be configured with two default routes that point to the two next-hop routers: 209.165.201.1 and 209.165.202.129. The link to 209.165.201.1 should be preferred and used, as long as the router 209.165.201.1 is alive and reachable; otherwise, the ASA should use the backup default route toward 209.165.202.129.

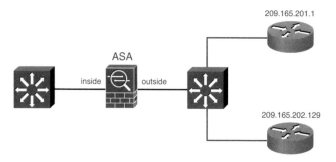

Figure 4-7   *Tracking a Static Route*

ASDM makes the tracked static route configuration quite easy. First, you must add a new static route by navigating to **Configuration > Device Setup > Routing > Static Routes** and clicking the **Add** button. Define the static route normally, but be sure to check the **Tracked** check box.

Then, in the same dialog box, you can define the SLA monitor test and the SLA target address. Click the **Monitoring Options** button to tune the SLA monitor test options, if needed. The options and their defaults are described in Table 4-4. Figure 4-8 shows how the example scenario from can be configured.

Note: Before you configure the ICMP echo target address, you might want to manually test the target's reachability with the **ping** *target* command.

Once you click **OK**, ASDM reminds you to define a backup route with a higher metric. Figure 4-9 shows a new static route being added with a metric of 100, which is higher than the tracked static route.

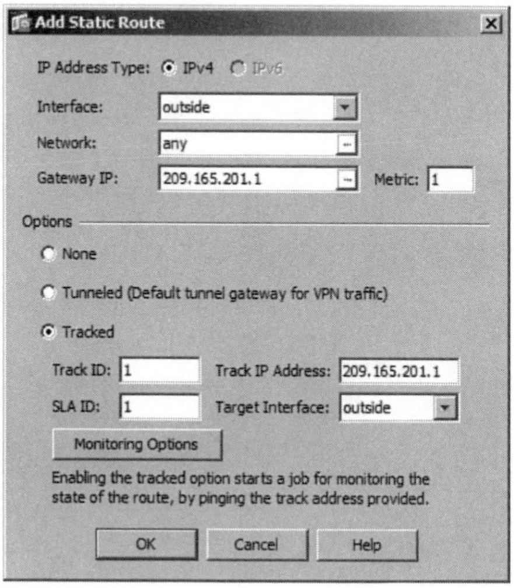

Figure 4-8   *Configuring a Tracked Static Route in ASDM*

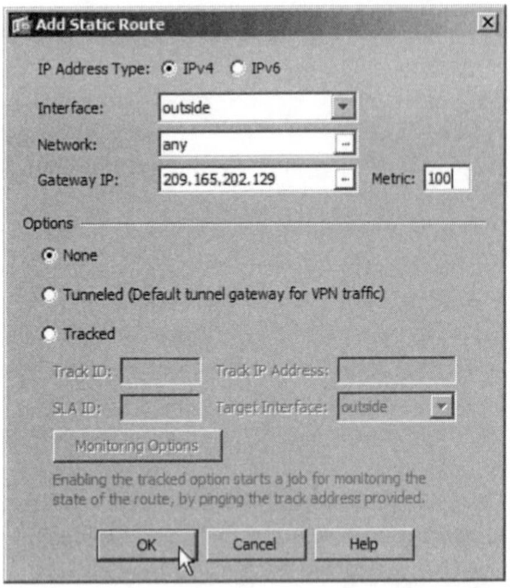

Figure 4-9   *Configuring a Backup Default Route in ASDM*

As an alternative, you can use the CLI to configure a tracked static route, though the process is a bit more complicated than ASDM. Use the following configuration steps to define an SLA process and then to bind it to a static route:

Step 1.   Define an SLA monitor process and an arbitrary process number:

```
ciscoasa(config)# sla monitor sla-id
```

Step 2.   Define the reachability test:

```
ciscoasa(config-sla-monitor)# type echo protocol ipIcmpEcho target
   interface interface-name
```

Although the command syntax seems lengthy, it really isn't too complex. The only test type is echo, which sends ICMP echo request packets to the target IP address found on the named ASA interface.

Step 3.   Tune optional test parameters.

An SLA test has several parameters that you can change to tune the test according to your environment. Table 4-4 lists the parameters along with their default values and command syntax.

Table 4-4   *Optional Parameters for an SLA Test*

Parameter	Command Syntax	Default
Test frequency	**frequency** *seconds*	60 sec
Number of ping packets	**num-packets** *number*	1 ICMP request packet
Size of ping packet	**request-data-size** *bytes*	28-byte payload
Type of Service	**tos** *number*	0
Test timeout interval	**timeout** *milliseconds*	5000 ms (5 sec)
Test threshold	**threshold** *milliseconds*	5000 ms

The test timeout interval is a rigid time period that determines when the echo test has failed. If the timeout interval has expired and no response has been received from the target, the target must be unresponsive.

An ASA also keeps track of a test threshold, which is used as an indicator that the target is getting increasingly hard to reach. The threshold isn't used to decide whether the target is reachable. Instead, it can give you an idea of how realistic your choice of the timeout interval is.

By default, the threshold interval is set to 5000 ms (5 sec). You can set a different threshold value, but keep in mind that it must always be less than or equal to the timeout interval value.

For example, suppose you choose a timeout interval of 10,000 ms (10 sec) and a threshold value of 5000 ms. After many echo tests are run, you can look at the test statistics to see how often the threshold is exceeded. If it is rarely exceeded, you might decide to reduce the timeout value to something at or below the current threshold value. If you decide to reduce the timeout value, you should also reduce the threshold value.

Step 4.   Schedule the SLA monitor test to run.

You can use the following command to run the SLA monitor test starting now and running continually forever:

```
ciscoasa(config)# sla monitor sla-id life forever now
```

The test continues to run until you manually remove it from the running configuration with the **no sla monitor** *sla-id* command.

Note: The **sla monitor** command has a much more complex syntax, as follows:
```
ciscoasa(config)# sla monitor schedule sla-id [life {forever|seconds}]
  [start-time {hh:mm[:ss] [month day|day month]|pending|
  now|after hh:mm:ss}] [ageout seconds] [recurring]
```

SLA monitor tests are meant to be more versatile than static route tracking requires. Be aware that you can set specific starting times and durations, although the **life forever now** keywords are most commonly used so that the test will always be running.

Step 5.   Enable reachability tracking.

To use the SLA monitor test, you must identify the test as a trackable object using the following configuration command:

```
ciscoasa(config)# track track-id rtr sla-id reachability
```

The SLA monitor test identified by *sla-id* will be used to track reachability information. Each track process is known by its *track-id* index, an arbitrary value from 1 to 500. You should define a unique track index for each SLA monitor test that you configure, so that each test can be tracked independently.

Note: Don't be confused by the **rtr** keyword in the command. The SLA feature originally was known as Response Time Reporter (RTR), but the keyword has not been updated to reflect the new naming scheme.

Step 6.   Apply tracking to a static route:

```
ciscoasa(config)# route if_name ip_address netmask gateway_ip
   [distance] track track-id
```

Notice that the normal **static route** command syntax is used, but the **track** keyword is added to make the static route conditional upon a tracked object (the SLA monitor test). If the test target is reachable (it returns ICMP echo replies to the ASA as expected), the static route will remain active in the routing table. If the target is not reachable (ICMP echo replies are not received as expected), the static route will remain in the running configuration, but will have a higher distance value and be less desirable than other identical routes in the routing table.

Therefore, be sure to give the tracked static route a very low distance value so that it will be preferred over any similar backup or secondary static routes while it is active. A distance value of 1 (the default) is commonly used.

Step 7.   Define a backup static route:

```
ciscoasa(config)# route if_name ip_address netmask gateway_ip distance
```

Finally, you should define a backup route that will be preferred whenever the tracked static route becomes inactive. The backup and tracked static routes should be identical except for their distance values. The tracked static route should have a low distance so that it is normally preferred, while the backup static route should have a higher, less preferred, distance value.

Example 4-3 lists the commands that can be used to configure the ASA for the scenario shown in Figure 4-7. SLA monitor test 1 is configured to perform ICMP echo tests on the 209.165.201.1 router. Notice that the default route pointing toward 209.165.201.1 has a distance of 1, while the backup default route pointing toward 209.165.202.129 has a higher (less preferred) distance of 100.

Example 4-3 *Static Route Tracking Configuration for Figure 4-7*

```
ciscoasa(config)# sla monitor 1
ciscoasa(config-sla-monitor)# type echo protocol ipIcmpEcho 209.165.201.1
  interface outside
ciscoasa(config-sla-monitor-echo)# exit
ciscoasa(config)# sla monitor schedule 1 life forever now

ciscoasa(config)# track 1 rtr 1 reachability
ciscoasa(config)# route 0.0.0.0 0.0.0.0 209.165.201.1 1 track 1
ciscoasa(config)# route 0.0.0.0 0.0.0.0 209.165.202.129 100
```

Static route tracking is a rather silent process, and an ASA won't give you any obvious signs that it is actually testing the reachability. However, you can monitor the status of a tracking process with the **show track** EXEC command. You can also display details about the SLA monitor test with the **show sla monitor configuration** command. Example 4-4 shows the output from each of these commands.

Example 4-4 *Displaying Information About Static Route Tracking*

```
ciscoasa# show track
Track 1
  Response Time Reporter 1 reachability
  Reachability is Down
  2 changes, last change 03:50:24
  Latest operation return code: Timeout
  Tracked by:
    STATIC-IP-ROUTING 0
ciscoasa#
ciscoasa# show sla monitor configuration
SA Agent, Infrastructure Engine-II
Entry number: 1
Owner:
Tag:
Type of operation to perform: echo
Target address: 209.165.201.1
Interface: outside
Number of packets: 1
Request size (ARR data portion): 28
Operation timeout (milliseconds): 5000
Type Of Service parameters: 0x0
Verify data: No
Operation frequency (seconds): 60
Next Scheduled Start Time: Start Time already passed
Group Scheduled : FALSE
Life (seconds): Forever
```

```
Entry Ageout (seconds): never
Recurring (Starting Everyday): FALSE
Status of entry (SNMP RowStatus): Active
Enhanced History:
ciscoasa#
```

Routing with RIPv2

The Routing Information Protocol (RIP) is a distance-vector routing protocol that uses a simple router hop count to select the best path to a destination route. Routers running RIP exchange routing information broadcasts at regular intervals and when changes to the network topology occur.

RIP exists as two versions; by default, an ASA sends routing updates as RIPv1, but receives updates in either RIPv1 or RIPv2. RIPv1 supports only classful networks, and its routing advertisements are broadcast in the clear. With RIPv2, classless networks and authenticated advertisements are supported, making it the more flexible and secure version. In fact, the CCNP Security FIREWALL exam covers only RIPv2. The ASA supports automatic route summarization, where subnets are summarized into networks that fall on classful boundaries.

If you have routers running RIPv2 in your network, you might consider running RIPv2 on an ASA so that it can exchange routing information dynamically. Be aware that RIP is limited to a maximum hop count of 16 routers, so it is more suited to smaller networks. RIP is also relatively slow to converge when a network topology changes due to a failed link or router.

As an example, suppose you are asked to configure an ASA to participate in RIPv2 with another router on the inside interface. Only routes that begin with 192.168.x.x should be learned from the other router. The inside ASA interface is connected to the 192.168.1.0/24 network. MD5 authentication should be used for any routing information exchanges.

To configure the scenario in ASDM, navigate to **Configuration > Device Setup > Routing > RIP**. In the **Setup** section, you can check the box to enable RIP, disable auto-summarization, enable RIPv2, enable default information originate, and specify any passive interfaces, as shown in Figure 4-10.

Next, go to the **Interface** section, select an interface that will participate in RIPv2, and then click the **Edit** button. In Figure 4-11, the inside interface is configured to use MD5 authentication and an authentication key.

Next, click the **Filter Rules** section to configure any route filtering that is needed. In Figure 4-12, an access list has been configured to permit only routes containing the 192.168 prefix in the inbound direction.

As an alternative, you can use the following steps to configure RIPv2 on an ASA with the CLI:

Step 1.   Enable RIPv2:

```
ciscoasa(config)# router rip
ciscoasa(config-router)# version 2
```

By default, automatic route summarization is enabled. To disable it, use the following command:

```
ciscoasa(config-router)# no auto-summary
```

If the ASA has a default route and you want it to be advertised to other RIPv2 routers, use the following command:

```
ciscoasa(config-router)# default-information originate
```

Step 2.   Identify directly connected networks to advertise:

```
ciscoasa(config-router)# network ip-address
```

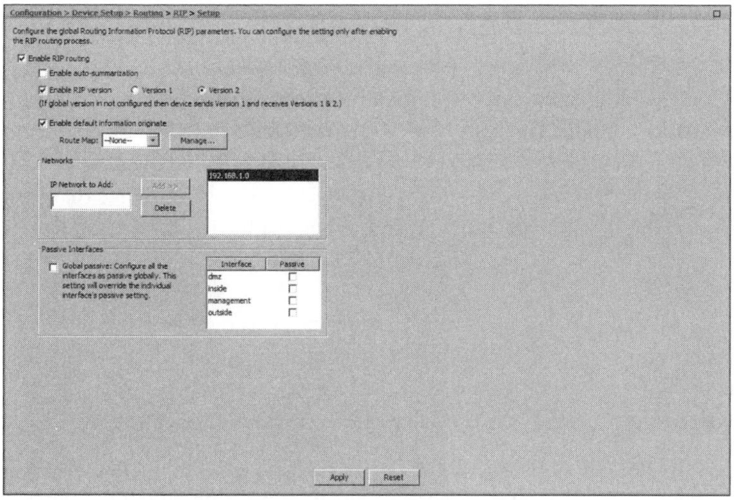

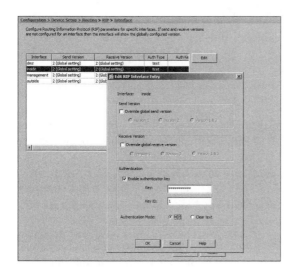

Figure 4-10   *Configuring the RIPv2 Setup Section in ASDM*

Figure 4-11   *Configuring the RIPv2 Interface Section in ASDM*

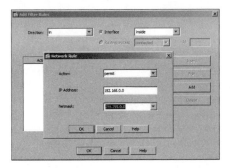

Figure 4-12   *Configuring the RIPv2 Filter Rules Section in ASDM*

Once RIPv2 is enabled, the ASA will not advertise any of its own directly connected networks. In fact, the ASA won't even participate in RIPv2 on any of its interfaces until you identify which networks it should use. By using the **network** command, you tell the ASA to enable RIPv2 on the interface that is connected to the IP subnet *ip-address* and to begin advertising that subnet.

Step 3.   Identify any passive interfaces.

If there are ASA interfaces where routing information should be received but not transmitted, you can identify them as passive interfaces with the following command:

ciscoasa(config-router)# **passive-interface** {**default** | *interface*}

If you use the **default** keyword, all the firewall interfaces will become passive. Then, to explicitly permit an interface to actively participate in RIP, you must use the **no passive-interface** *interface* command.

Step 4.   Optionally, filter routing information.

You can filter RIPv2 routing information that is sent or received on an ASA interface by applying a distribute list. In a nutshell, a distribute list uses a standard IP access list to identify specific routes; routes matching a **permit** statement are allowed to be used, whereas routes matching a **deny** statement are filtered out.

First, configure an access list that will identify the routes, and then bind the access list to a distribute list in the RIPv2 configuration, using the following commands:

ciscoasa(config)# **access-list** *acl-id* **standard** {**permit** | **deny**} *ip-address*
  mask
ciscoasa(config-router)# **distribute-list** *acl-id* {**in** | **out**} **interface**
  interface

Notice that the distribute list is applied in either the inbound or outbound direction, allowing routes to be filtered as they are received or transmitted, respectively.

Step 5. Use RIPv2 authentication on ASA interfaces.

Whenever you enable RIPv2 on an ASA, take every precaution to make sure that the routing information is coming from a trusted source. An ASA can support either cleartext or MD5 authentication to accomplish this. The same authentication method and key must be configured on each pair of RIPv2 peers. Because the cleartext key is passed along in the clear with routing updates, it is easily overheard and can be abused. Instead, you should use MD5 authentication, which passes an MD5 hash value that is computed on each routing advertisement and a hidden secret key.

RIPv2 authentication is configured on a per-interface basis. You can use the following interface configuration commands to select the authentication method and key:

```
ciscoasa(config-if)# rip authentication mode {text | md5}
ciscoasa(config-if)# rip authentication key key-string key_id id
```

The key-string field is a string of up to 16 characters. The key ID is a unique key identifier; although only one key can be used for RIPv2 authentication, you can define a different key number if you need to change keys periodically.

The commands listed in Example 4-5 can be used to configure the example scenario.

Example 4-5 *RIPv2 Example Configuration*

```
ciscoasa(config)# access-list ripfilter standard permit 192.168.0.0 255.255.0.0
ciscoasa(config)# router rip
ciscoasa(config-router)# version 2
ciscoasa(config-router)# no auto-summary
ciscoasa(config-router)# default-information originate
ciscoasa(config-router)# network 192.168.1.0
ciscoasa(config-router)# distribute-list ripfilter in interface inside
ciscoasa(config-router)# exit
ciscoasa(config)# interface ethernet0/1
ciscoasa(config-if)# rip authentication mode md5
ciscoasa(config-if)# rip authentication key myb1gs3cr3t key_id 1
```

Routing with EIGRP

The Enhanced Interior Gateway Routing Protocol (EIGRP) uses a complex routing metric that is based on a combination of delay, bandwidth, reliability, load, and MTU. EIGRP combines the advantages of link-state and distance-vector routing protocols, making it a hybrid of both methods.

EIGRP uses a neighbor discovery mechanism that works by sending hello messages to directly connected neighboring routers. Neighbors can be dynamically discovered or statically configured. All EIGRP messages, including the hello protocol, are sent as multicast packets to address 224.0.0.10, the "all EIGRP routers" address, using IP protocol 88.

EIGRP supports variable-length subnet masks (VLSM) and route summarization, providing plenty of flexibility in its routing information. It also uses the Diffusing Update

Key Topic

Algorithm (DUAL) to compute and maintain routing information from all of its neighbors. The ASA (or any other EIGRP router) always uses a feasible successor or a neighboring router with the lowest cost path to a destination.

EIGRP routers do not send periodic routing updates. Rather, routing information is exchanged only when a route's metric changes, based on information from neighboring routers. If you have routers running EIGRP in your network, you might want to run EIGRP on your ASA too, so that the ASA can benefit from dynamic routing information. Be aware that an ASA can run only one EIGRP process.

As an example, suppose that an ASA has its Ethernet0/0 interface facing the outside, public network, while Ethernet0/1 faces the inside, protected network, as shown in Figure 4-13. EIGRP is being used on the internal network, due to the network's size. The ASA will participate in EIGRP so that it can receive dynamic updates about internal IP subnets.

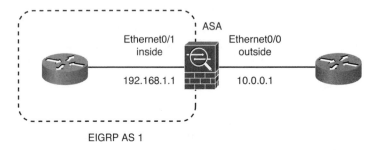

Figure 4-13 *Example EIGRP Scenario*

Because the ASA has only a single path to the outside world, it can become an EIGRP stub router. As well, there is no need for the outside interface to participate in routing updates because there is no trusted EIGRP neighbor there.

To configure the example scenario using ASDM, navigate to **Configuration > Device Setup > Routing > EIGRP**. Begin with the **Setup** option, where you enable EIGRP and set the autonomous system number, as shown in Figure 4-14. EIGRP routers can exchange routing information if they each belong to the same autonomous system. Make sure the autonomous system number (1 to 65,535) matches that of other EIGRP routers in your network.

Figure 4-14 *Configuring EIGRP Setup Parameters in ASDM*

You can also click the **Advanced** button to configure autosummarization, set the default metric values, configure EIGRP stub routing, and tune the administrative distance.

Next, click the **Networks** tab within the Setup window and add any IP networks that will participate in EIGRP routing updates and which subnets to advertise, as shown in Figure 4-15.

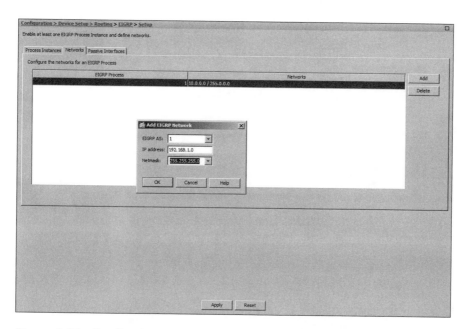

Figure 4-15   *Configuring EIGRP Networks in the ASDM EIGRP Setup*

Next, click the **Passive Interfaces** tab to identify any EIGRP passive interfaces. The subnet on a passive interface will be advertised, but the interface will not participate in EIGRP routing exchanges In Figure 4-16, the outside interface is configured to be passive.

To configure route filtering, choose **Routing > EIGRP > Filter Rules** and add any rules to a specific interface. Although route filtering is not used in the example scenario, the process is shown in Figure 4-17.

Next, you can configure EIGRP authentication by choosing **Routing > EIGRP > Interface**, selecting an ASA interface, and then clicking **Edit**. You should always make sure that an ASA receives trusted routing information from neighboring routers by configuring MD5 authentication. Once authentication is enabled, any EIGRP neighbors that fail to present the correct key will be ignored. You can enable MD5 authentication and enter a key string and key identifier, as shown in Figure 4-18.

An ASA can redistribute routes that it has learned from other sources into its EIGRP process. Directly connected and static routes, as well as routes learned from RIP or OSPF processes, can be redistributed. As a best practice, you should configure a route map to filter routing information from one routing protocol into EIGRP to prevent routing loops.

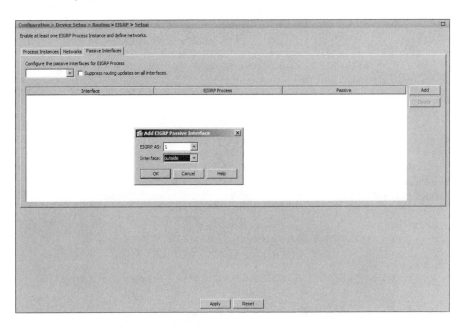

Figure 4-16 *Configuring EIGRP Passive Interfaces in ASDM*

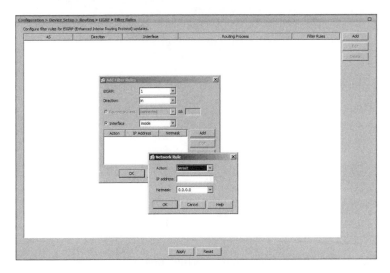

Figure 4-17 *Configuring EIGRP Route Filtering in ASDM*

You should also define default metric values for all routes that are redistributed into EIGRP, because metrics from the different route sources are not equivalent. You can do this for each redistributed source or you can define a single set of default metrics for all sources that do not have explicit values defined.

To configure redistribution into EIGRP, navigate to **Routing > EIGRP > Redistribution**, click the **Add** button to add a routing source, and fill in the necessary parameters, as shown in Figure 4-19.

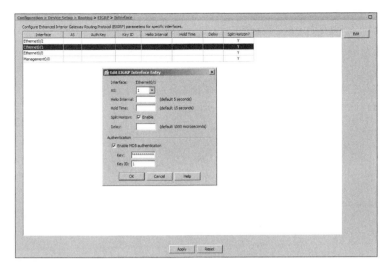

Figure 4-18 *Configuring EIGRP Authentication in ASDM*

Figure 4-19 *Configuring Route Redistribution into EIGRP from ASDM*

You can configure any summary addresses by choosing **Routing > EIGRP > Summary Address** and then adding the network address, subnet mask, and interface, as shown in Figure 4-20. No summary addresses are used in the example scenario.

Figure 4-20 *Configuring EIGRP Summary Addresses in ASDM*

You can configure EIGRP with the CLI as well by using the following steps:

Step 1. Enable an EIGRP process:

```
ciscoasa(config)# router eigrp as-num
```

Step 2. Associate a network with the EIGRP process:

```
ciscoasa(config-router)# network ip-addr [mask]
```

EIGRP must know which interfaces will participate in routing updates and which interface subnets to advertise. If an interface address falls within the subnet ip-addr and mask, EIGRP will use it in its operation.

If you want the interface subnet to be advertised, but you don't want the interface to participate in EIGRP routing exchanges, you can use the following command:

```
ciscoasa(config-router)# passive-interface interface
```

Step 3. Control route summarization.

By default, EIGRP will automatically summarize subnet routes into classful network routes when they are advertised. If you have contiguous subnets that are separated across ASA interfaces or across EIGRP routers, you should disable route summarization with the following EIGRP configuration command:

```
ciscoasa(config-router)# no auto-summary
```

Otherwise, you can configure a summary address that is advertised on a specific interface. This can be handy if you need a summary address that doesn't fall cleanly within a network boundary. In addition, if you have already disabled automatic summarization, the firewall can still advertise a summary address that is manually configured. You can configure a summary address, the EIGRP autonomous system number, and an optional administrative distance, with the following commands:

```
ciscoasa(config)# interface interface
ciscoasa(config-if)# summary-address eigrp as-num address mask
  [distance]
```

Step 4. Redistribute routing information from other sources.

To redistribute routes that were learned by RIP, that are statically defined, or that are directly connected, use the following EIGRP configuration command:

```
ciscoasa(config-router)# redistribute {rip|static
  | connected} [metric bandwidth delay reliability load mtu]
  [route-map map_name]
```

To redistribute routes learned from OSPF, use the following EIGRP configuration command:

```
ciscoasa(config-router)# redistribute ospf pid [match
  {internal|external [1|2]|nssa-external [1|2]}]
  [metric bandwidth delay reliability load mtu] [route-map map_name]
```

Identify the OSPF process as *pid*. You can match against OSPF internal, type 1 or 2 OSPF external, or external type 1 or 2 not-so-stubby area (**nssa-external**) routes.

You can define a set of default redistribution metric values with the following EIGRP configuration command:

```
ciscoasa(config-router)# default-metric bandwidth delay reliability
   loading mtu
```

Specify the composite default metric as the combination of bandwidth (1 to 4,294,967,295 kbps), delay (1 to 4,294,967,295 in tens of microseconds), reliability (0 to 255, ranging from low to high), loading (1 to 255, ranging from low to high link usage), and mtu (1 to 65,535 bytes).

Step 5.   Use stub routing for an ASA with a single exit point.

If the ASA has a single connection to the outside world through a neighboring router, it can become an EIGRP stub router. As a stub, it can receive routes (usually a default route) from its neighbor, but will advertise only specific routes of its own. The command syntax follows:

```
ciscoasa(config-router)# eigrp stub {receive-only | [connected]
   [redistributed] [static] [summary]}
```

With the **receive-only** keyword, the ASA will receive updates but will not advertise anything; otherwise, you can specify one or more route types to advertise. Use the **connected** keyword to advertise routes that are directly connected to the ASA, the **redistributed** keyword to advertise any routes that the ASA has redistributed into its EIGRP process, the **static** keyword to advertise static routes defined on the ASA, or the **summary** keyword to advertise summary addresses defined on the ASA.

Step 6.   Secure EIGRP updates with neighbor authentication.

You should always make sure that an ASA receives trusted routing information from neighboring routers by configuring MD5 authentication. EIGRP authentication is configured on a per-interface basis and must be associated with the EIGRP autonomous system number. Once authentication is enabled, any EIGRP neighbors that fail to present the correct key will be ignored. The command syntax follows:

```
ciscoasa(config)# interface interface
ciscoasa(config-if)# authentication mode eigrp as-num md5
ciscoasa(config-if)# authentication key eigrp as-num key-string
   key-id key-id
```

Step 7.   Optionally, filter EIGRP updates to suppress specific networks.

First, configure a standard access list that will permit only certain routes or subnets. Then, apply that access list to an EIGRP distribute list with the following EIGRP configuration command. The **in** keyword filters the routes as they are received from other EIGRP routers, whereas the **out** keyword filters the routes in EIGRP advertisements from the firewall. You can add the **interface** keyword to filter routes only on a specific interface:

```
ciscoasa(config-router)# distribute-list acl-id {in|out} [interface
    interface]
```

To configure the ASA for EIGRP operation with the example scenario, you can use the commands listed in Example 4-6.

Example 4-6 *Configuration Commands Used for EIGRP Scenario*

```
ciscoasa(config)# router eigrp 1
ciscoasa(config-router)# network 10.0.0.0
ciscoasa(config-router)# network 192.168.1.0
ciscoasa(config-router)# eigrp stub
ciscoasa(config-router)# passive-interface ethernet0/0
ciscoasa(config-router)# exit
ciscoasa(config)# route outside 0.0.0.0 0.0.0.0 10.0.1.2 1
ciscoasa(config)# interface ethernet 0/1
ciscoasa(config-if)# authentication mode eigrp 1 md5
ciscoasa(config-if)# authentication key eigrp 1 myb1gs3cr3t key-id 1
ciscoasa(config-if)# exit
```

You can verify EIGRP operation by displaying any active EIGRP neighbor routers and the EIGRP routing topology using the following EXEC commands:

```
ciscoasa# show eigrp neighbors
ciscoasa# show eigrp topology
```

Routing with OSPF

OSPF is a link-state routing protocol that can partition a network into a hierarchy of distinct numbered areas. Area 0 is always considered the backbone area of the OSPF domain or autonomous system, which must connect to all other areas.

When an OSPF router connects to two or more different areas, it is called an Area Border Router (ABR). When an OSPF router connects an area to a non-OSPF domain and it imports routing information from other sources into OSPF, it is called an Autonomous System Boundary Router (ASBR).

OSPF routers build a common database of the status of all links in the area by exchanging link-state advertisements (LSA). The routers build their routing tables by computing the shortest path first (SPF) algorithm based on that database. OSPF uses a path cost value, which is based on link bandwidth, as a routing metric. An ASA can support at most two different OSPF processes.

An Example OSPF Scenario

A firewall is situated so that it connects to OSPF area 0 on its inside interface and to OSPF area 4 on its outside interface. Therefore, the firewall is an ABR. The inside interface is configured as 192.168.1.1/24, and the outside interface as 10.1.4.1/24. The subnets on the inside network fall within 172.16.0.0/16 and 192.168.0.0/16.

Network 10.1.4.0/24 falls in OSPF area 4 on the outside, whereas 192.168.0.0/16 falls in OSPF area 0 on the inside, as shown in Figure 4-21. MD5 authentication is used for both the inside and outside OSPF areas.

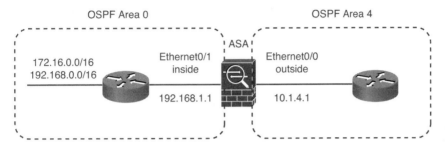

Figure 4-21   *Example OSPF Scenario*

The ASA is configured to allow any inside subnet except 192.168.99.0/24 to be advertised into OSPF area 4 on the outside.

You can use ASDM to configure the OSPF. Navigate to **Configuration > Device Setup > Routing > OSPF > Setup**. On the **Process Instances** tab, you can enable OSPF and configure the OSPF instance with a process ID, as shown in Figure 4-22. OSPF is identified by a unique, arbitrary process ID. Up to two separate OSPF processes can be run on a firewall. This allows each process to exchange routing information independently, although a single routing table is maintained in the firewall. (The process ID is only locally significant; it is not passed or matched among routers and firewalls.)

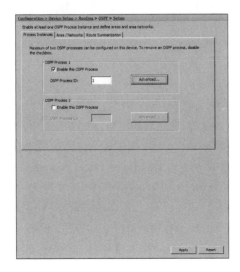

Figure 4-22   *Configuring the OSPF Process in ASDM*

By clicking the **Advanced** button, you can set the router ID, configure OSPF logging, adjust the administrative distance, tune the OSPF timers, and enable default information originate.

On the **Area/Networks** tab, you can define the IP networks in which OSPF will participate. Figure 4-23 shows the 192.168.1.0/24 network being added as OSPF area 0. Once all of the directly connected networks have been added, you can click the **Route Summarization** tab to add any summary routes that should be advertised.

Figure 4-23 *Configuring OSPF Networks in ASDM*

Next, you can choose **Routing > OSPF > Filtering** to configure any route filtering. You can click the **Add** button to add a new rule to the route filter. Specify the OSPF process number and OSPF area where the rule will be applied. You can also specify the IP network, filter direction, filter sequence number, and action. In Figure 4-24, network 172.16.0.0/16 is permitted by the filter.

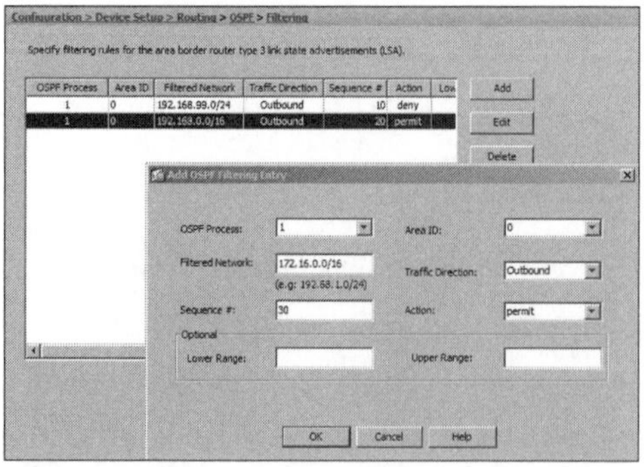

Figure 4-24 *Configuring OSPF Route Filtering in ASDM*

You can choose **Routing > OSPF > Interface** to configure any interface-related parameters. For example, Figure 4-25 shows the outside interface being configured for MD5 authentication, with key ID 1 and key string myoutsidekey.

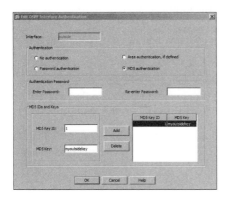

Figure 4-25 *Configuring OSPF Interface Parameters in ASDM*

If you have configured another routing information source besides OSPF, you might want to configure route redistribution. You can do this by choosing **Routing > OSPF > Redistribution**, although the example scenario does not require redistribution.

OSPF is a complex, robust routing protocol. This means that it is flexible but can be tedious to configure, especially through the CLI. You can configure OSPF by using the following steps:

Step 1.   Define an OSPF process:

`ciscoasa(config)# router ospf pid`

Step 2.   Configure Advanced options.

By default, OSPF uses the highest IP address defined on any ASA interface as the router ID, used to identify the ASA in any OSPF exchanges with neighboring routers. You can override that by using the following command:

`ciscoasa(config-router)# router-id ip_address`

By default, an ASA generates logging messages to indicate when an OSPF neighbor adjacency goes up or down. You can change the logging behavior with the following command:

`ciscoasa(config-router)# log-adj-changes [detail]`

An ASA can advertise a default route as an external route by using the following command:

`ciscoasa(config-router)# default-information originate [always]`
`  [metric value] [metric-type {1|2}] [route-map name]`

If you use the **always** keyword, a default route is advertised even if one has not been specifically configured. The route is advertised with a metric of *value* (0 to 16777214; the default is 1). By default, the route is advertised as an external Type 2 route (metric-type 2); you can override that behavior with the

metric-type keyword. You can also configure a route map separately and apply it with the **route-map** keyword to filter the default route that is advertised.

By default, all OSPF routes have an administrative distance of 110. This is consistent with Cisco routers. You can use the following command to change the distance values:

```
ciscoasa(config-router)# distance ospf [intra-area d1] [inter-area d2]
  [external d3]
```

Use the **intra-area** keyword to set routes within an OSPF area to *d1*, the **inter-area** keyword to set routes from one area to another to *d2*, and the **external** keyword to set routes from another routing protocol into the OSPF area to *d3*.

You can adjust the OSPF route calculation timers with the following command:

```
ciscoasa(config-router)# timers {spf spf_delay spf_holdtime | lsa-group-
  pacing seconds}
```

The OSPF process will wait a delay time of *spf_delay* (default 5 sec) after receiving a topology change before starting the SPF calculation. OSPF will wait *spf_holdtime* (default 10 sec) between two consecutive calculations. You can also tune the calculation process with the **lsa-group-pacing** keyword. LSAs are gathered and processed at regular intervals (the default is 240 sec).

Step 3. Associate a network with an OSPF area:

```
ciscoasa(config-router)# network ip_address netmask area area_id
```

The OSPF process exchanges routing information on any ASA interface that falls within the address range specified here. As well, the network assigned to that interface is advertised by OSPF.

An OSPF area can be referred to by a decimal number or by a subnet notation. For example, area 5 can also be written as 0.0.0.5, area 100 as 0.0.0.100, and area 0 as 0.0.0.0. Using subnet notation for OSPF areas is handy when you have a specific subnet by itself in one area. Also remember that OSPF must have one backbone area, called area 0 or area 0.0.0.0.

Step 4. Authenticate OSPF neighbors in an area.

OSPF peers can authenticate information from each other using cleartext passwords or MD5 hash values, although using MD5 is a best practice. If authentication is enabled on one device, it must be enabled on all the neighboring devices in the same area. Enable authentication with the following command:

```
ciscoasa(config-router)# area area_id authentication [message-digest]
```

In addition, the actual authentication keys must be defined on each OSPF interface with the following commands:

```
ciscoasa(config)# interface interface
ciscoasa(config-if)# ospf message-digest-key key-id md5 key
ciscoasa(config-if)# ospf authentication message-digest
```

If authentication has been enabled for an OSPF area, you must also set up the authentication key on each interface in that area. You can define several keys by repeating the command. Each key is known by a *key-id* index, ranging from 1 to 255. The actual MD5 key is a string of up to 16 text characters.

The key string found at index *key-id* on one router or firewall must match the same key at *key-id* on all other neighboring routers or firewalls. You can change the keys periodically by defining a new key at a new key-id index. The old key continues to be used even though a new one has been defined. As soon as all neighboring routers have the new key too, OSPF rolls over and uses the new authentication key. At that time, you should remove the old MD5 keys with the **no ospf message-digest** *key-id* interface configuration command.

Step 5.   Optionally, define a special case area.

You can define an OSPF area as a stub area if there is only one path into and out of the area. All OSPF neighbors in a stub area must configure it as a stub. You can use the following command to configure a stub area:

```
ciscoasa(config-router)# area area_id stub [no-summary]
```

Include the **no-summary** keyword to create a totally stubby area, where OSPF prevents the introduction of any external or interarea routes into the stub area.

You can configure an area as a not-so-stubby area (NSSA), where external routes are allowed to be transported through. In the following command, you can use the **no-redistribution** keyword on an ABR ASA if you want external routes to be redistributed only into normal areas, but not into any NSSAs:

```
ciscoasa(config-router)# area area_id nssa [no-redistribution]
[default-information-originate [metric-type 1|2] [metric
   metric_value]]
```

Use the **default-information-originate** keyword to generate a default route into the NSSA. If that is used, you can define the default route as an external route type 1 (route cost plus the internal OSPF metric) or 2 (route cost without the internal OSPF metric). You can also specify a default route metric.

Step 6.   Optionally, configure route filtering.

If an ASA is configured as an ABR, it sends type 3 LSAs between the areas it touches. This means that the networks in each area are advertised into other areas. Naturally, you wouldn't want private networks to be advertised toward the outside, for security and network translation reasons. You can define a prefix list to filter routes that are advertised:

```
ciscoasa(config)# prefix-list list_name [seq seq_number] {permit|deny}
   prefix/len [ge min_value] [le max_value]
```

Note: Unlike RIPv2 and EIGRP, OSPF does not use a distribute list to filter routes that are advertised. This is because every OSPF router maintains its own snapshot of the entire routing topology.

The prefix list is given a text string name. You can repeat this command to add more conditions to the list. By default, prefix list entries are automatically numbered in increments of 5, beginning with sequence number 5. Routes are evaluated against the prefix list entries in sequence, starting with the lowest defined sequence number. By giving a specific sequence number here, you can wedge a new statement between two existing ones.

A prefix list entry can either permit or deny the advertisement of matching routes in type 3 LSAs. A prefix list entry matches an IP route address against the *prefix* (a valid IP network address) and *len* (the number of leftmost bits in the address) values. The **ge** (greater than or equal to a number of bits) and **le** (less than or equal to a number of bits) keywords can also be used to define a range of the number of prefix bits to match. A range can provide a more specific matching condition than the *prefix/len* values alone.

For example, to permit advertisements of routes with a prefix of 172.16.0.0/16, but having any mask length between 16 and 24 bits, you could use the following command:

```
ciscoasa(config)# prefix-list LIST permit 172.16.0.0/16 ge 16 le 24
```

Next, apply the prefix list to filter LSAs into or out of an area with the following command:

```
ciscoasa(config-router)# area area_id filter-list prefix list_name
   [in | out]
```

If you want to suppress advertisement of an internal network, you can apply the prefix list for LSAs going **in** or **out** of the area *area_id*. This means you can stop the advertisements from leaving a private area by applying the prefix list to the private *area_id* in the **out** direction. Or you can filter the advertisements on the public area *area_id* side in the **in** direction.

Step 7. Summarize routes between areas.

An ABR can reduce the number of routes it sends into an area by sending a summary address instead. The summary address is sent in place of any route that falls within the range defined by *ip_address* and *netmask* in the following command:

```
ciscoasa(config-router)# area area_id range ip_address netmask
   [advertise | not-advertise]
```

The **advertise** keyword is assumed by default; if you don't want the summary address advertised, use the **not-advertise** keyword.

Step 8. Optionally, redistribute routes from another source.

When a firewall redistributes routes from any other source into OSPF, it automatically becomes an ASBR by definition. You can (and should) use a route map to control which routes are redistributed into OSPF. You can define a route map with the following command:

```
ciscoasa(config)# route-map map_tag [permit | deny] [seq_num]
```

The route map named *map_tag* (an arbitrary text string) either permits or denies a certain action. You can repeat this command if you need to define several actions for the same route map. In this case, you should assign a sequence number *seq_num* to each one.

Use the **permit** keyword to define an action that redistributes routes into OSPF. The **deny** keyword defines an action that is processed but does not redistribute routes.

Next, define one or more matching conditions with the **match** command. If you configure multiple **match** statements, all of them must be met. Table 4-5 lists the possible **match** commands.

Table 4-5 *Route Map match Commands*

Match Condition	Command Syntax
Next-hop outbound interface	ciscoasa(config-route-map)# **match interface** *interface*
OSPF metric value	ciscoasa(config-route-map)# **match metric** *metric_value*
Route IP address, permitted by a separate access list	ciscoasa(config-route-map)# **match ip address** *acl_id*
Route type	ciscoasa(config-route-map)# **match route-type** {**local** | **internal** | [**external** [**type-1** | **type-2**]]}
NSSA external routes	ciscoasa(config-route-map)# **match nssa-external** [**type-1** | **type-2**]
Next-hop router IP address, permitted by one or more separate access lists	ciscoasa(config-route-map)# **match ip next-hop** *acl_id* [...*acl_id*]
Advertising router IP address, permitted by one or more separate access lists	ciscoasa(config-route-map)# **match ip route-source** *acl_id* [...*acl_id*]

For each match in a route map, you can configure one or more attributes to be set by using the **set** commands listed in Table 4-6.

Table 4-6 *Route Map set Commands*

Attribute to Set	Command Syntax
Next-hop router IP address	ciscoasa(config-route-map)# **set ip next-hop** *ip-address* [*ip-address*]
Route metric value	ciscoasa(config-route-map)# **set metric** *value*
OSPF metric type	ciscoasa(config-route-map)# **set metric-type** {**internal** | **external** | **type-1** | **type-2**}

Finally, you can use the following command to redistribute routes from another source into the OSPF process:

```
ciscoasa(config-router)# redistribute {static | connected
  | rip | eigrp as_num} [metric metric_value] [metric-
  type metric_type] [route-map map_name] [tag tag_value] [subnets]
```

Either static routes (configured with the **route** command), connected routes (subnets directly connected to firewall interfaces), or routes learned through RIPv2 or EIGRP can be redistributed into the OSPF process. Use the **connected** keyword only when you have ASA interfaces that aren't configured to participate in OSPF. Otherwise, OSPF automatically learns directly connected interfaces and their subnets from the OSPF configuration.

If you configure a route map for redistribution, you should specify it with the **route-map** keyword. If the **route-map** keyword is omitted, all routes are distributed.

You can also set fixed values for the OSPF metric_value (0 to 16777214), the metric_type (**internal**, **external**, **type-1**, or **type-2**), and the route tag value (an arbitrary number that can be used to identify and match routes on other ASBRs) for all routes, not just ones matched by a route map.

By default, only routes that are not subnetted (classful routes) are redistributed into OSPF unless the **subnets** keyword is given.

Because an ASA can have two independent OSPF processes running, you can also redistribute routes from one OSPF process into the other. You can use the following command to identify the source OSPF process ID:

```
ciscoasa(config-router)# redistribute ospf pid [match
  {internal | external [1 | 2] | nssa-external [1 | 2]}]
  [metric metric_value] [metric-type metric_type]
  [route-map map_name] [tag tag_value] [subnets]
```

If you do not use a route map, you can still redistribute only routes with specific metric types by using the **match** keyword. The types include **internal** (internally generated), **external** (OSPF type 1 or 2), and **nssa-external** (OSPF type 1 or 2 coming into an NSSA).

You can use the commands listed in Example 4-7 to build the example scenario.

Example 4-7 *Configuration Commands Used for the Figure 4-21 Scenario*

```
ciscoasa(config)# interface ethernet0
ciscoasa(config-if)# nameif outside
ciscoasa(config-if)# security-level 0
ciscoasa(config-if)# ip address 10.1.4.1 255.255.255.0
ciscoasa(config-if)# ospf authentication message-digest
ciscoasa(config-if)# ospf message-digest-key 1 md5 myoutsidekey
ciscoasa(config-if)# exit
```

```
ciscoasa(config)# interface ethernet1
ciscoasa(config-if)# nameif inside
ciscoasa(config-if)# security-level 100
ciscoasa(config-if)# ip address 192.168.1.1 255.255.255.0
ciscoasa(config-if)# ospf authentication message-digest
ciscoasa(config-if)# ospf message-digest-key 1 md5 myinsidekey
ciscoasa(config-if)# exit

ciscoasa(config)# prefix-list InsideFilter 10 deny 192.168.99.0/24
ciscoasa(config)# prefix-list InsideFilter 20 permit 192.168.0.0/16
ciscoasa(config)# prefix-list InsideFilter 30 permit 172.16.0.0/16

ciscoasa(config)# router ospf 1
ciscoasa(config-router)# network 192.168.1.0 255.255.255.0 area 0
ciscoasa(config-router)# network 10.1.4.0 255.255.255.0 area 4
ciscoasa(config-router)# area 0 filter-list prefix InsideFilter out
ciscoasa(config-router)# exit
```

Verifying the ASA Routing Table

You can display the routes in an ASA's routing table in ASDM by navigating to
Monitoring > Routing > Routes. Figure 4-26 shows the routing table, which lists the
directly connected and static routes.

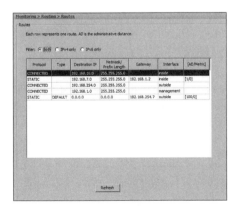

Figure 4-26 *Displaying the Routing Table in ASDM*

Through the CLI, you can verify the routes in an ASA's routing table by using the **show
route** command. The output shows routes learned by any possible means, whether
directly connected, through static configuration, or through a dynamic routing protocol.

Example 4-8 lists the contents the routing table on an ASA that has only directly connected and static routes.

Example 4-8 *Displaying the Routing Table Contents with* **show route**

```
ciscoasa# show route
Codes: C - connected, S - static, I - IGRP, R - RIP, M - mobile, B - BGP
       D - EIGRP, EX - EIGRP external, O - OSPF, IA - OSPF inter area
       N1 - OSPF NSSA external type 1, N2 - OSPF NSSA external type 2
       E1 - OSPF external type 1, E2 - OSPF external type 2, E - EGP
       i - IS-IS, L1 - IS-IS level-1, L2 - IS-IS level-2, ia - IS-IS inter area
       * - candidate default, U - per-user static route, o - ODR
       P - periodic downloaded static route

Gateway of last resort is 192.168.254.7 to network 0.0.0.0

C    192.168.10.0 255.255.255.0 is directly connected, inside
S    192.168.7.0 255.255.255.0 [1/0] via 192.168.1.2, inside
C    192.168.254.0 255.255.255.0 is directly connected, outside
C    192.168.1.0 255.255.255.0 is directly connected, management
S*   0.0.0.0 0.0.0.0 [100/0] via 192.168.254.7, outside
ciscoasa#
```

Notice the legend of route codes in the first several lines. Directly connected routes are displayed with a C code in the left column. Static routes are displayed with an S code. This ASA has one static route for a subnet located on the inside interface. It also has one static default route pointing toward a next-hop router on the outside interface.

Static routes and routes learned from a dynamic routing protocol are shown with square brackets containing two values. The first value is the administrative distance, and the second value is the metric derived or used by the routing protocol.

Notice that the default route in Example 4-8 has an administrative distance of 100, not the normal distance of 1 that a static route should have by default. In this case, static route tracking is involved; the tracked route must be down, so the backup (less preferable, greater distance) route is active in the routing table. You can display all the configured static routes with the **show running-config route** command, as demonstrated in Example 4-9.

Example 4-9 *Displaying Configured Static Routes*

```
ciscoasa# show running-config route
route outside 0.0.0.0 0.0.0.0 192.168.254.2 1 track 1
route outside 0.0.0.0 0.0.0.0 192.168.254.7 100
route inside 192.168.7.0 255.255.255.0 192.168.1.2 1
ciscoasa#
```

You can use the EXEC commands listed in Table 4-7 to verify dynamic routing protocol operation.

Table 4-7 *Useful Commands for Verifying Dynamic Routing Protocols*

Goal	CLI	ASDM
Display RIPv2 information.	ciscoasa# **show rip database**	—
Display EIGRP peers.	ciscoasa# **show eigrp neighbors**	**Monitoring > Routing > EIGRP Neighbors**
Display EIGRP information.	ciscoasa# **show eigrp topology**	—
Display OSPF status.	ciscoasa# **show ospf** *pid*	—
Display OSPF interface status.	ciscoasa# **show ospf interface** [*interface*]	—
Display OSPF peers.	ciscoasa# **show ospf neighbor**	**Monitoring > Routing > OSPF Neighbors**
Display OSPF information.	ciscoasa# **show ospf database**	**Monitoring > Routing > OSPF LSAs**

Exam Preparation Tasks

As mentioned in the section, "How to Use This Book," in the Introduction, you have a couple of choices for exam preparation: the exercises here, Chapter 17, "Final Preparation," and the exam simulation questions on the CD-ROM.

Review All Key Topics

Review the most important topics in this chapter, noted with the Key Topic icon in the outer margin of the page. Table 4-8 lists a reference of these key topics and the page numbers on which each is found.

Key Topic

Table 4-8   *Key Topics for Chapter 4*

Key Topic Element	Description	Page Number
Paragraph	Describes the DHCP relay agent feature	117
Paragraph	Describes the DHCP server feature	119
Table 4-2	Lists routing considerations	123
Table 4-3	Lists administrative distance values	124
Paragraph	Describes static routing	124
Paragraph	Explains static route tracking	126
Paragraph	Describes RIPv2	132
Paragraph	Describes EIGRP	135
Paragraph	Describes OSPF	142
Paragraph	Explains how to display the routing table	151
Table 4-7	Lists commands for verifying dynamic routing protocols	153

Define Key Terms

Define the following key terms from this chapter and check your answers in the glossary:

DHCP relay, DHCP server, static route, RIPv2, EIGRP, OSPF, administrative distance, SLA monitor

Command Reference to Check Your Memory

This section includes the most important configuration and EXEC commands covered in this chapter. It might not be necessary to memorize the complete syntax of every command, but you should be able to remember the basic keywords that are needed.

To test your memory of the commands, cover the right side of Tables 4-9 through 4-13 with a piece of paper, read the description on the left side, and then see how much of the command you can remember.

The FIREWALL exam focuses on practical, hands-on skills that are used by a networking professional. Therefore, you should be able to identify the commands needed to configure and test an ASA feature.

Table 4-9   *Commands Related to DHCP Service Configuration and Verification*

Task	Command Syntax
Enable DHCP relay agent	ciscoasa(config)# **dhcprelay server** *ip-address interface*
Enable DHCP relay agent interface	ciscoasa(config)# **dhcprelay enable** *interface*
Override default gateway with ASA interface address	ciscoasa(config)# **dhcprelay setroute** *interface*
Enable DHCP server	ciscoasa(config)# **dhcpd enable** *interface*
Define an address pool	ciscoasa(config)# **dhcpd address** *ip1*[-*ip2*] *interface*
Define a DHCP option	ciscoasa(config)# **dhcpd option** *code* {**ascii** *string*	**ip** *ip_address*	**hex** *hex_string*}
Define global DHCP parameters	ciscoasa(config)# **dhcpd dns** *dns1* [*dns2*]
	ciscoasa(config)# **dhcpd wins** *wins1* [*wins2*]
	ciscoasa(config)# **dhcpd domain** *domain_name*
	ciscoasa(config)# **dhcpd lease** *lease_length*
	ciscoasa(config)# **dhcpd ping_timeout** *timeout*
Display the DHCP server status	ciscoasa# **show dhcpd state**
Display DHCP lease bindings	ciscoasa# **show dhcpd binding all**

Table 4-10   *Commands Related to Static Route Configuration and Verification*

Task	Command Syntax
Define a static route	ciscoasa(config)# **route** *interface ip_address netmask gateway_ip* [*distance*]
Define an SLA monitor process	ciscoasa(config)# **sla monitor** *sla-id*
Define a reachability test	ciscoasa(config-sla-monitor)# **type echo protocol ipIcmpEcho** *target* **interface** *interface-name*

Table 4-10   *Commands Related to Static Route Configuration and Verification*

Task	Command Syntax
Tune the SLA monitor test	ciscoasa(config-sla-monitor)# **frequency** *seconds*
	ciscoasa(config-sla-monitor)# **num-packets** *number*
	ciscoasa(config-sla-monitor)# **request-data-size** *bytes*
	ciscoasa(config-sla-monitor)# **tos** *number*
	ciscoasa(config-sla-monitor)# **timeout** *milliseconds*
	ciscoasa(config-sla-monitor)# **threshold** *milliseconds*
Schedule the SLA monitor test	ciscoasa(config)# **sla monitor** *sla-id* **life forever now**
Enable reachability tracking	ciscoasa(config)# **track** *track-id* **rtr** *sla-id* **reachability**
Apply tracking to a static route	ciscoasa(config)# **route** *if_name ip_address netmask gateway_ip* [*distance*] **track** *track-id*
Define a backup static route	ciscoasa(config)# **route** *if_name ip_address netmask gateway_ip bigdistance*
Display static route tracking status	ciscoasa# **show track** [*track-id*]
Display SLA monitor test configuration	ciscoasa# **show sla monitor configuration**
Display SLA monitor test state	ciscoasa# **show sla monitor operation-state**

Table 4-11   *Commands Related to RIPv2 Configuration and Verification*

Task	Command Syntax
Enable RIPv2	ciscoasa(config)# **router rip**
	ciscoasa(config-router)# **version 2**
Disable automatic route summarization	ciscoasa(config-router)# **no auto-summary**
Advertise default route information	ciscoasa(config-router)# **default-information originate**
Identify a network to participate in RIPv2	ciscoasa(config-router)# **network** *ip-address*
Identify a passive interface	ciscoasa(config-router)# **passive-interface** {**default**	*interface*}
Use route filtering	ciscoasa(config-router)# **distribute-list** *acl-id* {**in**	**out**} **interface** *interface*
Use RIPv2 peer authentication	ciscoasa(config-if)# **rip authentication mode** {**text**	**md5**}
	ciscoasa(config-if)# **rip authentication key** *key-string* **key_id** *id*

Table 4-12 *Commands Related to EIGRP Configuration and Verification*

Task	Command Syntax
Enable EIGRP	ciscoasa(config)# **router eigrp** *as-num*
Associate a network with EIGRP	ciscoasa(config-router)# **network** *ip-addr* [*mask*]
Identify a passive interface	ciscoasa(config-router)# **passive-interface** *interface*
Disable automatic route summarization	ciscoasa(config-router)# **no auto-summary**
Advertise a summary address	ciscoasa(config)# **interface** *interface* ciscoasa(config-if)# **summary-address eigrp** *as-num address mask* [*distance*]
Redistribute routing information	ciscoasa(config-router)# **redistribute** {**rip** | **static** | **connected**} [**metric** *bandwidth delay reliability load mtu*] [**route-map** *map_name*]
Redistribute OSPF routing information	ciscoasa(config-router)# **redistribute ospf** *pid* [**match** {**internal** | **external** [**1** | **2**] | **nssa-external** [**1** | **2**]}] [**metric** *bandwidth delay reliability load mtu*] [**route-map** *map_name*]
Define default metrics	ciscoasa(config-router)# **default-metric** *bandwidth delay reliability loading mtu*
Configure a stub router	ciscoasa(config-router)# **eigrp stub** {**receive-only** | [**connected**] [**redistributed**] [**static**] [**summary**]}
Configure EIGRP peer authentication	ciscoasa(config)# **interface** *interface* ciscoasa(config-if)# **authentication mode eigrp** *as-num* **md5** ciscoasa(config-if)# **authentication key eigrp** *as-num key-string* **key-id** *key-id*
Use route filtering	ciscoasa(config-router)# **distribute-list** *acl-id* {**in** | **out**} [**interface** *interface*]
Display EIGRP peers	ciscoasa# **show eigrp neighbors**
Display EIGRP routing information	ciscoasa# **show eigrp topology**

Table 4-13   *Commands Related to OSPF Configuration and Verification*

Task	Command Syntax
Enable an OSPF process	ciscoasa(config)# **router ospf** *pid*
Set the OSPF router ID	ciscoasa(config-router)# **router-id** *ip_address*
Log adjacency changes	ciscoasa(config-router)# **log-adj-changes** [detail]
Advertise default information	ciscoasa(config-router)# **default-information originate** [**always**] [**metric** *value*] [**metric-type** {1 | 2}] [**route-map** *name*]
Set the administrative distance	ciscoasa(config-router)# **distance ospf** [**intra-area** *d1*] [**inter-area** *d2*] [**external** *d3*]
Adjust the OSPF timers	ciscoasa(config-router)# **timers** {**spf** *spf_delay spf_holdtime* | **lsa-group-pacing** *seconds*}
Associate a network with an OSPF area	ciscoasa(config-router)# **network** *ip_address netmask* **area** *area_id*
Enable peer authentication	ciscoasa(config-router)# **area** *area_id* **authentication** [*message-digest*]
Define MD5 authentication and key	ciscoasa(config)# **interface** *interface* ciscoasa(config-if)# **ospf message-digest-key** *key-id* **md5** *key* ciscoasa(config-if)# **ospf authentication message-digest**
Define a stub area	ciscoasa(config-router)# **area** *area_id* **stub** [**no-summary**]
Define a not-so-stubby area	ciscoasa(config-router)# **area** *area_id* **nssa** [**no-redistribution**] [**default-information-originate** [**metric-type** 1 | 2] [**metric** *metric_value*]]
Use route filtering	ciscoasa(config)# **prefix-list** *list_name* [**seq** *seq_number*] {**permit** | **deny**} *prefix/len* [**ge** *min_value*] [**le** *max_value*] ciscoasa(config-router)# **area** *area_id* **filter-list prefix** *list_name* [**in** | **out**]
Summarize routes between areas	ciscoasa(config-router)# **area** *area_id* **range** *ip_address netmask* [**advertise** | **not-advertise**]
Redistribute routing information	ciscoasa(config-router)# **redistribute** {**static** | **connected** | **rip** | **eigrp** *as_num*} [**metric** *metric_value*] [**metric-type** *metric_type*] [**route-map** *map_name*] [**tag** *tag_value*] [**subnets**]
Redistribute routes between OSPF processes	ciscoasa(config-router)# **redistribute ospf** *pid* [**match** {**internal** | **external** [1 | 2] | **nssa-external** [1 | 2]}] [**metric** *metric_value*] [**metric-type** *metric_type*] [**route-map** *map_name*] [**tag** *tag_value*] [**subnets**]
Display OSPF status	ciscoasa# **show ospf** *pid*

Table 4-13   *Commands Related to OSPF Configuration and Verification*

Task	Command Syntax
Display OSPF interface status	ciscoasa# **show ospf interface** [*interface*]
Display OSPF peers	ciscoasa# **show ospf neighbor**
Display OSPF information	ciscoasa# **show ospf database**

This chapter covers the following topics:

- **Basic Device Settings:** This section describes configuration of basic device settings, such as hostname, domain, enable password, and Telnet password.

- **Configuring DNS Resolution:** This section describes configuration of a Domain Name System (DNS) server group.

- **File System Management:** This section describes how to manage the file system in flash memory on a Cisco ASA, including where the ASA keeps its configuration, system software, and auxiliary files.

- **Managing Software and Feature Activation:** This section describes how to manage the activation of features within the operating system of an ASA and how to change the activation key of the security appliance.

- **Configuring Management Access:** This section describes how to configure an ASA for remote management, using Telnet, Secure Shell (SSH), a dedicated out-of-band interface, or HTTP over SSL/TLS (HTTPS) using Cisco Adaptive Security Device Manager (ASDM).

- **Controlling Management Access with AAA:** This section describes how to configure an ASA to perform authentication, authorization, and accounting, using the local database, a remote AAA server, or a combination of the two.

- **Configuring Monitoring Using SNMP:** This section describes how to configure an ASA to send SNMP traps to a management console for monitoring purposes.

- **Troubleshooting Remote Management Access:** This section describes common methods for troubleshooting remote management access problems.

- **Cisco ASA Password Recovery:** This section describes how to perform password recovery on an ASA to regain access after the loss of all administrative passwords.

CHAPTER 5

Managing a Cisco ASA

A Cisco Adaptive Security Appliance (ASA), like any other networking device, offers several ways for an administrative user to connect to and interact with it. The ASA supports in-band management (using a traffic-passing interface) and out-of-band management (using a dedicated management-only interface). You can access the ASA using Telnet, Secure Shell (SSH), and HTTPS protocols (after the ASA is configured to allow such access), as well as SNMP (versions 1, 2c, and 3) for monitoring purposes. You can achieve highly granular control over such access using authentication, authorization, and accounting (AAA) features of the ASA.

"Do I Know This Already?" Quiz

The "Do I Know This Already?" quiz allows you to assess whether you should read this entire chapter thoroughly or jump to the "Exam Preparation Tasks" section. If you are in doubt about your answers to these questions or your own assessment of your knowledge of the topics, read the entire chapter. Table 5-1 lists the major headings in this chapter and their corresponding "Do I Know This Already?" quiz questions. You can find the answers in Appendix A, "Answers to the 'Do I Know This Already?' Quizzes."

Table 5-1 *"Do I Know This Already?" Section-to-Question Mapping*

Foundation Topics Section	Questions
Basic Device Settings	1
File System Management	2
Managing Software and Feature Activation	3
Configuring Management Access	4
Controlling Management Access with AAA	5–7
Configuring Monitoring Using SNMP	8
Troubleshooting Remote Management Access	9
Cisco ASA Password Recovery	10

Caution: The goal of self-assessment is to gauge your mastery of the topics in this chapter. If you do not know the answer to a question or are only partially sure of the answer, you should mark that question as wrong for purposes of the self-assessment. Giving yourself credit for an answer you correctly guess skews your self-assessment results and might provide you with a false sense of security.

1. Which two commands establish a fully qualified domain name (FQDN) that can be used by an ASA for certificate generation? (Choose two answers.)

   a. **crypto ca trustpoint ASA-Self-Signed**

   b. **hostname FIREWALL**

   c. **ip domain-name CISCOPRESS.CCNP**

   d. **domain-name CISCOPRESS.CCNP**

2. Why would you issue the command **delete FSCK*.REN?**

   a. To delete "junk" files created by the ASA during a file system integrity check

   b. Because your ASA is running out of memory blocks

   c. To delete the autogenerated backup configuration files, which are named FSCKx.REN, where x is a number, beginning at 0 and incrementing to 4

   d. To delete all directories in flash named FSCKx.REN, where x is one or more characters

3. Which of the following are displayed by using the **show version** command? (Choose all that apply.)

   a. The device flash BIOS serial number

   b. The current value of the config-register

   c. The running activation key

   d. The number of active security contexts

   e. The type and amount of system flash memory

4. When does the ASA generate a self-signed X.509 certificate used to authenticate the device during ASDM use?

   a. On initial boot only, the ASA generates a persistent self-signed certificate.

   b. Upon each boot, the ASA generates a self-signed certificate, but you can create a persistent self-signed certificate.

   c. After you delete and regenerate the RSA key pair, upon the next boot only, the ASA generates a persistent self-signed certificate.

   d. The ASA does not use a certificate for ASDM access.

5. Which of the following is not a supported server type for AAA?

    a. TACACS+

    b. Kerberos

    c. LDAP

    d. SQL

    e. SecurID

    f. All of these are supported server types.

6. What is the default privilege level for users created with the **username** command?

    a. 0

    b. 1

    c. 2

    d. 5

    e. 15

    f. There is no default privilege level; you must explicitly assign one.

7. Where in Cisco Secure ACS are Shell Command Authorization Sets created?

    a. Administration Control

    b. Network Access Profiles

    c. Group Setup > TACACS+

    d. Shared Profile Components

    e. Shell Command Authorization Sets are not created in ACS; they are created locally on the ASA.

8. Which of the following SNMP trap types are enabled by default? (Choose all that apply.)

    a. Link Up

    b. Link Down

    c. Cold Start

    d. Authentication

    e. Session Threshold Exceeded

    f. All of the answers are correct.

9. What would happen during the initiation of an SSH connection that would generate the following system log message?

```
%ASA-3-315011: SSH session from 192.168.1.8 on interface management for user ""
disconnected by SSH server, reason: "Internal error" (0x00)
```

   a. The user's SSH client does not support SSH version 2.

   b. The user is attempting an SSH version 2 connection, and the ASA is configured to accept version 1 only.

   c. The ASA does not have an RSA key pair configured.

   d. The ASA is not configured to accept SSH connections from the indicated source address.

10. What value do you set the config-register to in order to perform password recovery?

   a. 0x01

   b. 0x02

   c. 0x41

   d. 0x24

   e. 0xFF

Foundation Topics

To properly integrate a Cisco ASA into your local network, you need to be able to configure the ASA with appropriate information about itself and the local environment. Before you can perform these basic management tasks, you will need to gather information about the local network environment into which the ASA will be integrated, such as the local Domain Name System (DNS) servers, Network Time Protocol (NTP) servers (and, if using authenticated NTP, their authentication credentials), file servers that are used by network devices to store files remote to themselves, and syslog servers for logging event information. Additionally, you will need to know which features are required for the ASA to satisfy the security requirements of your business. This information is necessary in order to choose the correct software image and activation key.

The FIREWALL exam focuses on practical, hands-on skills that are used by a networking professional. You will be expected to be familiar with how to configure various features either from the ASDM GUI or from the CLI, and to be able to use either for verification and troubleshooting. This being the case, this book will show the use of both tools, primarily configuring an ASA using ASDM, and recapping the equivalent CLI commands for each section.

Basic Device Settings

An ASA can operate with default settings for many items. For instance, it is possible to secure a network and pass traffic to and from the Internet without configuring items like the hostname, domain name, enable password, and local time parameters. However, if you want to provide the ASA with protection from unauthorized access, allow Secure Shell (SSH) management, write syslog messages with correct time stamps, register your device for a digital certificate that properly identifies it as an asset of your organization, and otherwise integrate the ASA into your local environment, you will have to perform some or all of the following tasks:

- Configure device identify (host and domain name)

- Configure basic authentication (enable and Telnet passwords)

Configuring Device Identity

Providing the ASA with information identifying itself is more than just a matter of seeing a unique device name in a CLI prompt. The device hostname and domain name together construct the fully qualified domain name (FQDN) of the ASA, which is used to generate a self-signed digital certificate upon boot. This certificate is used when authenticating the device for HTTPS (ASDM) management and can be used, if a certificate from another certificate authority (CA) is not configured, to authenticate the ASA for IP Security (IPsec) or Secure Sockets Layer (SSL) Virtual Private Network (VPN) operations (a certificate from a public CA is highly preferable). The hostname can also be sent by the ASA as part of syslog messages, to make it easier to identify their source, and can be registered in local DNS records, if so desired.

You can configure both hostnames and domain names (each limited to 63 characters maximum) within ASDM, but the following examples use the CLI to demonstrate a change in the command prompt. To configure the hostname of the ASA, use the **hostname** command from global configuration mode, as demonstrated here:

```
ciscoasa(config)# hostname FIREWALL
FIREWALL(config)#
```

Notice that the ASA changes the command prompt to show the newly configured hostname.

To complete the FQDN, a domain name is needed to complement the hostname. This is optional under most circumstances, but it is necessary when deploying any kind of X.509 digital certificates (which can be used for HTTPS access, SSL VPN, or IPsec VPN). To configure a domain name for the ASA, use the **domain-name** command from global configuration mode:

```
FIREWALL(config)# domain-name CISCOPRESS.CCNP
```

Note: The domain name CISCOPRESS.CCNP is used strictly for illustrative purposes, as no such top-level domain exists.

Configuring Basic Authentication

By default, a Cisco ASA requires no password to enter privileged EXEC (enable) mode. Because initial access to the console port necessitates physical access, this is understandable. However, if an ASA is going to enter production, it is unacceptable to provide access without requiring at least basic authentication. Also, although an ASA does require a password for remote Telnet access, it is set to "cisco" by default, which should be changed before the ASA enters a production network. By default, this password is also used for SSH access (with the username being "pix") in the absence of AAA authentication being configured. It is therefore critical to configure a strong password or configure AAA.

The hostname, domain name, enable password, and Telnet password are all configured within the same ASDM window. After launching ASDM, navigate to **Configuration > Device Setup > Device Name/Password** to make changes to these settings, as demonstrated in Figure 5-1.

Figure 5-1 shows the ASA with the hostname and domain name already set. To change the enable password, check the **Change the Privileged Mode Password** check box. Because there is no enable password on the device prior to this, leave the Old Password field under Enable Password blank and enter the new password twice, the second time to ensure you entered it correctly. To change the Telnet password, first check the **Change the Password to Access the Console of the Security Appliance** check box. Because the ASA has a default Telnet password, you need to enter **cisco** in the **Old Password** field under Telnet Password, and then enter a new password twice, to set a new password. Click **Apply** to send the changes to the ASA.

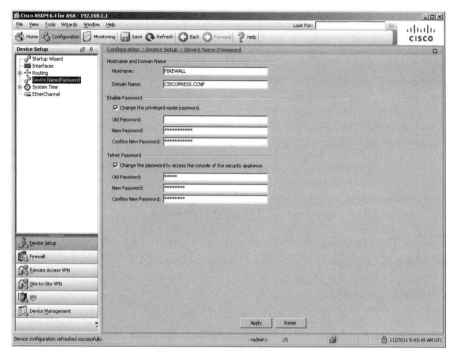

Figure 5-1 *Configuring Identity and Basic Passwords in ASDM*

The CLI commands generated by the changes made are as follows:

```
enable password sH5punHtqaLcqj3E level 15 encrypted
passwd w8iLGf/6z5hYvVsP encrypted
```

If you are configuring the ASA from the CLI, you can enter these commands directly in global configuration mode.

If you are configuring from the CLI, use the **enable password** command to set the privileged mode password. The ASA automatically converts the password to an MD5 hash when storing it. The keyword **encrypted** at the end of output line specifies that the password is shown in encrypted form (actually, an MD5 hash) rather than in plain text. You would not type this when configuring the enable password, but if you want to copy this password to another ASA, copy the entire line, including this keyword, to enable the new ASA to recognize that you are not entering a plain-text password.

Note: If entering the **enable password** command from the CLI in cleartext, simply enter the command as **enable password** *string* **level** *privilege_level*. The absence of the **encrypted** keyword is interpreted by the ASA as meaning that the string represents the new password in plain text. Subsequent **show** output, however, always displays the password in it MD5 hashed form.

Use the **passwd** (or **password**) command to set the Telnet password of the ASA. The ASA automatically converts the password to an MD5 hash when storing it.

Note: In the absence of AAA authentication (discussed later in this chapter), the Telnet password is also used for SSH authentication, coupled with the username "pix."

The configured enable password is used for access to Cisco Adaptive Security Device Manager (ASDM) in the absence of other HTTP authentication (covered later in the section, "Controlling Management Access with AAA"). Although you have set a Telnet password, accessing the ASA with Telnet is not currently possible. Enabling Telnet access is covered in the section, "Configuring Remote Access Using Telnet."

When you create passwords, write them down and store them in a manner consistent with your site security policy. You cannot view these passwords using **show** commands on the ASA because they are stored as Message Digest 5 (MD5) hashes. The **show running-config** command lists the encrypted form of the passwords.

Verifying Basic Device Settings

Device identity configuration can be verified using two commands, **show hostname** and **show running-config domain-name** (there is no **show domain-name** command), as demonstrated in Example 5-1.

Example 5-1   *Displaying Device Identity*

```
FIREWALL# show hostname
FIREWALL
FIREWALL# show running-config domain-name
CISCOPRESS.CCNP
```

The enable password can be verified by exiting privileged mode and then re-entering it, as demonstrated in Example 5-2.

Example 5-2   *Verifying Basic Authentication*

```
FIREWALL# disable (or logout or exit)
FIREWALL> enable
Password: **********
FIREWALL#
```

Configuring DNS Resolution

Because people have trouble remembering complex numbers, trying to remember multiple IP addresses would be impractical. Fortunately, the Domain Name System (DNS) enables you to use logical names for IP addresses by resolving those names to the IP addresses they represent.

Configuring DNS Server Groups

To configure the ASA to use DNS for name-to-address resolution, you create or modify the default DNS server group. To do so using ASDM, navigate to **Configuration > Device Management > DNS > DNS Client**, as shown in Figure 5-2.

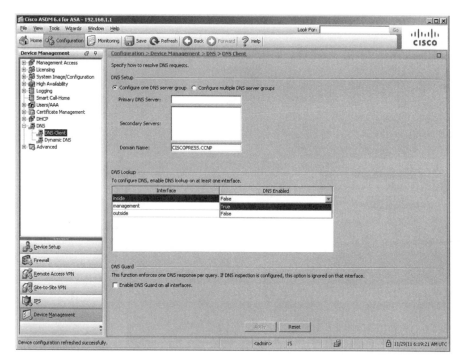

Figure 5-2   *Activating DNS on an Interface*

In the DNS Lookup area, as shown in Figure 5-2, you must enable DNS on at least one interface before you can add a DNS server to a DNS server group. You should enable DNS lookup on all interfaces from which the configured DNS servers are reachable. In Figure 5-3, DNS has been enabled on the inside interface, and you are ready to define specific DNS servers.

After DNS is enabled on at least one interface, you can configure a primary DNS server and any secondary DNS servers you want the ASA to use. In Figure 5-3, a primary DNS server (IP address 10.0.0.3) and one secondary DNS server (IP address 10.0.0.4) are configured. Note that the domain name suffix is assumed to be that configured earlier, CISCO-PRESS.CCNP. If you enter a different domain name suffix when configuring the default DNS server group, it will also change the ASA's domain name. Optionally, you can enable DNSGuard on all interfaces to enforce a one-to-one balance of DNS replies to DNS queries to guard against DNS spoofing attacks. If you use DNS servers on networks outside your domain of control, this is highly recommended.

Note: The explicit definition of DNS servers is required in order to use the Botnet Traffic Filtering function, as well as if you need the ASA to be able to resolve URLs when using clientless SSL VPN.

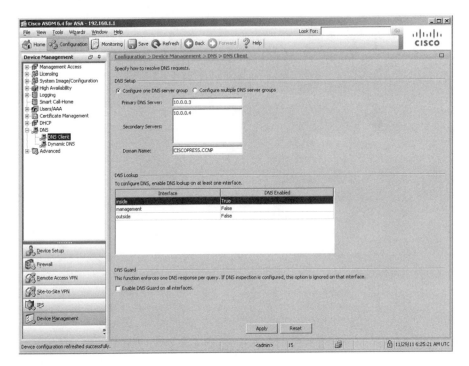

Figure 5-3   *Defining DNS Server Group Members*

The CLI commands generated by the changes made are as follows:

```
dns domain-lookup inside
dns server-group DefaultDNS
  name-server 10.0.0.3
  name-server 10.0.0.4
```

If you are configuring the ASA from the CLI, you can enter these commands in global configuration mode.

The **dns domain-lookup** command enables the ASA DNS client to query DNS servers over a particular interface. The **dns server-group** command defines a set of DNS resolver settings, including server IP addresses and the domain suffix used in lookups that lack a FQDN (for example, typing ROUTER instead of ROUTER.CISCOPRESS.CCNP). The DefaultDNS server group is the set of DNS settings the ASA uses by default.

Verifying DNS Resolution

There are a variety of ways to verify DNS functionality. Perhaps the easiest way is to simply ping a destination by name, as demonstrated in Example 5-3.

Example 5-3   *Verifying DNS Resolution*

```
FIREWALL# ping time.nist.gov
Type escape sequence to abort.
Sending 5, 100-byte ICMP Echos to 192.43.244.18, timeout is 2 seconds:
!!!!!
Success rate is 100% (5/5), round-trip min/avg/max = 127/130/133 ms
```

To troubleshoot DNS resolution, use the **debug dns resolver** command. You can also use this command with other options to see more than just resolver messages. The full syntax and options are shown here:

```
debug dns [resolver | all] [level]
```

The parameters for this command are described as follows:

- **resolver:** (Optional) Shows only DNS resolver messages.

- **all:** (Default) Shows all messages, including messages about the DNS cache.

- **level:** (Optional) Sets the debug message level to display, between 1 and 255. The default is 1. To display additional messages at higher levels, set the level to a higher number.

File System Management

A Cisco ASA uses built-in flash memory (flash: or disk0:) to store its configuration files, operating system binaries, and several auxiliary files used to provide system features (for example, AnyConnect client and Cisco Secure Desktop images). You can also install additional CompactFlash memory in the provided slot to expand storage capability (disk1:).

The flash memory is structured into a file system similar to that used by other operating systems, and supports the use of common file management commands and functions. You can manage the file system either from ASDM or from the CLI.

File System Management Using ASDM

To open the ASDM file system management interface, click **Tools > File Management** in the ASDM menu. The File Management window opens, as shown in Figure 5-4.

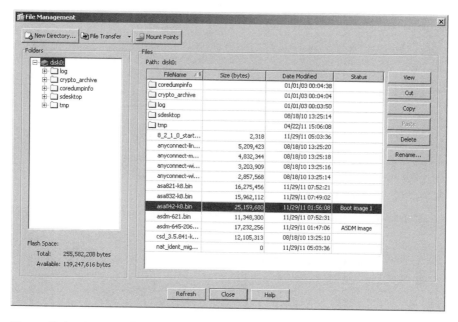

Figure 5-4 *ASDM File Management Window*

Note: File management using ASDM offers unique capabilities not accessible from the CLI: the capability to move files directly to or from the host on which ASDM is running, without a server protocol such as FTP or HTTP running on that host, or download updated images directly from Cisco.com.

Figure 5-4 shows the File Management window of a typical ASA. From this window, you can view, copy, move, delete, or rename files in flash memory, transfer files to the host running ASDM or remote servers using a variety of protocols, and manage files on remote mount points (remote storage devices). The window is split into two panes:

■ **Folders:** This pane (on the left) allows quick navigation through available folders.

■ **Files:** By default, this pane displays the contents of built-in flash memory (disk0:).

The buttons on the right side of the File Management window give immediate access to various file management functions: View (which opens a selected file in a browser window), Cut, Copy, Paste, Delete, and Rename.

Additionally, across the top of the File Management window are three buttons:

■ **New Directory:** Creates a new directory on the file system

■ **File Transfer:** Opens the File Transfer window, from which you can copy files to or from the computer running ASDM using the HTTPS connection of ASDM, or copy a file to or from a remote HTTP, HTTPS, FTP, or TFTP server

■ **Mount Points:** Opens the Manage Mount Points window, enabling you to configure remote storage for file systems using a Common Internet File System (CIFS) or FTP connection

File System Management Using the CLI

The ASA CLI has equivalent file management functions. Although the sections that follow present some samples, full details on all possible parameters will not be covered in this book. Full information on the meaning and use of all available parameters is available in the *Cisco ASA 5500 Series Command Reference*, 8.4 and 8.5, which is available at www. cisco.com/en/US/docs/security/asa/asa84/command/reference/cmdref.html.

dir

The **dir** command, used without parameters, displays the contents of the current directory. You can specify other locations by adding appropriate parameters to the **dir** command. The syntax for the **dir** command is as follows:

```
dir [/all] [all-filesystems] [/recursive] [disk0: | disk1: | flash: | system:] [path]
```

Note: On a Cisco ASA, the keyword **flash:** aliases to **disk0:** (internal flash).

more

The **more** command displays the contents of a file. The syntax for the **more** command is as follows:

```
more [/ascii | /binary | /ebcdic] [disk0: | disk1: | flash: | ftp: | http: |
  https: | smb: | system: | tftp:]filename
```

copy

The **copy** command is used to copy a file from one location to another. It can also be used to copy a file to your startup or running configuration. The syntax for the **copy** command is as follows:

```
copy [/noconfirm] [/pcap] {url | running-config | startup-config} {running-config
  | startup-config | url}
```

Note: A server parameter within a URL can be expressed as an IP address or a name to be resolved by DNS or local name-to-address mappings.

delete

The **delete** command allows you to delete a file from the local flash file system only. The syntax for the **delete** command is as follows:

```
delete [/noconfirm] [/recursive] {disk0: | disk1: | flash:}filename
```

rename

The **rename** command allows you to rename a file on the local flash file system only. The syntax for the **rename** command is as follows:

```
rename [/noconfirm] {disk0: | disk1: | flash:}source-path {disk0: | disk1: |
  flash:}destination-path
```

Example 5-4 demonstrates this command in action.

Example 5-4 *Renaming a File*

```
FIREWALL# rename disk0:/saved111010.cfg disk0:/test.cfg

Source filename [saved111010.cfg]? <press Enter>

Destination filename [test.cfg]? <press Enter>
FIREWALL#
```

mkdir

The **mkdir** command is used to create a new directory (make directory) in the file system. You are asked to confirm the creation, unless you specify the **noconfirm** parameter. If a directory with the specified name already exists, an error is generated and no new directory is created. The syntax for the **mkdir** command is as follows:

```
mkdir [/noconfirm] [disk0: | disk1: | flash:]path
```

In Example 5-5, an attempt is made to create a new directory named newdir, but this directory already exists.

Example 5-5   *Attempting to Create a Duplicate Directory Name*

```
FIREWALL# mkdir newdir

Create directory filename [newdir]?

%Error Creating dir disk0:/newdir (File exists)
FIREWALL#
```

rmdir

The **rmdir** command is used to delete a directory in the file system. You are asked to confirm the deletion, unless you specify the **noconfirm** parameter. The syntax for the **rmdir** command is as follows:

```
rmdir [/noconfirm] [disk0: | disk1: | flash:]path
```

Example 5-6 demonstrates this command in action.

Example 5-6   *Removing a Directory from the Local File System*

```
FIREWALL# rmdir newdir

Remove directory filename [newdir]?

Delete disk0:/newdir? [confirm]
FIREWALL#
```

cd

Use the **cd** command to change the current working directory to a specified location. If you do not specify a location, the working directory is changed to the root directory. The syntax for the **cd** command is as follows:

```
cd [disk0: | disk1: | flash:] [path]
```

pwd

Use the **pwd** command to display the current working directory (*pwd* stands for Print Working Directory).

In Example 5-7, an administrator changes the working directory to the "logs" directory. Note that the system prompt does not indicate the working directory location. Thus, the administrator uses the **pwd** command to confirm the current working directory. The example closes with a demonstration that using the **cd** command without parameters returns to the root directory.

Example 5-7 *Changing Directory and Confirming Location*

```
FIREWALL# cd logs
FIREWALL# pwd

disk0:/logs/
FIREWALL# cd
FIREWALL# pwd

disk0:/
FIREWALL#
```

fsck

If you suspect corruption in the local flash file system, you can use the **fsck** (file system check) command to check for it. If any is found, the ASA creates files with the name FSCK*xxxx*.REN, where *xxxx* is a sequential number starting with 0000. The ASA also performs a file system check every time it boots, so .REN files may appear in flash memory, even if you never use this command. These files sometimes contain a fraction of a file or even an entire file that was recovered by FSCK. In rare cases, you might need to inspect these files to recover data. Generally, these files are not needed and can be deleted. The syntax for the **fsck** command is as follows:

```
fsck [/noconfirm] {disk0: | disk1: | flash:}
```

Example 5-8 demonstrates this command in action.

Example 5-8 *Performing a File System Check and Deleting .REN Files*

```
FIREWALL# fsck disk0:
FIREWALL# delete FSCK*.REN

Delete filename [FSCK*.REN]? <press Enter>

Delete disk0:/FSCK0000.REN? [confirm] <press Enter>

Delete disk0:/FSCK0001.REN? [confirm] <press Enter>
FIREWALL#
```

Tip: The regular use of **fsck** to find and clear file system corruption is a good practice. Note that the ASA performs an **fsck** as part of its boot routine.

format or erase

You can completely erase all files in the local file system (including all hidden content such as startup-config, RSA private keys, and so on) using the **format** or **erase** command. The difference between these commands is that **format** rewrites the file allocation table, whereas **erase** overwrites all memory with the 0xFF pattern first. Therefore, using a raw disk read tool could see information deleted by **format** but not by **erase**. The syntax for the **format** and **erase** commands is as follows:

```
{format | erase} [disk0: | disk1: | flash:]
```

Caution: These commands should be used only in extraordinary circumstances because all data on the selected partition, including hidden system files, will be lost. Note also that use of either of these commands on disk0: (flash:) resets your device activation key to all zeros and removes licensing of all features beyond the standard feature set until a valid activation key is re-entered. This is because the activation key is stored in a hidden system file. Therefore, if you intend to use either of these commands, you should first execute the **show version** command and write down the displayed activation key. To delete only visible files (excluding hidden system files), use the **delete /recursive** command instead.

Managing Software and Feature Activation

Prior to software version 7.0, Cisco PIX Firewall allowed an administrator to place only three commonly used files on an ASA:

- One operating system binary
- One PDM file (the predecessor of ASDM)
- A startup-config file

Use of the **dir** command displayed cryptic information that didn't facilitate the identification of individual files. No directories could be created. In short, it was not a truly functional file system.

As of version 7.0, there is much more flexibility for managing the file system, including the ability to place multiple versions of operating system binaries and ASDM images, as well as multiple configuration files, in an organized file system in flash, limited only by how much flash memory is installed on your particular ASA. Commands have been added to specify which version of each of these files you want the firewall to use from one boot to another. The complication that comes along with this flexibility is the need to maintain proper organization and ensure that the version of ASDM you intend to use is compatible with the operating system binary that you intend to use.

Managing Cisco ASA Software and ASDM Images

To upgrade ASA software or an ASDM image, you must first download the appropriate files from Cisco.com. ASDM includes a wizard that enables you to download these files directly to the ASA itself. It is vital to always ensure that the ASDM file you upgrade to is compatible with the operating system binary you upgrade to. Information on which ASDM versions are compatible with which system binaries is available on Cisco.com. You also need to ensure that the ASDM version you want to use is compatible with your local desktop.

Additionally, you should always read the relevant release notes before implementing any new version of operating system or ASDM (to ensure hardware and software compatibility) and familiarize yourself with any factors that may influence operation of the proposed versions in your particular networking environment.

To use ASDM to specify which system image binary, ASDM image, and, optionally, nonstandard startup configuration file to load upon the next reboot, navigate to **Configuration > Device Management > System Image/Configuration > Boot Image/Configuration**. From this screen, you can add an image to the list of available choices and set the order in which these files will be selected upon next boot. The ASA will boot with the first image listed, unless it is either unavailable or determined to be corrupted upon next boot. On this same screen, you can specify a compatible version of ASDM to load. Figure5-5 shows a new image, asa823-k8.bin, being added to the list of choices. The Browse Flash dialog box is accessed by clicking **Add** and then clicking **Browse Flash** in the Add Boot Image dialog box.

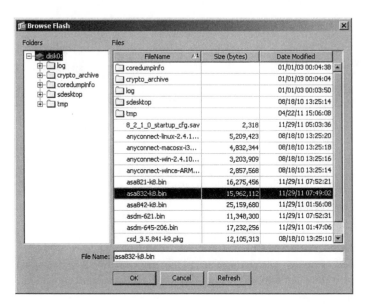

Figure 5-5 *Adding a New Boot Image to the Boot Order List*

Note: Whereas a change of operating system binary requires a reboot of the ASA, a change of ASDM image will be effective upon the next login to the ASA using ASDM.

Figure 5-6 shows the ASA boot order list after adding two additional image choices. You can adjust the order in which they will be searched by selecting an image name and clicking **Move Up** or **Move Down** to change the order.

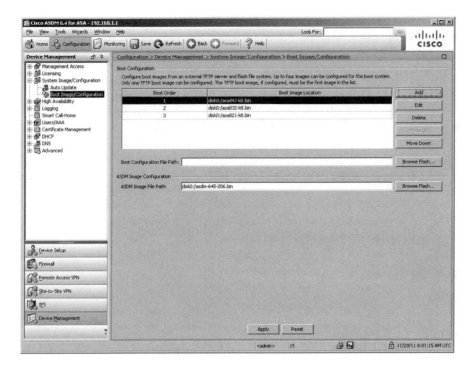

Figure 5-6 *ASDM Boot Configuration Pane with Three Binary Choices in the Boot Order List*

The CLI commands generated by the changes made are as follows:

```
boot system disk0:/asa832-k8.bin
boot system disk0:/asa821-k8.bin
```

If you are configuring the ASA from the CLI, you can enter these commands directly in global configuration mode. Note that because you are adding additional system images as fallback choices, these new commands appear below any existing **boot system** command in the ASA configuration.

Upgrading Files from a Local PC or Directly from Cisco.com

During normal operation, you can copy files to and from the flash file system and a TFTP, FTP, SMB, HTTP, or HTTPS server. As mentioned previously, if using ASDM, you can also transfer files directly to and from the host running ASDM or directly from Cisco.com. To do so, navigate to **Tools > Upgrade Software from Local Computer**. In the Upgrade Software dialog box, choose whether the upgrade will come from the local computer or from Cisco.com. Select the type of file you want to upload from the Image to Upload list, which includes the following choices:

- APCF file

- ASA image file

- ASDM image file

- Client Secure Desktop (CSD) file

- Cisco AnyConnect VPN Client file

Note: The APCF, CSD, and AnyConnect files are related to functions covered in the VPN course, and therefore are not covered in this book.

If you are upgrading from the local computer, enter a path to the source file and then enter the path to where in flash memory you want to copy the file. To execute the update, click **Upload Image**. Figure 5-7 shows an ASDM image selected for copying from the local computer.

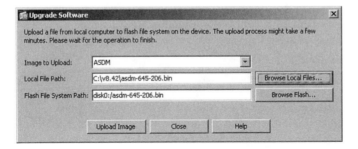

Figure 5-7   *Image Update from Local Computer*

As mentioned, you can also choose to upgrade directly from Cisco.com. To do so, navigate to **Tools > Check for ASA/ASDM Updates**, as shown in Figure 5-8.

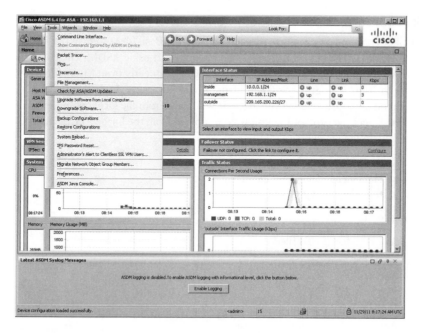

Figure 5-8 *Choosing to Check for Software Updates Directly on Cisco.com*

Note: To demonstrate this function, the ASA was temporarily downgraded to software version 8.3.2, and the 8.4.2 system binary was deleted from flash memory.

You are required to provide a valid Cisco.com username and password. Once you do, the Upgrade Software from Cisco.com Wizard opens. Complete the wizard to upgrade your ASA directly from Cisco.com. Figure 5-9 shows the wizard in action after selecting to upgrade the ASA to software version 8.4.2.

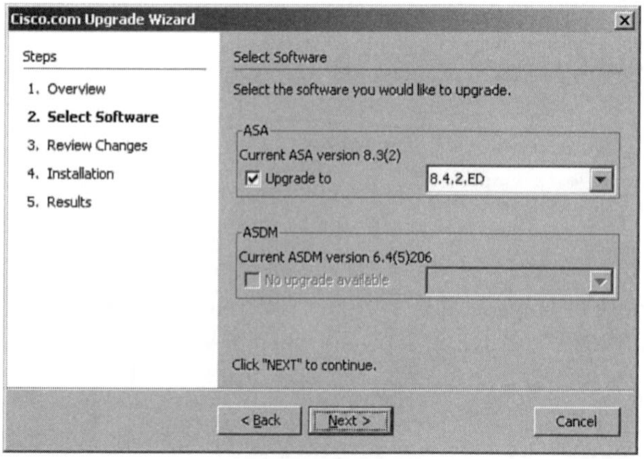

Figure 5-9 *Cisco.com Upgrade Wizard*

After upgrading images from either location, verify the correct boot order, as previously discussed, and reload the ASA. If using the Upgrade Wizard, you will be asked if you want to make the newly downloaded file the active system image, and reload the ASA. If you choose to do this, the wizard removes all existing **boot system** commands from the configuration and replaces them with a new list in the proper order, saves the changes to startup-config, and reloads the appliance.

Considerations When Upgrading from OS Version 8.2 to 8.3 or Higher

When upgrading an ASA to OS version 8.3 or higher for the first time, some items merit special attention.

Almost all ASA models have higher memory requirements for running these higher OS versions. Additionally, Cisco upgrading to versions 8.3 or higher only from version 8.2. It is important to consult the release notes for the version you intend to use to ensure your ASA meets the minimum memory requirements, and to ensure that your ASA is currently running software version 8.2 prior to performing a first upgrade to version 8.3 or higher.

Caution: It is possible that you could upgrade an ASA that contained less than the "required" amount of memory and it would function; however, any ASA containing less than the stated required minimum RAM is not supported by Cisco.

If you are upgrading an ASA from software version 8.2 to 8.3 or higher, and the ASA already has a configuration in place, the upgrade automatically updates the configuration to use the new NAT structure for versions 8.3 and higher. The version 8.2 configuration file and logs related to the migration process are saved as files in flash memory (as <version>_startup_cfg.sav and upgrade_startup_errors_<timestamp>.log, respectively).

If you are upgrading an ASA with a configuration, you should probably remove the **nat-control** command (covered in Chapter 7, in the sections, "Enforcing NAT" and "Configuring NAT Control"), if it is present in your configuration. Software versions 8.3 and higher do not support this command. If this command is present when the upgrade process migrates the configuration file, the ASA creates a NAT and ACL configuration that replicates the requirement that NAT take place in order for traffic to flow through the ASA between certain interfaces, which might add unnecessary complexity to your configuration.

The updating of the ASA to using the NAT structure required for versions 8.3 and higher also necessitates changes to any access lists, AAA rules, class maps, and so on that formerly made use of "mapped" IP addresses in versions prior to version 8.3. These features are all discussed elsewhere in this book. At this time, it is only important to know that these things will happen. You will see messages to this effect displayed on the ASA console the first time the ASA boots after being upgraded.

License Management

Key
Topic

The ASA activates licensed features based on the currently installed activation key, which is a hexadecimal string that identifies the feature set available on this particular ASA. Note that activation keys are not transferrable between ASAs. The activation key is bound to the flash BIOS serial number (shown in the **show version** command output, which is sometimes not the same as the chassis serial number that is engraved on the outside of the chassis). Some features are permanent, purchased features, while others can be temporary, test, and demonstration features.

You can view and update the ASA activation key and licensed feature set from ASDM or the CLI. In ASDM, navigate to **Configuration > Device Management > Licensing > Activation Key**. As shown in Figure 5-10, the Activation Key window has three areas:

- **Permanent Activation Key:** This area displays the ASA serial number and the Permanent Activation Key.

- **New Activation Key:** Enter a new activation key in this area to update the activation key running on the ASA.

- **Effective Running Licenses:** This area lists licensed features, the license value (whether the feature is active, or a quantity for items such as VLANs, security contexts, SSL VPN peers allowed, and so on), and a license duration, which is listed as "perpetual" for permanently licensed features.

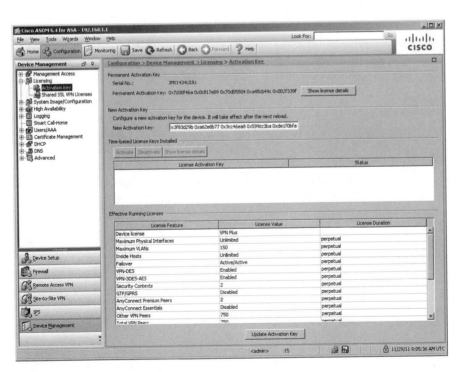

Figure 5-10   *Changing Activation Key with ASDM*

Note: Older versions of ASA software show blank License Duration for permanently licensed features.

Figure 5-10 shows an example of using ASDM to enter a new activation key on an ASA. Note that when typing an activation key, leading 0x is optional, as all values are assumed to be hexadecimal. Click **Update Activation Key**, and the new activation key is applied to the system image on the ASA. Note that the activation key is not part of the ASA configuration file but is stored in a hidden system file within flash memory.

The new activation key should not take effect until the next reboot of the ASA. You can verify this by using the CLI command **show activation-key**. The final line of output will state that the flash activation key is not the same as the running key. You can also use the command **show activation-key detail** to display both permanent and temporary activation keys with their enabled features, including all previously installed temporary keys and their expiration dates.

Upgrading the Image and Activation Key at the Same Time

Because an image upgrade will, and an activation key change should, require an ASA reboot, it is generally advisable, if changing both, to reboot as part of the same maintenance procedure.

Because the new key might be necessary to activate features not present in the current system image, the preferred method of doing this requires two reboots.

When you upgrade the system image file, the existing activation key is extracted from the original image and stored in a file in the ASA to be applied to the upgraded image. There is no need to change activation keys when updating system images, unless you are activating a new feature set.

To upgrade both the system image and activation key at the same time, first install the new image, and then reboot the system. Once rebooted, update the activation key, and reboot again.

If you are downgrading an image, you need to reboot only once, after installing the new image. The old key is both verified and changed with the current image.

Cisco ASA Software and License Verification

To verify the current system image software version and ASDM version used by the ASA, navigate to the **Home** view in ASDM, as shown in Figure 5-11.

As shown in Figure 5-11, the ASA system image and ASDM image versions, device type, and firewall and context modes are all listed. To view key licensed features, click the **License** tab, as shown in Figure 5-12.

As shown in Figure 5-12, key license information is displayed on the License tab. Clicking the **More Licenses** hyperlink opens the Activation Key window shown previously, in Figure 5-10.

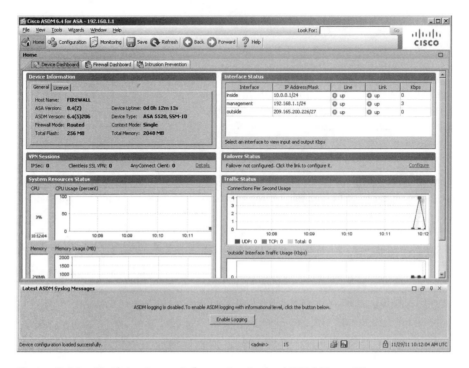

Figure 5-11   *Verifying Image Information in the ASDM Home View*

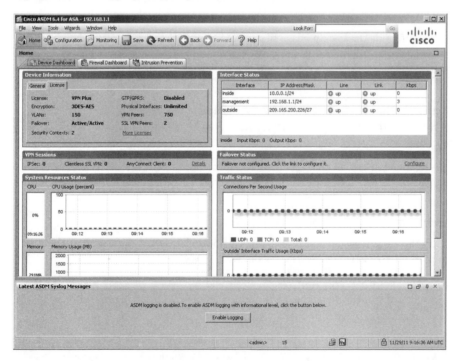

Figure 5-12   *Verifying License Information in ASDM*

The same information can be verified using the CLI **show version** command, as shown in Example 5-9. Key information discussed in this section is highlighted for easy reference.

Example 5-9 *Verifying Device Image and License Information*

```
FIREWALL# show version


Cisco Adaptive Security Appliance Software Version 8.4(2)
Device Manager Version 6.4(5)206

Compiled on Fri 26-Aug-11 14:59 by builders
System image file is "disk0:/asa842-k8.bin"
Config file at boot was "startup-config"

FIREWALL up 41 mins 32 secs

Hardware:   ASA5520, 2048 MB RAM, CPU Pentium 4 Celeron 2000 MHz
Internal ATA Compact Flash, 256MB
BIOS Flash M50FW016 @ 0xfff00000, 2048KB

Encryption hardware device : Cisco ASA-55x0 on-board accelerator (revision 0x0)
                            Boot microcode        : CN1000-MC-BOOT-2.00
                            SSL/IKE microcode     : CNLite-MC-SSLm-PLUS-2.03
                            IPSec microcode       : CNlite-MC-IPSECm-MAIN-2.06
                            Number of accelerators: 1

  0: Ext: GigabitEthernet0/0  : address is c84c.75be.15a8, irq 9
  1: Ext: GigabitEthernet0/1  : address is c84c.75be.15a9, irq 9
  2: Ext: GigabitEthernet0/2  : address is c84c.75be.15aa, irq 9
  3: Ext: GigabitEthernet0/3  : address is c84c.75be.15ab, irq 9
  4: Ext: Management0/0        : address is c84c.75be.15ac, irq 11
  5: Int: Internal-Data0/0     : address is 0000.0001.0002, irq 11
  6: Int: Internal-Control0/0 : address is 0000.0001.0001, irq 5


Licensed features for this platform:
Maximum Physical Interfaces    : Unlimited     perpetual
Maximum VLANs                  : 150           perpetual
Inside Hosts                   : Unlimited     perpetual
Failover                       : Active/Active perpetual
VPN-DES                        : Enabled       perpetual
VPN-3DES-AES                   : Enabled       perpetual
Security Contexts              : 2             perpetual
GTP/GPRS                       : Disabled      perpetual
AnyConnect Premium Peers       : 2             perpetual
AnyConnect Essentials          : Disabled      perpetual
Other VPN Peers                : 750           perpetual
```

```
Total VPN Peers                      : 750              perpetual
Shared License                       : Disabled         perpetual
AnyConnect for Mobile                : Disabled         perpetual
AnyConnect for Cisco VPN Phone       : Disabled         perpetual
Advanced Endpoint Assessment         : Disabled         perpetual
UC Phone Proxy Sessions              : 2                perpetual
Total UC Proxy Sessions              : 2                perpetual
Botnet Traffic Filter                : Disabled         perpetual
Intercompany Media Engine            : Disabled         perpetual

This platform has an ASA 5520 VPN Plus license.

Serial Number: JMX1434L0JU
Running Permanent Activation Key: 0x7d30f46a 0x0c817e89 0x70d05504 0xa45cb49c
   0x002f339f
Configuration register is 0x1
Configuration last modified by enable_15 at 09:02:08.259 UTC Tue Nov 29 2011
```

Configuring Management Access

There are several access methods available for managing a Cisco ASA. The management interface can be accessed locally; using the console port; or remotely using Telnet, SSH, or
HTTPS if the ASA is configured to accept these remote connection types. Additionally,
the ASA supports the use of SNMP, but SNMP for management is limited to read-only access to the ASA, so it is used only for monitoring. The use of SNMP for monitoring is
covered later in the chapter in the section, "Configuring Monitoring Using SNMP."

If you are using remote access for management, it is imperative that you securely configure such access, to ensure the integrity of the ASA, particularly if you are using in-band
management access (the management path uses an untrusted network, which includes any
network bearing nonmanagement traffic, such as user or application traffic) instead of
out-of-band (OOB) access (using a dedicated management network).

The sections that follow describe how to configure management access to the ASA, how
to configure remote management access, how to configure AAA features, and how to
troubleshoot management access.

Securing the local console port beyond the use of an enable password requires the use of
AAA, as covered in the section, "Controlling Management Access with AAA."

Overview of Basic Procedures

When designing and implementing local or remote management access to the ASA, you
need to perform some or all of the following main configuration tasks:

- Configure remote management channels to the ASA, choosing optimal protocols and
  using proper access control to limit the possible sources of remote management connections. Give preference to secure protocols such as SSH and SSL, even if using
  OOB networks for management access.

- Configure appropriately strong authentication for remote management access to gain assurance of remote administrator identity before allowing access to the ASA management interface.

- Configure authorization for the use of management features and commands, to differentiate various management roles and provide a policy where each administrator has the minimal required rights to perform their assigned job tasks (least-privilege Role-Based Access Control [RBAC] policy).

- Configure accounting for management access, to establish an audit trail for the purposes of intrusion detection, monitoring of management practices, and documentation required for compliance with various directives.

Note that these configuration tasks might not all be necessary in every environment, depending on the local organizational requirements, security policy, and management practices and capabilities.

Before deploying these management functions, you should consider several factors, including the following:

- **Existing administrator computing platforms (operating systems and applications) and the software available to administrators to perform management tasks:** These need to be verified for their compatibility with the ASA management functions.

- **Existing authentication methods and infrastructures present in the network, such as existing AAA servers, and their supported protocols:** This information is necessary to properly integrate the ASA into the existing infrastructure. Sometimes it might not be feasible to integrate the ASA into an existing infrastructure or to create a new centralized AAA infrastructure. In such a case, you might need to deploy the local AAA subsystem of the ASA and use a local user authentication and authorization database. Note that there is no local accounting database for administrative actions.

- **Existing security policies related to infrastructure management processes:** These policies might dictate the use of particular security controls for management access, particular management protocols, or a particular workflow process when managing devices.

- **The trustworthiness and type of management paths between administrators and the ASA:** This is necessary to determine the need for strongly authenticated, cryptographically protected management protocols that can operate over untrusted networks, and/or to choose between in-band or out-of-band management paths.

When deploying remote management access to the ASA, consider the following general deployment guidelines:

- Analyze all paths between administrators and the ASA end to end. If any part of such paths is routed across untrusted networks, use only encrypted management protocols coupled with strong authentication.

- Give preference to centralized AAA infrastructures rather than local AAA on the ASA. Centralized systems are more manageable and scalable and allow for centralized auditing.

- Group administrators into role-based groups and grant each group only the minimal privileges required for that particular administrative role (least-required privileges model).

- Use an administrative model in which no one person is allowed to make changes to security-critical settings. For example, you could let several people each know only a portion of a required passphrase, or you could implement a management system requiring review cycles for change control, where a configuration change created by one person needs to be approved by another (known as "dual control").

Configuring Remote Management Access

The Cisco ASA provides three remote access management protocols to access management functions: Telnet, Secure Shell (SSH), and HTTP over SSL/TLS (HTTPS).

Unlike some networking platforms that allow management access by default, the Cisco ASA must be configured to accept management access from specific source IP ranges, on specific interfaces, on a per-management-protocol basis, before any remote management access will succeed.

Telnet is a clear-text (and thus inherently unsecured) access protocol that authenticates access to the ASA based on the IP address of the session source (hence its strength is bounded by the resistance of the intermediate network path to IP spoofing) and authenticates administrators based on passwords or one-time passwords (OTP). If AAA is in use, usernames can also be required (covered later). The Telnet protocol should never be used over untrusted networks, and is generally considered obsolete for security device management. You should instead use SSH wherever possible.

The SSH protocol is a strongly encrypted and strongly authenticated protocol, allowing CLI terminal access to the ASA. The SSH protocol authenticates the ASA to the administrator using public-key-based authentication, and authenticates administrators to the ASA based on a combination of username and password or OTP. In the absence of AAA, a default username of "pix" is used. The SSH protocol can be used over untrusted networks, provided appropriate care is taken when managing the ASA's public key (not accepting it over an untrusted network without using some OOB verification mechanism, or having a preprovisioned authentic copy already stored on the client system).

The HTTPS protocol is also a strongly encrypted and strongly authenticated protocol, allowing access to the ASA using ASDM. The HTTPS protocol authenticates the ASA to the administrator using public-key-based authentication in the form of X.509 certificates (a self-signed certificate is used by default), and authenticates administrators to the ASA using a password, OTP, or client X.509 certificate. The HTTPS protocol can be used over untrusted networks, provided appropriate care is taken when managing the ASA's public key, similar to that previously detailed for SSH.

Configuring an Out-of-Band Management Interface

The first, optional task when configuring remote management access to the Cisco ASA is to dedicate one of its network interfaces as a management-only interface. You would typically use a dedicated management interface only in environments using a dedicated, out-of-band management network to access management interfaces of network devices and systems.

An ASA interface configured as a management-only interface can accept and respond to traffic where the ASA itself is the destination (PING, management session, and so on), but cannot pass any transit traffic through the ASA to or from another interface. Despite this restriction, you still need to specify in the ASA configuration exactly which systems can access the ASA using remote management protocols over the dedicated management network. Additionally, you might need to configure routes to remote management systems through the dedicated management interface.

If you are using OOB management, recommended practice dictates that you use the Management0/0 physical interface of the ASA for this function, as it is the lowest-bandwidth interface of the ASA. Additionally, as a precaution, consider applying a high security level to this interface and placing a deny-all transit access list on the interface (interface access lists are covered in Chapter 8, "Controlling Access Through the ASA"), in case the management-only setting is ever accidentally removed.

Note: Although the Cisco ASA 5500 Series appliances have a physical interface named Management0/0, this interface does not have to be used as an OOB management interface. Additionally, any other interface could be designated as a management-only interface.

To configure any ASA routed interface as a dedicated management interface, navigate to **Configuration > Device Setup > Interfaces**. Select an interface from the interfaces pane, and then click **Edit** to open the Edit Interface dialog box, shown in Figure 5-13.

Figure 5-13 shows the Edit Interface dialog box for the Management0/0 interface. To set the selected interface to be an OOB management interface, check the **Dedicate This Interface for Management Only** check box, click **OK**, and then click **Apply**.

The CLI commands generated by the changes made are as follows:

```
interface Management0/0
   management-only
```

If you are configuring the ASA from the CLI, you can enter these commands directly in global configuration mode.

Note: The Management0/0 physical interface is assigned a security level of 0 by default, so the details shown in Figure 5-13 are based on alterations previously made in compliance with the best practices mentioned earlier, of assigning a high security level to this interface, in case the management-only parameter was ever removed accidentally.

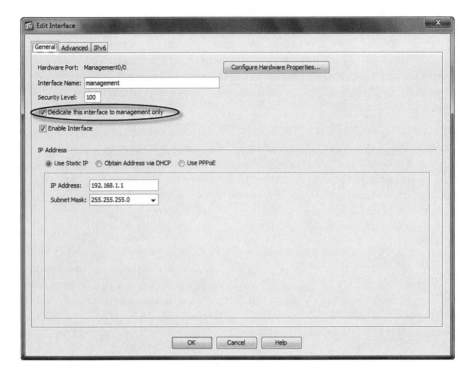

Figure 5-13   *Configuring an OOB Management Interface*

Configuring Remote Access Using Telnet

Although the use of Telnet is generally not recommended, you might prefer it on occasion. For example, you might require Telnet if you are using a client that does not support SSH; if you are managing a device on a secure OOB network, where there is no possibility of rogue sniffers being present; or if you are managing a device through a VPN tunnel that already provides encryption for the management session. In such a case, you can enable the Telnet server of a Cisco ASA by specifying the IP addresses that can connect to the ASA using Telnet, along with the interface that such source addresses are allowed to use Telnet to reach.

By configuring Telnet access, you can allow a maximum of five concurrent Telnet connections to an ASA (or per context, if using multicontext mode, with a maximum of 100 connections divided among all contexts).

To configure Telnet access to the ASA, navigate to **Configuration > Device Management > Management Access > ASDM/HTTPS/Telnet/SSH**. In the ASDM/HTTPS/Telnet/SSH window, click **Add** to add an access rule. The Add Device Access Configuration dialog box opens, as shown in Figure 5-14.

As shown in Figure 5-14, you can configure a Telnet access rule in the Add Device Access Configuration dialog box by selecting **Telnet** as the access type and then specifying the IP address and mask of the source of permitted access sessions, along with the incoming interface where the session will reach the ASA. Click **OK** to finish defining the rule. The example in Figure 5-14 allows incoming Telnet sessions from the 192.168.1.0/24 network to arrive on the management (Management0/0) interface. Because the management network is OOB in the example network, and thus secure from other network segments, it is the only interface for which allowing an unsecured protocol might be acceptable.

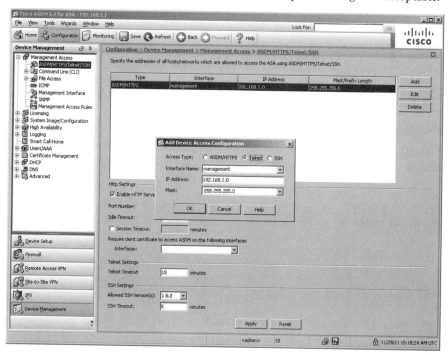

Figure 5-14 *Configuring a Telnet Access Rule*

To set the maximum time, in minutes, that a Telnet session can be idle before being logged out by the ASA, enter a value from 1 to 1440 in the **Telnet Timeout** field. By default, Telnet sessions are closed after being idle for 5 minutes. Figure 5-14 shows a setting of 15 minutes. Click **Apply** to apply the completed Telnet access rule to the configuration.

The CLI commands generated by the changes made are as follows:

```
telnet timeout 15
telnet 192.168.1.0 255.255.255.0 management
```

If you are configuring the ASA from the CLI, you can enter these commands directly in global configuration mode.

Tip: Although it is possible to configure a Telnet access rule on any interface of the ASA, Telnet traffic will be refused at the lowest security level (usually "outside") interface, unless it arrived at the ASA under the protection of an IP Security (IPsec) tunnel. This works only with IPsec, not with an SSL VPN tunnel. It is generally preferred to enable Telnet sessions to the inside interface and designate this as the management interface for sessions coming through an encrypted tunnel, using the **management-access inside** command. Note that this method works over both IPsec and SSL VPN tunnels. For more information, refer to the *Cisco ASA 5500 Series Command Reference*, 8.4 and 8.5, which is located at www.cisco.com/en/US/docs/security/asa/asa84/command/reference/cmdref.html.

To view or clear Telnet sessions, you can use the following commands:

- **who:** Displays which IP addresses are currently accessing the ASA console via Telnet.

- **kill** *session id*: Terminates a designated Telnet session (the *session id* number is obtained with the **who** command). When you kill a Telnet session, any active commands terminate normally, and then the ASA drops the connection, without warning the user.

Configuring Remote Access Using SSH

Key Topic

The SSH protocol provides an option for secure remote management of the ASA. Like Telnet, the ASA allows up to five concurrent SSH connections per context, with up to 100 total SSH sessions across all security contexts, when in multicontext mode.

Before you can enable the SSH server on the ASA, you must provide the ASA with a public-private pair of RSA keys. You can create an RSA key pair (or replace an existing pair) by using the **crypto key generate rsa** command from CLI global configuration mode. The full syntax and options are as follows:

```
crypto key generate rsa [usage-keys | general-keys] [label key-pair-label]
  [modulus size] [noconfirm]
```

- **general-keys:** Generates a single pair of general-purpose keys. This is the default key-pair type.

- **label key-pair-label:** Specifies the name to be associated with the key pair(s). This key pair must be uniquely labeled. If you attempt to create another key pair with the same label, the ASA displays a warning message. If no label is provided when the key is generated, the key pair is statically named <Default-RSA-Key>.

- **modulus size:** Specifies the modulus size of the key pair(s): 512, 768, 1024, or 2048. The default modulus size is 1024.

- **noconfirm:** Suppresses all interactive prompting.

- **usage-keys:** Generates two key pairs, one for signature use and one for encryption use. This implies that two certificates for the corresponding identity are required.

The default key-pair type is general-keys. SSH connections always use this key pair. The default modulus size is 1024. If replacing an existing pair, first use the **crypto key zeroize rsa default** command to delete the existing pair, as demonstrated in Example 5-10.

Example 5-10 *Creating a Default RSA Key Pair*

```
FIREWALL(config)# crypto key zeroize rsa default
FIREWALL(config)# !Use to delete an existing default RSA key pair
FIREWALL(config)# copy running-config startup-config
FIREWALL(config)# !Save the configuration with no default RSA key pair
```

```
FIREWALL(config)# crypto key generate rsa modulus 2048
INFO: The name for the keys will be: <Default-RSA-Key>
Keypair generation process begin. Please wait...
FIREWALL(config)# copy running-config startup-config
```

Once an RSA key pair exists for use, configuring SSH access is almost exactly the same as configuring Telnet access, with the exception that it is also possible to limit which SSH version can be used by clients to initiate management sessions. Whenever possible, you should use SSH version 2 only because it has stronger methods of key management and message integrity checking. Additionally, the idle time can be set from 1 to 60 minutes, whereas Telnet allows a range from 1 to 1440.

To configure SSH access to the ASA, navigate to **Configuration > Device Management > Management Access > ASDM/HTTPS/Telnet/SSH** and click **Add**, as shown in Figure 5-15.

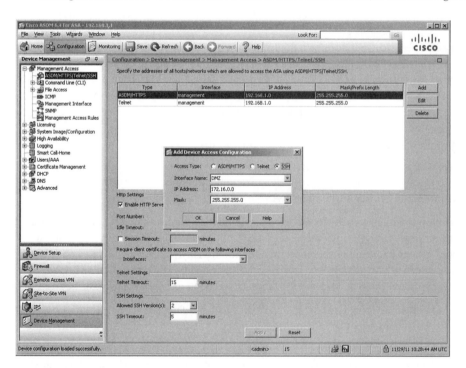

Figure 5-15 *Configuring an SSH Access Rule*

The example in Figure 5-15 allows incoming SSH sessions from the 172.16.0.0/24 network to arrive on the DMZ interface. Additionally, only SSH version 2 is permitted. The idle timeout is left at the default of 5 minutes.

The CLI commands generated by the changes made are as follows:

```
ssh version 2
ssh 172.16.0.0 255.255.255.0 DMZ
```

If you are configuring the ASA from the CLI, you can enter these commands directly in global configuration mode.

To view or clear SSH sessions, you can use the following commands:

- **show ssh sessions:** Displays which IP addresses are currently accessing the ASA console via SSH, as well as the SSH version used, the encryption algorithm used for the session, the session state, and the username that is logged in.

- **ssh disconnect** *session id*: Terminates a designated SSH session (the session id number is obtained with the **show ssh sessions** command), similarly to the **kill** command.

Configuring Remote Access Using HTTPS

HTTPS management access is used by ASDM. To configure HTTPS access to the ASA, the ASA must have an HTTPS X.509 server certificate. The ASA uses this certificate to authenticate itself to the client (browser or ASDM Launcher application). By default, the ASA will generate a self-signed server certificate each time it is rebooted, for this purpose. However, this changing certificate leads to a lot of browser security warnings because it cannot be verified. Therefore, you might want to generate a permanent self-signed certificate or, better yet, enroll the ASA in a Public Key Infrastructure (PKI) and obtain a server certificate in this manner. Generating a permanent self-signed certificate is simpler, and acceptable if accessing the ASA over a secure network, but enrolling the ASA in a PKI is more scalable, and thus the recommended solution.

Creating a Permanent Self-Signed Certificate

By creating a self-signed server certificate that is persistent across reboots, you can save the certificate on the administrator's client computer and thus avoid further browser security warnings when administering the ASA using HTTPS.

To deploy a permanent self-signed certificate, you must first set the ASA hostname and domain name (covered earlier in the section, "Configuring Device Identity") to insert a proper subject name in the server certificate. Additionally, you must generate an RSA key pair (you can use the default key pair, or generate a labeled key pair, for use with the server certificate, so that SSH and HTTPS access rely on different RSA keys).

To configure a permanent self-signed certificate using ASDM, navigate to **Configuration > Device Management > Certificate Management > Identity Certificates** and click **Add**. The Add Identity Certificate dialog box opens, as shown in Figure 5-16.

In the Add Identity Certificate dialog box, a trustpoint name is defined (which is how this certificate can be referenced in configuring features that use certificates). The ASA auto-generates trustpoint names, although you can also define your own name. In Figure 5-16, the default name is replaced with a new name of ASA-Self-Signed to clearly identify this certificate as self-signed.

You can import an identity certificate from a file, but in Figure 5-16, the choice is made to add a new identity certificate. You can then either select a key pair or create one by clicking the **New** button. In Figure 5-16, the default RSA key pair is selected.

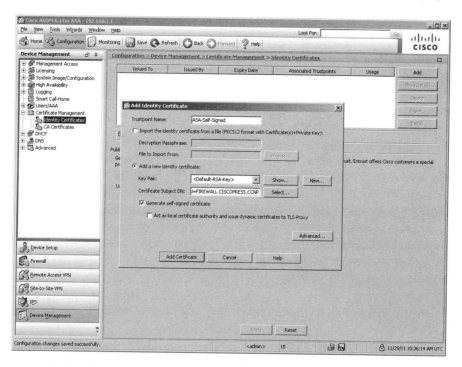

Figure 5-16 *Creating a Permanent Self-Signed Certificate*

Certificates must be bound to a specific identity. In X.509 certificates, the identity is known as the Subject Name. The ASA prefills the Certificate Subject DN (Distinguished Name) field with the device hostname. Generally, you will want to enter the common name of the ASA in the form CN=hostname.domainname for an identity certificate. If you want to construct a more complex Subject DN, click the **Select** button and create the desired string in the Certificate Subject DN dialog box. Figure 5-16 shows the Subject DN of CN=FIREWALL.CISCOPRESS.CCNP.

Because the purpose is to create a self-signed certificate, check the **Generate Self-Signed Certificate** check box, as shown in Figure 5-16. Click the **Add Certificate** button to finish creating the certificate. Finally, click **Apply** to send the generated commands to the ASA.

The CLI commands generated by the changes made are as follows:

```
crypto ca trustpoint ASA-Self-Signed
  id-usage ssl-ipsec
  no fqdn
  subject-name CN=FIREWALL.CISCOPRESS.CCNP
  enrollment self
crypto ca enroll ASA-Self-Signed noconfirm
```

If you are configuring the ASA from the CLI, you can enter these commands directly in global configuration mode.

Obtaining an Identity Certificate by PKI Enrollment

Instead of using a self-signed certificate, you could enroll the ASA in a Public Key Infra-structure (PKI) and deploy the PKI-provisioned certificate to the ASA. This is the pre-ferred and more scalable method. It is similar to the creation of a self-signed certificate, except that you have to forward your certificate enrollment request (containing identify-ing information and the ASA's public RSA key) to a PKI enrollment server (a registration authority [RA] or a certificate authority [CA]).

Enrollment with a PKI can be done using one of two methods:

■ Manually, wherein you copy and paste your certificate information into the RA or CA interface as instructed.

■ Simple Certificate Enrollment Protocol (SCEP), wherein you define an Enrollment URL (provided to you by the CA) and any relevant password, and the remainder of the process happens automatically, essentially without further human intervention. Note that this depends on the configuration of the CA server.

To enroll with a PKI for a certificate using ASDM, navigate to **Configuration > Device Management > Certificate Management > Identity Certificates** and click **Add**. In the Add Identity Certificate dialog box (shown previously in Figure 5-16), accept the autogen-erated trustpoint name, click the **Add a New Identity Certificate** radio button, choose an RSA key pair, and construct a Subject DN, as detailed previously for self-signed certifi-cates. Leave the Generate Self-Signed Certificate check box unchecked. To enroll in a PKI, next click the **Advanced** button. The Advanced Options dialog box opens, as shown in Figure 5-17.

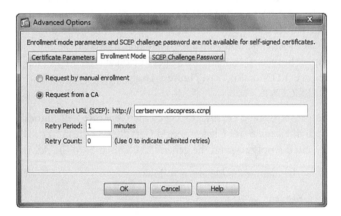

Figure 5-17 *Enrolling in a PKI for an Identity Certificate*

Click the **Enrollment Mode** tab, and click the **Request from a CA** radio button to specify the enrollment method. The Enrollment URL (SCEP) field is already prepended with "http://" and is completed in Figure 5-17 with **certserver.ciscopress.ccnp**. In this exam-ple, no SCEP challenge password is required, so you can simply click **OK** to finish defin-ing advanced options. Finally, click **Apply** to send the generated commands to the ASA.

The CLI commands generated by the changes made are as follows:

```
crypto ca trustpoint ASDM_TrustPoint0
  id-usage ssl-ipsec
  no fqdn
  subject-name CN=FIREWALL.CISCOPRESS.CCNP
  enrollment url http://certserver.ciscopress.ccnp
crypto ca authenticate ASDM_TrustPoint0 nointeractive
crypto ca enroll ASDM_TrustPoint0 noconfirm
```

If you are configuring the ASA from the CLI, you can enter these commands directly in global configuration mode.

Deploying an Identity Certificate

After you have obtained an identity certificate for the ASA, you must next bind the self-signed or PKI-obtained identity certificate to the interface(s) on which you want the ASA to accept HTTPS management sessions. To do so, navigate to **Configuration > Device Management > Advanced > SSL Settings.**

In the SSL Settings window, go to the Certificates area (bottom) and select an interface on which you want the ASA to accept HTTPS management connections. Then, click **Edit** to open the Select SSL Certificate dialog box, shown in Figure 5-18.

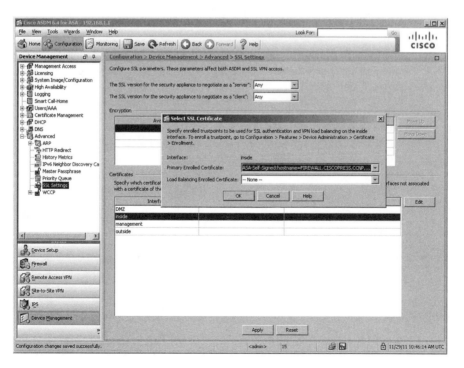

Figure 5-18 *Binding an Identity Certificate to an ASA Interface*

In the Primary Enrolled Certificate drop-down box, the self-signed or PKI-obtained certificate is selected. In Figure 5-18, the ASA-Self-Signed certificate is selected for use on the inside interface. Repeat these steps to activate the self-signed certificate on the management interface.

The CLI commands generated by the changes made are as follows:

```
ssl encryption rc4-sha1 aes128-sha1 aes256-sha1 3des-sha1
ssl trust-point ASA-Self-Signed inside
ssl trust-point ASA-Self-Signed management
```

If you are configuring the ASA from the CLI, you can enter these commands directly in global configuration mode.

Note: If you want a particular identity certificate associated with all interfaces to which a specific certificate is not bound, you can select it in the Fallback Certificate field at the bottom of the SSL Settings window. The fallback certificate is used on all interfaces not associated with a certificate of their own. Note also that this includes the outside interface, so strong authentication of users is exceptionally important.

After you have bound a server certificate to an ASA interface connected to a trusted network, browse to the ASA from the Administrator client and permanently install the ASA self-signed certificate in the browser. The specific steps differ depending on the browser used.

After you have created or obtained an identity certificate and bound it to an interface of the ASA, you need to configure the ASA to accept HTTPS administrative sessions, in the same manner as for Telnet or SSH.

To configure HTTPS access to the ASA, navigate to **Configuration > Device Management > Management Access > ASDM/HTTPS/Telnet/SSH**, and then click **Add** to open the Add Device Access Configuration dialog box, as shown in Figure 5-19.

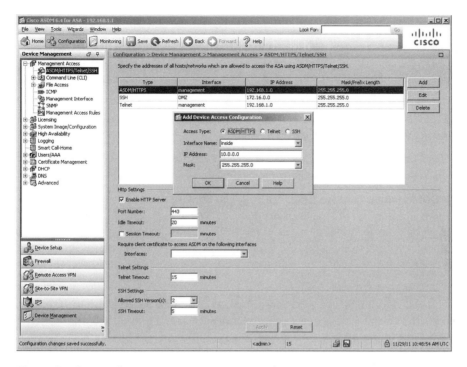

Figure 5-19 *Configuring an HTTPS Access Rule*

In Figure 5-19, HTTPS access is configured for the inside interface, with potential source IPs in the 10.0.0.0/24 network. Also, in the ASDM/HTTPS/Telnet/SSH window, ensure that the **Enable HTTP Server** check box is checked (it is by default). Additional options are available to change the TCP port on which the ASA listens for HTTPS connections, set an idle time for session closure, or set a session timeout value, which limits the maximum connection time even for sessions that are not idle. Repeat these steps to allow ASDM access from the network attached to the management interface.

The CLI command generated by the changes made is as follows:

```
http 10.0.0.0 255.255.255.0 inside
http 192.168.1.0 255.255.255.0 management
```

If you are configuring the ASA from the CLI, you can enter these commands directly in global configuration mode.

Configuring Management Access Banners

An ASA has the capability to display various configured banners both before and after login using various types of access to its management interface. These banners can contain whatever information is deemed appropriate in your environment, based on your local security policy. They are generally used to inform users of terms of use, warn of the consequences of unauthorized access, or display important maintenance-related information. Occasionally, they contain administrator contact information.

The banners supported by the ASA are as follows:

- **Message-of-the-day (MOTD) banner:** The first banner displayed when connecting to the console port, or remotely using Telnet or SSH. This banner is displayed before the CLI login banner and is generally where messages such as contact information are displayed.

- **Login banner:** Displayed before the CLI login prompt and is generally used to warn users against unauthorized access attempts.

- **Exec banner:** Displayed after CLI login and is generally used for messages such as maintenance-related information or reminders for all administrators.

- **ASDM banner:** Displayed after ASDM login. Because ASDM is an alternate management interface, and this banner is the only one seen by users logging in through ASDM, it should include all the same information as the login banner, at a minimum. It might be used to include all the information in all the other banners, as some information shown to CLI users might otherwise be missed by ASDM users.

Note: Although various urban legends exist of hackers who were acquitted of penetrating networks by courts who ruled that, because a management access banner used words such as "welcome," the organization had invited such access, no credible references to any such court action exist. However, various attorneys seem to agree on the following guidelines for what should definitely be included in a login banner: It must clearly identify which organization owns the asset, so connecting users cannot claim they accidentally logged in to the wrong network; it must clearly state that only authorized access is acceptable; it should clearly state that a user should disconnect if not authorized; it should clearly state what actions the organization will take in response to unauthorized access (generally, prosecution to the full extent of the law); and, if actions taken during access are logged, the banner must clearly state this, and that accessing the system provides both user acknowledgment and acceptance of this fact.

All of these banners are configured in the same window within ASDM. Navigate to **Configuration > Device Management > Management Access > Command Line (CLI) > Banner**, as illustrated in Figure 5-20, and enter appropriate text in the provided banner fields.

In Figure 5-20, all banner types are configured. Note the explicit nature of the warnings in the login banner, which include giving a connecting user the opportunity to disconnect immediately.

The CLI commands generated by the changes made are as follows:

```
no banner motd
banner motd You may contact the owner of this system by email at administra
  tor@ciscopress.ccnp, or by phone at (123) 555-1212.
no banner exec
banner exec This firewall is running v8.4(2) of the ASA OS. This
system is scheduled for maintenance on Saturday at 11 PM CST, and is anticipated
to be unavailable for approximately 2 hours.
no banner login
```

```
banner login WARNING: This system is the property of Cisco Press, and is
intended for <...output omitted...>
no banner asdm
banner asdm WARNING: This system is the property of Cisco Press, and is intended
for <...output omitted...>
```

If you are configuring the ASA from the CLI, you can enter these commands directly in global configuration mode.

Figure 5-20 *Configuring Management Access Banners*

Note: The banners configured are merely examples and are not intended to imply "best practices." For instance, the MOTD banner is seen by connecting users prior to successful login, so it is highly unlikely it would contain the administrator's phone number. The login banner, on the other hand, contains all the elements previously discussed as desirable for full legal protection.

Controlling Management Access with AAA

The ASA uses its AAA subsystem to provide a user-based security model for access to its management interface, to user sessions crossing the firewall (cut-through proxy), and for remote access VPNs. This chapter discusses the first of those, using AAA to control management access.

The ASA has the capability to use a locally defined database for authentication and authorization purposes (note that there is no local accounting). It also supports a wide variety of external server types and protocols for full AAA support. External servers provide many potential benefits, such as centralized control, scalability (you have to create only one database of users to support a theoretically unlimited number of client systems), improved manageability, database mirroring, mass import/export of records, and integration with advanced and existing AAA methods.

The AAA server types supported by the ASA are as follows:

- Local database

- TACACS+

- RADIUS

- NTLM

- Kerberos

- LDAP

- SecurID

Although it is possible to use simpler administrative access control methods, it is strongly recommended that you use the AAA subsystem to control management access to the ASA. The use of the AAA subsystem allows you to use stronger authentication methods (with the use of external servers), implement a Role-Based Access Control (RBAC) system using authorization, reuse existing user authentication databases, implement strong auditing of management access (important for compliance with various regulations), and centralize all AAA functions.

AAA authorization requires an existing authentication configuration (it is not possible to know which privileges you have if the ASA cannot identify you). AAA accounting is possible without authentication, but it is of limited value without it (although it is possible to know that something was done without knowing who did it, it is certainly much more useful to know who did it).

To use the AAA subsystem to control management access to the ASA, you need to perform some or all of the following tasks:

- Create user objects in the local database. You can do this if you are using only locally defined administrator accounts, or as a fallback for times when communication to a central AAA database is not possible. (Having such a fallback is strongly recommended, as you might otherwise be unable to administer the ASA.)

- Configure local or remote administrator authentication information. At a minimum, this will include username, password, and associated privilege level.

- Configure a remote AAA server group and populate it with members. Available AAA features will depend on which type of server is defined. TACACS+ is preferred when configuring management access control due to its robust support for command authorization and accounting.

- Configure local or remote administrator authorization information. This allows you to control access to specific device management features and commands.

- Configure remote accounting for maintenance of a central auditing database.

Because there are so many possible combinations available within AAA configuration, this discussion is limited to a reasonable subset, to provide sufficient, albeit not exhaustive, coverage. As such, this section demonstrates how to configure the following scenario:

- An administrator account with a strong password and level 15 (highest level) access in the local database. This will be for fallback use if the remote AAA infrastructure is not available to the ASA, or for accessing the ASA via the Serial console.

- Authentication against the local database only, if accessing the Serial console port of the ASA. This is for illustration only, as centralized AAA would still be preferable for console access.

- Authentication against a TACACS+ server at 192.168.1.5, reachable through the "management" interface, for all remote management access sessions, with a fallback to the local database if this server is unreachable.

- Command and session authorization against the TACACS+ server, for all management access sessions (console or remote), with a fallback to the local database if this server is unreachable.

- Command and session accounting to the TACACS+ server, for all management access sessions.

Creating Users in the Local Database

To use local AAA authentication, or for local fallback in case remote, centralized AAA servers become unavailable, you must configure at least one user in the local database. The local database supports only password authentication (and not OTPs, tokens, and so on) and can be used to assign a privilege level to all locally defined users. A privilege level is a simple mechanism that allows differentiation of user access privileges and provides a simple method for multiple levels of management access. A privilege level defines which management functions and commands are available to a user. Privilege levels range from 0 (no access) to 15 (full administrative control). More information on privilege levels appears later, in the section, "Configuring AAA Command Authorization."

It is recommended that you create at least one local administrator account, even if you intend to use remote AAA authentication on a regular basis. You will use this account in emergencies if communication to the central AAA servers fails, either because the servers are experiencing problems or because of network issues. This one account should be granted full administrative access, to ensure that it is not limited in its functionality should its use become necessary.

To create a local user database object, navigate to **Configuration > Device Management > Users/AAA > User Accounts**. The Add User Account window opens, as shown in Figure 5-21.

Figure 5-21 shows creation of a user account. Enter a username—in this case, **Administrator**—in the Username field, and enter a sufficiently strong password in the Password and Confirm Password fields. Next, select the correct radio button for the level of access you want to give the user account. Because this example is configuring a full administrative access account, to be used as a fallback in case of remote AAA communication failure, click **Full Access**. When you choose Full Access, you should also set a specific **Privilege Level**. The default is 2, and in the absence of AAA command authorization, this level will provide full administrative access. Remember, however, that you want to ensure that this account is not limited in functionality, because it is intended for use in emergencies. Setting the level to 15 ensures that, even if AAA command authorization is configured on the ASA, this account will continue to have full administrative access. Therefore, the level is set to 15 in Figure 5-21.

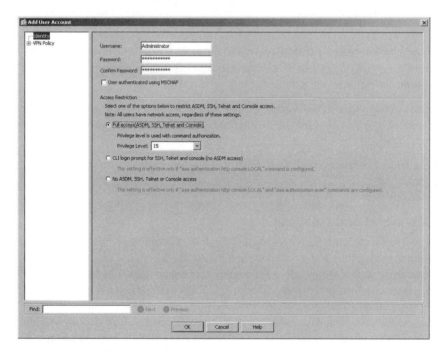

Figure 5-21   *Adding User Accounts to Local AAA Database*

Note that ASDM contains reminders that the other two settings are effective only if certain other commands are part of the ASA's configuration. Assuming the correct commands are present, choosing CLI Login Prompt for SSH, Telnet and Console (No ASDM Access) is fairly self-explanatory—you are giving this local account access to the terminal, but not to ASDM. This might be necessary if you are using local command authorization (discussed later, in the section "Configuring AAA Command Authorization") because an authenticated ASDM user has de facto level 15 access to the ASA. If you want to limit users to CLI access so you can limit their access to specific commands, this would be an appropriate setting.

The third option, No ASDM, SSH, Telnet or Console Access, might seem strange at first. Why create a local user account that has no access? The answer is, in case you use the local user database to authenticate VPN users. VPN support is not a subject covered in the

FIREWALL exam, so it will not be discussed in this book, but that would be the purpose of a local user account with no administrative access.

To complete the creation of the local user account, click **OK**, and then click **Apply** to send the changes to the ASA.

The CLI command generated by the changes made is as follows:

```
username Administrator password loLkxe5el7hVzl6M encrypted privilege 15
```

If you are configuring the ASA from the CLI, you can enter this command directly in global configuration mode.

Note: Again, this is merely an example. In a production network, it is strongly recommended that you create a username that does not in itself identify this account as having super-user privileges. Therefore, usernames like "Admin," "Administrator," or "root" are strongly discouraged because they tend to be the first target for attackers.

Using Simple Password-Only Authentication

If there is no AAA authentication of any kind configured for the Telnet, SSH, or HTTP (ASDM) consoles, the ASA supports a simple password authentication method where all administrators use the same password (and in the case of SSH, the same username) to access the ASA. This is strongly discouraged as a mode of authentication. Setting the default Telnet and SSH passwords was already covered earlier in this chapter. By default, the configured enable password is used, without a username, for ASDM access.

Configuring AAA Access Using the Local Database

You can configure AAA authentication to any of the following five "consoles" for interactive management access to an ASA:

- Serial (the physical console port)

- Telnet

- SSH

- HTTP (actually HTTPS using ASDM)

- Enable (Setting AAA authentication on the Enable console requires a user to provide a username and password when moving from unprivileged mode to privileged mode and is an integral part of command authorization, as discussed later in the section, "Configuring AAA Command Authorization.")

To enable AAA authentication on the consoles using the local database, navigate to **Configuration > Device Management > Users/AAA > AAA Access**. Figure 5-22 shows the resulting window.

Recall that the scenario in this section is that administrative access using the Serial console will be controlled using the local AAA database, as an illustration. As such, Figure 5-22 shows setting only the Serial console to use the local database for authentication. To do this, check the **Serial** check box, and then choose **LOCAL** in the drop-down box for the AAA server group. Click **Apply** to send the change to the ASA.

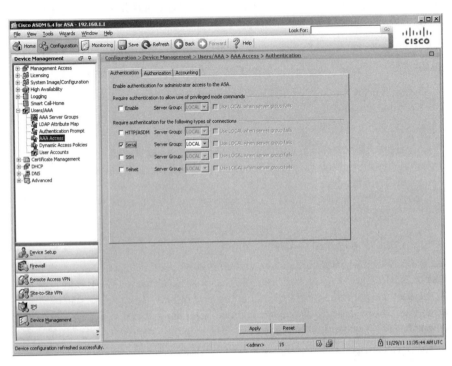

Figure 5-22   *Configuring AAA Serial Console Authentication*

The LOCAL server group is the name used to refer to the locally configured user database. The LOCAL server group can never fail to be reached (similar to a router loopback interface). As such, it can only accept or reject authentication based on whether the usernames and passwords entered are correct. You can edit the properties of the LOCAL server group and set a maximum number of failed logins, after which the ASA can lock a local user account. To do so, navigate to **Configuration > Device Management > Users/AAA > AAA Server Groups**. Select the LOCAL server group, and click **Edit** to open the Edit LOCAL Server Group dialog box, shown in Figure 5-23.

Figure 5-23 demonstrates enabling local user lockout. Check the **Enable Local User Lockout** check box, and set the number of failed attempts that will trigger locking of an account (the valid range is from 1 to 16). In Figure 5-23, this value is set to **3**. Click **OK**, and then click **Apply** to send these changes to the ASA. This setting is available only for the LOCAL server group, as account locking following failed attempts is configured on the remote server if you are using remote AAA services.

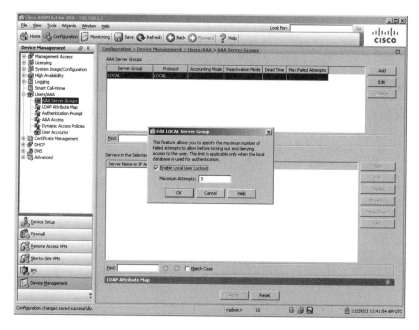

Figure 5-23   *Enabling Local User Lockout*

The CLI commands generated by the changes made are as follows:

```
aaa authentication serial console LOCAL
aaa local authentication attempts max-fail 3
```

If you are configuring the ASA from the CLI, you can enter these commands directly in global configuration mode.

Note: The name LOCAL is case sensitive. Only LOCAL in all caps is recognized by the ASA as a reference to the local user database. Other database names can be in any mixture of case, at your discretion.

At this point, it is a good idea to test the user authentication using the LOCAL database, to ensure it works properly, before moving on to securing other management access channels. Remember, this is your fallback for situations where remote AAA server communication fails. If you fail to test it to ensure it works, and remote AAA server communication fails, you could end up locked out of your firewall, requiring password recovery to regain access. By performing this test prior to securing other management access channels, if anything goes wrong, you will temporarily be locked out from the Serial console port, but you will still have access to the ASA via Telnet, SSH, or HTTP/ASDM (depending on which is configured as allowed).

Testing of remote AAA servers is possible either from within ASDM or from the CLI using the **test aaa-server** command. Unfortunately, this is not supported for the LOCAL database. So, to test the LOCAL database, you need to connect to the ASA (in our example) using the Serial console and see if your authentication is successful.

Configuring AAA Access Using Remote AAA Server(s)

Key
Topic

As mentioned earlier in this chapter, using a centralized server (or set of servers) for AAA control is preferable to using the local database. Configuring the use of remote AAA authentication on the ASA is a three-step process (additional configuration is necessary on the servers to be used for this function):

Step 1.   Create a AAA server group, if none already exists, and configure how servers in the group are accessed (protocol, port, and how to determine if a server is failing communication).

Step 2.   Populate the server group with member servers. Define the location of each server and assign a symmetric password, which will be used to encrypt the communication session (or portions thereof, depending on the protocol used) between the ASA and the remote AAA server. This same password must be configured on the server when defining the ASA as a AAA client.

Step 3.   Enable user authentication for each remote management access channel (the consoles). Define which authentication server group will be used for each console upon which AAA authentication is enabled (note that you define a group here, not a specific server).

The sections that follow describe these steps in more detail.

Step 1: Create a AAA Server Group and Configure How Servers in the Group Are Accessed

To create a new AAA server group, navigate to **Configuration > Device Management > Users/AAA > AAA Server Groups** and click **Add.** The Add AAA Server Group dialog box opens, as shown in Figure 5-24.

Figure 5-24   *Creating a AAA Server Group*

Figure 5-24 shows a new server group named CP-TACACS being created. TACACS+ is selected as the communication protocol to use with this server group. All other settings are left at their default settings.

If you choose a AAA accounting method, to be used if AAA accounting is configured (covered later, in the section, "Configuring Remote AAA Accounting"), the choices are Simultaneous, which means any accounting messages are sent to all servers in the selected group, and Single, which means one server in the group will act as the sole recipient of all AAA accounting records.

If a server is declared "dead" by the ASA, you can choose a Reactivation Mode for determining when it will be put back into the group's active list of servers, for the ASA to attempt communication to it again. The default mode is Depletion, which means as soon as all servers that are members of this group are declared dead, they are all reactivated, and the ASA once again attempts to reach member servers in the order in which they are defined within the group. The other choice is Timed, which means a server will be declared dead for a predefined number of minutes and then automatically reactivated within the group. You define this time period in the Dead Time field.

At the bottom of the configurable fields is Max Failed Attempts. You can change the number of times the ASA should retry a member server before declaring the server dead. You configure on a per-server basis the number of seconds the ASA waits per attempt before a retry, as discussed later. Click **OK** to complete the creation of the new server group.

Step 2: Populate the Server Group with Member Servers

To populate the server group with member servers, select the **AAA Server Group** in the AAA Server Groups area, and then click **Add** in the Servers in the Selected Group area. The Add AAA Server dialog box opens, as shown in Figure 5-25.

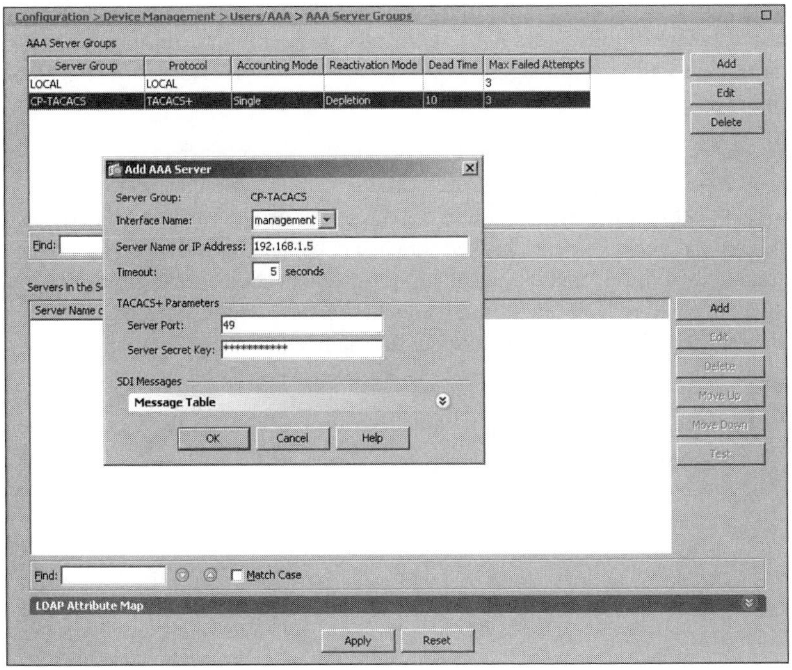

Figure 5-25   *Adding a New AAA Server*

For each server in a group, you must specify a location, IP address, and a symmetrical password used for session encryption. (This is a TACACS+ example; if you are using RADIUS, only user passwords are encrypted in the ASA-AAA server communication.) Optionally, you can adjust the default timeout per request, and set the port on which the server listens for AAA requests.

In Figure 5-25, a new server is defined as a member of the CP-TACACS group. The server is reachable through the ASA interface named management and has an IP address of 192.168.1.5. The timeout is set to 5 seconds per request, instead of 10. The default TCP port of 49 for TACACS+ is left unaltered, and the symmetrical password is set (the string is masked in the ASDM interface). Click **OK**, and then click **Apply** to complete the creation of the new member server.

The CLI commands generated by the changes made are as follows:

```
aaa-server CP-TACACS protocol tacacs+
aaa-server CP-TACACS (management) host 192.168.1.5 key **********
 timeout 5
```

If you are configuring the ASA from the CLI, you can enter these commands directly in global configuration mode.

Step 3: Enable User Authentication for Each Remote Management Access Channel

The final step is to configure AAA authentication using the new server group for each of the management access methods. In this scenario, it was decided to use remote AAA services for all consoles other than Serial and to set the use of the LOCAL server group for fallback, in case of failure of the remote AAA server group. To complete this process, navigate to **Configuration > Device Management > Users/AAA > AAA Access** once again, as shown in Figure 5-26.

In Figure 5-26, AAA authentication is configured on all consoles other than the Serial console, which was configured previously. In addition to enabling AAA authentication for each console, and selecting the newly configured AAA server group, the Use LOCAL When Server Group Fails check box is checked for each console. This means that if communication attempts by the ASA fail with all member servers in the selected group, remote AAA will be deemed to have failed, and the local database will be used for authentication. Note that the entry of an incorrect username or password is a failed authentication, not a failure of communication to the AAA server.

In Figure 5-26, the Enable console is set up to use server group LOCAL, due to the command authorization example in the next section.

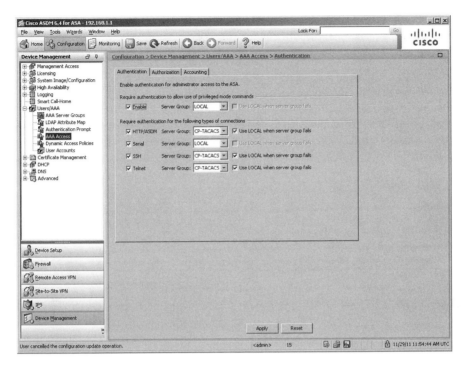

Figure 5-26 *Configuring AAA Authentication*

> **Note:** To authenticate console access, you may use any authentication protocol that is supported by the ASA AAA server groups, except the HTTP Form protocol, which is supported only in clientless SSL VPNs.

The CLI commands generated by the changes made are as follows:

aaa authentication enable console LOCAL
aaa authentication http console CP-TACACS LOCAL
aaa authentication ssh console CP-TACACS LOCAL
aaa authentication telnet console CP-TACACS LOCAL

If you are configuring the ASA from the CLI, you can enter these commands directly in global configuration mode.

Although the ASA is now configured to use a remote TACACS+ server for console authentication, this obviously will not function until you configure a remote TACACS+ server to accept such requests from the ASA, as described next.

Configuring Cisco Secure ACS for Remote Authentication

In the example, ASA is configured to use a remote TACACS+ server to perform authentication of remote management access. This server will be a Cisco Secure Access Control Server version 4.2. Because this book is focused on firewall configuration and troubleshooting, it covers only minimal information on Cisco Secure ACS—just enough to function as a server for AAA requests being sent by the firewall.

Figure 5-27 shows the Cisco Secure ACS window in which an ASA is defined as a AAA client. To access this window, navigate to the Network Configuration page in ACS, click the **Not Assigned** hyperlink under Network Device Groups, and then click **Add Entry** under the (Not Assigned) AAA Clients section of the resulting screen. Alternatively, you can create a network device group (NDG) for AAA clients if your organization chooses to use a NDG organization structure. The Add AAA Client pane opens.

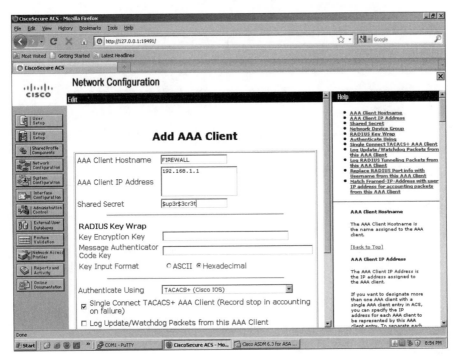

Figure 5-27   *Defining a AAA Client in ACS*

In the **AAA Client Hostname** box, enter the name for your ASA. Although this field does not have to match the configured hostname on your ASA, it is generally good practice to do so. In the **AAA Client IP Address** box, enter the IP address of the ASA interface that will generate AAA requests. For instance, if this AAA server is on the OOB management network connected to the Management0/0 interface of the firewall (as is the case in our example), enter the IP address 192.168.1.1, the ASA's interface IP.

In a production environment, the symmetrical Shared Secret configured on the ASA and the AAA server should be very long and random. The reason is that this value is used as a seed to create the session encryption key used to safeguard communication between the ASA and this server. In our example, for the sake of expediency, it is set to a much simpler value of $up3r$3cr3t (SuperSecret, with common character substitutions).

In the Authenticate Using field, select the protocol used for communication of AAA requests/responses. In our example, select **TACACS+ (Cisco IOS)** for an ASA. Optionally, to create a persistent connection that will be used for future AAA requests (rather than renegotiating a new TCP handshake for each request), check the **Single Connect TACACS+ AAA Client** check box. Note that this applies only to TACACS+, not RADIUS, as RADIUS is a UDP protocol. When complete, click the **Submit + Apply** button at the bottom of the screen. (You must scroll down to see it.)

Now that the ASA is configured as a client on the AAA server, you must populate the AAA database with usernames, their passwords, and access privileges. To do so, click the **User Setup** button in Cisco Secure ACS 4.2.

Enter a new username in the User field, and click the **Add/Edit** button to open the User Setup screen, where you define a user database object, as shown in Figure 5-28.

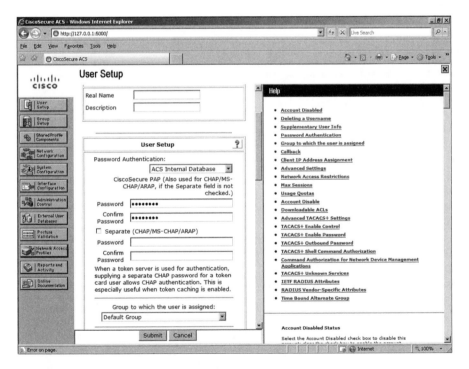

Figure 5-28   *Adding a User in ACS*

Add any optional details you choose, such as a real name and description. Select **ACS Internal Database** in the Password Authentication field. Enter and verify the password in plain text in the section labeled CiscoSecure PAP.

It is strongly recommended that you also configure password complexity rules within Cisco Secure ACS, to enforce the creation of strong passwords. For information on how to do this, consult the documentation for the Cisco Secure ACS product.

There are many other options that could be set for a user, and several become important if you are performing AAA command authorization using a remote AAA server. For now, however, you have configured everything necessary to perform AAA authentication for remote management access to the ASA, so click the **Submit** button at the bottom of the screen.

There are two ways to test communication with the remote AAA server from the ASA. From the CLI, use the **test aaa-server** command, entering the proper parameters for server group name, username, and password. You will be separately prompted for a specific server IP address. If you are using ASDM, navigate to the **Configuration > Device Management > Users/AAA > AAA Server Groups** window. Select a server from the lower pane, and click the **Test** button to the right. The Authentication radio button is selected by default. Enter a username and password, and click **OK** to test. Ensuring that configured users are successfully authenticated by your AAA servers is critical prior to configuring command authorization (covered in the next section).

Example 5-11 shows both a successful test and a failed test of AAA authentication.

Example 5-11   *Testing AAA Authentication*

```
FIREWALL# test aaa-server authentication CP-TACACS username Dave password
  Z3br@Gr@yT
Server IP Address or name: 192.168.1.5
INFO: Attempting Authentication test to IP address <192.168.1.5> (timeout: 10
  seconds)
INFO: Authentication Successful

FIREWALL# test aaa-server authentication CP-TACACS username Bob password Z3br@Gr@y
Server IP Address or name: 192.168.1.5
INFO: Attempting Authentication test to IP address <192.168.1.5> (timeout: 10
  seconds)
ERROR: Authentication Rejected: Unspecified
```

Tip: If remote AAA communication fails when a user is authenticating for administrative access, the user attempting access is given no notification. As such, it can be difficult to determine that failure of remote AAA communication is the issue. If authenticating to the Serial, Telnet, or SSH console, the key is to watch carefully and note how long it takes to receive the Username prompt, how long after you enter your username you are prompted to enter your password, and how quickly you receive an Authentication Failure message after entering your password. If the Username prompt takes a long time to be displayed, but the Password prompt is immediate, and you get a failed authentication response almost instantaneously, your ASA is failing to communicate with the remote AAA server.

Configuring AAA Command Authorization

There are a number of approaches you can use for authorizing management functions on an ASA. Like AAA authentication, this can be done using either a local or remote authorization database, or by using both, with the local database acting as a fallback for the remote database. In our example, we will first configure the local authorization method, and then later change it to a fallback method after we've configured remote authorization.

All CLI commands (which are mapped to ASDM user interface functions) have an associated privilege level. Privilege levels are integers, between 0 and 15. Most commands by default are either privilege level 1 (commands executable from unprivileged mode) or privilege level 15 (commands requiring privileged mode for execution). An administrative user with a particular privilege level can execute all commands having a level up to and including the privilege level assigned to that user. For instance, a user with privilege level 15 can execute all commands (which is why we assigned user Administrator privilege level 15 in the previous section), but a user with privilege level 8 could only execute commands having levels 1 through 8.

By setting command privilege levels in a planned manner, you can therefore create multiple levels of administrative access, allowing you to implement an RBAC policy. Creating users and assigning privilege levels to them was covered in a previous section, "Creating Users in the Local Database." Recall that the default privilege level for any newly created user is 2. The default behavior of privilege levels is as follows:

- **Privilege level 0:** Denies all access to management functions

- **Privilege level 1:** Allows CLI access only

- **Privilege level 2:** Allows CLI and ASDM access

Configuring Local AAA Command Authorization

To enable AAA authorization using the LOCAL database, you can use a wizard function in ASDM to quickly set up RBAC privilege levels to most commands, while still being able to make manual customizations to each command. To do so, navigate to **Configuration > Device Management > Users/AAA > AAA Access** and click the **Authorization** tab, shown in the background in Figure 5-29.

First, check the **Enable** check box. Enabling AAA command authorization has the effect that every time an administrative user enters a command (or attempts to use a feature in ASDM), the firewall will check that user's privilege level against the configured level of the command they are attempting to use. If the user has sufficient privileges, the command will execute. If not, the user will receive a Command Authorization Failed error.

Leave LOCAL as the server group (which it is by default). To invoke the wizard, click the **Set ASDM Defined User Roles** button. Figure 5-29 shows the resulting dialog box. The three predefined roles, and their associated privilege levels, are as follows:

- **Admin:** Privilege level 15

- **Read Only:** Privilege level 5

- **Monitor Only:** Privilege level 3

As you can see, a wide range of ASA commands will be set to privilege level 3 (and a few to privilege level 5) if you click **Yes**, mapping them to the Monitor Only or Read Only roles, respectively. All other commands remain at their default privilege level.

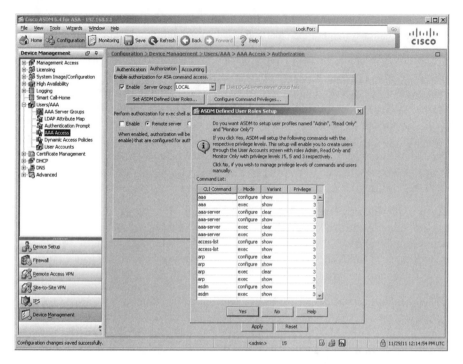

Figure 5-29 *Defined User Roles Wizard*

Note: It is important that the database used for command authorization be the same as that used to authenticate to the Enable console. This is critical, as commands entered in privileged mode will be deemed to have been entered by the user who authenticated to the Enable console. If user Dave authenticated to the SSH console using server group CP-TACACS, but then authenticated as Administrator to the Enable console, using server group LOCAL, user Administrator is seen by the ASA as the issuer of commands being authorized.

After you have set up command privilege levels by using the wizard, you can customize command privilege levels by clicking the **Configure Command Privileges** button on the Authorization tab of the AAA Access window, which opens the Command Privilege Setup dialog box, shown in Figure 5-30.

From the list of configurable commands, select a command to alter, and click **Edit**. In the resulting dialog box, also shown in Figure 5-30, click the selection arrow and choose a privilege level. The figure shows selecting a privilege level of 8 for the access list cmd variant (creating or editing an access list). Click **OK** twice, and then click **Apply** to complete the command customization.

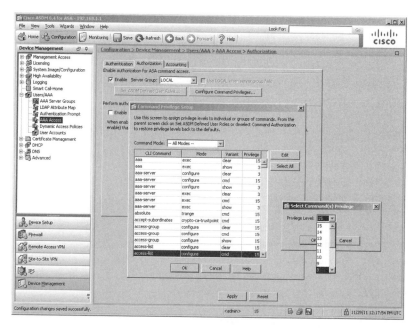

Figure 5-30   *Customizing Command Privilege Levels*

The CLI commands generated by the changes made are as follows:

```
aaa authorization command LOCAL
privilege show level 3 mode configure command aaa
privilege show level 3 mode exec command aaa
privilege clear level 3 mode configure command aaa-server
privilege show level 3 mode configure command aaa-server
privilege clear level 3 mode exec command aaa-server
privilege show level 3 mode exec command aaa-server
privilege cmd level 8 mode configure command access-list
privilege show level 3 mode configure command access-list
privilege show level 3 mode exec command access-list
privilege clear level 3 mode configure command arp
privilege show level 3 mode configure command arp
privilege clear level 3 mode exec command arp
privilege show level 3 mode exec command arp
privilege show level 5 mode configure command asdm
privilege show level 3 mode exec command asdm
privilege show level 3 mode exec command asp
privilege show level 3 mode exec command blocks
privilege show level 3 mode configure command clock
privilege show level 3 mode exec command clock
privilege show level 3 mode exec command compression
privilege show level 3 mode exec command cpu
privilege clear level 3 mode configure command crypto
privilege show level 3 mode configure command crypto
```

```
privilege clear level 3 mode exec command crypto
privilege show level 3 mode exec command crypto
privilege show level 3 mode configure command dhcpd
privilege show level 3 mode exec command dhcpd
privilege clear level 3 mode exec command dns-hosts
privilege show level 3 mode exec command dns-hosts
privilege clear level 3 mode exec command dynamic-filter
privilege show level 3 mode exec command dynamic-filter
privilege show level 3 mode exec command eigrp
privilege cmd level 3 mode configure command failover
privilege show level 3 mode configure command failover
privilege cmd level 3 mode exec command failover
privilege show level 3 mode exec command failover
privilege show level 3 mode exec command firewall
privilege show level 5 mode exec command import
privilege show level 3 mode configure command interface
privilege show level 3 mode exec command interface
privilege show level 3 mode configure command ip
privilege show level 3 mode exec command ip
privilege show level 3 mode exec command ipv6
privilege clear level 3 mode configure command logging
privilege show level 3 mode configure command logging
privilege clear level 3 mode exec command logging
privilege cmd level 3 mode exec command logging
privilege show level 3 mode exec command logging
privilege show level 3 mode exec command mode
privilege show level 3 mode exec command module
privilege show level 3 mode exec command ospf
privilege cmd level 3 mode exec command packet-tracer
privilege cmd level 3 mode exec command perfmon
privilege cmd level 3 mode exec command ping
privilege show level 5 mode configure command privilege
privilege show level 3 mode exec command reload
privilege show level 3 mode configure command route
privilege show level 3 mode exec command route
privilege show level 5 mode exec command running-config
privilege show level 3 mode configure command ssh
privilege show level 3 mode exec command ssh
privilege show level 3 mode exec command uauth
privilege show level 3 mode exec command vlan
privilege show level 3 mode exec command vpn
privilege show level 3 mode exec command vpn-sessiondb
privilege show level 3 mode exec command wccp
privilege show level 3 mode exec command webvpn
privilege cmd level 3 mode exec command who
```

If you are configuring the ASA from the CLI, you can enter these commands directly in global configuration mode. The customized command is highlighted for reference.

Note: If you set command privilege levels for the configuration command (mode config-ure), it is imperative that the users have sufficient privileges to execute the **configure terminal** command. By default, this remains a level 15 command, so even if a user has privilege level 8, for example, and the **configure access-list** privilege level is set to 8, as in the example, the user cannot configure access lists until you first make **configure terminal** a level 8 or lower command. The required syntax to do so is **privilege cmd level 8 mode exec command configure.**

Configuring Remote AAA Command Authorization

You can also enable command authorization using a remote TACACS+ server group. You should first configure all command authorization parameters on the AAA server because once you activate this feature on the ASA, any commands that you try to issue are imme-diately rejected if not part of the authorized command set configured on the AAA server. It is also recommended that you configure the use of the LOCAL database as a fallback, and configure at least one username in the local database with privilege level 15 access, in case of remote server communication failure. Note that only the TACACS+ protocol sup-ports command authorization.

The configuration of command authorization on a Cisco Secure ACS server will not be covered in detail in this book. However, it can be reached in ACS by navigating to **Shared Profile Components > Shell Command Authorization Sets.** One Shell Command Autho-rization Set is created per profile (for example, Admin, View Only, and so on). Within each set, you are allowed to specify commands and command parameters to be explicitly permitted or denied, and also whether to permit or deny any commands or command pa-rameters not explicitly configured.

Note: It might seem odd that you use Shell Command Authorization Sets, and not PIX/ASA Command Authorization Sets, which is an available option under Shared Profile Components. PIX/ASA Command Authorization Sets were used with software versions prior to 8.0. With software versions 8.0 and higher, Shell Command Authorization Sets are used.

After you have configured command authorization sets, you edit user or group records within ACS, granting them shell access (authorization to enter privileged mode) and as-signing them a Shell Command Authorization Set, which defines which commands they are allowed to use. This can be done for all AAA clients of the ACS server (firewalls, routers, switches, and so on), or by sorting AAA clients into network device groups. Figure 5-31 shows an example of assigning a shell command authorization set for all AAA client devices.

It is recommended that you always apply permissions to groups, rather than to individual users, for scalability and ease of use, unless you have specific requirements for some users to have specialized access rights. In the figure, a group has been granted Shell access and assigned the shell command authorization set named CiscoPress.

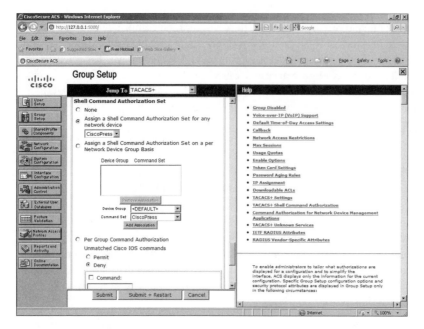

Figure 5-31 *Assigning a Shell Command Authorization Set to Group*

Note: Preliminary configuration of the Cisco Secure ACS interface options is necessary before these options will become available for configuration. Please refer to documentation for the ACS product for complete instructions. Also, other options on ACS are relevant to command authorization. Although not relevant to the FIREWALL exam, this is one of the most maddeningly difficult configuration issues that the author has repeatedly been asked about. Therefore, the following ACS configuration is necessary for remote AAA command authorization to function properly:

1. Click the **Interface Configuration** button, and then **TACACS+ (Cisco)**.

2. Scroll down and check the **Advanced TACACS+ Features** check box, and then click **Submit**.

3. Return to Group Setup, select the correct group, and click **Edit Group Settings**.

4. Under the Enable Options heading, set the Max Privilege Level to 15, either for any AAA client, or per Network Device Group, if you are using them. Finally, click the **Submit + Restart** button at the bottom of the screen.

5. For each user you want to use Command Authorization, edit his profile on the ACS Server. After the Interface Configuration changes are made, there will be a new section available: Advanced TACACS+ Settings. Within this section, under the TACACS+ Enable Control heading, select the **Use Group Level Setting** radio button. Then, under the TACACS+ Enable Password heading, select what password this user will use to enter privileged mode. Finally, click the **Submit** button at the bottom of the screen.

Only after all these steps are completed will remote AAA Command Authorization function properly.

After you have configured the remote AAA server with proper settings, you must configure the ASA to check for user authorizations, using the appropriate AAA server group. To do so, return to **Configuration > Device Management > Users/AAA > AAA Access**, and then click the **Authorization** tab, as shown in Figure 5-32.

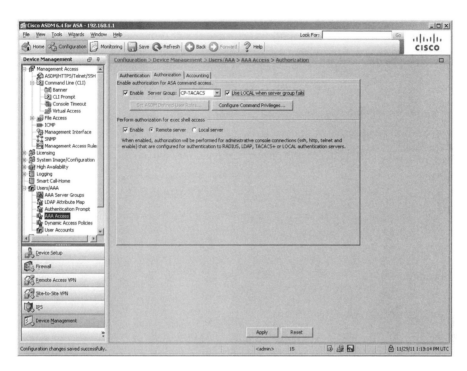

Figure 5-32   *Configuring Remote AAA Command Authorization*

Figure 5-32 shows the changes from the previous example that are necessary to redirect command authorization queries to a remote AAA server group instead of to the local database. The box is still checked to enable command authorization, but this time, the CP-TACACS server group is selected, and the local database is selected as a fallback method.

In addition to performing command authorization, it is possible to separately authorize shell access. This feature allows you to prevent users without the shell access privilege from being able to log into the ASA and gain CLI access (the ability to distinguish network users from device administrators). Note that gaining access is different from being able to execute commands, which is why this is a separate feature. Figure 5-32 also shows this separate authorization check being enabled, and the selection of the remote server to perform the check. This automatically performs the check against the same server group that performed the original user authentication. If only this option is enabled, then remotely defined user privilege levels are used along with locally defined command privilege levels, to determine user command authorization.

If you configure the ASA to perform command authorization using a TACACS+ server, it is imperative that the Enable console authentication be performed using TACACS+. If a TACACS+ server is not used for Enable console authentication, then the user successfully gaining access to privileged EXEC mode is known to the ASA only as the "enable_15" (system default privileged username) user. The ASA would thus send authorization requests to the TACACS+ server as user enable_15 attempting to perform commands. Because it is highly unlikely that a TACACS+ server would have an enable_15 user defined, all command authorization requests would fail. Configuring Enable console authentication to use TACACS+ would ensure the proper username is sent to the TACACS+ server for subsequent command authorization requests.

Once these changes are made, click **Apply** to finish activating remote command authorization.

The CLI commands generated by the changes made are as follows:

```
aaa authorization command CP-TACACS LOCAL
aaa authorization exec authentication-server
```

If you are configuring the ASA from the CLI, you can enter these commands directly in global configuration mode.

Configuring Remote AAA Accounting

The ASA remote AAA accounting feature supports recording of specific events to a centralized AAA server or group of servers. You can audit access to privileged mode (enable console access), audit when administrative users gain Serial, Telnet, or SSH console access to the ASA via RADIUS or TACACS+, or audit the execution of individual commands via TACACS+ only. If auditing command execution, you set a privilege level to be recorded. All executions of commands having the configured privilege level or a higher level are recorded to the AAA Accounting log. To configure AAA accounting, navigate to **Configuration > Device Management > Users/AAA > AAA Access** and then click the **Accounting** tab, shown in Figure 5-33.

In Figure 5-33, all accounting options are enabled, with log messages being sent to the CP-TACACS server group. Remember that whether accounting messages are sent to a single server or to all group members is configured as part of creating the server group.

Check the **Enable** check box in the Require Accounting to Allow Accounting of User Activity area, which activates accounting of access to the Enable console (entry into privileged mode). Access to the Serial, SSH, and Telnet consoles can be logged by checking the appropriate check boxes.

To record successful or failed attempts to execute specific commands (incomplete or otherwise invalid commands and "typos" are not logged), check the **Enable** check box in the Require Command Accounting for ASA area. When this option is enabled, you will also want to select a Privilege Level option, which will record all desired command execution.

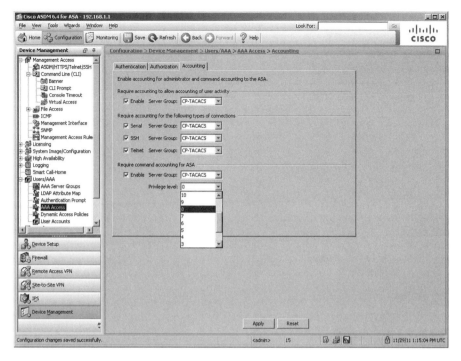

Figure 5-33   *Configuring AAA Accounting*

In Figure 5-33, privilege level 8 is selected, which will cause all commands having privilege level 8 or higher to be logged. The selected level should be based on your local security policy. For instance, most organizations would want to record only commands that change the ASA configuration, and not commands that only monitor activity (such as **show** commands). Other organizations require the recording of all command activity.

The CLI commands generated by the changes made are as follows:

```
aaa accounting enable console CP-TACACS
aaa accounting serial console CP-TACACS
aaa accounting ssh console CP-TACACS
aaa accounting telnet console CP-TACACS
aaa accounting command privilege 8 CP-TACACS
```

If you are configuring the ASA from the CLI, you can enter these commands directly in global configuration mode.

Verifying AAA for Management Access

When using AAA servers, you can easily verify successful communication between your ASA and the AAA server by observing the AAA server status and statistics, using the **show aaa-server** command. As Example 5-12 demonstrates, this command displays the server group to which a server belongs, the protocol used by the server group for AAA exchanges, the IP address of the server, the current status (active or inactive) of the AAA server, and statistics about AAA exchanges (requests and responses).

Example 5-12 *Viewing AAA Server Statistics*

```
FIREWALL# show aaa-server
Server Group:    LOCAL
Server Protocol: Local database
Server Address:  None
Server port:     None
Server status:   ACTIVE, Last transaction at 13:07:14 UTC Tue Nov 29 2011
Number of pending requests           0
Average round trip time              0ms
Number of authentication requests    33
Number of authorization requests     0
Number of accounting requests        0
Number of retransmissions            0
Number of accepts                    4
Number of rejects                    29
Number of challenges                 0
Number of malformed responses        0
Number of bad authenticators         0
Number of timeouts                   0
Number of unrecognized responses     0


Server Group:    CP-TACACS
Server Protocol: tacacs+
Server Address:  192.168.1.5
Server port:     49
Server status:   ACTIVE, Last transaction at 13:36:34 UTC Tue Nov 29 2011
Number of pending requests           0
Average round trip time              3ms
Number of authentication requests    47
Number of authorization requests     115
Number of accounting requests        4
Number of retransmissions            0
Number of accepts                    125
Number of rejects                    38
Number of challenges                 15
Number of malformed responses        0
Number of bad authenticators         0
Number of timeouts                   3
Number of unrecognized responses     0
```

The **test aaa-server** command is the other principal method of verifying AAA functionality. Due to the importance of verifying successful authentication prior to configuring command authorization, this command was discussed and demonstrated earlier in this chapter.

Configuring Monitoring Using SNMP

The Cisco ASA supports network monitoring using SNMP versions 1, 2c, and 3 (not supported prior to OS version 8.2), and supports any combination of those being used simultaneously (that is, different monitoring platforms using different versions). As stated earlier, the ASA supports SNMP read-only access through the use of SNMP GET requests. SNMP write access is not allowed, so using SNMP SET requests or attempting to modify the configuration in any way using SNMP is not permitted.

The ASA can be configured to send *SNMP traps*, which are unsolicited messages from the managed device to a network management system (NMS) for certain events (event notifications). You can also use an NMS to browse the Management Information Bases (MIB) on the ASA. A MIB is a collection of information definitions, and the ASA maintains a database of values for each definition. Browsing a MIB requires using an NMS to determine values by issuing a series of GET-NEXT and/or GET-BULK requests of the MIB tree.

SNMP on the ASA requires client authentication. With SNMP version 1 or 2c, this is done by the NMS sending the proper community string (a password, sent in clear text) with its request. Such community strings can be set either as a default or uniquely per NMS IP address. SNMP version 3 can use strong, cryptographic protection for its information exchanges, and/or a combination of username and key for authentication.

To configure the ASA to permit NMS polling or sending of SNMP traps to an NMS, navigate to **Configuration > Device Management > Management Access > SNMP** to open the SNMP configuration window, shown in Figure 5-34.

If the Community String (Default) field is left blank, this ASA will be configured with specific community strings on a per-IP-address basis. Contact and location information is entered only once, if completed, because this information refers to the ASA itself and does not change on a per-management-station basis. This ASA will listen on the default SNMP polling port of UDP 161, unless changed.

To add an NMS definition, click the **Add** button in the SNMP Management Stations area. This opens the Add SNMP Host Access Entry dialog box. If you are editing or deleting existing configured NMS definitions, use the **Edit** or **Delete** key. When adding or editing, configure the NMS definition according to the settings in your network. In Figure 5-34, the OOB management network attached to interface management is selected. The NMS IP address of 192.168.1.14 is defined. The default SNMP trap port of UDP 162 is left unaltered, a unique community string is defined for this NMS host, and the SNMP version is selected as version 2c.

Note that you can configure an SNMP host to perform polling, receive traps, or both by checking the appropriate box in this dialog box. Both choices are checked by default, as shown in Figure 5-34. Complete the NMS definition by clicking **OK**. If you select an interface other than "inside" for the sending of SNMP traps, you receive a warning message that this might be insecure. Acknowledge the message and complete the configuration by clicking **Apply**.

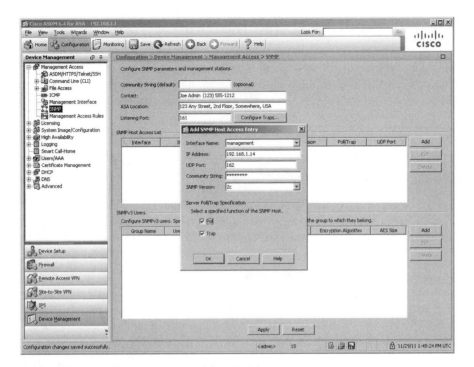

Figure 5-34   *SNMP Configuration Window*

The CLI commands generated by the changes made are as follows:

snmp-server location 123 Any Street, 2nd Floor, Somewhere, USA
snmp-server contact Joe Admin (123) 555-1212
snmp-server host management 192.168.1.14 **community** SNMP1234 **version** 2c

If you are configuring the ASA from the CLI, you can enter these commands directly in global configuration mode.

The ASA can be configured to send several types of SNMP traps. If your local policy dictates, click the **Configure Traps** button in the SNMP configuration window to open the SNMP Trap Configuration dialog box, shown in Figure 5-35.

In Figure 5-35, in addition to the four standard SNMP traps (which are enabled by default), traps are enabled for IPsec Start and Stop and for Remote Access Session Threshold Exceeded. Complete the traps configuration by clicking **OK** and then clicking **Apply**. If you want to send SNMP traps as syslog messages, in addition to enabling syslog traps within the SNMP Trap Configuration screen, you need to configure a logging filter and destination in order to send traps (as syslog messages) to a configured syslog server. Configuration of logging is covered in Chapter 6, "Recording ASA Activity."

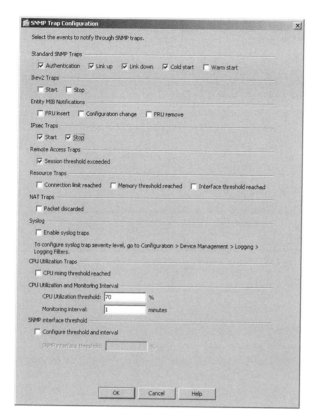

Figure 5-35 *IDS and IPS Operational Differences*

The CLI commands generated by the changes made are as follows:

```
snmp-server enable traps ipsec start
snmp-server enable traps ipsec stop
snmp-server enable traps remote-access session-threshold-exceeded
```

If you are configuring the ASA from the CLI, you can enter these commands directly in global configuration mode.

If you are using SNMP version 3, you will need to configure SNMPv3 users and groups. This is the major difference between SNMPv3 and earlier versions. Groups define the protection model used for communication between the ASA and the NMS. The definition of groups and users allows for highly granular control over access to the SNMP agent and MIB objects.

Three SNMPv3 group definitions are supported by the ASA:

- **No Authentication, No Encryption:** Cleartext communication between the ASA and NMS

- **Authentication Only:** Communication is authenticated but unencrypted

- **Authentication and Encryption:** Authentication and full encryption for communication between the ASA and NMS

To use authenticated and/or encrypted communication, you need to configure the cryptographic keys and choose algorithms to authenticate and/or encrypt SNMP packets. These are symmetric keys and must be defined on both the ASA and the NMS.

To configure new SNMPv3 user information, from the SNMP configuration window, click **Add** in the SNMPv3 Users area to open the Add SNMP User Entry dialog box, shown in Figure 5-36. If you are editing or deleting existing configured users, use the **Edit** or **Delete** button.

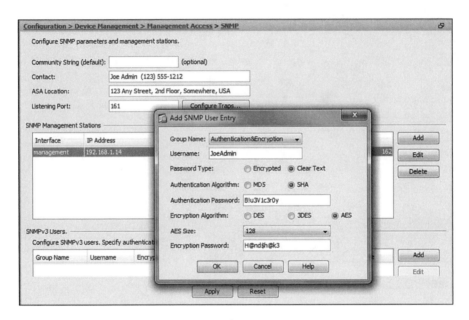

Figure 5-36 *Adding SNMPv3 User Information*

In this case, an SNMPv3 group name of Authentication and Encryption is selected. The remote username is configured, and Clear Text is selected for Password Type. If Encrypted is selected here, both password fields must be completed with hexadecimal strings, in the format xx:xx:xx:.... Because Clear Text is selected, a plaintext password is entered for the password to be used with the selected Authentication Algorithm (you should prefer SHA over MD5). If AES is selected as the Encryption Algorithm, you must also select the size of the AES key, either 128-, 192-, or 256-bit (AES or 3DES is recommended). The encryption password is then entered, either in plaintext or hexadecimal format, once again depending on the Password Type selected. A maximum of 64 characters is allowed for either password. Complete the addition of the new user by clicking **OK** and then clicking **Apply**.

The CLI commands generated by the changes made are as follows:

```
snmp-server group Authentication&Encryption v3 priv
snmp-server user JoeAdmin Authentication&Encryption v3 auth B!u3V1c3r0y priv AES
    128 H@nd$h@k3
```

If you are configuring the ASA from the CLI, you can enter these commands directly in global configuration mode.

The full syntax and options of the **snmp-server group** command are as follows:

```
snmp-server group group-name {v3 {auth | noauth | priv}}
```

- **auth:** Specifies packet authentication without encryption.

- **group-name:** Defines the name of the group.

- **noauth:** Specifies no packet authentication or encryption.

- **priv:** Specifies both packet authentication and encryption.

- **v3:** Specifies the group is using the SNMP v3 security model, which is the most secure of the supported security models. This version allows you to explicitly configure authentication characteristics.

The full syntax and options of the **snmp-server user** command are as follows:

```
snmp-server user username group-name {v3 [encrypted] [auth {md5 | sha} auth-pass
    word]} [priv {des | 3des | aes {128 | 192 | 256}} priv-password]
```

- **128 | 192 | 256:** Specifies the number of bits used by the AES algorithm for encryption.

- **auth:** Specifies which authentication algorithm should be used, when using authentication.

- *auth-password*: Specifies the string that enables the agent to receive packets from the ASA. The maximum length is 64 characters. You can specify a plaintext password or localized digest. The digest must be formatted as xx:xx:xx..., where xx are hexadecimal values. The digest should be exactly 16 octets in length.

- **des | 3des | aes:** Specifies encryption algorithm.

- **encrypted:** Specifies that the passwords appear in digest format, rather than plaintext.

- *group-name*: Specifies the name of the group to which the user belongs.

- **md5 | sha:** Specifies the authentication algorithm.

- *priv-password*: Specifies a string as the privacy user password. The maximum length is 64 characters. You can specify a plaintext password or a localized digest. The digest must be formatted as xx:xx:xx..., where xx are hexadecimal values. The digest should be exactly 16 octets in length.

- *username*: Specifies the name of the user on the host that connects to the agent.

- **v3:** Specifies that the SNMP Version 3 security model should be used. Allows the use of the **encrypted, priv,** and **auth** keywords.

Troubleshooting Remote Management Access

Most issues with remote management access appear in the ASA system log (or remote syslog server) depending on the severity level. Use the **show logging** command, use the ASDM real-time log viewer, or examine your centralized log files for such messages.

Some examples follow:

```
%ASA-3-710003: TCP access denied by ACL from 10.10.5.12/6724 to
  inside:10.0.0.1/22
```

The preceding message indicates that management access rules do not permit the management session.

```
%ASA-3-315004: Fail to establish SSH session because RSA host key retrieval failed.
%ASA-3-315011: SSH session from 192.168.1.8 on interface management for user ""
disconnected by SSH server, reason: "Internal error" (0x00)
```

This message pair indicates that the local RSA key pair has not been generated, as required for the ASA SSH server.

If system log messages do not pinpoint the issue, consider debugging management protocols on the ASA, such as the following (note that some of these commands support different levels of debugging):

- **debug ssh:** Debugs the SSH daemon to determine low-level protocol failures, such as algorithm or version incompatibility

- **debug http:** Debugs HTTP exchanges to determine problems with the ASDM image

- **debug snmp:** Debugs SNMP exchanges to help determine problems with SNMP authentication and OIDs

To troubleshoot AAA for management access, you have to troubleshoot activity on both the ASA and, in the case of remote AAA, the AAA server.

The recommended troubleshooting task flow when troubleshooting local or remote AAA is as follows:

Step 1. For remote AAA, verify mutual reachability between the ASA and the server using **ping, traceroute, show aaa-server**, or similar tools. Also, verify that symmetrical session keys (shared secret) are used in the AAA protocol association.

Step 2. Verify the status of AAA authentication requests. Use **show logging, debug aaa authentication, debug tacacs**, and **debug radius** on the ASA. On the remote server, view failure reports and check for locked user accounts.

Step 3. Verify the AAA authorization process. In addition to the previously mentioned commands, use **debug aaa authorization**. Check the failure reports and verify user or group privileges on remote AAA servers.

Step 4. Verify that AAA accounting messages are properly being sent by the ASA, using the **debug aaa accounting** command, and received on the AAA server, by viewing its accounting reports.

The ASA logs many system messages related to the AAA subsystem. By using the **show logging** command, using the ASDM real-time log viewer, or examining logs in a centralized logging or management system, you may be able to pinpoint the cause of AAA issues.

Some examples follow:

```
%ASA-6-113015: AAA user authentication Rejected : reason = Invalid password :
  local database : user = Administrator
```

The preceding message indicates that authentication failed due to bad credentials.

```
%ASA-6-113014: AAA authentication server not accessible : server = 192.168.1.5 :
  user = Dave
%ASA-2-113022: AAA Marking TACACS+ server 192.168.1.5 in aaa-server group CP-
  TACACS as FAILED
```

This message pair indicates that user authentication failed due to server communication failure.

```
%ASA-6-113004: AAA user authentication Successful : server = 192.168.1.5 :
  user = Dave
%ASA-6-113005: AAA user authorization Rejected : reason = User was not found :
  user = Dave
```

This message pair indicates that the user was not found in the authorization database (note that remote AAA was used for authentication, but authorization is checked against the local database).

Finally, you can debug protocol-level details to troubleshoot possible compatibility issues between your ASA and a remote AAA server by using the **debug tacacs** or **debug radius** commands. You can specify conditional debugging (such as limiting to a single username) to avoid excessive output and performance issues. Because much of the output uses terms that are unique to TACACS+ ("verbs") and RADIUS ("attributes"), knowledge of these terms are necessary to properly interpret the debug output.

Unlocking Locked and Disabled User Accounts

A user account is normally locked when a configurable threshold of successive and unsuccessful login attempts have been made using that account.

If a local database user account becomes locked, and you need to unlock it, within ASDM, navigate to **Monitor > Properties > Device Access > AAA Local Locked Out Users**, as shown in Figure 5-37.

If any local user accounts appear in the list of locked accounts, you may either select one account name and click the **Clear Selected Lockout** button to unlock a single account, or simply click the **Clear All Lockouts** button to remove the lock from all accounts.

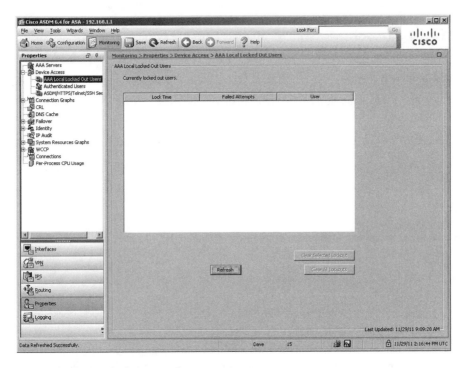

Figure 5-37   *Unlocking Local User Accounts*

Cisco ASA Password Recovery

If you lose the ability to gain management access to the ASA, either due to loss of necessary passwords or due to accidental lockout from the incorrect application of AAA functions, you can regain access to the ASA using a special procedure that can be performed only through the Serial console. Although this procedure is referred to as *password recovery*, it is not actually possible to "recover" lost passwords. Instead, you replace previously set passwords with new ones of your choosing.

Performing Password Recovery

To perform password recovery, connect to the serial console port of the ASA. Power cycle the ASA and watch the messages during boot. Two messages will appear, as follows:

```
Use BREAK or ESC to interrupt boot.
Use SPACE to begin boot immediately.
```

A 10-second countdown appears directly below these messages. Press the **Esc** key to interrupt the boot process and enter ROM Monitor (ROMMON) mode. From ROMMON mode, you set the configuration register value to instruct the ASA to bypass its startup configuration file (where passwords and AAA commands are stored), and reboot it. Example 5-13 shows the full procedure.

Example 5-13 *Performing Password Recovery*

```
rommon #0> confreg 0x41
rommon #1> boot
Loading disk0:/asa823-k8.bin...
<...output omitted...>
ciscoasa> enable
Password: <press Enter>
ciscoasa# copy startup-config running-config
FIREWALL# configure terminal
FIREWALL (config)# password NEWPASSWORD
FIREWALL (config)# enable password NEWPASSWORD
FIREWALL (config)# username Administrator password NEWPASSWORD
FIREWALL (config)# no aaa authorization command
FIREWALL (config)# config-register 0x1
FIREWALL (config)# exit
FIREWALL# copy running-config startup-config
FIREWALL# reload noconfirm
```

In ROMMON mode, you can use the **confreg** command, without specifying a value, to go through a prompted series of questions that will set the configuration register value. You can also use the **reset** command where the example shows the **boot** command.

In configuration mode, you can change whichever passwords or AAA commands need to be changed to ensure access to the ASA is regained. Example 5-13 shows some typical changes, but is not intended to imply that all those changes will be needed. It is important to remember to reset the configuration register back to the value of 0x1, so the ASA will return to the normal boot procedure.

Enabling or Disabling Password Recovery

Password recovery is enabled by default on the Cisco ASA. The **no service password-recovery** command prevents users from entering ROMMON mode with the ASA configuration intact. If this command is used to disable the password recovery feature, a user entering ROMMON mode is prompted to erase all flash file systems. The user cannot enter ROMMON mode without performing this erasure. If a user declines to perform the erasure, the ASA reboots.

Password recovery requires the use of ROMMON mode to reset the value of the configuration register while retaining the ASA configuration. Confirming the erasure of all files deletes the configuration files, and thus prevents the resetting of passwords without loss of the remaining configuration. However, by disabling password recovery, you also ensure that unauthorized users cannot view the configuration or change passwords, despite having physical access to the ASA. The only way to recover the ASA to an operating state, without password recovery, is to load a new image and a backup configuration file, if available.

The **service password-recovery** command appears in the configuration file for informational purposes only. When you enter the command, or its **no** form, at the CLI prompt, the setting is saved in flash memory. The only way to change this setting is to enter the command at the CLI prompt. Loading a new configuration that contains the command does not change the setting.

If you disable password recovery while the ASA is configured to ignore the startup configuration at startup (as in password recovery), the ASA changes the setting to boot the startup configuration file as usual.

To re-enable password recovery after it has been disabled, enter the **service password-recovery** command in global configuration mode.

Exam Preparation Tasks

As mentioned in the section, "How to Use This Book," in the Introduction, you have a couple of choices for exam preparation: the exercises here, Chapter 17, "Final Preparation," and the exam simulation questions on the CD-ROM.

Review All Key Topics

Review the most important topics in this chapter, noted with the Key Topic icon in the outer margin of the page. Table 5-2 lists a reference of these key topics and the page numbers on which each is found.

Table 5-2   *Key Topics for Chapter 5*

Key Topic Element	Description	Page Number
Paragraph	Describes storage and viewing of the enable password	167
Section	Describes file system management CLI commands	172
Section	Describes license management process	182
Section	Describes configuration of an out-of-band management interface	189
Section	Describes configuration of SSH remote access	192
Section	Describes digital certificate enrollment	196
Section	Describes configuring AAA access with remote AAA servers	208
Section	Describes configuring Cisco Secure ACS to support AAA features	211
Section	Describes configuration of AAA command authorization	214
Section	Describes ASA password recovery procedure	232

Command Reference to Check Your Memory

This section includes the most important configuration and EXEC commands covered in this chapter. It might not be necessary to memorize the complete syntax of every command, but you should be able to remember the basic keywords that are needed.

To test your memory of the commands, cover the right side of Tables 5-3 through 5-10 with a piece of paper, read the description on the left side, and then see how much of the command you can remember.

The FIREWALL exam focuses on practical, hands-on skills that are used by a networking professional. Therefore, you should be able to identify the commands needed to configure and test an ASA feature.

Table 5-3 *Basic Device Settings Commands*

Task	Command Syntax
Set the ASA hostname	ciscoasa(config)# **hostname** *name*
Set the default domain name	ciscoasa(config)# **domain-name** *name*
Set the enable password	ciscoasa(config)# **enable password** *password* [**level** *level*] [**encrypted**]
Set the login password	ciscoasa(config)# **passwd** *password* [**encrypted**]
Display the ASA hostname	ciscoasa# **show hostname**
Display the default domain name	ciscoasa# **show running-config domain-name**
Exit privileged EXEC mode and return to un-privileged EXEC mode	ciscoasa# **disable**
Enter privileged EXEC mode from unprivileged EXEC mode	ciscoasa> **enable**

Table 5-4 *Commands Related to Name-to-Address Mapping*

Task	Command Syntax
Associate a name with an IP address	ciscoasa(config)# **name** *ip_address name* [**description** *text*]]
Enable the use of the **name** command	ciscoasa(config)# **names**
Disable the display of names in place of IP addresses	ciscoasa(config)# **no names**
Enable the ASA to send DNS requests to a DNS server through an interface	ciscoasa(config)# **dns domain-lookup** *interface-name*
Enter DNS server-group mode	ciscoasa(config)# **dns server-group** *name*
Specify from 1 to 6 DNS server IP addresses in server-group	ciscoasa(config)# **name-server** *ip_address* [*ip_address2*] [...] [*ip_address6*]
Display debug messages for DNS	ciscoasa# **debug dns** [**resolver** | **all**] [*level*]

Table 5-5   *File System Management Commands*

Task	Command Syntax
Display directory contents	ciscoasa# **dir** [/all] [all-filesystems] [/recursive] [cdisk0: | disk1: | flash: | system:] [*path*]
Display contents of a file	ciscoasa# **more** [/ascii | /binary | /ebcdic] [disk0: | disk1: | flash: | ftp: | http: | https: | smb: | system: | tftp:]*filename*
Copy a file from one location to another	ciscoasa# **copy** [/noconfirm] [/pcap] {*url* | **running-config** | **startup-config**} {**running-config** | **startup-config** | *url*}
Delete a file	ciscoasa# **delete** [/noconfirm] [/recursive] {disk0: | disk1: | flash:}*filename*
Rename a file	ciscoasa# **rename** {disk0: | disk1: | flash:}*filename* {disk0: | disk1: | flash:}*filename*
Create a new directory	ciscoasa# **mkdir** [/noconfirm] [disk0: | disk1: | flash:]*path*
Remove an existing directory	ciscoasa# **rmdir** [/noconfirm] [disk0: | disk1: | flash:]*path*
Change the current directory	ciscoasa# **cd** [disk0: | disk1: | flash:] [*path*]
Display the current directory	ciscoasa# **pwd**
Perform a file system check and repair corruptions	ciscoasa# **fsck** [/noconfirm] {disk0: | disk1: | flash:}
Erase all files and reformat the file system	ciscoasa# {**format** | **erase**} [disk0: | disk1: | flash:

Table 5-6   *Commands Related to Managing Software and Feature Activation*

Task	Command Syntax
Specify which image file the ASA loads on next reboot	ciscoasa(config)# **boot system**
Display the running activation key and licensed features	ciscoasa# **show activation-key** [detail]
Display the software version, hardware configuration, license key, and related uptime data	ciscoasa# **show version**

Table 5-7 *Commands Related to Management Access*

Task	Command Syntax
Set an interface to accept management traffic only	ciscoasa(config-if)# **management-only**
Add Telnet access to the console and set the idle timeout	ciscoasa(config)# **telnet** {{*hostname* / *ip_address mask interface_name*} / {*ipv6_address interface_name*} / {**timeout** *number*}}
Display active Telnet administration sessions	ciscoasa# **who**
Terminate a Telnet session	ciscoasa# **kill** *telnet_id*
Generate RSA key pairs for identity certificates	ciscoasa(config)# **crypto key generate rsa** [**usage-keys** / **general-keys**] [**label** *key-pair-label*] [**modulus** *size*] [**noconfirm**]
Remove the key pairs of the indicated type (rsa or dsa)	ciscoasa(config)# **crypto key zeroize** {**rsa** / **dsa**} [**label** *key-pair-label*] [**default**] [**noconfirm**]
Restrict the version of SSH accepted by the ASA	ciscoasa(config)# **ssh version** {**1** / **2**}
Add SSH access to the ASA	ciscoasa(config)# **ssh** {*ip_address mask* / *ipv6_address/prefix*} *interface*
Display information about the active SSH session(s)	ciscoasa# **show ssh sessions** [*ip_address*]
Disconnect an active SSH session	ciscoasa# **ssh disconnect** *session_id*
Enter the trustpoint configuration mode for the specified trustpoint	ciscoasa(config)# **crypto ca trustpoint** *trustpoint-name*
Specify how the enrolled identity of a trustpoint can be used	ciscoasa(ca-trustpoint)# **id-usage** {**ssl-ipsec** / **code-signer**}
Ask the CA not to include an FQDN in the Subject Alternative Name extension of the certificate	ciscoasa(ca-trustpoint)# **no fqdn**
Ask the CA to include the specified Subject DN in the certificate	ciscoasa(ca-trustpoint)# **subject-name** *X.500 name*
Specify enrollment that generates a self-signed certificate	ciscoasa(ca-trustpoint)# **enrollment self**
Specify SCEP enrollment to enroll with this trustpoint and configure the enrollment URL (url)	ciscoasa(ca-trustpoint)# **enrollment url** *url*

Table 5-7   *Commands Related to Management Access*

Task	Command Syntax
Install and authenticate the CA certificates associated with a trustpoint	ciscoasa(ca-trustpoint)# **crypto ca authenticate** *trustpoint* [**fingerprint** *hexvalue*] [**nointeractive**]
Start the enrollment process with the CA	ciscoasa(ca-trustpoint)# **crypto ca enroll** *trustpoint* [**noconfirm**]
Specify the encryption algorithms that the SSL/TLS protocol uses	ciscoasa(config)# **ssl encryption** [*3des-sha1*] [*des-sha1*] [*rc4-md5*] [*aes128-sha1*] [*aes256-sha1*] [*possibly others*]
Specify the certificate trustpoint that represents the SSL certificate for an interface	ciscoasa(config)# **ssl trust-point** {*trustpoint* [*interface*]}
Specify hosts that can access the internal HTTP server	ciscoasa(config)# **http** *ip_address subnet_mask interface_name*
Configure the ASDM, session, login, or message-of-the-day banner	ciscoasa(config)# **banner** {asdm l exec l login l motd *text*}
Add a user to the local database	ciscoasa(config)# **username** *name* {**nopassword** l **password** *password* [**mschap** l **encrypted** l **nt-encrypted**]} [**privilege** *priv_level*]
Authenticate users who access the ASA CLI over a serial, SSH, HTTPS (ASDM), or Telnet connection, or authenticate users who access privileged EXEC mode using the **enable** command	ciscoasa(config)# **aaa authentication** {serial l enable l telnet l ssh l http} **console** {LOCAL l *server_group* [LOCAL]}
Limit the number of consecutive failed local login attempts that the ASA allows any given user account (with the exception of users with a privilege level of 15; this feature does not affect level 15 users)	ciscoasa(config)# **aaa local authentication attempts max-fail** *number*
Create a AAA server group and configure AAA server parameters that are group-specific and common to all group hosts	ciscoasa(config)# **aaa-server** *server-tag* **protocol** *server-protocol*
Configure a AAA server as part of a AAA server group and configure AAA server parameters that are host-specific	ciscoasa(config)# **aaa-server** *server-tag* [(*interface-name*)] **host** {*server-ip* l *name*} **key** [*key*] [**timeout** *seconds*]

Table 5-7 *Commands Related to Management Access*

Task	Command Syntax
Check whether the ASA can authenticate or authorize users with a particular AAA server	ciscoasa# **test aaa-server** {**authentication** *server_tag* [**host** *ip_address*] [**username** *username*] [**password** *password*] | **authorization** *server_tag* [**host** *ip_address*] [**username** *username*]}
Configure command privilege levels for use with command authorization	ciscoasa(config)# **privilege** [**show** | **clear** | **configure**] **level** *level* [**mode** {**enable** | **configure**}] **command** *command*
Enable management authorization, and enable support of administrative user privilege levels from RADIUS	ciscoasa(config)# **aaa authorization exec authentication-server**
Enable support for AAA accounting for administrative access	ciscoasa(config)# **aaa accounting** {**serial** | **telnet** | **ssh** | **enable**} **console** *server-tag*

Table 5-8 *SNMP Monitoring Commands*

Task	Command Syntax
Set the ASA location for SNMP	ciscoasa(config)# **snmp-server location** *text*
Set the SNMP server contact name	ciscoasa(config)# **snmp-server contact** *text*
Specify the NMS that can use SNMP	ciscoasa(config)# **snmp-server host** {*interface* {*hostname* | *ip_address*}} [**trap** | **poll**] [**community** 0 | 8 *community-string*] [**version** {1 | 2c | 3 *username*}] [**udp-port** *port*]
Clear local host table entries	ciscoasa(config)# **snmp-server enable traps** [**all** | **syslog** | **snmp** [*trap*] [...] | **entity** [*trap*] [...] | **ipsec** [*trap*] [...] | **remote-access** [*trap*]]
Configure a new SNMP group	ciscoasa(config)# **snmp-server group** *group-name* {**v3** {**auth** | **noauth** | **priv**}}
Configure a new SNMP user	ciscoasa# **snmp-server user** *username group-name* {**v3** [**encrypted**] [**auth** {**md5** | **sha**} *auth-password*]} [**priv** {**des** | **3des** | **aes** {**128** | **192** | **256**}} *priv-password*]

Table 5-9 *Troubleshooting Commands*

Task	Command Syntax
Display debug information and error messages associated with SSH	ciscoasa(config)# **debug ssh**
Display detailed information about HTTP traffic	ciscoasa(config)# **debug http**
Clear local host table entries	ciscoasa(config)# **show aaa-server**
Show the logs in the buffer or other logging settings	ciscoasa(config)# **show logging** [**message** [*syslog_id* | **all**] | **asdm** | **queue** | **setting**]
Show debug messages for AAA	ciscoasa# **debug aaa** [**accounting** | **authentication** | **authorization** | **common** | **internal** | **vpn** [*level*]]
Show debug messages for TACACS+	ciscoasa# **debug tacacs** [**session** | **user** *username*]
Show debug messages for RADIUS	ciscoasa# **debug radius** [**all** | **decode** | **session** | **user** *username*]]

Table 5-10 *Commands Related to Password Recovery*

Task	Command Syntax
Set the configuration register value that is used the next time you reload the ASA while in ROMMON mode	rommon> **confreg 0x41**
Reboot the ASA from ROMMON mode	rommon> **boot** OR rommon> **reset**
Set the configuration register value that is used the next time you reload the ASA	ciscoasa(config)# **config-register** *hex_value*
Clear local host table entries	ciscoasa(config)# **reload** [**at** *hh:mm* [*month day* | *day month*]] [**cancel**] [**in** [*hh:*]*mm*] [**max-hold-time** [*hh:*]*mm*] [**noconfirm**] [**quick**] [**reason** *text*] [**save-config**]
Disable password recovery	ciscoasa(config)# **no service password-recovery**

This chapter covers the following topics:

- **System Time:** This section describes configuration of system time, both locally on the ASA and through the use of NTP.

- **Managing Event and Session Logging:** This section gives an overview of the ASA logging subsystem, including event destinations, severity levels, and NetFlow support.

- **Configuring Event and Session Logging:** This section describes the configuration of logging on the ASA. It covers the setting of global parameters, the creation of event lists and filters, and the details on configuring a number of event destinations.

- **Verifying Event and Session Logging:** This section covers commands used to verify proper functioning of logging on the ASA.

- **Troubleshooting Event and Session Logging:** This section covers commands used to troubleshoot logging functionality.

CHAPTER 6

Recording ASA Activity

Effective troubleshooting of network or device activity, from the perspective of the Cisco Adaptive Security Appliance (ASA), requires accurate information. Many times, the best source of accurate and complete information will be various logs, if logging is properly configured to capture the necessary information. An ASA has many potential destinations to which it can send logging information.

"Do I Know This Already?" Quiz

The "Do I Know This Already?" quiz allows you to assess whether you should read this entire chapter thoroughly or jump to the "Exam Preparation Tasks" section. If you are in doubt about your answers to these questions or your own assessment of your knowledge of the topics, read the entire chapter. Table 6-1 lists the major headings in this chapter and their corresponding "Do I Know This Already?" quiz questions. You can find the answers in Appendix A, "Answers to the 'Do I Know This Already?' Quizzes."

Table 6-1 *"Do I Know This Already?" Section-to-Question Mapping*

Foundation Topics Section	Questions
System Time	1–4
Managing Event and Session Logging	5–7
Configuring Event and Session Logging	8–12
Verifying Event and Session Logging	13
Troubleshooting Event and Session Logging	14

Caution: The goal of self-assessment is to gauge your mastery of the topics in this chapter. If you do not know the answer to a question or are only partially sure of the answer, you should mark that question as wrong for purposes of the self-assessment. Giving yourself credit for an answer you correctly guess skews your self-assessment results and might provide you with a false sense of security.

1. Which are two of the most important reasons for ensuring accurate time on an ASA? (Choose two.)

   a. Synchronization with AAA servers

   b. Use of digital certificates

    c. Time-based Modular Policy Framework rules

    d. Time stamps in log messages

2. Where in ASDM do you configure NTP authentication and servers?

    a. **Configuration > Device Setup > System Time > NTP**

    b. **Configuration > Device Management > System Time > NTP**

    c. **Configuration > Device Management > System Time > NTP > Parameters**

    d. **Configuration > Device Setup > System Time > NTP > Parameters**

3. Consider the following command:

`ntp authentication-key 1 md5 UEB34mid@#9C`

What does this command mean?

    a. This is the first authentication key in a key ring, and the MD5 hash value is the value UEB34mid@#9C.

    b. The key number is 1, which will be sent by the NTP server in all packets. The key of UEB34mid@#9C is used to create an MD5 keyed hash value to verify the server message.

    c. The key number is 1, which is locally significant and allows the creation of multiple trusted keys per server. The key of UEB34mid@#9C is used to create an MD5 keyed hash value to verify the server message.

    d. None of these answers are correct. This is not a valid command string.

4. Consider the following command:

`ntp server 10.0.0.5 key 1 source inside prefer`

What is the meaning of the word "prefer" in this command?

    a. This NTP server is preferred over all other time sources.

    b. The ASA prefers the use of NTP authentication key 1 over other keys in the key ring.

    c. The ASA prefers the use of NTP authentication using key 1, but is willing to accept unauthenticated NTP messages from this server.

    d. This NTP server is preferred over other time sources of similar accuracy, but can be overridden by a more accurate time source.

    e. None of these answers are correct. This is not a valid command string.

5. What are the two major classifications of ASA events? (Choose two.)

    a. System events

    b. Security events

    c. Network events

    d. Syslog events

    e. None of these answers are correct. This is not a valid command string.

6. Consider the following partial event message:

```
Jan 5 2011 09:27:16 FIREWALL : %ASA-6-725002: Device completed ...
```

What is the severity level of this event message?

a. Notifications

b. Informational

c. Warnings

d. Debugging

e. Errors

7. Which version of NetFlow is supported by the ASA?

a. 9

b. 2

c. 7.2

d. 5

8. If the internal buffer logging destination becomes full, which two locations can its contents be copied to, to ensure no loss of information?

a. An HTTP server

b. An FTP server

c. Internal flash memory

d. A TFTP server

e. An SCP server

9. How are time stamps enabled/disabled for logging event messages to destinations?

a. Once, globally, by navigating to **Configuration > Device Management > Logging > Syslog Setup**.

b. Once, globally, by navigating to **Configuration > Device Management > Logging > Logging Setup**.

c. Once, globally, but this can be done only from the CLI.

d. Per log destination, by navigating to **Configuration > Device Management > Logging >** *screen for destination being configured*.

e. Per log destination, but this can be done only from the CLI interface

10. You want to change the level at which message 106018 is logged to Notifications, from its default setting. The message will be sent to your syslog server destination. Which of the following is the correct command syntax?

a. **logging trap message 106018 level Notifications**

b. **message 106018 syslog level Notifications**

c. **logging message 106018 level Notifications**

d. **logging level Notifications message 106018**

e. **logging message 106018 new level Notifications**

11. What is an event list? (Choose all that apply.)

   a. A grouping of messages, based on which logging subsystem generated the events in the list.

   b. A reusable group of messages, selected by a combination of event class, event severity, and separately by message IDs.

   c. A filter, used to determine which messages generated by the logging subsystem are forwarded to a particular log destination.

   d. All of these answers are correct.

12. You want to configure logging so that email messages are sent to administrators when events of maximum level Errors are generated by the system. Which of the following is the correct syntax for the command you need to use?

   a. logging smtp Errors

   b. logging trap smtp Errors

   c. logging email Errors

   d. logging trap email Errors

   e. logging mail Errors

   f. logging trap mail Errors

13. You want to verify that the ASA is sending NetFlow v9 records to the configured NetFlow collector. Which of these items will do that?

   a. Use the **show logging** command and look for a nonzero number as **messages logged** for the NetFlow destination.

   b. Use the **show logging** command and look for a nonzero number as **packets sent** for the NetFlow destination.

   c. Use the **show flow-export counters** command and look for a non-zero number as **messages logged**.

   d. Use the **show flow-export counters** command and look for a nonzero number as **packets sent**.

14. You suspect your syslog server is not receiving all messages generated by the ASA, possibly due to excessive logging leading to a queue overflow. What command would you use to verify your suspicions?

   a. show logging

   b. show logging queue

   c. show logging drops

   d. show logging queue drops

Foundation Topics

This chapter discusses methods for gathering information on network or device activity, including the use of system event logs. It also discusses how to ensure accurate time on the system clock because accurate time stamps on gathered information are critical to properly analyzing that information.

The FIREWALL exam focuses on practical, hands-on skills that are used by a networking professional. You are expected to be familiar with how to configure various features either from the ASDM GUI or from the CLI and to be able to use either for verification and troubleshooting. This being the case, this book shows the use of both tools, primarily configuring an ASA using ASDM, and recapping the equivalent CLI commands for each section.

System Time

Having a correct time set on a Cisco ASA is important for a number of reasons. Possibly the most important reason is that digital certificates compare this time to the range defined by their Valid From and Valid To fields to define a specific validity period. Having a correct time set is also important when logging information with the **timestamp** option. Whether you are sending messages to a syslog server, sending messages to an SNMP monitoring station, or performing packet captures, time stamps have little usefulness if you cannot be certain of their accuracy.

The default ASA time zone is set to UTC (Coordinated Universal Time), but you can add local time zone information so that the time displayed by the ASA is more relevant to those who are viewing it. Even if you set local time zone information, the ASA internally tracks time as UTC, so if it is interacting with hosts in other time zones (which is fairly common when using digital certificates for VPN connectivity, for example), they have a common frame of reference.

To set the time locally on the ASA (that is, not using Network Time Protocol [NTP]), first navigate to **Configuration > Device Setup > System Time > Clock** to display the Clock settings window, shown in Figure 6-1. If you want to set the clock to UTC time, simply enter a new date and time, as UTC is the default time zone. If you prefer to set the clock using your local time zone, choose that time zone from the drop-down list before you enter a new date and time. (Figure 6-1 shows the North American Central Time Zone being selected.)

You can then set the date and time accordingly. Time is set as hours, minutes, and seconds, in 24-hour format. Optionally, you can click the Update Displayed Time button to update the time shown in the bottom-right corner of the Cisco ASDM status bar. The current time updates automatically every ten seconds. The example assumes that the current time is manually set. Click **Apply** to complete the setting of the internal clock.

The configured time is retained in memory when the power is off, by a battery on the ASA motherboard.

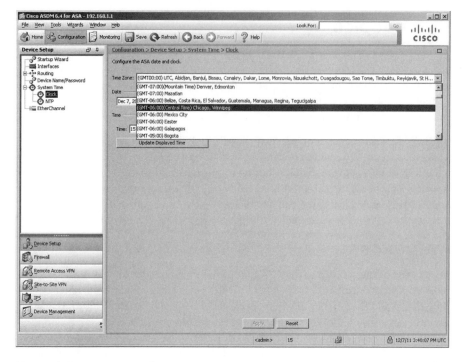

Figure 6-1 *Setting Local Time Parameters*

The CLI commands generated by the changes made are as follows:

```
clock set 09:58:26 DEC 7 2011
clock timezone CST -6 0
clock summer-time CDT recurring 2 Sun Mar 2:00 1 Sun Nov 2:00 60
```

If you are configuring the ASA from the CLI, you can enter these commands directly in global configuration mode. (The **clock set** command can actually be entered from privileged mode as well.)

The **clock set** command is used to manually set the ASA date and time information. It can be used from the CLI in privileged EXEC mode (use of configuration mode is not necessary). When setting from the CLI, the date can be specified as MONTH DAY YEAR or DAY MONTH YEAR—whichever you prefer.

The **clock timezone** command defines a name for your local time zone (in Standard Time) and its offset from UTC in hours (the -6 in the example) and in minutes (the 0 in the example) if you live in a time zone with an offset that is not in whole hours.

The **clock summer-time** command defines a name for your local time zone (in DST), and uses the keyword **recurring** to set a recurring range, defined as a day and time of a given month, rather than a specific date, so that you do not need to alter the setting yearly. Use it to set the beginning and ending days and times for DST in your time zone (in the example, DST begins on the second Sunday in March at 2 a.m. and ends on the first Sunday of November at 2 a.m.) and the DST offset from Standard Time (in the example, 60 minutes).

Note: Because of the change in dates on which Daylight Savings Time (DST) begins and ends in the United States, effective 2007, the beginning and ending dates when using the **recurring** keyword are different for older OS versions and might not align with DST periods in other countries. You might want to consider verifying the configured period for DST, especially for ASAs that will be operated outside of the United States. You may do so by using the **show clock detail** command.

NTP

Of course, to ensure precise synchronization of the ASA's clock to the rest of your network, you should configure the ASA to obtain time information from a trusted NTP server. To do so, navigate to **Configuration > Device Setup > System Time > NTP**. The NTP settings window opens. To define a new NTP time source, click **Add** to open the Add NTP Server Configuration dialog box, as shown in Figure 6-2. Define the IP address of the new NTP time source, the ASA interface through which this NTP server can be reached, whether this is a preferred time source, and any information relevant to the use of authenticated NTP communication.

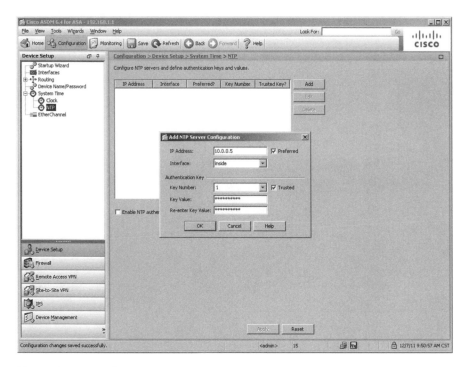

Figure 6-2 *Configuring an NTP Server*

Figure 6-2 shows the configuration of an internal NTP server, 10.0.0.5, which is preferred to other NTP sources and uses NTP authentication for added security. To use NTP authentication, both the server and any clients must be configured with the same trusted key number and key (effectively, a password). The key number must be included in NTP packets from the server in order for the ASA to accept synchronization to that server. The key is used to create a keyed hash for verification that NTP advertisements are from an authorized source, and have not been tampered with. You must check the **Trusted** check box for the configured key ID for authentication to work. You must also check the **Enable NTP Authentication** box at the bottom of the NTP server window (shown in the background in Figure 6-2).

Note: The ASA can act only as an NTP client, not as an NTP server.

You can configure additional NTP servers (a minimum of three associations is recommended for optimal accuracy and redundancy). Figure 6-3 shows the result of configuring 192.43.244.18 (time.nist.gov) as an additional NTP server. (It is not set as preferred and does not use authentication.) Note that you can enter only IP addresses when defining NTP servers, not logical names to be resolved to IP addresses via DNS.

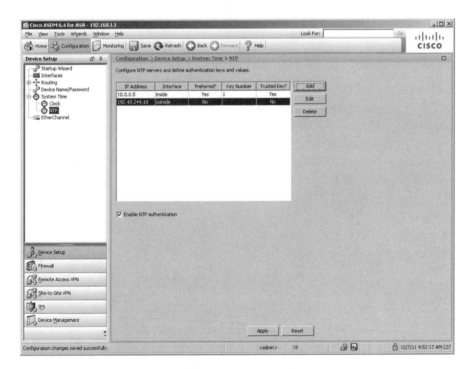

Figure 6-3 *Configuring Multiple NTP Servers*

Using an NTP server reachable through the outside interface, and not using authentication, is inherently subject to potential compromise, so it should be done only as a backup to an internal NTP server, if available. Note also that, because NTP Authentication is enabled on this ASA, time would not currently be accepted from the TIME.NIST.GOV server, because it is not configured for authenticated NTP messaging. Thus, the addition of this server is for example purposes only.

Time derived from an NTP server overrides any time set manually in the Clock pane. However, in the unlikely event of an extended period of unavailability of any configured NTP servers, the local clock can serve as a fallback mechanism for maintaining time on the ASA. Setting a server as preferred does not guarantee that the ASA will accept the time advertised by such a server. The ASA will choose the NTP server with the lowest stratum number and synchronize to that server. A stratum number indicates the distance from the reference clock, so a lower stratum number implies that a server is more reliable than others with a higher stratum number. The atomic clock at NIST, for instance, is considered stratum 0. If several servers have similar accuracy, the preferred server is used. If another server is significantly more accurate than the preferred server, however, the ASA uses the more accurate one.

Key Topic

The CLI commands generated by the changes made are as follows:

```
ntp server 10.0.0.5 key 1 source inside prefer
ntp server 192.43.244.18 source outside
ntp authenticate
ntp authentication-key 1 md5 UEB34mid@#9C
ntp trusted-key 1
```

If you are configuring the ASA from the CLI, you can enter these commands directly in global configuration mode.

Note that if you set the time zone using ASDM, the use of Daylight Saving Time (DST) is automatically enabled, if appropriate, with the correct date and time parameters for the selected time zone. To alter the start and end dates of DST, should they be incorrect, you would need to make the change from the CLI.

The **ntp server** command defines a server to be used as a time source by the ASA. This command sets the server IP address, authentication key number (if used), source interface, and whether or not it is a preferred server.

To enable authentication with an NTP server, you must use the **ntp authenticate** command from global configuration mode. The **ntp authentication-key** command ties the key number to the specific key used to create an MD5 keyed hash for source validation and integrity check. For NTP authentication to succeed, any key ID to be accepted by the ASA must be defined as trusted. This is done using the **ntp trusted-key** command.

Key Topic

Verifying System Time Settings

System time can be verified using two commands, **show clock** and **show ntp associations**. Both have an optional keyword of **detail**. Example 6-1 shows the use of both the standard and detailed version of the **show clock** command.

Example 6-1 *Verifying System Time with* **show** clock

```
FIREWALL# show clock

10:03:16.309 CST Wed Dec 7 2011
```

```
FIREWALL# show clock detail

10:03:55.129 CST Wed Dec 7 2011
Time source is NTP
UTC time is:  16:03:55 UTC Wed Dec 7 2011
Summer time starts 02:00:00 CST Sun Mar 11 2012
Summer time ends 02:00:00 CDT Sun Nov 4 2012
```

As shown in the example, using the **detail** keyword with the **show clock** command adds information on the time source, and the local time zone DST information. Using **show clock detail** also adds the display of UTC time, as a non-local reference. (This is a recent change and was not the case in earlier versions of the OS.) Note the source of NTP in this example.

Example 6-2 shows the use of the **show ntp associations** command, which displays the configured NTP server and whether the ASA is successfully synced.

Example 6-2   *Verifying System Time with show ntp associations*

```
FIREWALL# show ntp associations

      address        ref clock    st  when  poll reach  delay  offset   disp
*~10.0.0.5         0.0.0.0         4    87  1024  377    2.5   -0.23    1.8
-~192.43.244.18    .ACTS.          1   147  1024  377   41.5   -1.08   16.5
* master (synced), # master (unsynced), + selected, - candidate, ~ configured
```

Managing Event and Session Logging

The ASA supports a full audit trail of system log messages that describe its activities and security events. The two major classifications of events are *system events*, such as resource depletion, and *network events*, such as denied sessions or packets. These messages are used to create log files, which can be filtered and sent to a number of different destinations for storage, display, or analysis.

Figure 6-4 provides a graphical illustration of the ASA logging subsystem, showing the two major event classifications as sources, and the eight possible destinations.

The ASA supports sending log messages to the following destinations:

■ **Console:** The ASA console, a low-bandwidth serial connection to which messages can be sent for display on a console CLI session. This mode is useful for limited debugging, or in production environments with limited traffic or a lack of centralized management tools.

Logging Sources and Destinations

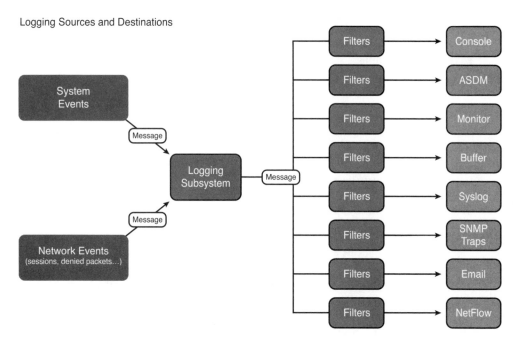

Figure 6-4   *ASA Logging Subsystem*

- **ASDM:** The ASDM graphical user interface, which provides a powerful real-time event viewer useful for troubleshooting issues or monitoring network activity.

- **Monitor:** Telnet or SSH administrative sessions. This mode is useful to receive real-time debugging information when troubleshooting.

- **Buffered:** The internal in-memory buffer on the ASA. Although useful for storage and analysis of recent activity, the internal buffer is limited in size, and it is not persistent across appliance reboots. The buffer can optionally be archived to an external FTP server or to the ASA's internal flash memory.

- **Host:** Remote syslog servers, using the standard syslog protocol. Use the **logging host** command in conjunction with the **logging trap** command to define both a destination server and a logging level.

- **SNMP:** Remote network management servers, using the standard Simple Network Management Protocol (SNMP) Trap to send event messages. This mode is configured with the **snmp-server enable traps syslog** command, rather than directly with a **logging** *destination* command.

- **Mail:** Remote email systems, using the standard Simple Mail Transfer Protocol (SMTP) to send event messages to a defined SMTP server, or set of SMTP servers.

- **Flow-export-syslogs:** Remote NetFlow collectors, using the standard NetFlow v9 protocol to send event messages to the defined collector.

NetFlow Support

Cisco NetFlow efficiently provides a key set of services for IP applications, including network traffic accounting, usage-based network billing, network planning, security, denial-of-service monitoring capabilities, and network monitoring. NetFlow provides valuable information about network users and applications, peak usage times, and traffic routing.

The basic output of NetFlow is known as a flow record. Several different formats for flow records have existed as NetFlow has evolved and matured. The current version of NetFlow formatting is known as NetFlow version 9. The ASA supports providing NetFlow Secure Event Logging (NSEL), beginning with version 8.2(1). NSEL allows specific, high-volume, traffic-related events to be exported from the ASA in a more efficient and scalable manner than that provided by standard syslog logging. You may use any NetFlow v9–capable collector to receive ASA NetFlow data.

The ASA implementation of NSEL is a stateful, IP flow tracking method that exports only those records that indicate significant events in a flow. In stateful flow tracking, tracked flows go through a series of state changes. NSEL events are used to export data about flow status, and are triggered by the events that cause state changes. Examples of events that are tracked include flow-create, flow-teardown, and flow-denied (excluding flows that are denied by EtherType ACLs, which are discussed in Chapter 12, "Using Transparent Firewall Mode"). Each NSEL record has an event ID and an extended event ID field, which describe the flow event.

The ASA supports multiple NetFlow export destinations and can therefore store its NetFlow information on multiple NetFlow collectors.

For a detailed discussion on ASA NetFlow event generation, consult "Cisco ASA 5500 Series Implementation Note for NetFlow Collectors, 8.2," at www.cisco.com/en/US/docs/security/asa/asa82/netflow/netflow.html.

Logging Message Format

Most ASA messages generated by the logging subsystem are simple text messages that conform to a particular message format, as demonstrated here:

```
Jan 5 2011 09:27:16 FIREWALL : %ASA-6-725002: Device completed SSL handshake with
    client management:192.168.1.108/49287
```

This message consists of the following:

■ An optional **timestamp** (disabled by default)

■ An optional **device-id** (disabled by default), which can include the interface name, IP address, hostname, context name, or a custom string up to 16 characters, if configured

■ A message identifier (**%ASA-6-725002** in the example), which identifies the device type (ASA), the message severity level (6, Informational), and the event message number (725002)

■ The message text (**Device completed SSL handshake...**)

Additional data may be added to the message, depending on its destination. For example, a time stamp and hostname may be added for the syslog destination.

Message Severity

Each log message is assigned a severity level that indicates its relative importance. Lower numbers are of higher severity than higher numbers. Possible number and string values for message severity are shown in Table 6-2.

Table 6-2 *Message Severity Levels*

Key
Topic

Numeric Level	Equivalent String	Definition
0	Emergencies	Extremely critical "system unusable" messages
1	Alerts	Messages that require immediate administrator action
2	Critical	A critical condition
3	Errors	An error message (also the level of many access list deny messages)
4	Warnings	A warning message (also the level of many other access list deny messages)
5	Notifications	A normal but significant condition (such as an interface coming online)
6	Informational	An informational message (such as a session being created or torn down)
7	Debugging	A debug message or detailed accounting message

Note: Take care in setting the severity level of messages being sent to various destinations, particularly the console. Too low a severity (a high number), when coupled with a lot of traffic, can severely impact system performance, or potentially exhaust system resources, and make it difficult or impossible to regain access to the device CLI. It is important to remember that the ASA will send all messages of the selected level and all higher severity (lower number) messages, not just messages of the configured level.

Configuring Event and Session Logging

Configuring event and session logging consists of some or all of the following tasks:

- Globally enabling system logging and configuring global logging properties

- Optionally, disabling logging of specific messages

- Optionally, changing the severity level of specific messages

- Optionally, configuring message event filters that will govern which system messages to send to particular destinations

- Configuring event destinations and specifying message filters that apply to each of those destinations

Configuring Global Logging Properties

To globally enable system logging and set general logging properties, navigate in ASDM to **Configuration > Device Management > Logging > Logging Setup**. The Logging Setup pane opens, as shown in Figure 6-5. In this pane, you can set several global logging properties.

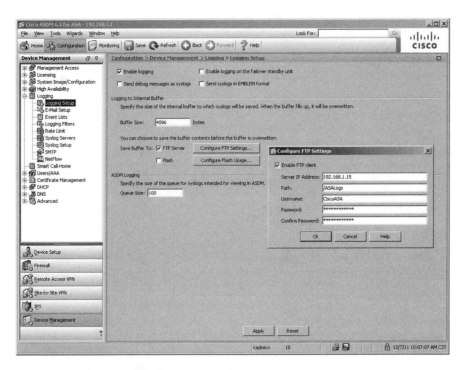

Figure 6-5 *Setting Global Logging Parameters*

In Figure 6-5, the Enable Logging check box is selected. This is necessary because, by default, all logging on the ASA is disabled. Options within this same pane, none of which are selected in the figure, are as follows:

- **Enable logging on the failover standby unit:** Check this box to enable logging for a standby ASA, if one exists. By default, if this box is not checked, only severity level 1 messages are available on the standby unit (severity level 1 messages on the standby unit are related to failover events). Failover configurations are discussed in Chapter 14, "Deploying High Availability Features."

- **Send debug messages as syslogs:** Check this box to redirect all debug output to system logs. By default, debug output is not included in system log messages. Checking this box redirects debug messages to logs as syslog message 711001, with severity level 7. Use care with this option because it can generate a tremendous amount of logging information, depending on what is being debugged.

- **Send syslogs in EMBLEM format:** Check this box to enable Cisco EMBLEM format for all log destinations other than syslog servers. EMBLEM format is designed to be consistent with the Cisco IOS format. Many event management solutions will not recognize EMBLEM format messages, however. It is used primarily for the CiscoWorks Resource Manager Essentials (RME) Syslog Analyzer.

In Figure 6-5, the Buffer Size setting is left at the default of 4096 bytes (valid sizes are from 4096 to 1,048,576 bytes). This pertains to the internal buffer, maintained in memory. When this buffer gets full, it is overwritten in circular fashion, with each new message overwriting the oldest message in the buffer. If you do not want to lose information to these overwrites, there are two options for preserving buffered log messages: sending the buffer contents to an FTP server or saving them to internal flash memory. In Figure 6-5, the check box for FTP Server is checked, and the Configure FTP Settings button has been clicked, opening the Configure FTP Settings dialog box, seen on the right side of the figure.

To enable saving of buffer contents to an FTP server, in the Configure FTP Settings dialog box, check the **Enable FTP Client** check box and configure information on the FTP server address, directory path for storing buffer log contents, and a username and password used to log in to the FTP server. In Figure 6-5, a server is defined in the out-of-band (OOB) management network, at IP address 192.168.1.15; the /ASALogs directory of the FTP server is used for storage; the username is set to CiscoASA; and a password of CCNPSecurity is entered twice, the second time to verify it is entered correctly. Clicking OK would complete the FTP server definition.

If you were saving buffered log contents to internal flash memory, you would need to define two parameters: the maximum amount of flash memory to be used for storing log information, and the minimum free space to be preserved in flash memory. Selecting this option creates a directory named "syslog" on the device disk on which messages are stored.

Finally, Figure 6-5 leaves the default queue size of 100 for messages retained in the ASDM log buffer. The ASDM log buffer is a different buffer than the internal log buffer.

Once the FTP server window is completed and saved, clicking Apply in the Logging Setup pane will send the new settings to the ASA.

The CLI commands generated by the changes made are as follows:

```
logging enable
logging ftp-bufferwrap
logging ftp-server 192.168.1.15 /ASALogs CiscoASA CCNPSecurity
```

If you are configuring the ASA from the CLI, you can enter these commands directly in global configuration mode.

Two other settings that are global for syslog messages are the syslog Facility Code and whether messages carry a time stamp when sent by the ASA. These settings are not made in the same pane in which the other settings are made.

To modify these settings, navigate to **Configuration > Device Management > Logging > Syslog Setup**. This pane is shown in Figure 6-6. In the Syslog Format area, at the top of the pane, you can set the Facility Code and enable/disable time stamps.

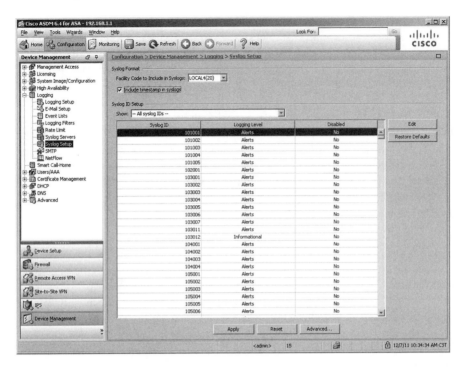

Figure 6-6 *Syslog Setup Pane*

In Figure 6-6, the default syslog Facility Code of LOCAL4(20) is left unchanged. Syslog Facility Codes are included in messages sent to syslog servers. The codes are used by syslog servers to organize event messages as they arrive. Eight logging facilities are available, LOCAL0 to LOCAL7 (if set in decimal only, 16–23). LOCAL4(20) is the default setting for all ASA syslog events. In the figure, the check box to enable time stamps is selected. Click **Apply** to send the change to the ASA.

The CLI command generated by the change is as follows:

```
logging timestamp
```

If you are configuring the ASA from the CLI, you can enter this command directly in global configuration mode.

Altering Settings of Specific Messages

Sometimes, a default system message does not contain any useful information, or the default severity assigned to a message is not suitable to a particular environment. In such cases, you can tune individual system messages by globally suppressing them or by altering their default severity. You tune these aspects in the Syslog Setup pane, too.

The Syslog ID Setup area comprises most of the Syslog Setup pane. The first option available is to change what message IDs are displayed in the main portion of this area. The default option is to display all syslog message IDs. Other options available in the Show drop-down list are as follows:

■ **Disabled syslog IDs:** Display only message IDs that have been explicitly suppressed.

■ **Syslog IDs with changed logging:** Display only message IDs with severity levels that have been changed from their default values.

■ **Syslog IDs that are suppressed or with a changed logging level:** Display all message IDs that have been modified by being suppressed or having their default level modified.

To modify a specific message ID, still in the Syslog Setup window, click the message to select it, and then click the **Edit** button to open the Edit Syslog ID Settings dialog box, shown in Figure 6-7. In this dialog box, you can suppress (disable) a particular message or change its configured logging level.

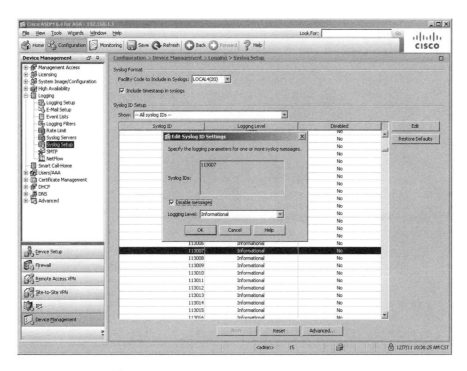

Figure 6-7   *Disabling a Message ID*

In Figure 6-7, message ID 113007 has been selected for editing, and the Disable Messages check box has been selected. Clicking **OK** will configure global suppression of this particular message. Message 113007 is generated when a locked user account is unlocked by an administrator, and in this scenario, it has been decided that this information is unimportant—what is important is to log when an account is locked for excessive incorrect password attempts.

Note: There is a difference between suppressing a message ID and filtering it (covered later). If a message ID is disabled, the ASA will not generate that particular message to any logging destination. Filtering a message is a means of not delivering a particular message to a particular logging destination, but the ASA still generates the message, and can deliver it to other destinations.

There are times when you may want to log a particular message ID, but alter the severity level at which it is reported. You do so from the same Edit Syslog ID Settings dialog box. Click a message to select it, and then click the **Edit** button. Figure 6-8 shows an example of modifying the severity level of a syslog message.

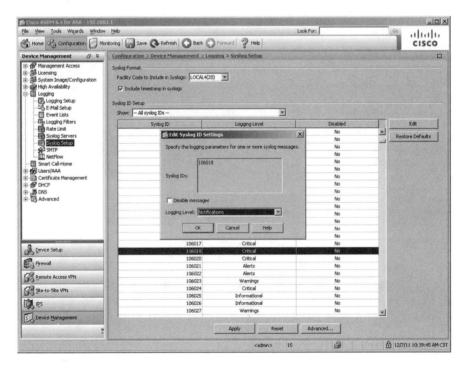

Figure 6-8   *Modifying a Syslog Message Severity Level*

In Figure 6-8, message ID 106018 has been selected for modification. As you can see in the background, the default setting for this message ID is Critical (2). This particular message is generated if an ICMP packet is denied by an outgoing access list. Because outgoing filters do not exist by default on the ASA, this means an administrator explicitly configured the ASA to block such packets. However, given that an internal user generating a ping that is dropped by the ASA would generate such a message, in this scenario it has been decided to alter the level from Critical to Notifications (5). Click **OK** to complete the modification of this message, and then click **Apply** to send these changes to the ASA.

The CLI commands generated by the changes made are as follows:

```
logging message 106018 level Notifications
no logging message 113007
```

If you are configuring the ASA from the CLI, you can enter these commands directly in global configuration mode.

Configuring Event Filters

For each logging destination, you can configure filters (known as *event lists*) that determine which subset of all generated messages will be forwarded to that destination. You can configure such filters based on the following:

- **Event (message) severity only:** For example, by specifying a maximum severity of 4 (Warnings), all messages with a severity of Warnings or higher (severity levels 0 through 4) would be forwarded to the logging destination. All messages with severities of 5 through 7 would be dropped.

- **Event classes:** All system messages are grouped into event classes based on the subsystem that created the messages. For example, there is an event class for the Authentication subsystem.

- **A combination of event class and event severity:** For example, all Authentication messages with a maximum severity of 4 (Warnings).

- **The message ID:** Each message has a unique message ID. Therefore, you can select individual messages for forwarding to particular logging destinations.

Event lists are reusable groups of messages, which can be selected by a combination of event class and severity, or individually by message ID. When you create an event list, you can apply that same event list to multiple logging destinations, thus simplifying the configuration of message filters.

To create an event list, navigate to **Configuration > Device Management > Logging > Event Lists.** Click **Add** to create a new event list. This opens the Add Event List dialog box, which is shown in Figure 6-9. You assign a unique name to each event list, and then configure the parameters that define your desired filter.

In Figure 6-9, a name of ALERT-ADMIN-BY-EMAIL has been defined. The Add button in the Event Class/Severity Filters area was clicked to open the Add Class and Severity Filter dialog box, in which a specific class and severity can be defined. In this example, All Event Classes has been selected, and a severity level of Alerts (1) has been selected. In this scenario, it has been determined that any syslog message of severity 0 or 1 should generate an immediate email notification to an administrator (setup of the SMTP log destination is covered in the "Email" section of this chapter). This event list will accommodate such a configuration. Click **OK** twice to complete the configuration of the event class filter and the creation of the event list. Finally, click **Apply** to send the configuration to the ASA.

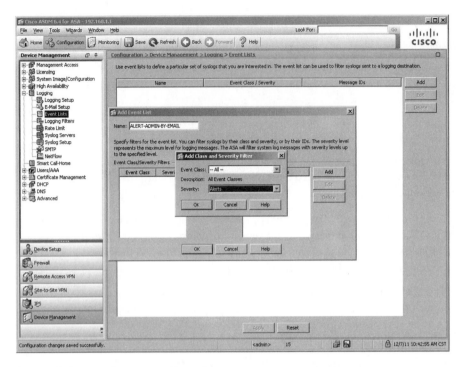

Figure 6-9   *Configuring an Event List*

The CLI command generated by the change is as follows:

```
logging list ALERT-ADMIN-BY-EMAIL level Alerts
```

If you are configuring the ASA from the CLI, you can enter this command directly in global configuration mode.

Configuring Individual Event Destinations

After you have enabled logging globally, optionally set up global logging properties, and optionally configured event lists, you can configure the ASA to send logging messages to one or more logging destinations. For each destination, you specify a filter that will select a subset of generated messages to be forwarded to that destination.

To configure logging destinations and filters, navigate to **Configuration > Device Management > Logging > Logging Filters**. In the Logging Filters pane that opens, you can activate logging to any of the eight available destinations and configure filters that determine which generated messages are forwarded to each.

Internal Buffer

The first example will be to configure the internal buffer as a logging destination. In the Logging Filters pane, select the **Internal Buffer** destination, and click **Edit** to open the Edit Logging Filters dialog box, as shown in Figure 6-10.

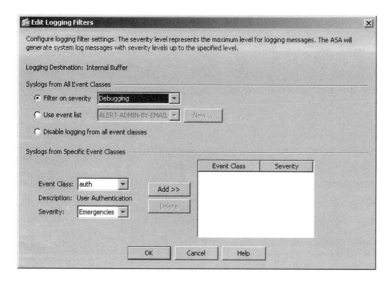

Figure 6-10 *Configuring the Internal Buffer Logging Filter*

As you can see in Figure 6-10, you have several options for determining the logging filter for a particular log destination. To create a filter that applies to all event classes, choose one of the following radio buttons in the top, Syslogs from All Event Classes area:

- **Filter on severity:** Filters system log messages by their severity level, and allows you to specify the level of messages that should be forwarded to the log destination. In Figure 6-10, this choice is selected, and the filter level is set to Debugging, which sends all system messages to the destination being configured (internal buffer). Depending on traffic, this particular choice can overwhelm the destination service (especially the console) or the user attempting to analyze events. You should carefully consider the impact of your choice before applying the configuration to the ASA. If you wish to log all messages from all severity levels, it is strongly recommended that you do so to the internal buffer, and never to the console. In fact, it is generally recommended to leave console logging disabled.

- **Use event list:** Filters system log messages based on a previously defined event list, and allows you to specify which event list to use, or create a new event list.

- **Disable logging from all event classes:** Disables all forwarding of system messages to the destination being configured.

You can also create specific logging filters in this dialog box by entering the filter criteria in the Syslogs from Specific Event Classes area. This is equivalent to creating an event list for just this specific logging destination.

Click **OK** to complete the configuration of a logging filter to the internal buffer logging destination. Click **Apply** to send the modified settings to the ASA.

The CLI command generated by the change made is as follows:

```
logging buffered Debugging
```

If you are configuring the ASA from the CLI, you can enter this command directly in global configuration mode.

ASDM

Cisco ASDM contains a powerful event viewer that you can use to display a real-time message feed from the ASA. This event viewer is particularly useful when you are troubleshooting ASA software and configuration issues, or when you are monitoring real-time activity over the ASA.

You enable logging to the internal ASDM event viewer by configuring the ASDM logging destination and specifying a logging filter, in the same manner as for other logging destinations. Messages are forwarded to ASDM over the HTTPS session and are displayed in a log viewer window at the bottom of the ASDM Home page.

This example assumes that the ASDM logging destination has been configured to receive messages from all event classes, containing a maximum severity level of Informational. Click **Apply** to send the modified settings to the ASA.

The CLI command generated by the change made is as follows:

```
logging asdm Informational
```

If you are configuring the ASA from the CLI, you can enter this command directly in global configuration mode.

Key Topic

To use the full event viewer functionality, start the viewer by navigating in ASDM to **Monitoring > Logging > Real-Time Log Viewer**, selecting a logging level, and clicking the **View** button. The ASDM Real-Time Log Viewer opens in a dedicated window and starts displaying log messages as selected by the configured message filter. Figure 6-11 shows an example of the Real-Time Log Viewer.

In the Real-Time Log Viewer, you can set additional keyword-based filtering by entering a keyword in the Filter By field in the log viewer toolbar. Above this field are toolbar icons that can be used to pause, resume, and clear the event display, copy individual messages to the clipboard, and set message colors.

The log viewer interface also allows you to select a particular message, and invoke various options by right-clicking it. You can, for example, show or even create specific access rules based on log messages. For example, if a log message showed that a packet had been denied by an access rule, you could immediately create a rule to allow such packets in the future. Or, for all session-related messages, you could right-click the interface and select Show Access Rule to jump immediately to the table of access rules and to the exact rule permitting or denying this particular connection.

At the bottom of the Real-Time Log Viewer, a context-sensitive help window shows message descriptions, recommends actions to administrators, and offers full message details. This is the only tool in ASDM that provides an administrator with such detailed explanations of log messages. Additionally, the suggestion of remedies is an invaluable aid in rapid troubleshooting and resolution of identified problems.

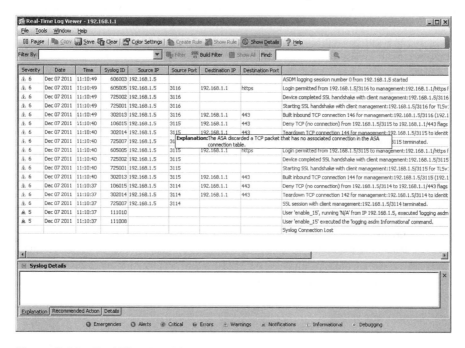

Figure 6-11   *Real-Time Log Viewer*

You can also use ASDM to view a snapshot of the current appliance internal log buffer, by navigating to **Monitor > Logging > Log Buffer**, selecting a maximum severity level, and clicking View.

Syslog Server(s)

Probably the most common destination to configure for log messages is one or more syslog servers in your network. Configuring the ASA to send log messages to syslog servers enables you to easily archive logs, limited only by the available disk space on the remote syslog server. You can specify up to 16 syslog servers as log destinations. Further, the ASA can deliver syslog messages to servers using either UDP (standard syslog) or TCP (specialized for firewall syslog) as transport protocols.

Prior to ASA software version 8.0, all syslog messages were transferred in clear text. Beginning with software version 8.0(2), support was introduced for secure logging, using a SSL/TLS transport layer between the ASA and syslog servers. Certificate-based authentication and encrypted data transfer help mitigate security threats to the logging service when messages are crossing an untrusted network. To use secure logging, you must set up an SSL/TLS connection between the ASA and a remote syslog server supporting SSL/TLS. Also, the SSL syslog server must be added to the ASA as a certificate trust point. Configuration of secure logging is not covered in this book, but more information can be obtained from the *Cisco ASDM User Guide* available at Cisco.com.

Key Topic

When an ASA is configured to use TCP-based syslog to at least one syslog server, by default, the ASA will drop all traffic attempting to go through the appliance if the TCP-based syslog server is down or unable to record further messages in its logs (that is, it is out of disk space). This feature is designed to prevent traffic from traversing an ASA that is unable to log security events, a common requirement in high-security networks. Use this feature if your local security policy requires this level of risk control.

Note: Even if an ASA is dropping all transit traffic because of the failure of TCP-based syslog connectivity, it still allows traffic terminating at the ASA itself. For instance, you can still SSH into the ASA and execute commands that allow you to determine this as the cause of all traffic being dropped.

To configure (non-SSL/TLS) syslog servers as log destinations, navigate to **Configuration > Device Management > Logging > Syslog Servers**. In the Syslog Servers pane, click **Add** to define a new syslog server log destination. The Add Syslog Server dialog box opens, as shown in Figure 6-12. Here, you define which interface the ASA uses to reach the server, the server's IP address, whether to use TCP or UDP as the transport protocol, the destination port on the server, and, optionally, the use of EMBLEM format (only if using UDP) or SSL/TLS encryption (only if using TCP).

Figure 6-12   *Adding a Syslog Server Destination*

In Figure 6-12, a syslog server is defined, reachable through the management interface (in the OOB management network), using IP address 192.168.1.7, and standard UDP-based syslog transport to port 514 (the default UDP port; the default TCP port is 1470). Click **OK** to complete the configuration of this server.

If you are using TCP-based syslog, you have the option to allow user traffic to traverse the ASA even when the TCP syslog server is down. To do so, in the main Syslog Servers pane, check the **Allow User Traffic to Pass when TCP Syslog Server Is Down** check box and then click **Apply** to send the new server definitions to the ASA. Selecting this option generates the **logging permit-hostdown** command in the ASA configuration.

After you have defined one or more syslog servers, you must configure a logging filter for the destination syslog servers, before the ASA actually sends event messages to the configured servers. You do this the same way as covered previously. This example assumes that you have configured a logging filter to send all event classes, with a maximum severity of Warnings (4) to the logging destination of syslog servers.

The CLI commands generated by the changes made are as follows:

```
logging trap Warnings
logging host management 192.168.1.7
```

If you are configuring the ASA from the CLI, you can enter these commands directly in global configuration mode.

In most cases, using remote syslog servers as the primary method of reporting events to a central repository is recommended, as syslog is a widely supported and easily deployed logging protocol. Because UDP transport does not guarantee delivery, and should be used only over trusted or OOB networks, you should consider the use of TCP-based syslog when operating over a congested network subject to frequent packet loss. Also, consider the use of SSL/TLS if you are using untrusted ("sniffable") transport networks between the ASA and the syslog server.

Email

Sending log messages to an email system is useful, as it provides a simple way to integrate event notification with many messaging solutions, including simple email, mobile email, and SMS or pager systems, using appropriate gateways.

Configuring the ASA to send email notifications is similar to configuring syslog servers, in that you must first define how the ASA reaches intended recipients (sender and receiver addresses, SMTP servers, and so on), and then create a logging filter instructing the ASA to use email as a logging destination and what events to send.

To configure email sender and recipient addresses, navigate to **Configuration > Device Management > Logging > E-Mail Setup**. Enter a source email address in the provided field, and then click the **Add** button to add recipient information. Figure 6-13 shows an example, where a source address of ASA@CiscoPress.CCNP has been entered in the Source E-Mail Address field.

In the Add E-Mail Recipient dialog box, the Destination E-Mail Address field has been completed with Admin@CiscoPress.CCNP as the recipient. Finally, the maximum severity of event messages that should generate an email to this recipient is configured in the Syslog Severity field, as Alerts.

After you have configured recipients, you must configure the ASA with information about the SMTP server(s) through which the ASA will send email notifications. To do this, navigate to **Configuration > Device Management > Logging > SMTP**. The SMTP pane, as shown in Figure 6-14, is where you configure a primary and, optionally, secondary SMTP server address for the ASA to send email through.

Figure 6-14 shows an example where two SMTP servers on the inside network—10.0.0.15 as primary and 10.0.0.16 as secondary—are configured.

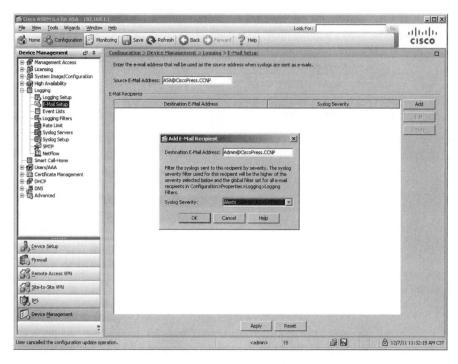

Figure 6-13 *Adding an Email Recipient*

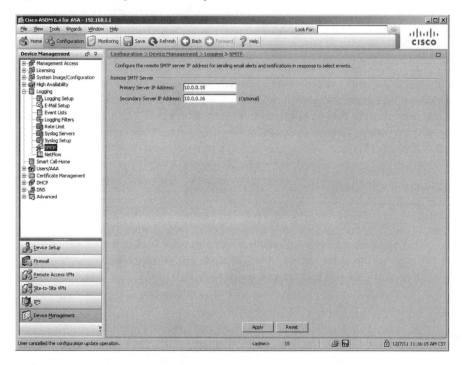

Figure 6-14 *Defining SMTP Servers*

After configuring sender and recipient addresses and SMTP servers, you configure email notifications just like any other logging destination. In this example, however, rather than simply setting a maximum severity for all event classes, Figure 6-15 shows the configuration of a logging filter for the E-Mail destination, using the previously created event list named ALERT-ADMIN-BY-EMAIL.

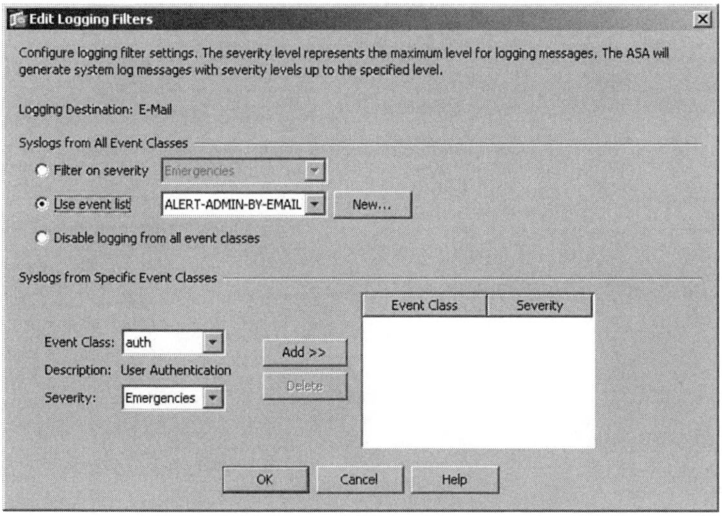

Figure 6-15 *Configuring Email Logging Filter*

It is important to limit the amount of notifications sent via email, so use this destination only for exceptional events of critical importance. In this example, recall that event list ALERT-ADMIN-BY-EMAIL was defined with a maximum severity level of Alerts (1). This example might be overly restrictive, so use an appropriate level based on your local security policy.

Click **OK** in the Edit Logging Filters dialog box, and then click **Apply** in the Logging Filters pane, to complete the configuration of email as a logging destination.

The CLI commands generated by the changes made are as follows:

```
logging mail ALERT-ADMIN-BY-EMAIL
smtp-server 10.0.0.15 10.0.0.16
logging from-address ASA@CiscoPress.CCNP
logging recipient-address Admin@CiscoPress.CCNP level Alerts
```

If you are configuring the ASA from the CLI, you can enter these commands directly in global configuration mode.

NetFlow

To configure NSEL in the ASA, you must first configure NetFlow export destinations by defining the location of NetFlow collectors. To do so, navigate to **Configuration > Device Management > Logging > NetFlow**. In the NetFlow window, shown in Figure 6-16, you can configure NetFlow destinations, and also some options that might impact performance with NetFlow export enabled.

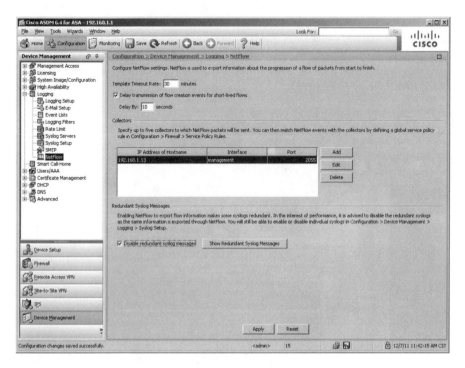

Figure 6-16   *Configuring NetFlow Settings*

In Figure 6-16, a NetFlow collector has been defined through the management interface, with IP address 192.168.1.13, and the default NetFlow port of UDP 2055. Additionally, the option Delay Transmission of Flow Creation Events for Short-Lived Flows has been enabled, and the delay set to 10 seconds. Finally, because use of NetFlow makes some syslog messages redundant, the option to Disable Redundant Syslog Messages has been selected. (Neither of the preceding options is enabled by default.)

Defining flows to be exported to NetFlow collectors is unique among logging destinations. With NSEL, you can granularly select which flows through the ASA are exported using NetFlow, based on flow properties such as IP addresses, protocols, and ports. You configure this selection using Cisco Modular Policy Framework (MPF) service policies, which are covered in Chapter 9, "Inspecting Traffic."

The CLI commands generated by the changes made are as follows:

```
no logging message 106015
no logging message 106023
...output omitted...
flow-export delay flow-create 10
flow-export destination management 192.168.1.13 2055
```

If you are configuring the ASA from the CLI, you can enter these commands directly in global configuration mode.

Telnet or SSH Sessions

To enable the ASA to display system event messages in Telnet or SSH sessions, you can configure a logging filter for the Telnet and SSH Sessions destination, like any other destination. This generates the **logging monitor** command in the ASA's configuration file. Although these messages are sent to the Telnet or SSH session, the user must also use the **terminal monitor** command to see the messages displayed in their remote terminal session.

Verifying Event and Session Logging

Only a few commands are used to verify the configuration and functionality of logging. Example 6-3 shows the use of the **show logging** command to see a summary of the logging configuration, along with any internally buffered log messages.

Example 6-3   *Verifying Logging*

```
FIREWALL# show logging

Syslog logging: enabled
     Facility: 20
     Timestamp logging: enabled
     Standby logging: disabled
     Debug-trace logging: disabled
     Console logging: disabled
     Monitor logging: disabled
     Buffer logging: level debugging, 5548 messages logged
     Trap logging: level warnings, facility 20, 2145 messages logged
         Logging to management 192.168.1.7
     History logging: disabled
     Device ID: disabled
     Mail logging: list ALERT-ADMIN-BY-EMAIL, 0 messages logged
     ASDM logging: level informational, 802 messages logged
Dec 07 2011 16:10:13 FIREWALL : %ASA-7-609001: Built local-host
  management:192.168.1.15
Dec 07 2011 16:10:23 FIREWALL : %ASA-7-609002: Teardown local-host
  management:192.168.1.15 duration 0:00:10
...output omitted...
```

The output shows several important pieces of information, which are shaded for easy reference. Logging is globally enabled. Time stamps are enabled. Console logging is disabled, as it should be on production devices, except in rare circumstances. For each configured destination, you can see the number of logged messages. Additionally, if you are using a TCP syslog server, the connection from the ASA to the syslog server will be shown.

At the end of the configuration summary, you will see the full contents of the internal log buffer. This output is truncated in the example.

To verify NetFlow export operation, use the **show flow-export counters** command, as shown in Example 6-4. A non-zero packets sent count will prove that the ASA is sending NetFlow v9 records to the configured NetFlow collector.

Example 6-4   *Verifying NetFlow Export*

```
FIREWALL# show flow-export counters

destination: management 192.168.1.13 2055
  Statistics:
    packets sent                                    14327
  Errors:
    block allocation failure                        0
    invalid interface                               0
    template send failure                           0
    no route to collector                           0
```

Implementation Guidelines

When implementing event and session logging, consider the following implementation guidelines:

- Depending on the requirements of your local security policy, some events can be deleted, archived, or partially archived. This depends on the amount of event history available for online retrieval, the need for long-term reporting, and regulatory and legal requirements, which might require a specific retention period or, conversely, not allow certain types of personal information to be stored in an event database or event archives. Therefore, you should create a log retention policy that will enable you to store appropriate logs for an appropriate amount of time.

- It is generally best to log too much information as opposed to too little. Gathering too much information typically is harmless, unless it causes performance or capacity issues, whereas gathering too little information might prevent you from having information necessary to respond effectively to incidents or to meet regulatory requirements.

- Tune logging to exclude duplicate information. Some events might be redundant or not needed in your local environment. Make sure you analyze the event feed thoroughly to review and confirm these duplicates.

- Use multiple destinations for logging, to increase reliability of the information gathered.

- Try to handle boundary conditions, such as excessive event rate and lack of storage space, appropriately and without interruptions to service. Monitoring should be regularly tested and validated for accuracy, to ensure that changes to the system have not disabled desired functionality.

- Synchronize the ASA clock to a reliable time source, to ensure trustworthy logging of time stamps.

■ Transport events over the network using reliable and secure channels, if possible. Use a trusted network, or at least authenticate and verify the integrity of messages. To ensure reliability and no packet loss, consider using TCP transport for log messages to remote servers.

■ To provide the most scalable remote event export in high-connection-rate environments, consider using NetFlow instead of syslog to report on network events.

■ Limit access to the ASA logging subsystem (so that logging cannot be disabled without detection), the central event database, and long-term event archives. Implement mechanisms to prevent or detect changes to stored event data.

■ Consider using an appliance-based logging server, especially when output from multiple sources will be collected, or where real-time event parsing along with event correlation might be required.

Troubleshooting Event and Session Logging

The recommended troubleshooting task flow when troubleshooting remote logging is as follows:

■ For remote logging, verify mutual connectivity between the ASA and the server using **ping**, **traceroute**, or similar tools.

■ If you are using a TCP syslog server with a fail-closed policy (the default), use the **show logging** command (shown in Example 6-3) to determine if the host is reachable.

■ Use **show logging** on the ASA to determine the configuration of the event source. Verify logging filters to ensure that they are not filtering out desired event messages. You can also use the **capture** command to verify that events are actually being sent through ASA interfaces. On the remote log destination, view stored logs and consider running a network analyzer to determine if events are arriving properly at the destination.

■ Finally, there could be a performance problem at the ASA that prevents it from sending messages to a destination. Use **show logging queue** (detailed in the next section) to examine the logging queue length and any drops, to determine if such a problem exists.

Troubleshooting Commands

Oversubscription of the logging queue indicates local performance issues. If you encounter oversubscription, consider logging less, rate-limiting a logging destination, tuning the logging queue, or using alternative logging methods such as NetFlow.

Example 6-5 shows the use of the **show logging queue** command to look for performance issues. A large number of discarded event messages is indicative of a logging subsystem performance problem.

Example 6-5 *Verifying Logging Queue Performance*

```
FIREWALL# show logging queue

        Logging Queue length limit : 512 msg(s)
        412366 msg(s) discarded due to queue overflow
        10 msg(s) discarded due to memory allocation failure
        Current 216 msg on queue, 512 msgs most on queue
```

The logging queue is where messages wait to be dispatched to their destinations. This queue is 512 messages long by default, but can be made larger or smaller. Rare drops due to queue overflow might not be indicative of a serious problem. Frequent drops due to queue overflow is a sign that the ASA is not able to keep up with the number of messages being generated, and cannot dispatch them all to their intended destinations. If this occurs, first consider extending the size of the logging queue, using rate-limiting or more efficient logging methods (such as NetFlow), and reducing the amount of information being logged.

You can use the **logging queue** command to extend the size of the queue. Valid values range from 0 to 8192 messages. The following command doubles the size of the queue from the default value of 512 to a new value of 1024:

```
FIREWALL (config)# logging queue 1024
```

If a TCP-based syslog server is being used as a destination, with a fail-closed policy, and the server is not reachable, this will be indicated in the output of the **show logging** command, and will also appear as a recurring syslog message in an available destination (such as Internal Buffer or ASDM):

```
Dec 07 2011 18:49:56 FIREWALL : %ASA-3-414003: TCP Syslog Server management:
   192.168.1.7/1470 not responding, New connections are denied based on logging
   permit-hostdown policy
```

Exam Preparation Tasks

As mentioned in the section, "How to Use This Book," in the Introduction, you have a couple of choices for exam preparation: the exercises here, Chapter 17, "Final Preparation," and the exam simulation questions on the CD-ROM.

Review All Key Topics

Review the most important topics in this chapter, noted with the Key Topic icon in the outer margin of the page. Table 6-3 lists a reference of these key topics and the page numbers on which each is found.

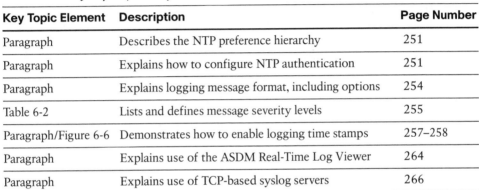

Table 6-3   *Key Topics for Chapter 6*

Key Topic Element	Description	Page Number
Paragraph	Describes the NTP preference hierarchy	251
Paragraph	Explains how to configure NTP authentication	251
Paragraph	Explains logging message format, including options	254
Table 6-2	Lists and defines message severity levels	255
Paragraph/Figure 6-6	Demonstrates how to enable logging time stamps	257–258
Paragraph	Explains use of the ASDM Real-Time Log Viewer	264
Paragraph	Explains use of TCP-based syslog servers	266

Command Reference to Check Your Memory

This section includes the most important configuration and EXEC commands covered in this chapter. It is not necessary to memorize the complete syntax of every command, but you should be able to remember the basic keywords that are needed.

To test your memory of the commands, cover the right side of Tables 6-4 and 6-5 with a piece of paper, read the description on the left side, and then see how much of the command you can remember.

The FIREWALL exam focuses on practical, hands-on skills that are used by a networking professional. Therefore, you should be able to identify the commands needed to configure and test an ASA feature.

Table 6-4   *ASA Time-Related Commands*

Task	Command Syntax
Set system time	ciscoasa# **clock set** *hh:mm:ss* {*month day* | *day month*} *year*
Set system time zone	ciscoasa(config)# **clock timezone** *zone* [-]*hours* [*minutes*]

Table 6-4 *ASA Time-Related Commands*

Task	Command Syntax
Set Daylight Saving Time parameters	ciscoasa(config)# **clock summer-time** *zone* **recurring** [*week weekday month hh:mm week weekday month hh:mm*] [*offset*] OR ciscoasa(config)# **clock summer-time** *zone* **date** {*day month*	*month day*} *year hh:mm* {*day month*	*month day*} *year hh:mm* [*offset*]
Configure an NTP server	ciscoasa(config)# **ntp server** *ip_address* [**key** *key_id*] [**source** *interface_name*] [**prefer**]
Enable NTP authentication	ciscoasa(config)# **ntp authenticate**
Set a key to authenticate with an NTP server	ciscoasa(config)# **ntp authentication-key** *key_id* **md5** *key*
Specify that a key is trusted (required for NTP authentication)	ciscoasa(config)# **ntp trusted-key** *key_id*
Display system time	ciscoasa# **show clock** [**detail**]
Display NTP associations	ciscoasa# **show ntp associations** [**detail**]

Table 6-5 *ASA Logging Configuration Commands*

Task	Command Syntax
Globally enable logging	ciscoasa(config)# **logging enable**
Configure save of buffered log to an FTP server before wrapping, and define an FTP server	ciscoasa(config)# **logging** ftp-bufferwrap ciscoasa(config)# **logging** ftp-server *ftp_server path username* [*0*	*8*] *password*
Include a time stamp on logged messages	ciscoasa(config)# **logging timestamp**
Include a device identifier on logged messages	ciscoasa(config)# **logging device-id** {**context-name**	**hostname**	**ipaddress** *interface_name*	**string** *text*}
Disable a system message	ciscoasa(config)# **no logging message** *syslog_id*
Change the severity level of a system message	ciscoasa(config)# **logging message** *syslog_id* **level** *level*
Create a logging list to be used with other commands	ciscoasa(config)# **logging list** *name* {**level** *level* [**class** *event_class*]	**message** *start_id*[-*end_id*]}

Table 6-5 *ASA Logging Configuration Commands*

Task	Command Syntax
Log event messages to a particular destination	ciscoasa(config)# **logging** [**asdm** | **buffered** | **console** | **mail** | **monitor** | **trap**] [*logging_list* | *level*]
Define a syslog server	ciscoasa(config)# **logging host** *interface_name syslog_ip* [**tcp**/*port* | **udp**/*port*] [**format emblem**] [**secure**] [**permit-hostdown**]
Define an SMTP server	ciscoasa(config)# **smtp-server** {*primary_server*} [*backup_server*]
Configure source and destination email addresses	ciscoasa(config)# **logging from-address** *from-email-address* ciscoasa(config)# **logging recipient-address** *address* [**level** *level*]
Delay export of NetFlow flow-create events	ciscoasa(config)# **flow-export delay flow-create** *seconds*
Define a NetFlow collector	ciscoasa(config)# **flow-export destination** *interface-name ipv4-address* | *hostname udp-port*
Display log settings and buffered messages	ciscoasa# **show logging**
Display NetFlow counters	ciscoasa# **show flow-export counters**
Display logging queue statistics	ciscoasa# **show logging queue**
Adjust logging queue size	ciscoasa(config)# **logging queue** [*size*]

This chapter covers the following topics:

- **Understanding How NAT Works:** This section describes the functionality of Network Address Translation (NAT), its benefits, and required information for implementing address translation on a Cisco ASA.

- **Implementing NAT in ASA Software Versions 8.2 and Earlier:** This major section covers the use of NAT in software versions 8.2 and earlier.

  - **Enforcing NAT:** This section describes the difference between enabling NAT and requiring NAT on a Cisco ASA.

  - **Address Translation Deployment Options:** This section describes the many various forms of address translation on a Cisco ASA, gives examples of NAT versus Port Address Translation (PAT), and describes which form of address translation is appropriate for various network scenarios, and in what situations NAT or PAT should not be used.

  - **Configuring NAT Control:** This section demonstrates how to configure NAT control to require all transit traffic to be addressed by translation rules (and exemptions).

  - **Configuring Dynamic Inside NAT:** This section demonstrates how to configure dynamic inside NAT, create global address pools, and alter the default system translation slot idle timer value.

  - **Configuring Dynamic Inside PAT:** This section demonstrates how to configure dynamic inside PAT, allowing multiple internal hosts to share a single global IP address.

  - **Configuring Dynamic Inside Policy NAT:** This section demonstrates how to configure dynamic inside policy NAT to create conditional translation rules based on the contents of access control lists.

CHAPTER 7

Using Address Translation

- **Verifying Dynamic Inside NAT and PAT:** This section shows commands used to verify NAT and PAT configuration on an ASA using dynamic inside NAT or PAT.

- **Configuring Static Inside NAT:** This section demonstrates how to configure static inside NAT to create permanent mappings between internal hosts and global IP addresses.

- **Configuring Network Static Inside NAT:** This section demonstrates how to configure network static inside NAT, which allows for the creation of multiple static mappings with a single command.

- **Configuring Static Inside PAT:** This section demonstrates how to configure static inside PAT, which allows multiple servers, using unique ports, to share a single global IP address. Static inside PAT can also be used to perform port redirection for servers using custom ports (where the port the connection is directed to by the client, and the port the server is actually listening on, are different).

- **Configuring Static Inside Policy NAT:** This section demonstrates how to configure static inside policy NAT to create conditional translation rules based on the contents of access control lists, for servers requiring only outbound connectivity.

- **Verifying Static Inside NAT and PAT:** This section shows commands used to verify NAT and PAT configuration on an ASA using static inside NAT or PAT.

- **Configuring No-Translation Rules:** This section demonstrates how to configure dynamic and static identity NAT, or NAT bypass, for hosts that do not require translation.

- **NAT Rule Priority:** This section discusses the priority in which address translation rules are applied to traffic.

- **Configuring Outside NAT:** This section discusses and demonstrates how to configure outside NAT, for use when external hosts require translation when communicating with hosts on more secure interfaces.

- **Other NAT Considerations:** This section discusses effects of NAT on other elements of ASA configuration, and demonstrates how to configure DNS Rewrite.

- **Troubleshooting Address Translation:** This section discusses the steps in troubleshooting address translation issues.

- **Implementing NAT in ASA Software Versions 8.3 and Later:** This major section covers the use of NAT in software versions 8.3 and later.

  - **Major Differences in NAT Beginning in Software Version 8.3:** This section provides a brief discussion of the major changes in how NAT is handled between current versions of the OS and older versions.

  - **NAT Table:** This section discusses the structure of the NAT Table in OS versions 8.3 and higher and how the ASA determines which NAT rule to apply to individual packet flows.

  - **Configuring Auto (Object) NAT:** This section demonstrates how to configure various NAT rule types for use with auto (object) NAT to include static address translations, static port mappings, dynamic NAT (one-to-one), and dynamic PAT (many-to-one).

  - **Verifying Auto (Object) NAT:** This section shows the commands used to verify translation configuration and operation on an ASA using auto NAT.

  - **Configuring Manual NAT:** This section discusses and demonstrates the configuration of manual NAT to include NAT exemptions and twice NAT.

  - **When Not to Use NAT:** This section discusses times when the use of NAT is inappropriate with OS versions 8.3 and higher.

  - **Tuning NAT:** This section discusses adjusting the translation slot global timer and activating DNS Rewrite.

  - **Troubleshooting NAT:** This section discusses the common commands and consideration to troubleshoot problems with NAT when using OS versions 8.3 and higher.

The Cisco Adaptive Security Appliance (ASA) is frequently deployed at the border between a network using a private IP addressing scheme and the public Internet address space. To solve addressing issues when interconnecting these networks, the Cisco ASA supports Network Address Translation (NAT) and Port Address Translation (PAT).

This chapter discusses methods for configuring, verifying, and troubleshooting NAT and PAT deployed on a Cisco ASA.

The methods of performing address translation on a Cisco ASA were completely reworked beginning with OS version 8.3. Because the FIREWALL exam might include questions about address translation using both 8.2-and-before and 8.3-and-later versions of the OS, this chapter contains major sections for both 8.2-and-before and 8.3-and-later address translation. So this book serves as a valuable reference and provides, it provides full coverage for both methods; however, the exam will likely emphasize the methods used in OS versions 8.3 and later, so pay particularly close attention when studying that portion of this chapter.

"Do I Know This Already?" Quiz

The "Do I Know This Already?" quiz allows you to assess whether you should read this entire chapter thoroughly or jump to the "Exam Preparation Tasks" section. If you are in doubt about your answers to these questions or your own assessment of your knowledge of the topics, read the entire chapter. Table 7-1 lists the major headings in this chapter and their corresponding "Do I Know This Already?" quiz sections. You can find the answers in Appendix A, "Answers to the 'Do I Know This Already?' Quizzes."

Table 7-1   *"Do I Know This Already?" Section-to-Question Mapping*

Foundation Topics Section	Questions
Understanding How NAT Works	1
Enforcing NAT	2
Address Translation Deployment Options	3–4
Configuring Dynamic Inside NAT	5–6
Configuring Dynamic Inside PAT	7–8
Configuring Static Inside NAT	9
Configuring Static Inside PAT	10
Configuring Static Inside Policy NAT	11
Configuring No-Translation Rules	12
Other NAT Considerations	13
Major Differences in NAT Beginning in Software Version 8.3	14
NAT Table	15–16
Configuring Auto (Object) NAT	17–20
Verifying Auto (Object) NAT	21
Configuring Manual NAT	22

Caution: The goal of self-assessment is to gauge your mastery of the topics in this chapter. If you do not know the answer to a question or are only partially sure of the answer, you should mark that question as wrong for purposes of the self-assessment. Giving yourself credit for an answer you correctly guess skews your self-assessment results and might provide you with a false sense of security.

1. Which of the following is not a benefit of NAT?

   a. Hides internal addressing and topology from hosts on the Internet.

   b. Allows multiple hosts to share the same globally unique IP address.

   c. Mitigates global address depletion.

   d. Allows change of ISP without internal re-addressing.

   e. All of the above are benefits of NAT.

2. Which of the following is true when NAT control is enabled on an ASA running an OS version before 8.2?

   a. Translation rules are not required but will be performed if configured.

   b. Configuration of translation rules is not permitted.

   c. Translation rules are required for all transit traffic.

   d. Translation rules are required only for sessions initiated on a higher security interface bound for a lower security interface.

3. Your ASA is running OS version 8.2 and is configured for dynamic inside PAT. Hosts on the 10.0.0.0/24 internal network share global IP address 209.165.200.254. As hosts initiate TCP connections to external servers, what happens?

   a. The source IP address is translated to 209.165.200.254. The source port is retained, unless that port is already in use, in which case it is translated.

   b. The source IP address is translated to 209.165.200.254. If the original source port is 1024 or greater, it is translated to a seemingly random port number in the range 1024–65535.

   c. The source IP address is translated to 209.165.200.254. Each host is then allocated ten port numbers for its use. These ports are assigned to subsequent connections from the source host and return to availability as sessions are terminated.

   d. The described configuration is invalid.

4. An application embeds IP addresses at the application layer and uses end-to-end encryption. Which "flavor" of address translation should be used in this situation on an ASA running OS version 8.2?

   a. Dynamic inside NAT

   b. Static inside policy NAT

   c. Dynamic inside policy NAT

   d. Static outside NAT

   e. NAT bypass

5. Which of the following commands changes the translation slot idle timer value to 1 hour?

   a. **translation idle timer 01:00:00**

   b. **xlate idle timer 01:00:00**

   c. timeout xlate 01:00:00

   d. **timer xlate 01:00:00**

   e. None of these answers are correct.

6. An ASA is running OS version 8.2. Given the following partial ASA configuration, with all translation slots cleared, to which address will host 10.0.0.101 be translated when initiating a session to web server 172.16.0.5 on the DMZ network?

```
access-list NO_NAT permit ip host 10.0.0.101 172.16.0.32 255.255.255.224
nat-control
nat (inside) 5 access-list NO_NAT
nat (inside) 1 10.0.0.0 255.255.255.0 tcp 0 0 udp 0
nat (inside) 2 0.0.0.0 0.0.0.0 tcp 0 0 udp 0
global (outside) 1 209.165.200.235-209.165.200.254 netmask 255.255.255.224
global (DMZ) 2 172.16.0.101-172.16.0.254 netmask 255.255.255.0
global (DMZ) 5 interface
```

   a. 209.165.200.235

   b. 172.16.0.101

   c. 172.16.0.1 (the ASA DMZ interface IP)

   d. None of these answers are correct because the translation attempt will fail.

7. Your ASA is running OS version 8.2. You are tasked to configure dynamic inside PAT for hosts on the inside network when they communicate with the DMZ network. The DMZ network is 172.16.0.0/24. The PAT address will be 172.16.0.254. Which subnet mask should you enter in the NAT Rules configuration window?

   a. 255.255.255.0

   b. 255.255.255.255

   c. 0.0.0.255

   d. 0.0.0.0

   e. None of the answers are correct. There is no subnet mask field in the NAT Rules configuration window.

8. Your ASA is running OS version 8.2. You are tasked to configure dynamic inside PAT for hosts on the inside interface when communicating with external hosts (through the outside interface). Because of a lack of IP addresses, you will use the IP address of the ASA's outside interface, 209.165.200.226, as the PAT address. Which of the following configurations is correct?

   a.
```
nat (inside) 5 0.0.0.0 0.0.0.0
global (outside) 5 209.165.200.226
```

   b.
```
nat (inside) 1 10.0.0.0 255.255.255.0
global (outside) 1 209.165.200.226
```

   c.
```
nat (inside) 0 10.0.0.0 255.255.255.0
global (outside) 0 interface
```

   d.
```
nat (inside) 300 10.0.0.0 255.255.255.0
global (outside) 300 interface
```

   e. None of the answers provide a valid configuration.

9. Your ASA is running OS version 8.2. You have a web server on the DMZ network, address 172.16.0.5. You are tasked with granting access to this server to all Internet-based hosts, using global address 209.165.200.228. Which of the following shows the correct command or commands to accomplish this, assuming access lists are already configured to permit this traffic?

   a. `nat (DMZ) 4 172.16.0.5 255.255.255.255`
          `global (outside) 4 209.165.200.228 netmask 255.255.255.255`

   b. `static (DMZ,outside) 172.16.0.5 209.165.200.228 netmask 255.255.255.255`

   c. `access-list WEB permit tcp any host 209.165.200.228 eq www`
          `static (DMZ,outside) access-list WEB`

   d. `static (DMZ,outside) 209.165.200.228 172.16.0.5 netmask 255.255.255.255`

10. Your ASA is running OS version 8.2. You have an SMTP email server on the DMZ, address 172.16.0.20. This host must be reachable from the Internet using port 25, and from the PartnerNet (172.18.10.0/24) using port 2525. Additionally, a web server on the DMZ, address 172.16.0.5, shares the global IP address 209.165.200.235 with the email server, for the outside interface. Which of the following configurations would work?

   a. `static (DMZ,outside) tcp 209.165.200.235 25 172.16.0.20 25`
          `static (DMZ,outside) tcp 209.165.200.235 80 172.16.0.5 80`
          `static (DMZ,PartnerNet) tcp 172.18.10.20 2525 172.16.0.20 25`

   b. `static (DMZ,outside) 209.165.200.235 25 172.16.0.20 25`
          `static (DMZ,outside) 209.165.200.235 80 172.16.0.5 80`
          `static (DMZ,PartnerNet) 172.18.10.20 2525 172.16.0.20 25`

   c. `static (DMZ,outside) tcp 172.16.0.20 25 209.165.200.235 25`
          `static (DMZ,outside) tcp 172.16.0.5 80 209.165.200.235 80`
          `static (DMZ,PartnerNet) tcp 172.16.0.20 25 172.18.10.20 2525`

   d. `static (DMZ,outside) tcp 209.165.200.235 2525 172.16.0.20 25`
          `static (DMZ,outside) tcp 209.165.200.235 80 172.16.0.5 80`
          `static (DMZ,PartnetNet) tcp 172.18.10.20 25 172.16.0.20 25`

11. An ASA is running OS version 8.2. When using static inside policy NAT, hosts on less secure interfaces are able to initiate communication with hosts on more secure interfaces that are subject to translation. True or false?

   a. True

   b. False

12. Your ASA is running OS version 8.2. Your inside network is 10.0.0.0/24. Your DMZ network is 172.16.0.0/24. You want to configure hosts on the inside network to reach the DMZ without being translated, while still maintaining the ability to communicate with the Internet through use of address translation. Which of the following configuration samples accomplishes this?

   a. `access-list NO_NAT permit ip 10.0.0.0 255.255.255.0 172.16.0.0 255.255.255.0`
          `nat (inside) 1 access-list NO_NAT`
          `nat (inside) 1 10.0.0.0 255.255.255.0`
          `global (outside) 1 209.165.200.235-209.165.200.254 netmask 255.255.255.224`

b.
```
access-list NO_NAT permit ip 10.0.0.0/24 172.16.0.0/24
nat (inside) 1 10.0.0.0/24
nat (inside) 0 access-list NO_NAT
global (outside) 1 209.165.200.235-209.165.200.254/27
```

c.
```
access-list NO_NAT permit ip 10.0.0.0 255.255.255.0 172.16.0.0 255.255.255.0
nat (inside) 1 10.0.0.0 255.255.255.0
nat (inside) 0 access-list NO_NAT
global (outside) 1 209.165.200.235-209.165.200.254 netmask 255.255.255.224
```

d.
```
access-list NO_NAT permit ip 10.0.0.0 255.255.0.0 172.16.0.0 255.255.255.0
nat (inside) 1 10.0.0.0 255.255.255.0
nat (inside) 0 access-list NO_NAT
global (outside) 1 209.165.200.235-209.165.200.254 netmask 255.255.255.224
```

13. Your ASA is running OS version 8.2. Hosts on the inside network need to reach a web server on the DMZ. However, they use an Internet-based DNS server for name resolution. How would you configure the ASA to ensure that these connections are successful?

a. `static (DMZ,outside) 209.165.200.228 172.16.0.5 dns`

b.
```
nat (inside) 1 10.0.0.0 255.255.255.0 dns
global (outside) 1 interface
```

c. `static (DMZ,inside) 172.16.0.5 172.16.0.5 dns`

d. `None of the answers are correct.`

14. An ASA is running OS version 8.3. Where in the configuration would you create an auto NAT rule?

a. In global configuration mode

b. As part of the NAT Table configuration

c. In network object group configuration mode

d. In NAT configuration mode

e. In network object configuration mode

15. An ASA is running OS version 8.3. Which of the following is the correct order for determining which NAT rule to apply to a packet?

a. Manual NAT, auto NAT, twice NAT, manual NAT after auto NAT

b. Static inside NAT, dynamic inside policy NAT, dynamic inside NAT

c. Manual NAT, auto NAT, manual NAT after auto NAT

d. NAT 0 with access list, static inside NAT, static inside policy NAT, auto NAT

e. NAT exemption, manual NAT, auto NAT, dynamic inside NAT

16. An ASA is running OS version 8.3. How many auto NAT rules can the NAT Table contain for a single network object?

   a. One

   b. Two

   c. Three

   d. Limited only by memory

17. An ASA is running OS version 8.3. You are using ASDM to add a new network object. What four values are available settings in the Type field?

   a. host

   b. pool

   c. range

   d. subnet

   e. FQDN

   f. network

18. An ASA is running OS version 8.3. All translation slots are cleared. The host 10.0.0.101 initiates a connection using source port 49151 to the DMZ web server, 172.16.0.5. What are the values in the source address and source port fields when this packet is forwarded onto the DMZ segment?

```
object network INSIDE-SEGMENT
  subnet 10.0.0.0 255.255.255.0
object network IT-SEGMENT
  subnet 10.0.1.0 255.255.255.0
object network OUTSIDE-NAT-POOL
  range 209.165.200.235 209.165.200.254
object network INSIDE-SEGMENT
  nat (any,outside) dynamic OUTSIDE-NAT-POOL interface
object network IT-SEGMENT
  nat (any,DMZ) dynamic 172.16.0.254
```

   a. 172.16.0.254/49151

   b. 209.165.200.235/A seemingly random port, 1024 or higher, based on an internal ASA algorithm

   c. 10.0.0.101/1024

   d. 172.16.0.254/A seemingly random port, 1024 or higher, based on an internal ASA algorithm

   e. 10.0.0.101/49151

   f. 10.0.0.101/A seemingly random port, 1024 or higher, based on an internal ASA algorithm

19. An ASA is running OS version 8.3. Given the following configuration, on what port is the DMZ HTTPS server actually listening for incoming connections?

```
object network DMZ-HTTPS-PRIV
  nat (DMZ,outside) static DMZ-PAT-OUTSIDE service tcp 8443 443
```

   a. 8443

   b. 443

   c. Neither 8443 nor 443

   d. There is not enough information in the sample configuration to make a determination.

20. An ASA is running OS version 8.3. In what ASDM window would you define source and destination interface settings when creating an auto NAT rule?

   a. Add Network Object

   b. Add NAT Rule

   c. Advanced NAT Settings

   d. Network Object NAT Settings

21. You see the following in the output of the **show xlate** command:

```
TCP PAT from DMZ:172.16.0.15 8443-8443 to outside:209.165.200.230 443-443
     flags sr idle 0:25:53 timeout 0:00:00
```

What is the meaning of the **s** and **r** flags?

   a. **r** means sequence number randomization is enabled, and **s** means static NAT is being used.

   b. **r** means port mapping is being used, and **s** means static NAT is being used.

   c. **r** means sequence number randomization is enabled, and **s** means SYN flood protection is enabled.

   d. **r** means port mapping is being used, and **s** means SYN flood protection is enabled.

22. An ASA is running OS version 8.3. What is the effect of the following manual NAT rule?

```
nat (inside,outside) 1 source dynamic INSIDE-SEGMENT VENDOR-SERVER-PAT
    destination static VENDOR-SERVER VENDOR-SERVER service HTTPS
    VENDOR-PORTMAP
```

   a. Hosts in the INSIDE_SEGMENT object will have their addresses translated to VENDOR-SERVER-PAT only when connecting to the VENDOR-SERVER address using the port 443.

   b. Hosts in the INSIDE_SEGMENT object will have their addresses translated to VENDOR-SERVER-PAT only when connecting to the VENDOR-SERVER address using the port defined in the service object named VENDOR-PORTMAP.

   c. Hosts in the INSIDE_SEGMENT object will have their addresses translated to VENDOR-SERVER-PAT only when connecting to the VENDOR-SERVER address using the port defined in the service object named HTTPS.

   d. None of these answers are correct.

Foundation Topics

This chapter describes how IP addresses can be altered or translated as packets move through an ASA. The various types of Network Address Translation (NAT) and Port Address Translation (PAT) are covered.

NAT performs the translation of source and/or destination IP addresses in packets traversing the ASA. PAT, in addition to translating IP addresses, translates source port numbers in TCP or UDP packets, thus allowing many-to-one translation of source IP addresses. This allows numerous internal hosts to share a single public IP address when communicating with external networks.

The methods of performing address translation on a Cisco ASA were completely reworked beginning with OS version 8.3. Because the FIREWALL exam includes questions about address translation using both pre- and post-8.3 versions of the OS, this chapter contains major sections for both pre- and post-8.3 address translation.

Understanding How NAT Works

Network Address Translation (NAT) was developed to overcome IP addressing problems that occurred when the ARPANet, which interconnected only a few dozen large institutions, became the Internet, which had the ability to interconnect networks and computers globally, leading to massive growth. There simply were not enough addresses available in the originally designed IP addressing scheme to accommodate universal connectivity, especially given the manner in which addresses were originally assigned. Therefore, a system of "private" IP addresses was developed, first in RFC 1597, which was then superseded by the better-known RFC 1918, which allows multiple networks around the world to deploy the exact same IP addresses for addresses that require only local uniqueness. This eliminates the need to maintain globally unique addresses for every connected host worldwide.

Because private IP addresses are intended for local use only and are considered "non-routable" on the public Internet, NAT is required to translate these private (local) IP addresses to public (global), routable addresses when hosts on a private network need to communicate with hosts outside of that private network.

Additionally, because many organizations can deploy the same private IP addresses, due to local significance, NAT is required if hosts on these networks with overlapping addresses need to communicate with each other.

NAT thus provides the following benefits:

- NAT mitigates public IP address depletion because, when used in combination with PAT, many private hosts can share a single public IP address, while using unique private addresses internally.

- NAT allows an organization to undergo a change of Internet service provider (ISP), with provider-dependent public IP addresses, without having to change its internal, private addressing plan.

■ As a security measure, NAT hides the internal IP addressing scheme and network topology from the public Internet, even while it allows interconnectivity.

In its simplest form, for an ASA to perform NAT or PAT, four pieces of information are required:

■ Original source IP address (and port) in the packet

■ Interface where the original packet enters the ASA (ingress interface)

■ Interface where the packet will exit the ASA (egress interface)

■ Translated address (and, optionally, port) to insert into the packet

Understanding this concept is important because these four pieces of information are required in each of the many variations of NAT and PAT. If any of these four items is unknown, an ASA cannot perform address translation. Also, these items are all recorded in the translation table (xlate table) maintained by the ASA for tracking address translation that it is performing.

Beginning in OS version 8.3, NAT is organized in an object-oriented manner, rather than being interface-dependent. Although it is still technically necessary to include both ingress and egress interfaces in NAT rules, there is an option to use "any" as the ingress or egress interface definition, so translation rules are not necessarily applied between only a single pair of interfaces. Furthermore, it is possible, with a single rule, to translate both source and/or destination addresses in a packet, so NAT is no longer limited to source address only. Finally, NAT rules are no longer determined in an interface-sorted manner, according to a priority scheme, but rather in a NAT table that is not sorted by interface. All these items are covered in the section, "Implementing NAT in ASA Software Versions 8.3 and Later."

Figure 7-1 shows a basic example of NAT implementation. An internal host, with private IP address 10.0.0.101, needs to communicate with a web server on the Internet.

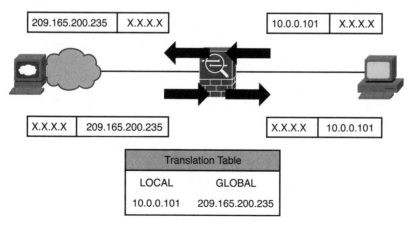

Translation Table	
LOCAL	GLOBAL
10.0.0.101	209.165.200.235

Figure 7-1 *Basic Address Translation Example*

When the NAT-enabled Cisco ASA in Figure 7-1 receives a packet from the internal host, it translates the source IP address of the packet before forwarding the packet to the Internet. This is necessary because the private IP address assigned to the host is not allowed to be routed through the Internet. In the figure, the host's address is translated to the public IP address 209.165.200.235. When a host on the Internet receives this packet, it sends its reply to 209.165.200.235 as the destination IP address. This packet arrives at the Cisco ASA, which consults its address translation table and, finding the entry related to the translation being performed, translates this destination IP address back to 10.0.0.101 before forwarding it onto the internal network to the originating host.

So, in the example shown in Figure 7-1, the four required pieces of information are

- **10.0.0.101:** Original source IP address

- **inside:** Ingress interface

- **outside:** Egress interface (determined by routing decision)

- **209.165.200.235:** Translated source IP address

Implementing NAT in ASA Software Versions 8.2 and Earlier

Beginning with software version 8.3, Cisco radically altered the manner in which address translation is configured on an ASA. To understand how this new method of configuring address translation differs from earlier versions, and the benefits it brings, it is important to understand how NAT worked before these changes. Also, the FIREWALL exam expects you to be familiar with both methodologies, and possibly expects you to be able to compare different configurations that actually achieve the same result—one using "legacy" syntax and another using current syntax.

Enforcing NAT

The basic example of NAT just detailed stated that a "NAT-enabled" ASA received packets. So, what makes an ASA NAT-enabled? Simply put, any ASA that is configured to perform NAT is NAT-enabled. However, if an organization uses RFC 1918 private addresses, NAT is required to permit communication with external networks. You must therefore be able to distinguish between *performing* NAT and *enforcing* NAT. As already stated, any ASA configured to perform NAT will do so. What, then, does it mean to configure an ASA to enforce NAT?

Prior to OS version 7.0, there was no way for a PIX firewall to forward packets from a higher-security interface to a lower-security interface ("outbound" traffic) without being configured with rules for address translation. Thus, it was a requirement of passing traffic that all outbound packets be matched to a translation rule (even if such a rule were to exempt a packet from translation). The use of NAT was thus *enforced*, not merely *permitted*. Starting with OS version 7.0, and the introduction of the Cisco ASA, an ASA does not enforce the use of NAT, by default.

It is important to note that if an organization's network already contains enough globally unique IP addresses to accommodate all internal hosts, NAT is not necessary to permit that network to intercommunicate with the rest of the world. The internal hosts could be configured with globally unique addresses, and the ASA could simply forward traffic without any address translation. However, even in such a case, some organizations choose to assign private, RFC 1918 addresses to their internal network, especially if their IP addresses were allocated to them by an ISP rather than registered to them directly. If such an organization decides to change ISPs, it does not need to re-address its entire internal network, which it would otherwise have to do if it had allocated the globally unique IPs directly to internal hosts. It is important to remember the security implications of NAT (hiding internal address and topology information) before making such a decision.

Even if an organization used private IP addresses, it would not be necessary to perform NAT on the ASA. The ASA would simply forward packets with the original addresses intact. The assumption would be that another inline device would perform NAT. Otherwise, the packets would be dropped as nonroutable traffic when they entered the Internet space.

With OS versions 7 and later, it is still possible to enforce the use of NAT. Essentially, the ASA functions much as a pre-OS version 7 firewall would, and drops any outbound packets not addressed by configured translation rules. Enforcing NAT is considered a security enhancement, as it can create another layer of access control (dropping packets that have no translation rule), and is thus widely used, even at the cost of increased configuration complexity.

The function used to enforce NAT is known as *NAT control*, and its configuration is covered later in this chapter alongside the configuration of NAT rules.

Address Translation Deployment Options

As previously mentioned, there are many variations of address translation that can be performed by a Cisco ASA. One of the deployment options, just covered, is whether to enforce the use of NAT as a security enhancement.

If you are using NAT, there are many further options to consider, such as whether to perform fixed or temporary address translation. Fixed translation, where an original address is permanently assigned the translated IP address, is known as *static NAT*. Temporary translation, where an original host is assigned an address from an available pool, and that address is returned to the pool after a configurable idle time, is known as *dynamic NAT*. Static NAT is typically used with servers, and dynamic NAT is typically used with client hosts.

There are two "directions" for NAT usage, known as inside NAT and outside NAT. If the packets arriving at the ASA from a host subject to translation ingress an interface with a higher security level than the interface they egress, the address translation performed is known as *inside NAT*. Conversely, if packets arriving from a host subject to translation ingress an interface with a lower security level than the interface they egress, the address translation performed is known as *outside NAT*. Recall that the assigned security level of an interface determines whether that interface, and networks reachable through that interface, is considered more or less secure relative to the other interface involved in a traffic flow.

Note: It is always important to remember which host is subject to translation. For instance, packets originating on the Internet and destined for an internal web server do not constitute the use of outside NAT. It is not the originating host that is subject to address translation, but rather the internal web server. Thus, packets from the host subject to translation (the internal web server) ingress the ASA on an interface that has a higher security level than the interface they egress, and the translation performed is inside NAT.

The implementation of NAT or PAT can be further enhanced by making it conditional (based on a policy). Generally, the need for this arises based on access restrictions at the destination host, but there are many reasons it may be necessary in practice. Such implementation is accomplished by using an access control list (ACL) to define the policy. Traffic flows defined as permitted in the ACL become those subject to the policy NAT implementation.

Thus, when performing NAT, you have the choices of dynamic inside NAT, static inside NAT, dynamic outside NAT, and static outside NAT. Each of these deployment options can further be subdivided into policy versus nonpolicy options.

A final option to consider is to exempt certain traffic from NAT. If NAT control is not enabled (NAT is not being enforced), this is unnecessary. However, if NAT control is enabled, and there are traffic flows that you do not want to undergo address translation, you must configure NAT exemption rules.

NAT Versus PAT

It is important to understand the difference in implementation between NAT and PAT so that you understand when each choice is appropriate for your particular network environment.

When you use inside NAT, only the source IP address of the internal host is translated, and a one-to-one mapping is made between the original (local) IP address and the translated (global) address assigned to the host. The global address can be assigned in either a static (fixed and permanent) or dynamic (from a pool and temporary) manner. If there are not enough global IP addresses to support all internal hosts, some hosts will not be able to communicate through the ASA.

Figure 7-2 illustrates the use of NAT with an example of inside NAT. Recall that inside NAT means that traffic from the host subject to translation ingresses the ASA on a more secure interface than it egresses the ASA. In the figure, two hosts connected to the inside interface of the ASA both need to communicate with destinations on the Internet.

In Figure 7-2, hosts on the internal 10.0.0.0/24 network share a pool of global addresses, 209.165.200.235-254, from which addresses are dynamically allocated to hosts as they make connections, and to which addresses are returned after an idle period. Host 10.0.0.101 is assigned the first address from the pool, 209.165.200.235, when it makes the first outbound connection. Host 10.0.0.102, upon making its connection, is assigned the next address from the pool, 209.165.200.236. This is merely an example, although it also illustrates how the ASA allocated pool addresses prior to OS version 8.0(3). As of version 8.0(3), a seemingly random address is allocated from the pool based on an internal ASA algorithm.

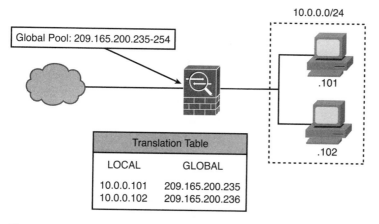

Figure 7-2 *Dynamic Inside NAT Scenario*

Note: The example deliberately uses a pool that is not congruent with the boundaries of subnetting, such as 209.165.200.240/28 would be. Although the command that creates a global pool optionally uses a subnet mask parameter, it does not perform subnetting of the network attached to the ASA. This is an important concept for you to understand to maximize the efficiency of address allocation within your own network environment.

Figure 7-3 illustrates the use of NAT with an example of inside PAT. When you use inside NAT, only the source IP address of the internal host is translated, and a one-to-one mapping is made between the original (local) IP address and the translated (global) address assigned to the host. With PAT, however, both the source IP address and source port (for TCP and UDP packets) are translated, which creates a many-to-one mapping, with multiple internal hosts sharing a single global IP address, and each of their TCP or UDP connections being assigned a unique port number, tracked by the ASA for the duration of the connection. This allows for maximum efficiency in conserving global IP addresses, but is not compatible with all applications.

In Figure 7-3, hosts on the internal 10.0.0.0/24 network share a single global address, 209.165.200.254. When host 10.0.0.101 initiates a TCP connection to a web server on the Internet, it is assigned the 209.165.200.254 address, and its original TCP source port of 49501 is translated to port 46224. When host 10.0.0.102 makes its connection to the same web server, it also uses global IP address 209.165.200.254, and is assigned the translated port 27645. Subsequent connections from any host on the 10.0.0.0/24 network (including .101 and .102) are assigned seemingly random source port numbers, based on an internal ASA algorithm.

Input Parameters

With these considerations in mind, we can now more fully define the overall input parameters that you will need to consider in determining how NAT or PAT functionality needs to be defined for your particular environment.

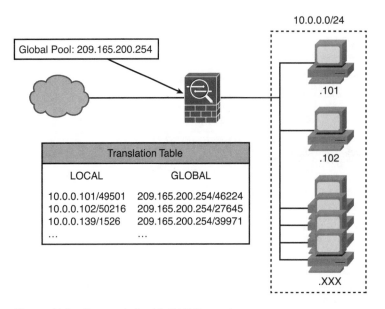

Figure 7-3   *Dynamic Inside PAT Scenario*

Table 7-2 lists and describes input parameters. You must understand and fully enumerate these parameters to correctly deploy address translation rules for your environment.

Table 7-2   *Address Translation Input Parameters*

Input Parameter	Description
Local (original) IP addressing	Required to determine which hosts should be subjected to translation
Pool of available global IP addresses	Required to determine to which addresses such hosts should be translated
Role of systems requiring translation	Required to choose between static and dynamic NAT
Specification of flows requiring NAT	Required to choose between policy and nonpolicy NAT, and between inside and outside NAT
List of applications accessed through the NAT device	Required to determine application NAT compatibility
Defense-in-depth requirement	Required to determine the need for NAT control (enforcement of NAT)

It is important to remember that the terms "local" and "global," when related to NAT configuration on a Cisco ASA, really equate to "original" and "translated," respectively, because in the case of outside NAT, the local address is frequently that of a foreign network, and the global addresses to which the local addresses are translated are usually from an internal network.

Regarding system roles, each system can generally be defined as either a client (a system that only initiates connections) or a server (a system that accepts incoming connections, and can also initiate outgoing connections). Client hosts can generally operate successfully through dynamic NAT, but servers require static NAT, as the IP addresses to which their clients need to connect must be predictable and fixed.

It is important to know if your organization uses applications that do not work with NAT or PAT. Examples of such applications are presented later, in the section, "NAT Exemption."

Deployment Choices

The decision of whether to use inside or outside NAT, policy or nonpolicy NAT, or static or dynamic NAT may at first seem complex. Table 7-3 presents the various deployment choices, along with the criteria that normally make such a choice appropriate.

Table 7-3 *NAT Deployment Choices and Criteria*

Deployment Choice	Criteria
Dynamic NAT	Use for client systems when you have a large enough pool of available global IP addresses to support assignment to clients in a one-to-one manner.
Dynamic PAT	Use for client systems when your global pool contains fewer IP addresses than there are hosts requiring translation, and you therefore must perform assignment in a many-to-one manner.
Static NAT	Use for server systems that require inbound (or bidirectional) connectivity over NAT and you have enough global IP addresses to allow each server its own specific, fixed address.
Static PAT	Use for server systems that require only inbound connectivity over NAT and you do not have enough global IP addresses to allow each server its own specific, fixed address. Also use it when a single global IP address is shared by many internal servers, each supporting applications on different listening ports.
Policy NAT	Use when you need translation to depend on granularly defined policies for specific traffic flows.
NAT control	Use when you need NAT to become another layer of access control on your ASA, at the cost of increased configuration complexity.
NAT exemption	Use when you encounter situations covered in the upcoming "NAT Exemption" section. Also, it can be used in situations where NAT is not required, such as in a VPN between two networks without overlapping IP addresses.

On a single Cisco ASA, it is possible to deploy a combination of all the options in Table 7-3, depending on your needs.

When NAT is combined with access controls, on a Cisco ASA running an OS version prior to 8.3, NAT configuration necessarily influences the configuration of interface ACLs, AAA rules, and Modular Policy Framework (MPF) rules (each topic is covered in other chapters).

NAT Exemption

The last deployment choice for NAT is when *not* to use it. Remember, of course, that if NAT control is not enabled, then all traffic is exempted from NAT. That is, if NAT rules are configured, they are implemented, but traffic that is not subject to such rules is forwarded without the requirement for NAT (NAT is not enforced).

The following is a list of situations that would require you to exempt certain traffic from NAT on an ASA that otherwise enforces NAT:

- Do not use NAT or PAT with applications that embed IP addresses on the application layer and use end-to-end encryption. With encrypted traffic, the Cisco ASA cannot translate embedded addresses and allow such applications to work properly across NAT.

- Do not use NAT or PAT with applications that authenticate entire packets (such as IPsec Authentication Header [AH] or Border Gateway Protocol [BGP]). When a packet hash value is calculated, and then addresses and/or port numbers are translated later, the verification of the hash at the other end of the communication will fail, and the packet will be dropped.

- Do not use NAT or PAT with applications that establish additional dynamic sessions, and for which the ASA does not support protocol-specific inspection rules. Also, if the application uses an encrypted control channel, the ASA will not be able to inspect the packet contents and perform modifications allowing the application to work properly across NAT/PAT.

There are other situations in which you will typically choose to exempt traffic from NAT/PAT, but in such cases, it is a choice, whereas the list just presented shows when it is a requirement. The most frequent examples of this are traffic that will traverse a VPN connection (for more information on VPNs, consult the *CCNP Security VPN Official Certification Guide*), or traffic between two internal networks, such as from the inside network to the DMZ network. Although such traffic traverses the ASA, the private addresses in use are never seen in an external environment where they would be considered nonroutable, so address translation is not necessary.

Configuring NAT Control

As previously mentioned, *NAT control* is a feature that configures the ASA to enforce NAT usage—that is, to require a translation rule for each host on a more secure interface when it communicates with hosts on lower security interfaces. (NAT exemption is an acceptable translation rule.) NAT control is disabled by default.

When NAT control is enabled and a host on a more secure interface attempts communication through the ASA to a less secure interface, the ASA first checks to see if there is an existing entry in the translation table for the host in question. Such an entry would exist if the host had previously communicated through the ASA, there was a configured translation rule for the host, and a translation slot had been created for that host and had not yet expired due to the xlate timeout value being exceeded. If an entry exists, the ASA performs the same translation for the host as previously.

If there is not an existing entry, one will be created if a translation rule is configured for the host. If there is not an existing entry, and no translation rule exists to create one, the traffic is dropped.

Note: NAT is not required between same security level interfaces even if NAT control is enabled (as long as the ASA is configured to permit traffic between same security level interfaces). You can configure NAT if desired, and the ASA will perform address translation for the traffic passing between the same security level interfaces.

Figure 7-4 demonstrates how to enable NAT control (navigate to **Configuration > Firewall > NAT Rules**). NAT control is a global feature and is either on or off for the entire ASA, not specific interfaces or translation rules. However, it is configured in the NAT Rules window of the device configuration.

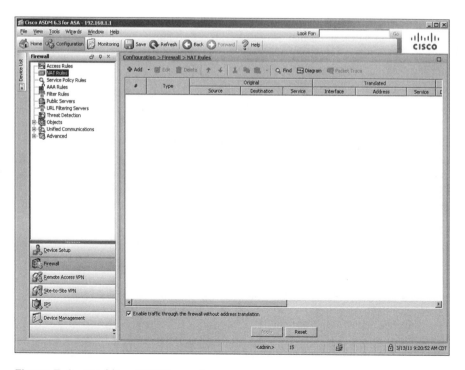

Figure 7-4 *Enabling NAT Control*

Note: All figures in the 8.2 and earlier NAT configuration examples use ASA OS version 8.23 with ASDM version 6.3. All figures in the 8.3 and later NAT configuration examples use ASA OS version 8.42 with ASDM version 6.45. Therefore, you might notice differences in some appearance and options.

At the bottom of the NAT Rules window is a check box that is checked by default. To enable NAT control, uncheck the **Enable Traffic Through the Firewall Without Address Translation** check box and click **Apply**.

The CLI command generated by the change made is as follows:

```
nat-control
```

If you are configuring the ASA from the CLI, you can enter this command directly in global configuration mode.

Configuring Dynamic Inside NAT

Dynamic inside NAT creates a temporary translation entry (slot) in the translation table when a host on a more secure interface sends traffic through the ASA to a less secure interface. Each local (original) address configured to use NAT on the ingress interface is translated to a global (translated) address selected from a configured pool on the egress interface. The translation is kept in place until a configurable idle timer expires (3 hours by default) or the translation slot is manually cleared by an administrator. Because these translations are dynamic, the same host, initiating connections at different times, is frequently translated to different global addresses.

Dynamic inside NAT should generally be used for client hosts that need outbound connectivity only. This is because, when using dynamic inside NAT, hosts on less secure interfaces cannot initiate connections to hosts on more secure interfaces that are configured to use dynamic NAT translation, unless the translation slot has already been created by outbound packets, and the interface access list on the less secure interface permits such a connection (interface access lists are discussed in Chapter 8, "Controlling Access Through the ASA"). Additionally, as previously mentioned, servers must have addresses that are fixed and predictable in order for their clients to connect to them successfully, so dynamic NAT is not an option for service-providing hosts.

Recall the four pieces of information necessary for an ASA to perform NAT:

- Original source IP address (and port) in the packet
- Interface where the original packet enters the ASA (ingress interface)
- Interface where the packet will exit the ASA (egress interface)
- Translated address (and, optionally, port) to insert into the packet

To configure an ASA to perform dynamic inside NAT, you must specify these four pieces of information. Also, you can optionally alter the default global translation slot idle timeout value (known as the xlate timer).

In demonstrating how to configure dynamic inside NAT, we will use the example introduced earlier. Figure 7-5 shows the scenario. Hosts on the 10.0.0.0/24 network, which is connected to the ASA inside interface, will share a pool of global addresses, 209.165.200.235-254, configured on the ASA outside interface. Additionally, this example will assume that the xlate timeout value needs to be adjusted from 3 hours to 1 hour.

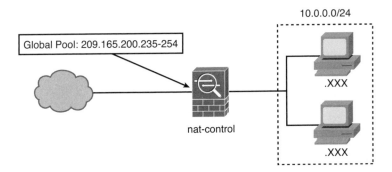

10.0.0.0/24

Global Pool: 209.165.200.235-254

.XXX

nat-control

.XXX

Figure 7-5   *Dynamic Inside NAT Scenario*

The configuration scenario assumes that routing between all involved networks has been properly configured, and that any access lists present on the ASA permit communication between the inside network and the Internet.

To configure the scenario in Figure 7-5, first navigate to **Configuration > Firewall > NAT Rules**. Click **Add** to open a drop-down menu, and choose **Add Dynamic NAT Rule**. Figure 7-6 shows the resulting Add Dynamic NAT Rule dialog box, in which you configure the specifics of the new NAT rule.

From the Interface drop-down list, select the ingress interface for this NAT rule. In Figure 7-6, the inside interface is selected. Next, in the Source field, enter the local IP address or address range that will be subject to this NAT rule. Optionally, click the ellipsis (...) button to choose an IP address or range that has already been defined within Cisco ASDM. If entered manually, define the address and subnet mask using prefix and length notation. Figure 7-6 shows the 10.0.0.0/24 address range being specified.

Note: If you enter an IP address with no mask, Cisco ASDM treats it as a host address, even if it ends with a 0 in the final octet.

Note: Although it is possible to define a source range of 0.0.0.0/0 (any IP address), this is poor security practice, as it would perform NAT translation for any source IP, whether or not that IP was a valid address in the range reachable through the ingress interface. This would only be overcome if you enable reverse-path verification with the **ip verify reverse-path interface** *intf_name* command.

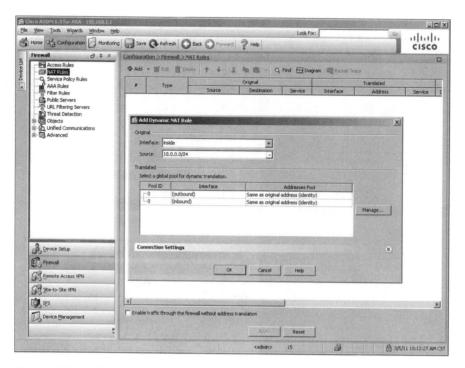

Figure 7-6   *Adding a Dynamic NAT Rule*

Finally, in the Translated area of the dialog box, any previously defined global pools are listed. You can select one to which you want to bind this NAT rule, and click **OK**. Because, in this example, only the system default NAT exemption rules are currently known, click the **Manage** button to begin the configuration of a new global pool. This will open the Manage Global Pool dialog box.

The Manage Global Pool dialog box allows you to select or edit a global address pool that has already been defined, or create a new global address pool. To create a new global pool, click the **Add** button, which opens the Add Global Address Pool dialog box, shown in Figure 7-7. This dialog box allows you to create address translation pools and bind them to ASA interfaces.

When you create a global pool, you must bind it to a particular ASA interface. This is because the same originating hosts that are subject to a NAT rule might, at any given time, be in communication with hosts reachable through different lower security interfaces. Recall that all translation rules require an original address, an ingress interface, a translated address, and an egress interface in order to completely define an address translation rule. You have already completed the definition of the first two factors—the creation of the global address pool defines the latter two.

To select an interface where the global pool will be used, from the Interface drop-down list, select the interface where traffic using this pool will egress the ASA. In Figure 7-7, the outside interface is selected.

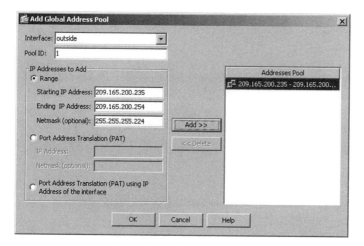

Figure 7-7 *Creating a Global Address Pool*

Next, enter a number between 1 and 2147483647 in the Pool ID field. Cisco ASDM and the ASA use this number to bind the local (original) addresses previously specified to this global pool. In Figure 7-7, a pool ID (also called a NAT ID) of 1 is used.

In the IP Addresses to Add area, click the **Range** radio button. The other options in this section are not used for dynamic NAT. Enter the first IP address for the pool in the Starting IP Address field. Enter the last IP address for the pool in the Ending IP Address field. In Figure 7-7, the pool range is defined as 209.165.200.235 through 209.165.200.254. When this pool of 20 addresses is exhausted, no further translations will occur until addresses are returned to the pool. Any outbound packets requiring translation in such a situation would be dropped.

Optionally, you might enter a network mask for the range defined. If the global pool range is part of the subnet to which the egress interface is connected (as it is in our example), you should enter the same mask configured on the interface itself. While not strictly necessary, this can be helpful when referring to the configuration. Because the IP address on the interface in this example is 209.165.200.226 with a 255.255.255.224 mask, the mask entered in Figure 7-7 is 255.255.255.224. Remember that this mask is for reference only and does not perform any subnetting function.

Note: You can specify more than one range of addresses with the same pool ID on the same interface. These ranges will be added together to form a single pool consisting of multiple ranges. Also, any addresses that are routed to the selected interface are acceptable, even if they are from different subnets than the ASA interface itself. For instance, the outside interface of our ASA is on the 209.165.200.224/27 subnet. However, assuming that the perimeter router also routed the 209.165.201.0/27 subnet to the ASA, you could configure all or any part of that address range as a global pool on the outside interface. Note that in such a case, it is not even necessary to "reserve out" the .0 and .31 addresses, which would normally be considered unusable because they would represent the network identifier and the local broadcast address. You could use all 32 addresses in the range for the global address pool.

To complete the definition of the new global address pool, click **Add** to move the defined range into the Addresses Pool list. Then, click **OK** in this dialog box, and click **OK** again in the Manage Global Pool dialog box. This returns you to the Add Dynamic NAT Rule dialog box. Figure 7-8 shows this, with the newly created global address pool now present in the Translated area of the dialog box.

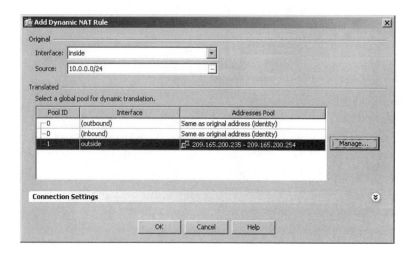

Figure 7-8 *Binding a Global Pool to a NAT Rule*

The final step to completing the definition of a NAT rule is to bind the original address and ingress interface to a particular translation pool defined on the egress interface for this traffic. You have defined as eligible for translation, original addresses of 10.0.0.0/24, which ingress the inside interface, and have created a global pool of 209.165.200.235-254 to be used when the outside interface is the egress interface. To bind these together, select the newly configured pool by clicking it, as shown in Figure 7-8, and then click the **OK** button.

Tip: When you are configuring from the CLI, where changes are immediate (whereas clicking **Apply** is necessary in Cisco ASDM), it is advisable to create the global pool first, and then enter the **nat** command, because as soon as you enter the **nat** command, eligible hosts may begin to attempt connections. When the ASA attempts to match these hosts to a global pool and finds none, it will drop the packets. Also, it will record the fact that the attempting host has no translation rule, and drop packets for the duration of the xlate timeout value, unless an administrator manually clears the translation slot.

The final step in this scenario is to adjust the global translation idle timer (the xlate timeout value) from the default of 3 hours to 1 hour. To do this, navigate to **Configuration > Firewall > Advanced > Global Timeouts**. Figure 7-9 shows the Global Timeouts window. There are many global timeout values tracked by a Cisco ASA.

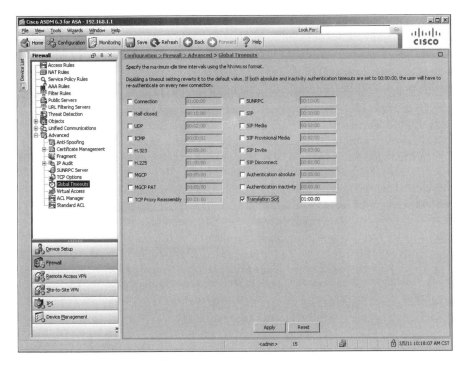

Figure 7-9   *Changing the xlate Timeout*

As shown Figure 7-9, to change the xlate (translation slot) timeout value, check the **Translation Slot** check box. The field will no longer be dimmed. Enter a new timeout value. The figure shows the new timeout value being set as 1 hour (01:00:00).

Click **OK** to save the changes made in this window. Finally, click **Apply** to send the configuration changes to your ASA.

The CLI commands generated by the changes made are as follows:

```
nat (inside) 1 10.0.0.0 255.255.255.0
global (outside) 1 209.165.200.235-209.165.200.254 netmask 255.255.255.224
timeout xlate 1:00:00
```

If you are configuring the ASA from the CLI, you can enter these commands directly in global configuration mode. Note that two commands exist to define dynamic NAT and are associated with each other through the use of the same NAT ID number, which is 1 in this example.

Any individual host can match only one NAT rule for any given connection. The practical significance of this is that any given original address can be bound to only one dynamic NAT ID at a time. So, in the example, a host on the 10.0.0.0/24 subnet would be bound to NAT ID 1, regardless of the egress interface. For example, if a host on the inside subnet were to communicate with the DMZ subnet, and such connections were dynamically translated, we would need a global address pool, with a NAT ID of 1, on the DMZ interface for the internal host to be successfully translated. This is perfectly

Key
Topic

acceptable—nothing implies that a NAT ID can be used on only one interface or must be unique in any way. Examples of multiple interfaces with NAT appear in the next section.

Configuring Dynamic Inside PAT

Dynamic inside NAT creates one-to-one translations of local IP addresses to global IP addresses. Dynamic inside PAT, by contrast, creates many-to-one translations, allowing numerous local IP addresses to share a single global IP address. It does so by creating a temporary translation of both the original IP address and the original source port number to a global IP address and unique global port number, for each translated session (the term *session* is used to indicate a unique, bidirectional communication and therefore is used even when referring to UDP, which is connectionless). These translations are created and added to the translation table for each outbound TCP or UDP session requiring PAT, and are deleted and removed from the table when the OSI Layer 4 session closes. The port numbers are assigned based on an internal algorithm and will appear random.

Note: Older versions of the OS on the Cisco PIX Firewall and ASA assigned PAT port numbers sequentially, beginning with 1024 and moving upward, for host connections initiated from port numbers 1024 and higher.

Because each OSI Layer 4 session uses a separate translation slot, the size of the translation table can grow very large in a production network.

To provide a global IP address for PAT, you can define an available IP address, or you can configure the use of the ASA's IP address on the egress interface. Using the ASA interface IP is particularly useful in environments where you are provided only one IP address, usually dynamically assigned, by an ISP, but it is not limited to such instances.

Like dynamic NAT, dynamic PAT is typically used for client hosts that need outbound connectivity only, and when there are not enough global IP addresses available to assign a unique global address to each local host.

The configuration of dynamic inside PAT is similar to that of dynamic inside NAT. The only difference, in fact, is that when defining the global address pool, instead of using a range of addresses, you specify a single IP address (or the ASA interface).

To present a multi-interface translation scenario, the PAT configuration example will proceed as if there are no current translation rules present on the ASA. You will define the use of PAT for hosts on the inside interface when they initiate communication with hosts reachable through either the outside or DMZ interfaces of the ASA. Further, there will be occasions when hosts on the DMZ need to initiate connectivity to the outside world, so this example will configure PAT for those connections as well.

To begin the process, once again navigate to **Configuration > Firewall > NAT Rules** and click **Add > Add Dynamic NAT Rule** to create a new rule and to define an original interface and IP address range that will be subject to translation. In our example, this would be the inside interface and the 10.0.0.0/24 subnet. In the Add Dynamic NAT Rule dialog box, click **Manage** to open the Manage Global Pool dialog box, and then click **Add** to open the

Add Global Address Pool dialog box, displayed in Figure 7-10. Here, you will define a single global address to be used for PAT.

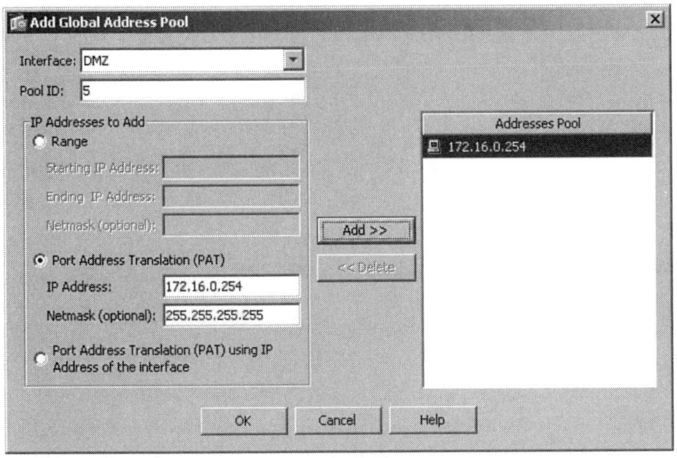

Figure 7-10 *Configuring a PAT Global Address*

In the Interface field, select the egress interface where the PAT address will be used. In Figure 7-10, the DMZ interface has been selected. Enter a valid NAT ID number in the Pool ID field. In the figure, the pool ID has been set to 5. To configure the use of PAT, in the IP Addresses to Add area, click the **Port Address Translation (PAT)** radio button.

In the IP Address field, enter the global IP address that will be used for PAT. In Figure 7-10, the address that will be used is 172.16.0.254. Even though PAT implies the use of a single IP address, there is an optional Netmask field. This should always be set to 255.255.255.255 for PAT, as it is in Figure 7-10.

Click the **Add** button to move the address you defined to the Addresses Pool list. Then, click **OK** to complete this PAT address creation and return to the Manage Global Pool dialog box.

Note: You can specify more than one PAT address with the same pool ID on the same interface. If port assignments are exhausted on the first address listed (which can occur in high-traffic environments where tens of thousands of concurrent sessions occur and use all ports in the 1024–65535 range), new port translations will occur using the second address in the list, and so on.

You have now configured the use of PAT when communicating with hosts reachable through the DMZ interface. To create another PAT rule, for use when communicating with hosts reachable through the outside interface, once again click **Add** to open the Add Global Address Pool dialog box, displayed in Figure 7-11. This time, you will configure the use of PAT by using the ASA interface address as the PAT address.

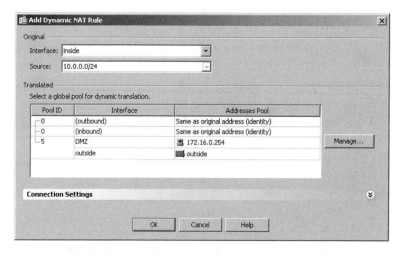

Figure 7-11   *Configuring PAT Using the Interface Address*

In Figure 7-11, the outside interface has been selected. Because the same local hosts will be using this translation rule, whether communicating through the DMZ or outside interface, the same NAT ID number must be used. Therefore, the figure shows this value once again being set to 5.

In the IP Addresses to Add area, click the **Port Address Translation (PAT) Using IP Address of the Interface** radio button instead of specifying a separate IP address.

Click **OK** in the Add Global Address Pool dialog box, and then click **OK** in the Manage Global Pool dialog box, to complete the definition of the new PAT addresses and return to the Add Dynamic NAT Rule dialog box.

Figure 7-12 shows the Add Dynamic NAT Rule dialog box, which now shows the two newly defined PAT addresses with the same NAT ID number listed in the Pool ID column.

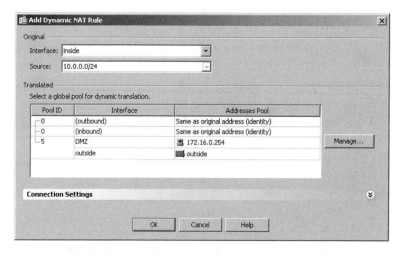

Figure 7-12   *Binding a PAT Address to a NAT Rule*

To complete the definition of the new PAT translation rules for hosts on the inside subnet, select the newly configured PAT "pool" by clicking it, and then click the **OK** button.

The final portion of this configuration scenario is to configure PAT translation for hosts on the DMZ subnet, when initiating communication to hosts on the outside. These hosts will use the same "pool" as the inside hosts—namely, the PAT rule using the outside interface IP address.

To associate a new set of original (local) host addresses with an existing pool, navigate once again to **Configuration > Firewall > NAT Rules** and then click **Add > Add Dynamic NAT Rule** to open the Add Dynamic NAT Rule dialog box. Figure 7-13 shows an example of defining a new source IP range to use an existing global pool.

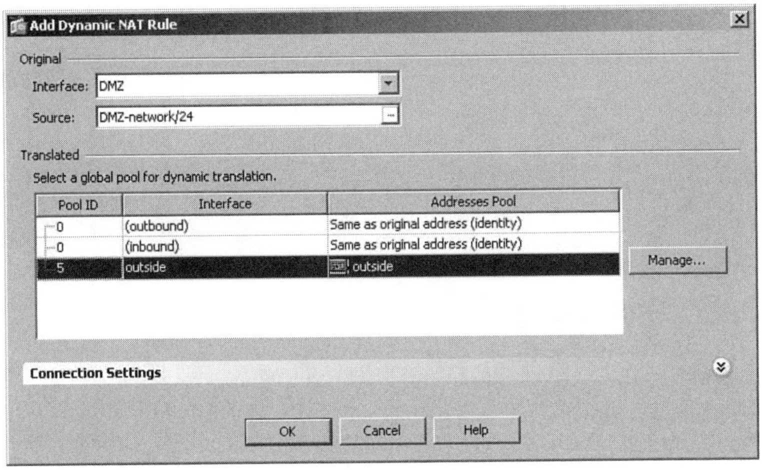

Figure 7-13   *Binding an Existing PAT Address to a NAT Rule*

In the Original area of the Add Dynamic NAT Rule dialog box, from the Interface drop-down list, select the ingress interface for this NAT rule. In Figure 7-13, the DMZ interface is selected.

Next, in the Source field, enter the local IP address or address range that will be subject to this NAT rule. Optionally, you may click the ellipsis (...) button to choose an IP address or range that has already been defined within Cisco ASDM. In Figure 7-13, the ellipsis was clicked and the DMZ network was selected.

The last step is to select Pool ID 5 in the Translated area. Click **OK** to complete the binding and return to the NAT Rules window. Figure 7-14 shows the results in the NAT Rules window.

Note the number column (column header #). The numbers shown here are a strict sequence, starting at 1, and show how many NAT rules exist on the interface. It is not related to the NAT ID number configured in the NAT rules.

Finally, click **Apply** to send the configuration changes to your ASA.

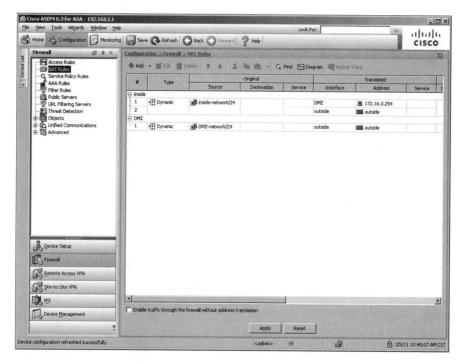

Figure 7-14 *Completed NAT Rules Display*

The CLI commands generated by the changes made are as follows:

```
nat (DMZ) 5 172.16.0.0 255.255.255.0 tcp 0 0 udp 0
nat (inside) 5 10.0.0.0 255.255.255.0 tcp 0 0 udp 0
global (outside) 5 interface
global (DMZ) 5 172.16.0.254 netmask 255.255.255.255
```

If you are configuring the ASA from the CLI, you can enter these commands directly in global configuration mode. For now, do not worry about the **tcp** and **udp** parameters; they are discussed elsewhere.

Note: Note the use of the keyword **interface** in the sample configuration. Not only is this convenient for situations where the ASA is dynamically addressed (as the PAT address will change when the interface address is changed), but is required, as attempting to enter the IP address of the ASA interface when entering this command would generate an error.

Configuring Dynamic Inside Policy NAT

In production networks, you might regularly encounter situations in which local hosts, communicating with different destinations through the same egress interface of the ASA, are required to have different translation rules for each set of destination addresses. In such situations, dynamic NAT or PAT as seen thus far is insufficient to handle the required translations. Examples of such situations include communication across a VPN tunnel to a network that has addressing conflicts with the local network (possibly even overlapping IP address spaces), or connections to application vendors that require your entire network to appear to the application as a single, authorized IP address, and the PAT address normally used for these originating hosts cannot be used for some reason (perhaps because only a subset of local hosts using dynamic PAT are authorized to use the application).

Cisco ASAs support a feature known as policy NAT (or policy PAT), which allows you to specify which specific traffic flows (rather than only which source IP addresses) will be subject to a translation rule. You do this by defining a policy using an ACL, wherein flows defined with a permit entry become eligible for the policy NAT rule you create. ACL configuration is covered in detail in Chapter 8, but this chapter presents some examples for the purpose of illustrating policy NAT rule creation. If you do not fully understand the examples because you do not understand the ACL used, feel free to return and read this section after you read Chapter 8.

You can combine policy NAT with dynamic inside NAT and create dynamic inside policy NAT rules. In this case, you will translate the source IP addresses of your local hosts dynamically, depending on the specific definition of traffic flows defined in an ACL.

To demonstrate a case where dynamic inside policy NAT could be used, we will use the following configuration scenario: The original dynamic NAT configuration from earlier in the chapter is configured on the ASA. The PAT rules from the last section are not present. Several hosts in the 10.0.0.0/24 inside subnet are authorized to connect to a vendor application server on the Internet. This vendor requires all users coming from your organization to appear to their server as a single IP address. Because you are using one-to-one dynamic inside NAT, each internal host has a unique global address when translated.

Thus, you need to create a dynamic inside policy NAT rule to translate internal hosts to use a configured PAT address if they are communicating with the vendor application server, but still use the previously defined NAT rule (pool ID 1) when connecting elsewhere on the Internet.

The configuration scenario presented is based on the scenario in the preceding text. It assumes that all required routing is properly configured and that access rules allow all required communication between these hosts and the outside world.

To configure a dynamic inside policy NAT rule, navigate to **Configuration > Firewall > NAT Rules** and then click **Add > Add Dynamic Policy NAT Rule** to open the Add Dynamic Policy NAT Rule dialog box, shown in Figure 7-15. From this dialog box, you will define your policy for traffic flows subject to this new translation rule.

In the Original area, from the Interface drop-down list, choose an interface that will be the ingress interface for hosts with local addresses to be translated. In Figure 7-15, the inside interface is selected.

In the Source field, enter local addresses, or use the ellipsis button to choose addresses already defined in Cisco ASDM. In the example, the inside-network object known to ASDM has been selected.

Next, in the Destination field, enter the destination address(es) to which these hosts will be connecting, to define specific traffic flows subject to translation. In Figure 7-15, the address 209.165.202.150 is entered (no mask is necessary because ASDM defaults to a /32 mask). This is the vendor application server address.

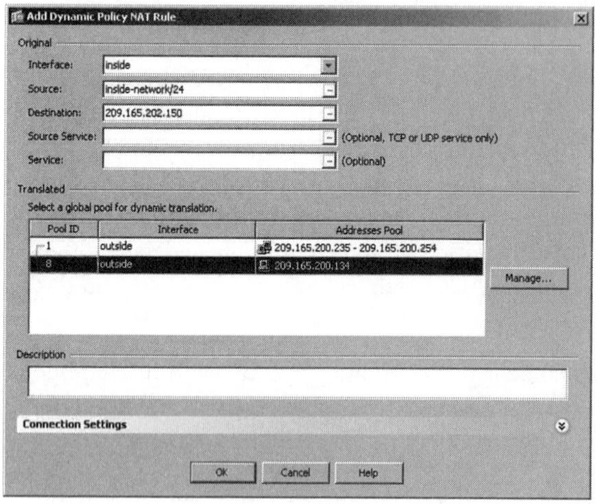

Figure 7-15 *Configuring Dynamic Policy NAT Rule*

Optionally, you can further refine the definition of traffic flows subject to translation by selecting a service in the Service field, to specify the destination service (destination port) that the local hosts are connecting to when they become subject to this translation rule. In Figure 7-15, no service is selected, so all traffic destined to the vendor application server will be subject to this translation rule.

Now that you have defined a policy to select traffic flows subject to this translation rule, assign a PAT global address to this rule, using the same procedure covered in earlier examples. Click the **Manage** button on the right side of the Translated area to define the PAT address. This scenario assumes a Pool ID of 8 was used, with a PAT address of 209.165.200.134. Traffic flows subject to this translation policy will have the source IP address of the local host translated to this PAT address when completing the connection.

Note: This demonstrates an important concept in translation rules. It was stated earlier that any local host could match only one translation rule for any particular traffic flow. Policy NAT rules are evaluated before "regular" NAT rules, so even though this rule uses a pool ID of 8, it will be used, rather than pool ID 1, when packets match the defined policy. The pool IDs do not dictate the order of evaluation.

Select the newly created PAT pool. Click **OK** in the Add Dynamic Policy NAT Rule dialog box to complete the definition of the policy NAT rule. Finally, click **Apply** to send the changes to the ASA.

The CLI commands generated by the changes made are as follows:

```
access-list POLICY-NAT-ACL line 1 extended permit ip 10.0.0.0 255.255.255.0 host
209.165.202.150
!
```

```
nat (inside) 8 access-list POLICY-NAT-ACL tcp 0 0 udp 0
global (outside) 8 209.165.200.134 netmask 255.255.255.255
```

The ACL name is changed from that assigned by ASDM for readability. If you are configuring the ASA from the CLI, you can enter these commands directly in global configuration mode.

Note: Deny access control entries (ACE) are not supported inside policy NAT ACLs. You should only define flows unidirectionally, using the local network as the source in the policy NAT ACL.

Verifying Dynamic Inside NAT and PAT

To examine existing translation table entries (translation slots), use the **show xlate** or **show xlate details** command.

Example 7-1 shows the use of the **show xlate** command based on the original configuration of dynamic inside NAT only. The output shows the number of translation slots currently in use, and the highest number of translation slots concurrently in use since the last reboot of the ASA. Finally, all active translation slots are displayed, with the keyword Global indicating the translated address and the keyword Local indicating the original address. Note that no interface information is contained in the output.

Example 7-1   show xlate *Command Output (NAT)*

```
FIREWALL# show xlate
1 in use, 3 most used
Global 209.165.200.235 Local 10.0.0.101
```

Example 7-2 shows the use of the **show xlate** command based on the PAT configuration created in the multi-interface scenario presented earlier in the chapter. For each translation slot entry, the keyword PAT appears before the Global keyword. Along with the global and local IP addresses, the number appearing in parentheses is the source port number in the packet, after translation (global) and prior to translation (local).

Example 7-2   show xlate *Command Output (PAT)*

```
FIREWALL# show xlate
3 in use, 10 most used
PAT Global 209.165.200.226(50595) Local 10.0.0.101(49298)
PAT Global 209.165.200.226(25788) Local 172.16.0.51(49297)
PAT Global 209.165.200.226(48335) Local 10.0.0.101(62474)
```

Example 7-3 shows the use of the **show xlate detail** command based on the configuration combining dynamic inside NAT with dynamic inside policy PAT. The **show xlate detail** command adds a table of Flag identifiers, for help in understanding the flags listed in the individual translation slot entries. Each translation slot entry also includes information on interfaces involved in the traffic flow. Each entry lists the ingress interface and original (local) address first, followed by the egress interface and translated (global) address. PAT entries indicate whether the protocol in use was TCP or UDP. Translations based on policies (ACLs) show the name of the ACL that defines the policy. Finally, entries contain flags denoting the type of NAT applied. Dynamic translations contain the **i** flag and PAT translations contain the **r** flag, for example.

Example 7-3   show xlate detail *Command Output*

```
FIREWALL# show xlate detail
2 in use, 8 most used
Flags: D - DNS, d - dump, I - identity, i - dynamic, n - no random,
       r - portmap, s - static
NAT from inside:10.0.0.101 to outside:209.165.200.240 flags i
TCP PAT from inside:10.0.0.101/49274 to outside(POLICY-NAT-ACL):209.165.200.134/
    17637 flags ri
```

To manually clear the translation table and return all allocated slots to the pool for assignment, use the **clear xlate** command. This is highly recommended (Cisco even uses the word "required," although this is not entirely accurate) whenever translation rules are changed. There are variations on this command (shown in the section, "Command Reference to Check Your Memory," at the end of this chapter) that allow you to clear only certain translation slots, instead of the entire table. Some active connections that require translation might fail if the underlying translation is cleared, so it is important, in production environments, to clear only those translation slots necessary for your purpose.

Configuring Static Inside NAT

Static inside NAT creates permanent, fixed translations between a local address and a global address. Translation slots created using static translation rules are always present in the translation table, and are persistent across reboots. They have no idle timer leading to expiration. If you delete a static NAT rule from the ASA, the associated entries in the translation table are automatically removed; however, existing sessions remain functional unless manually cleared by an administrator.

Because translation slots based on static translation rules are always active, hosts from less secure networks can initiate communications to the statically translated local hosts, as long as the access list rules on the ASA permit such traffic. These factors make static inside NAT ideal for servers that need to be accessed from less secure interfaces, where the address configured on the server needs to be translated.

Figure 7-16 shows an example of this concept. There are two application servers, a web server and an FTP server, located on the DMZ network.

The IP addresses configured on the hosts are private IP addresses—172.16.0.5 for the web server and 172.16.0.10 for the FTP server. These servers are regularly accessed by clients on the Internet. They must therefore have fixed IP addresses, which can be registered in DNS records that Internet-based hosts will use to find them. Because the private IP addresses configured on the servers cannot be registered in global DNS entries, these servers will use static inside NAT to provide fixed translations to global IP addresses.

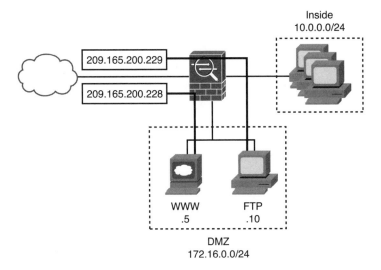

Figure 7-16 *Static Inside NAT Example*

Figure 7-16 shows an example where the web server's local IP address of 172.16.0.5 will be translated to a global IP address of 209.165.200.228, and the FTP server's local IP address of 172.16.0.10 will be translated to a global IP address of 209.165.200.229. When you create DNS records for these hosts, you will use those global addresses. When users on the Internet want to access these hosts, the packets they send will have one of those addresses as the destination IP address. The ASA will be responsible for translating that destination IP and forwarding the traffic to the correct server.

Note that static translations on a Cisco ASA are automatically bidirectional. In other words, unless you create translation rules that will supersede the static translations for these two hosts, if they were to initiate connectivity to hosts reachable through the outside interface of the ASA, their source IP address would be translated to the same global IP address at all times. For example, if the web server with local address 172.16.0.5 connected to an external host, perhaps to download updates for installed software packages, the source address in such packets would be translated to 209.165.200.228 before being forwarded by the ASA through the outside interface.

Recall the four pieces of information necessary for an ASA to perform NAT:

■ Original source IP address (and port) in the packet

■ Interface where the original packet enters the ASA (ingress interface)

■ Interface where the packet will exit the ASA (egress interface)

■ Translated address (and, optionally, port) to insert into the packet

When dynamic inside NAT was defined, the original IP address and interface were defined with the **nat** command, and the mapped (translated) IP address and interface were defined with the **global** command. These two commands were bound together by using the same **NAT ID** parameter in both.

Static inside NAT is different, in that all four required pieces of information are defined in a single command (and in a single ASDM window).

To begin the process, navigate to **Configuration > Firewall > NAT Rules**, and then click **Add > Add Static NAT Rule** to create a new rule. The Add Static NAT Rule dialog box will open, as shown in Figure 7-17, where you define a new static inside NAT rule.

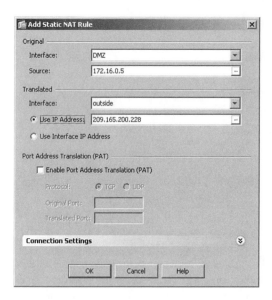

Figure 7-17   *Configuring a Static NAT Rule*

In the Original area, you define the actual IP address of the host being translated (some-times called *real_ip* in documentation) and the ingress interface for traffic arriving from that host (*real_ifc*). From the Interface drop-down list, select the ASA interface through which the host subject to translation is reached (where packets *from* said host will *ingress* to the ASA). In Figure 7-17, the DMZ interface is selected.

In the Source field, enter the local (real) IP address of the host that will be translated. In Figure 7-17, 172.16.0.5 is entered, defining the web server.

In the Translated area, you define the global address to which the host will be translated (called *mapped_ip*) when traffic *from* that host *egresses* the ASA on a selected interface (*mapped_ifc*). In this example, you are creating a mapping for the web server on the out-side interface, so, in the figure, the outside interface is selected from the Interface drop-down list.

Click the **Use IP Address** radio button and enter the global (translated/mapped) IP ad-dress in the field. It is important that you not use a global IP address that is also defined as part of a global address pool on the same interface. In Figure 7-17, the global IP address of 209.165.200.228 is entered.

Click **OK** to accept the new static translation definition and close the Add Static NAT Rule dialog box. Using the same procedure, define the static translation for the FTP server, from real interface DMZ and address 172.16.0.10 to mapped interface outside and address 209.165.200.229, per the scenario information. Then click **Apply** to send the changes to the ASA.

The CLI commands generated by the changes made are as follows:

```
static (DMZ,outside) 209.165.200.228 172.16.0.5 netmask 255.255.255.255 tcp 0 0
 udp 0
static (DMZ,outside) 209.165.200.229 172.16.0.10 netmask 255.255.255.255 tcp 0 0
 udp 0
```

If you are configuring the ASA from the CLI, you can enter these commands directly in global configuration mode.

Note: If you are configuring **static** commands from the CLI, it is important to remember that the order of the interfaces is *real* and then *mapped* (or local and then global, if you prefer), but the order of IP addresses is *mapped* and then *real* (global and then local). Also, there is no space after the comma when specifying interface names. Inserting a space will generate a syntax error.

Note: When you are configuring static translations, in the absence of a configured network mask, a /32 netmask is assumed (the translation is for a single host). Most other commands that have a netmask value as an available parameter default to a classful netmask if none is explicitly configured.

Configuring Network Static Inside NAT

Static inside NAT is not limited to defining host-specific translations. It is possible, with a single static translation, to statically translate an entire range of local addresses to a global address range of the same size.

Consider, for example, the network diagram shown in Figure 7-18. There are 32 servers located in the DMZ: 172.16.0.32–172.16.0.63. You have obtained from your ISP a global IP address block of 209.165.201.0/27, which is 32 addresses in size.

Note that the ASA IP address of 209.165.200.226 is not part of the same network as the addresses assigned by your ISP. This is perfectly acceptable. By default, the ASA will act as a proxy ARP responder for any global addresses configured on its interfaces—it does not need to be attached to the network itself.

Note: When using address blocks for translation, *as long as the ASA interface is not part of the defined network*, it is not necessary to reserve out the addresses that would normally represent the network identifier (.0) and the directed broadcast address (.31). As long as the addresses are routed toward the firewall, all addresses in the block can be used for host translations.

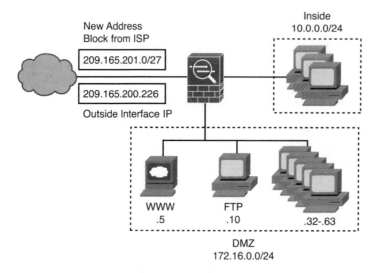

Figure 7-18   *Network Static Inside NAT Scenario*

So, you have 32 servers that will need static translations, and you have a block of 32 global addresses. If you were to use host-specific static translations, you would need to configure 32 of them. Is there a way to accomplish this with less configuration work? Yes! Network static translations (sometimes simply called "net statics") are the answer to this need.

To begin the process, navigate to **Configuration > Firewall > NAT Rules**, and then click **Add > Add Static NAT Rule** to create a new rule. The Add Static NAT Rule dialog box opens, as shown in Figure 7-19.

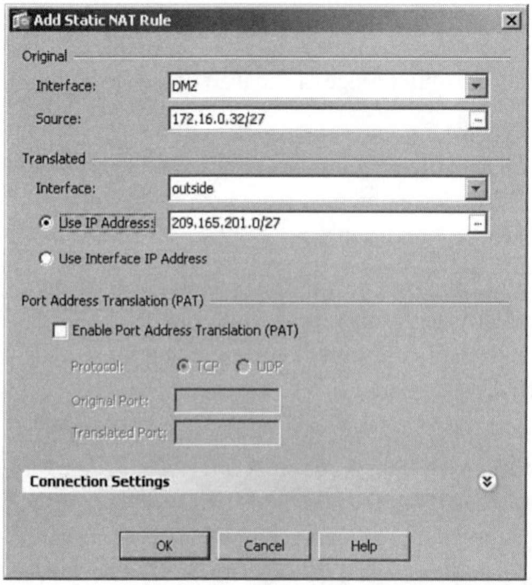

Figure 7-19   *Configuring a Network Static Inside NAT Rule*

In the Original area, from the Interface drop-down list, select the ASA interface through which the host range subject to translation is reached (where packets *from* said host range will *ingress* to the ASA). In Figure 7-19, the DMZ interface is selected.

In the Source field, enter the local (real) IP address range of the hosts that will be translated, *including a netmask value*. In Figure 7-19, 172.16.0.32/27 is entered, defining the range of addresses from 172.16.0.32 through 172.16.0.63.

In the Translated area, you define the global address range and interface used for this translation. In Figure7-19, the outside interface is selected from the Interface drop-down list.

Click the **Use IP Address** radio button and enter the global IP address range in the field, including a netmask value (the same as used to define the original address range). In Figure 7-19, the global IP address range of 209.165.201.0/27 is entered.

> **Note:** The netmask value defines both the size of the block being translated and the specific bits being translated. In this example, the host portion of the original IP addresses is 32–63, but the global address range is 0–31. However, you are translating only the first 27 bits of the original address. So, for example, 172.16.0.39 (**10101100.00010000.00000000.00100111**) is translated to 209.165.201.7 (**11010001. 10100101. 11001001.00000111**). The first 27 bits are translated to equal the first 27 bits of the address in the Use IP Address field, and the last 5 bits are left unchanged.

Click **OK** to accept the new static translation definition and close the Add Static NAT Rule dialog box. Then, click **Apply** to send the changes to the ASA.

The CLI command generated by the changes made is as follows:

```
static (DMZ,outside) 209.165.201.0 172.16.0.32 netmask 255.255.255.224 tcp 0 0
    udp 0
```

If you are configuring the ASA from the CLI, you can enter this command directly in global configuration mode.

> **Note:** It is not possible to define many-to-one static translations prior to OS version 8.3. For example, you can translate an original host address to a translated host address, or you can translate a block of original addresses to a block of translated addresses, as just demonstrated. You cannot, however, translate a block of original addresses to a single host translated address, statically (although you can perform port-redirection for inbound sessions only, as discussed in the following section, "Configuring Static Inside PAT"). This deficiency of function is addressed in OS versions 8.3 and later.

Configuring Static Inside PAT

Using static inside PAT, you can create a fixed translation from a local host IP address and local Layer 4 port (for TCP or UDP) to a global IP address and global Layer 4 port. Static inside PAT is useful when you want to allow inbound connectivity to a number of local servers, using a single global IP address. Remember, of course, that an interface access list on the ASA would still need to be configured to allow such connections (interface access lists are discussed in Chapter 8). It also allows you to reuse a global IP address that is used for dynamic inside NAT/PAT (because outgoing sessions will use port numbers of 1024 and higher) to also support inbound connectivity to servers on specific global ports (which will generally be 1023 and below), forwarded to specific local hosts, on specific local ports.

Static inside PAT has the following characteristics:

- It supports only incoming sessions to the configured global address and port. If the local host also needs to initiate outgoing sessions, you should use either inside NAT or PAT rules to accomplish this.

- It supports the use of the ASA interface as the global address.

- It allows port redirection from a well-known global port to a custom local port, or vice versa. For example, a local web-based application server listens on the well-known TCP port 80. Incoming connections use a custom TCP port of 8080, and the static inside PAT rule redirects these to TCP port 80 when forwarding to the local server.

- It allows port redirection so that multiple local servers, using unique local ports, can share a single global IP address. For example, assume you have two local servers: a web-based application server listening for HTTPS on customized TCP port 8443 and a mail server listening for SMTP on TCP port 25. You have only one global IP address available. Incoming connections to the global IP address, on well-known TCP port 443, are forwarded to the web server on the custom port. Incoming connections to the same global IP address, on port 25, are forwarded to the mail server, still using port 25.

Figure 7-20 shows a network diagram based on the example just described. This is the basis for the configuration scenario to demonstrate the use of static inside PAT.

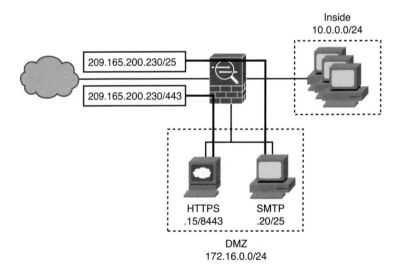

Figure 7-20 *Static Inside PAT Scenario*

You have two servers located on the DMZ segment. The first, with a local IP address of 172.16.0.15, hosts a secure web-based application and listens for HTTPS connections on customized TCP port 8443. The second is a mail server, with a local IP address of 172.16.0.20, and listens for SMTP connections on TCP port 25. You have only one global IP address available for use, 209.165.200.230.

You will configure static inside PAT so that the two local servers, listening on unique local ports, can share the single available global IP address.

To begin the process, navigate to **Configuration > Firewall > NAT Rules**, and then click **Add > Add Static NAT Rule** to create a new rule. The Add Static NAT Rule dialog box will open, as shown in Figure 7-21.

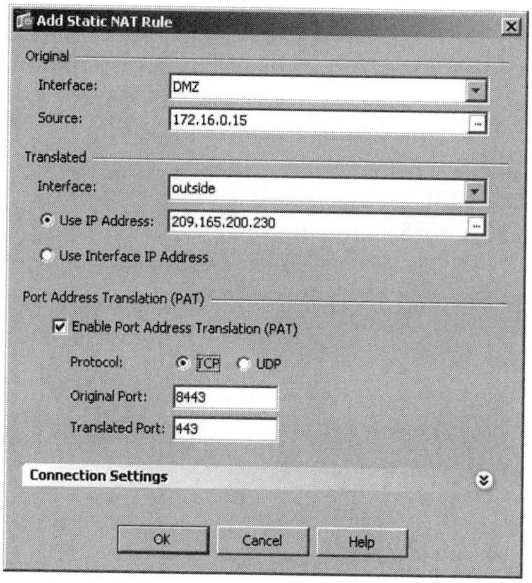

Figure 7-21   *Configuring a Static Inside PAT Rule*

In the Original area, from the Interface drop-down list, select the ASA interface through which the hosts subject to translation are reached (where packets *from* said hosts will *ingress* to the ASA). In Figure 7-21, the DMZ interface is selected.

In the Source field, enter the local (real) IP address of the first server that will be translated. In Figure 7-21, 172.16.0.15 is entered, defining the secure web-based application server.

In the Translated area, select the interface where you will map the global IP address used in this translation. In Figure 7-21, the outside interface is selected from the Interface drop-down list.

Click the **Use IP Address** radio button and enter the global IP address in the field. In Figure 7-21, the global IP address of 209.165.200.230 is entered.

Note: Optionally, you could click the Use Interface IP Address radio button to use the IP address of the selected interface (outside in this example) as the global IP address used for this translation rule.

In the Port Address Translation (PAT) area, check the **Enable Port Address Translation (PAT)** check box. This will make the fields below this available for editing.

Next, select the radio button for the protocol for which you are translating ports: **TCP** or **UDP**. In Figure 7-21, the TCP radio button is selected.

In the Original Port field, enter the actual port on which the server is configured to listen. In Figure 7-21, port 8443 is configured.

In the Translated Port field, enter the port that will be specified as the destination port for inbound connections. This server requires port redirection, and port 443 is configured in this field.

Click **OK** to accept the new static translation definition and close the Add Static NAT Rule dialog box. Using the same procedure, define the static translation for the mail server, from real interface DMZ and address 172.16.0.20 to mapped interface outside and address 209.165.200.230, this time using TCP port 25 as both the original and translated port, because port redirection is not used for the mail server. Then click **Apply** to send the changes to the ASA.

The CLI commands generated by the changes made are as follows:

```
static (DMZ,outside) tcp 209.165.200.230 443 172.16.0.15 8443 netmask
  255.255.255.255 tcp 0 0 udp 0
static (DMZ,outside) tcp 209.165.200.230 25 172.16.0.20 25 netmask
  255.255.255.255 tcp 0 0 udp 0
```

If you are configuring the ASA from the CLI, you can enter these commands directly in global configuration mode.

These translations allow outside hosts to access either server in the DMZ by connecting to their global IP address and global port (assuming that access rules have been created to permit such connections). To access the secure web-based application server, outside hosts would connect to 209.165.200.230, TCP port 443. To access the mail server, outside hosts would connect to 209.165.200.230, TCP port 25.

Note: Static PAT allows you to use the same global IP address for many different static rules, provided the port is unique for each rule. You cannot use the same global IP address for multiple static NAT rules.

Configuring Static Inside Policy NAT

As previously mentioned, in production networks, local hosts communicating with different destinations through the same egress interface of the ASA regularly are required to have different translation rules for each set of destination addresses. Dynamic inside policy NAT allows you to provide different translation rules depending on the specific traffic flows involved. Static inside policy NAT does the same thing, while providing a fixed, rather than dynamic, address translation for the original local host.

The most common example where static inside policy NAT would be required is communication across a VPN tunnel to a network that has addressing conflicts with the local network (possibly even overlapping IP address spaces).

As with dynamic policy NAT, this is done by defining a policy using an ACL, wherein flows defined with a permit entry become eligible for the static policy NAT rule you create. Permitted traffic flows will have their original source IP address statically translated to the global IP address provided in the static translation rule.

To demonstrate a case where static inside policy NAT could be used, consider the following configuration scenario: Your company, Company A, recently acquired another company, Company B, and you have established a VPN connection between the two sites. Users at Company B must be able to communicate with your mail server on the DMZ subnet (172.16.0.20:25), and your mail server must be able to communicate bidirectionally with the Company B mail server, which will eventually be phased out. However, Company B has a VPN with a vendor that also uses the 172.16.0.0/24 address space. Obviously, you cannot force the vendor to re-address its network.

Note: It is the fact that you need to allow bidirectional traffic initiation with the remote network that makes the use of static inside policy NAT necessary. The remote network must have a fixed IP address to which it connects in order to reach the local server, but the local server must also be able to initiate connectivity to the remote network. If only the remote network initiated connectivity, dynamic inside policy PAT could be used. If only the local host initiated connectivity, dynamic inside NAT might be able to be used.

Thus, you need to create a static inside policy NAT rule, which will allow these users to connect to your mail server using an address that will not conflict with their existing routing plan, while the server still uses the previously defined static PAT rule when connecting to the Internet.

Figure 7-22 presents a network diagram based on the scenario just described.

To begin the process, navigate to **Configuration > Firewall > NAT Rules**, and then click **Add > Add Static Policy NAT Rule** to create a new rule. The Add Static Policy NAT Rule dialog box will open, as shown in Figure 7-23.

In the Original area, from the Interface drop-down list, select the ASA interface through which the host subject to translation is reached. In Figure 7-23, the DMZ interface is selected.

In the Source field, enter the local IP address of the host that will be translated. In Figure 7-23, 172.16.0.20 is entered, defining the mail server.

Next, in the Destination field, enter the destination address(es) to which this host will be communicating, to define specific traffic flows subject to translation. In Figure 7-23, the address 10.10.10.0/24 is entered, specifying the internal network of Company B.

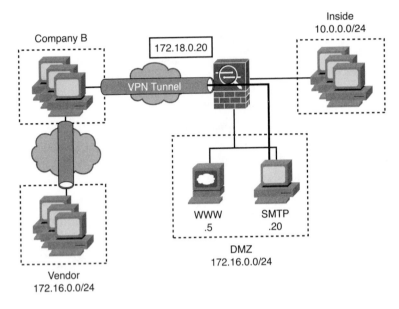

Figure 7-22   *Static Inside Policy NAT Scenario*

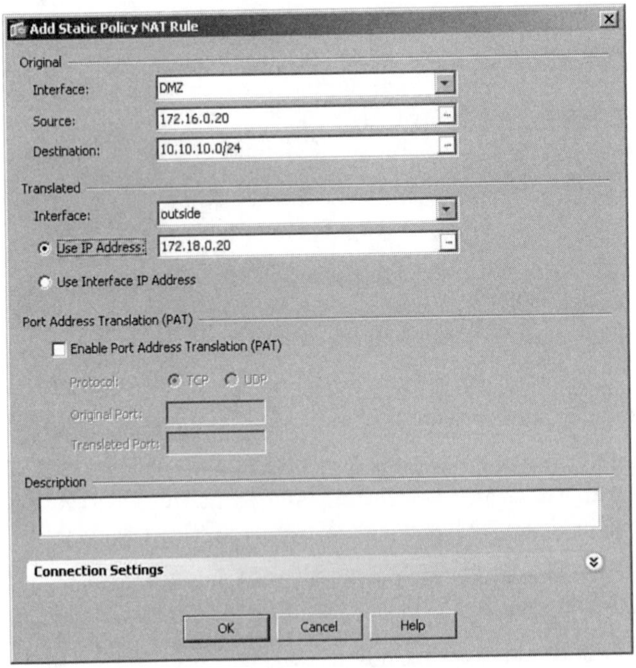

Figure 7-23   *Configuring a Static Inside Policy NAT Rule*

In the Translated area, select the interface where you will map the global IP address used in this translation. In Figure 7-23, the outside interface is selected from the Interface drop-down list.

Click the **Use IP Address** radio button and enter the global IP address in the field. In Figure 7-23, the global IP address of 172.18.0.20 is entered.

Click **OK** to accept the new static policy NAT definition and close the Add Static Policy NAT Rule dialog box. Then click **Apply** to send the changes to the ASA. Because the policy NAT rule just defined uses the same local address and same port pair as an existing static rule, Cisco ASDM will present you with a Warning message. Note that Warnings indicate an unusual condition that you should verify, whereas Errors indicate that the configuration is invalid.

The CLI commands generated by the changes made are as follows:

```
access-list POLICY-NAT-ACL2 line 1 extended permit ip host 172.16.0.20 10.10.10.0
  255.255.255.0
!
static (DMZ,outside) 172.18.0.20 access-list POLICY-NAT-ACL2 tcp 0 0 udp 0
```

The ACL name is changed from that assigned by ASDM for readability. If you are configuring the ASA from the CLI, you can enter these commands directly in global configuration mode.

Although the policy is configured for outgoing traffic, remember that the ASA will also apply the same condition to incoming traffic. That is, if mail server 172.16.0.20 is initiating connectivity to the 10.10.10.0/24 network, its source address will be translated to 172.18.0.20. Likewise, if hosts on the 10.10.10.0/24 network send traffic to 172.18.0.20, and this traffic is routed across the VPN to the ASA, after decryption, the destination address in the packets will be changed from 172.18.0.20 to 172.16.0.20, before being forwarded to the mail server on the DMZ.

Note: Static inside policy PAT can be defined in the same manner, by enabling PAT and specifying original and translated port numbers, after configuring the global IP address.

Verifying Static Inside NAT and PAT

As with dynamic inside NAT and PAT, static inside NAT and PAT can be verified using the **show xlate** or **show xlate detail** command.

The output of **show xlate** is the same regardless of whether translations are dynamic or static. There is nothing in the output that indicates a given xlate table entry is based on a static, rather than dynamic, translation rule.

Example 7-4, however, shows the use of the **show xlate detail** command. The **show xlate details** command adds a table of Flag identifiers, for help in understanding the flags listed in the individual translation slot entries. Each translation slot entry also includes information on interfaces involved in the traffic flow. Each entry lists the ingress interface and original (local) address first, followed by the egress interface and translated (global) address. PAT entries indicate whether the protocol in use was TCP or UDP. Translations based on policies (ACLs) show the name of the ACL that defines the policy. Finally, entries contain flags denoting the type of NAT applied. Static translations contain the **s** flag and PAT translations contain the **r** flag, for example.

Example 7-4 show xlate detail *Command Output*

```
FIREWALL# show xlate detail
6 in use, 6 most used
Flags: D - DNS, d - dump, I - identity, i - dynamic, n - no random,
       r - portmap, s - static
TCP PAT from DMZ:172.16.0.20/25 to outside:209.165.200.230/25 flags sr
TCP PAT from DMZ:172.16.0.15/8443 to outside:209.165.200.230/443 flags sr
NAT from DMZ:172.16.0.5 to outside:209.165.200.228 flags s
NAT from DMZ:172.16.0.10 to outside:209.165.200.229 flags s
NAT from DMZ:172.16.0.32 to outside:209.165.201.0 flags s
NAT from DMZ:172.16.0.20 to outside(POLICY-NAT-ACL2):172.18.0.20 flags s
```

To manually clear the translation table and return all allocated slots to the pool for assignment, use the **clear xlate** command. Because static translations are permanent, if you use the **clear xlate** command and then immediately use the **show xlate** command, all statically defined translation slots will appear in the xlate table.

Configuring No-Translation Rules

If you enable NAT control, you must configure translation rules for each host on a more secure interface that requires communication with hosts on less secure interfaces. There are many cases, however, where you will not require NAT for such communication.

For example, if a host on your inside network needs to communicate with a host on your DMZ network, there are no networks in the path that would consider either address nonroutable. As such, there is no reason why the original address of the host cannot remain as it is in the data packets. Other examples are when NAT will be performed by some other device in the data path of the traffic, so the ASA does not need to perform NAT.

Where NAT control is enabled but no translation is required or desired, you must configure no-translation rules to satisfy the requirement that you have addressed how NAT is to be handled for such communication—it is not to be performed.

The Cisco ASA provides three mechanisms that enable you to create translation rules that perform no actual translation:

■ **Dynamic identity NAT:** Creates dynamic identity translation slots in the translation table (where local and global addresses are the same) when hosts on a more secure interface communicate with hosts on less secure interfaces

■ **Static identity NAT:** Creates static identity translation slots in the translation table immediately as they are configured, which can support servers that do not require translation

- **NAT bypass (exemption):** Allows packets to completely bypass the ASA NAT engine, not creating translation slots at all

Configuring Dynamic Identity NAT

Dynamic identity NAT creates temporary translation slots in the translation table, which "translate" a local address on a specific interface to the same address on all lower-security interfaces. These slots are created by outbound packets from hosts configured for dynamic identity NAT arriving at the ASA. Because these slots come into existence only when outbound traffic occurs, this method is suitable to support only client systems, not servers.

When configuring dynamic identity NAT, you are not able to limit the non-translation to specific global interfaces. For example, you cannot perform normal translation for hosts when they access the outside, while performing identity NAT when the same hosts access the DMZ.

Note: Remember that any given traffic flow can match only a single translation rule. Dynamic identity NAT has the same precedence as any other dynamic NAT rule (non-zero NAT ID pool number). Because the NAT ID number is selected from the **nat** command that most specifically matches the traffic being analyzed, it is important to ensure that you properly define the source address(es) subject to translation. For example, suppose a host of 10.0.0.75 is the source of packets and the ASA contains the following **nat** commands:

```
nat (inside) 0 10.0.0.0 255.255.255.0 tcp 0 0 udp 0
nat (inside) 5 10.0.0.64 255.255.255.192 tcp 0 0 udp 0
```

The command with NAT ID 5 is a more specific match, based on prefix length, than the identity NAT rule. As such, NAT would be performed, using global pool 5 on the egress interface. It is important to remember that the NAT ID number exists only to bind a **nat** command to a global pool—it does not imply ordinality (that is, lower numbers are not processed for a match prior to higher numbers). It is not the NAT ID number that determines which **nat** rule is applied to the traffic, but rather the prefix length to which the **nat** command address matches the source address in the packets.

Dynamic identity NAT is configured the exact same way as any other dynamic NAT rule, with one exception. To configure dynamic identity NAT, navigate to **Configuration > Firewall > NAT Rules** and click **Add > Add Dynamic NAT Rule**. The Add Dynamic NAT Rule dialog box opens, as shown in Figure 7-24. Note that this example assumes that previously defined NAT rules for hosts on the inside interface are no longer in place.

Define the original interface and IP address(es) subject to this NAT rule as you would for any dynamic inside NAT rule. In Figure 7-24, the inside network 10.0.0.0/24 is defined. Then, in the Translated area, select the predefined pool with NAT Pool ID 0. Because this example is for traffic from a higher-security interface (inside) to a lower-security interface (DMZ), choose the NAT 0 pool with (outbound) listed in the Interface column. The NAT Pool ID of 0 in an outbound direction has special significance to the ASA. It means that specified host addresses will not be translated to any lower-security interfaces, and that translation slots can be created only by outbound communication. Because source addresses on lower-security interfaces are not, by default, translated when traversing the

ASA toward a higher-security interface (for example, Internet-sourced traffic trying to reach a web server in the DMZ), inbound identity NAT would be used only in the rare circumstances in which such translation was configured and you needed to override it.

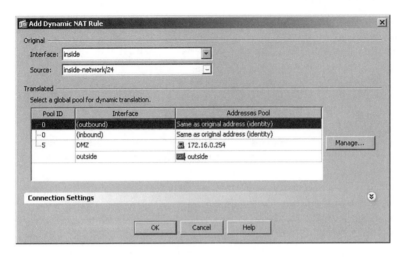

Figure 7-24   *Configuring a Dynamic Identity NAT Rule*

Click **OK** in the Add Dynamic NAT Rule dialog box to complete the definition of the no-NAT rule. Finally, click **Apply** to send the changes to the ASA.

The CLI command generated by the changes made follows:

```
nat (inside) 0 10.0.0.0 255.255.255.0 0 0 tcp 0 0 udp 0
```

If you are configuring the ASA from the CLI, you can enter this command directly in global configuration mode.

Note: Because the ASA is not performing NAT for the inside network in this example, hosts on the inside network would not be able to communicate with any hosts outside the local network (on the Internet, for example) unless another device in the traffic path, such as an edge (sometimes called perimeter) router, performed NAT.

Configuring Static Identity NAT

Static identity NAT creates permanent translation slots in the translation table that "translate" a local address on a specific interface to the same address on a specific lower-security interface. These slots are created immediately upon configuration. Because these slots always exist, this method is suitable to support servers accepting inbound connections.

When configuring static identity NAT, you are able to limit the non-translation to specific global interfaces. You can therefore perform normal translation for hosts when they access the outside, while performing identity NAT when the same hosts access the DMZ, for example.

The other significant difference with static (versus dynamic) identity NAT is that, access rules permitting, hosts on the less secure interface can access an identity-NAT "translated" server on the more secure interface, using its configured local IP address.

Consider the example shown in Figure 7-25. Your company has an SMTP gateway, 172.16.0.20, on the DMZ network. Mail must pass through this device when moving between the Internet and the internal network. When mail arrives from the Internet, it is passed through various security measures, such as filtering, virus checks, and so on, on the gateway device, and only then is forwarded to your company's internal mail server, 10.0.0.20, on the inside network. Because both servers are part of the private-address space, no translation is necessary, but because either server may initiate communication, identity NAT must be performed statically, not dynamically.

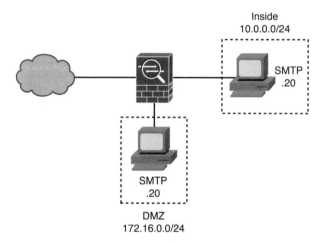

Figure 7-25 *Static Identity NAT Scenario*

Static identity NAT is configured the exact same way as any other static NAT rules. To configure static identity NAT, navigate to **Configuration > Firewall > NAT Rules** and click **Add > Add Static NAT Rule**. The Add Static NAT Rule dialog box opens, as shown in Figure 7-26.

The example that follows will configure the mail address scenario described in the preceding paragraphs.

Define the original interface and IP address(es) subject to this NAT rule as you would for any static NAT rule. In Figure 7-26, the inside interface is selected and the mail server address of 10.0.0.20 is specified.

In the Translated area, you define the interface where the global address to be configured will be used. In Figure 7-26, the DMZ interface is selected.

Click the **Use IP Address** radio button and enter the same IP address in this field as you did in the Source field. In Figure 7-26, the IP address 10.0.0.20 is entered in both fields.

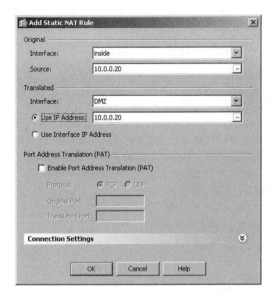

Figure 7-26 *Configuring a Static Identity NAT Rule*

Click **OK** to accept the new static translation definition and close the Add Static NAT Rule dialog box. Then click **Apply** to send the changes to the ASA.

The CLI command generated by the changes made follows:

```
static (inside,DMZ) 10.0.0.20 10.0.0.20 netmask 255.255.255.255 tcp 0 0 udp 0
```

If you are configuring the ASA from the CLI, you can enter this command directly in global configuration mode.

Configuring NAT Bypass (NAT Exemption)

The final, and most preferred, method to perform no translation in situations where NAT control is enabled is NAT bypass (commonly referred to as "NAT 0 with an ACL" or "policy identity NAT").

NAT bypass allows configured traffic flows to completely bypass the ASA's NAT engine. Clients and/or servers not requiring translation are thus allowed to communicate without the creation of any translation slots in the translation table (which reduces device processing overhead).

The most common use of NAT bypass is for traffic that will cross the Internet inside a VPN tunnel. Because the original source address is not visible to the Internet, where it would be considered nonroutable, it is generally preferred not to translate this traffic. The other time NAT bypass can be used is when hosts on a more secure interface need to communicate with hosts on a less secure interface, but do not need to accept inbound connections (where the use of static identity NAT is appropriate).

The configuration scenario will be to set up NAT bypass for traffic originating on the inside network and destined for the DMZ network. Because this traffic is contained inside the internal network space, no translation is necessary. Also, in this scenario, hosts on the DMZ never initiate connections to the inside—they are always the server part of the client/server pair.

To configure NAT bypass, navigate to **Configuration > Firewall > NAT Rules** and click **Add > Add NAT Exempt Rule**. The Add NAT Exempt Rule dialog box opens, as shown in Figure 7-27. In this dialog box, you will define a full traffic flow policy (which becomes an ACL, hence the common name "NAT 0 with an ACL") and enable the defined flow to bypass the NAT engine.

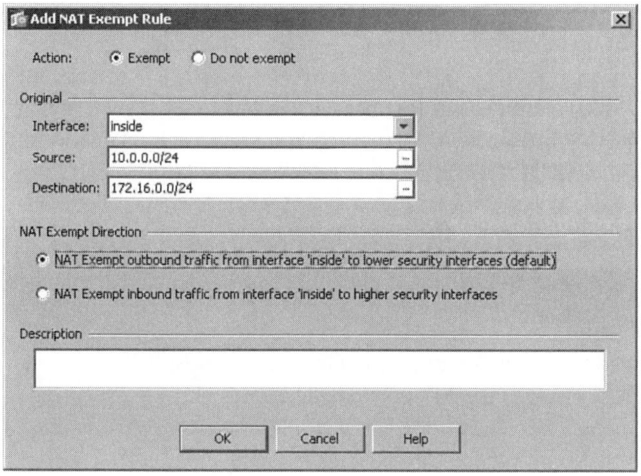

Figure 7-27   *Configuring a NAT Bypass Rule*

In the Original area, from the Interface drop-down list, select the ASA interface through which the host(s) subject to translation exemption can be reached. In Figure 7-27, the inside interface is selected.

In the Source field, enter the local IP address of the host(s) that will bypass NAT. In Figure 7-27, 10.0.0.0/24 is entered, defining the inside network.

Next, in the Destination field, enter the destination address(es) to which traffic that will bypass NAT will be destined, to define specific traffic flows subject to translation exemption. In Figure 7-27, the address 172.16.0.0/24 is entered, specifying the DMZ network.

Click the **NAT Exempt Outbound Traffic from Interface 'inside' to Lower Security Interfaces (Default)** radio button to enable NAT bypass.

Click **OK** to accept the new NAT bypass rule definition and close the Add NAT Exempt Rule dialog box. Then click **Apply** to send the changes to the ASA.

The CLI commands generated by the changes made are as follows:

```
access-list NO-NAT line 1 extended permit ip host 10.0.0.0 255.255.255.0
  172.16.0.0 255.255.255.0
!
nat (inside) 0 access-list NO-NAT tcp 0 0 udp 0
```

The ACL name is changed from that assigned by ASDM for readability. If you are configuring the ASA from the CLI, you can enter these commands directly in global configuration mode.

Note: You can apply only a single NAT bypass rule to any one interface. As such, all traffic to be exempted from NAT, when ingressing through a given interface, must be defined as part of the same ACL.

NAT Rule Priority

It has been mentioned more than once in this chapter that any specific traffic flow can match only one NAT rule. This is not to say that conflicting NAT rules cannot be configured, but rather that only one NAT rule can be applied to a packet as it ingresses the ASA through an interface where a NAT rule exists.

It is therefore important to know how, in the presence of conflicting rules, an ASA prioritizes the rules. The ASA will apply the NAT rule with the highest precedence that matches the packets being subjected to NAT control.

The order in which rules appear in the ASA configuration matters, as most NAT is applied to the first rule encountered that matches the packets being checked. The one exception is dynamic NAT, which, as has already been mentioned, will apply the rule with the best (longest bit pattern) match to the source address in the packets being checked.

The precedence of NAT rules, with NAT control enabled, is as follows:

Key Topic

1. **NAT bypass (exemption) (nat 0 access-list):** Supersedes all other translation rules, and searched in the order in which the rules appear in the configuration, with the first matching rule applied.
2. **Static NAT and static PAT (policy and regular):** Searched in the order in which the rules appear in the configuration, with the first matching rule applied.
3. **Policy dynamic NAT (nat *nat_id* access-list):** Searched in the order in which the rules appear in the configuration, with the first matching rule applied.
4. **Regular dynamic NAT (including dynamic identity NAT - NAT 0 without ACL):** Searches all dynamic NAT rules applied to the ingress interface, and applies the rule with the best (longest bit pattern) match to the local address.

If NAT control is enabled, and a packet does not match any of the rules listed, the packet is dropped. If NAT control is disabled (the default), packets not matching a translation rule are forwarded without translation, if permitted by security policy.

Configuring Outside NAT

All the NAT examples presented thus far have been inside NAT, which is applied to packets that ingress an interface that has a higher security level than the interface they egress. Outside NAT is exactly the opposite—it is applied to packets that ingress a lower security interface than they egress (inbound traffic).

Outside NAT is always optional (and actually fairly rare), even if NAT control is enabled. Consider the very common example of traffic entering an ASA from the Internet (presumably, through the outside interface). There is rarely a reason why the source address of such traffic would need to be altered.

Situations that would require outside NAT are generally due either to overlapping IP address spaces needing to communicate with each other (likely through a VPN) or to external hosts connecting to applications that are configured to service only specific client addresses (and the source address of the external host must therefore be translated to an authorized source address).

Occasionally, you will need to apply both inside NAT and outside NAT to the same traffic flow (almost always due to overlapping IP addresses on the network requiring communication). This is known as *bidirectional NAT*, sometimes also called *dual NAT*.

Configuration of outside NAT is exactly the same as configuration of inside NAT, with the exception that the Original or Source (policy NAT/PAT rules only) fields will refer to a lower-security interface, and the Translated or Destination (policy NAT/PAT rules only) fields will refer to a higher-security interface.

Note: Although it is possible to configure dynamic outside NAT, there are caveats to its use, and it is generally not recommended. You should, instead, use static outside NAT when outside NAT is necessary.

The configuration scenario has a server on the inside network that is configured to accept connection requests only from IP addresses on the 10.0.0.0/20 network. However, you have customers who will regularly access this server to obtain customized reports. These reports are based on information in the public domain, so they do not require encryption. One such customer is using PAT on their edge device, so all their users, when their traffic arrives at the ASA outside interface, appear to be coming from IP address 209.165.202.135. Figure 7-28 illustrates the network topology for this scenario.

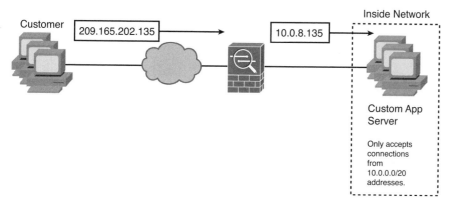

Figure 7-28   *Outside NAT Scenario*

Because the traffic arrives at the ASA with a public source IP address, but the application server will only accept connections from IP addresses in the 10.0.0.0/20 address space, you will need to perform static outside NAT on the incoming requests, before forwarding them to the application server.

To configure static outside NAT, navigate to **Configuration > Firewall > NAT Rules** and then click **Add > Add Static NAT Rule.** The Add Static NAT Rule dialog box will open, as shown in Figure 7-29, where you define a new static outside NAT rule.

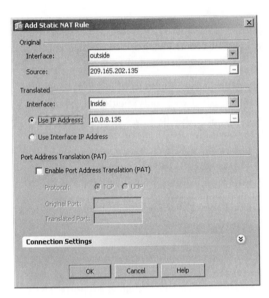

Figure 7-29 *Configuring a Static Outside NAT Rule*

In the Original area, you define the actual IP address(es) being translated, and the ingress interface for traffic arriving from such address(es). From the Interface drop-down list, select the ASA interface through which the host subject to translation is reached (where packets *from* said host will *ingress* the ASA). Because this is outside NAT, the original interface will be the less secure interface in the traffic path. In Figure 7-29, the outside interface is selected.

In the Source field, enter the real IP address of the host(s) that will be translated. In Figure 7-29, the customer PAT address of 209.165.202.135 is entered.

In the Translated area, you define the address to which the host(s) will be translated when traffic *from* such host(s) *egresses* the ASA on a selected interface. In our example, we are creating a mapping for the customer traffic on the inside interface, so, in Figure 7-29, the inside interface is selected.

Click the **Use IP Address** radio button and enter the translated (mapped) IP address in the field. In Figure 7-29, the IP address of 10.0.8.135 is entered, which is an address we have allocated for use by this customer.

Note: Although not used in this example, it is perfectly permissible to use an IP address that overlaps the internal 10.0.0.0/24 network, such as 10.0.0.135, so long as you have ensured that address will never be allocated to an actual internal host. For instance, you might exclude a range of IP addresses from assignment by local DCHP, and use such a range for outside NAT assignments.

Click **OK** to accept the new static translation definition and close the Add Static NAT Rule dialog box. Then, click **Apply** to send the changes to the ASA.

The CLI command generated by the changes made follows:

```
static (outside,inside) 10.0.8.135 209.165.202.135 netmask 255.255.255.255 tcp 0
  0 udp 0
```

If you are configuring the ASA from the CLI, you can enter this command directly in global configuration mode.

Note: The order in which interfaces and IP addresses are specified when using outside NAT is still *real, mapped, mapped, real*, just as in any other **static** command. Similarly, if you are using dynamic outside NAT (which is not recommended), the **nat** command would be bound to the less secure interface (outside in our example) and the **global** pool would exist on the more secure interface (inside in our example). The **nat** command must also include the keyword **outside** to indicate the use of outside NAT.

Other NAT Considerations

The performance of NAT was one of the principle functions of ASAs in most production networks. It is important to consider the ramifications that the changing of addresses has on other items in the ASA configuration. Several such items are discussed in this section.

DNS Rewrite (Also Known as DNS Doctoring)

Key Topic

Static inside NAT is normally performed for servers, so that external hosts, upon receiving the IP address of the server from an Internet-based DNS server, can route traffic to the server's global IP address. Such traffic will arrive at the ASA and then be redirected to the internal server based on the interface and IP address in the **static** command.

However, what if the client is on the internal network? If you are using an internal DNS server, this presents no problems, as the local IP address of the server would be returned to the client performing a DNS query.

Figure 7-30 illustrates a network where internal clients make DNS queries to an external DNS server when looking for an internal server. This would present a problem, which the DNS Rewrite feature is designed to solve.

The problem arises from the fact that the Internet-based DNS server does not know the private IP address of the server, or which DNS queries come from the same internal network as where the server is located. So, if client 10.0.0.103 were to send to the DNS server a DNS query looking for the server www.ciscopress.ccnp, the only address the server would know to respond with would be 209.165.200.228, the global IP address of the web server, as configured earlier. If the client were to attempt a connection to this address, it would be unsuccessful, as the server is actually located in the DMZ, but the global IP address would route through the outside interface.

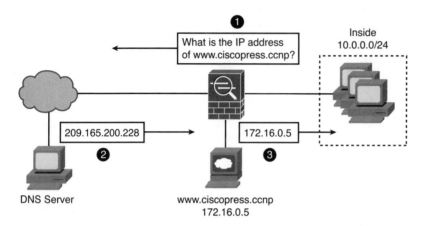

Figure 7-30 *DNS Rewrite Scenario*

Note: DNS Rewrite is supported for both static and dynamic NAT rules.

With DNS Rewrite enabled, the ASA inspects inbound DNS replies and, if the IP address being returned is a global IP address configured with a static inside NAT rule, translates the address inside the DNS reply to be the local IP address of the server. So, the 209.165.200.228 address embedded in the DNS reply would match the static inside NAT rule for the web server, and the ASA would translate this to the local IP address 172.16.0.5 before forwarding the reply to the requesting client. Client 10.0.0.103 would now attempt its connection to 172.16.0.5, which would be successful.

Note: DNS inspection must be enabled for DNS Rewrite to function.

To configure DNS Rewrite for hosts using static inside NAT translation, navigate to **Configure > Firewall > NAT Rules.** Click **Add > Add Static NAT Rule** if you are creating a new rule, or **Edit > Edit Static NAT Rule** if you are adding DNS Rewrite to an existing static translation rule. Click the expand symbol to the right of the words Connection Settings to make the DNS Rewrite option visible (it is hidden by default). Figure 7-31 shows an example of editing the static inside NAT rule previously configured for the web server. The Connection Settings area has already been expanded.

Check the **Translate the DNS Replies That Match the Translate Rule** check box to enable DNS Rewrite for this static translation rule.

Click **OK** to accept the change and close the Add/Edit Static NAT Rule dialog box. Then click **Apply** to send the changes to the ASA.

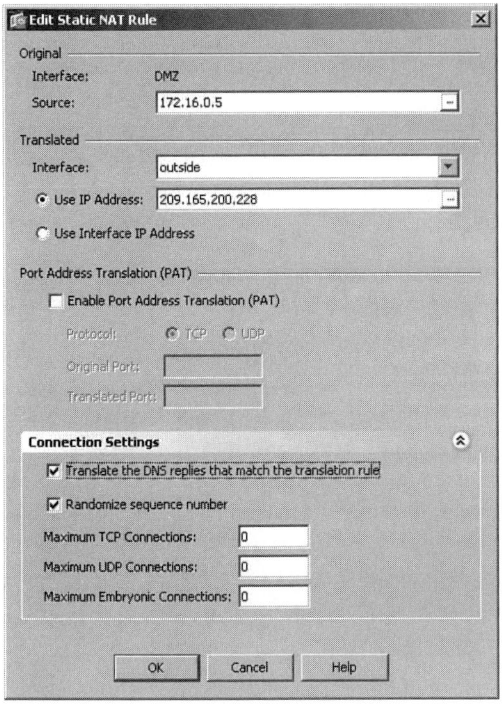

Figure 7-31   *Configuring DNS Rewrite*

The CLI commands generated by the changes made are as follows:

```
no static (DMZ,outside) 209.165.200.228 172.16.0.5 netmask 255.255.255.255
static (DMZ,outside) 209.165.200.228 172.16.0.5 netmask 255.255.255.255 dns tcp
  0 0 udp 0
```

If you are configuring the ASA from the CLI, you can enter these commands directly in global configuration mode. The **no** command is generated because you are editing an existing rule.

Integrating NAT with ASA Access Control

Configuring NAT rules on an ASA impacts the configuration of access control rules, including interface access rules (interface ACLs), which filter traffic, user AAA rules (for Cut-through Proxy services), and Modular Policy Framework service policies (which can affect traffic handling in a number of ways), as they all typically refer to IP addresses that may be subject to translation.

In the case of interface ACLs, you must keep the following in mind:

■   For inbound ACLs (applied to traffic as it ingresses the ASA through the interface), access rules are applied *before* NAT takes place. Therefore, an access control entry (ACE, a single line of an ACL) that filters source addresses must refer to the untranslated (original) address(es) of the source host(s). An access list that filters based on destination addresses must refer to the translated (mapped) address(es) of the destination host(s). This is true whether the traffic is moving from a higher-security interface to a lower-security interface (outbound flow) or vice versa (inbound flow).

Example 1: An ACL is applied inbound to the inside interface (more secure to less secure, or outbound connections). The source addresses referenced should be the local (untranslated) addresses. In our sample network, for example, you would permit or deny access from addresses in the 10.0.0.0/24 network.

Example 2: An ACL is applied inbound to the outside interface (less secure to more secure, or inbound connections). The destination addresses referenced should be the global (translated) addresses. In our sample network, for example, you would permit or deny access to the 209.165.200.228 address of the web server.

- For outbound ACLs (applied to traffic as it egresses the ASA through the interface), access rules are applied *after* NAT has taken place. Therefore, an ACE that filters source addresses must refer to the translated (global) address(es) of the source host(s). An access list that filters based on destination addresses must refer to the untranslated (original) address(es) of the destination host(s). This is true whether the traffic is moving from a higher-security interface to a lower-security interface (outbound flow) or vice versa (inbound flow).

  Example 1: An ACL is applied outbound to the outside interface (outbound connections). The source addresses referenced should be the global (translated) addresses. In our sample network, for example, such a rule would apply whether traffic originated on the inside or the DMZ networks, as both would egress through the outside interface to reach the Internet. You would permit or deny access from addresses in the 209.165.200.224/27 address range, which was used for our translation examples.

  Example 2: An ACL is applied outbound to the DMZ interface (which would be an inbound connection if originating on the outside interface, or an outbound connection if originating on the inside interface). The destination addresses referenced should be the local (untranslated) addresses of hosts on the DMZ. In our sample network, for example, you would permit or deny access to addresses in the 172.16.0.0/24 network.

Integrating NAT with MPF

If you apply Modular Policy Framework rules (discussed in Chapter 9, "Inspecting Traffic") to traffic flows subject to NAT, similar rules apply. MPF rules, like access lists, can apply to traffic either as it ingresses the ASA through an interface or as it egresses the ASA through an interface.

In the case of MPF rules, the same rules apply as for interface ACLs:

- For rules applied to traffic as it ingresses an interface:
  - The class flow specification must reference the untranslated IP address as the source IP address.
  - The class flow specification must reference the translated IP address as the destination IP address.

- For rules applied to traffic as it egresses an interface:

    - The class flow specification must reference the translated IP address as the source IP address.

    - The class flow specification must reference the untranslated IP address as the destination IP address.

Integrating NAT with AAA (Cut-Through Proxy)

AAA (cut-through proxy) rules applied to an interface only affect traffic ingressing the ASA through that interface. The same rules for ingress traffic apply as those listed for MPF rules:

- The AAA rule must reference the untranslated IP address as the source IP address.

- The AAA rule must reference the translated IP address as the destination IP address.

Troubleshooting Address Translation

Troubleshooting NAT requires that you observe activity on the ASA itself while generating traffic to or from a host subject to translation rules. The most common commands used for this purpose are **show xlate**, **show xlate detail**, and **clear xlate**, which have all been examined already in this chapter. It also requires reviewing log messages generated by the address translation process (or access rules).

Improper Translation

If traffic does not appear to be translated according to a configured NAT rule you are expecting to perform the translation, you should consider performing the following steps in troubleshooting:

Step 1.   Verify whether the traffic is being translated at all. Remember that if NAT control is enabled, and no translation rules are configured for a traffic flow, the traffic will be dropped. Use the **show xlate** or **show xlate detail** command to look for translations. Clear the translation table with **clear xlate** if recent changes have been made to translation rules.

Step 2.   If traffic is not being translated, look for missing **nat**, **global**, or **static** commands, **nat** and **global** commands that do not have the same NAT ID number, or incorrect interface pairs configured within a **static** command.

Step 3.   If traffic is being translated, but not by the correct NAT rule, check for overlapping translation rules. Keep in mind the order of precedence for NAT rules, from NAT bypass at the top to dynamic NAT at the bottom.

Protocols Incompatible with NAT or PAT

Some protocols encounter problems when running over NAT (and especially PAT). Ensure that any application traffic subject to translation rules on the ASA do not have the following features:

- Protocols that embed IP addresses at the application layer (within the data portion of packets, rather than the headers), unless the protocol is specifically supported by ASA packet inspection rules.

- Protocols that embed IP addresses at the application layer and use end-to-end encryption. If the payload of packets is encrypted when crossing through the ASA, even protocols supported by ASA packet inspection rules will not be properly translated.

- Protocols that include the IP or TCP/UDP headers as input to authentication hashing algorithms. These will not work with NAT or PAT, respectively, because NAT or PAT would be altering the headers subject to the integrity check. The AH protocol used within IPsec and authenticated BGP routing updates are examples of this.

In such cases, exempt application traffic using such protocols from NAT by using NAT bypass (preferred) or static identity NAT.

Proxy ARP

When address translation is configured on a Cisco ASA, the ASA performs proxy ARP for all global addresses in its translation table by default (note that this is for addresses *in the translation table*, not for addresses merely *configured* for NAT). In some cases, this is not desired because it might interfere with the proper operation of adjacent hosts.

You can disable proxy ARP behavior of the ASA on an interface by using the **sysopt noproxyarp** *interface_name* command in global configuration mode.

> **Caution:** Extreme care should be taken before disabling proxy ARP on an ASA interface when NAT control is enabled. For example, if it were disabled on the outside interface, the ASA would not reply to ARP requests for any of the global IP addresses of internal servers subject to static inside NAT, and no hosts from the Internet would be able to initiate connections to any such servers.

NAT-Related Syslog Messages

Problems performing address translation will be logged by the ASA. These messages can assist you in narrowing your troubleshooting focus. One of the most common NAT-related syslog messages occurs when the ASA cannot create a translation slot because it was either unable to find a matching global pool (on the correct interface, with the correct pool number) or the pool addresses are exhausted.

The following syntax shows the system message 305005. This message is generated when a packet does not match any of the configured translation rules, while NAT control is enabled. The same message is used whether the session should have matched dynamic or static translation rules:

```
%PIX|ASA-3-305005: No translation group found for protocol src
interface_name:source_address/source_port dst
  interface_name:dest_address/dest_port
```

The following syntax shows the system message 305006. There are several variations to this message, depending on which type of NAT rule and which protocol are involved. For instance, a static mapping "fails" if the ASA attempts to perform translation to an address that is a network identifier or broadcast address. A portmap failure indicates a problem applying PAT.

```
%PIX | ASA-3-305006: {outbound static | identity | portmap | regular}
translation creation failed for protocol src
  interface_name:source_address/source_port
dst interface_name:dest_address/dest_port
```

Implementing NAT in ASA Software Versions 8.3 and Later

Beginning with software version 8.3, Cisco has radically altered the manner in which address translation is configured on an ASA. Software versions 8.2 and earlier used a style of NAT configuration that had existed for several years. This style of NAT configuration had the potential to be cumbersome to configure and difficult to keep organized, particularly with the introduction of new capabilities on the ASA, such as support for a much higher number of interfaces than previously supported, or configurations where all interfaces have the same security level. Thus, Cisco introduced a new, object-oriented configuration for NAT rules, which lessens complexity, reduces configuration size, and reduces the likelihood of configuration error.

Major Differences in NAT Beginning in Software Version 8.3

There are a large number of differences in how NAT is configured and processed in OS versions 8.3 and later versus OS versions 8.2 and before. A few of the major differences are covered in the following sections.

Network Objects

The implementation of NAT on an ASA running software version 8.3 or later is done through the use of network objects (hence, "object-oriented"). The concept of a network object is new in ASA software version 8.3. A network object differs from an object group (described in Chapter 8), because it defines a single IP address, range of addresses, network, or FQDN (although this option is fairly uncommon).

Key Topic

The host, range, or subnet that's defined by a network object is used to identify the real, nontranslated, IP address in a NAT configuration. A network object can also be used to define any available translation addresses (similar to a global pool in versions 8.2 and earlier). You then refer to these objects in the NAT configuration.

By creating an object for each host, translated address, and service that is used in translation rules, it is easier to understand how the NAT configuration is being used, and "trace the logic" of the address translation that will be performed by the ASA. You can also configure complete translation definitions with one command, rather than having to link one or more **nat** commands to one or more **global** commands through the use of NAT ID numbers. The simplification of the NAT configuration and organization is the first step in the move toward "flow-based policies," where a user configures what actions to apply to a flow (inspection, NAT, IPS, and so on) all in one place in the ASA configuration.

NAT Control

One significant change in NAT with software versions 8.3 and higher is that NAT control (enforcing use of NAT, as previously described in the section, "Enforcing NAT") is no longer a supported option. If a connection finds no translation rules, it passes through the ASA without translation, as long as the connection is allowed by configured access rules and policies (including default behaviors).

Integrating NAT with Other ASA Functions

Perhaps the most significant change is that, when ACLs, MPF, AAA, Botnet Traffic Filter, and Web Cache Communications Protocol (WCCP) filters are applied to interfaces, they no longer need to refer to the translated addresses from NAT rules. All rules now refer to the network object by its native IP address or assigned identifier. Because a single host could have numerous translated addresses, depending on how many interfaces it communicated with, this radically reduces the complexity of configuration that was described in the section, "Other NAT Considerations," and its discussion of integrating NAT with these other functions.

NAT "Direction"

The security levels of interfaces no longer matter in the configuration of NAT rules. For example, there is no longer a concept of "outside NAT" versus "inside NAT." All NAT rules are configured the same way, regardless of whether the source is on a higher security or lower security interface than the destination.

NAT Rule Priority

NAT rules are now configured in an object-oriented manner instead of all being configured globally, so the NAT rule priority scheme for versions 8.2 and earlier (covered in the section, "NAT Rule Priority") no longer applies. Versions 8.3 and later now have a different structure for determining which NAT rule is applied to an address(es) in a packet. This is covered in the section, "NAT Table," later in this chapter.

New NAT Options in OS Versions 8.3 and Later

There is now an **any** option that can be used when defining ingress and egress interfaces in the NAT configuration. This enables the creation of single-line translation rules that will apply to all interfaces, rather than one or more lines of configuration for each interface where a host required translation, resulting in more compact and user-friendly configurations.

You can configure translations as part of network object definitions, which are added to the configuration. This is known as "auto NAT" and is described in the section, "Configuring Auto (Object) NAT." Auto NAT reduces configuration complexity when only one translation policy is required for a host.

You can configure a single NAT rule that will translate both the source and destination addresses in a packet. This is known as manual NAT or "twice NAT," because NAT can be performed twice—once on the source IP and once on the destination IP. Although all manual NAT rules are thus twice NAT rules, the term "twice NAT" is more commonly used only if translations actually occur to both source and destination addresses.

Starting in OS version 8.3, it is now possible to configure a static translation for many-to-one translation (PAT).

You can group translation network objects (address pools) into an object group (object groups are fully covered in Chapter 8), and use that object group in creating translation rules.

NAT rules can be defined as unidirectional, meaning only traffic sourced from a defined object can use the translation. Connections toward the object must match a different NAT rule, or they will not be translated.

NAT Table

As discussed earlier in the section, "NAT Rule Priority," OS versions 8.2 and earlier implemented various NAT rules in a structured order of operations that depended on what type of NAT rules existed in the configuration, with each having its own priority. Because several types of NAT rules could apply to the same source host, this leads to complexity, and frequently leads to troubleshooting scenarios where translation is being applied differently than the administrator intended.

Beginning in OS version 8.3, NAT rules are placed in a NAT Table, which has three sections. NAT rules are searched from top to bottom in the NAT Table, and the first rule that matches the packet being analyzed is always applied, regardless of whether it is a static or dynamic rule, a translation exemption, or whether the source is on a higher or lower security interface than the destination. This reduces the complexity of NAT configuration and troubleshooting. The sections in the NAT Table are as follows:

- **Manual NAT (1st section):** Default location for manual NAT statements.

- **Auto NAT (2nd section):** Also referred to as "object NAT" because the contents of this section come from NAT rules configured within network object definitions. This is the default location for auto NAT statements.

- **Manual NAT After Auto NAT (3rd section):** Manual NAT entries created using the **after-auto** keyword are located here.

The Manual NAT section allows an administrator to define translation rules to be compared before the remaining sections. These rules are usually very specific. For example, a rule could translate both source and destination addresses in a packet, which would require the packet to be addressed from a specific source to a specific destination in order to match the rule. This example is similar in function to the policy NAT rules created in OS versions 8.2 and earlier. You can also add entries to this section if a host requires multiple translation rules, which depend on the input or output interfaces or the destination address. For example, a server on the inside interface that retains its original address when communicating with the DMZ interface, but gets statically translated to a globally routable IP when communicating with the outside interface.

The Auto NAT section, also referred to as object NAT, contains translation rules defined as part of the network object definition itself. This allows each object definition to contain a single translation only. For example, a server allowing Internet-based clients to connect might contain a single static translation rule, or an inside network segment containing only clients might contain a single dynamic NAT or PAT rule, to allow connections to be initiated by the clients defined in the object.

The Manual NAT After Auto NAT section contains translation rules that could conflict with the entries in the prior two sections. These entries are configured the same way as other manual NAT rules (but are generally less specific) but are specified for use only after auto NAT. These translations are therefore used only if a packet does not match any translation rules from the first two sections of the NAT Table.

Example 7-5 shows a NAT Table displayed by using the **show nat** command on a newly rebooted ASA (as indicated by the 0 hit counts for all rules). It is inserted here for reference. The configuration that leads to this NAT Table is the subject of the next several sections. There is also a detailed variation of the command **show nat detail**.

Example 7-5 *NAT Table Displayed*

```
FIREWALL# show nat
Manual NAT Policies (Section 1)
1 (inside) to (outside) source dynamic INSIDE-SEGMENT VENDOR-SERVER-PAT
  destination static VENDOR-SERVER VENDOR-SERVER service HTTPS VENDOR-PORTMAP
    translate_hits = 0, untranslate_hits = 0
2 (inside) to (outside) source static INSIDE-SEGMENT INSIDE-SEGMENT   destination
  static SATELLITE-OFFICE SATELLITE-OFFICE
    translate_hits = 0, untranslate_hits = 0
3 (inside) to (outside) source static INSIDE-SEGMENT PARTNER-VPN-NAT-OUTBOUND
  destination static PARTNER-VPN-SEGMENT PARTNER-VPN-NAT-INBOUND
    translate_hits = 0, untranslate_hits = 0


Auto NAT Policies (Section 2)
1 (DMZ) to (outside) source static DMZ-WEB-PRIV DMZ-WEB-PUB
    translate_hits = 0, untranslate_hits = 0
2 (DMZ) to (outside) source static DMZ-FTP-PRIV DMZ-FTP-PUB
    translate_hits = 0, untranslate_hits = 0
3 (DMZ) to (outside) source static DMZ-HTTPS-PRIV DMZ-PAT-OUTSIDE   service tcp
  8443 https
    translate_hits = 0, untranslate_hits = 0
4 (DMZ) to (outside) source static DMZ-SMTP-PRIV DMZ-PAT-OUTSIDE   service tcp
  smtp smtp
    translate_hits = 0, untranslate_hits = 0
5 (any) to (outside) source dynamic INSIDE-SEGMENT OUTSIDE-NAT-POOL interface
    translate_hits = 0, untranslate_hits = 0
6 (any) to (DMZ) source dynamic IT-SEGMENT 172.16.0.254
    translate_hits = 0, untranslate_hits = 0


Manual NAT Policies (Section 3)
1 (any) to (outside) source dynamic IT-SEGMENT IT-OUTSIDE-PAT
    translate_hits = 0, untranslate_hits = 0
```

This method of matching a NAT rule might at first seem like it would have more overhead than that implemented in previous OS versions; however, it allows for more flexibility, for example, the **any** option for both input and output interfaces. Because traffic can match a rule no matter which interface it ingresses, the order of entries in the NAT Table becomes very important. The NAT Table must therefore be structured much like an ACL, with more specific entries at the top, and less specific entries at the bottom. Note that all entries are assigned a sequence number, per section of the NAT Table. Use this sequence number to ensure that NAT rules are applied in the order you intend.

Configuring Auto (Object) NAT

Auto NAT is the simplest form of NAT to configure on the ASA. With auto NAT, the NAT rule is configured in the same ASDM window as that used to create the object itself. Any single object can have only one auto NAT rule associated with it. The direction of any translation is defined by selecting the source object and the input (ingress) and output (egress) interfaces. The use of the **any** keyword for interface adds a broader scope to a translation definition.

Auto NAT allows for the definition of three basic NAT configurations for a network object:

- **Static NAT:** Creates a one-to-one translation for the object, which will never change. Similar to static NAT in previous OS versions, this type of rule creates a permanent entry in the NAT Table and allows for flows to be initiated in either direction (with the object as source or destination), as long as the initial packets in the flow are permitted by access policies on the ASA.

- **Dynamic NAT:** Creates a one-to-one translation for the object, but the NAT Table entry is created only after the host initiates a flow that matches the policy. This is similar to dynamic NAT in previous OS versions and allows the possibility for multiple hosts to reuse translated addresses. Dynamic NAT is typically configured when there are not enough translated addresses available to provide for one-to-one translations, but PAT is not used, either to conserve NAT Table entries (because PAT creates a translation entry for each individual flow that is translated, rather than one per source IP address) or because applications are in use that are incompatible with PAT. After a temporary translation entry is created by the host that initiated a connection, that translation can be used in both directions, as long as allowed by access policies. This is the same as the use of dynamic PAT in previous OS versions.

- **Dynamic PAT:** A many-to-one translation that allows multiple original addresses to simultaneously share one or more translated addresses. Although this provides for maximum conservation of globally routable IP addresses, it actually creates more translation entries in the NAT Table than dynamic NAT, as already mentioned, and is not compatible with all applications. Many common applications, such as FTP and SQLnet, are incompatible with PAT.

Note: The translation rules created in the following sections are not intended to convey "best practice" at all times. In many instances, the scenarios used are purposely chosen to be able to demonstrate various available options.

Configuring Static Translations Using Auto NAT

The configuration scenario used in this section will be the same as that used in the earlier section, "Configuring Static Inside NAT"—two application servers exist on the DMZ interface that require access from the Internet. A web server with native IP address 172.16.0.5 and an FTP server with native IP address 172.16.0.10. The web server will use translated IP address 209.165.200.228 when communicating with the outside interface (the Internet), and the FTP server will use translated IP address 209.165.200.229. If desired, you can refer to Figure 7-16 for a graphical representation of the network diagram.

To begin the process, navigate to **Configuration > Firewall > Objects > Network Objects/Groups** to open the Network Objects window. Then, from the Add drop-down menu, select **Network Object** to create a new network object. The Add Network Object window opens, as shown in Figure 7-32, where you define a new network object and the associated auto NAT rule.

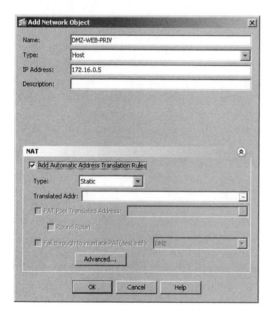

Figure 7-32   *Configuring a (Host) Network Object and Associated Static NAT Rule*

In the top part of this window, you define the network object (in this case, an individual host, and its original, non-translated, IP address).

In the Name field, enter the name to be used to refer to this network object. Remember that this name will be used in ACLs, MPF policies, and so on to refer to this object, so it should be short, yet adequately descriptive. In Figure 7-32, DMZ-WEB-PRIV is entered, which clearly defines the web server on the DMZ, private address.

Note: If your organization does not have a clearly defined naming convention, you may want to create one. As an alternative, you can give network objects names that include the native IP address, such as OBJ-172.16.0.5.

In the Type field, you define the type of object being created. In this case, select Host. The available choices are **Host**, **Range**, **Network**, or **FQDN**.

In the IP Address field, enter the original (native) IP address used by this object. In Figure 7-32, the IP address of 172.16.0.5 is entered.

You may optionally enter a description in the Description field. In our example, this is left blank.

If you were creating a network object with no NAT rules, you would be done at this point and would click **OK** to accept the new object definition and close the Add Network Object window. In this scenario, however, you want to create a static NAT entry for this host, as part of the network object definition. Therefore, expand the NAT portion of the window. It is shown expanded in Figure 7-32.

To create an auto NAT rule, rather than a manual NAT rule, check the **Add Automatic Address Translation Rules** box, and then select a translation type. In Figure 7-32, Static is selected as the translation type.

Because you will need to create a new network object for the translated address in this scenario, click the ellipsis (...) button to the right of the Translated Addr field to open the Browse Translated Addr window, as shown in Figure 7-33.

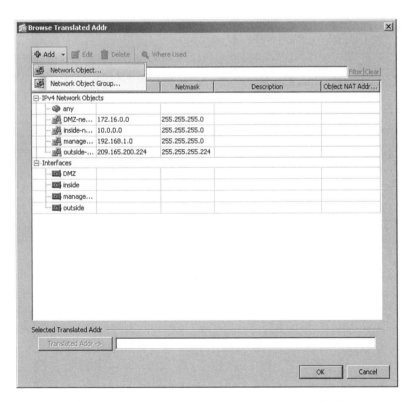

Figure 7-33   *Creating a New (Host) Translation Network Object*

This window functions much as the Network Objects window, so to add a translation network object, from the Add drop-down menu, select **Network Object** (as shown in the figure) to open the Add Network Object window once again, as shown in Figure 7-34.

Note: It is possible to create translation rules simply by typing a translated address into the Translated Addr field, but to maximize flexibility and fully demonstrate an object-oriented example, this chapter shows the creation of translation network objects.

This time, you will define a network object for the translated address, so enter the appropriate information for the translated object definition. Remembering that in our scenario, this translation will be used for communication through the outside interface. (In Figure 7-33, DMZ-WEB-PUB is entered in the Name field.) Because this is a host-specific static translation, Host is selected as the Type.

Note: FQDN is not an available option when creating a translation network object. This is because, although not all network objects have translation components and therefore an FQDN type is valid, a translation network object must by definition, reference an address (or range of addresses), and an FQDN is not a valid choice for this function.

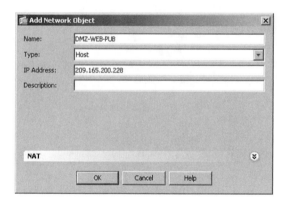

Figure 7-34 *Configuring a Translation Network Object*

Finally, in the IP Address field, 209.165.200.228 is entered. Click **OK** to complete the creation of the translation network object and return to the Browse Translated Addr window, as shown in Figure 7-35. The newly created translation object appears in the list of IPv4 network objects and is highlighted, but it has not yet been assigned as the translated address.

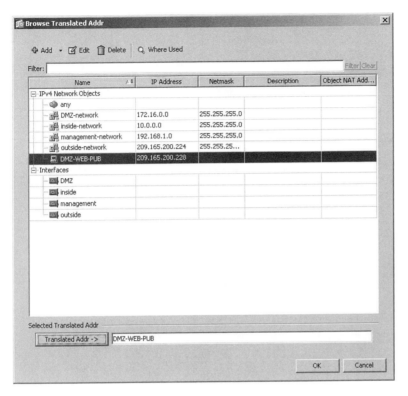

Figure 7-35 *Assigning a Translated Addr Network Object*

To assign this new object as the translated address for the original network object being created, while the translation object is highlighted, click the **Translated Addr** button at the bottom of this window (as done in Figure 7-35). Then, click **OK** to complete the assignment and return to the original network object definition window. The Translated Addr field is now populated with information for the translation object just created (shown on the left side of Figure 7-36).

You're almost finished. Because this particular translation is intended to occur only between a specific pair of interfaces (DMZ and outside, in this case), it is necessary to define the "direction" of this translation rule. To do so, click the **Advanced...** button at the bottom of the Add Network Object window. This opens the Advanced NAT Settings window, as shown on the right side of Figure 7-36.

In the Interface section of this window, you have the ability to choose a source and destination interface. Both are set to "any" by default. The source interface should be set to the actual location of the host for which this translation is being created (in our case, DMZ, which is selected in Figure 7-36). The destination interface should be set to any interface where the host in question will be referred to by the translated address (in our case, outside, which is selected in Figure 7-36).

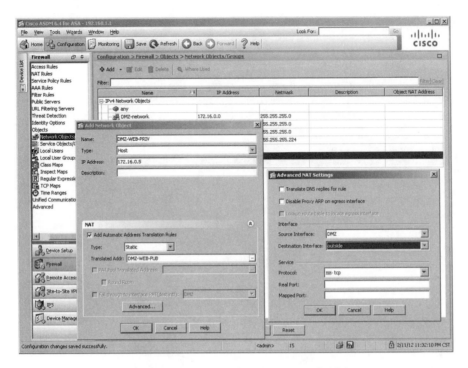

Figure 7-36 *Completing the Creation of a New Network Object*

After setting the interface choices, click **OK** to complete the settings of Advanced NAT Settings. Then, click **OK** again to complete the definition of the new network object for the DMZ web server.

Follow the same procedure to create a network object for the DMZ FTP server, using appropriate information. Then, click **Apply** to send the changes to the ASA.

The CLI commands generated by the changes made are as follows (spacing inserted for readability):

```
object network DMZ-FTP-PRIV
  host 172.16.0.10
!
object network DMZ-FTP-PUB
  host 209.165.200.229
!
object network DMZ-WEB-PRIV
  host 172.16.0.5
!
object network DMZ-WEB-PUB
  host 209.165.200.228
!
object network DMZ-FTP-PRIV
  nat (DMZ,outside) static DMZ-FTP-PUB
```

```
!
object network DMZ-WEB-PRIV
  nat (DMZ,outside) static DMZ-WEB-PUB
```

If you are configuring the ASA from the CLI, you can enter these commands directly in global configuration mode.

If using ASDM, the definition of the network object will be split into two parts: one defining the host address and a separate one defining the NAT rule. The reason for this is that, although there will only be one network object defined for a host—for example, DMZ-WEB-PRIV—there may be multiple translation rules applied to that host (for example, the static just created, a NAT exemption for communicating across a VPN, and so on). All such translation rules will be grouped together under the object in the section of the configuration showing translation rules, which makes it easier to examine all the rules to which a host is subject.

It is not necessary to split the definition this way if configuring from the CLI; however, it is necessary to create the translation objects first, so that you can use their names when configuring the NAT rule for the original network object, as shown here:

```
object network DMZ-FTP-PUB
  host 209.165.200.229
!
object network DMZ-FTP-PRIV
  host 172.16.0.10
  nat (DMZ,outside) static DMZ-FTP-PUB
!
object network DMZ-WEB-PUB
  host 209.165.200.228
!
object network DMZ-WEB-PRIV
  host 172.16.0.5
  nat (DMZ,outside) static DMZ-WEB-PUB
```

Configuring Static Port Translations Using Auto NAT

You can use auto NAT to configure static port translations, similar to what was called static inside PAT in OS versions 8.2 and before. To demonstrate this, we once again use a previously demonstrated example. If desired, refer to Figure 7-20 for a graphical depiction of the network diagram.

In this scenario, you have two servers located on the DMZ segment. The first, with a native IP address of 172.16.0.15, hosts a secure web-based application and listens for HTTPS connections on customized TCP port 8443. The second is a mail server, with a native IP address of 172.16.0.20, and listens for SMTP connections on the standard TCP port 25. You have only one global IP address available for use: 209.165.200.230.

Using the same methods just demonstrated, create network object definitions for the HTTPS and SMTP servers. Also, create a translation network object named DMZ-PAT-OUTSIDE, using the 209.165.200.230 address.

To configure static port translations for the two servers, it is necessary to edit the Advanced NAT Settings for each of these objects. To do so, navigate to **Configuration > Firewall > Objects > Network Objects/Groups** to open the Network Objects window. Select one of the new server objects (this scenario will show the HTTPS server), and click the **Edit** button at the top of the window to open the Edit Network Object window. Click the **Advanced...** button at the bottom of this window to open the Advanced NAT Settings window. Figure 7-37 shows this sequence.

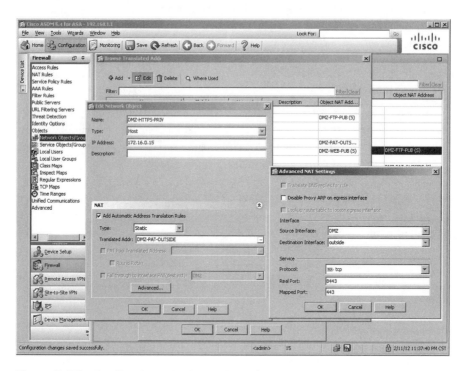

Figure 7-37   *Configuring a Static Port Translation*

In the interfaces section of this window, select the Source and Destination interfaces of DMZ and outside, respectively, as before, because this static port translation is unique to that interface pair. Figure 7-37 shows these selections.

Static port translations are created in the Service section of the Advanced NAT Settings window. The default protocol setting is TCP, which is what this scenario requires. In the Real Port field, enter the port that the server is natively configured to listen on (in this case, 8443). In the Mapped Port field, enter the port that connections will be made to on the Destination interface (in this case, 443). Figure 7-37 shows these settings.

Click **OK** to accept the changes and close the Advanced NAT Settings window. Click **OK** again to do the same in the Edit Network Object window. Repeat this procedure for the SMTP server—this time setting both the real port and mapped port to a value of 25. Then, click **Apply** to send the changes to the ASA.

The CLI commands generated by the changes made are as follows (spacing inserted for readability):

```
object network DMZ-HTTPS-PRIV
  host 172.16.0.15
!
object network DMZ-PAT-OUTSIDE
  host 209.165.200.230
!
object network DMZ-SMTP-PRIV
  host 172.16.0.20
!
object network DMZ-HTTPS-PRIV
  nat (DMZ,outside) static DMZ-PAT-OUTSIDE service tcp 8443 443
!
object network DMZ-SMTP-PRIV
  nat (DMZ,outside) static DMZ-PAT-OUTSIDE service tcp 25 25
```

If you are configuring the ASA from the CLI, you can enter these commands in global configuration mode.

Examine the following CLI commands to understand the structure:

```
object network DMZ-HTTPS-PRIV
 nat (DMZ,outside) static DMZ-PAT-OUTSIDE service tcp 8443 443
```

In the **nat** command, the interface names are listed as original first, and then translated. The word **static** defines the translation type. The translated address is then defined (in this case, **DMZ-PAT-OUTSIDE**). The keyword **service** is new and indicates that the ASA is to perform static port translation. Finally, the ports are listed in the order real (actually configured on the server), and then mapped (translated). These two port numbers can be the same, as they are for the SMTP server, or different, as they are for the HTTPS server.

Comparing Static NAT Configurations from OS Versions 8.2 and 8.3

Key Topic

From the preceding examples, it might not be immediately apparent how the method of defining translations in OS versions 8.3 and later reduces the size of the configuration when compared to a similar configuration in OS versions 8.2 and earlier, as claimed. This is because of the simplistic examples, where each server object has had only one translation rule associated with it. Consider the following example, where a server on the inside interface is statically translated to another address on an ASA with seven interfaces (inside, outside, DMZ, and four other interfaces). The translated address used is the same on all interfaces, which makes it possible to use the "any" interface option on the 8.3 ASA. Example 7-6 shows the version 8.2 configuration, and Example 7-7 shows the corresponding 8.3 configuration that accomplishes the same translations.

Example 7-6 *Sample Static Configuration from OS Version 8.2*

```
static (inside, outside) 209.165.200.231 10.0.0.10
static (inside, DMZ) 209.165.200.231 10.0.0.10
static (inside, INTF4) 209.165.200.231 10.0.0.10
static (inside, INTF5) 209.165.200.231 10.0.0.10
static (inside, INTF6) 209.165.200.231 10.0.0.10
static (inside, INTF7) 209.165.200.231 10.0.0.10
```

Example 7-7 *Sample Static Configuration from OS Version 8.3*

```
object network INSIDE-SVR-PUB
 host 209.165.200.231
object network INSIDE-SVR-PRIV
 host 10.0.0.10
 nat (inside,any) static INSIDE-SVR-PUB
```

As the examples demonstrate, the translations are configured with a single line. Even the total number of configuration lines is reduced, despite first creating the two network objects.

Configuring Dynamic Translations Using Auto NAT

Creating dynamic translations with auto NAT is done using the same ASDM screens as static translations. One important difference in functionality, however, is that while static translations never expire, translation slots created by a dynamic NAT rule expire after being idle for 3 hours, by default (not seeing any traffic that uses the translation slot). The presented scenario will once again use a familiar example (with a slight modification) to begin. You will configure a dynamic translation for the inside network, 10.0.0.0/24, to a range of translated addresses, 209.165.200.235–254, for use on the outside interface. These translations will be one-to-one (NAT, not PAT). If this pool of addresses is exhausted, you want to "back up" this translation range by using PAT with the interface address of the ASA acting as the PAT translation address. If desired, refer to Figure 7-5 for a graphic representation of the network diagram. In pre-8.3 versions of the OS, this was done with the following configuration:

```
nat (inside) 1 10.0.0.0 255.255.255.0
global (outside) 1 209.165.200.235-209.165.200.254 netmask 255.255.255.224
global (outside) 1 interface
```

Remember that the concept of NAT ID numbers no longer exists. It is not necessary in OS versions 8.3 and later to map the **nat** and **global** commands together.

To begin the process, navigate to **Configuration > Firewall > Objects > Network Objects/Groups** to open the Network Objects window. Then, from the Add drop-down menu, select **Network Object** to create a new network object. The Add Network Object window opens, as shown in Figure 7-38.

In Figure 7-38, INSIDE-SEGMENT is entered in the Name field, because it is short, yet adequately descriptive of the original network object to be created. In the Type field, Network is selected.

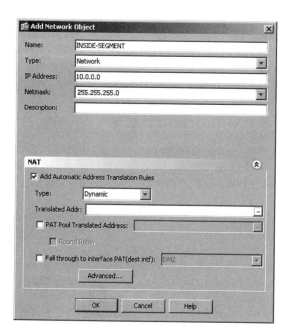

Figure 7-38 *Configuring a (Network) Network Object and Associated Dynamic NAT Rule*

Note: When Network is selected as the object type, a Netmask field is added to the window. This is shown is Figure 7-38. If you refer to Figure 7-32, where a host object was defined, there was no Netmask field.

In the IP Address field, enter the original (native) IP address of this object. In Figure 7-38, the IP address of 10.0.0.0 is entered. In the Netmask field, enter the appropriate netmask value or select one from the drop-down list. In this case, 255.255.255.0 is selected from the drop-down list.

Expand the NAT portion of the window. It is shown expanded in Figure 7-38. Check the **Add Automatic Address Translation Rules** box, and then select a translation type. In Figure 7-38, dynamic is selected as the translation type.

Because you will need to create a new network object for the translated address in this scenario, click the ellipsis (...) button to the right of the Translated Addr field to open the Browse Translated Addr window. From the Add drop-down menu, select **Network Object** to open the Add Network Object window once again, as shown in Figure 7-39.

In the Name field, enter a name for the object to be created. In Figure 7-39, OUTSIDE-NAT-POOL is entered. Select **Range** as the Type. Doing this alters the appearance of the window to show fields of Start Address and End Address. This has already been done in Figure 7-39.

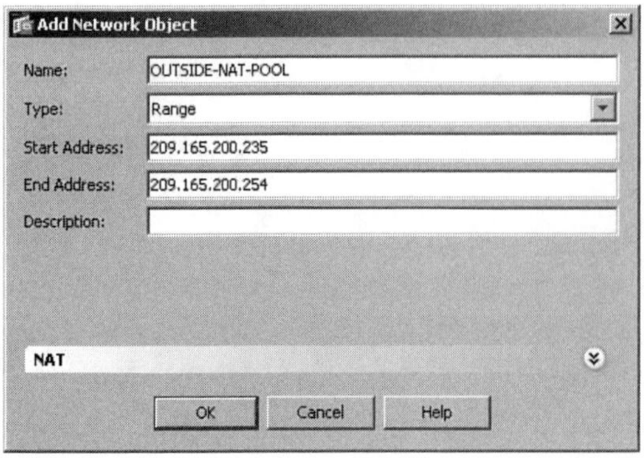

Figure 7-39   *Configuring a New (Range) Translation Network Object*

Note: A name is optional for some translation objects, but required for others. This can be seen by observing how the Add Network Object window changes depending on your selections. For example, the label for the Name field is **Name (optional):** in many cases, but depending on selections (such as selecting a Type of Range), the label will change to **Name:**, indicating it is a required field.

In the Start Address and End Address fields, enter the first and last addresses in the pool range. In Figure 7-39, 209.165.200.235 and 209.165.200.254 are entered, respectively.

Using the same procedures as already demonstrated, assign this object as the Translated Addr for the INSIDE-SEGMENT object being created and return to the Add Network Object window, as shown in Figure 7-40.

At the bottom of this window, check the **Fall Through to Interface PAT (Dest Intf)** button and select the outside interface from the drop-down list. Doing this also sets the outside interface as the destination interface for this rule, as if you had entered the Advanced NAT Settings window and made such a change. Finally, click **OK** to complete the creation of the new Network Object.

Note: Although it might seem necessary to go to the Advanced NAT Settings window and select inside as the source interface, this is not the case. In this scenario, source addresses of 10.0.0.0/24 exist through only one interface; however, leaving the source interface setting at the default of **any** provides great flexibility. An example of this is shown in the section, "Comparing Dynamic NAT Configurations from OS versions 8.2 and 8.3."

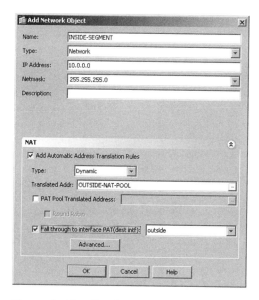

Figure 7-40 *Configuring Interface PAT to Back Up a NAT Pool*

To demonstrate an example of the use of PAT only (also referred to as "PAT Hide"), we will continue the scenario as follows: You will create a network object named IT-SEGMENT, using address 10.0.1.0/24.

You will then create a PAT translation rule for communication from the IT-SEGMENT object to the DMZ network using the address 172.16.0.254 as the translated address.

Note: Because there is no concept of NAT control is OS versions 8.3 and later, this is not necessary in the sample network to get traffic through the firewall. The scenario assumes the existence of software firewalls on the DMZ servers, which allow connectivity only from the PAT address, 172.16.0.254. Also, you have not configured the ASA to be able to route to the 10.0.1.0/24 subnet. Therefore, this scenario continuation is primarily for purposes of illustration.

Using procedures already demonstrated, create the IT-SEGMENT object, assigning the appropriate name, type, and address. Figure 7-41 shows a partially configured Add Network Object window.

Expand the NAT section of this window and check the box to enable auto NAT, as shown in Figure 7-42.

Select **Dynamic PAT (Hide)** in the Type field, as shown in Figure 7-42. Then, in the Translated Addr field, directly enter the PAT address. Figure 7-42 shows the scenario PAT address of 172.16.0.254. Using procedures already described, enter the Advanced NAT Settings window and set the Destination interface to DMZ. Click **OK** to accept this change and return to the Add Network Object window. Then, click **OK** to complete the creation of the new object and translation rule. Finally, click **Apply** to send the changes to the ASA.

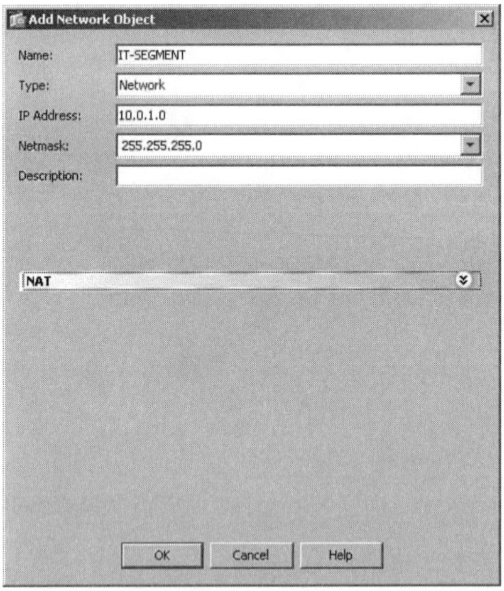

Figure 7-41   *Partially Configured Network Object*

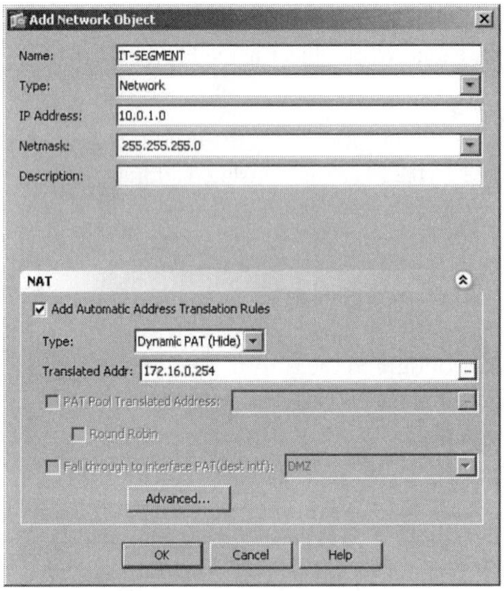

Figure 7-42   *Configuring a Static PAT Rule*

The CLI commands generated by the changes made are as follows. Note the new options demonstrated here, of defining both a range and a subnet, rather than only a host address as network objects (spacing inserted for readability):

```
object network INSIDE-SEGMENT
  subnet 10.0.0.0 255.255.255.0
!
```

```
object network IT-SEGMENT
  subnet 10.0.1.0 255.255.255.0
!
object network OUTSIDE-NAT-POOL
  range 209.165.200.235 209.165.200.254
!
object network INSIDE-SEGMENT
  nat (any,outside) dynamic OUTSIDE-NAT-POOL interface
!
object network IT-SEGMENT
  nat (any,DMZ) dynamic 172.16.0.254
```

If you are configuring the ASA from the CLI, you can enter these commands in global configuration mode.

Using Object Groups in NAT Rules

The creation and use of object groups is covered in Chapter 8. However, it is not necessary to understand all the options available with object groups to understand how they can be used in NAT rules.

Recall the scenario just covered in the section, "Configuring Dynamic Translations Using Auto NAT." You configured the INSIDE-SEGMENT network object to use first a pool of addresses using NAT, then to fall back on a single PAT address, if these NAT addresses were all in use. For this topic, we extend that scenario as follows: Following rapid growth of your organization, you determine that the pool of NAT addresses is not large enough to accommodate your needs. Furthermore, because of the use of some applications incompatible with PAT, you need more addresses available for NAT. You therefore obtain from your ISP a second block of addresses for your use: 209.165.201.0/27. You want to assign 20 of these addresses into a pool for use with NAT, and one address as a PAT fallback, prior to the use of the ASA interface address for PAT.

You are attempting to configure the following:

1. Hosts in the INSIDE-SEGMENT object will first use the NAT pool addresses of 209.165.200.235-254. These will be assigned in a seemingly random manner, based on an internal ASA algorithm, until all are in use.

2. You want hosts in the INSIDE-SEGMENT object to use addresses in a new range, 209.165.201.10-29, assigned in the same manner.

3. If both these pools are fully utilized, you want further connections from INSIDE-SEGMENT hosts to use PAT, utilizing the address 209.165.201.30.

4. In the unlikely scenario that the previous PAT address has all ports utilized, you want remaining connections from INSIDE-SEGMENT hosts to use PAT, utilizing the ASA's interface address.

Using procedures already demonstrated, you need to create new network objects, as follows:

1. An object OUTSIDE-NAT-POOL2, defined as the range 209.165.201.10-29
2. An object OUTSIDE-PAT, defined as the host address 209.165.201.30

To refer to the combination of all these addresses as a single logical pool to be used for translation, you must create a network object group. To begin the process, navigate to **Configuration > Firewall > Objects > Network Objects/Groups** to open the Network Objects window. Then, from the Add drop-down menu, select **Network Object Group** to create a new network object group. The Add Network Object Group window opens, as shown in Figure 7-43.

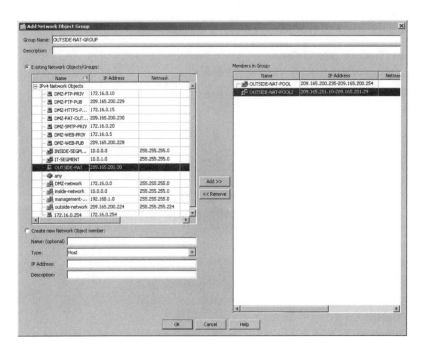

Figure 7-43   *Configuring a Network Object Group*

In the Group Name field, enter a brief but descriptive name for this group. In Figure 7-43, OUTSIDE-NAT-GROUP is entered. Then, in the Existing Network Objects/Groups list, select the three network objects that will comprise this group, and click the **Add >>** button to move their names to the Members in Group list. Figure 7-43 shows the two NAT pools already added, and the PAT object name selected, to demonstrate what the process looks like.

After you add all desired members to the group, click **OK** to complete the creation of the new object group.

Next, select the INSIDE-SEGMENT network object and click the **Edit** button to open the Edit Network Object window, as shown in Figure 7-44.

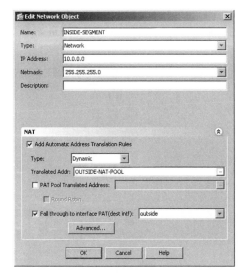

Figure 7-44   *Editing a Network Object*

In the NAT portion of the window, you see the previously configured value of OUTSIDE-NAT-POOL in the Translated Addr field. Click the ellipsis (...) button to the right of this field to open the Browse Translated Addr window, as shown in Figure 7-45.

Select the newly created object group, and click the **Translated Addr ->** button at the bottom of the window to change the assignment of translated addresses for the object. Figure 7-45 shows this completed. Then, click **OK** to complete this assignment.

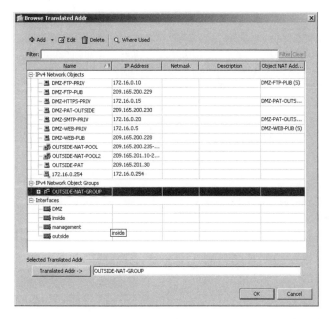

Figure 7-45   *Assigning an Object Group as a Translated Addr*

Verify that the object group name now appears in the Translated Addr field, and click **OK** to complete the editing of the network object. Finally, click **Apply** to send the changes to the ASA.

The CLI commands generated by the changes made are as follows (spacing inserted for readability):

```
object network OUTSIDE-NAT-POOL2
  range 209.165.201.10 209.165.201.29
!
object network OUTSIDE-PAT
  host 209.165.201.30
!
object-group network OUTSIDE-NAT-GROUP
  network-object object OUTSIDE-NAT-POOL
  network-object object OUTSIDE-NAT-POOL2
  network-object object OUTSIDE-PAT
!
object network INSIDE-SEGMENT
  nat (any,outside) dynamic OUTSIDE-NAT-GROUP interface
```

If you are configuring the ASA from the CLI, you can enter these commands directly in global configuration mode.

Note that the translated address shown in the **nat** command is the new object group, followed by the interface address. When an object group is used in a **nat** command in this way, the ASA will use the individual members of the object group, in the listed order, to assign translated addresses for connections.

Comparing Dynamic NAT Configurations from OS Versions 8.2 and 8.3

In comparing dynamic NAT configurations, let us again consider the example of an ASA with seven interfaces (inside, outside, DMZ, and four other interfaces). All internal interfaces will share the same pool of NAT addresses (backed up by PAT using the ASA interface address) on the outside interface, which makes it possible to use the "any" interface option on the 8.3 ASA. Servers on the DMZ are statically translated, so they do not need dynamic NAT rules. Example 7-8 shows the version 8.2 configuration, and Example 7-9 shows the corresponding 8.3 configuration that accomplishes the same translations.

Example 7-8 *Sample Dynamic Configuration from OS Version 8.2*

```
nat (inside) 1 10.0.0.0 255.255.255.0
nat (INTF4) 1 10.0.4.0 255.255.255.0
nat (INTF5) 1 10.0.5.0 255.255.255.0
nat (INTF6) 1 10.0.6.0 255.255.255.0
nat (INTF7) 1 10.0.7.0 255.255.255.0
global (outside) 1 209.165.200.235-209.165.200.254 netmask 255.255.255.224
global (outside) 1 interface
```

Example 7-9   *Sample Dynamic Configuration from OS Version 8.3*

```
object network OUTSIDE-NAT-POOL
  range 209.165.200.235 209.165.200.254
object network INTERNAL-SEGMENTS
 subnet 10.0.0.0 255.255.248.0
 nat (any,outside) dynamic OUTSIDE-NAT-POOL interface
```

As the examples demonstrate, the translations are configured with a single line, as opposed to the seven lines required in previous OS versions. This demonstrates the power and flexibility of the new "any" option for NAT rules, which did not exist before OS version 8.3. The repeated use of NAT ID 1 in the older versions can also lead to confusion, especially for an inexperienced administrator. This new approach leads to a more compact, and more easily understood, configuration.

Verifying Auto (Object) NAT

You can use several commands to verify the configuration and operation of NAT on an ASA running OS versions 8.3 and later.

Example 7-10 shows the use of the **show running-config nat** command to examine the configured NAT rules in the ASA configuration. Note that this displays only the NAT rules configured for each object, and not the object definition. You might recall it was mentioned earlier that the network object configuration appeared in two places in the configuration: one for the actual definitions and another for the NAT rules.

Example 7-10   show running-config nat *Command Output*

```
FIREWALL# show running-config nat
!
object network DMZ-FTP-PRIV
 nat (DMZ,outside) static DMZ-FTP-PUB
object network DMZ-HTTPS-PRIV
 nat (DMZ,outside) static DMZ-PAT-OUTSIDE service tcp 8443 https
object network DMZ-SMTP-PRIV
 nat (DMZ,outside) static DMZ-PAT-OUTSIDE service tcp smtp smtp
object network DMZ-WEB-PRIV
 nat (DMZ,outside) static DMZ-WEB-PUB
object network INSIDE-SEGMENT
 nat (any,outside) dynamic OUTSIDE-NAT-GROUP interface
object network IT-SEGMENT
 nat (any,DMZ) dynamic 172.16.0.254
```

If you want to see the definitions of objects from the configuration, there are several ways of doing so. Example 7-11 shows the use of two variants of the **show running-config object** command. The first, **show running-config object id**, displays the object configuration of a single object, in the same way it would appear in the output of a **show running-config** command. If you prefer, you can use the new **in-line** option to display the entire object configuration in a single line of output, as shown in the second part of the example.

Example 7-11 *Displaying Object Definitions*

```
FIREWALL# show running-config object id INSIDE-SEGMENT
object network INSIDE-SEGMENT
 subnet 10.0.0.0 255.255.255.0

FIREWALL# show running-config object in-line|include INSIDE-SEGMENT
object network INSIDE-SEGMENT subnet 10.0.0.0 255.255.255.0
```

To display the NAT Table, use the **show nat** command, as shown in Example 7-12. Note that so far, only auto NAT policies have been configured, but the output still labels this as Section 2 of the NAT Table. Also, network object names are shown, if configured. Although not shown here, there is also a **show nat detailed** version of this command.

Example 7-12 **show nat** *Command Output with Auto NAT Only*

```
FIREWALL# show nat
Auto NAT Policies (Section 2)
1 (DMZ) to (outside) source static DMZ-WEB-PRIV DMZ-WEB-PUB
    translate_hits = 5824, untranslate_hits = 3196
2 (DMZ) to (outside) source static DMZ-FTP-PRIV DMZ-FTP-PUB
    translate_hits = 2531, untranslate_hits = 138
3 (DMZ) to (outside) source static DMZ-HTTPS-PRIV DMZ-PAT-OUTSIDE   service tcp
  8443 https
    translate_hits = 82, untranslate_hits = 105
4 (DMZ) to (outside) source static DMZ-SMTP-PRIV DMZ-PAT-OUTSIDE   service tcp
  smtp smtp
    translate_hits = 1477, untranslate_hits = 1253
5 (any) to (outside) source dynamic INSIDE-SEGMENT OUTSIDE-NAT-POOL interface
    translate_hits = 71, untranslate_hits = 149
6 (any) to (DMZ) source dynamic IT-SEGMENT 172.16.0.254
    translate_hits = 26, untranslate_hits = 26
```

To display the list of currently active translations, use the **show xlate** command, as shown in Example 7-13.

Example 7-13   show xlate *Command Output*

```
FIREWALL# show xlate
6 in use, 6 most used
Flags: D - DNS, i - dynamic, r - portmap, s - static, I - identity, T - twice
NAT from DMZ:172.16.0.5 to outside:209.165.200.228
    flags s idle 0:00:38 timeout 0:00:00
NAT from DMZ:172.16.0.10 to outside:209.165.200.229
    flags s idle 0:02:12 timeout 0:00:00
TCP PAT from DMZ:172.16.0.15 8443-8443 to outside:209.165.200.230 443-443
    flags sr idle 0:25:53 timeout 0:00:00
TCP PAT from DMZ:172.16.0.20 25-25 to outside:209.165.200.230 25-25
    flags sr idle 0:05:47 timeout 0:00:00
NAT from any:10.0.0.123 to outside:209.165.200.244 flags i idle 0:00:28 timeout
  3:00:00
NAT from any:10.0.0.101 to outside:209.165.200.251 flags i idle 0:10:11 timeout
  3:00:00
```

With OS version 8.3 and later, there is no longer a **show xlate detail** command, but the **show xlate** command contains the same output as used to be shown with the **show xlate detail** command in earlier OS versions. PAT rules will display the protocol, TCP or UDP, in the output of the xlate table. All PAT xlate slots, whether created statically or dynamically, will include the r flag for port mapping. Static translations are listed with a timeout value of 0:00:00, meaning they never expire. The dynamic translations in this output show the system default of 3 hours for dynamic translation slots. Note that object names are not shown—only addresses.

Additionally, you can examine the configured NAT rules from within ASDM by navigating to the **Configuration > Firewall > NAT Rules** window. An example of this window is shown in the next section, "Configuring Manual NAT."

Configuring Manual NAT

A production network will frequently need more options than are provided by auto NAT alone. Recall that, with auto NAT, there can be only one NAT rule for any network object. There may also be a need to define exceptions to the configured auto NAT rules. In either of these situations, it will be necessary to configure manual NAT rules, which offer the capability of defining rules with much more granular details, and can also be configured to be checked either before or after the auto NAT rules which are configured.

Manual NAT rules are, by default, checked before auto NAT rules, because they appear in Section 1 of the NAT Table. If configured with the **after-auto** keyword, manual NAT rules appear in Section 3 of the NAT Table, and will have effect only if no previous matches occur in the NAT Table for the packet being examined. This can be used as a fallback option, where translation is required, but specific options failed to match.

Using manual NAT, you can configure more than one NAT option per network object, based on different matching criteria (for example, the same source communicating with different destinations).

As previously mentioned, manual NAT allows you to configure the translation of both the source and destination addresses in a packet, referred to as *twice NAT*. This makes it possible to handle situations where the source and destination networks use overlapping private IP addresses (a fairly common occurrence in VPN setups between networks under different administrative domains).

The configuration scenario to be used in the following examples has the following requirements:

1. All auto NAT rules created in the previous section of this chapter are still in use.

2. Several hosts in the 10.0.0.0/24 inside subnet are authorized to connect to a vendor application server, 192.0.2.50, port 8443, on the Internet. This vendor requires all users coming from your organization to appear to their server as a single IP address: 209.165.200.234. Because you are using one-to-one dynamic NAT, each internal host has a unique global address when translated. Thus, you need to configure a manual NAT rule to translate internal hosts to use a configured PAT address if they are communicating with the vendor application server, but still use the previously defined auto NAT rule when connecting elsewhere through the outside interface.

3. You need to configure NAT for a VPN between your inside segment and a satellite office, which uses the IP address 10.10.10.0/24. Because the satellite office also belongs to your company, and you use internal DNS servers, traffic across this VPN needs to be exempted from address translation. Because you already have an auto NAT rule configured to dynamically translate all traffic from the inside segment through the outside interface, a manual NAT rule is required to accomplish this exemption.

4. You need to configure NAT for a second VPN between your inside network 10.0.0.0/24, and a partner site, which also uses the 10.0.0.0/24 network for its address. This requires twice NAT being configured. The two networks require full bidirectional (any-to-any) connectivity.

Note: VPN configuration is not a subject in the FIREWALL course or exam, so the full VPN configuration will not be dealt with here. This chapter will only discuss the NAT rule configuration for the scenarios just described.

Requirement 2 from this list is similar to that seen previously in this chapter, in the section, "Configuring Dynamic Inside Policy PAT," and in fact, manual NAT rules are the replacement for all policy NAT/PAT rules from OS versions 8.2 and earlier. To configure the necessary rule, begin by navigating to **Configuration > Firewall > NAT Rules** to open the NAT Rules window, as shown in Figure 7-46.

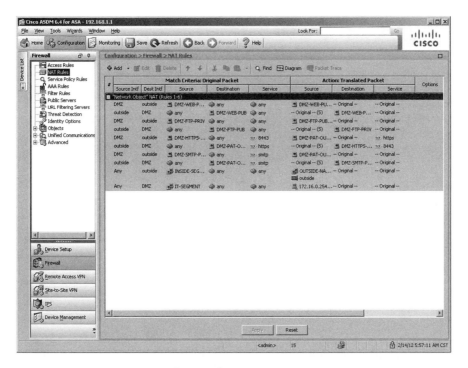

Figure 7-46 *ASDM NAT Rules Window*

To add the new manual NAT rule, click **Add > Add NAT Rule Before "Network Object" NAT** to open the Add NAT Rule dialog box, as shown in Figure 7-47.

As you can see in Figure 7-47, there are a wide variety of configuration options within this one window. The Match Criteria section allows you to define a traffic flow, as an access list did in OS versions 8.2 and earlier when creating policy NAT/PAT rules. The Action section allows you to specify that the source, destination, or both addresses from a matching packet be altered to new values. Finally, in the Options section, in addition to being able to quickly enable or disable (without deleting) the rule, you can activate DNS Rewrite (which functions as previously described in the section, "Other NAT Considerations"), and a new option, Direction, which can make NAT rules unidirectional. (Translation occurs in only one direction; no translation occurs in the other direction.)

In the Match Criteria section, from the drop-down list as the Source Interface (ingress), select the inside interface. Then, click the ellipsis (...) button for the Source Address field, and using procedures previously demonstrated, assign the network object INSIDE-SEGMENT as the source address, as shown in Figure 7-47.

For the destination interface (egress), select outside from the drop-down list. In the Destination Address field, you might think you could simply type the vendor server address of 192.0.2.50, but this is not the case. In manual NAT rules, you can specify only **any**, an object or object group name, or an interface name. Therefore, click the ellipsis button and, using procedures already demonstrated, create a new network object named VENDOR-SERVER, defined as the host 192.0.2.50, and assign it as the destination address. These changes are shown in Figure 7-47.

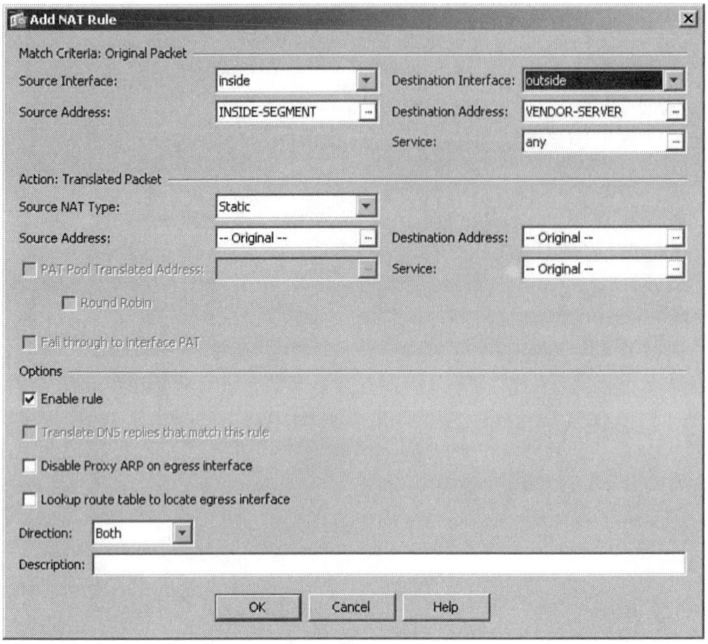

Figure 7-47 *Configuring a Manual NAT Rule (Dynamic PAT)*

To demonstrate the syntax of port mapping in a manual NAT rule, this scenario had the vendor server listening on port 8443. Rather than make users on the inside network specify this port when attempting to connect, you decide to create port mapping in the ASA's NAT rule to handle the redirection automatically from an original destination port of 443 (used by the inside clients by specifying an HTTPS URL in their browser) to port 8443, the actual listening port on the vendor server. Although creation of service object groups is covered in Chapter 8, Figure 7-48 shows an example for purposes of this scenario. Click the ellipsis button for the Service field, and then click **Add > Service Object** to open the Add Service Object dialog box, as shown in Figure 7-48.

Enter a name for the service object in the Name field. Figure 7-48 shows the creation of the object HTTPS. Leave the service type set to the default of TCP. In the Destination Port/Range field, enter the original destination port value of 443. Click **OK** to complete the creation of the service object, and assign it as the original destination service using the procedures already demonstrated.

Figure 7-49 shows the continuation of configuration in the Add NAT Rule dialog box, following the creation of the new service object.

In the Action section of the window, set the Source NAT Type to Dynamic PAT (Hide), because the scenario specified translation to a single IP address. In the Source Address field, once again, only an object or object group name, or an interface name, are allowed as inputs. So, create and assign a new network object named VENDOR-SERVER-PAT, defined as the host address 209.165.200.234, as shown in Figure 7-49. Leave the Destination Address field at its default value of "— Original —", indicating no translation is to occur to the destination address in matching packets. Then, using procedures already demonstrated, create and assign a service object named VENDOR-PORTMAP, defined as destination port 8443, in the Service field. These changes are all shown in Figure 7-49.

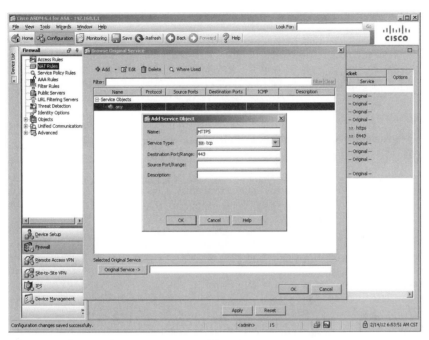

Figure 7-48 *Configuring a Service Object*

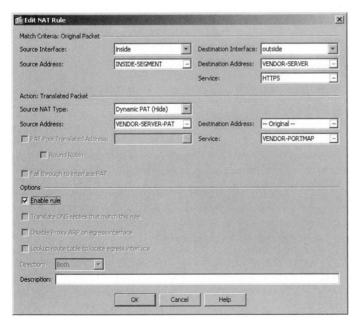

Figure 7-49 *Completing the Manual NAT Rule Configuration*

All newly created rules are enabled by default, so no further changes are necessary (although you can optionally enter a description for this rule, if desired). Click **OK** to complete the definition of the new manual NAT rule.

Note: Because this example alters both source and destination information in subject packets, the equivalent configuration in OS versions 8.2 and earlier require multiple rules using a combination of dynamic inside policy NAT and static outside PAT, as those versions are limited to altering only source information in packets.

Verify that the new rule appears in the NAT Rules window, above the "Network Object" NAT section, and click **Apply** to send the changes to the ASA.

The CLI commands generated by the changes made are as follows (spacing inserted for readability):

```
object network VENDOR-SERVER
  host 192.0.2.50
!
object network VENDOR-SERVER-PAT
  host 209.165.200.234
!
object service HTTPS
  service tcp destination eq https
!
object service VENDOR-PORTMAP
  service tcp destination eq 8443
!
nat (inside,outside) 1 source dynamic INSIDE-SEGMENT VENDOR-SERVER-PAT destination
  static VENDOR-SERVER VENDOR-SERVER service HTTPS VENDOR-PORTMAP
```

If you are configuring the ASA from the CLI, you can directly enter these commands in global configuration mode.

Note: Although the modification of destination information in the scenario just presented would technically make this a twice NAT rule, that term is more typically used when both source and destination addresses are being altered.

Examining the Syntax of the Manual NAT Command

The syntax of the manual NAT **nat** command is somewhat complex at first glance, so it warrants a close examination:

```
nat (inside,outside) 1
```

The initial section specifies that the rule applies for packets sourced from the inside and destined to the outside interface. Thus, it specifies both ingress and egress interfaces. Also, the number 1 indicates the order in which this rule is to appear in the Manual NAT section of the NAT Table. Recall that manual NAT allows for multiple translation rules for the same network object, with different matching conditions, and that NAT is applied from top to bottom in the NAT Table, so the order of rules becomes important.

For example, assume one manual NAT rule specified that traffic from source A to destination B, with destination port 80, were to be translated a particular way. Another specifies that all other traffic from source A to destination B is to be translated differently. It is obvious that these rules must appear in the correct order or they would not function as intended.

Auto NAT rules did not require ordering, because auto NAT only allows a single NAT rule per network object.

```
source dynamic INSIDE-SEGMENT VENDOR-SERVER-PAT
```

This section specifies how the source (original) address in a matching packet is to be translated (in this case, dynamically). It also specifies the original address, which defines the matching condition (in this case, the network object INSIDE-SEGMENT), and the source address after translation (in this case, the network object VENDOR-SERVER-PAT) in that order.

```
destination static VENDOR-SERVER VENDOR-SERVER
```

This section specifies how the destination address in a matching packet is to be translated, if at all. In this case, to indicate that no translation is to occur, the rule specifies that the destination address is to be "statically translated to itself."

```
service HTTPS VENDOR-PORTMAP
```

The final section specifies the configured portmap rule. If a manual NAT rule does not contain port mapping, this section would simply not exist, and the command would end with the destination address mapping information. Also, note that port mapping is only available for destination, not source, information. The service objects are listed in the order of original port, then translated port, so this example will translate a destination port of 443 to a destination port of 8443 for packets from the INSIDE-SEGMENT object to the VENDOR-SERVER object.

Configuring a NAT Exemption Using Manual NAT

Returning to the configuration scenario, requirement 3 is the equivalent of a policy NAT exemption in OS versions 8.2 and earlier. This configuration is actually quite straightforward.

First, using procedures already demonstrated, create a new network object named SATELLITE-OFFICE, defined as the network 10.10.10.0/24. Then, from the NAT Rules window, click **Add > Add NAT Rule Before "Network Object" NAT** to open the Add NAT Rule window, as shown in Figure 7-50.

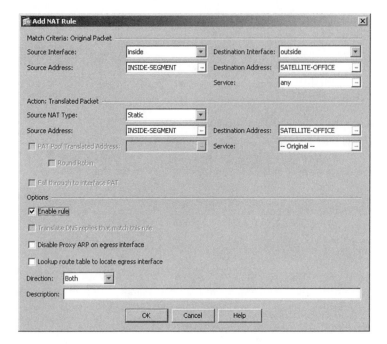

Figure 7-50 *Configuring a Manual NAT Exemption Rule*

In the Match Criteria section of the dialog box, select the inside interface, and the object INSIDE-SEGMENT as the source of packets subject to the rule. Select the outside interface and the new object SATELLITE-OFFICE as the destination, as shown in Figure 7-50.

In the Action section, choose static as the source NAT type, and then repeat the selections of INSIDE-SEGMENT and SATELLITE-OFFICE as the source and destination addresses, respectively. These changes are also shown in Figure 7-50.

Click **OK** to complete the definition of this new NAT rule. Figure 7-51 shows the NAT Rules screen following this configuration. Note that the new NAT rule appears on two lines: one for traffic from inside to outside and one from outside to inside. Both lines specify "Original" in all the columns under the Action: Translated Packet header, indicating neither source nor destination addresses are to be altered in the packets that match this rule.

Configuring Twice NAT

Requirement 4 in our NAT scenario introduces the need for twice NAT, because of the overlapping IP addresses involved. Prior to OS version 8.3, such a scenario was usually handled by performing inside policy NAT at each end of a VPN tunnel with overlapping addresses.

Figure 7-52 provides an illustration of the situation.

With OS versions 8.3 and higher, twice NAT makes it possible to handle the necessary address translations entirely on one ASA. Because all NAT rules now have the capability to specify destination interfaces, a routing decision is no longer necessary to select an egress interface, so overlapping addresses no longer present the difficulty they once did.

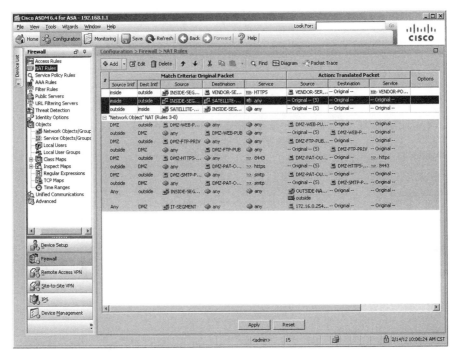

Figure 7-51 *NAT Rules Window Showing New Manual NAT Rules*

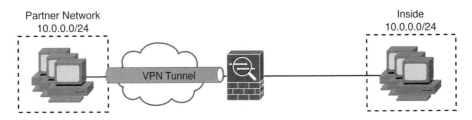

Figure 7-52 *VPN with Overlapping Address Ranges*

To configure this solution, using procedures already demonstrated, open the Add NAT Rule dialog box, as shown in Figure 7-53.

Specify the inside interface and object INSIDE-SEGMENT as the source information for this twice NAT rule. Select the outside interface as the destination interface. Although you could, because the addresses are the same, define the INSIDE-SEGMENT object as the destination address, this might cause confusion when reading the configuration. Therefore, using procedures already demonstrated, create and apply a new object named PARTNER-VPN-SEGMENT, defined as the network 10.0.0.0/24. These settings are shown in Figure 7-53.

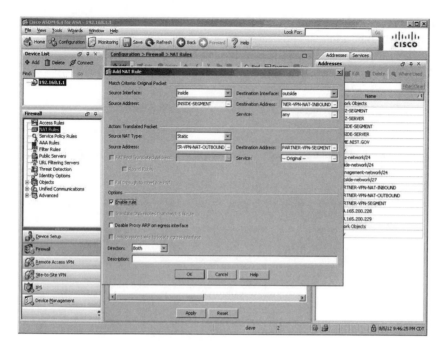

Figure 7-53 *Configuring a Twice NAT Rule*

In the Match Criteria section of the dialog box, specify the inside interface and object IN-SIDE-SEGMENT as the source information for this twice NAT rule. Select the outside interface as the destination interface.

Recall that our requirement was for full bidirectional (any-to-any) connectivity. Therefore, each internal host in the INSIDE-SEGMENT object must be uniquely identifiable from the partner network, and vice versa. Therefore, you must use static NAT, and not PAT, to accomplish this objective. The administrators of the partner network requested that you translate traffic to use source address 192.168.10.0/24 for this VPN.

In the Action section of the dialog box, select **Static** as the Source NAT Type. Then, using procedures already demonstrated, create and assign a network object named PARTNER-VPN-NAT-OUTBOUND, defined as the network 192.168.10.0/24, in the Source Address field, as shown in Figure 7-53. This completes the configuration of translation for your internal network. You must now configure the translation for the partner network.

Because the partner network uses overlapping addressing to your own, it is also necessary to translate the destination address in packets. For indysnvr, if one of your inside hosts were to attempt to send packets to the destination address 10.0.0.50, it would be considered local segment traffic and would not be routed to the ASA as the default gateway for the inside host. Therefore, inside hosts must use a destination address that requires routing the packet to the ASA, which then translates that address into the corresponding 10.0.0.0 address used on the partner network.

You have decided to use the network address, 192,168,20.0/24, to represent the partner network. This means that internal hosts will use that address space as the destination address in packets intended to be transmitted to the partner site. Because this network is non-local, internal hosts will route such packets to the ASA, where they will have their destination address translated to the actual 10.0.0.0/24 addresses in use at the partner site. They will then be sent across the VPMN tunnel, having had both source and destination addresses translated.

Therefore, using procedures already demonstrated, in the Destination Address field within the Match Criteria section of the dialog box, create and assign a new object named PARTNER-VPN-NAT-INBOUND, defined as the network 192.168.20.0/24.

Finally, to specify the translated destination address for selected packets, using procedures already demonstrated, in the Action section of the dialog box, create and assign a new network object named PARTNER-VPN-SEGMENT, defined as the network 10.0.0.0/24, in the Destination Address field. These settings are shown in Figure 7-53.

Figure 7-54 provides an illustration of the functionality of this new twice NAT rule.

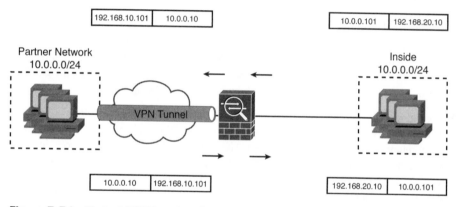

Figure 7-54 *Twice NAT Functionality*

To complete the configuration of this scenario, click **OK** to complete the new twice NAT rule, and then click **Apply** to send the changes to the ASA.

The CLI commands generated by the changes made are as follows (spacing inserted for readability):

```
object network PARTNER-VPN-NAT-INBOUND
  subnet 192.168.20.0 255.255.255.0
!
object network PARTNER-VPN-NAT-OUTBOUND
  subnet 192.168.10.0 255.255.255.0
!
object network PARTNER-VPN-SEGMENT
  subnet 10.0.0.0 255.255.255.0
!
object network SATELLITE-OFFICE
```

```
   subnet 10.10.10.0 255.255.255.0
!
nat (inside,outside) 2 source static INSIDE-SEGMENT INSIDE-SEGMENT destination
  static SATELLITE-OFFICE SATELLITE-OFFICE
!
nat (inside,outside) 3 source static INSIDE-SEGMENT PARTNER-VPN-NAT-OUTBOUND
  destination static PARTNER-VPN-NAT-INBOUND-PARTNER-VPN-SEGMENT
```

If you are configuring the ASA from the CLI, you can enter these commands directly in global configuration mode.

Note the order of objects in the **nat** command generated by this configuration. While the source objects are listed in the order real, hen mapped, the destination objects are listed in the order mapped, hen real. This is because the original source packets generated by internal hosts would have the real source, and mapped destination IP addresses in them, prior to translation. Following translation, it has the mapped source, and real destination IP addresses. Thus, the pre-translation objects are both listed first, and the post-translation objects second, in each section of the command.

Configuring Translations Using Manual NAT After Auto NAT

Manual NAT "after auto NAT" allows for translations to occur in packets that do not match any more specific translation rules in the NAT Table. They are configured in the same way as other manual NAT rules, with the exception that they are specifically configured to be placed in Section 3 of the NAT Table, rather than Section 1.

The configuration scenario for this example is as follows: Recall that the object IT-SEGMENT has an auto NAT rule defined, performing PAT whenever a host on that segment communicates with the DMZ segment. The ASA is configured to allow a combination of NAT/PAT for internal hosts communicating to the outside interface. A perimeter router at the edge of your network has access rules which drop any packets from the inside network destined to specific web sites, due to the presence of "hacking tools" on those sites. It is well known that what is a hacking tool in the wrong hands is frequently, in the hands of a properly trained administrator, an excellent network auditing tool. Therefore, you need to create a manual NAT after auto NAT rule, which will translate the source address of packets from the IT-SEGMENT to a different PAT address than other internal hosts use, so that the IT-SEGMENT will have access to the restricted web sites. You will use the translated source address 209.165.200.233 for this purpose.

Using the procedures already demonstrated, create a translation object named IT-OUT-SIDE-PAT defined as the host address 209.165.200.233. Then, navigate to the NAT Rules screen. **Click Add > Add NAT Rule After "Network Object NAT Rules"**, as shown in Figure 7-55.

This opens the Add NAT Rule After "Network Object" NAT Rules window, as shown in Figure 7-56.

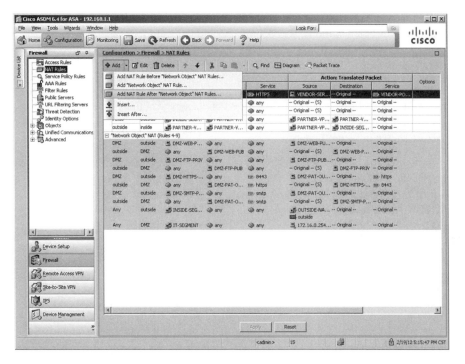

Figure 7-55 *Adding a Manual NAT After Auto NAT Rule*

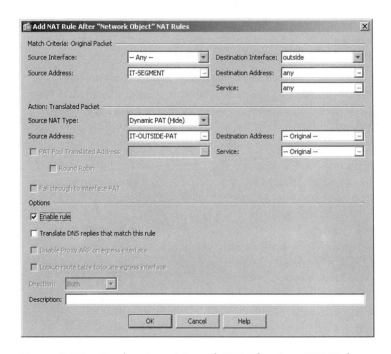

Figure 7-56 *Configuring a Manual NAT After Auto NAT Rule*

Naturally, this window is organized exactly the same way as the Add NAT Rule window previously shown. A few options, because they would only apply to specific rules that would need to appear in Section 1 of the NAT Table are not present, but the window is laid out the same way.

Under Match Criteria, leave the Source Interface field at the default value of **Any** and se-lect the IT-SEGMENT object previously defined as the source address. Select **outside** as the destination interface, and leave the destination address and service set as **any**. These changes are shown in Figure 7-56.

In the Action section, set the Source NAT Type to Dynamic PAT (Hide). For the source ad-dress, select and assign the object IT-OUTSIDE-PAT you just created. Leave all other fields at their defaults, and click **OK** to complete the configuration of this new rule. Finally, click **Apply** to send the changes to the ASA.

The CLI commands generated by the changes made are as follows (spacing inserted for readability):

```
object network IT-OUTSIDE-PAT
  host 209.165.200.233
nat (any,outside) after-auto 1 source dynamic IT-SEGMENT IT-OUTSIDE-PAT
```

If you are configuring the ASA from the CLI, you can enter these commands directly in global configuration mode.

Note the keyword **after-auto**, which is inserted into the **nat** command. This option speci-fies that the NAT rule will be placed after the auto NAT section of the NAT Table and is the only syntax that differentiates a manual NAT from a manual NAT after auto NAT rule.

Configuring a Unidirectional Manual Static NAT Rule

There are occasions when address translations should not be bidirectional (the default). For example, when connections sourced from a defined object should translate to a partic-ular address, but connections initiated toward that same object, as a destination, should not use that same translated address to refer to the host. To gain access, such connections must match a translation rule that works in both directions.

Unidirectional translation rules are also useful if you want a host to be able to initiate out-bound connectivity, but under no circumstances should inbound connections to the host be possible, even if access rules are misconfigured to allow such inbound connections.

Note: Make sure to check the specific release you will be running on your ASA in your production environment, because the **unidirectional** keyword is considered deprecated in the latest versions of the OS. For the version upon which the FIREWALL exam is based, the **unidirectional** keyword is still a supported option, however.

The configuration scenario is as follows: You decided, for security reasons, to create a uni-directional translation for an internal server, which will use translated address 209.165.200.231 when communicating with the outside interface. You want it to be able to initiate outbound connections, but inbound connection attempts to the 209.165.200.231 address should not be translated and forwarded to the host, regardless of access rules.

Using procedures already demonstrated, create two new network objects, INSIDE-SVR-PRIV, defined as host 10.0.0.10, and INSIDE-SVR-PUB, defined as host 209.165.200.231.

Navigate to the NAT Rules window and click **Add > Add** to open the Add NAT Rule window, as shown in Figure 7-57.

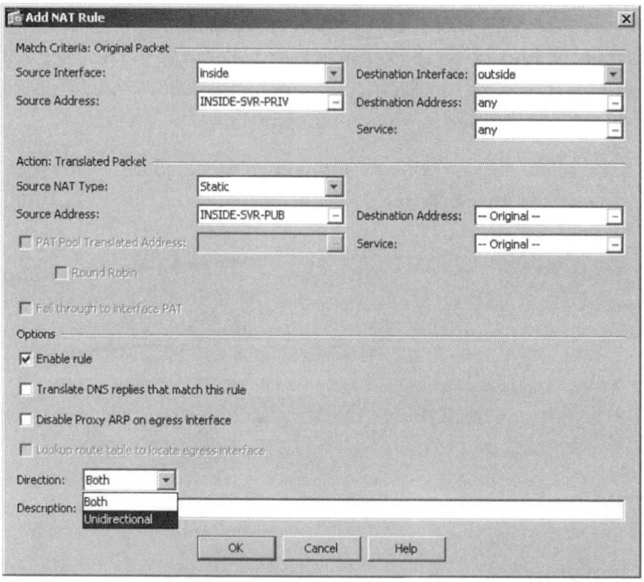

Figure 7-57   *Configuring a Unidirectional Manual Static NAT Rule*

In the Match Criteria section, select **inside** as the source interface, and define the object INSIDE-SVR-PRIV as the source address. Select outside as the destination interface. Leave other fields at their defaults. These settings are shown in Figure 7-57.

In the Action section, set the source NAT type as static. Set the source address to the object INSIDE-SVR-PUB. These settings are also shown in Figure 7-57.

Near the bottom of the Options section, locate the Direction field. This field is set to Both (bidirectional) by default. Change the setting to Unidirectional, as shown in Figure 7-57. Then, click **OK** to complete the creation of the new rule and **Apply** to send the changes to the ASA.

The CLI commands generated by the changes made are as follows (spacing inserted for readability):

```
object network INSIDE-SVR-PUB
 host 209.165.200.231
!
object network INSIDE-SVR-PRIV
 host 10.0.0.10
nat (inside,outside) 4 source static INSIDE-SVR-PRIV INSIDE-SVR-PUB unidirectional
```

If you are configuring the ASA from the CLI, you can enter these commands directly in global configuration mode.

Inserting a Manual NAT Rule in a Specific Location

Recall that NAT rules are applied to packets by searching the NAT Table, top to bottom, and applying the first rule that matches the packet being analyzed. Because the order of manual NAT rules thus has a specific impact on the operation of NAT on an ASA, it is sometimes necessary to insert a new rule into a specific location in the list. Figure 7-58 shows the NAT Rules window in ASDM with the Add menu expanded.

As you can see in Figure 7-58, there are two options for inserting a rule into a specific location within an existing list: **Insert** and **Insert After**.

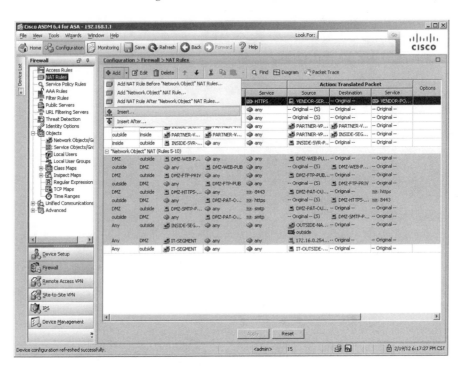

Figure 7-58 *Inserting a Manual NAT Rule in a Specific Location*

To insert a new rule above a specific rule, highlight that rule, and then choose **Insert** from the Add menu. Likewise, to insert a new rule below a specific rule, highlight that rule, and then choose **Insert After** from the Add menu.

NAT rules can also be inserted into specific locations when using the CLI. Recall that each manual NAT rule created has a number that dictates its position within the NAT Table. To insert a new rule between existing rules 3 and 4, for example, assign the new rule position number 4. Existing rules 4 and above will have their position numbers automatically increased by 1.

Comparing Manual NAT Configurations from OS versions 8.2 and 8.3

In comparing manual NAT configurations, consider the configuration just completed for the NAT scenario requirements 2 and 3. It's been a while since these requirements were presented, so they are repeated here for reference:

1. Several hosts in the 10.0.0.0/24 inside subnet are authorized to connect to a vendor application server, 192.0.2.50, port 8443, on the Internet. This vendor requires all users coming from your organization to appear to their server as a single IP address: 209.165.200.234. Because you are using one-to-one dynamic NAT, each internal host has a unique global address when translated. Thus, you need to configure a manual NAT rule to translate internal hosts to use a configured PAT address if they are communicating with the vendor application server, but still use the previously defined auto NAT rule when connecting elsewhere through the outside interface.

2. You need to configure NAT for a VPN between your inside segment and a satellite office, which uses the IP address 10.10.10.0/24. Because the satellite office also belongs to your company, and you use internal DNS servers, traffic across this VPN needs to be exempted from address translation. Because you already have an auto NAT rule configured to dynamically translate all traffic from the inside segment through the outside interface, a manual NAT rule is required to accomplish this exemption.

Because there are already many things occurring in these examples, we assume a simple two-interface firewall: inside and outside. Example 7-14 shows the version 8.2 configuration, and Example 7-15 shows the corresponding 8.3 configuration that accomplishes the same translations.

Example 7-14   *Sample Hybrid NAT Configuration from OS Version 8.2*

```
access-list POLICY-NAT permit tcp 10.0.0.0 255.255.255.0 host 192.0.2.50 eq 443
access-list VPN permit ip 10.0.0.0 255.255.255.0 10.10.10.0 255.255.255.0
static (outside,inside) tcp 192.0.2.50 443 192.0.2.50 8443 netmask 255.255.255.255
nat (inside) 0 access-list VPN
nat (inside) 1 10.0.0.0 255.255.255.0
nat (inside) 200 access-list POLICY-NAT
global (outside) 1 209.165.200.235-209.165.200.254 netmask 255.255.255.224
global (outside) 1 interface
global (outside) 200 209.165.200.234
```

Example 7-15   *Sample Hybrid NAT Configuration from OS Version 8.3*

```
object network INSIDE-SEGMENT
  subnet 10.0.0.0 255.255.255.0
object network OUTSIDE-NAT-POOL
  range 209.165.200.235 209.165.200.254
object network SATELLITE-OFFICE
  subnet 10.10.10.0 255.255.255.0
object network VENDOR-SERVER
  host 192.0.2.50
object network VENDOR-SERVER-PAT
  host 209.165.200.234
object service HTTPS
  service tcp destination eq https
object service VENDOR-PORTMAP
  service tcp destination eq 8443
nat (inside,outside) 1 source dynamic INSIDE-SEGMENT VENDOR-SERVER-PAT destination
  static VENDOR-SERVER VENDOR-SERVER service HTTPS VENDOR-PORTMAP
nat (inside,outside) 2 source static INSIDE-SEGMENT INSIDE-SEGMENT destination static
  SATELLITE-OFFICE SATELLITE-OFFICE
object network INSIDE-SEGMENT
  nat (any,outside) dynamic OUTSIDE-NAT-POOL interface
```

Although the 8.3 configuration is actually more lines in total, the vast majority of it is the configuration of the objects themselves. The translations are configured with only three lines, as compared to the nine lines required in previous OS versions.

The configuration for older OS versions contains a mixture of static and dynamic translations operating on the same packets (in different directions). Nothing in the configuration makes it readily apparent these rules have any relationship to each other, much less that they will be manipulating packets in the same flow. Either of these two facts can also lead to confusion. Furthermore, you need a thorough understanding of NAT rule priority to realize that the rules are actually applied in the order (refer to the section, "NAT Rule Priority," if desired, to review why this is the order of application):

1. NAT 0 w/ACL
2. Static translation
3. Dynamic NAT rule with NAT ID 200
4. Dynamic NAT rule with NAT ID 1

The combination of these factors presents a real challenge for understanding the configuration, even for experienced administrators. Imagine expanding such an example to the multiple-interface firewalls used in previous examples.

Although the initial creation of the necessary network objects takes some time, the new format rules are much more easily understood and clearly tie together the manipulations occurring to both source and destination information in affected packets.

When Not to Use NAT

Just as with OS versions 8.2 and earlier, there are times when you should not use NAT with OS versions 8.3 and later:

■ Do not use NAT or PAT with applications that embed IP addresses on the application layer and use end-to-end encryption, or embed IP addresses on the application layer, and are not specifically supported by ASA advanced protocol inspection.

■ Do not use NAT or PAT with applications that authenticate entire packets (such as IPsec Authentication Header [AH] or Border Gateway Protocol [BGP]).

■ Do not use NAT or PAT with applications that establish additional dynamic sessions, and for which the ASA does not support protocol-specific inspection rules. Also, if the application uses an encrypted control channel, the ASA will not be able to inspect the packet contents and perform modifications allowing the application to work properly across NAT/PAT.

Tuning NAT

It is sometimes necessary to adjust parameters that affect how the ASA performs NAT and the creation of translation slots. The ASA has many configuration options that can modify behavior. Two that are used fairly commonly are to adjust the global translation slot idle timer and activate DNS rewrite.

Both topics were discussed previously, in the section related to OS versions 8.2 and earlier. Adjusting the global translation slot timer is done exactly the same way in current OS versions as has already been covered. Refer to Figure 7-9 if you want to review this procedure.

The functionality of DNS rewrite was discussed in the section, "Other NAT Considerations." Activating DNS rewrite on a NAT rule is still done by activating an option with the NAT Rule configuration screen. For this scenario, you will activate DNS rewrite for the auto NAT rule for the DMZ web server.

Using procedures already demonstrated, open the Edit NAT Rule window for the auto NAT rule for the DMZ-WEB-PRIV object. From the Edit NAT Rule window, click the **Advanced...** button to open the Advanced NAT Settings window, as shown in Figure 7-59.

To activate DNS rewrite for a NAT rule, in the Options section of the window, check the box titled **Translate DNS Replies for Rule**. Click **OK** to accept the new setting, and then click **OK** again to finish the rule modification. Finally, click **Apply** to send the changes to the ASA. As was the case with earlier OS versions, this change simply adds the keyword **dns** to the end of the translation command, as shown here.

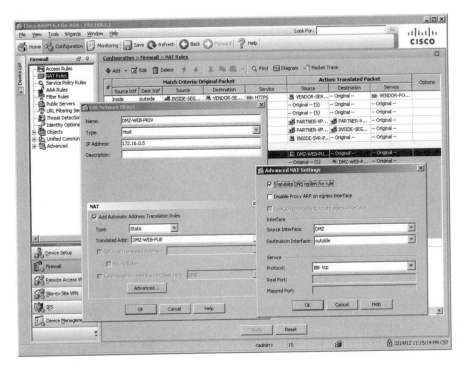

Figure 7-59   *Activating DNS Rewrite*

The CLI commands generated by the changes made are as follows (spacing inserted for readability):

```
object network DMZ-WEB-PRIV
  no nat (DMZ,outside) static DMZ-WEB-PUB
  nat (DMZ,outside) static DMZ-WEB-PUB dns
```

If you are configuring the ASA from the CLI, you can enter these commands in global configuration mode.

Note: For manual NAT rules, the DNS rewrite option is on the main window for the NAT rule. (There is no Advanced NAT Settings tab for manual NAT rules.) The checkbox is titled **Translate DNS Replies That Match This Rule.**

Troubleshooting NAT

Troubleshooting NAT requires that you observe activity on the ASA itself while generating traffic to or from a host subject to translation rules. The most common commands used for this purpose are **show xlate**, **show nat**, **show nat detail**, and **clear xlate**, which have all been examined already in this chapter. It also requires reviewing log messages generated by the address translation process (or access rules).

Improper Translation

If traffic does not appear to be translated according to a configured NAT rule you are expecting to perform the translation, consider performing the following steps in troubleshooting:

Step 1.   Verify whether the traffic is being translated at all. Remember that there is no concept of NAT control in OS versions 8.3 and higher, so if NAT rules are improperly configured, traffic might be getting forwarded with no translation occurring. Use the **show xlate** command to look for translations. Clear the translation table with **clear xlate** if recent changes have been made to translation rules.

Step 2.   If traffic is not being translated, look for missing **nat** rules by examining the NAT Table. Use the **show nat** (or **show nat detail**) command to verify a NAT rule exists for the traffic in question.

Step 3.   If traffic is being translated, but not by the correct NAT rule, check for overlapping translation rules. Keep in mind that the NAT Table is examined from top to bottom. If there are conflicting rules, you may need to alter the order of rules in the NAT Table so traffic matches the correct rule.

Example 7-16 shows sample output from the **show nat** and **show nat detail** commands for a newly rebooted ASA (noted by all the hit counts being zero). Note more verbose output regarding source and destination addresses and services when using the **detail** option.

Example 7-16   show nat detail *Command Output*

```
FIREWALL# show nat
Manual NAT Policies (Section 1)
1 (inside) to (outside) source dynamic INSIDE-SEGMENT VENDOR-SERVER-PAT
  destination static VENDOR-SERVER VENDOR-SERVER service HTTPS VENDOR-PORTMAP
    translate_hits = 0, untranslate_hits = 0
2 (inside) to (outside) source static INSIDE-SEGMENT INSIDE-SEGMENT   destination
  static SATELLITE-OFFICE SATELLITE-OFFICE
    translate_hits = 0, untranslate_hits = 0
3 (inside) to (outside) source static INSIDE-SEGMENT PARTNER-VPN-NAT-OUTBOUND
  destination static PARTNER-VPN-SEGMENT PARTNER-VPN-NAT-INBOUND
    translate_hits = 0, untranslate_hits = 0

Auto NAT Policies (Section 2)
```

```
1 (DMZ) to (outside) source static DMZ-WEB-PRIV DMZ-WEB-PUB
    translate_hits = 0, untranslate_hits = 0
2 (DMZ) to (outside) source static DMZ-FTP-PRIV DMZ-FTP-PUB
    translate_hits = 0, untranslate_hits = 0
3 (DMZ) to (outside) source static DMZ-HTTPS-PRIV DMZ-PAT-OUTSIDE   service tcp
  8443 https
    translate_hits = 0, untranslate_hits = 0
4 (DMZ) to (outside) source static DMZ-SMTP-PRIV DMZ-PAT-OUTSIDE   service tcp
  smtp smtp
    translate_hits = 0, untranslate_hits = 0
5 (any) to (outside) source dynamic INSIDE-SEGMENT OUTSIDE-NAT-POOL interface
    translate_hits = 0, untranslate_hits = 0
6 (any) to (DMZ) source dynamic IT-SEGMENT 172.16.0.254
    translate_hits = 0, untranslate_hits = 0


Manual NAT Policies (Section 3)
1 (any) to (outside) source dynamic IT-SEGMENT IT-OUTSIDE-PAT
    translate_hits = 0, untranslate_hits = 0



FIREWALL# show nat detail
Manual NAT Policies (Section 1)
1 (inside) to (outside) source dynamic INSIDE-SEGMENT VENDOR-SERVER-PAT
  destination static VENDOR-SERVER VENDOR-SERVER service HTTPS VENDOR-PORTMAP
    translate_hits = 0, untranslate_hits = 0
    Source - Origin: 10.0.0.0/24, Translated: 209.165.200.234/32
    Destination - Origin: 192.0.2.50/32, Translated: 192.0.2.50/32
    Service - Origin: tcp destination eq https , Translated: tcp destination eq 8443
2 (inside) to (outside) source static INSIDE-SEGMENT INSIDE-SEGMENT   destination
  static SATELLITE-OFFICE SATELLITE-OFFICE
    translate_hits = 0, untranslate_hits = 0
    Source - Origin: 10.0.0.0/24, Translated: 10.0.0.0/24
    Destination - Origin: 10.10.10.0/24, Translated: 10.10.10.0/24
3 (inside) to (outside) source static INSIDE-SEGMENT PARTNER-VPN-NAT-OUTBOUND
  destination static PARTNER-VPN-SEGMENT PARTNER-VPN-NAT-INBOUND
    translate_hits = 0, untranslate_hits = 0
    Source - Origin: 10.0.0.0/24, Translated: 192.168.10.0/24
    Destination - Origin: 10.0.0.0/24, Translated: 192.168.20.0/24
4 (inside) to (outside) source static INSIDE-SVR-PRIV INSIDE-SVR-PUB
  unidirectional
    translate_hits = 0, untranslate_hits = 0
    Source - Origin: 10.0.0.10/32, Translated: 209.165.200.231/32


Auto NAT Policies (Section 2)
1 (DMZ) to (outside) source static DMZ-WEB-PRIV DMZ-WEB-PUB
    translate_hits = 0, untranslate_hits = 0
    Source - Origin: 172.16.0.5/32, Translated: 209.165.200.228/32
```

```
 2 (DMZ) to (outside) source static DMZ-FTP-PRIV DMZ-FTP-PUB
     translate_hits = 0, untranslate_hits = 0
     Source - Origin: 172.16.0.10/32, Translated: 209.165.200.229/32
 3 (DMZ) to (outside) source static DMZ-HTTPS-PRIV DMZ-PAT-OUTSIDE    service tcp
 8443 https
     translate_hits = 0, untranslate_hits = 0
     Source - Origin: 172.16.0.15/32, Translated: 209.165.200.230/32
     Service - Protocol: tcp Real: 8443 Mapped: https
 4 (DMZ) to (outside) source static DMZ-SMTP-PRIV DMZ-PAT-OUTSIDE    service tcp
 smtp smtp
     translate_hits = 0, untranslate_hits = 0
     Source - Origin: 172.16.0.20/32, Translated: 209.165.200.230/32
     Service - Protocol: tcp Real: smtp Mapped: smtp
 5 (any) to (outside) source dynamic INSIDE-SEGMENT OUTSIDE-NAT-POOL interface
     translate_hits = 0, untranslate_hits = 0
     Source - Origin: 10.0.0.0/24, Translated: 209.165.200.235-209.165.200.254,
 209.165.200.226/27
 6 (any) to (DMZ) source dynamic IT-SEGMENT 172.16.0.254
     translate_hits = 0, untranslate_hits = 0
     Source - Origin: 10.0.1.0/24, Translated: 172.16.0.254/32

 Manual NAT Policies (Section 3)
 1 (any) to (outside) source dynamic IT-SEGMENT IT-OUTSIDE-PAT
     translate_hits = 0, untranslate_hits = 0
     Source - Origin: 10.0.1.0/24, Translated: 209.165.200.233/32
```

Proxy ARP and Syslog Messages

Both of these topics were covered in the "Troubleshooting Address Translation" section in the portion of this chapter covering OS versions 8.2 and earlier. There are no significant differences in these troubleshooting steps when using OS versions 8.3 and higher.

Egress Interface Selection

The ASA uses both the routing table and the xlate table to make routing decisions. In older OS versions, a routing decision was made in order to select the egress interface. Therefore, overlapping address spaces and such could cause significant complication when trying to configure address translation rules.

Now, to manage destination IP translated traffic, the ASA searches for an existing xlate slot (including static translation) to select the egress interface. Recall that ALL translation slots, as of OS version 8.3, include an egress interface. Refer, if desired, to Figure 7-13, the **show xlate** command output, for the illustration of this fact. Packets are then virtually forwarded to the egress interface. After packets are at the egress interface, an interface route lookup is performed to find the correct next hop(s) that belong to the selected egress interface. Only routes that point out the selected egress interface are eligible. Thus, conflicting IP addressing on local and remote networks can be adequately overcome. Use the **show route** command to assist with determining if the ASA has correct routes in its configuration.

Exam Preparation Tasks

As mentioned in the section, "How to Use This Book," in the Introduction, you have a couple of choices for exam preparation: the exercises here, Chapter 17, "Final Preparation," and the exam simulation questions on the CD-ROM.

Review All Key Topics

Review the most important topics in this chapter, noted with the Key Topic icon in the outer margin of the page. Table 7-4 lists a reference of these key topics and the page numbers on which each is found.

Table 7-4 *Key Topics for Chapter 7*

Key Topic Element	Description	Page Number
Bulleted list	Lists the benefits of NAT	288
Paragraph	Explains NAT control operation	296
Paragraph	Explains dynamic inside NAT operation	298
Paragraph	Describes matching NAT ID between NAT and global commands	303
Section	Describes commands to verify NAT and PAT operation	311
Section	Explains configuring static inside NAT	312
Section	Explains how to configure NAT bypass	328
Numbered list	Lists NAT rule priority with NAT control enabled	330
Section	Explains how to configure DNS Rewrite	333
Paragraph	Explains concept of network objects for NAT	339
Section	Describes the NAT Table and its sections	341
Bulleted list	Explains the types of rules that can be created with auto NAT	343
Section	Compares static NAT translations between OS versions	351
Section	Breaks down the syntax of manual NAT command	368
Section	Explains how to configure twice NAT	370

Define Key Terms

Define the following key terms from this chapter and check your answers in the glossary:

ingress interface, egress interface, NAT, PAT, xlate table, static NAT, dynamic NAT, inside NAT, outside NAT, dynamic inside NAT, static inside NAT, dynamic outside NAT, static outside NAT, NAT exemption, NAT control, bidirectional NAT, DNS Rewrite, proxy ARP, auto NAT, manual NAT, twice NAT, network object, NAT Table, unidirectional manual static NAT

Command Reference to Check Your Memory

This section includes the most important configuration and EXEC commands covered in this chapter. It might not be necessary to memorize the complete syntax of every command, but you should be able to remember the basic keywords that are needed.

To test your memory of the commands, cover the right side of Table 7-5 with a piece of paper, read the description on the left side, and then see how much of the command you can remember.

The FIREWALL exam focuses on practical, hands-on skills that are used by a networking professional. Therefore, you should be able to identify the commands needed to configure and test an ASA feature.

Table 7-5 *Commands Related to ASA Translation Using OS Versions 8.2 and Earlier*

Task	Command Syntax
Enable NAT control	ciscoasa(config)# **nat-control**
Configure use of dynamic inside NAT (some parameters covered in other chapters)	ciscoasa(config)# **nat** (*real_ifc*) *nat_id real_ip* [*mask* [**dns**] [[**tcp**] *tcp_max_conns* [*emb_limit*]] [**udp** *udp_max_conns*] [**norandomseq**]]
Configure use of dynamic policy NAT (configuration of access lists is covered in Chapter 8)	ciscoasa(config)# **nat** (*real_ifc*) *nat_id* **access-list** *access_list_name* [**dns**] [[**tcp**] *tcp_max_conns* [*emb_limit*]] [**udp** *udp_max_conns*] [**norandomseq**]]
Configure use of dynamic identity NAT	ciscoasa(config)# **nat** (*real_ifc*) **0** *real_ip* [*mask* [**dns**] [[**tcp**] *tcp_max_conns* [*emb_limit*]] [**udp** *udp_max_conns*] [**norandomseq**]]
Configure use of dynamic policy identity NAT	ciscoasa(config)# **nat** (*real_ifc*) **0 access-list** *access_list_name* [**dns**] [[**tcp**] *tcp_max_conns* [*emb_limit*]] [**udp** *udp_max_conns*] [**norandomseq**]]
Configure use of dynamic outside NAT	ciscoasa(config)# **nat** (*real_ifc*) *nat_id* **access-list** *access_list_name* [**dns**] [**outside**] [[**tcp**] *tcp_max_conns* [*emb_limit*]] [**udp** *udp_max_conns*] [**norandomseq**]]

Table 7-5   *Commands Related to ASA Translation Using OS Versions 8.2 and Earlier*

Task	Command Syntax
Create a pool of global addresses for use by NAT or PAT	ciscoasa(config)# **global** (*mapped_ifc*) *nat_id* {*mapped_ip*[*-mapped_ip*] [**netmask** *mask*] | **interface**}
Configure use of static inside NAT	ciscoasa(config)# **static** (*real_ifc,mapped_ifc*) {*mapped_ip* | **interface**} {*real_ip* [**netmask** *mask*]} [**dns**] [[**tcp**] *max_conns* [*emb_lim*]] [**udp** *udp_max_conns*] [**norandomseq** [**nailed**]]
Configure use of static inside PAT	ciscoasa(config)# **static** (*real_ifc,mapped_ifc*) {**tcp** | **udp**} {*mapped_ip* | **interface**} *mapped_port* {*real_ip real_port* [**netmask** *mask*]} [**dns**] [[**tcp**] *max_conns* [*emb_lim*]] [**udp** *udp_max_conns*] [**norandomseq** [**nailed**]]
Configure use of static inside policy NAT	ciscoasa(config)# **static** (*real_ifc,mapped_ifc*) {*mapped_ip* | **interface**} {**access-list** *access_list_name*} [**dns**] [[**tcp**] *max_conns* [*emb_lim*]] [**udp** *udp_max_conns*] [**norandomseq** [**nailed**]]
Configure use of static inside policy PAT	ciscoasa(config)# **static** (*real_ifc,mapped_ifc*) {**tcp** | **udp**} {*mapped_ip* | **interface**} *mapped_port* {**access-list** *access_list_name*} [**dns**] [[**tcp**] *max_conns* [*emb_lim*]] [**udp** *udp_max_conns*] [**norandomseq** [**nailed**]]
Change the default translation slot idle timer value	ciscoasa(config)# **timeout xlate** *hh:mm:ss*
Display translation table (terse)	ciscoasa# **show xlate**
Display translation table (detailed)	ciscoasa# **show xlate detail**
Clear translation table	ciscoasa# **clear xlate**
Disable proxy ARP	ciscoasa(config)# **sysopt noproxyarp** *interface_name*

Table 7-6 *Commands Related to ASA Translation Using OS Versions 8.3 and Later*

Task	Command Syntax
Enable NAT control	ciscoasa(config)# **nat-control**
Display translation table	ciscoasa# **show xlate**
Display NAT Table (terse)	ciscoasa# **show nat**
Display NAT Table (detailed)	ciscoasa# **show nat detail**
Create a network object	ciscoasa(config)# **object network** obj_name	[**rename** new_obj_name] [**description** text]
Configure an auto NAT static NAT rule or static PAT rule	ciscoasa(config-network-object)# **nat** [(*real_ifc,mapped_ifc*)] **static** {*mapped_inline_ip*	*mapped_obj*	**interface**} {**dns**	**service** {**tcp**	**udp**} *real_port mapped_port*]
Configure an auto NAT dynamic NAT rule	ciscoasa(config-network-object)# **nat** [(*real_ifc,mapped_ifc*)] **dynamic** {*mapped_inline_host_ip* [**interface**]	*mapped_obj* [**interface**]	**interface**} [**dns**]
Display NAT rules configuration	ciscoasa# **show running-config nat**
Display object configuration	ciscoasa# **show running-config object id** obj_name
Display object configuration on single line	ciscoasa# **show running-config object in-line**	**include** *obj_name*
Create a service object	ciscoasa(config)# **object service** *object name* [**rename** *new_obj_name*] {*protocol*	**icmp** *icmp-type*	**icmp6** *icmp6-type*	**tcp**	**udp**	[**source** [*operator*] *begin-port* [*end-port*]] [[*operator*] *begin-port* [*end-port*]]}
Configure a manual NAT (twice NAT) static NAT rule	ciscoasa(config)# **nat** [(*real_ifc,mapped_ifc*)] [*line*	{**after-auto** [*line*]}] **source static** {*real_obj*	**any**} {*mapped_obj*	**interface**	**any**}} [**destination static** {*mapped_obj*	**interface**} {*real_obj*	**any**}] [**service** {*real_src_mapped_dest_svc_obj*	**any**} *mapped_src_real_dest_svc_obj*] [**dns**] [**unidirectional**] [**inactive**] [**description** *desc*]
Configure a manual NAT (twice NAT) dynamic NAT rule	ciscoasa(config)# **nat** [(*real_ifc,mapped_ifc*)] [*line*	{**after-autot** [*line*]}] **source dynamic** {*real_obj*	**any**} {*mapped_obj* [**interface**]	**interface**} [**destination static** {*mapped_obj*	**interface**} {*real_obj*	**any**}] [**service** {*mapped_dest_svc_obj real_dest_svc_obj*] [**dns**] [**unidirectional**] [**inactive**] [**description** *desc*]

This chapter covers the following topics:

- **Understanding How Access Control Works:**
  This section provides a brief introduction to the information necessary to implement effective access control.

- **State Tables:** This section describes the two state tables (connection and local host) used by the Cisco ASA to determine if connections should be allowed through the ASA without the need to consult interface access rules, and how to view their contents.

- **Understanding Interface Access Rules:** This section describes the functionality of interface access rules, the most common access control method deployed on Cisco ASAs.

- **Default Access Rules:** This section describes the default interface access rules present on an ASA.

- **The Global ACL:** This section discusses the global ACL, a new concept in OS version 8.3, created to make it easier to configure and manage the access policy configuration.

- **Configuring Interface Access Rules:** This section demonstrates how to configure interface access rules (ACLs in the CLI), including how to create and edit rules. It also discusses how to activate system logging for specific rules, add comments to your list of access rules, modify logging levels of syslog messages generated by packets matching access rules, and perform ACL creation and editing from the CLI.

CHAPTER 8

Controlling Access Through the ASA

- **Time-Based Access Rules:** This section explains how to create access rules that are applied only at specific times, by creating time ranges and then referencing them in access rules.

- **Verifying Interface Access Rules:** This section describes methods to verify the content and functionality of interface access rules, including methods of managing access rules from both Cisco ASDM and the CLI.

- **Organizing Access Rules Using Object Groups:** This section describes the concept of object groups in the Cisco ASA, including the types of object groups, how they are used, and why they are used.

- **Verifying Object Groups:** This section describes how to verify membership within object groups, as well as in access rule sets (access lists), both in Cisco ASDM and the CLI.

- **Configuring and Verifying Other Basic Access Controls:** This section describes how to implement and verify the use of Unicast Reverse Path Forwarding and host shunning.

- **Troubleshooting Basic Access Control:** This section describes how to use various tools effectively on the ASA to troubleshoot issues with access control.

This chapter reviews access control lists (ACL) and host shunning, and how these features can be configured to control traffic movement through a Cisco Adaptive Security Appliance (ASA).

"Do I Know This Already?" Quiz

The "Do I Know This Already?" quiz allows you to assess whether you should read this entire chapter thoroughly or jump to the "Exam Preparation Tasks" section. If you are in doubt about your answers to these questions or your own assessment of your knowledge of the topics, read the entire chapter. Table 8-1 lists the major headings in this chapter and their corresponding "Do I Know This Already?" quiz questions. You can find the answers in Appendix A, "Answers to the 'Do I Know This Already?' Quizzes."

Table 8-1 *"Do I Know This Already?" Section-to-Question Mapping*

Foundation Topics Section	Questions
State Tables	1–3
Understanding Interface Access Rules	4–8
Configuring Interface Access Rules	9–11
Time-Based Access Rules	12–13
Verifying Interface Access Rules	14
Organizing Access Rules Using Object Groups	15
Configuring and Verifying Other Basic Access Controls	16–17
Troubleshooting Basic Access Control	18

1. Which of the following are state tables maintained by the ASA? (Choose two.)

   a. Host table

   b. Connection table

   c. Session table

   d. Local host table

   e. Xlate table

2. Which of the following would be tracked for a TCP connection? (Choose all that apply.)

   a. Source IP address

   b. Destination port number

   c. Sequence number (in both directions)

   d. Acknowledgment number (in both directions)

   e. Idle time

   f. TCP window size

3. Consider this entry from the connection table:

```
TCP outside 192.0.2.223:3122 DMZ 172.16.0.10:8400, idle 0:03:13, bytes
  244335, flags UIOB
```

What do the flags UIOB indicate? (Choose all that apply.)

    a. This connection is currently up.

    b. This connection is currently idle.

    c. This connection has seen both inbound and outbound data.

    d. This connection was initiated from a lower-security interface to a higher security interface.

    e. This connection was initiated from a higher-security interface to a lower security interface.

    f. This connection is currently half-closed.

4. If a packet arrives at an ASA interface and is associated with an already-existing connection object, how will it be processed by the interface access rules?

    a. In order, until first match.

    b. Entire list, applying best match.

    c. In order, until first match, but after any address translation is applied.

    d. It is not processed by the interface access rules.

5. The initial packet in an SSH session destined for the ASA itself arrives at the ASA interface. How will it be processed by the interface access rules?

    a. In order, until first match.

    b. Entire list, applying best match.

    c. In order, until first match, but after any address translation is applied.

    d. It is not processed by the interface access rules.

6. What do all access lists contain as the final rule?

    a. Explicit deny all

    b. Implicit deny all

    c. Transparent deny all

    d. Implicit permit all

7. If no interface access rules are applied, what will happen to traffic ingressing the ASA through the DMZ interface, security level 50, and destined for the DMZ2 interface, security level 60?

    a. It will be permitted.

    b. It will be denied.

    c. There is not enough information given to know for certain.

    d. It will be permitted only if it passes a uRPF check.

8. Consider the following configuration:

```
access-list INSIDE-IN permit ip object INSIDE-SEGMENT any
access-list OUTSIDE-OUT permit tcp 10.0.0.0 255.255.255.0 any eq https
access-list GLOBAL-ACL deny ip any any
object network INSIDE-SEGMENT
 subnet 10.0.0.0 255.255.255.0
 nat (inside,any) dynamic 209.165.200.254 interface
access-group INSIDE-IN in interface inside
access-group OUTSIDE-OUT out interface outside
access-group GLOBAL-ACL global
```

If host 10.0.0.108 on the inside interface initiates an HTTP connection to server 192.0.2.150 on the Internet, will it be permitted through the ASA?

a. Yes, it will be permitted.

b. No, it will be denied.

9. Consider the following configuration: Which of the following access list statements will allow Internet-based hosts to reach the web server on the DMZ, assuming access list OUTSIDE-IN is applied inbound on the outside interface?

```
object network DMZ-WEB-SVR
  host 172.16.0.5
  nat (DMZ,outside) static 209.165.200.228
object-group network WEB-SVRS
 network-object host 172.16.0.5
 network-object host 172.16.0.10
```

a. `access-list OUTSIDE-IN permit tcp any host DMZ-WEB-SVR eq 80`

b. `access-list OUTSIDE-IN permit ip any object WEB-SVRS eq http`

c. `access-list OUTSIDE-IN permit tcp any object DMZ-WEB-SVR eq www`

d. `access-list OUTSIDE-IN permit tcp any object WEB-SVRS eq http`

e. `access-list OUTSIDE-IN permit ip any object DMZ-WEB-SVR eq http`

10. If you include a description when configuring an access rule in Cisco ASDM, what effect does this have on the access list when viewed from the CLI?

a. None; access rule descriptions are not made part of the configuration file.

b. It will create an **access-list remark** statement with its own line number, placed directly before the access rule being configured.

c. It will create an **access-list remark** statement with its own line number, placed directly after the access rule being configured.

d. It will create an **access-list remark** statement with the same line number as the access rule being configured, placed directly before the access rule being configured.

e. It will create an **access-list remark** statement with the same line number as the access rule being configured, placed directly after the access rule being configured.

11. When an access rule denies traffic, this is a security event, and the ASA generates which syslog message for each denied packet, by default?

    a. 106100

    b. 106015

    c. 106023

    d. 106123

12. July 1, 2012 at midnight through September 31, 2012 at 11:59 p.m. is an example of what type of time range?

    a. Definite

    b. Periodic

    c. Absolute

    d. Temporary

13. Where in Cisco ASDM are time ranges configured?

    a. **Configuration > Firewall > Access Rules > Time Ranges**

    b. **Configuration > Firewall > Advanced > Time Ranges**

    c. **Configuration > Firewall > Time Ranges**

    d. Configuration > Firewall > Objects > Time Ranges

14. The **show access-list brief** command displays which of the following? (Choose all that apply.)

    a. The access-list id of all access lists configured

    b. The number of ACEs in each ACL

    c. The hit count for each ACE in each ACL

    d. A hexadecimal hash identifier for each access list

15. What are the four types of object groups that can be created on the Cisco ASA?

    a. Network

    b. ICMP

    c. Service

    d. Port Range

    e. Protocol

    f. Server

    g. ICMP-type

    h. Encryption Domain

16. Where in Cisco ASDM is uRPF enabled?

   a. Configuration > Firewall > Access Rules > Anti-Spoofing

   b. Configuration > Firewall > Advanced > uRPF

   c. Configuration > Firewall > Access Rules > uRPF

   d. Configuration > Firewall > Advanced > Anti-Spoofing

   e. Configuration > Firewall > Interfaces > Anti-Spoofing

   f. Configuration > Firewall > Interfaces > uRPF

17. How can you clear only a single host from the shunning list?

   a. clear shun *ip_address*

   b. clear shun *interface ip_address*

   c. clear shun *ip_address interface*

   d. You cannot clear only one entry from the shunning list.

18. What command would create a packet capture consisting only of packets dropped by interface access rules?

   a. capture ACL-DROPS type acl-drop

   b. capture ACL-DROPS type asp-drop acl-drop

   c. capture ACL-DROPS asp-drop acl-drop

   d. capture ACL-DROPS acl-drop

   e. capture ACL-DROPS interface outside acl-drop

   f. capture ACL-DROPS interface outside asp-drop acl-drop

Foundation Topics

Access control is at the heart of the Cisco ASA. The ASA provides an administrator with a full-featured set of access control methods, allowing access between network segments to be tightly controlled.

This chapter discusses the most fundamental of these control mechanisms: interface access rules that enforce Layer 3–4 policy, permanent automatic antispoofing mechanisms, and temporary host-blocking mechanisms that may be required for incident response. These mechanisms are the most common types of access controls deployed in most production networks.

Understanding How Access Control Works

Before implementing the access controls demonstrated in this chapter, you should gather some important input parameters from your network environment. Items you will need to know include the following:

- **The desired OSI Layer 3–4 access policy:** This information should be based on your local security policy and should specify which hosts are allowed to communicate with each other, using which specific applications. Based on this information, you will build an optimal, least-required-privilege access policy that allows only the required connectivity through the ASA.

- **Details of the network topology:** This information enables you to properly and optimally design routing on the ASA and deploy automatic antispoofing using the Unicast Reverse Path Forwarding (uRPF) feature.

- **Whether there is a need for fast, temporary blocking of specific hosts:** This feature may be required by organizations whose policies dictate temporary blocking of hosts that are involved in security incidents, such as denial-of-service attacks. The shunning feature covered in this chapter fulfills such a need.

State Tables

The Cisco ASA is, at its foundation, a stateful packet filtering device that is application-aware, and is capable of verifying the legitimacy and correctness of packets arriving at its interfaces by using various state tables combined with configured access policies. If a packet arrives at an ASA interface, it either must match expected traffic definitions from an existing session or will be compared against the inbound interface security policy applied to that interface.

To determine whether the interface security policy will be applied to packets, therefore, the ASA must be able to determine if arriving packets match expected traffic from an existing connection. The ASA does this by maintaining state tables, as just mentioned. State tables act as short-term memory for the device on active connections. Essentially, the state tables describe the device's environment; traffic the device has seen in the past, combined with its knowledge of networking protocols and applications, allows it to predict what correct future traffic within the same session will look like.

Connection Table

The most fundamental state table used by the ASA is the connection table (sometimes also called the session table). In the connection table, the ASA tracks all connections that were permitted across the device.

Note: As a reminder, do not confuse the generic term "connection," which is used to indicate an active communication, for the specific term "connection-oriented." The connection table maintains information not only on connection-oriented Transmission Control Protocol (TCP) sessions, but also on all active communications, whether TCP, User Datagram Protocol (UDP), or based on advanced protocol inspection capabilities discussed in other chapters.

Key
Topic

All packets belonging to existing connections that arrive at an ASA interface must match the currently expected packet properties for that particular connection, as recorded in the connection table. If arriving packets belong to an existing session but do not match the expected properties from the connection table, the ASA will drop the packets.

The connection table is constantly updated based on properties observed in permitted packets. When a packet is permitted to cross through the ASA, the associated connection's state information is adjusted appropriately, based on the protocol in use for that session. If it is the first packet in a session, a new connection object is created in the connection table. If it is not the first packet, the connection object is updated appropriately. For example, a TCP connection object would have its sequence numbers updated with each permitted packet.

The Cisco ASA tracks various connection properties, depending on the transport protocol on which the tracked session is based. These properties are summarized in Table 8-2 and detailed in the following paragraphs. Note that TCP and UDP are tracked by default, but Internet Control Message Protocol (ICMP) and Encapsulating Security Payload (ESP) are tracked only if specifically configured.

Table 8-2   *Statefully Tracked Protocol Information*

Protocol	Extent of Stateful Tracking
TCP	Source and destination addresses and ports, TCP flags, sequence numbers (in both directions), and idle time
UDP	Source and destination addresses and ports, idle time, and for some applications, request identifiers
ICMP (PING)	Source and destination addresses, ICMP type, ICMP code, idle time, and ICMP packet ID
ESP (IPsec)	Source and destination addresses, IPsec Security Parameter Index (SPI), and idle time

For *TCP connections*, the ASA tracks a full set of connection parameters, source and destination IP addresses and ports, the TCP state machine (also called TCP flags, to track when a connection is establishing, established, or closing), and the TCP sequence number in both directions. Additionally, by default, for each new connection, the ASA will randomize the initial sequence number of the connection in each direction, and cache the difference between the initial and randomized sequence number, so that all subsequent packets can have the sequence number adjusted accordingly. Finally, the idle time of all TCP connections is tracked so that abandoned or dead connections can be timed out.

A TCP connection object is created in the connection table if the ASA security policy permits its initial synchronization (SYN) packet. If either endpoint closes the connection with a reset (RST), or the endpoints mutually close the connection by exchanging finish (FIN) packets, the connection object is deleted from the connection table. TCP flows can also be deleted by the ASA if they are idle for longer than the configurable TCP idle timer. The ASA also tracks half-closed flows (only one side has sent a FIN), and uses a separate idle timer to delete them if they remain in the half-closed state for that amount of time.

For *UDP flows*, the ASA tracks source and destination IP addresses and ports and the idle time since the last packet of the flow was seen by the ASA. For certain applications (such as DNS), the ASA also tracks request identifiers, to help it defend against packet-spoofing attacks. A UDP flow connection object is created in the connection table if the ASA security policy permits it. Because UDP flows have no state machine, UDP flows are deleted only when they are idle for longer than the configurable UDP idle timer.

For *ICMP pings* (for example, ICMP echo and echo reply transactions), the ASA tracks source and destination IP addresses, ICMP type and code, the ICMP packet identifier, and the idle time of the request. An ICMP connection object is created in the connection table if the ASA security policy permits it. When a response is received (e.g., an echo reply from the target, an unreachable message from a router, and so forth), the ICMP connection object is deleted from the connection table. However, by default, the ASA treats ICMP traffic as stateless. Despite being in the connection table, expected ICMP replies will not be permitted through the ASA by default. You must either permit them using an access list or, preferably, enable ICMP inspection, to allow replies to return through the ASA and to enforce the request-response packet-for-packet balance.

For *IPsec Encapsulating Security Payload (ESP) tunnel flows* through the ASA (the ASA is not an endpoint of the tunnel), the ASA tracks source and destination IP addresses, the Security Parameters Index (SPI, or tunnel ID), and the idle time of the tunnel flow. An IPsec ESP flow connection object is created in the connection table if the ASA security policy permits it. If the tunnel flow is idle for more than the configurable idle time, it is deleted from the connection table. By default, the ASA treats ESP flows as stateless, and does not enter ESP flows into the connection table. To allow returning packets through the ASA "statefully," you must enable IPsec inspection of pass-through traffic.

Because determinations on which flows to allow through the ASA statefully (without need for an access rule to permit the return session flow) are based on the presence of a connection object in the connection table, it is important to know how to view the contents of the connection table. You can display the current contents of the connection table using the **show conn** command (which also has several optional parameters, such as **detail**).

Examples 8-1 and 8-2 show the use of the **show conn** and **show conn detail** commands, respectively.

Example 8-1   show conn *Command Output*

```
FIREWALL# show conn
352 in use, 5985 most used
UDP DMZ 172.16.0.25:161 inside 10.0.0.30:1879, idle 0:00:27, bytes 706509, flags -
UDP outside 192.0.2.18:123 inside 10.0.0.108:123, idle 0:00:34, bytes 79, flags -
TCP outside 192.0.2.150:80 DMZ 172.16.0.5:59512, idle 0:00:00, bytes 0, flags Uf
TCP outside 192.0.2.150:80 inside 10.0.0.102:59559, idle 0:00:03, bytes 1488,
    flags UfFRIO
TCP outside 192.0.2.150:80 inside 10.0.0.108:59393, idle 0:00:06, bytes 123013,
    flags UIO
TCP outside 192.0.2.150:80 inside 10.0.0.107:59498, idle 0:00:06, bytes 1021,
    flags UIO
TCP outside 192.0.2.223:3122 DMZ 172.16.0.10:8400, idle 0:03:13, bytes 244335,
    flags UIOB
TCP outside 192.0.2.74:45781 inside 10.0.0.10:389, idle 0:04:01, bytes 9419,
    flags UIOB
UDP outside 192.0.2.146:5440 inside 10.0.0.10:5440, idle 0:00:20, bytes 761933,
    flags -
TCP outside 192.0.2.6:1047 inside 10.0.0.10:389, idle 0:00:00, bytes 2253, flags UIOB
ICMP outside 192.0.2.37:512 inside 10.0.0.10:0, idle 0:00:00, bytes 0
... output omitted ...
```

Example 8-2   show conn detail *Command Output*

```
FIREWALL# show conn detail
368 in use, 5985 most used
Flags: A - awaiting inside ACK to SYN, a - awaiting outside ACK to SYN,
       B - initial SYN from outside, b - TCP state-bypass or nailed, C - CTIQBE
         media,
       D - DNS, d - dump, E - outside back connection, F - outside FIN, f -
         inside FIN,
       G - group, g - MGCP, H - H.323, h - H.225.0, I - inbound data,
       i - incomplete, J - GTP, j - GTP data, K - GTP t3-response
       k - Skinny media, M - SMTP data, m - SIP media, n - GUP
       O - outbound data, P - inside back connection, p - Phone-proxy TFTP
         connection,
       q - SQL*Net data, R - outside acknowledged FIN,
       R - UDP SUNRPC, r - inside acknowledged FIN, S - awaiting inside SYN,
       s - awaiting outside SYN, T - SIP, t - SIP transient, U - up,
       V - VPN orphan, W - WAAS,
       X - inspected by service module
UDP DMZ: 172.16.0.25/161 inside:10.0.0.30/1879,
    flags -, idle 0s, uptime 1D22h, timeout 2m0s, bytes 706983
UDP outside: 192.0.2.18/61840 DMZ:172.16.0.15/22936,
    flags -, idle 29s, uptime 29s, timeout 2m0s, bytes 128
```

```
TCP outside:192.0.2.150/80 inside:10.0.0.102/59512,
    flags Uf, idle 4s, uptime 9s, timeout 1h0m, bytes 0
TCP outside: 192.0.2.150/80 inside:10.0.0.108/59315,
    flags UfFRIO, idle 6m4s, uptime 6m4s, timeout 10m0s, bytes 1493
TCP outside: 192.0.2.150/80 inside:10.0.0.107/59393,
    flags UIO, idle 10s, uptime 20s, timeout 1h0m, bytes 123013
UDP outside:192.0.2.146/5440 inside:10.0.0.10/5440,
    flags -, idle 24s, uptime 3D23h, timeout 2m0s, bytes 762029
TCP outside: 192.0.2.150/43089 DMZ:172.16.0.5/443,
    flags UIOB, idle 2s, uptime 11s, timeout 1h0m, bytes 2296
... output omitted ...
```

The **show conn** command displays the number of active connections and information about each. In Example 8-1, there are 11 connections displayed in the connection table output: 3 UDP, 7 TCP, and 1 ICMP.

For each flow, you can see the ASA interfaces involved in the flow, source and destination IP addresses and ports (for TCP and UDP), or session IDs (shown in the same position as the source port field, for GRE and ICMP flows), the current idle time, and the cumulative byte count for traffic flowing between the two endpoints. For TCP connections, connection tracking flags (internal tracking flags used by the ASA, not TCP flags from the packet) are also shown.

Example 8-2 shows similar connections in the connection table. By using the **detail** keyword, additional information is shown about each connection.

TCP Connection Flags

Table 8-3 shows 12 of the most common connection states (flags) seen in the connection table. There are other connection states for specific applications, but the ones shown are valid for any TCP connection in the table.

Table 8-3   *Basic TCP Connection States*

Flag	Description
a	Awaiting outside ACK to SYN
A	Awaiting inside ACK to SYN
B	Initial SYN from outside
f	Inside FIN
F	Outside FIN
I	Inbound data
O	Outbound data
r	Inside acknowledged FIN

Table 8-3   *Basic TCP Connection States*

Flag	Description
R	Outside acknowledged FIN
s	Awaiting outside SYN
S	Awaiting inside SYN
U	Up (connection established)

Note: For a complete list of **show conn** flag descriptions, consult ASA documentation available on Cisco.com.

Analyzing the TCP flags from the connection table is useful, particularly during troubleshooting, as they can indicate various issues. For example, a connection "stuck" in a state with the flags saA showing indicates an unresponsive host on the interface with the lower security level, and might indicate a routing problem. A connection "stuck" in a state with the flags aB might even indicate a denial-of-service attack is in progress, targeting an internal host. If almost all connections show the UIO (up, inbound data, outbound data) or UIOB (the same, but also indicates that the TCP session was initiated from a lower-security to a higher-security-level direction), this would typically indicate normal ASA operation.

The **clear conn** command and its variants can be used to delete entries from the connection table. This can be for a single connection, all the way up to all current connections in the table, depending on the parameters you specify.

If you clear a TCP connection, the application using that connection will be disconnected, and may not recover automatically. For other connection types, such as UDP and ICMP, traffic flows will typically re-create the connection object automatically.

Example 8-3 shows a typical use of the **clear conn** command. In this example, the intent is to clear all connections involving the external host 192.0.2.146, which has recently been the source address on intrusion prevention alerts for servers inside your network. Full parameter options are presented in the section, "Command Reference to Check Your Memory," at the end of this chapter.

Example 8-3   clear conn *Command Usage*

```
FIREWALL# clear conn address 192.0.2.146
12 connection(s) deleted.
```

Note: Although the *Cisco ASA Command Reference Guides* state that the **clear conn** command was introduced as early as OS version 7.0(8), it was included only in specific subreleases of code versions prior to 8.2. As of 8.2, it is fully supported.

Inside and Outside, Inbound and Outbound

The descriptions in Table 8-3 use the terminology of inside/outside or inbound/outbound when describing connections. These terms portray the security levels of the involved interfaces relative to one another and should not be confused with the interfaces actually named "inside" and "outside" (if such interface names exist). They should instead be interpreted as follows:

- Every connection across the ASA is initiated by an endpoint reachable through one ASA interface and terminates on an endpoint reachable through a different ASA interface. Each ASA interface has an assigned security level, which is a numeric value from 0 to 100, indicating the "trustworthiness" of networks reachable through that interface. The higher the number, the more trust is implied. For example, interface "inside" is given a security level of 100 by default, whereas interface "outside" is assigned a security level of 0.

- For each connection, the *inside* interface is the interface with the higher assigned security level, and the *outside* interface is the interface with the lower assigned security level.

- Traffic flowing from an endpoint on a higher-security interface to an endpoint on a lower-security interface is considered *outbound*. Conversely, traffic flowing from an endpoint on a lower security interface to an endpoint on a higher security interface is considered *inbound*.

Local Host Table

Another state table maintained by the Cisco ASA is the *local host table*, where the ASA tracks all IP addresses that have connections established through the ASA. Each individual host (IP address) is tracked with a local host object, where the ASA maintains per-host statistics, such as current connection count. Each local host object references connection objects in the connection table that involve that particular host address. Thus, by viewing the local host table, you can also see the relevant entries from the connection table to which it is linked.

You can view the local host state table using the **show local-host** command. Because the local host table can be quite extensive, it is very common to filter this output by specifying additional parameters. The most common parameter to specify is the IP address for which you are seeking information. Remember that in the connection table, and therefore the local host table, internal hosts are always represented with their *real* IP address, and not any *mapped* IP address from a translation rule, even if the connection is initiated from a less secure interface and the original packets were therefore using a mapped IP address as a destination address. Example 8-4 shows a typical output, where a specific IP address was added as a parameter. Full parameter options are presented in the "Command Reference to Check Your Memory" section at the end of this chapter.

Example 8-4   show local-host *Command Output*

```
FIREWALL# show local-host 10.0.0.108
Interface management: 0 active, 0 maximum active, 0 denied
Interface DMZ: 2 active, 69 maximum active, 0 denied
Interface inside: 130 active, 320 maximum active, 0 denied
local host: <10.0.0.108>,
    TCP flow count/limit = 15/unlimited
    TCP embryonic count to host = 0
    TCP intercept watermark = unlimited
    UDP flow count/limit = 10/unlimited

  Xlate:
    NAT from any:10.0.0.108 to outside:209.165.200.238 flags I idle 0:00:00
        timeout 3:00:00

  Conn:
    TCP outside 192.0.2.65:22 inside 10.0.0.108:50124, idle 0:00:58, bytes 443,
        flags UIO
    ... output omitted ...
Interface outside: 120 active, 1940 maximum active, 0 denied
```

In Example 8-4, internal host 10.0.0.108 has established a Secure Shell (SSH) connection to external host 192.0.2.65. Because the ASA in this example allowed the connection, it will create two objects in the local host table (local host 10.0.0.8 and local host 192.0.2.65) and one object in the connection table (TCP 10.0.0.8:50124 > 192.0.2.65:22), which will be linked to both of the local host table objects.

The local host table is organized by ASA interface, and then by host IP address. For each listed interface, a current connection count and the highest connection count seen since the last reboot are listed, along with a count of any denied connection requests.

The **clear local-host** command and its variants can be used to delete objects from the local host table. This can be for a single object, a group of objects, or all current objects in the table, depending on the parameters you specify.

If you clear a local host object, all connections associated with that object are also deleted. As with clearing connection objects, some flows may recover automatically, while others may not. Additionally, using the **clear local-host** command reinitializes per-client runtime states such as connection and embryonic connection limits. As a result, using this command removes any connections that use those limits.

The following syntax shows a typical use of the **clear local-host** command:

```
FIREWALL# clear local-host all
```

In this example, the intent is to clear the entire local host table. It is also possible to clear the local host entry for a single host. This syntax appears in the section, "Command Reference to Check Your Memory," at the end of this chapter.

State Table Logging

When system logging is enabled on the ASA, it will by default log events associated with the creation and deletion of objects in the connection and local host tables. By default, creation and deletion of local host objects is logged at the debugging (7) level, while creation and deletion of connection objects is logged at the informational (6) level.

The sample output in Example 8-5 shows typical log messages associated with the setup and teardown of a TCP session.

Example 8-5 *Log Messages for TCP Session Setup and Teardown*

```
%ASA-7-609001: Built local-host outside:192.0.2.65
%ASA-6-302013: Built outbound TCP connection 977 for outside:192.0.2.65/22
   (192.0.2.65/22) to inside:10.0.0.108/55198 (209.165.200.238/55198)
%ASA-6-302014: Teardown TCP connection 977 for outside:192.0.2.65/22 to
   inside:10.0.0.108/55198 duration 0:04:06 bytes 156 TCP FINs
%ASA-7-609002: Teardown local-host outside:192.0.2.65 duration 0:04:06
```

Understanding Interface Access Rules

Interface access rules are the most commonly used access control mechanism on the Cisco ASA. Interface access rules permit or deny the *establishment* of connections *through* the ASA, based on the traffic flow's input and output ASA interfaces, OSI Layer 3 criteria (such as source and destination IP addresses), and OSI Layer 4 criteria (such as source and/or destination TCP or UDP ports).

It should be noted that while the Cisco ASA has supported both standard and extended access lists since version 7.0, all access lists are assumed to be extended (have the capability to specify protocol and both source and destination addresses and ports), unless you specify otherwise. Although standard ACLs do exist on an ASA, they are used for things such as route update filters or VPN split-tunneling definitions and cannot be used for interface access rules.

Effectively, interface access rules determine which *new* connections can enter the connection state table. If a packet arrives at an ASA interface and is associated with an already existing connection object, it is not operated upon by the interface access rules. If a packet is not associated with an existing connection entry, however, the ASA will compare the packet to the interface access rules. If the rules permit the packet, an object associated with the connection initiated by this packet is created in the connection table, and if the host addresses involved were not previously in the local host table, relevant objects will be created there as well.

Interface access rules control only *transit traffic through the ASA*—that is, traffic that passes between ASA interfaces but initiates and terminates at endpoints other than the ASA itself. Interface access rules do not control traffic terminating on the ASA itself, such as management connections to the ASA using SSH or HTTPS, ICMP traffic destined for the ASA itself, or traffic associated with VPN tunnels that terminate at the ASA. To control these connections, you must use separate management access rules, discussed in other chapters. Additionally, all traffic sourced by the ASA itself is not subject to interface access rules, and is permitted by default.

Note: Internet Security Association and Key Management Protocol/Internet Key Exchange (ISAKMP/IKE) packets and Encapsulating Security Payload (ESP) packets are always permitted to enter any ASA interface on which ISAKMP is enabled. By default, data packets arriving through a VPN tunnel are also not examined by the interface access rules. However, if you disable the **sysopt connection permit-vpn** command, packets arriving through a VPN tunnel will be examined by the interface access rules. Even in this case, it is not necessary to explicitly permit ISAKMP/IKE or ESP packets in interface access rules. VPN traffic is covered in detail in a different course and exam from what this book is intended to address, so consult those resources for more detailed coverage of this topic.

Interface access rules are an ordered list of permit and deny statements, evaluated sequentially from the top down. The first rule that matches the new connection packet being evaluated will permit or deny the connection. Once a rule matches an evaluated packet, all subsequent rules are ignored, so order of entries is very important. All access rule sets, which contain explicit rules, contain an **implicit deny** (an "invisible" deny all) rule as the final rule. Therefore, if a new connection does not match any of the explicit permit rules in an interface rule set, it will be denied (dropped) by default.

Note: Default interface access rule sets, covered in the section, "Default Access Rules," do not contain any explicit rules, and therefore have no implicit deny. This is critical for understanding the functioning of the global ACL, which is also covered later, in the section, "The Global ACL."

Stateful Filtering

Because the Cisco ASA is a stateful packet filtering device, interface access rules rely on the presence of the state tables previously described to simplify rule creation. Interface access rules only need to permit the initial packet of a connection, for all protocols and applications that are handled statefully by the ASA. This means your interface access rules do not have to account for the following:

- Any traffic flowing in the reverse direction (return traffic) of that connection. For example, if an internal host initiates a connection to a web server on the Internet, the web content returned does not need to be explicitly permitted in the access rule applied to the outside interface. Because these packets are associated with a flow for which a connection table object exists, they will be automatically permitted by the ASA, as long as they match the properties expected from them by the connection table (for instance, a sequence number within an expected range).

- Any additional connections/flows established by an application. Because the ASA is application-aware for most applications that establish dynamic sessions (such as FTP data channels, Session Initiation Protocol (SIP) voice channels, SQL redirect connections, and so forth), it will automatically permit any additional connections established by the same application session, if you permit the initial packet of the application's session (sometimes called the "control channel").

Consider the example illustrated in Figure 8-1. Host 10.0.0.108, attached to the inside interface of the ASA, wants to initiate an HTTP connection to web server 192.0.2.150, somewhere in the Internet.

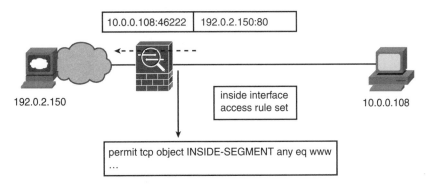

Figure 8-1 *Access Rules Example*

When the initial packet of the session arrives at the inside interface of the ASA, the ASA compares the packet to the connection table and determines that this packet is not associated with any existing connection entries. Therefore, the packet is compared to the interface access rules. The rule shown in Figure 8-1 permits the connection, so the ASA creates two local host objects and a connection object, in those respective state tables. All subsequent packets associated with this session are allowed through the ASA without regard to the contents of interface access rules.

Figure 8-2 shows the continuation of this session, with emphasis on the stateful handling of the now-established connection.

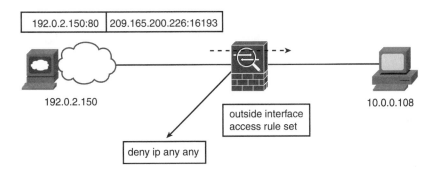

Figure 8-2 *Stateful Connection Example*

Figure 8-2 shows an example where the access rules on the outside interface of the ASA deny all traffic (for the sake of simplicity). Because of the stateful nature of inspection on the ASA, the return traffic from server 192.0.2.150 is permitted because it matches the connection entry created when the session was established.

If a protocol is not handled statefully by the ASA (for example, applications that do not use TCP or UDP for transport, or ICMP or ESP transit packets, if appropriate inspection is not configured), the ASA is not able to bidirectionally track the session. For such flows to transit the ASA, you will need to explicitly permit the flow's packets using the access rules applied to all ASA interfaces involved in the traffic flow.

Interface Access Rules and Interface Security Levels

Although it is typically recommended to apply access rules to all ASA interfaces, this is optional. In the absence of a specific set of access rules on an interface, the ASA will apply its *default access policy* to packets arriving at the interface, as detailed here:

■ All *outbound* connections (initial packet ingresses the ASA through an interface with a higher security level than that of the egress interface selected by routing) are permitted.

■ All *inbound* connections (initial packet ingresses the ASA through an interface with a lower security level than that of the egress interface selected by routing) are denied.

Connections between interfaces with the same security level are denied by default; however, if you use the **same-security-traffic permit inter-interface** global configuration command (covered in Chapter 3, "Configuring ASA Interfaces"), the handling of connection requests depends on whether the interface receiving the initial packet has an access rule applied:

■ If no access rule is applied, traffic between interfaces with the same security level is permitted, based on the **same-security-traffic** command.

■ If an access rule is applied, then traffic between interfaces with the same security level must be explicitly permitted in the access rule, in addition to the global **same-security-traffic** command.

The other case to consider is when a packet will ingress and egress the ASA through the same interface (needed in certain VPN configurations). By default, the ASA does not allow packets to ingress and egress through the same interface. If you need to allow such traffic flows, you can use the **same-security-traffic permit intra-interface** global configuration command (covered in Chapter 3). As with inter-interface traffic, the flows will be permitted in the absence of an access rule on the interface being used. However, if an access rule is in place, it may need to permit the required connections, depending on your VPN configuration.

Interface Access Rules Direction

An access rule can be applied to an interface in either an inbound (traffic ingresses the ASA through the interface) or an outbound (traffic egresses the ASA through the interface) direction. This use of the terms *inbound* and *outbound* in this case is thus specific to the interface where the ACL is applied, and should not be confused with the terms *inbound* and *outbound* used earlier to refer to relative interface security levels.

To be permitted to transit the ASA, an initial packet in a flow must be permitted through all access rules it encounters in its initiating direction. Figure 8-3 shows an example of this.

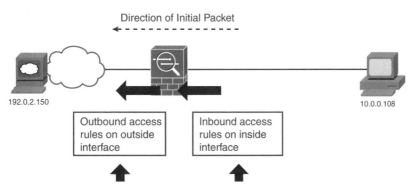

Figure 8-3   *Inbound and Outbound Access Rules in Flow Path*

In Figure 8-3, an application session is initiated by a host on the inside interface, destined for a host on the Internet (reachable through the outside interface). For this session to be permitted and a connection object to be created in the connection table, the initial packet in the session would have to be permitted both by the access rules applied to the inside interface in an inbound direction and by any access rules applied to the outside interface in an outbound direction.

A common strategy used with Cisco ASAs is to apply only inbound access rules to the various ASA interfaces. This simplifies configuration by using a consistent approach no matter whether controlling access from higher- to lower-security interfaces or vice versa. If access rules are applied to every ASA interface, this approach guarantees that each initial packet of a session is processed by exactly one set of interface access rules, on the interface where the packet ingresses the ASA. Thus, you need only ensure that an application's traffic is permitted by one set of access rules to ensure it is allowed through the ASA.

In rare situations, it can be useful to also use outbound interface access rules. Figure 8-4 shows such an example.

In Figure 8-4, the ASA has an outside interface, with security level 0, and three internal interfaces, one each for the Sales, Accounting, and Engineering departments, all having security level 100. Because all three interfaces have the same security level, they are by default isolated from each other. If the goal is to keep them isolated from each other, but to provide all three with access to the Internet through the outside interface, simply applying one set of access rules, outbound on the outside interface (to govern what connectivity is allowed from all three departments) might be easier than applying three separate inbound interface access rules, one on the interface for each department. Obviously, this would depend on what other security policies are in place and how they would be affected by this approach.

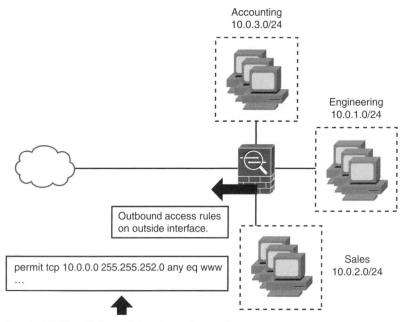

Permits HTTP traffic from all three internal networks.

Figure 8-4   *Outbound Interface Access Rule Example*

Default Access Rules

Before any user-configured access rules are defined or applied, the ASA begins with a default set of interface access rules. If you are using Cisco ASDM to create your access rules, you will use the Cisco ASDM Access Rules table. You can find this table, with its default set of rules, by navigating to **Configuration > Firewall > Access Rules**, with results similar to those shown in Figure 8-5.

The Cisco ASDM Access Rules table is a consolidated view of all interface access rules that are configured and applied on the ASA interfaces. The default rules operate under the strategy mentioned previously, wherein one rule set is applied to each interface, in an inbound direction. The default rule set shown is therefore the default set of rules applied to traffic as it ingresses the ASA through the indicated interface. Note that all rules shown have a description that states they are "implicit" rules. This means that if you were to access the CLI and execute the **show access-lists** command, you would not see any output, as none of these rules are explicitly defined, but rather are representations of how the ASA handles traffic based on default rules regarding interface security levels. Note the presence of the global access rule, which is discussed in the next section.

By default, the Access Rules table displays both IPv4 and IPv6 access rules on all interfaces. You can use the Access Rule Type selector at the bottom of the window to declutter the display by choosing to show only IPv4 or only IPv6 rules, which is generally recommended if you use a large rule set or only use one IP version within your environment. Figure 8-6 shows the default rule set, with only IPv4 rules displayed.

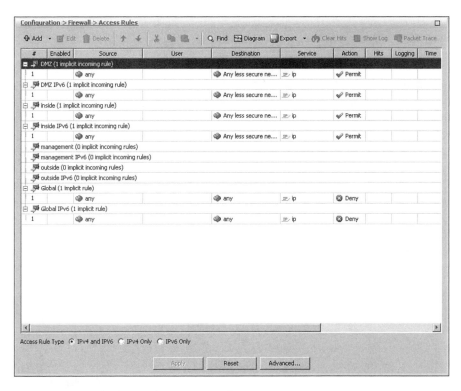

Figure 8-5 *Default Interface Access Rules*

The Global ACL

The global ACL is a new concept, introduced in OS version 8.3, to make it easier to configure and manage the access policy configuration of an ASA.

Any traffic ingressing any ASA interface and not matching a rule in the interface-specific access rule set (including implicit rules) is compared to the global ACL looking for a match. Thus, the global ACL can be thought of as being logically appended to each interface access rule set.

Access rules for the global ACL are configured in the same manner as for an interface rule set; however, if you define any explicit rules within the global ACL, all implicit interface access rules (which permit all traffic flows destined for lower security-level interfaces) are removed, and the global ACL is used to evaluate all traffic ingressing that interface. This is probably a good idea from a security "best practices" viewpoint; however, it can wreak havoc on a network in which the ASA was configured to take advantage of the implicit permit rules. Therefore, carefully review the full impact before defining explicit rules within the global ACL.

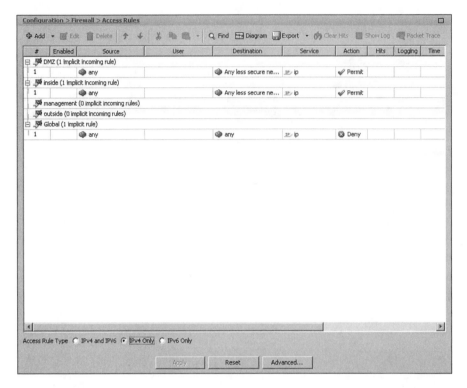

Figure 8-6   *Default IPv4 Interface Access Rules*

As shown in Figure 8-6, with no explicit rules defined, the inside and DMZ interfaces, because they have security levels other than zero and are not configured for management-only, have a default rule set that permits all traffic to less secure networks (lower-security interfaces). Because the outside interface has security level zero, it is not possible for it to access any less secure networks, so it has no interface-specific default rule set. Finally, because the management interface is configured for management only, it does not allow any transit traffic. Each rules set then has the global ACL "deny any any" rule logically appended to them. Therefore, the outside interface, with no interface-specific rule set, has an effective rule set of "deny any any" based on all packets being compared to the global ACL.

Configuring Interface Access Rules

After you have a comprehensive understanding of the methods of applying interface access rules, along with the security policy you intend to implement with them, you can begin configuring interface access rules. The major tasks you need to perform are as follows:

1. Configure individual rules within a commonly named rule set.

2. Optionally, if you plan to use objects or object groups in access rules, configure object and/or object group definitions.

3. Optionally, if you are using objects or object groups in access rules, configure rules that use the configured objects or object groups.

4. Optionally, if you plan to use time-based access rules, configure time range definitions.

5. Optionally, if you are using time-based access rules, configure rules that use the configured time ranges.

6. Apply the rule set to an interface in an inbound or outbound direction.

> **Note:** Network objects were discussed in Chapter 7, "Using Address Translation." Object groups are discussed in the section, "Organizing Access Rules Using Object Groups." Time ranges are discussed in the section, "Time-Based Access Rules."

The configuration scenario used in the examples that follow implement the following security policy features:

■ Permit any host on the inside network to reach any host on a less secure interface using HTTP.

■ Log all denied flows on the outside interface, using an alternate syslog message ID (reasons for this are explained later in this section). Note that, because you cannot activate logging on an "implicit" line in an ACL, you must enter an explicit deny all rule to accomplish this objective.

■ Permit any host on the outside to reach the DMZ web server using HTTP.

■ Allow the DMZ Simple Mail Transfer Protocol (SMTP) (email) server to reach any host, through any interface, using SMTP.

Although this might seem fairly extensive for an example, it is actually a basic beginning security policy, and will allow for demonstration of a number of important items regarding implementation of interface access rules on the Cisco ASA.

The first requirement in the preceding list is to permit all hosts on the inside network to reach any host on a less-secure interface using HTTP. Because there are currently no rules other than implicit rules on the ASA, you need to add the first rule to the inside interface. To do so, navigate to **Configuration > Firewall > Access Rules** and expand the **Add** drop-down menu. Figure 8-7 shows the resulting menu.

From the menu, click **Add Access Rule**. The Add Access Rule dialog box opens, as shown in Figure 8-8.

Because this rule will be implemented on the inside interface, first choose the **inside** interface from the Interface drop-down list, as shown in Figure 8-8. Next, choose the action to be applied to matching packets by clicking either the **Permit** or **Deny** radio button. In the figure, Permit is selected.

In the Source field, you can enter an IP address or click the ellipsis (...) button to choose from a list of addresses and objects known to ASDM (as explained in Chapter 7). Because the inside network is known to ASDM, click the ellipsis button to open the Browse Source dialog box, which is shown in Figure 8-9.

There are actually two objects in this list, which both refer to the inside network: INSIDE-SEGMENT and inside-network. Either could be used for the purposes of creating this rule. To demonstrate the differences in resulting syntax, as shown in Figure 8-9, select the

inside-network object and then, to choose it as the source, click the **Source ->** button, so that inside-network/24 appears in the field at the bottom of the dialog box. Then, click **OK** to finalize the choice.

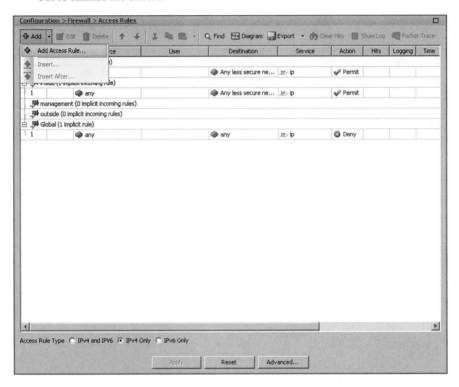

Figure 8-7   *Add Access Rule Menu*

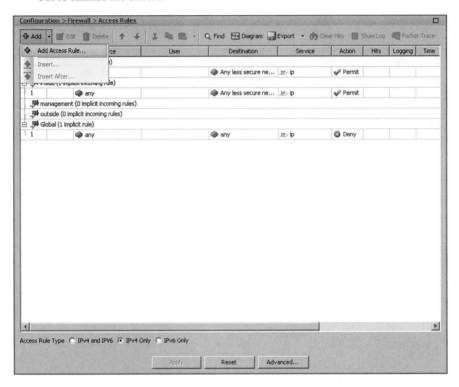

Figure 8-8   *Add Access Rule Dialog Box*

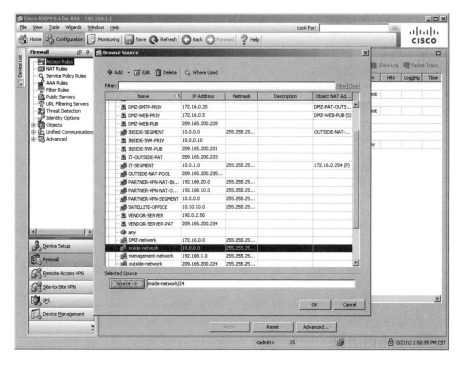

Figure 8-9 *Browse Source Dialog Box*

The scenario is to allow access to any destination on a less secure interface, so leave the keyword **any** in the Destination field of the Add Access Rule dialog box (refer to Figure 8-8). To specify HTTP as the destination service, click the ellipsis button to the right of the Service field. The Browse Service dialog box opens, as shown in Figure 8-10.

The predefined services listed in the Browse Service dialog box are organized first by protocol (TCP, UDP, TCP&UDP, IP, and so on) and then alphabetically within the protocol. In Figure 8-10, the TCP/HTTP service is selected. First, select the desired service, and then click the **Service ->** button at the bottom of the dialog box, so the selected service(s) appear in the field. Finalize the choice by clicking **OK**.

Figure 8-11 shows the rule as just configured.

Other options are explored later in this chapter. For now, complete the addition of this new access rule by clicking **OK**. The rule definition is complete, and you are returned to the Access Rules window. Figure 8-12 shows the newly created access rule in the Access Rules window.

Note that the addition of an explicit permit entry has caused the removal from the inside interface of the implicit permit any to lower-security interface rule. This is very important, as all access that was previously implicitly permitted will now be denied, unless explicit permit entries are added to the inside interface access rules. Remember, it is only in the complete absence of an interface access rule set that traffic is implicitly permitted from higher-security to lower-security interfaces. The moment an explicit rule is defined, the implicit permit will no longer exist, but the implicit deny all from the global ACL remains. Therefore, it is important to apply your entire rule set at the same time, to avoid disruptions in service. The example here is highly simplistic, and only for educational purposes. It would not likely be a realistic policy to apply to the inside interface of an ASA in a production network.

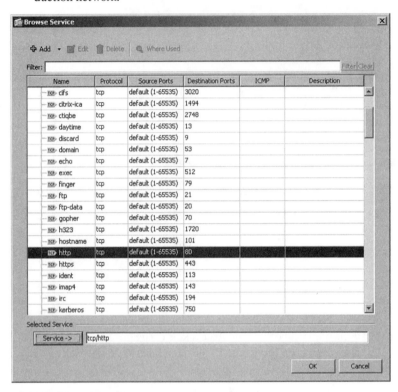

Figure 8-10 *Browse Service Dialog Box*

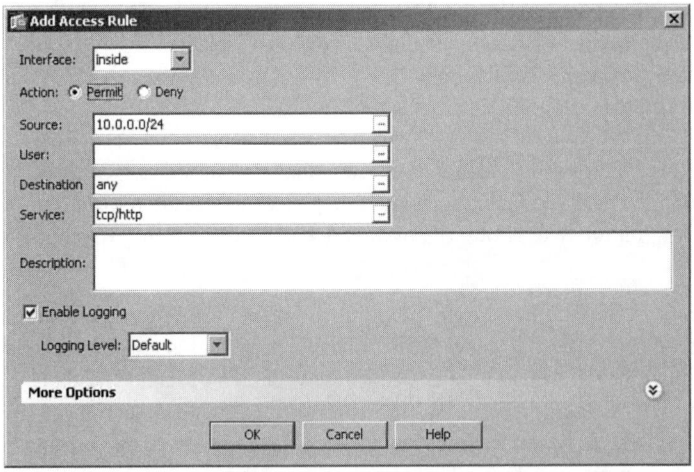

Figure 8-11 *Inside Interface Completed Access Rule*

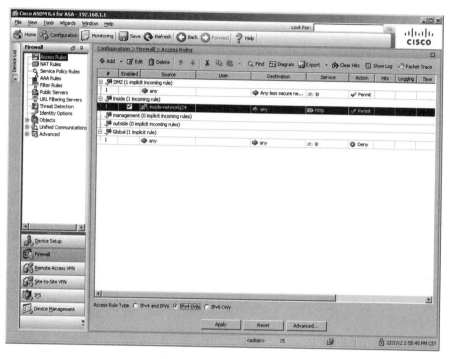

Figure 8-12 *Access Rules Table with New Entry*

Access Rule Logging

By default, the Cisco ASA logs all security events. When an access rule denies traffic, this is a security event, and the ASA generates syslog message 106023 for each denied packet. Severity level is dependent on which type of packet is denied. A separate log message for each denied flow setup attempt can quickly become burdensome if even a small attack is launched against the networks protected by the ASA.

Although it is possible to disable logging entirely for an access rule, and this might be permissible for permit entries (which sometimes are logged only for troubleshooting purposes), logging should never be disabled for deny rules, as they indicate a security event.

It is therefore recommended that you consider altering the default logging settings for your access rules and setting them to use system message ID 106100 instead. This message ID provides statistics for each access rule, but also lets you limit the number of system messages produced and how often they are reported.

The Cisco ASA generates syslog message 106100 for every matching permit or deny access rule flow that passes through the ASA, and is explicitly configured to generate interval logging messages, instead of the default of one message per "hit." The first match flow is cached. Subsequent matches increase the hit count for the access rule, rather than creating new syslog messages. If the number of hits is not zero, new 106100 messages are generated at an interval you specify.

When you add an access rule in Cisco ASDM, the Enable Logging check box is checked by default, and the word "Default" is displayed as the selected logging level in the Logging Level drop-down list. These default settings will lead to syslog message 106023 being generated when an IP packet is denied by the access rule.

Key Topic

To enable logging via syslog message 106100 instead of message 106023, you must choose an option other than Default from the Logging Level drop-down list. The choices are the standard syslog levels 0–7 (Emergencies through Debugging). When this is done, and a reporting interval is defined (the default is every 300 seconds), the ASA will generate the 106100 messages at the selected level and report them at the selected interval.

The scenario describes a requirement to log all denied flows on the outside interface. You want to use syslog message 106100 at intervals to avoid excessive log messages; however, it is not possible to edit the definition of the implicit deny all rule in the global ACL. Therefore, to meet this requirement, you need to add an explicit deny all rule on the outside interface, so that you can alter the selected logging level and define a logging interval. You will also enter a description for this rule to explain why you are including it in the access rules.

To begin, from the Access Rules window, choose to add a new access rule, as before. The Add Access Rule dialog box opens. Figure 8-13 shows the rule configuration.

To create an explicit deny all entry on the outside interface, choose the **outside** interface from the Interface drop-down list. Then, click the **Deny** radio button as the Action, leave the keyword **any** in both the Source and Destination fields, and enter **ip** in the Service field. These options are configured as described in Figure 8-13.

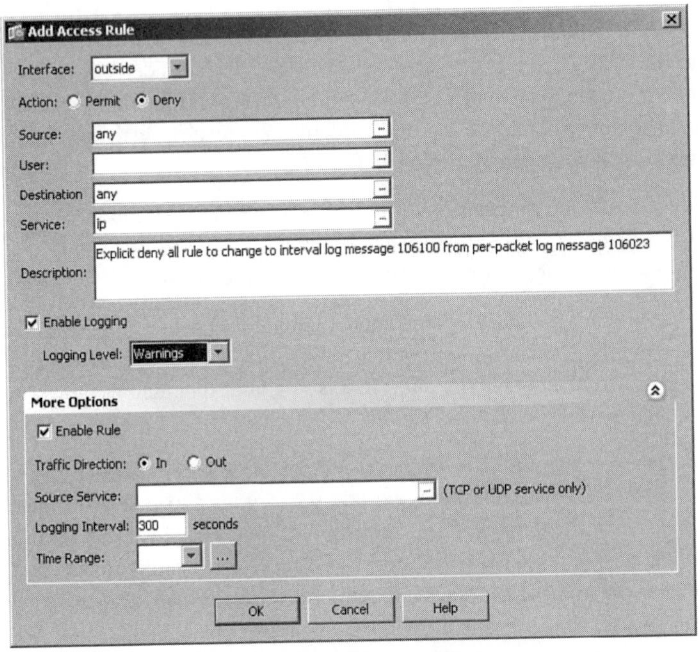

Figure 8-13 *Altered Logging and Description in an Access Rule*

Next, you want to add a description, explaining why you are creating an explicit deny all rule, when the implicit deny all rule already exists. Figure 8-13 shows the Description field containing an explanation about the use of syslog message 106100.

Note: Entering a description for an access rule will cause the creation of a separate **access-list remark** entry (access rule), with its own line number, when viewing the access list (rule set) from the CLI. Although this is useful documentation, it should be used judiciously to avoid the creation of overly large access lists. Therefore, use it when creating a rule that is in some way unusual or in need of explanation, but not for rules whose purpose or reason is already clear.

Click the **More Options** arrow to expand the access rule options area. Note when you do that the Logging Interval field is dimmed and thus cannot be edited.

As explained previously, to alter logging to the use of syslog message 106100, you must choose a specific level in the Logging Level field, rather than leaving it at the default. As shown in Figure 8-13, change the setting in this field to Warnings (4) as the desired level. When this is done, the Logging Interval field in the More Options area becomes editable. Enter an appropriate interval, from 1 to 600 seconds, in this field. Figure 8-13 shows an entry of 300 seconds, which is the default. Finally, click **OK** to complete the addition of this new access rule.

The next requirement in the scenario is to permit access from any source on the outside interface to the DMZ web server, using HTTP. This rule needs to be added before the explicit deny all rule just configured. If you were to use the Add Access Rule function, as previously, the new rule defined would end up below other existing rules, and above only the implicit deny all rule from the global ACL.

The menu contains options to Insert (with a + sign above a line, meaning the new rule will be inserted above the currently selected rule) or Insert After (with the + sign below a line, meaning the new rule will be inserted below the currently selected rule). Choose the **Insert** option to open the Insert Access Rule dialog box, as shown in Figure 8-14.

Figure 8-14 shows the choice of the outside interface, permit as an action, and any as a source address. When you permit access from the outside world, "any" is frequently the source address. Next, you must specify the DMZ web server as the destination. This server has the configured IP address of 172.16.0.5 and was previously defined as the network object DMZ-WEB-PRIV. With OS versions 8.3 and higher, all access rules, on all interfaces, whether applied inbound or outbound, refer to the native addresses of hosts or networks. Therefore, you can enter this IP, or the object name, as the destination in this access rule.

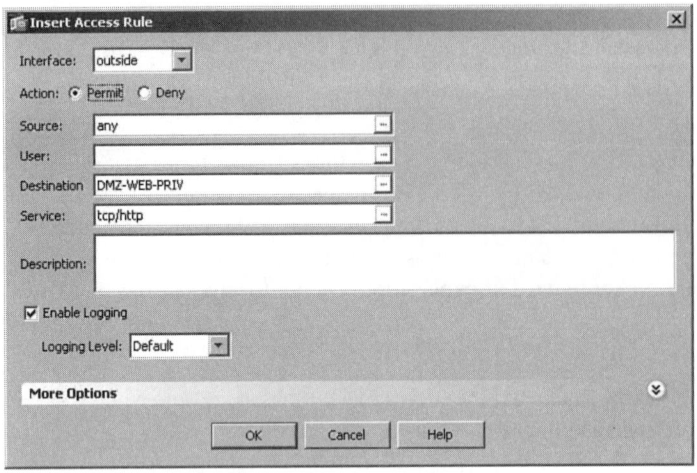

Figure 8-14   *Inserting a Permit Web Server Access Rule*

Recall, however, the discussion of address translation in Chapter 7, and its effect on inter-face access rules, if using OS versions 8.2 or earlier. With those OS versions, when an ac-cess rule is applied inbound on an interface, the access rule condition is checked before address translation occurs. Thus, when configuring access rules that permit traffic from a less secure interface to reach a destination on a more secure interface, you must use a des-tination address of the global (translated) IP address of the destination host, not its local (untranslated) IP address. The DMZ web server had a global IP address of 209.165.200.228 assigned to it, so if using earlier OS versions, you need to enter that address in the Desti-nation field.

This fact means that access rule configuration is now much simpler with OS versions 8.3 and higher, because you do not need to remember address translation rules (which are fre-quently different on different interfaces) to properly configure access rules.

Therefore, to configure this access rule, click the ellipsis (...) button for the Destination field and, using procedures already demonstrated, select the object name DMZ-WEB-PRIV and assign it as the destination address for this rule. This assignment is reflected in Figure 8-14.

Note: If entering IP addresses directly in either the Source or Destination field, it is not necessary to enter the /32 after the address to indicate a host-specific netmask, if you want to define an individual host. If no netmask value is specified, ASDM defaults to a host-specific mask when creating access rules.

Next, specify the destination service, as previously demonstrated. Figure 8-14 shows TCP/HTTP as the configured service. Optionally, enter a description. Because the pur-pose of this rule is readily apparent, no description is shown in Figure 8-14. Finalize the insertion of this access rule by clicking **OK**.

The final access rule in the scenario is to permit the DMZ SMTP server to reach any host through any interface, using SMTP.

Note: Although this example serves to demonstrate how the destination of "any" will apply to both higher- and lower-security interfaces as destinations, a more appropriate configuration for a production network is shown later in the chapter, in the section, "Managing Access Rules from the CLI."

Because this will be the initial rule on the DMZ interface, go through the steps to add a new access rule, as previously described. Figure 8-15 shows the Add Access Rule dialog box, where the new rule is configured.

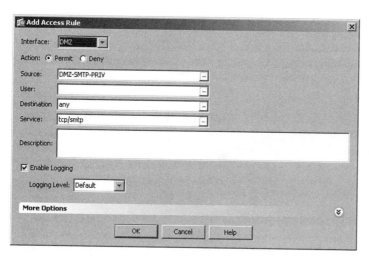

Figure 8-15 *Adding an Access Rule to the DMZ Interface*

As shown in Figure 8-15, first choose **DMZ** from the Interface drop-down list as the interface where the rule will be applied, and then click the **Permit** radio button as the Action. Using procedures previously demonstrated, select the network object DMZ-SMTP-PRIV in the Source field.

The SMTP server needs to be able to reach other SMTP servers on any other ASA interface, whether more secure or less secure. Therefore, Figure 8-15 shows leaving the keyword any in the Destination field (notice that "any" does not mean "the Internet"). Specifying services and entering descriptions has already been explained. The figure shows TCP/SMTP as the selected service. Finalize the rule configuration by clicking **OK**.

Configuring the Global ACL

Because all interface access rule sets now contain explicit entries, it is possible to enter explicit rules in the global ACL, without adversely impacting functionality by "silently" removing implicit rules from other interface rule sets.

This configuration scenario is based on the decision to use NTP for time synchronization throughout your network. You have decided to use the National Institute of Standards and

Technology (NIST) publicly available NTP server. You want any host, on any interface, to be able to reach this time server for synchronization.

As previously mentioned, the creation of rules in the global ACL is performed in the same manner as the creation of any access rule. Therefore, from the Access Rules window, select to add a new access rule. Figure 8-16 shows the Add Access Rule window where this new rule is defined.

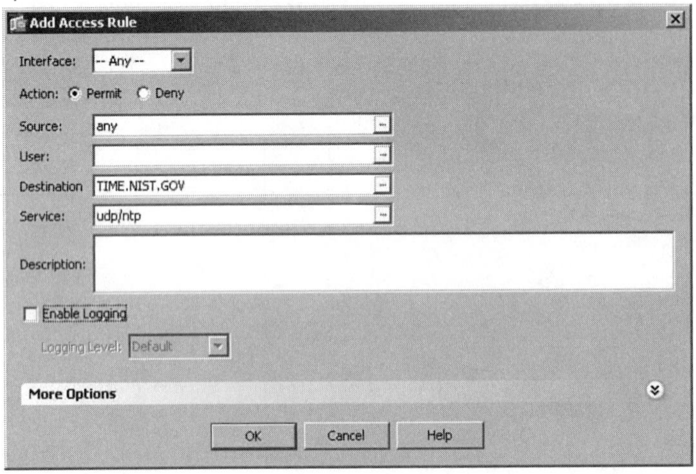

Figure 8-16   *Configuring a Global Access Rule*

To insert a rule in the global ACL, set the Interface to **Any**, rather than a specific interface name, as shown in Figure 8-16.

Because this rule will be applied to any interface, leave the source address set to any. Then, using procedures previously demonstrated, create a new network object named TIME.NIST.GOV, defined as the host IP 192.43.244.18, and assign it as the destination address. Using procedures previously demonstrated, assign UDP/NTP as the service. Finally, because this is a permit access rule for traffic that is not significant to track, uncheck the Enable Logging check box to disable logging for this specific rule. All these settings are shown in Figure 8-16.

Click **OK** to complete the addition of the global ACL rule. Figure 8-17 shows the Access Rules window, including all the newly created rules.

Finally, click **Apply** to send all changes made thus far to the ASA.

The CLI commands generated by the changes made are as follows. The access list names are altered from what ASDM would assign (spacing has been added for readability):

```
object network TIME.NIST.GOV
  host 192.43.244.18
!
access-list INSIDE-IN line 1 extended permit tcp 10.0.0.0 255.255.255.0 any eq http
!
```

```
access-list DMZ-IN line 1 extended permit tcp object DMZ-SMTP-PRIV any eq smtp
!
access-list OUTSIDE-IN line 1 extended permit tcp any object DMZ-WEB-PRIV eq http
access-list OUTSIDE-IN line 2 remark Explicit deny all rule to change to interval
    log message 106100 from per-packet log message 106023
access-list OUTSIDE-IN line 3 extended deny ip any any  log 4 interval 300
!
access-list GLOBAL-ACL line 1 extended permit udp any object TIME.NIST.GOV eq ntp
    log disable
!
access-group DMZ-IN in interface DMZ
access-group INSIDE-IN in interface inside
access-group OUTSIDE-IN in interface outside
access-group GLOBAL-ACL global
```

If you are configuring the ASA from the CLI, you can enter these commands in global configuration mode.

Access-list commands define access rules, and the CLI **access-group** command applies access rules to interfaces. The **access-group** command, which applies the global ACL contains neither a direction nor an interface name, but simply the keyword **global**. Despite the lack of a directional indicator, the global ACL is applied only in the inbound direction on all interfaces.

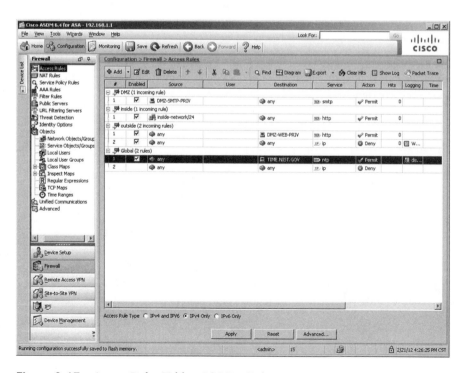

Figure 8-17 *Access Rules Table with New Rules*

Note the syntax in the INSIDE-IN ACL refers to the IP network 10.0.0.0 with mask. This is because the example selected the inside-network as the source. If you had instead selected the object INSIDE-SEGMENT, as objects were used in the other rules, the access list would have instead appeared as follows. The use of objects makes the purpose and meaning of the rules much clearer, assuming a good naming convention is used:

```
access-list INSIDE-IN line 1 extended permit tcp object INSIDE-SEGMENT any eq http
```

Cisco ASDM Public Server Wizard

Key Topic

It has been explained that allowing access to a server from a lower security interface (when the server is located on a network connected to a higher security interface) requires both the creation of a static translation and an interface access rule on the lower-security interface, to allow the session to be established.

Cisco ASDM contains a feature, called the Public Server Wizard, which creates a static NAT rule for a specified host, as well as an interface access rule for that host using a particular service, by completing information on a single screen within ASDM. The commands generated are those that have already been covered separately, but this wizard consolidates those separate configuration steps into one, thus reducing the complexity involved in separately configuring the required parameters.

For this example, assume a new web server is being configured, which will be located in the DMZ segment. Translation and access rules will be created using the ASDM Public Server Wizard. Also, to demonstrate alternative naming methods, a different object naming method will be used for the translation objects.

To begin, navigate to **Configuration > Firewall > Public Servers**, and then click the **Add** button in the Public Servers window. The Add Public Server dialog box opens. Figure 8-18 shows the rule configuration.

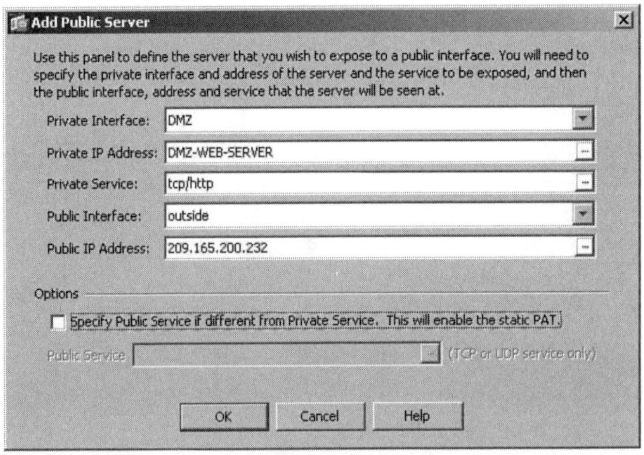

Figure 8-18 *Using the ASDM Public Server Wizard*

As shown in Figure 8-18, complete the fields with the necessary information. In the Private Interface field, select the interface through which the actual server is reachable—in this case, DMZ. Next, using procedures previously demonstrated in Chapter 7, click the ellipsis button for the Private IP Address field, and create a new network object named DMZ-WEB-SERVER, defined as the host address 172.16.0.23. Do not define any NAT rules when creating the object. In the Service field, enter (or choose by clicking the ellipsis button to open a list) the service (port) on which the server is to be reachable from the less secure interface—in this case, TCP/HTTP. For public interface, select outside. Finally, in the Public IP Address field, directly enter the IP address 209.165.200.232.

> **Note:** Because translations no longer have an impact on addresses used in access rules, AAA rules, MPF, and so on, this example does not create a –PRIV and –PUB object for the server, as was done in Chapter 7 examples. The public address appears in the ASA configuration only once—in the NAT command, so the network object for the server is simply the server name, with no indication of the fact that it is defining the private address. Similarly, the translated address is entered, with no indication of what server it refers to, because the server object name will appear as part of the same **nat** command.

Finalize the rule configuration by clicking **OK**. Finally, click **Apply** to send the changes to the ASA.

The CLI commands generated by the changes made are as follows:

```
object network DMZ-WEB-SERVER
  host 172.16.0.23
object network DMZ-WEB-SERVER
  nat (DMZ,outside) static 209.165.200.232
access-list OUTSIDE-IN line 1 extended permit tcp any object DMZ-WEB-SERVER eq http
```

If you are configuring the ASA from the CLI, you can enter these commands directly in global configuration mode. Note that the Public Server Wizard created the new access rule in position number 1 in the list of rules applied to the selected public interface (outside in this example). If this is not the desired location, reorder to access rules as described later, in the section, "Managing Rules in Cisco ASDM."

Configuring Access Control Lists from the CLI

You configure interface access rules in the CLI by creating access control lists (ACL) using the **access-list** command to configure individual rules. ACLs are made up of one or more access control entries (ACE), each represented by one line in the ACL, that specify a permit or deny rule, or remark.

> **Note:** An ACE in an ACL is the equivalent of an interface access rule in the Cisco ASDM Access Rules table.

If you are configuring access control lists from the CLI, Cisco ASA ACLs use network masks, and not the wildcard masks used in Cisco router ACLs, whenever masks are specified. The keywords **any** and **host** work in ASA access rules as they do in other Cisco ACLs.

Key Topic

After an ACL is configured, it must be activated and applied to an interface using the CLI **access-group** command. This command specifies which ACL is being applied, to which interface, and in which direction (inbound or outbound). The command specifies the keyword **in** or **out** to specify the direction in which traffic is flowing through the interface, where the ACL is to be applied. Only one ACL can be applied to an interface, per direction. So, you could have one ACL applied inbound and another applied outbound on the same interface, but you could not apply two different ACLs inbound on the same interface.

> **Note:** When an access rule is configured using Cisco ASDM, it creates both the **access-list** and **access-group** commands in the ASA configuration.

If you create a remark in an ACL for documentation purposes, you can place it before or after the ACE to which it refers. You should, however, place remarks consistently so that it is clear to which ACE remarks are referring. When an access rule remark is configured using Cisco ASDM, it is always placed above the access rule to which it refers, so this is probably the best choice in order to maintain consistency in an environment where administrators use both ASDM and the CLI to manage the ASA.

When you are creating ACLs from the CLI, entering line numbers and the keyword **extended** is optional. Line numbers are automatically assigned to all ACEs in order, one number at a time (you cannot specify an interval, as you can on Cisco routers, when renumbering ACLs). Also, remember that all access lists are assumed to be extended (have the ability to specify protocol and both source and destination addresses and ports), unless you specify they are standard ACLs. Although standard ACLs do exist on an ASA, they are used for things such as route update filters or VPN split-tunneling definitions, and cannot be used for interface access rules. Full syntax options are presented in the "Command Reference to Check Your Memory" section at the end of this chapter.

Implementation Guidelines

When implementing interface access rules to provide access control, consider the following implementation guidelines:

- Consider applying interface access rules to all ASA interfaces and permitting only the minimal required set of services. This is in keeping with a minimal access policy, which is both effective for preventing network attacks and required by some regulatory standards. Some organizations might configure a less stringent access methodology, to increase manageability, if the number of rules would otherwise become cumbersome. This approach generally will increase the risk of attack against protected networks.

- Generally, the simplest strategy to implement effective access control is to use only inbound interface access rules (applied as packets ingress the ASA through an interface) that are applied to all ASA interfaces. This guarantees that every connection always passes through one, and only one, set of interface access rules as it crosses the ASA. It also prevents rule duplication on multiple interfaces. If a rule is required on multiple interfaces, consider whether it is appropriate to make it a global access rule.

- As with any sequential rule set, you should place your most specific rules (for example, specific to host 10.0.0.5 vs. network 10.0.0.0/24) toward the top of the rule set, to avoid overriding them with more general rules. Also, as long as more specific rules are not overridden, you should also consider placing rules that you anticipate will be matched most frequently toward the top of the rule set, to minimize required processing.

- In all interface access rules, it is recommended that you add an explicit deny all statement at the end of the rule set, to gather statistics on denied traffic and to be able to observe how many connection attempts are being denied by this explicit catch-all rule (the hit count). You may or may not follow this recommendation, depending on you use of the global ACL.

Time-Based Access Rules

In some instances, entering a permanent access rule is inappropriate, and you'll want more granular control over when a rule is enforced and what it enforces. Examples include access rules for contract workers, who have a defined end date and time to their access privileges, access rules for applications that function only during specific time frames, and access rules for corporate environments with multiple shifts of workers, each with unique access permissions. The Cisco ASA accommodates these needs by offering time-based access rules.

You can define *absolute* and/or *recurring* time ranges. An example of an absolute time range would be July 1, 2012 at midnight through September 31, 2012 at 11:59 p.m. An example of a recurring time range would be weekdays (M–F), from 8:00 a.m. to 5:00 p.m.

Note: If a **time-range** command has both **absolute** and **periodic** values specified, then the **periodic** commands are evaluated only after the **absolute start** time is reached, and are not further evaluated after the **absolute end** time is reached. For example, if both the time ranges mentioned in the preceding paragraph are defined within a single time range definition, then applied to an ACE, the rule would be active only from July 1, 2012 to September 31, 2012, and within that time range, only on weekdays between 8 a.m. and 5 p.m.

To the configuration scenario, the following two requirements have been added:

- Permit a contractor FTP access to the DMZ web server, beginning April 1, 2012 and expiring June 30, 2012, for the purpose of updating content, and log all access.

- Allow regional offices in the United States to post files to/pull files from the DMZ FTP server on weekdays, from midnight until 4:59 a.m. local time.

Note: Time ranges are enforced based on what time it is at the ASA's location, not based on the time at the source of a connection. Keep this in mind if configuring an ASA for an organization with users distributed across multiple time zones.

Configuring time-based access rules is a two-step process:

Step 1.   Configure an absolute and/or recurring time range.

Step 2.   Configure an access rule and reference a defined time range for this rule. Thus, the rule is active only during the defined time range. At all other times, it is present in the configuration, but inactive. Initial packets of a flow are evaluated by time-based access rules only while those rules are active.

To configure a time range, navigate to **Configuration > Firewall > Objects > Time Ranges**. The Time Ranges window is displayed. This list is initially blank. To create the first time range, for contractor access, click **Add** to open the Add Time Range dialog box, shown in Figure 8-19.

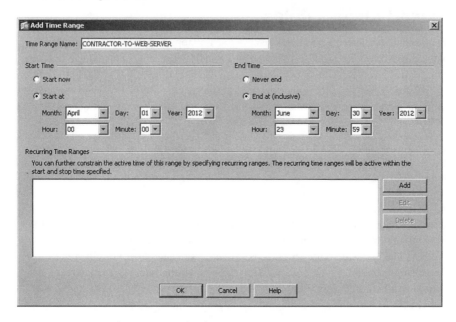

Figure 8-19   *Configuring an Absolute Time Range*

First, give the time range a name. Figure 8-19 shows a name of CONTRACTOR-TO-WEB-SERVER entered.

Note: Spaces are not allowed in time range names.

To define an absolute time range, enter information in both the Start Time and End Time areas. Figure 8-19 shows a Start At value of April 1, 2012 at 00:00 (midnight), and an End At (Inclusive) value of June 30, 2012 at 23:59 (11:59 p.m.). Remember that midnight is the beginning of a day, not the end, so this time range runs from April 1 through June 30, including all 24 hours of both those days. Finalize the definition of this absolute time range by clicking **OK**.

The next required time range is for the purpose of allowing remote offices to access the DMZ FTP server on weekdays from midnight to 4:59 a.m. This is an ongoing requirement, with no beginning or ending dates, so a recurring time range is the proper choice.

To define a recurring time range, navigate to the Time Ranges window as before, and click **Add** to open the Add Time Range dialog box once again, as shown in Figure 8-20.

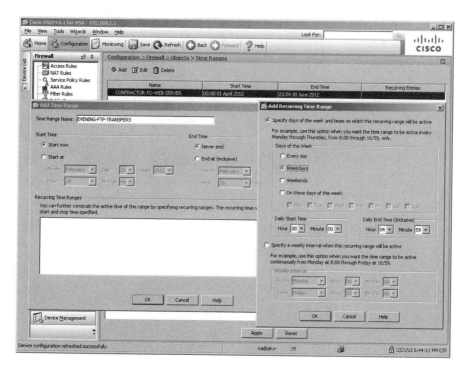

Key Topic

Figure 8-20 *Configuring a Recurring Time Range*

Enter a name for the time range as before. Figure 8-20 shows a name of EVENING-FTP-TRANSFERS entered. For recurring time ranges, select the **Start Now** radio button under Start Time, and select the **Never End** radio button under End Time. Then, at the right side of the Recurring Time Ranges area, click the **Add** button to open the Add Recurring Time Range dialog box, which is shown in the right side of Figure 8-20.

When defining a recurring time range, you might choose to either specify days of the week and times when the range is active (for instance, weekdays from 8 a.m. to 5 p.m.) or specify a weekly interval (such as Monday at 8 a.m. through Friday at 5 p.m.). Note that these are very different choices, although they both have the same beginning and ending times.

The configuration example requires daily time ranges, so Figure 8-20 shows that option chosen. Next, define the specific daily time range. In the figure, Weekdays is chosen for the Days of the Week parameter. Then, specify the Daily Start Time and Daily End Time

(Inclusive). Figure 8-20 shows a Daily Start Time of 00:00 and a Daily End Time of 04:59. Click **OK** to complete the definition of the daily time range, and then click **OK** again to complete the definition of the recurring time range.

Now that the necessary time ranges have been defined, it is time to create the time-based access rules that refer to them. Navigate to the Access Rules window as before. Specify that you will be inserting the time-based access rule above the explicit deny all rule on the outside interface, as before. Figure 8-21 shows the Insert Access Rule dialog box, where the contractor access rule is defined.

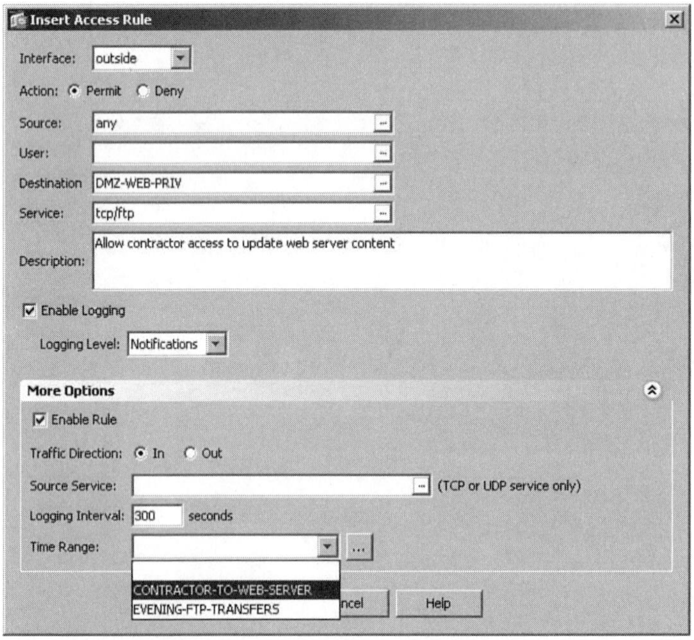

Figure 8-21   *Configuring a Time-Based Access Rule*

Figure 8-21 shows the choice of the outside interface, permit as the action, and a source of any, because you cannot predict the contractor's IP address in advance. Do not worry that this would appear to let anyone in the world access the web server using FTP. The server itself will enforce login credentials, to ensure only authorized access.

Click the ellipsis button for the Destination Address field. Select and assign the network object DMZ-WEB-PRIV as the destination. Then, specify TCP/FTP as the destination service, as previously demonstrated. Optionally, enter a description to create a remark ACE. Figure 8-21 shows the specified changes.

Because the stated requirement includes the logging of all access, verify that the **Enable Logging** check box is checked (it is by default). Set the Logging Level and Logging Interval, if desired. Figure 8-21 shows a Logging Level of Notifications (5) and the default Logging Interval of 300 seconds.

To make this access rule time-based, at the bottom of the More Options area, click the drop-down arrow next to Time Range and choose the time range defined for the contractor access rule. Figure 8-21 shows this time range being chosen. Finalize the configuration of this time-based access rule by clicking **OK**.

Using the same procedures, insert a rule above the explicit deny all rule in the outside interface rule set, which allows access from any source IP address to the network object DMZ-FTP-PRIV using the TCP/FTP service. Use default logging settings and apply the time range named EVENING-FTP-TRANSFERS.

Figure 8-22 shows the complete Access Rules table, containing all rules created thus far.

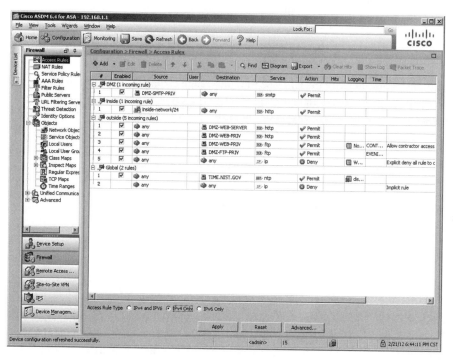

Figure 8-22   *Completed Access Rules Table*

Note that the Hits field is automatically updated to show the number of times an initial packet in a flow has matched a particular access rule. Only the initial packet in a flow matches a rule and causes the hit counter to increment—traffic does not match a rule on a per-packet basis.

Click **Apply** to send the changes to the ASA.

The CLI commands generated by the changes made are as follows (spacing inserted for readability):

```
time-range CONTRACTOR-TO-WEB-SERVER
  absolute start 00:00 01 April 2012 end 23:59 30 June 2012
```

```
!
time-range EVENING-FTP-TRANSFERS
  periodic weekdays 00:00 to 04:59
!
access-list OUTSIDE-IN line 3 remark Allow contractor access to update web server
  content
access-list OUTSIDE-IN line 4 extended permit tcp any object DMZ-WEB-PRIV eq ftp
  log 5 interval 300 time-range CONTRACTOR-TO-WEB-SERVER
access-list OUTSIDE-IN line 5 extended permit tcp any object DMZ-FTP-PRIV eq ftp
  time-range EVENING-FTP-TRANSFERS
```

If you are configuring the ASA from the CLI, you can enter these commands directly, beginning in global configuration mode.

Configuring Time Ranges from the CLI

To configure a time range in the CLI, use the **time-range** command, followed by the range name, to enter time range configuration mode. Use the keyword **absolute** or **periodic** to define the type of time range being configured. To specify a time-based condition within an ACE, simply append the keyword **time-range** and the range name at the end of the rule definition. Full syntax options are presented in the section, "Command Reference to Check Your Memory," at the end of this chapter.

Verifying Interface Access Rules

Use the **show access-list** command to view configured ACLs. The **show access-list** command displays all configured ACLs, the ACEs within each ACL, hit counts for each ACE, and a unique hexadecimal identifier for each ACE (the identifiers are system-created and not configurable). By contrast, the **show running-config access-list** command shows only the configured ACLs, without expanding object-groups, showing hit counts, and so on.

To know whether time-based ACEs should be active, use the **show clock** command to display the current time, according to the ASA. Remember that it is the ASA clock that determines whether time-based access rules are active, not the time where the user is located.

Example 8-6 shows the use of the **show clock** command to verify ASA time.

Example 8-6   show clock *Command Usage*

```
FIREWALL# show clock
10:22:38.829 CST Sat Feb 18 2012
```

Example 8-7 shows the use of the **show access-list** command, using the argument of an ACL name to limit the output to only that ACL, rather than all ACLs. (Spacing has been inserted between each ACE to enhance readability.)

Example 8-7   show access-list *Command Output*

```
FIREWALL# show access-list OUTSIDE-IN
access-list OUTSIDE-IN; 5 elements; name hash: 0x9ccc1a31

access-list OUTSIDE-IN line 1 extended permit tcp any object DMZ-WEB-SERVER eq www
  (hitcnt=8) 0x40178d02
 access-list OUTSIDE-IN line 1 extended permit tcp any host 172.16.0.23 eq www
  (hitcnt=8) 0x40178d02

access-list OUTSIDE-IN line 2 extended permit tcp any object DMZ-WEB-PRIV eq www
  (hitcnt=4571) 0xccb8bc5d
 access-list OUTSIDE-IN line 2 extended permit tcp any host 172.16.0.5 eq www
  (hitcnt=4571) 0xccb8bc5d

access-list OUTSIDE-IN line 3 remark Allow contractor access to update web server
  content

access-list OUTSIDE-IN line 4 extended permit tcp any object DMZ-WEB-PRIV eq ftp log
  notifications interval 300 time-range CONTRACTOR-TO-WEB-SERVER (hitcnt=0)
  (inactive) 0xcef8e373
access-list OUTSIDE-IN line 4 extended permit tcp any host 172.16.0.5 eq ftp log
  notifications interval 300 time-range CONTRACTOR-TO-WEB-SERVER (hitcnt=0)
  (inactive) 0xcef8e373

access-list OUTSIDE-IN line 5 extended permit tcp any object DMZ-FTP-PRIV eq ftp
  time-range EVENING-FTP-TRANSFERS (hitcnt=92) (inactive) 0xf40023a7
 access-list OUTSIDE-IN line 5 extended permit tcp any host 172.16.0.10 eq ftp time-
  range EVENING-FTP-TRANSFERS (hitcnt=92) (inactive) 0xf40023a7

access-list OUTSIDE-IN line 6 remark Explicit deny all rule to change to interval log
  message 106100 from per-packet log message 106023

access-list OUTSIDE-IN line 7 extended deny ip any any log warnings interval 300
  (hitcnt=11244) 0x502c4bfb
```

Notice that neither of the time-based access rules is currently active—the contractor rule because the defined time period for that rule has not yet begun, and the file transfer rule because it is a Saturday, and would be outside the defined time range even on a weekday.

When using the **show access-list** command (but not when using the **show running-config access-list** command), access list entries that contain an object or object group name will be "expanded" to show the IP addresses involved on individual lines, with the same line number as the entry containing the object or object group name. Note the indented items under each line containing an object name in Example 8-7, showing the IP addresses associated with those network objects.

The commands in Example 8-7 are listed by ACL line number. The line numbers displayed in the **show access-list** output are optional when you are configuring an ACL from the CLI. If you do not specify a line number when entering an **access-list** command, it will be assigned by the system, and the line will be placed at the end of the ACL. Each ACE (including remarks) will be given a unique line number within the ACL. By specifying a line number when you are defining an ACE from the CLI, it is possible to insert an ACE at a specific position in an ACL (which is covered in the section, "Managing Access Rules from the CLI").

If you only want to see the identifier (name or number) of all the ACLs configured on your ASA, along with the number of ACEs they contain and their name hash (a non-configurable internal value for tracking the ACL), use the **show access-list brief** command. Example 8-8 shows the usage of this command, which specifies two access list names as arguments to limit output to only those ACLs.

Example 8-8   show access-list brief *Command Output*

```
FIREWALL# show access-list INSIDE-IN OUTSIDE-IN brief
access-list INSIDE-IN; 1 elements; name hash: 0xf1656621
access-list OUTSIDE-IN; 5 elements; name hash: 0x9ccc1a31
```

Managing Rules in Cisco ASDM

The Cisco ASDM Access Rules table contains several features that enable you to quickly and efficiently manage it. Figure 8-23 shows the Access Rules table after a specific rule has been right-clicked to open the options menu.

Notice that from this menu, you can choose to add an access rule or insert access rules (previously demonstrated using the Add button at the top of the window), or edit or delete a rule (also available through buttons at the top of the window). You can also easily copy (clone) a rule, for instance, when you add another web server—just clone the existing web server rule, and then edit it to change the destination address.

You can change the order of rules, using either the Cut, Copy, and Paste (or Paste After) options or the Move Up and Move Down arrows (to the right of the Delete button at the top of the window). Remember that because access rules are evaluated in order, positioning within the rule set applied to an interface can be critical to functionality.

From within ASDM, you can also clear the hit counter for a specific rule (right-click menu) or all access rules (button on the toolbar), which is commonly required during troubleshooting. You can also show log messages generated by a chosen rule (right-click menu) or by all access rules (button on the toolbar). Additionally from the right-click menu, you can export the contents of the Access Rules table to a comma-separated value (CSV) format file.

You can edit a rule in place (rather than opening the Edit Access Rule dialog box) by clicking in a field such as Source or Destination and altering the contents within the Access Rules window. Rules can also be temporarily disabled (if you want to permanently remove a rule, simply delete it). Figure 8-24 shows such an example. The DMZ web server is going to be undergoing maintenance, so you want to temporarily disable the rule that permits access to the server.

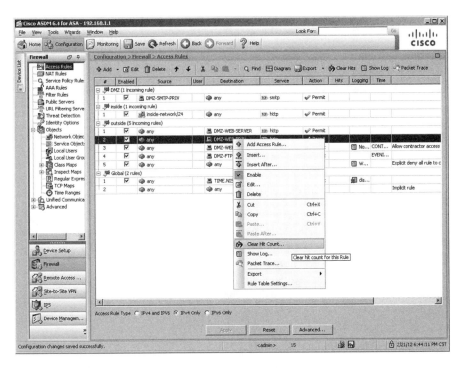

Figure 8-23 *Managing Access Rules in ASDM*

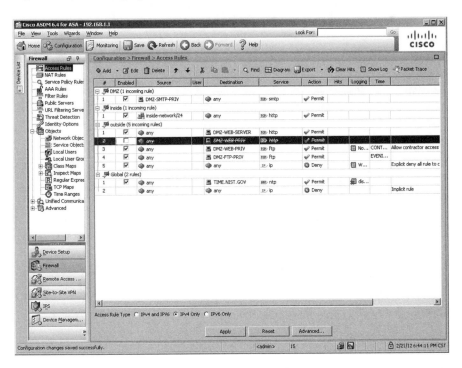

Figure 8-24 *Temporarily Disabling an Access Rule*

Figure 8-24 shows the access rule that permits access to the web server selected (high-lighted). To temporarily disable the rule, simply uncheck the **Enabled** check box and click **Apply**. Note that several of the columns are "crossed out" graphically when a rule is disabled in this way, as shown in Figure 8-24. When the maintenance on the web server is complete, re-enable the rule by checking the **Enabled** check box and clicking **Apply**.

The CLI command generated by the changes made is as follows:

```
access-list OUTSIDE-IN line 2 extended permit tcp any object DMZ-WEB-PRIV eq http
  inactive
```

If you are configuring the ASA from the CLI, you can enter this command directly in global configuration mode. Note that you are simply appending the keyword **inactive** to the existing ACE.

Another helpful feature within ASDM is the display of a diagram to visually represent the function of an access rule. The Diagram feature is a toggle; click the **Diagram** button in the toolbar to enable it, and it will remain on until you click that button again to disable the feature. Figure 8-25 shows the altered view of the Access Rules window with the Diagram feature enabled, after having re-enabled the web server access rule.

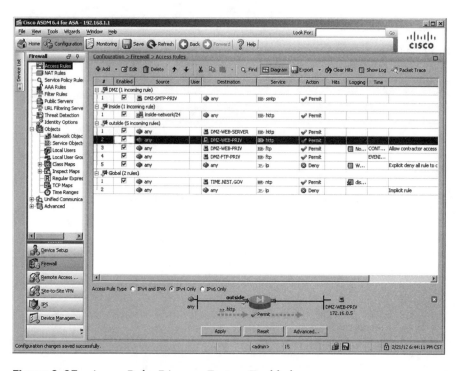

Figure 8-25 *Access Rules Diagram Feature Enabled*

The Diagram feature causes a visual representation of the selected access rule to display at the bottom of the window. In Figure 8-25, the access rule permitting access to the DMZ web server is selected. The diagram shows that any source can send TCP/HTTP packets into the outside interface of the ASA, and they will be permitted to reach the destination object name of the DMZ web server's native address.

Managing Access Rules from the CLI

Several commands are available to manage ACLs and their component ACEs from the CLI. To delete an ACE, use the keyword **no** and specify the complete rule in the CLI (you do not have to include the line number or keyword **extended**, but the command will still work if you do), as shown in the following command:

```
FIREWALL(config)# no access-list OUTSIDE-IN permit tcp any object DMZ-WEB-PRIV eq
  http
```

Only the single ACE is deleted, and remaining ACEs are appropriately renumbered. You can delete an entire access list from the configuration by using the **clear configure access-list** [*ACL-name*] command, as demonstrated here:

```
FIREWALL(config)# clear configure access-list INSIDE-IN
```

The use of this command will also automatically remove the associated **access-group** command if the ACL was applied to an interface at the time of deletion.

Note: The previous two commands are for purposes of illustration only, and are not accounted for in further configuration examples in this chapter.

Caution: If you delete all entries from an ACL, *all references to that ACL are removed from the configuration*. This is especially important for access lists used for purposes other than interface access rules. For example, in Chapter 7, translation rules were created that referenced ACLs. If such an ACL were deleted in its entirety, the translation rules that referred to it would be automatically deleted as well. You are not given any warning or acknowledgment message stating that this has occurred.

Furthermore, using the **clear configure access-list** command without any arguments will delete all ACLs on the ASA, no matter how they were applied. Therefore, exercise great care when using any variation of the **clear configure access-list** command.

You can insert an ACE at a specific position in an ACL by specifying a line number when configuring the ACE. The ACE will be inserted above the ACE that currently has that line number, and all subsequent ACEs will be renumbered automatically. Consider the following existing ACL:

```
access-list DMZ-IN line 1 remark Allow mail server to both inside and Internet
access-list DMZ-IN line 2 extended permit tcp object DMZ-SMTP-PRIV any eq smtp
```

Suppose you want to implement more effective security, while still permitting the SMTP server to reach all required destinations, so you decide to limit SMTP access to the inside network to only the internal mail server. Example 8-9 shows the required configuration, along with a **show** command that verifies the changes. An appropriate object definition is assumed to exist for the internal mail server.

Example 8-9   *Inserting ACEs into an Existing ACL*

```
FIREWALL(config)# access-list DMZ-IN line 2 permit tcp object DMZ-SMTP-PRIV object
   INSIDE-SMTP-SERVER eq smtp
FIREWALL(config)# access-list DMZ-IN line 3 deny tcp object DMZ-SMTP-PRIV object
   INSIDE-SEGMENT eq smtp
FIREWALL(config)# exit
FIREWALL# show running-config access-list DMZ-IN
access-list DMZ-IN line 1 remark Allow mail server to both inside and Internet
access-list DMZ-IN line 2 extended permit tcp object DMZ-SMTP-PRIV object INSIDE-
   SMTP-SERVER eq smtp
access-list DMZ-IN line 3 deny tcp host object DMZ-SMTP-PRIV object INSIDE-
   SEGMENT eq smtp
access-list DMZ-IN line 4 extended permit tcp object DMZ-SMTP-PRIV any eq smtp
```

Organizing Access Rules Using Object Groups

The access rules demonstrated thus far have been manageable. When only one source, one destination, and one service exist, only a minimal number of access rules are needed in an interface rule set. However, as the number of clients (sources), servers (destinations), and services increase, the number of access rules required to manage a security policy may increase uncontrollably.

Consider, for example, a situation where a company maintains 50 servers on a DMZ network, which provide four services each to the outside world (perhaps HTTP, HTTPS, FTP, and SMTP), and also act as clients for connections to five database servers in the inside network, on one destination port. Using the methods shown thus far, you would need to create 200 access rules for the outside interface and 5 more for the DMZ interface.

One solution for this dilemma is to group specific hosts into networks and allow entire networks to access resources. You could also allow complete TCP, UDP, or even IP connectivity between hosts. These approaches are not recommended, however, as they depart from the minimal-access approach to network security and increase risk by allowing unnecessary connectivity. What is needed is a way to reduce configuration complexity, while maintaining a minimal access security design.

Key Topic

The solution is *object grouping*. Object grouping allows you to group arbitrarily into a single access rule, hosts, resources, or services that share the same policy requirements, thereby minimizing the number of rules you must create. Furthermore, adding or removing hosts or services from object groups will automatically add or remove them to or from any access rule that references the object group, thus greatly simplifying ongoing changes to security policy.

For instance, continuing with the example previously stated, you could group the 50 servers in the DMZ into a group named DMZ-SERVERS, group the five database servers on the inside network into a group named DB-SERVERS, and group the four services (HTTP/S, FTP, and SMTP) into a group named PUBLIC-SERVICES. Instead of 205 access rules, you could now implement the same security policy using two access rules. That's right—a better than 100:1 reduction in access rules, through the use of object groups.

Note: You can also nest object groups, by making one or more object groups members of another object group of the same type. For instance, if you had network object groups for regional offices in the United States and Canada, you could make these two groups members of an object group called NORTH-AMERICAN-OFFICES. The individual groups could be referenced in access rules that apply only to one country or the other, and the nested object group could be referenced in access rules that apply to both.

Creation of object groups is entirely optional, although it should be clear by now why you might want to use them. There are four types of object groups you can create on the ASA:

■ **Network object groups:** These groups consist of any combination of individual host addresses and network addresses, and can be used in the source or destination address fields of ACLs, as well as in the definition of network objects, as demonstrated in Chapter 7.

■ **Service object groups:** These groups consist of any combination of individual ports or port ranges, and can be used in the source or destination port fields of ACLs. In versions 8.2 and later of the OS, service object groups can also include ICMP types and IP protocols, which makes them a "super-set" type of object group, including items that previously had to be defined in separate object group types.

■ **ICMP-type object groups:** These groups consist of ICMP message types, and can be used in the ICMP message type field of ACLs.

■ **Protocol object groups:** These groups consist of protocols within the Internet Protocol suite, and can be used in the protocol field of ACLs.

Recall from the configuration scenario that the following requirement has not yet been completed:

Allow regional offices in the United States to post files to/pull files from the DMZ FTP server on weekdays, from midnight until 4:59 a.m. local time.

Additionally, the following requirement has been added:

In addition to HTTP, permit all hosts on the inside network to access servers on all other interfaces, using HTTPS and FTP.

In the preceding section of this chapter, the time range needed for the first of these requirements was created. Using object groups, you must now create a group defining the remote regional offices.

Although optional, the first step demonstrated will be to create network objects and assign them names, one per regional office. To create these objects, navigate to **Configuration > Firewall > Objects > Network Objects/Groups**. Click the arrow next to the **Add** button to display the menu shown in Figure 8-26.

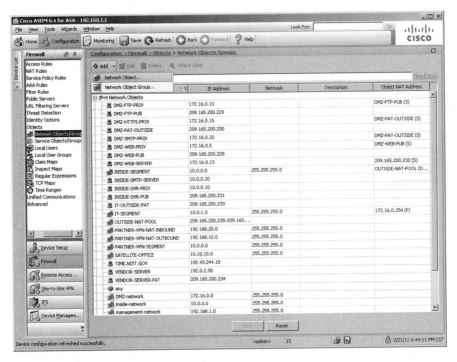

Figure 8-26 *Add Network Objects/Groups Menu*

From this menu, click **Network Object** to open the Add Network Object dialog box, shown in Figure 8-27.

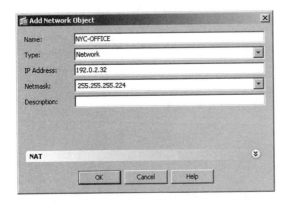

Figure 8-27 *Add Network Object Dialog Box*

Defining a network object is straightforward: Assign a name to the object (optional), enter an IP address and netmask, and add a description of the object (optional).

Note: If you define a network object without a name, the name assigned will be the IP address you enter when defining the object.

In Figure 8-27, the name NYC-OFFICE is assigned. The IP address of 192.0.2.32 is entered, with a netmask of 255.255.255.224. Complete the definition of the new network object by clicking **OK**.

Repeat these steps and define 192.0.2.64/27 as LA-OFFICE, 192.0.2.96/27 as CHI-OFFICE, and 192.0.2.128/27 as HOU-OFFICE.

After you create these individual network objects, you are returned to **Configuration > Firewall > Objects > Network Objects/Groups.** Click the arrow next to the **Add** button, and this time click **Network Object Group** to open the Add Network Object Group dialog box, shown in Figure 8-28.

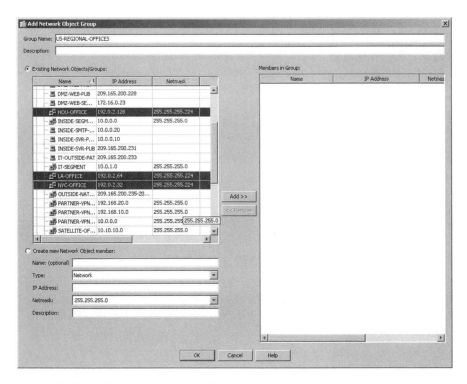

Figure 8-28 *Add Network Object Group Dialog Box*

In the Group Name field, assign a name for this new network object group. The group name can be up to 64 characters in length (spaces are not allowed). The name must be unique for each object group, no matter what type (that is, a network object group cannot have the same name as a service object group). In Figure 8-28, the name US-REGIONAL-OFFICES is assigned. You may optionally enter a description.

Because you have predefined the network objects that will be members of this group, click the **Existing Network Objects/Groups** radio button. Within that listing, select the objects representing the four regional offices, as shown in Figure 8-28 (you can select multiple objects simultaneously by using Ctrl-click or, if contiguous, Shift-click). Then click the **Add >>** button in the middle of the window, to move these objects into the Members in Group list. The resulting display is shown in Figure 8-29.

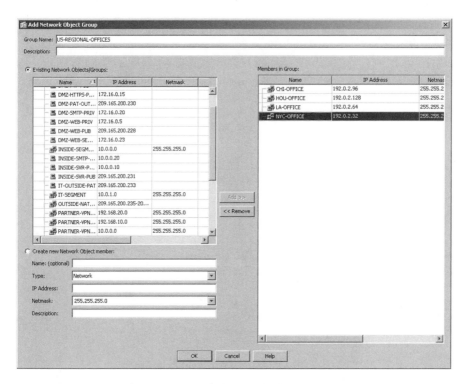

Figure 8-29   *New Object Group Members Added*

Note: As shown in Figure 8-29, you can optionally create new network objects as group members directly from this window, by clicking the **Create New Network Object Member** radio button, defining network object parameters in the designated fields, and then clicking the **Add >>** button.

After you verify that the Members in Group list is correct, finalize the creation of this new object group by clicking **OK**. The display returns to the Network Objects/Groups window, which shows all network objects at the top of the window and object groups below that. Figure 8-30 shows this display, including the object group just created.

You can expand the view to show the membership of an object group by clicking the **+** sign to the left of the group name. In Figure 8-30, this has been done for the group US-REGIONAL-OFFICES.

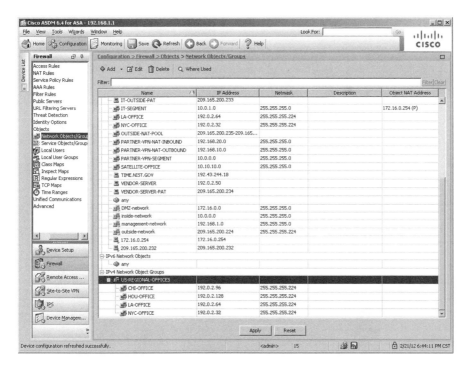

Figure 8-30 *Expanded Object Group View*

Note that the four network objects that are members of this group remain in the list of network objects. Network objects can be reused in a number of ways in the ASA configuration, to include membership in multiple object groups, NAT rules, MPF, and so on. Adding objects to a group does not remove them from the list of network objects, but rather references the original object.

The next requirement in the configuration scenario is to allow multiple services to be reached by any host on the inside network. Previously, only HTTP access had been permitted. Because the source (the inside network) and destination (any other interface) are the same as a previously created rule, the easiest way to accomplish this new requirement is to create a service object group, containing all the desired services, and then edit the existing access rule.

You therefore need to create a service object group, which will include the TCP protocols HTTP, HTTPS, and FTP as members. To demonstrate an alternate method of doing so, navigate to **Configuration > Firewall > Access Rules** to return to the Access Rules window. Next, from the ASDM menu, choose **View > Services**. This opens the Services panel on the far right side of the ASDM window, as shown in Figure 8-31.

Note: Similar panels may be activated from the View menu for Addresses (which allows the creation of network object groups) and Time Ranges.

Figure 8-31   *Services Panel Expanded*

Within the Services panel, click **Add > TCP Service Group**. Doing so opens the Add TCP Service Group dialog box, which is shown in Figure 8-32.

Assign a name to the Service object group in the Group Name field. You may optionally enter a description. In Figure 8-32, the name EXTERNAL-SERVICES-ALLOWED is entered, along with a brief description of the group's purpose.

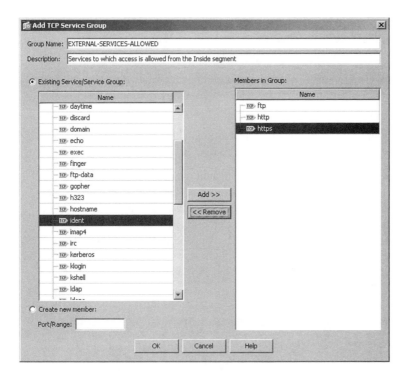

Figure 8-32 *Add TCP Service Group Dialog Box*

Because you chose to create a TCP Service Group, all the predefined TCP service names are listed in the Existing Service/Service Group list. This is a list of services (in alphabetical order) associated with known port numbers, and allows you to quickly build service groups without having to memorize associated port numbers. If you need to add a service that is not in the predefined list, click the **Create New Member** radio button and enter a port number or range in the provided field.

For our configuration scenario, using the same method described earlier, add the HTTP, HTTPS, and FTP services to the group, as shown completed in Figure 8-32. Finalize the creation of this Services object group by clicking **OK**. Note that the newly created group will now appear at the bottom of the Services panel.

Object group types that can be created from within the Services panel are as follows:

- **Service Group:** Creates an IP service object group, which groups services based on arbitrary protocols

- **TCP Service Group:** Creates a TCP service object group, which groups services that use only the TCP protocol

- **UDP Service Group:** Creates a UDP service object group, which groups services that use only the UDP protocol

- **TCP-UDP Service Group:** Creates a TCP and UDP service object group, which allows you to group services that use the same destination port over both the TCP and UDP protocols (for example, DNS on port 53)

- **ICMP Group:** Creates an ICMP-type object group, which allows you to group various ICMP service types (for example, echo-reply, unreachable, and time-exceeded in a "response" group)

- **Protocol Group:** Creates a Protocol object group, which allows you to group IP protocols (for example, EIGRP and OSPF in a "routing protocols" group)

Now that the required object groups have been created, you can reference them when creating or editing access rules. To change the existing access rule on the inside interface, from allowing only outbound HTTP to allowing all three protocols in the object group just created, close the Services panel and return to the Access Rules window. Then, to demonstrate the "edit in place" feature of ASDM, double-click the field for Service within the existing access rule for the inside interface. It currently shows a value of tcp/http. The field transitions to edit mode, and an ellipsis button appears to the right of the field, as shown in Figure 8-33.

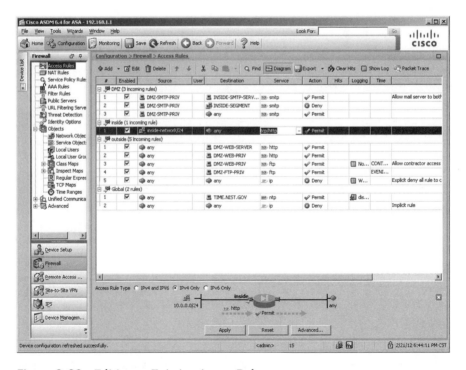

Figure 8-33   *Editing an Existing Access Rule*

Click the ellipsis button to open the Browse Service dialog box, as shown in Figure 8-34.

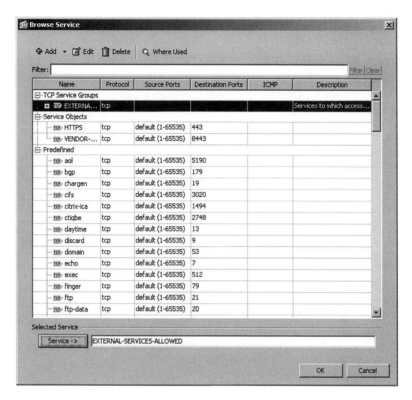

Figure 8-34   *Browse Service Dialog Box*

Note in Figure 8-34 that all user-defined object groups are listed at the top of the Browse Service dialog box, above the list of predefined services.

First, you need to delete the current setting of TCP/HTTP as the destination service. Simply delete the value from the Service field at the bottom of the window. Then, select the EXTERNAL-SERVICES-ALLOWED object group, and click the **Service ->** button to assign the object group as the selected service. This is shown in Figure 8-34. Finalize the assignment of the object group as the selected service by clicking **OK**. This returns the view to the Access Rules window, and the object group name is now displayed in the Service column of the inside interface access rule.

The final requirement in the configuration scenario is to permit the four U.S. regional offices to access the DMZ FTP server from midnight to 4:59 a.m. on weekdays. The current rule on the outside interface permits any source address to do so, so you will once again need to edit an existing access rule to change this requirement.

Using the same method as before, select the Source field of the existing access rule for editing by double-clicking it. Click the ellipsis button to open the Browse Source dialog box, as shown in Figure 8-35.

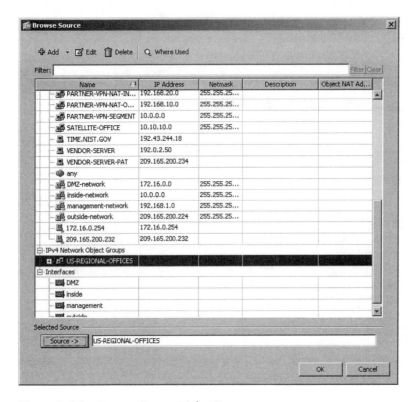

Figure 8-35 *Browse Source Dialog Box*

You will notice that network object groups are listed below network objects in this view. First, delete the "any" entry in the Source field, then select the object group US-RE-GIONAL-OFFICES, and assign it as the new source by clicking the **Source ->** button. Click **OK** to finalize the assignment and return to the Access Rules window. Figure 8-36 shows the revised contents of the ASA Access Rules.

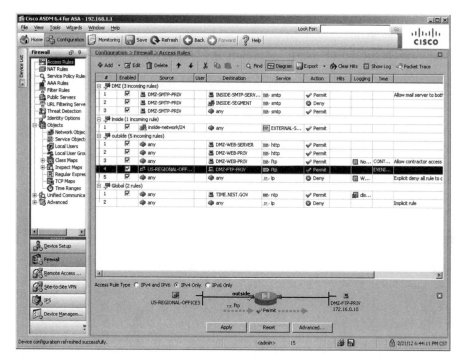

Figure 8-36   *Modified Access Rules with Object Groups*

Finally, click **Apply** to send the changes to the ASA, and then click **Save** to store the revised configuration as the startup-config file.

The CLI commands generated by the changes made are as follows (spacing is inserted for increased readability):

```
object network CHI-OFFICE
  subnet 192.0.2.96 255.255.255.224
object network HOU-OFFICE
  subnet 192.0.2.128 255.255.255.224
object network LA-OFFICE
  subnet 192.0.2.64 255.255.255.224
object network NYC-OFFICE
  subnet 192.0.2.32 255.255.255.224
!
object-group network US-REGIONAL-OFFICES
  network-object object CHI-OFFICE
  network-object object HOU-OFFICE
  network-object object LA-OFFICE
  network-object object NYC-OFFICE
!
object-group service EXTERNAL-SERVICES-ALLOWED tcp
  description Services to which access is allowed from the Inside segment
```

```
    port-object eq ftp
    port-object eq http
    port-object eq https
!
access-list INSIDE-IN line 1 extended permit tcp 10.0.0.0 255.255.255.0 any object-
    group EXTERNAL-SERVICES-ALLOWED
!
no access-list INSIDE-IN line 2 extended permit tcp 10.0.0.0 255.255.255.0 any eq
    http
!
no access-list OUTSIDE-IN line 5 extended permit tcp any object DMZ-FTP-PRIV eq
    ftp time-range EVENING-FTP-TRANSFERS
!
access-list OUTSIDE-IN line 5 extended permit tcp object-group US-REGIONAL-OFFICES
    object DMZ-FTP-PRIV eq ftp time-range EVENING-FTP-TRANSFERS
```

If you are configuring the ASA from the CLI, you can enter these commands directly in global configuration mode.

Note that, to replace an element in an ACE with an object group, you place the keyword **object-group** in front of the group name, in the ACE syntax. You may freely mix object-group-based ACE conditions with classic, single-service or single-address ACE conditions.

Verifying Object Groups

At their core, object groups are for our consumption as human administrators—they allow us to easily create or edit access rule entries and allow us to use easily understood logical names to refer to groups of addresses, ports, protocols, or ICMP types that would otherwise need to be enumerated within the ASA configuration. They do not, however, actually alter the functionality of access rules, from the ASA's point of view.

You can verify the application of object groups within access rules by opening the Services panel (shown previously in Figure 8-31) or Addresses panel and cross-referencing them with the Access Rules table. You can also verify group membership by expanding the view of any object group within either of these panels. Figure 8-37 shows the Addresses panel (choose **View > Addresses**), with the US-REGIONAL-OFFICES object group membership expanded.

Editing the membership of an object group automatically updates any access rule that references the object group. This makes the editing of underlying ACLs far easier than manually locating rules for deletion or inserting new ACEs in the correct position within a long and complex ACL.

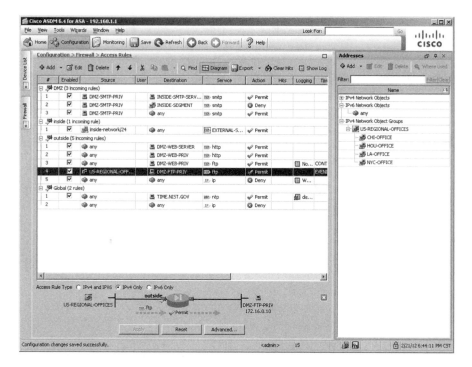

Figure 8-37   *Verifying Object Groups in ASDM*

The difference between how you might edit access rules containing object groups and how the ASA operates on them can be demonstrated using **show** commands. Example 8-10 shows a "logical" view of the configured access lists, which is how administrators edit ACLs. Note how short and concise this listing is.

Example 8-10   show running-config access-list *Output with Object Groups*

```
FIREWALL# show running-config access-list
access-list INSIDE-IN extended permit tcp 10.0.0.0 255.255.255.0 any object-group
  EXTERNAL-SERVICES-ALLOWED
access-list DMZ-IN remark Allow mail server to both inside and Internet
access-list DMZ-IN extended permit tcp object DMZ-SMTP-PRIV object INSIDE-SMTP-SERVER
  eq smtp
access-list DMZ-IN extended deny tcp object DMZ-SMTP-PRIV object INSIDE-SEGMENT eq smtp
access-list DMZ-IN extended permit tcp object DMZ-SMTP-PRIV any eq smtp
access-list OUTSIDE-IN extended permit tcp any object DMZ-WEB-SERVER eq www
access-list OUTSIDE-IN extended permit tcp any object DMZ-WEB-PRIV eq www
access-list OUTSIDE-IN remark Allow contractor access to update web server content
access-list OUTSIDE-IN extended permit tcp any object DMZ-WEB-PRIV eq ftp log
  notifications time-range CONTRACTOR-TO-WEB-SERVER
access-list OUTSIDE-IN extended permit tcp object-group US-REGIONAL-OFFICES object DMZ-
  FTP-PRIV eq ftp time-range EVENING-FTP-TRANSFERS
```

```
access-list OUTSIDE-IN remark Explicit deny all rule to change to interval log message
  106100 from per-packet log message 106023
access-list OUTSIDE-IN extended deny ip any any log warnings
access-list GLOBAL-ACL extended permit udp any object TIME.NIST.GOV eq ntp log disable
```

Example 8-11 shows the same access lists, as the ASA actually operates on them, by using the **show access-list** command, without the **running-config** argument. As previously mentioned, when using this command, the ASA will expand all object groups to display individual ACEs for each combination of object group members in a rule.

Example 8-11 show access-list *Output with Object Groups*

```
FIREWALL# show access-list
access-list cached ACL log flows: total 0, denied 0 (deny-flow-max 4096)
            alert-interval 300
access-list INSIDE-IN; 3 elements; name hash: 0xf1656621
access-list INSIDE-IN line 1 extended permit tcp 10.0.0.0 255.255.255.0 any object-
  group EXTERNAL-SERVICES-ALLOWED (hitcnt=0) 0xe86dade4
 access-list INSIDE-IN line 1 extended permit tcp 10.0.0.0 255.255.255.0 any eq ftp
  (hitcnt=0) 0x5f8d3c2c
 access-list INSIDE-IN line 1 extended permit tcp 10.0.0.0 255.255.255.0 any eq www
  (hitcnt=0) 0x31ef50e1
 access-list INSIDE-IN line 1 extended permit tcp 10.0.0.0 255.255.255.0 any eq https
  (hitcnt=0) 0xc6f6c701
access-list DMZ-IN; 3 elements; name hash: 0x33999acc
access-list DMZ-IN line 1 remark Allow mail server to both inside and Internet
access-list DMZ-IN line 2 extended permit tcp object DMZ-SMTP-PRIV object INSIDE-SMTP-
  SERVER eq smtp (hitcnt=0) 0xa283a3e0
 access-list DMZ-IN line 2 extended permit tcp host 172.16.0.20 host 10.0.0.20
  eq smtp (hitcnt=0) 0xa283a3e0
access-list DMZ-IN line 3 extended deny tcp object DMZ-SMTP-PRIV object INSIDE-
  SEGMENT eq smtp (hitcnt=0) 0x89a59184
 access-list DMZ-IN line 3 extended deny tcp host 172.16.0.20 10.0.0.0
  255.255.255.0 eq smtp (hitcnt=0) 0x89a59184
access-list DMZ-IN line 4 extended permit tcp object DMZ-SMTP-PRIV any eq smtp
  (hitcnt=0) 0x3b8b87ca
 access-list DMZ-IN line 4 extended permit tcp host 172.16.0.20 any eq smtp (hitcnt=0)
  0x3b8b87ca
access-list OUTSIDE-IN; 8 elements; name hash: 0x9ccc1a31
access-list OUTSIDE-IN line 1 extended permit tcp any object DMZ-WEB-SERVER eq www
  (hitcnt=0) 0x40178d02
 access-list OUTSIDE-IN line 1 extended permit tcp any host 172.16.0.23 eq www
  (hitcnt=0) 0x40178d02
access-list OUTSIDE-IN line 2 extended permit tcp any object DMZ-WEB-PRIV eq www
  (hitcnt=0) 0xccb8bc5d
```

```
access-list OUTSIDE-IN line 2 extended permit tcp any host 172.16.0.5 eq www
  (hitcnt=0) 0xccb8bc5d
access-list OUTSIDE-IN line 3 remark Allow contractor access to update web server
  content
access-list OUTSIDE-IN line 4 extended permit tcp any object DMZ-WEB-PRIV eq ftp log
  notifications interval 300 time-range CONTRACTOR-TO-WEB-SERVER (hitcnt=0)
  (inactive) 0xcef8e373
 access-list OUTSIDE-IN line 4 extended permit tcp any host 172.16.0.5 eq ftp
  log notifications interval 300 time-range CONTRACTOR-TO-WEB-SERVER (hitcnt=0)
  (inactive) 0xcef8e373
access-list OUTSIDE-IN line 5 extended permit tcp object-group US-REGIONAL-
  OFFICES object DMZ-FTP-PRIV eq ftp time-range EVENING-FTP-TRANSFERS (inactive)
  0xc53e606d
 access-list OUTSIDE-IN line 5 extended permit tcp 192.0.2.96 255.255.255.224 host
  172.16.0.10 eq ftp time-range EVENING-FTP-TRANSFERS (hitcnt=0) (inactive)
  0x30426396
 access-list OUTSIDE-IN line 5 extended permit tcp 192.0.2.128 255.255.255.224 host
  172.16.0.10 eq ftp time-range EVENING-FTP-TRANSFERS (hitcnt=0) (inactive)
  0x04fec957
 access-list OUTSIDE-IN line 5 extended permit tcp 192.0.2.64 255.255.255.224 host
  172.16.0.10 eq ftp time-range EVENING-FTP-TRANSFERS (hitcnt=0) (inactive)
  0xbdf6d167
 access-list OUTSIDE-IN line 5 extended permit tcp 192.0.2.32 255.255.255.224 host
  172.16.0.10 eq ftp time-range EVENING-FTP-TRANSFERS (hitcnt=0) (inactive)
  0xae58cf00
access-list OUTSIDE-IN line 6 remark Explicit deny all rule to change to interval log
  message 106100 from per-packet log message 106023
access-list OUTSIDE-IN line 7 extended deny ip any any log warnings interval 300
  (hitcnt=0) 0x502c4bfb
access-list GLOBAL-ACL; 1 elements; name hash: 0xf07a8f76
access-list GLOBAL-ACL line 1 extended permit udp any object TIME.NIST.GOV eq ntp log
  disable (hitcnt=0) 0xebbdaf93
 access-list GLOBAL-ACL line 1 extended permit udp any host 192.43.244.18 eq ntp log
  disable (hitcnt=0) 0xebbdaf93
```

Obviously, this output is far more lengthy. Observe that, in line 1 of access list INSIDE-IN, the object group EXTERNAL-SERVICES-ALLOWED is expanded into its individual membership. All entries use the same line number, but this view is helpful, as you can see hit counts for each object group member, which is especially helpful when troubleshooting.

Configuring and Verifying Other Basic Access Controls

In addition to interface access rules, the ASA supports Unicast Reverse Path Forwarding (uRPF) and shunning of hosts or connections.

Creating per-interface access rules to protect against IP masquerade packets (spoofed source address) can be very labor-intensive. Because the ASA can refer to its own routing table to determine which networks are reachable through which interface, it can use the same method to validate source addresses of incoming packets. This is known as Unicast Reverse Path Forwarding (uRPF), and the ASA supports strict uRPF, where packets must arrive at a correct interface to be accepted.

When a packet arrives at an interface where uRPF has been enabled, the ASA performs the following checks:

1. Does the packet belong to an existing connection? If a packet belongs to a connection in the connection table, its source address is considered valid and it is passed to the inspection engines. The ASA always tracks both interfaces that a transit connection is using, and will deny packets that arrive at an unexpected interface for an existing connection.

2. Is the source address valid for the ingress interface? If a packet does not belong to an existing connection (or uses a stateless protocol, in which case every packet in the flow must be validated), the ASA extracts the source address from the packet and performs a uRPF check. The routing table is consulted to determine if the network to which the address belongs is reachable through the interface where the packet is arriving. If it is, the packet is forwarded to the inspection engines.

3. If the packet fails the uRPF check, the packet is dropped and a violation is logged, using the message ID 106021, which distinguishes this type of drop from the "generic" drop message of 106023.

By default, uRPF is disabled on all interfaces. You should consider enabling it unless you know of legitimate asymmetric flows that will transit the ASA. The application of uRPF will break asymmetric flows, and if such flows exist, properly configured interface access rules should be used instead.

Note: Because uRPF relies on the ASA routing table, it is only as trustworthy as the routing table itself. That is, if routing is not properly secured (using routing protocol authentication and filtering when using dynamic routing protocols), uRPF will be unreliable. Additionally, all packets from addresses not explicitly in the ASA routing table will match a configured default route, so although enabling uRPF on the interface used by the default route (usually the outside interface) will prevent spoofing of source addresses the ASA knows to be located through other interfaces, it will not prevent spoofing of invalid source IP addresses that are not known to the ASA.

Because the examples are for a small network, you will not enable uRPF on the outside interface; the vast majority of packets will match the default route, so it is not likely worth the processing overhead to use uRPF instead of interface access rules to prevent spoofed sources from the outside in this particular network. To enable uRPF on some or all remaining ASA interfaces, navigate to **Configuration > Firewall > Advanced > Anti-Spoofing**. The Anti-Spoofing window opens, as shown in Figure 8-38.

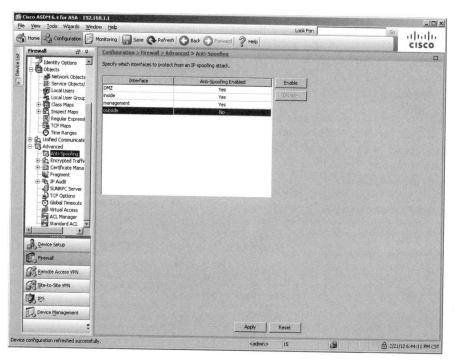

Figure 8-38   *Enabling uRPF*

Select the interface on which you want to enable uRPF, and click **Enable**. Figure 8-38 shows uRPF enabled on all but the outside interface. Then, click **Apply** to send the change to the ASA.

The CLI commands generated by the changes made are as follows:

```
ip verify reverse-path interface inside
ip verify reverse-path interface DMZ
ip verify reverse-path interface management
```

If you are configuring the ASA from the CLI, you can enter these commands directly in global configuration mode.

Shunning

Packet shunning is an ASA feature that allows you to quickly block all packets from a particular IP address at the ASA, regardless of ingress interface, interface access rules, or even existence of a connection in the connection state table. In short, it overrides all methods by which a packet might be permitted to traverse the ASA.

Shunning is configured in one of three ways: manually by an administrator; automatically by a Cisco Intrusion Prevention System (IPS) sensor (including the ASA AIP-SSM module, described in Chapter 15, "Integrating ASA Service Modules"), which can automatically deploy shunning rules in response to detected attacks; or automatically as a result of configuring the scanning threat-detection feature. You should generally use shunning to quickly respond to the occurrence of a security incident. Because shuns do not become part of the ASA configuration file, and are therefore not persistent across reboots, the feature allows you to isolate traffic from a particular host without modifying the permanent access policy configured on the ASA. This gives you the ability to immediately protect your network from an apparently hostile host, and then take the time to analyze the situation to determine if adding a permanent block of the host to the ASA's access rules is appropriate.

Shunning can be configured only through the CLI, and not from within ASDM. Use the **shun** command and specify a source IP address to shun. Example 8-12 shows the usage of the **shun** command, first to block all traffic from a source host, and second to block only a single TCP connection.

Example 8-12   shun *Command Usage*

```
FIREWALL# shun 192.0.2.153
Shun 192.0.2.153 added in context: single_vf
Shun 192.0.2.153 successful


FIREWALL# shun 192.0.2.231 209.165.200.228 40000 80 6
Shun 192.0.2.231 added in context: single_vf
Shun 192.0.2.231 successful
```

Shunning of individual connections is usually performed by a Cisco Intrusion Prevention Sensor, rather than manually. However, full support for manual connection shunning is now supported. In some older OS versions, the options showed up in output, but you could not manually shun a connection—you could only shun a source address. Note, however, that only a single shun entry can exist for any one source host at any time. Therefore, if you shun a single connection, and the host launches an attack from a different source port, the shun would have no effect on that subsequent attack—you cannot add multiple shun entries for the same host.

Use the **show shun** command to display the list of all currently blocked hosts. Note that the ASA automatically applies the shun only to the interface through which the shunned address is reachable, according to its routing table. You can alternately use the **show shun statistics** command to observe the number of packets dropped because of host shunning. Example 8-13 shows the usage of the **show shun** and **show shun statistics** commands.

Example 8-13   show shun *Command Usage*

```
FIREWALL# show shun
shun (outside) 192.0.2.153 0.0.0.0 0 0 0
```

```
FIREWALL# show shun statistics
outside=ON, cnt=3
inside=OFF, cnt=0
DMZ=OFF, cnt=0
management=OFF, cnt=0

Shun 192.0.2.153 cnt=3, time=(0:00:49)
```

Use the **clear shun** command to disable all shunning rules currently enabled. You may also use the **clear shun statistics** command to clear only the packet counters.

Troubleshooting Basic Access Control

You can use a combination of CLI commands and Cisco ASDM verification and debugging tools to troubleshoot issues related to basic access control. Typically, you will be seeking to determine why a particular session cannot be established through the ASA when you believe it should be. Occasionally, you will need to determine why sessions you believe should be denied are being permitted through the ASA.

There are a number of tools available for troubleshooting basic access control issues, including ASA logs, a packet capture capability, and the Packet Tracer tool, available both from the CLI and within ASDM.

Examining Syslog Messages

The following shows an example of syslog messages created by the ASA when a connection is permitted. If you see these messages, but your connection does not get established, you should verify the routing information in your network, especially if connection slots are inactivated with a SYN timeout, when using TCP.

```
%ASA-7-609001: Built local-host inside:10.0.0.108
%ASA-7-609001: Built local-host outside:192.0.2.150
%ASA-6-305011: Built dynamic TCP translation from inside:10.0.0.108/49334 to
   outside:209.165.200.226/46683
%ASA-6-302013: Built outbound TCP connection 237 for outside:192.0.2.150/80
   (192.0.2.150/80) to inside:10.0.0.108/49334 (209.165.200.226/46683)
```

If the ASA denies a new connection based on interface access rules, you will see either the standard 106023 messages or, if you altered the default logging (as demonstrated earlier in this chapter), 106100 messages:

```
%ASA-4-106100: access-list OUTSIDE-IN denied tcp outside/192.0.2.232(49314) ->
   DMZ/172.16.0.10(80) hit-cnt 1 first hit [0x2c1c6a65, 0x0]
```

You might also see the 106015 message, which would indicate that a noninitial packet has arrived at an ASA interface but does not match any existing connections in the connection table. This usually indicates either a reconnaissance attack attempt or legitimately delayed packets that were not received until after their transport connection had been closed.

If a packet is denied by uRPF on an interface, you will see this type of syslog message:

```
%ASA-1-106021: Deny UDP reverse path check from 172.27.25.42 to 172.27.25.255 on
    interface inside
```

Finally, if a packet is denied by shunning, you will see this type of syslog message:

```
%ASA-4-401004: Shunned packet: 192.0.2.232 ==> 209.165.200.228 on interface outside
```

You can view the syslog messages in the ASA log using the CLI **show logging** command (if buffered logging is enabled), or you can use the Cisco ASDM Real-Time Log Viewer. To use the Real-Time Log Viewer, both system logging and ASDM logging must be enabled. You can access the Real-Time Log View by navigating to **Monitoring > Logging > Real-Time Log Viewer** and clicking **View** to open the Real-Time Log Viewer window, shown in Figure 8-39.

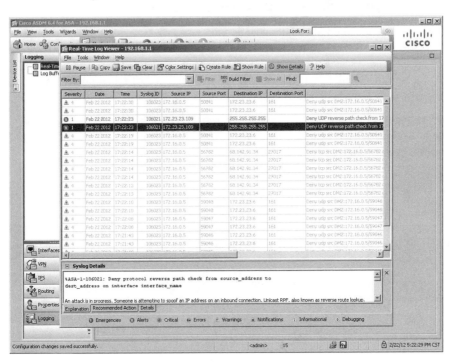

Figure 8-39 *ASDM Real-Time Log Viewer*

The Real-Time Log Viewer contains tabs at the bottom of the window that offer explanations, recommended actions, or detailed information on a selected message within the log. You can also filter the displayed messages, or search them, using the Filter By and Find fields at the top of the window.

You can use the Cisco ASDM rule-to-log correlation feature to observe syslog messages that are generated by packets matching a specific interface access rule. To do so, navigate to **Configuration > Firewall > Access Rules** and right-click a specific rule to open the Access Rule menu. From this menu, choose the **Show Log** option, as shown in Figure 8-40. This will cause the Real-Time Log Viewer to open, displaying only messages that match the selected access rule.

Figure 8-40   *Access Rule-to-Log Correlation Feature*

An additional tool offered by the Cisco ASDM Real-Time Log Viewer is the ability to create a permit access rule from a deny syslog message. Select a log message that indicates that a desired connection has been denied, and click the **Create Rule** button at the top of the Real-Time Log Viewer window. An interface access rule will be automatically created, which will permit this connection in the future, and you are given an opportunity to review the rule before it is applied.

Packet Capture

The packet capture utility is covered in detail in Chapter 16, "Traffic Analysis Tools"; however, it is possible to use a variation of the **capture** command to capture only those packets that were denied by interface access rules. You do so by adding the **type asp-drop acl-drop** parameter to the **capture** command. Example 8-14 shows an example of creating such a packet capture and displaying the resulting captured packets.

Example 8-14   capture *Command Limited to ACL Drops*

```
FIREWALL# capture ACL-DROPS type asp-drop acl-drop
FIREWALL# show capture ACL-DROPS

13 packets captured

   1: 04:21:58.081584 209.165.200.245.56838 > 192.168.100.3.161:  udp 77 Drop-reason:
      (acl-drop) Flow is denied by configured rule
   2: 04:21:58.611189 209.165.200.245.49368 > 209.165.200.229.80: S
      2739424558:2739424558(0) win 8192 <mss 1460,nop,wscale 2,nop,nop,sackOK>
      Drop-reason:
(acl-drop) Flow is denied by configured rule

...output omitted...
  13: 04:22:21.878662 209.165.200.245.49369 > 209.165.200.228.443: S
      2330381003:2330381003(0) win 8192 <mss 1460,nop,nop,sackOK> Drop-reason:
      (acl-drop)
      Flow is denied by configured rule
13 packets shown
```

Packet Tracer

When troubleshooting basic access control, the Packet Tracer tool, also covered in Chapter 16, allows you to quickly pinpoint possible reasons for connectivity issues through the ASA. The Packet Tracer tool is available through either the CLI or Cisco ASDM. Within ASDM, you access it from the Tools menu. When the Packet Tracer window opens, specify the connection parameters you want to simulate and test, the input interface, and the source and destination IP addresses and ports, and then click **Start**. Figure 8-41 shows an example of a completed Packet Tracer test.

Figure 8-41 shows a sample test using the outside interface as the ingress interface for the packet. The source address tested is 192.0.2.73, with a source port of 49252. The destination is the translated address assigned to the DMZ web server, 209.165.200.228, with a destination port of HTTP. The ACCESS-LIST section of the output is expanded to show the specific rule that permitted the packet, and the RESULT line of the output is selected for easy reference.

Note: When using packet tracer with the outside interface as a source, you must enter the translated address for an internal server to run the test. Packet tracer simulates the arrival of a packet containing the exact information you specify in all address/port fields. Therefore, you must enter information as it would appear in the packet BEFORE arriving at the ASA and being subjected to translation rules. This differs from how you configure rules, always referring to an internal host by its native address. Note, however, that although the example tests a destination IP of 209.165.200.228, the access list line that shows as a match is the one which permits access to DMZ-WEB-PRIV, which was defined as 172.16.0.5. You may also want to consider unchecking the Show Animation option to increase the speed of the test when using the GUI Packet Tracer utility.

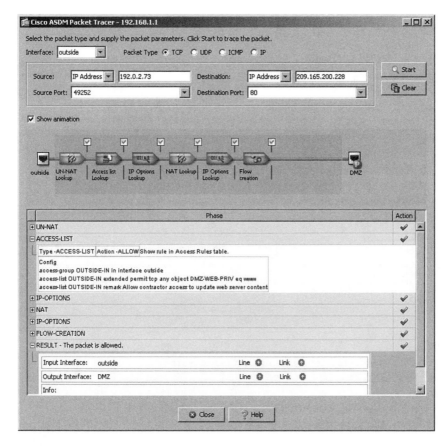

Figure 8-41   *Packet Tracer Utility Results*

Example 8-15 shows an example of invoking the Packet Tracer tool from the CLI. You supply the same connection information as in the ASDM tool. This example shows the same source and destination addresses as the preceding example, but the destination service is changed to port 443, which is not allowed by the interface access rules.

Example 8-15   packet-tracer *Command Usage*

```
FIREWALL# packet-tracer input outside tcp 192.0.2.73 49252 209.165.200.228 443

Phase: 1
Type: UN-NAT
Subtype: static
Result: ALLOW
Config:
object network DMZ-WEB-PRIV
 nat (DMZ,outside) static DMZ-WEB-PUB dns
```

```
Additional Information:
NAT divert to egress interface DMZ
Untranslate 209.165.200.228/443 to 172.16.0.5/443

Phase: 2
Type: ACCESS-LIST
Subtype: log
Result: DROP
Config:
access-group OUTSIDE-IN in interface outside
access-list OUTSIDE-IN extended deny ip any any log warnings
Additional Information:

Result:
input-interface: outside
input-status: up
input-line-status: up
output-interface: DMZ
output-status: up
output-line-status: up
Action: drop
Drop-reason: (acl-drop) Flow is denied by configured rule
```

Suggested Approach to Access Control Troubleshooting

An orderly approach to access control troubleshooting follows. This is a suggested guide only, and not all steps will be appropriate in all situations. This example is based on troubleshooting a connection that is not establishing when you think it should.

Step 1. Determine if the interface on which the connection is arriving uses an inbound set of access rules (ACL). You can accomplish this by using the CLI **show running-config access-group** command or examining the ASDM Access Rules window. If the interface on which the connection is arriving does use an inbound set of access rules, verify that the access rule set permits this connection by using the CLI or ASDM Packet Tracer tool, by examining ASA log files for denied connections, or by using the packet capture tool to view dropped packets. Do not forget to consider the contents of the global ACL in your review. If no issues are revealed by these checks, proceed to Step 3. If the rule set is found not to permit the connection, create a permit rule to permit it.

Step 2. If the ingress interface does not use an inbound rule set, you should determine if the egress interface to which the connection is routed has a lower security level. If it does, the connection should be automatically permitted, and you can proceed to Step 3. If the connection is routed to an egress interface with a higher security level, you will need to create an interface access rule set (ACL) to permit such a connection. Depending on your network addressing, you might also need to create a static translation for the destination host. For example, packets inbound to the outside interface, and trying to reach a server on the DMZ with an RFC 1918 private IP address natively assigned.

Step 3. Determine whether the egress interface to which the connection is routed uses an outbound access rule set (an outbound ACL). You can verify this by using the CLI **show running-config access-group** command or by examining the ASDM Access Rules window. If it does, verify that the access rule set permits this connection using the same methods described in Step 1. If no issues are revealed by these checks, proceed to Step 4. If the rule set is found not to permit the connection, create a permit rule to permit it.

Step 4. Verify whether uRPF is enabled on the ingress interface by using the **show running-config ip verify reverse-path** command. If it is not, proceed to Step 6.

Step 5. If uRPF is enabled on the ingress interface, verify that it does not block the connection. Use the **show logging** command or the ASDM Real-Time Log Viewer to find possible denied packets. Use the **show route** command to examine the routing table and verify whether the route for the source address points to the correct interface.

Step 6. Verify that the connection is not shunned by the ASA. Use the **show shun** command to display currently shunned hosts and connections. If the host is in the shunning list, consider removing the host from the shunning list using the **no shun** *host ip* command, if this is acceptable and does not increase risk.

Exam Preparation Tasks

As mentioned in the section, "How to Use This Book," in the Introduction, you have a couple of choices for exam preparation: the exercises here, Chapter 17, "Final Preparation," and the exam simulation questions on the CD-ROM.

Review All Key Topics

Review the most important topics in this chapter, noted with the Key Topic icon in the outer margin of the page. Table 8-4 lists a reference of these key topics and the page numbers on which each is found.

Table 8-4   *Key Topics for Chapter 8*

Key Topic Element	Description	Page Number
Paragraph	Describes connection table packet matching requirements	398
Table 8-3	Identifies basic TCP connection states from the **show conn detail** command	401
Section	Explains the terms inside and outside, inbound and outbound	403
Paragraph	Explains access rules that apply only to new connections	405
Paragraph	Explains access rules that apply only to transit traffic	405
Paragraph	Explains that access rules are an ordered list, and the implicit deny all	406
Bulleted list	Explains the effects of stateful packet handling on access rules	406
Paragraph	Explains how to implement interval ACL logging versus per-packet logging	418
Section	Introduces the new ASDM Public Server Wizard	424
Paragraph	Explains how to apply access rules from the CLI	426
Figure 8-20	Shows how to configure a time range in Cisco ASDM	429
Paragraph	Explains that altering object groups automatically alters access rules	438
Bulleted list	Describes the various types of nonnetwork object groups	445

Command Reference to Check Your Memory

This section includes the most important configuration and EXEC commands covered in this chapter. It might not be necessary to memorize the complete syntax of every command, but you should be able to remember the basic keywords that are needed.

To test your memory of the commands, cover the right side of Tables 8-5 through 8-14 with a piece of paper, read the description on the left side, and then see how much of the command you can remember.

The FIREWALL exam focuses on practical, hands-on skills that are used by a networking professional. Therefore, you should be able to identify the commands needed to configure and test an ASA feature.

Table 8-5 *Commands Related to State Tables*

Task	Command Syntax
Display connection table entries	ciscoasa# **show conn** [count | [all] [detail] [long] [state *state_type*] [protocol {tcp | udp}] [address *src_ip*[-*src_ip*] [netmask *mask*] [port *src_port*[-*src_port*]] [address *dest_ip*[-*dest_ip*] [netmask *mask*] [port *dest_port*[-*dest_port*]]
Clear connection table entries	ciscoasa# **clear conn** [all] [protocol {tcp | udp}] [address *src_ip* [-*src_ip*] [netmask *mask*] [port *src_port*[-*src_port*]] [address *dest_ip*[-*dest_ip*] [netmask *mask*] [port *dest_port*[-*dest_port*]]
Display local host table entries	ciscoasa# **show local-host** [*IP_address*] [detail] [all] [brief] [connection {tcp *start*[-*end*] | udp *start*[-*end*] | embryonic *start* [-*end*]}]
Clear local host table entries	ciscoasa# **clear local-host** [*IP_address*] [all]

Table 8-6 *Optional* **show conn** *and* **clear conn** *Parameters*

Parameter	Description
all	Displays (or clears) connection to the device or from the ASA, in addition to transit-traffic connections. Without the **all** keyword, only transit connections are displayed/cleared.
count	Displays the number of active connections.
detail	Displays connections in detail, including translation type and interface information.
long	Displays connections in long format.

Table 8-7 *Optional* show local-host *and* clear local-host *Parameters*

Parameter	Description
all	Includes local hosts that connect to and from the ASA. Without the **all** keyword, only hosts connecting through the box are displayed/cleared.
brief	Displays information on local hosts in brief format.
connection	Displays three types of filters based on the number and type of connections: TCP, UDP, and embryonic. These filters can be used individually or jointly.
detail	Displays the detailed network states of local host information, including more information about active xlates and network connections.

Table 8-8 *Commands Related to Access Lists*

Task	Command Syntax
Create an extended access list entry (Do not be intimidated that this syntax looks highly complex. You will see that most of it is simply various options that were explored in the chapter materials.)	ciscoasa(config)# **access-list** *id* [**line** *line-number*] [**extended**] {**deny** | **permit**} {*protocol* | **object-group** *protocol_obj_grp_id*} {*src_ip mask* | **interface** *ifc_name* | **object-group** *network_obj_grp_id*} [*operator port* | **object-group** *service_obj_grp_id*] {*dest_ip mask* | **interface** *ifc_name* | **object-group** *network_obj_grp_id*} [*operator port* | **object-group** *service_obj_grp_id* | **object-group** *icmp_type_obj_grp_id*] [**log** [[*level*] [**interval** *secs*] | **disable** | **default**]] [**inactive** | **time-range** *time_range_name*]
Embed a remark within an access list	ciscoasa(config)# **access-list** *id* [**line** *line-number*] **remark** *text*
Bind an access list to an interface	ciscoasa(config)# **access-group** *access-list* {**in** | **out**} **interface** *interface_name*
Display contents of one or all access list(s), as they appear in the configuration	ciscoasa# **show run access-list** [*id*]
Display contents of one or all access list(s), as they are operated upon by the ASA	ciscoasa# **show access-list** *id_1* [..[*id_2*]] [**brief**] Note: This will include hit counts and an internal hexadecimal ACE identifier.
Delete one or all access list(s)	ciscoasa# **clear configure access-list** [*id*]

Table 8-9   access-list extended *Parameters*

Parameter	Description
default	(Optional) Sets logging to the default method, which will generate syslog message 106023 for each denied packet.
disable	(Optional) Disables logging for this ACE.
inactive	(Optional) Disables an ACE. To re-enable it, enter the entire ACE without the **inactive** keyword. This command allows you to temporarily disable an ACE without losing its position in your permanent configuration, which makes re-enabling it easier.
interface *ifc_name*	Specifies that the ASA interface is the source or destination address. This is normally used in conjunction with policy translations that use an ASA interface as the global address. Note that when using an ASA interface address as source or destination, you must specify the **interface** keyword. Entering the IP address of the interface will generate an error.
interval *secs*	(Optional) Specifies the log interval at which to generate system log message 106100. The valid range is from 1 to 600 seconds. The default is 300 seconds.
level	(Optional) Sets the system log message 106100 severity level. Valid values are from 0 to 7. The default level is 6 (Informational).
log	(Optional) Sets logging options when an ACE matches a packet for network access (an access list applied with the **access-group** command).
operator	(Optional) Matches the port numbers used by the source or destination. The permitted operators are as follows: ■ **lt:** less than ■ **gt:** greater than ■ **eq:** equal to ■ **neq:** not equal to ■ **range:** an inclusive range of values (specify two port numbers; for example: **range 100 200**)

Table 8-10　*Commands Related to Time Range*

Task	Command Syntax
Create a time range and enter time range configuration mode	ciscoasa(config)# **time-range** *name*
Define a recurring (weekly) time range	ciscoasa(config-time-range)# **periodic** *days-of-the-week time* **to** [*days-of-the-week*] *time*
Define an absolute time range	ciscoasa(config-time-range)# **absolute** [**start** *time date*] [**end** *time date*] Note: For time ranges that begin immediately, only an end time needs to be specified. For time ranges that never end, only a start time needs to be specified.

Table 8-11　*Time-Range* periodic *Parameters*

Parameter	Description
days-of-the-week	(Optional) The first occurrence of this argument is the starting day or day of the week that the associated time range is in effect. The second occurrence is the ending day or day of the week the associated statement is in effect. This argument is any single day or combinations of days: Monday, Tuesday, Wednesday, Thursday, Friday, Saturday, and Sunday. Other possible values are ■ **daily:** Monday through Sunday ■ **weekdays:** Monday through Friday ■ **weekend:** Saturday and Sunday If the ending days of the week are the same as the starting days of the week, you can omit them.
time	Specifies the time in the format HH:MM. For example, 8:00 is 8:00 a.m. and 20:00 is 8:00 p.m.
to	Entry of the **to** keyword is required to complete the range "from start-time to end-time."

Table 8-12 *Commands Related to Object Groups*

Task	Command Syntax
Associate a name with an IP address and create a network object	ciscoasa(config)# **name** *ip_address name* [**description** *text*]]
Create an object group of a specific type and enter object-group configuration mode (each type of object group has its own configuration mode prompt)	ciscoasa(config)# **object-group** {**protocol** | **network** | **icmp-type**} *obj_grp_id* -OR- ciscoasa(config)# **object-group service** *obj_grp_id* [**tcp** | **udp** | **tcp-udp**]
Add a network object to a network object group	ciscoasa(config-network)# **network-object host** *host host_addr* | *host_name* -OR- ciscoasa(config-network)# **network-object** *net_addr netmask*
Add a protocol object to a protocol object group	ciscoasa(config-protocol)# **protocol-object** *protocol*
Add an ICMP message type to an icmp-type object group	ciscoasa(config-icmp)# **icmp-object** *icmp_type*
Add a port or port range object to a TCP, UDP, or TCP-UDP service object group	ciscoasa(config-service)# **port-object eq** *service* -OR- ciscoasa(config-service)# **port-object range** *begin_service end_service*
Define an object group as a member of another object group of the same type (object group nesting)	ciscoasa(config-*type*)# **group-object** *obj_grp_id*

Table 8-13 *Object Group Parameters*

Parameter	Description
icmp-type	Defines a group of ICMP types such as echo and echo-reply. After entering the main **object-group icmp-type** command, add ICMP objects to the ICMP type group with the **icmp-object** and the **group-object** commands.
Network	Defines a group of hosts or subnet IP addresses. After entering the main **object-group network** command, add network objects to the network group with the **network-object** and the **group-object** commands.
Protocol	Defines a group of protocols such as TCP and UDP. After entering the main **object-group protocol** command, add protocol objects to the protocol group with the **protocol-object** and the **group-object** commands.
service	An enhanced service object group defines a mix of TCP services, UDP services, ICMP-type services, and any protocol if **tcp**, **udp**, or **tcp-udp** is not specified on the command line. After entering the main **object-group service** command, add service objects to the service group with the **service-object** and the **group-object** commands.
	When **tcp**, **udp**, or **tcp-udp** is optionally specified on the command line, **service** defines a standard service object group of TCP/UDP port specifications such as "eq smtp" and "range 2000 2010." In this case, after entering the main **object-group service** command, add port objects to the service group with the **port-object** and the **group-object** commands.

Table 8-14 *Commands Related to Other Access Controls*

Task	Command Syntax
Activate uRPF on an ASA interface	ciscoasa(config)# **ip verify reverse-path interface** *interface_name*
Display uRPF statistics	ciscoasa# **show ip verify statistics**
Implement host shunning	ciscoasa# **shun** *src_ip* [*dst_ip src_port dest_port* [*protocol*]] [**vlan vlan_id**]
Display shunning list or shun statistics	ciscoasa# **show shun** [*src_ip* | *statistics*]
Clear the shunning list or shun statistics	ciscoasa# **clear shun** [*statistics*]
Use the Packet Tracer tool to test connectivity and access rule policies	ciscoasa# **packet-tracer input** [*src_int*] *protocol src_addr src_port dest_addr dest_port* [**detailed**] [**xml**]
	Note: ASDM automatically displays the trace capture in XML format.

Table 8-14 *Commands Related to Other Access Controls*

Task	Command Syntax
Use the packet capture tool to capture only packets dropped by access rules (ACLs)	ciscoasa# **capture** *capture_name* **type asp-drop acl-drop**
Display packets captured using the packet capture tool	ciscoasa# **show capture** *capture_name*

This chapter covers the following topics:

- **Understanding the Modular Policy Framework:** This section provides an overview of a flexible and organized method you can use to configure security policies for a variety of Cisco ASA features.

- **Configuring the MPF:** This section explains the modular approach to configuring and enforcing security policies. Traffic can be matched with one type of policy module and acted on within another policy module. The whole hierarchy of policies is then applied to firewall interfaces and traffic inspection.

- **Configuring a Policy for Inspecting OSI Layers 3 and 4:** This section explains how you can leverage the MPF to define security policies that operate on Layer 3 (IP header) and Layer 4 (UDP or TCP header) information.

- **Configuring Dynamic Protocol Inspection:** This section covers the ASA inspection engines that can be used to inspect protocols that use a fixed control port to set up subsequent connections on ports that are determined dynamically.

- **Configuring a Policy for Inspecting OSI Layers 5–7:** This section explains how to use the MPF to define security policies that inspect and analyze application traffic.

- **Detecting and Filtering Botnet Traffic:** This section explains how an ASA can be configured to detect malicious botnet traffic as it occurs.

- **Using Threat Detection:** This section covers the threat detection feature that can be used to gather statistics about network objects and to discover abnormal activity that might be related to security attacks.

CHAPTER 9

Inspecting Traffic

A Cisco Adaptive Security Appliance (ASA) can maintain the state of connections passing through it in order to provide effective security. Connection state involves parameters such as address translation, connection direction and flow, and limits on the connection itself. In addition, an ASA must be able to inspect various protocols as they pass through, so that the protocols themselves meet criteria defined in the security policies.

Traffic inspection can be one of the most complex functions to perform and configure. This chapter covers the tools and features you can use to configure a variety of inspection policies, with an emphasis on the Modular Policy Framework (MPF).

"Do I Know This Already?" Quiz

The "Do I Know This Already?" quiz allows you to assess whether you should read this entire chapter thoroughly or jump to the "Exam Preparation Tasks" section. If you are in doubt about your answers to these questions or your own assessment of your knowledge of the topics, read the entire chapter. Table 9-1 lists the major headings in this chapter and their corresponding "Do I Know This Already?" quiz questions. You can find the answers in Appendix A, "Answers to the 'Do I Know This Already?' Quizzes."

Table 9-1   *"Do I Know This Already?" Section-to-Question Mapping*

Foundation Topics Section	Questions
Understanding the Modular Policy Framework	1–4
Configuring the MPF	5–9
Configuring a Policy for Inspecting OSI Layers 3 and 4	10–13
Configuring Dynamic Protocol Inspection	14–15
Configuring a Policy for Inspecting OSI Layers 5–7	16–17
Detecting and Filtering Botnet Traffic	18–19
Using Threat Detection	20–21

Caution: The goal of self-assessment is to gauge your mastery of the topics in this chapter. If you do not know the answer to a question or are only partially sure of the answer, you should mark that question as wrong for purposes of the self-assessment. Giving yourself credit for an answer you correctly guess skews your self-assessment results and might provide you with a false sense of security.

1. Which one of the following should be applied to one or more ASA interfaces to implement a security policy?

   a. A class map

   b. A policy map

   c. A service policy

   d. An access policy

2. Which one of the following contains the actions that are taken to enforce a security policy?

   a. A class map

   b. A policy map

   c. A service policy

   d. An access policy

3. Which one of the following contains definitions of traffic flows that should be identified so that an action can be taken?

   a. A class map

   b. A policy map

   c. A service policy

   d. An access policy

4. Which one of the following is the name of the default security policy that is applied to all ASA interfaces?

   a. global_policy

   b. default_policy

   c. policy_all

   d. inspection_default

5. When using the Modular Policy Framework to build a security policy, which one of the following should you configure first from the CLI?

   a. A class map

   b. A policy map

   c. A service policy

   d. An access policy

6. To make configuration changes to the default global security policy, which one of the following commands should be entered?

   a. ciscoasa(config)# **service-policy global_policy global**

   b. ciscoasa(config)# **global_policy**

   c. ciscoasa(config)# **policy-map global_policy**

   d. ciscoasa(config)# **class-map global_policy**

7. In a class map, which one of the following command keywords should you use to classify traffic?

   a. ciscoasa(config-cmap)# **classify**

   b. ciscoasa(config-cmap)# **permit**

   c. ciscoasa(config-cmap)# **match**

   d. ciscoasa(config-cmap)# **access-list**

8. Suppose you enter the **service-policy p1 global** command to apply a policy map to all ASA interfaces. Then you enter the **service-policy p2 global** command to apply a second policy map to all interfaces. Which of the following describes the correct outcome?

   a. Neither command will be accepted; it isn't possible to apply policy maps globally.

   b. Policy p1 will be applied globally, but p2 will not; only one global policy is supported.

   c. Policy p2 will overwrite policy p1.

   d. Both policy maps will be applied to all interfaces.

9. Refer to the following figure. Which policy has been applied to the inside and outside ASA interfaces?

   a. Policy p1

   b. Policy anything

   c. Policy voice

   d. Policy global_policy

10. By default, how long will an ASA permit an idle TCP connection to stay open? (Hint: **set connection timeout tcp**)

   a. Unlimited time

   b. 30 seconds

   c. 1 minute

   d. 1 hour

11. Which one of the following commands can be used to configure the TCP Intercept feature to limit the number of embryonic TCP connections to a total of ten for a traffic class?

   a.   set connection embryonic-conn-max 10

   b.   tcp-intercept embryonic 10

   c.   embryonic tcp 10

   d.   set connection timeout embryonic 10

12. Which one of the following policy map configuration commands should be used to detect defunct idle TCP connections?

   a.   ciscoasa(config-pmap-c)# set connection tcp

   b.   ciscoasa(config-pmap-c)# set connection idle

   c.   ciscoasa(config-pmap-c)# set connection dcd

   d.   ciscoasa(config-pmap-c)# set connection tcp detect

13. Suppose you want to configure a security policy to clear the TCP options field in TCP packets. Which one of the following represents the most appropriate ASA feature and initial configuration command that you could use?

   a.   TCP Intercept; tcp-intercept

   b.   TCP Normalizer; tcp-map

   c.   TCP Verifier; tcp-verify

   d.   TCP Guard; tcp-guard

14. Consider the following configuration:

```
ciscoasa(config)# class-map M1
ciscoasa(config-cmap)# match port tcp eq 8080
ciscoasa(config-cmap)# exit
ciscoasa(config)# policy-map global_policy
ciscoasa(config-pmap)# class M1
ciscoasa(config-pmap-c)# inspect http
ciscoasa(config-pmap-c)# exit
```

Which one of the following is a correct statement?

   a.   HTTP will be inspected on TCP port 80 only.

   b.   HTTP will be inspected on a nonstandard port.

   c.   No HTTP traffic will be inspected because class M1 matches TCP port 8080, while the inspect http command uses TCP port 80.

   d.   Only traffic with source TCP port 8080 will be inspected.

15. The **established** command is used for what one purpose?

   a. To inspect only TCP connections that are fully open and established

   b. To permit traffic from hosts that are known on a whitelist

   c. To inspect a custom dynamic protocol

   d. To permit return traffic from an outbound connection

16. Which of the following answers correctly describes inspection of ICMP traffic? (Choose all that apply.)

   a. It isn't possible because ICMP is a stateless protocol.

   b. ICMP can be inspected with the **inspect icmp** command.

   c. ICMP connections stay open for 30 seconds before being closed.

   d. ICMP connections stay open until the first reply is received.

17. Which one of the following partial commands can be used to minimize the HTTP protocol during inspection?

   a. match not request method get

   b. minimize request method

   c. no match http

   d. match http protocol-violation

18. Which of the following are valid sources of information for the Botnet Traffic Filtering databases?

   a. A statically configured whitelist

   b. A statically configured blacklist

   c. A dynamic database downloaded from Cisco

   d. A dynamic database downloaded from flash memory

19. Which one of the following command keywords is used to configure Botnet Traffic Filtering?

   a. ciscoasa(config)# **botnet-filter**

   b. ciscoasa(config)# **attack-filter**

   c. ciscoasa(config)# **traffic-filter**

   d. ciscoasa(config)# **dynamic-filter**

20. Which one of the following sources of information does the threat detection feature use?

   a. A dynamic database downloaded from Cisco

   b. A blacklist that you can configure

   c. Statistics collected from network activity

   d. A database of IPS signatures

21. Which one of the following ASA features can actively shun attacking hosts?

    a. Basic threat detection

    b. Advanced threat detection

    c. Aggressive threat detection

    d. Scanning threat detection

Foundation Topics

A Cisco ASA offers many robust traffic inspection features that you can leverage to secure a network in a variety of ways. The key to using these features lies in understanding the modular approach to configuring security policies. This chapter begins by introducing the Modular Policy Framework of configuration, and then builds on that foundation by covering inspection engines and other, more specific inspection features.

Understanding the Modular Policy Framework

Chapter 8, "Controlling Access Through the ASA," covered interface access control lists (ACL) and how you can use them to control access through an ASA. With ACLs alone, packets are permitted or denied based on the information that can be found in the packet headers. Although that approach does offer granular control over things such as source and destination addresses and Layers 3 and 4 protocols and port numbers, it still treats all types of traffic identically once the packets are permitted or denied.

A robust security appliance should also be able to identify specific traffic flows and apply the appropriate security policies to them. For example, suppose you need to prioritize one type of traffic flow over another. You might also need to examine specific application protocols with a deep packet inspection, to make sure that hosts are using the protocols correctly. Sometimes, you might want to funnel certain traffic flows through an intrusion prevention system (IPS) process to detect and prevent any malicious activity. Functions such as these are not possible with simple interface ACLs.

Fortunately, the ASA offers much more flexibility through its Modular Policy Framework (MPF). In a nutshell, the MPF provides an organized and scalable means of defining inspection policies for network traffic flows. With the MPF feature, you can define a set of policies that identifies traffic and then takes some specific actions on it. The MPF doesn't replace the use of ACLs—it simply augments ACLs with additional functionality.

The MPF concept might be confusing at first, especially when you begin trying to configure it or reverse engineer it for the first time. Think of the MPF as a set of three nested items:

- **Service policy:** An entire set of policies that is applied to one or all ASA interfaces, configured with the **service-policy** command

Key
Topic

- **Policy map:** Where an action is taken on matched traffic, configured with the **policy-map** command

- **Class map:** Where specific traffic flows are identified or classified, configured with the **class-map** command

Because the MPF is designed to be modular, a service policy can contain one or more policy maps, which can, in turn, contain one or more class maps. As well, any class maps you define can be referenced in multiple policy maps and service policies.

To get an idea of the MPF structure, you can look at the policies that are configured by default in an ASA. First, you can use the **show running-config service-policy** command to see which service policies have been defined and applied to the ASA interfaces. Example 9-1 shows a default service policy that refers to something called global_policy, which has been applied globally to all ASA interfaces. A service policy always references a policy map—the next level down in the MPF hierarchy.

Example 9-1   *Displaying the Default Service Policies*

```
ciscoasa# show running-config service-policy
service-policy global_policy global
ciscoasa#
```

Now you know that the name of the policy map is global_policy, but what does it do? Next, you can look for the policy map configuration to find out. Use the **show running-config policy-map global_policy** command to display its contents, as shown in Example 9-2.

Example 9-2   *Displaying a Policy Map Configuration*

```
ciscoasa# show running-config policy-map global_policy
!
policy-map global_policy
 class inspection_default
  inspect dns preset_dns_map
  inspect ftp
  inspect h323 h225
  inspect h323 ras
  inspect rsh
  inspect rtsp
  inspect esmtp
  inspect sqlnet
  inspect skinny
  inspect sunrpc
  inspect xdmcp
  inspect sip
  inspect netbios
  inspect tftp
  inspect ip-options
!
ciscoasa#
```

Notice how the policy map named global_policy begins with a **class** command and then contains a long list of **inspect** commands. A policy map must always classify or identify traffic first and then take some action on it. The **class** command references a class map that does the actual traffic classification, while the **inspect** commands define each of the actions that must be taken on the matching traffic.

The individual commands shown in Example 9-2 are covered later in this chapter. For now, just notice that the ASA is classifying traffic on all of its interfaces and subjecting that traffic to a variety of robust inspection engines.

One more thing—what sort of traffic is being classified in the policy map? To find out, you need to look at the configuration of a class map called inspection_default. You can do that by using the **show running-config class-map inspection_default** command, as demonstrated in Example 9-3.

Example 9-3 *Displaying a Class Map Configuration*

```
ciscoasa# show running-config class-map inspection_default
!
class-map inspection_default
 match default-inspection-traffic
!
ciscoasa#
```

The class map contains a single **match** command that identifies the appropriate traffic. Although there are many **match** commands that can be used, the **match default-inspection-traffic** command identifies a default list of protocols and port numbers—traffic that would commonly be inspected in most networks. The entire set of match commands is covered in the "Configuring the MPF" section in this chapter.

The default MPF configuration shown in Examples 9-1 through 9-3 forms the simple hierarchy shown in Example 9-4. The service policy references a single policy map, which references a single class map. Keep in mind that you can leverage the MPF to create much more robust or complex policy configurations, where a list of policy maps can use multiple class maps and actions to treat many different traffic flows in unique ways.

Example 9-4 *Simple Hierarchy of the Default MPF Configuration*

```
service-policy pmap1
policy-map pmap1
              class cmap1
              action ...

 class-map cmap1
              match ...
```

Cisco Adaptive Security Device Manager (ASDM) displays the MPF in a much simpler fashion. To view the MPF configuration, navigate to **Configuration > Firewall > Service Policy Rules**. Figure 9-1 shows the default ASA MPF configuration. You can see evidence of a global policy (applied to all interfaces), a name inspection_default, a match any-any condition, a service called default-inspections, and a list of 15 inspection actions. However, you don't see the underlying concept of service policy, policy maps, and class maps.

You can also click the **Diagram** button at the top of the Service Policy Rules window to display a functional diagram of any highlighted MPF policy. In Figure 9-1, the diagram for the default policy is shown at the bottom of the window. A global policy is shown for the ASA, along with any-to-any traffic matching and default-inspection service.

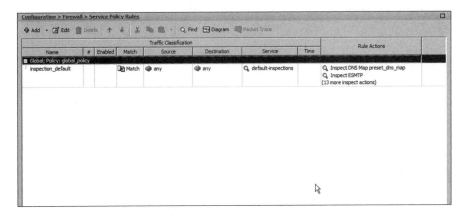

Figure 9-1 *Displaying the MPF Configuration in ASDM*

Note: The CLI and ASDM provide two different views of the same MPF configuration. The FIREWALL exam blueprint does not specify which user interface you might have to use to configure or verify MPF on the exam. Therefore, you should be sure to understand both perspectives.

Configuring the MPF

The default MPF configuration takes care of several common functions, but you have to add to the configuration to leverage the full potential. The MPF is a bit of a double-edged sword. On one hand, it is a very versatile means of defining robust security policies. On the other hand, it is so versatile that it can be confusing to configure.

As you begin to configure your security policies, you should outline the complete policy structure as a list of the individual policies. Be sure to show how the default global policy fits into the whole picture. To see what policies are already in place, you can display the running configuration or use the **show** commands that were presented in the previous section to find individual portions of the policies.

You can configure security policies by modifying an existing policy map or by creating a new one. Policy maps are applied to ASA interfaces by referencing them in service policies. Each interface can have only one service policy specifically applied to it; in addition, one global policy can be applied to all interfaces.

Exactly what can you configure in a policy map? Remember that a policy map consists of a series of actions that is taken on matched traffic. The following list describes the actions that an ASA can take on traffic it encounters:

- **Apply application inspection engines:** You can tailor the stateful inspection process that is performed on a specific type of traffic. Different sets of traffic can be inspected differently.

- **Set connection limits:** The ASA can control the volume of UDP and TCP connections that are initiated for matched traffic.

- **Adjust TCP parameters:** Values carried in the TCP header can be inspected, changed, or normalized to conform to configured limits in very specific ways. This can be done differently for each set of traffic identified.

- **Limit management traffic:** Connections that terminate on the ASA itself can be limited, just like other types of connections that pass through the ASA. Configuring limits on management traffic can help prevent unnecessary strain on the ASA's CPU.

- **Send traffic to a Security Services Module (SSM):** Specific traffic can be diverted to an embedded Advanced Inspection and Prevention (AIP) module or an embedded Content Security and Control (CSC) module.

- **Limit the bandwidth used:** You can tailor traffic policers to limit the bandwidth used by predefined sets of traffic. For example, mission-critical applications might be allowed to use any available bandwidth, whereas peer-to-peer file sharing applications are limited to a small portion of interface bandwidth.

- **Provide priority handling:** Specific types of traffic can be given priority over other types as packets are sent out an interface. This allows time-critical applications to receive premium service as those packets are inspected and passed through the ASA.

It might seem intuitive to start configuring the actions first. Keep in mind that each action in a policy map must be performed on traffic that has matched some condition. Therefore, you have to define the matching condition first, then the action. In a sense, you will have to work backwards, so planning the security policies ahead of time often makes the process less confusing.

As a rule, remember the following security policy building blocks and their functions:

- **Class map:** *Which* traffic will be matched?

- **Policy map:** *What* action will be taken on each class of traffic?

- **Service policy:** *Where* will the policy map be applied?

Figure 9-2 shows how the MPF building blocks all fit together and build upon each other to make up a single service policy.

While the MPF offers a general framework for creating security policies, you can construct policies for specific purposes—often based on the content of the traffic being inspected. You can configure security policies according to the following broad categories:

- **OSI Layers 3 and 4:** Match and take action based on information found in the Layer 3 and 4 headers, such as IP address, protocol, and port numbers

- **OSI Layers 5–7:** Match and take action on traffic flows, based on information found in the application layer content of packets

- **Management traffic:** Match and take action on traffic that terminates on the ASA itself, rather than passing through the ASA

Each of these categories is covered in subsequent sections.

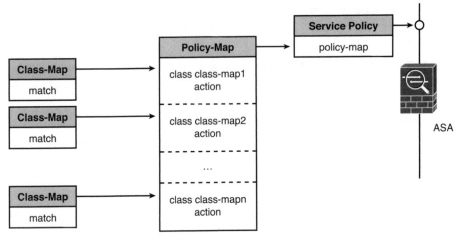

Match Conditions:
• Match Port Number
• Match Through an Access List
• Match Traffic Flow
• Match IP Precedence
• Match DSCP
• Match RTP Port Range
• Match VPN Tunnel Group

• Match Anything
• Match default-inspection-traffic

Actions:
• Inspect Traffic
• Set Connection Options
• Send to AIP or CSC SSM
• Police or Shape Traffic
• Send to Priority Queue
• Export NetFlow Data

Figure 9-2 *MPF Organization and Structure*

Configuring a Policy for Inspecting OSI Layers 3 and 4

With the MPF, you can configure a class map that identifies a specific type of traffic according to parameters found in OSI Layers 3 and 4, or the IP and UDP packet headers or TCP packet headers, respectively. You can apply that class map to a policy map that can take action on the matching traffic.

You can use the following steps to configure a security policy:

Step 1.   Define a Layers 3–4 class map.

Step 2.   Define a Layers 3–4 policy map.

Step 3.   Apply the policy map to the appropriate interfaces.

The sections that follow examine each step of configuring a security policy in more detail, beginning with the CLI and ending with ASDM. Be aware that the configuration order is somewhat different between the two methods.

Step 1: Define a Layers 3–4 Class Map

As traffic moves through an ASA, it can be identified or classified according to the matching conditions defined in a class map. You can configure multiple class maps to identify several different classes of traffic, if needed. Then a different policy can be applied to each traffic class.

First, identify the class map with the **class-map** command, as follows:

```
ciscoasa(config)# class-map class_map_name
ciscoasa(config-cmap)# description text
```

Give the class map an arbitrary name as *class_map_name*, and then use the **description** command to describe the purpose of the class map. If the class map does not already exist, a new one will be created.

Next, choose one of the following ways to match or classify the Layers 3–4 traffic:

- **All traffic:** All packets passing through an ASA interface

- **Default traffic:** Packets that belong to a predefined set of protocols and port numbers

- **Traffic flow:** Packets destined for a unique IP address, where the policy action will be applied on a per-flow basis

- **Destination port:** Packets being sent to a destination port number or range of port numbers

- **Access list:** Packets that are permitted by an access list, matched according to protocol, IP addresses, and port numbers

- **QoS values:** Packets that contain up to four matching IP precedence values or up to eight matching Differentiated Services Code Point (DSCP) values

- **RTP port range:** Real-time Transport Protocol (RTP) packets that fall within a range of UDP port numbers

- **VPN group:** Packets that pass through a specific VPN tunnel group name

Choose the corresponding **match** command from Table 9-2 and enter it as the matching condition. You can define only one matching condition in a class map. End the class map configuration by entering the **exit** command.

Table 9-2   *Match Commands Used in a Class Map*

Key Topic

Matching Condition	Command Syntax
Any traffic	ciscoasa(config-cmap)# **match any**
Default traffic types	ciscoasa(config-cmap)# **match default-inspection-traffic**
Traffic flow	ciscoasa(config-cmap)# **match flow ip destination-address**
Destination port number	ciscoasa(config-cmap)# **match port** {tcp | udp} {eq *port* | **range** *start end*}
Access list	ciscoasa(config-cmap)# **match access-list** *acl_name*
QoS: IP precedence	ciscoasa(config-cmap)# **match precedence** *value1* [*value2* [*value3* [*value4*]]]

Table 9-2   *Match Commands Used in a Class Map*

Matching Condition	Command Syntax
QoS: DSCP	ciscoasa(config-cmap)# **match dscp** *value1* [*value2* ...[*value8*]]
RTP port number range	ciscoasa(config-cmap)# **match rtp** *starting_port range*
VPN tunnel group name	ciscoasa(config-cmap)# **match tunnel-group** *name*

Note: The **match tunnel-group** command is one exception—it can accept one additional **match flow ip** command to match individual traffic flows within a VPN tunnel.

Example 9-5 shows the commands that can be used to configure three different class maps:

- A class map named anything that matches against any traffic

- A class map named voice that matches against RTP port numbers 2000 through 2100

- A class map named data-center that matches against destination addresses in the 10.100.0.0/16 subnet

Example 9-5   *Configuring Three Class Maps*

```
ciscoasa(config)# class-map anything
ciscoasa(config-cmap)# match any
ciscoasa(config-cmap)# exit
!
ciscoasa(config)# class-map voice
ciscoasa(config-cmap)# match rtp 2000 100
ciscoasa(config-cmap)# exit
!
ciscoasa(config)# access-list extended dc permit ip any 10.100.0.0 255.255.0.0
ciscoasa(config)# class-map data-center
ciscoasa(config-cmap)# match access-list dc
ciscoasa(config-cmap)# exit
```

Step 2: Define a Layers 3–4 Policy Map

Security policies are defined in a policy map as a sequence of match-action pairs. Each security policy references a class map to match traffic, followed by one or more actions to take on the matched traffic.

First, identify the policy map with the **policy-map** command, as follows:

```
ciscoasa(config)# policy-map policy_map_name
ciscoasa(config-pmap)# description text
```

Give the policy map an arbitrary name as *policy_map_name*, and then use the **description** command to describe the purpose of the policy map.

Next, use the **class** command to identify a class map that will be used to match or classify traffic, as follows:

```
ciscoasa(config-pmap)# class {class_map_name | class-default}
```

You can use the **class-default** keyword to use the default class map. This is a handy way to identify all the traffic that hasn't been classified in any other class map. The **class-default** class map is automatically configured by default, and contains only the **match any** command. Therefore, this class map should be the last one defined in a policy.

Next, choose an action to take on any traffic that is matched or classified by the class map. The following list summarizes the actions that are possible; each of them, except for NetFlow data export, is covered in a different section or chapter in this book, as noted.

- **Set connection limits:** Covered in the "Tuning Basic Layer 3–4 Connection Limits" section in this chapter

- **Adjust TCP options:** Covered in the "Inspecting TCP Parameters with the TCP Normalizer" section in this chapter

- **Inspect the traffic with an application inspection engine:** Covered in the "Configuring Dynamic Protocol Inspection" section in this chapter

- **Inspect the traffic with an intrusion prevention system (IPS) or Content Security and Control (CSC) module:** Covered in Chapter 15, "Integrating ASA Service Modules"

- **Police or shape the traffic to control the bandwidth used:** Covered in Chapter 11, "Handling Traffic"

- **Give the traffic priority handling through the ASA:** Covered in Chapter 11

- Export information about the traffic as NetFlow export data

Choose the corresponding command from Table 9-3 to enter into the policy map. Some of the commands in the table are abbreviated because of their complexity, but are covered in their entirety in other sections or chapters. You should be able to get a good idea of the possible actions and their command keywords here, without getting lost in more complex functions.

Table 9-3 *Actions to Take on Traffic Matched by a Class Map*

Action	Command Syntax
Set connection limits	ciscoasa(config-pmap-c)# **set connection ...**
Adjust TCP options	ciscoasa(config-pmap-c)# **set connection advanced-options ...**

Key Topic

Table 9-3 *Actions to Take on Traffic Matched by a Class Map*

Action	Command Syntax
Inspect applications	ciscoasa(config-pmap-c)# **inspect** *engine_name*
Send to IPS module	ciscoasa(config-pmap-c)# **ips** {**inline**	**promiscuous**} {**fail-open**	**fail-close**}
Send to CSC module	ciscoasa(config-pmap-c)# **csc** {**fail-open**	**fail-close**}
Police the traffic	ciscoasa(config-pmap-c)# **police** {**output**	**input**} *conform_rate* [*burst_bytes*] [**conform-action** {**drop**	**transmit**}] [**exceed-action** {**drop**	**transmit**}]
Shape the traffic	ciscoasa(config-pmap-c)# **shape** *bps* [*bpi*]
Apply priority handling	ciscoasa(config-pmap-c)# **priority**
Export NetFlow data	ciscoasa(config-pmap-c)# **flow-export** ...

You can enter more than one action for any given security policy in a policy map. In other words, after you enter the **class** command to reference a class map, you can enter any number of action commands to be performed on the matching traffic.

Note: Be aware that the actions might not be carried out in exactly the same order you enter them in the configuration. If multiple actions are found in a security policy, they are performed in the following order:

1. QoS policing of ingress traffic
2. Set connection limits and TCP options
3. Send traffic to the CSC module
4. Application inspection
5. Send traffic to the IPS module
6. QoS policing of egress traffic
7. QoS priority handling
8. QoS traffic shaping

Remember that you can add another security policy to a policy map by simply configuring another **class** command followed by one or more action commands. In this fashion, you can build up a whole list of match-action policies, each taking some specific action on a different type of traffic. As well, you can add new policies to an existing policy map as needed in the future.

As an example, a policy map named p1 is configured in Example 9-6. Three security poli-cies are configured within the policy map, each referencing a class map configured in Example 9-5. The three policies can be described as follows:

1. Match any traffic with class map anything, and then set some connection volume pa-rameters and subject the traffic to some application inspection engines.

2. Match RTP traffic with class map voice, and then flag the resulting traffic for priority handling.

3. Match traffic destined for the data center with class map data-center, and then set connection timeout parameters.

Example 9-6   *Configuring a Policy Map with Three Security Policies*

```
ciscoasa(config)# policy-map p1
ciscoasa(config-pmap)# class anything
ciscoasa(config-pmap-c)# set connection ...
ciscoasa(config-pmap-c)# inspect ...
ciscoasa(config-pmap-c)# class voice
ciscoasa(config-pmap-c)# priority
ciscoasa(config-pmap-c)# exit
ciscoasa(config-pmap)# class data-center
ciscoasa(config-pmap-c)# set connection timeout ...
ciscoasa(config-pmap)# exit
```

What happens if a certain type of traffic ends up matching multiple class maps within a policy map? For instance, packets that are destined for the data center will be matched by class map data-center in the third security policy in Example 9-6. However, that same traf-fic can also be matched by class map anything in the first security policy.

When multiple matches occur, the ASA will make sure that each type of action is per-formed only once. For the data center traffic scenario with Example 9-6, the ASA would perform the **set connection** and **inspect** actions found in the first security policy. The **set connection timeout** action in the third security policy would also be performed because it is unique and different from the **set connection** in the first policy. If the third policy also had a similar **set connection** or **inspect** action, then that action would be skipped.

Also keep in mind that the ASA will not duplicate actions taken on traffic that falls within the same traffic flow, as long as the traffic is either UDP, TCP, or ICMP, and is subject to stateful inspection. This becomes important when similar security policies are applied on multiple interfaces, where packets from the same traffic flow pass through two different interfaces: one on ingress and another on egress. If identical actions are configured on two interfaces, only the first action that is encountered is performed.

When you have entered the final security policy in the policy map, use the **exit** command to end the policy map configuration.

Step 3: Apply the Policy Map to the Appropriate Interfaces

The entire policy map is applied to one or all ASA interfaces, where the classifications and actions are carried out. Use the following command to define a service policy that binds a policy map to an interface:

```
ciscoasa(config)# service-policy policy_map_name {global | interface if_name}
```

You can use the **global** keyword to apply the policy map globally, to all ASA interfaces. The ASA supports only one global service policy. Remember that a global service policy is configured by default. Therefore, you cannot add a second global service policy; you can edit the existing one or you can remove it and add a different one in its place.

In Example 9-7, the policy map named p1, configured in Example 9-6, is applied as a service policy to the outside ASA interface.

Example 9-7 *Applying a Policy Map as a Service Policy*

```
ciscoasa(config)# service-policy p1 interface outside
```

The actions taken in a policy map (and the service policy that references it) can be limited to a specific traffic direction, depending on how the service policy is applied. Table 9-4 lists the traffic directions that are affected by each type of action. Notice that most actions can act on traffic in both the ingress and egress direction when the service policy is applied to a single interface, but only in the ingress direction if applied globally. Actions related to QoS functions (policing, shaping, and priority handling) are the exceptions, controlling traffic in only one direction—usually traffic leaving the ASA.

Table 9-4 *Traffic Directions Affected by Policy Map Actions*

Action	Applied to Interface	Applied Globally
Set connection limits	Bidirectional	Ingress only
Adjust TCP options	Bidirectional	Ingress only
Inspect with application engines	Bidirectional	Ingress only
Offload to IPS or CSC module	Bidirectional	Ingress only
Policing (input)	Ingress only	Ingress only
Policing (output)	Egress only	Egress only
Shaping	Egress only	Egress only
Priority handling	Egress only	Egress only

Creating a Security Policy in ASDM

Notice how the Layers 3–4 service policy configuration unfolds in three distinct steps using the CLI: class map, policy map, and then service policy. In contrast, ASDM integrates all three steps into one smooth process. The CLI functions are all present, but ASDM provides a layer of abstraction.

To create a new service policy, navigate to **Configuration > Firewall > Service Policy Rules**. Select the ASA interface where the service policy will be applied and enter a name for the policy map. In Figure 9-3, the service policy is applied to the outside interface and is associated with policy map p1, following the same scenario presented in Examples 9-5 through 9-7.

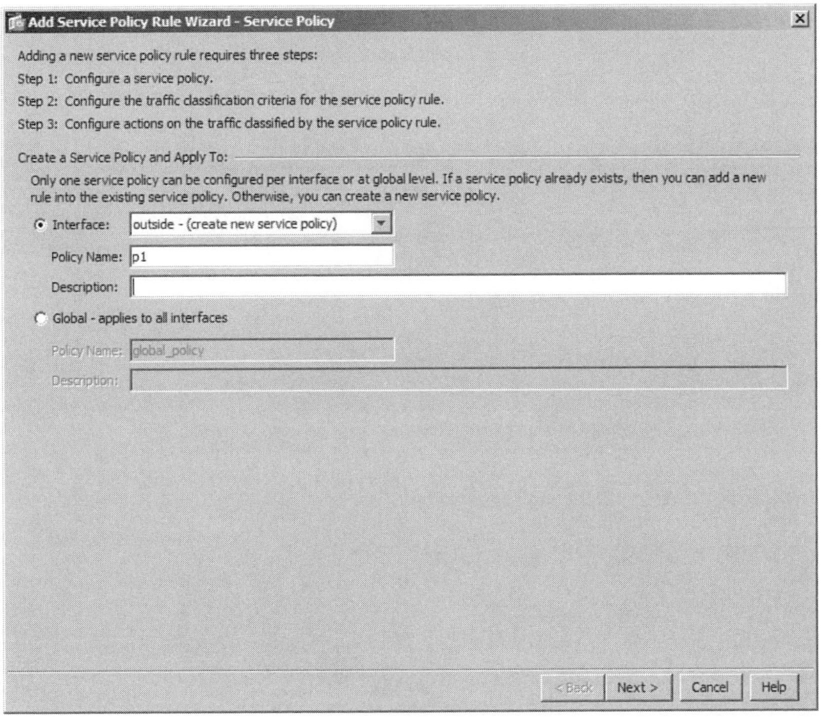

Figure 9-3   *Configuring a New Service Policy in ASDM*

Click the **Next** button to move on to define matching conditions. In Figure 9-4, the first security policy of Example 9-5 is defined—a new traffic class (class map) called anything is created. In the Traffic Match Criteria area, the Any Traffic check box is checked.

Click the **Next** button to define the actions that will be taken on the classified or matched traffic. ASDM organizes actions into Protocol Inspection, Connection Settings, QoS, and NetFlow tabs. In Figure 9-5, the first action configured is to set a TCP connection timeout limit of 30 minutes.

Because you can define multiple actions in a policy map, you can also click a different tab in the Rule Actions dialog box and identify further actions there. Following the scenario in Example 9-6, Figure 9-6 shows the Protocol Inspection tab with HTTP inspection checked to create a second action. After you define all the actions for the traffic class, click the **Finish** button.

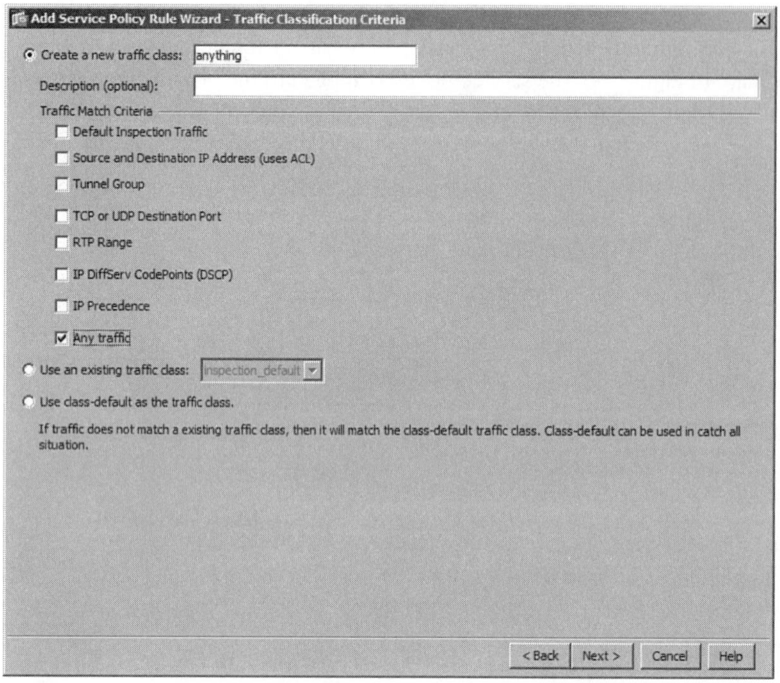

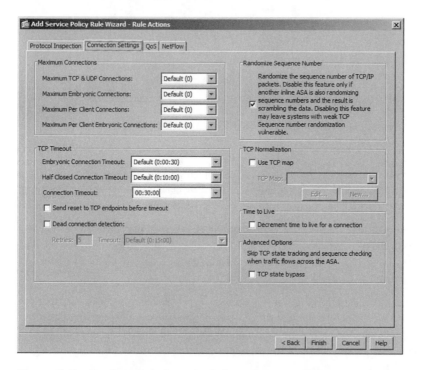

Figure 9-4 *Defining Traffic Classification Criteria in ASDM*

Figure 9-5 *Configuring a Security Policy Action in ASDM*

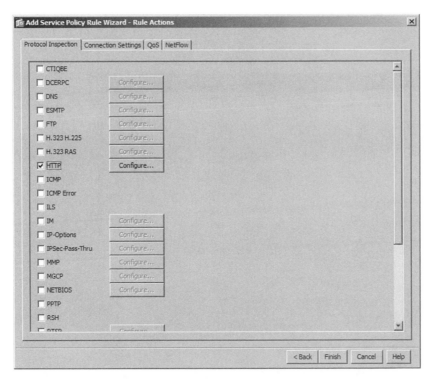

Figure 9-6 *Configuring a Second Rule Action in ASDM*

Once you finish configuring a service policy rule, ASDM will display it in a summary list of all service policy rules. Figure 9-7 shows the newly created rule named anything under the outside interface policy p1, along with the global policy named inspection_default. From this list, you can verify the interface, the rule name, the matching conditions (source and destination addresses and service port numbers), and a list of actions to be taken.

Notice that only the first security policy from Examples 9-5 through 9-7 has been configured in Figure 9-7. To configure the remaining two policies, click the **Add** button and repeat the service policy rule process. The interface and policy should be identical to the values used in the previous rule configuration. Figure 9-8 shows the final service policy rule configuration, complete with all three policies from the scenario.

Notice that the third service policy rule, which is selected in Figure 9-8, has a check box in the Enabled column. This is because the rule has been configured with an access list as a matching condition. The access list has been configured with a single entry, permitting traffic destined for the 10.100.0.0/16 subnet. Like any access list, it could be expanded to include other entries. ASDM shows each line of the access list with its own check box so that you can make each entry active (enabled) or inactive.

Finally, you can use ASDM to verify that a service policy rule is configured correctly. Begin by selecting a rule from the list. Then, above the rule list, select **Packet Trace** instead of Diagram. A Packet Tracer window will appear, as shown in Figure 9-9. ASDM will simulate traffic passing into an interface and through the service policy rule you have selected.

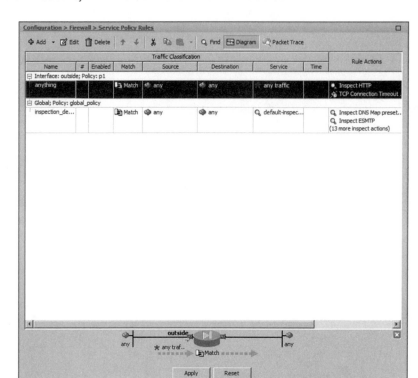

Figure 9-7 *Viewing a Summary of Service Policy Rules in ASDM*

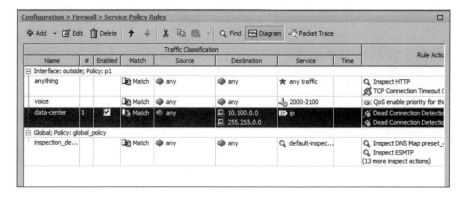

Figure 9-8 *Service Policy Rules*

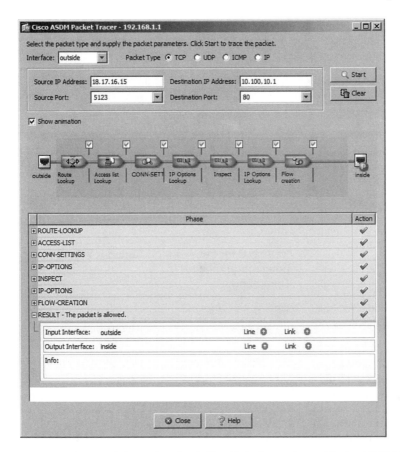

Figure 9-9   *Verifying a Service Policy Rule Operation with the ASDM Packet Tracer*

You can specify the protocol and source and destination addresses of the simulated packet. Once you are ready to begin the test, click the **Start** button.

ASDM will show what happens to the packet at every step of the ASA's inspection processes. In Figure 9-9, the test packet uses TCP port 80 and has a destination address of 10.100.10.1, which should trigger one of the security policy rules that have been configured. Packet Tracer shows the results of a route lookup, an access list lookup, connection settings, IP options lookup, an application inspection engine, another IP options lookup, and a flow creation process. These are all normal processes that could be encountered, although only some of them are actually configured in the service policy rule. A check mark beside each process indicates that the packet has successfully been handled.

Tuning Basic Layers 3–4 Connection Limits

As an ASA inspects traffic, it can also impose limits on the Layers 3–4 connections that form. The following two basic types of connection limits are available:

■ **Connection timeouts:** The duration of TCP connections in various states

■ **Connection volumes:** The number of simultaneous connections

You can configure both types of connection limits with the **set connection** command, as an action within a policy map. The subsequent keywords and options determine the specific connection limit that will be applied.

Connection time limits are set globally with the **timeout** configuration command. However, you can set TCP connection timeout limits that will be applied to only the connections that are matched within a policy map by using the following policy map action command:

```
ciscoasa(config-pmap-c)# set connection timeout [embryonic {hh:mm:ss | 0}]
  [half-closed {hh:mm:ss | 0}] [tcp {hh:mm:ss | 0} [dcd [retry_interval
  [max_retries]]
```

Table 9-5   *TCP Connection Timeout Limit Options*

Description	Keyword for set connection timeout Command	Timeout Values
Automatically close embryonic (not completely opened) connections after a timeout	**embryonic** {*hh:mm:ss* | **0**}	Default: 30 seconds Minimum: 5 seconds
Automatically close half-closed (partially closed, or incomplete FIN-FIN handshake) connections after a timeout	**half-closed** {*hh:mm:ss* | **0**}	Default: 10 minutes Minimum: 5 minutes
Automatically close TCP connections that have been idle after a timeout	**tcp** {*hh:mm:ss* | **0**}	Default: 1 hour Minimum: 5 minutes
Use dead connection detection (DCD) to probe for defunct idle connections	**dcd** [*retry_interval* [*max_retries*]]	retry_interval = 15 seconds max_retries = 5

Table 9-5 provides details of each type of connection timeout and its associated keyword. With most of the timeout keywords, you can give a specific amount of time as *hh:mm:ss* (24-hour format) or as **0** for an unlimited amount of time.

With the **tcp** keyword, the firewall will identify any TCP connection that has been idle for longer than the timeout value, and will automatically close it. Although this is a handy housekeeping function, it will close any TCP connection that has been idle more than a fixed amount of time.

Some TCP connections can remain idle for an extended period of time, but still be valid. For example, suppose the TCP idle timeout is set to 5 minutes. A Telnet session through the firewall to a host could very easily stay idle for more than 5 minutes, while the user answered a telephone call or got up to do something else. Closing idle, but valid, connections would become a nuisance to the end users.

Instead, you can use the **tcp** and **dcd** keywords together to add some intelligence into the whole TCP connection timeout process. Once a TCP connection has been idle for the **tcp** timeout duration, the ASA will begin to actively send probes to the client and server to see whether they are still responsive. The probes are used to stimulate the hosts to answer; if they both answer, the connection must still be valid and should not be closed for being idle.

DCD probes are sent at *retry_interval* seconds. If no response is received, the probes are resent for *max_retries* times. If there still is no response at that point, the connection is presumed to be idle and is automatically closed.

Note: A DCD probe is just a minimum size packet with the ACK bit set, using the same IP addresses and TCP ports that the actual TCP connection uses. In this way, the client and server each think it is simply answering a TCP ACK sent by its peer. No data changes hands, other than basic acknowledgments.

By default, an ASA will allow an unlimited number of simultaneous UDP and TCP connections to be built to and from specific hosts. Because hosts cannot support an unlimited number of connections without exhausting their resources, you can use the following forms of the **set connection** policy map configuration command as an action to limit the volume or number of connections that can be built:

```
ciscoasa(config-pmap-c)# set connection [conn-max n] [embryonic-conn-max n]
  [per-client-embryonic-max n] [per-client-max n]
```

The connection volume limits configured in a policy map with **set connection** are very similar to the limits set in address translation commands such as **static** and **nat**. If connection limits are configured with both methods, and a traffic flow applies to both conditions, the lower connection limit will be enforced.

Table 9-6 shows each type of connection volume limit and its associated keyword.

With the **conn-max** and **per-client-max** options, when the maximum number of connections is reached, the ASA will begin dropping any new connections.

Table 9-6 *Connection Volume Limit Options*

Description	Keyword for set connection Command	Values
Limit the total simultaneous connections (UDP and TCP) in use by all traffic matching the policy	conn-max *n*	Default: 0 (unlimited) Maximum: 65535
Limit the total number of simultaneous connections in use on a per-client or host basis	per-client-max *n*	Default: 0 (unlimited) Maximum: 65535
Limit the total number of TCP embryonic connections opened for all traffic matching the policy	embryonic-conn-max *n*	Default: 0 (unlimited) Maximum: 65535
Limit the total number of TCP embryonic connections opened on a per-client or host basis	per-client-embryonic-max *n*	Default: 0 (unlimited) Maximum: 65535

The **embryonic-conn-max** and **per-client-embryonic-max** options limit TCP connections that are only partially open. This can happen when a host initiates a TCP connection with a SYN handshake, but is waiting on the rest of the three-way handshake (SYN-ACK and ACK) to be completed. Sometimes, this happens under normal conditions, but it can be exploited as a SYN attack, where an attacking host initiates multiple TCP connections toward a target host, but uses spoofed source addresses. The target host will try to respond to the spoofed source addresses with the next stage of handshaking, but the TCP connections will never open properly. As a result, the target host can become overwhelmed with embryonic connections that exhaust its resources.

The ASA can help alleviate this attack. As soon as one of the embryonic connection limits is reached, the ASA will begin intercepting new TCP connections and acting as a proxy for the target host. This is known as the *TCP Intercept* feature. The ASA will respond to the initial SYN on the target host's behalf, but will return a "SYN cookie" as the TCP sequence number. The cookie is a hash that is computed from the TCP and IP header information and a secret password known only to the ASA. If the TCP connection is legitimate and a source host actually answers with the final handshake, the ASA can recognize the incremented sequence number. Otherwise, the ASA can freely ignore any further attempts to initiate more connections without impacting the target host.

An ASA can also apply the following two connection controls that are not related to connection volume or limits:

- TTL decrementing

- Randomize initial sequence number

IP packets carry a time-to-live (TTL) field that serves as a counter for the number of router hops that have been traversed. Normally, the TTL value begins with a high number and is decremented by each router along the network path. An ASA, however, does not by default decrement the TTL value of packets it handles. Because the TTL value remains unchanged, hosts in the network are not able to see an ASA as a router hop in traceroute packets. In effect, this keeps the ASA somewhat invisible.

You can configure the ASA to "uncloak" itself and decrement the TTL value for specific types of traffic. First, match the traffic with a class map, and then enter the following command as an action in a policy map:

```
ciscoasa(config-pmap-c)# set connection decrement-ttl
```

When a new TCP connection is negotiated between two hosts, an initial sequence number (ISN) is used as a starting point for TCP connection sequence numbers. Ideally, the ISN should be a random number so that it can never be predicted and leveraged in TCP spoofing attacks. In practice, the ISN can sometimes be predicted based on the behavior of certain host TCP stacks, giving malicious users a foothold to hijack the connection.

By default, an ASA will compute a random ISN for each new TCP connection that is negotiated through it. Random ISN generation occurs only for connections that are initiated by hosts located on the more secure interface of the ASA. Because the ASA sits in the middle of the two negotiating hosts, it can intercept the proposed ISN and substitute its own random number.

Sometimes, you might not want an ASA to change the ISNs of certain TCP connections. For example, if a protocol or application computes an authentication or hash code based on TCP packets as they leave a host, altering the ISN along the way will cause the packet authentication to fail at the destination host. You can disable random ISN generation on an ASA by entering the following command as an action in a policy map:

```
ciscoasa(config-pmap-c)# set connection random-sequence-number {enable | disable}
```

You can also configure connection limits in ASDM. First, either create a new service policy rule or edit an existing one. Define a matching condition, and then click the **Connection Settings** tab in the Rule Actions dialog box, as shown in Figure 9-10. The TCP connection timeouts are presented in the lower-left quadrant of the dialog box, while the connection volume limits are located in the upper-left quadrant. You can also enable the TCP random sequence number function by checking the box in the upper-right area of the dialog box.

Inspecting TCP Parameters with the TCP Normalizer

An ASA can inspect individual packets containing TCP segments to make sure that they conform to the TCP protocol specification. Any packets that do not are "normalized" or changed so that they do conform. You can leverage the TCP normalizer feature to prevent malformed packets or packets that are crafted to evade stateful inspection from reaching protected hosts.

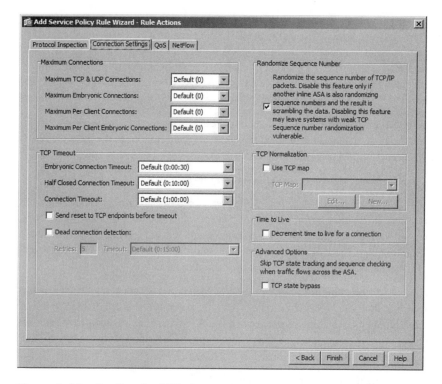

Figure 9-10 *Configuring TCP Connection Timeout Limits in ASDM*

The TCP normalizer has many TCP parameters that you can configure, each defined in a TCP map. You can invoke the TCP normalizer through the MPF by matching traffic with a class map and then referencing the TCP map in a **set connection advanced-options** *tcp-map* command within a policy map.

To configure the TCP normalizer, begin by defining a TCP map with the following command:

```
ciscoasa(config)# tcp-map tcp-map-name
```

The TCP map will act as a template for modifying various options in the TCP header of matched packets. You can enter one or more of the TCP normalizer actions listed in Table 9-7 as part of the TCP map configuration.

Table 9-7 *TCP Normalizer Actions*

Action	Command Syntax
Verify that TCP retransmissions are consistent with the originals. Packets must arrive in sequential order. (Default: Disabled)	ciscoasa(config-tcp-map)# **check-retransmission**

Table 9-7 *TCP Normalizer Actions*

Action	Command Syntax
Verify TCP checksum; drop the packet if it fails. (Default: Disabled)	ciscoasa(config-tcp-map)# **checksum-verification**
Check the maximum segment size (MSS); take action if it exceeds the value set when the TCP connection began. (Default: Drop the packet.)	ciscoasa(config-tcp-map)# **exceed-mss** {**allow** | **drop**}
Check for packets that have an invalid ACK flag, and then take action. (Default: Drop the packet.)	ciscoasa(config-tcp-map)# **invalid-ack** {**allow** | **drop**}
Check the reserved bits in the TCP header, which should always be cleared to 0. If not, take action. (Default: Allow the packet as is.)	ciscoasa(config-tcp-map)# **reserved-bits** {**allow** | **clear** | **drop**}
Keep *number* of out-of-order packets in a queue for inspection. Drop them after *seconds* time has elapsed. (Default: 0 packets in queue.)	ciscoasa(config-tcp-map)# **queue-limit** *number* [**timeout** *seconds*]
Check for TCP sequence numbers that fall outside the window, and then take action. (Default: Allow the packet.)	ciscoasa(config-tcp-map)# **seq-past-window** {**allow** | **drop**}
Check to see whether SYN packets contain payload data; if so, take action. (Default: Allow the packet.)	ciscoasa(config-tcp-map)# **syn-data** {**allow** | **drop**}
Check to see whether SYN-ACK packets contain payload data; if so, take action. (Default: Allow the packet.)	ciscoasa(config-tcp-map)# **synack-data** {**allow** | **drop**}
Check for packets that masquerade as retransmissions of prior packets that passed inspection but were dropped because of TTL expiration, and then take action. (Default: Enabled.)	ciscoasa(config-tcp-map)# **ttl-evasion-protection**
Check the contents of the TCP URG (urgent) flag and pointer, and then take action. (Default: Clear the URG field.)	ciscoasa(config-tcp-map)# **urgent-flag** {**allow** | **clear**}
Check for packets that advertise a TCP window size that is greatly different for no apparent reason, and then take action. (Default: Drop the packet.)	ciscoasa(config-tcp-map)# **window-variation** {**allow-connection** | **drop-connection**}

The TCP normalizer can also inspect the contents of the TCP options field to make sure that they conform to limits you set in the TCP map. You can enter one or more of the commands listed in Table 9-8.

Table 9-8   *TCP Normalizer Actions on the TCP Options Field*

Action	Command Syntax
Check to see whether the Selective ACK (SACK, TCP option 4) is set, and then take action. (Default: Allow the packet.)	ciscoasa(config-tcp-map)# **tcp-options selective-ack** {**allow** | **clear**}
Check to see whether the time stamp (TCP option 8) is used, and then take action. (Default: Allow the packet.)	ciscoasa(config-tcp-map)# **tcp-options timestamp** {**allow** | **clear**}
Check to see whether the window scale (TCP option 3) flag is set to expand the TCP window field from 16 to 32 bits, and then take action. (Default: Allow the packet.)	ciscoasa(config-tcp-map)# **tcp-options window-scale** {**allow** | **clear**}
Check to see whether the TCP option numbers are within the specified range; if so, take action. (Default: Clear all TCP option numbers except 2, 3, 4, 5, and 8.)	ciscoasa(config-tcp-map)# **tcp-options range** *lower upper* {**allow** | **clear** | **drop**}

With so many TCP parameters to inspect and so many different **tcp-map** commands available, should you memorize them all for the exam? Probably not, but you should at least become familiar with the basic functions that are at your disposal.

Along the same lines, you might experiment with a command or its settings and then forget what the default configuration is. You can return any of the TCP normalizer commands to the default by entering the **default** keyword followed by the normalizer command keyword. For example, if you entered the **reserved-bits clear** command, but you can't remember if the default should be **allow**, **clear**, or **drop**, simply enter **default reserved-bits** instead.

Once you configure a TCP map, you can configure the TCP normalizer by defining a service policy using the MPF. Be sure to match the traffic that will be normalized by defining a class map. Reference the class map in a policy map, and then define the policy action with the following command:

```
ciscoasa(config-pmap-c)# set connection advanced-options tcp-map-name
```

Use Example 9-8 as a guideline for your MPF configuration.

Example 9-8   *MPF Structure for the TCP Normalizer*

```
ciscoasa(config)# class-map class_map_name
ciscoasa(config-cmap)# match condition
ciscoasa(config-cmap)# exit

ciscoasa(config)# policy-map policy_map_name
ciscoasa(config-pmap)# class class_map_name
```

```
ciscoasa(config-pmap-c)# set connection advanced-options tcp-map
ciscoasa(config-pmap-c)# exit
ciscoasa(config-pmap)# exit

ciscoasa(config)# service-policy policy_map_name interface interface
```

As a sample exercise, suppose you need to configure an ASA to support a protocol that uses a specific TCP options value. A common scenario is with authenticated BGP connections, where two routers use TCP option 19 to negotiate an MD5 hash value exchange in order to peer. If the TCP option field is cleared, the BGP authentication will never take place.

Example 9-9 lists the configuration commands that can be used to allow TCP option 19 between peers 192.168.10.10 and 192.168.20.20. The TCP map TCP-BGP allows option 19 to remain intact. Access list ACL-BGP matches against BGP packets (TCP port 179) between the routers, in both directions. Class map BGP references the access list to match the BGP traffic. Policy map MyPolicy references the class map to match the traffic and leverages the TCP normalizer through the TCP map.

Example 9-9   *Commands Used to Configure the TCP Normalizer*

```
ciscoasa(config)# tcp-map TCP-BGP
ciscoasa(config-tcp-map)# tcp-options range 19 19 allow
ciscoasa(config-tcp-map)# exit
!
ciscoasa(config)# access-list ACL-BGP permit tcp host 192.168.10.10 host
  192.168.20.20 eq 179
ciscoasa(config)# access-list ACL-BGP permit tcp host 192.168.20.20 host
  192.168.10.10 eq 179
!
ciscoasa(config)# class-map BGP
ciscoasa(config-cmap)# match access-list ACL-BGP
ciscoasa(config-cmap)# exit
!
ciscoasa(config)# policy-map MyPolicy
ciscoasa(config-pmap)# class BGP
ciscoasa(config-pmap-c)# set connection advanced-options TCP-BGP
ciscoasa(config-pmap-c)# exit
ciscoasa(config-pmap)# exit
ciscoasa(config)# service-policy MyPolicy interface outside
```

By default, an ASA will inspect TCP packets and apply the default TCP normalizer actions to it. In some rare cases, you might need to exempt some TCP traffic from the stateful inspection and modification. For example, a traffic flow might be routed asymmetrically, where packets in one direction flow through an ASA, but packets in the other direction do not. In that case, the ASA will not be able to maintain its stateful inspection because it cannot see all of the TCP traffic that is occurring in both directions.

You can allow some traffic to bypass the TCP normalizer by matching it with a class map and entering the following command as an action in the policy map:

```
ciscoasa(config-pmap-c)# set connection advanced-options tcp-state-bypass
```

Be aware that this command also exempts the traffic from other important inspection processes—not just the TCP normalizer. You should configure TCP state bypass only when absolutely necessary.

You can also use ASDM to configure the TCP normalizer. First, either create a new service policy rule or edit an existing one. Specify the ASA interface where the service policy will be applied, and then define the traffic matching condition. For the rule action, click the **Connection Settings** tab. In the TCP Normalization area, check the **Use TCP Map** check box. To create a new TCP map, click the **New** button. All of the default values will be shown in the Add TCP Map dialog box; edit any values and click **OK**. Figure 9-11 shows how the scenario from Example 9-9 can be configured.

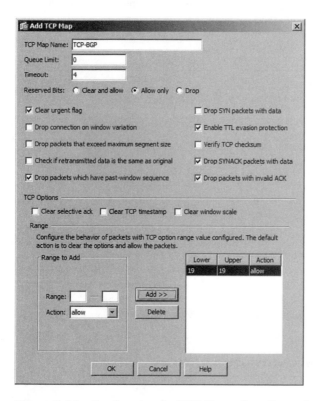

Figure 9-11 *Configuring the TCP Normalizer Scenario of Example 9-6 in ASDM*

After you configure the TCP map, it will be referenced in the TCP Normalizer area of the Connection Settings tab in the Rule Actions dialog box, as shown in Figure 9-12.

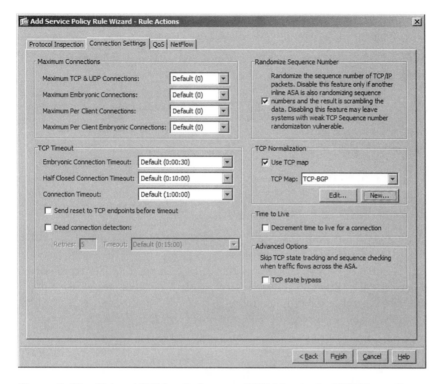

Figure 9-12   *Using ASDM to Reference a TCP Map in the TCP Normalizer*

Configuring ICMP Inspection

Internet Control Message Protocol (ICMP) is used in a variety of ways to test and exchange network parameters between devices. For example, the ping "application" can be used to send echo requests from one host to another; the target host is expected to return echo replies. This tests the hosts' livelihood and the network's connectivity.

By default, ICMP traffic is denied passage from a lower-security ASA interface to one with a higher security level. To permit ICMP traffic, you could add a **permit icmp any any** access list rule that is applied to the outside interface. Such a broad rule might also permit open access for misuse of ICMP and abuse of protected hosts.

A better solution is to enable the ICMP inspector. ICMP is not a stateful protocol at all, but the ASA can infer enough information to make it seem stateful. The ICMP inspector can selectively (and automatically) open a "connection" to permit return traffic based on the original outbound requests. It will permit only one response to return for every request that is sent out. The ICMP sequence numbers must also match between a request and a reply packet. With "stateful" ICMP inspection, the ICMP connections and xlate entries can be quickly torn down as soon as the appropriate reply is received.

You can enable ICMP inspection as an action within a policy map by using the **inspect icmp** command. By default, the ICMP inspector does not permit any ICMP error packets to return. This is because an ICMP error message can be sent from an address other than the original ICMP target. In the CLI, you can use the **inspect icmp error** command to enable ICMP error processing as part of ICMP inspection.

Example 9-10 shows how ICMP and ICMP error inspection can be enabled globally, within the global_policy policy map.

Example 9-10   *Enabling ICMP and ICMP Error Inspection Globally*

```
ciscoasa(config)# policy-map global_policy
ciscoasa(config-pmap)# class inspection_default
ciscoasa(config-pmap-c)# inspect icmp
ciscoasa(config-pmap-c)# inspect icmp error
ciscoasa(config-pmap-c)# exit
ciscoasa(config-pmap)# exit
ciscoasa(config)#
```

You can also control ICMP inspection from within ASDM. Navigate to **Configuration > Firewall > Service Policy Rules,** then select a service policy to edit or create. Select the **Rule Actions** tab, then select the **Protocol Inspection** tab, where you can use the ICMP and ICMP Error checkboxes as shown in Figure 9-13.

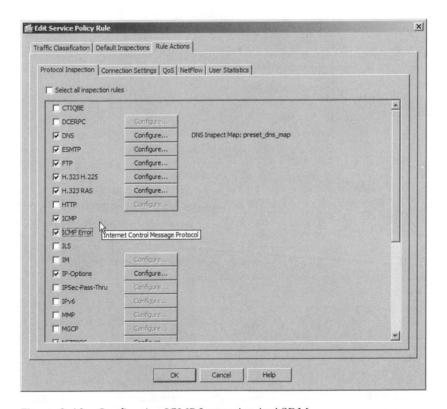

Figure 9-13   *Configuring ICMP Inspection in ASDM*

Configuring Dynamic Protocol Inspection

An ASA inherently inspects UDP and TCP packets to make sure that some form of connection state is followed. These two types of protocol inspection are enabled by default and cannot be disabled.

With UDP, sessions are not negotiated between two hosts. As such, packets might not necessarily be sent in both directions in a predictable fashion. Therefore, the ASA keeps track of the sessions in its connection table by monitoring the source and destination UDP port numbers. UDP "connections" simply age out after they become idle for a fixed amount of time (default 2 minutes). DNS "connections" are not subject to this timeout, as they are handled by a separate inspection engine.

In contrast, TCP is connection-based, so the ASA can follow the source and destination port numbers, as well as other information in the TCP packet headers, to inspect for proper TCP connection use. The TCP normalizer adds additional control over the TCP header information.

Many protocols and applications don't simply stick with a consistent source and destination port number throughout the lifetime of their TCP connections. Instead, the initial connection serves as a control session by which additional sessions are set up. The additional sessions use different port numbers that are negotiated dynamically.

To effectively inspect the entire session between two hosts, the ASA must inspect the original control connection and understand the underlying protocol so that it can learn when new connections are being negotiated and then inspect them in turn. This process moves beyond simple UDP or TCP header inspection, to look further into the UDP or TCP packet payloads to understand their contents. This is commonly called *deep packet inspection (DPI)*, and is implemented with individual *dynamic protocol inspectors* or *inspection engines*.

Protocol inspectors are enabled and configured within a policy map or an ASDM service policy rule configuration. As with any MPF definition, traffic must first be matched or classified and then have some action applied to it. To apply a protocol inspector as the policy action, you can use the **inspect** command. Example 9-11 shows the basic MPF structure that you can follow. Notice that the **inspect** command is followed by the name of a specific protocol inspector.

Example 9-11 *MPF Structure for Protocol Inspection*

```
ciscoasa(config)# class-map class_map_name
ciscoasa(config-cmap)# match condition
ciscoasa(config-cmap)# exit

ciscoasa(config)# policy-map policy_map_name
ciscoasa(config-pmap)# class class_map_name
ciscoasa(config-pmap-c)# inspect inspect_name [options]

ciscoasa(config-pmap-c)# exit
```

```
ciscoasa(config-pmap)# exit

ciscoasa(config)# service-policy policy_map_name interface interface
```

The ASA platform offers 26 unique dynamic protocol inspectors. Of those, 15 of them are enabled by default and applied to all traffic passing through the device. This is done in a policy map called global_policy, which is applied in a global service policy to all ASA interfaces. First, the class map inspection_default is used to match against all traffic on the default well-known port numbers, and then the various inspectors are invoked using the **inspect** commands. Statistics from this default configuration can be displayed with the **show service-policy** command, as shown in Example 9-12.

Example 9-12 *Displaying the Activity of the Default Dynamic Protocol Inspectors*

```
ciscoasa# show service-policy
Global policy:
  Service-policy: global_policy
    Class-map: inspection_default
      Inspect: dns preset_dns_map, packet 0, drop 0, reset-drop 0
      Inspect: ftp, packet 0, drop 0, reset-drop 0
      Inspect: h323 h225 _default_h323_map, packet 0, drop 0, reset-drop 0
              tcp-proxy: bytes in buffer 0, bytes dropped 0
      Inspect: h323 ras _default_h323_map, packet 0, drop 0, reset-drop 0
      Inspect: rsh, packet 0, drop 0, reset-drop 0
      Inspect: rtsp, packet 0, drop 0, reset-drop 0
              tcp-proxy: bytes in buffer 0, bytes dropped 0
      Inspect: esmtp _default_esmtp_map, packet 0, drop 0, reset-drop 0
      Inspect: sqlnet, packet 0, drop 0, reset-drop 0
      Inspect: skinny , packet 0, drop 0, reset-drop 0
              tcp-proxy: bytes in buffer 0, bytes dropped 0
      Inspect: sunrpc, packet 0, drop 0, reset-drop 0
              tcp-proxy: bytes in buffer 0, bytes dropped 0
      Inspect: xdmcp, packet 0, drop 0, reset-drop 0
      Inspect: sip , packet 0, drop 0, reset-drop 0
              tcp-proxy: bytes in buffer 0, bytes dropped 0
      Inspect: netbios, packet 0, drop 0, reset-drop 0
      Inspect: tftp, packet 0, drop 0, reset-drop 0
      Inspect: ip-options _default_ip_options_map, packet 0, drop 0, reset-drop 0
```

To see the concise configuration commands, however, you need to focus on the global_policy policy map. You can use the **show running-config policy-map global_policy** command, as shown in Example 9-13.

Example 9-13 *Displaying the Default Dynamic Protocol Inspector Configuration*

```
ciscoasa# show running-config policy-map global_policy
!
policy-map global_policy
 class inspection_default
  inspect dns preset_dns_map
  inspect ftp
  inspect h323 h225
  inspect h323 ras
  inspect rshD
  inspect rtsp
  inspect esmtp
  inspect sqlnet
  inspect skinny
  inspect sunrpc
  inspect xdmcp
  inspect sip
  inspect netbios
  inspect tftp
  inspect ip-options
!
ciscoasa#
```

You can configure a dynamic protocol inspector by using one of the commands listed in Table 9-9. The inspectors that are enabled by default are shown in shaded text. Notice how some inspector commands end with an option that references a special type of policy map, while others do not. In general, the commands without the *policy-map* option are dynamic protocol inspectors. Most of the commands with a policy map are application layer inspectors and are described in subsequent sections in this chapter.

Table 9-9 *Dynamic Protocol Inspectors and Command Syntax*

Protocol Name	Command Syntax	Default Protocol and Port
CTIQBE	inspect ctiqbe	TCP 2748
DCERPC	inspect dcerpc [*dcerpc-policy-map*]	
DNS	inspect dns [*dns-policy-map*] [dynamic-filter-snoop]	UDP 53
ESMTP	inspect esmtp [*esmtp-policy-map*]	TCP 25
FTP	inspect ftp [strict] [*ftp-policy-map*]	TCP 21
H323	inspect h323h225 [*h323-policy-map*]	TCP 1720
	inspect h323ras [*h323-policy-map*]	TCP 1718–1719
HTTP	inspect http [*http-policy-map*]	TCP 80

Table 9-9   *Dynamic Protocol Inspectors and Command Syntax*

Protocol Name	Command Syntax	Default Protocol and Port
ICMP	inspect icmp [error]	ICMP
ILS	inspect ils	TCP 389
IM	inspect im *im-policy-map*	
IP Options	inspect ip-options [*ip-options-policy-map*]	RSVP
IPsec passthru	inspect ipsec-pass-thru [*ipsec-policy-map*]	
MGCP	inspect mgcp [*mgcp-policy-map*]	UDP 2427–2727
MMP	inspect mmp [tls-proxy *proxy-name*]	
NetBIOS	inspect netbios [*netbios-policy-map*]	UDP 137–138
PPTP	inspect pptp	
RSH	inspect rsh	TCP 514
RTSP	inspect rtsp [*rtsp-policy-map*]	TCP 554
SIP	inspect sip [*sip-policy map*] [{phone-proxy	tls-proxy} *proxy-name*]	TCP 5060
Skinny	inspect skinny [*skinny-policy-map*][{phone-proxy	tls-proxy} *proxy-name*]	TCP 2000
SNMP	inspect snmp [*snmp-policy-map*]	
SQLnet	inspect sqlnet	TCP 1521
SunRPC	inspect sunrpc	
TFTP	inspect tftp	UDP 69
WAAS	inspect waas	TCP 1–65535
XDMCP	inspect xdmcp	UDP 177

You can configure an inspector as part of your own policy map, to inspect only certain matched traffic on a specific interface. To do that, configure a policy map, reference a class map, and then enter the appropriate **inspect** command as the policy action. In Example 9-14, the HTTP inspector has been configured as an action to inspect only the traffic destined for the 172.16.1.0/24 subnet on TCP port 80. A custom class map called CMAP_HTTP matches the traffic, while the policy map called MYPOLICY applies the HTTP inspector to the traffic.

Example 9-14 *Configuring HTTP Inspection for Specific Traffic on an Interface*

```
ciscoasa(config)# access-list MYHTTP extended permit tcp any 172.16.1.0
  255.255.255.0 eq www
ciscoasa(config)# class-map CMAP_HTTP
ciscoasa(config-cmap)# match access-list MYHTTP
ciscoasa(config-cmap)# exit
ciscoasa(config)# policy-map MYPOLICY
ciscoasa(config-pmap)# class CMAP_HTTP
ciscoasa(config-pmap-c)# inspect http
ciscoasa(config-pmap-c)# exit
ciscoasa(config-pmap)# exit
ciscoasa(config)# service-policy MYPOLICY interface outside
```

A more common scenario is to configure an inspector as part of the global policy to inspect all traffic passing through the ASA on any interface. To do this, you can simply make changes to the global_policy policy map that is configured by default. As an example, the commands listed in Example 9-15 can be used to enable HTTP inspection on a global basis. The **class inspection_default** command is also configured by default, but you will have to enter it again as the matching condition before you can configure an inspector as a policy action.

Example 9-15 *Configuring Global HTTP Inspection*

```
ciscoasa(config)# policy-map global_policy
ciscoasa(config-pmap)# class inspection_default
ciscoasa(config-pmap-c)# inspect http
```

You can also use ASDM to configure dynamic protocol inspectors. Navigate to **Configuration > Firewall > Service Policy Rules**. To configure the scenario presented in Example 9-15, select the global policy and inspection_default, and then click **Edit**. Next, click the **Rule Actions** tab and then the **Protocol Inspection** tab. Check the **HTTP** check box, as shown in Figure 9-14, and then click the **OK** button.

Notice that Table 9-9 lists a default protocol and port number for each dynamic protocol inspector. The ASA will use that protocol and port to eavesdrop on control sessions. If your environment uses an application that is configured for a nondefault or nonstandard port number, you can define additional command session ports for the ASA to use.

First, define a class map that will be used to match traffic on the new, nonstandard port number. In the class map, use the **match port** command along with the protocol and port number. Next, configure the policy map and reference your new class map, followed by the appropriate **inspect** command.

Key Topic

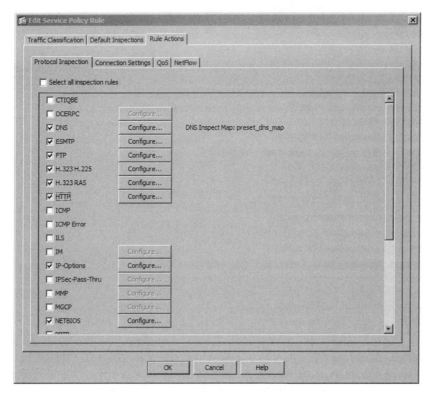

Figure 9-14 *Using ASDM to Configure Example 9-11*

Suppose you need to configure HTTP inspection for servers that use TCP port 8080. Example 9-16 lists the commands you can use. Class map CMAP_NEW_HTTP is configured to match against TCP port 8080. In the global policy map global_policy, the class map is referenced just prior to the **inspect http** command.

Now suppose the commands in Example 9-16 are entered after those in Example 9-15. Which HTTP inspector will be active? Actually, both of them will be active within the global_policy policy map. One instance of the **inspect http** command follows the inspection_default class map, which uses the default TCP port 80. The other instance follows the CMAP_NEW_HTTP class map, which matches TCP port 8080.

Example 9-16 *Configuring HTTP Inspection on a Nonstandard Port*

```
ciscoasa(config)# class-map CMAP_NEW_HTTP
ciscoasa(config-cmap)# match port tcp eq 8080
ciscoasa(config-cmap)# exit
ciscoasa(config)# policy-map global_policy
ciscoasa(config-pmap)# class CMAP_NEW_HTTP
ciscoasa(config-pmap-c)# inspect http
ciscoasa(config-pmap-c)# exit
```

You can also use ASDM to accomplish the same results. As an example, suppose you want to configure the scenario from Example 9-16. Navigate to **Configuration > Firewall > Service Policy Rules**. Select the policy line that shows Global; Policy; global_policy, and then click **Add** to add a new policy rule into the global default policy.

In the first Add Service Policy Rule Wizard window, make sure to click the **Global - Applies to All Interfaces** radio button, as shown in Figure 9-15. Click **Next**.

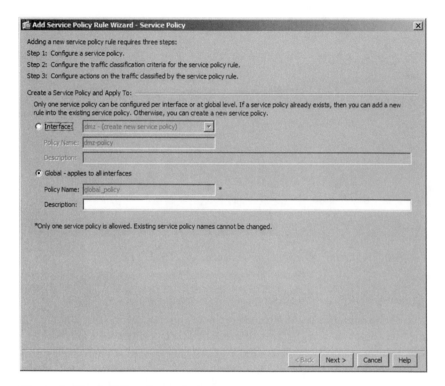

Figure 9-15   *Building Example 9-12 in ASDM*

Next, select **Create a New Traffic Class** that will match against the nonstandard HTTP traffic, and then give the class a name. In Figure 9-16, the new class is called CMAP_NEW_HTTP. Choose **TCP or UDP Destination Port** as the match criteria. Click the **Next** button.

Next, specify the protocol and destination port where the ASA should expect to find the control sessions for the nonstandard protocol. In Figure 9-17, TCP port 8080 is entered. Click the **Next** button.

Finally, choose the dynamic protocol inspector that will be used for traffic that uses the nonstandard port. In Figure 9-18, only the HTTP inspector is chosen. Click the **Finish** button to complete the service policy configuration.

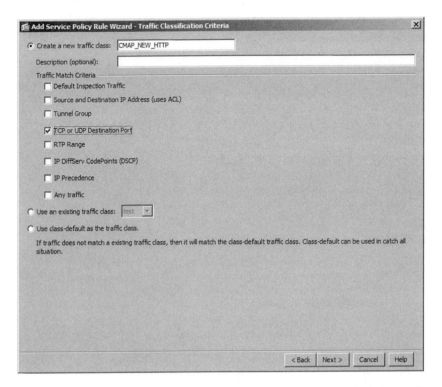

Figure 9-16   *Defining a Matching Criteria for the Nonstandard HTTP Traffic*

Configuring Custom Protocol Inspection

Suppose you need to configure an ASA to support a dynamic application that is not included in the list of stock dynamic protocol inspectors. The application uses a control session with a predictable destination port to negotiate and maintain subsequent connections on dynamic port numbers. Because the ASA doesn't have a protocol inspector that can interpret the underlying session negotiation, it isn't able to permit the additional connections as they occur dynamically.

One solution is to add a rule to an access list that permits traffic between the two hosts that are using the application. First, you would have to permit packets that are destined for the control session protocol and port number. What about any other sessions that are dynamically negotiated? You might add an access list rule to permit each subsequent session, if you know each protocol and port number ahead of time. If not, your access list rule would need to be more general to encompass every possible port number.

As an example, suppose the client machines are located in the 10.10.0.0/16 subnet on the outside ASA interface, while the server is located at 192.168.1.100 on the inside interface. The application always uses TCP port 4001 for its control session. Other dynamic sessions can use any UDP port between 4000 and 5000.

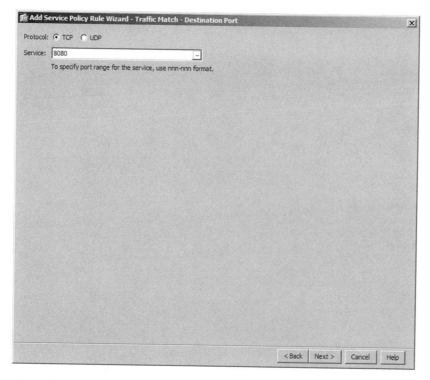

Figure 9-17   *Specifying the Nonstandard Protocol and Destination Port Number*

A naive approach might be to create an access list rule that will permit any inbound traffic to reach the 192.l68.1.100 server, as demonstrated here:

```
ciscoasa(config)# access-list OUTSIDE extended permit ip any host 192.168.1.100
```

Such a rule might make quick work of setting up the server access, but it also leaves the server exposed. The access rule doesn't limit the inbound traffic at all; rather, it opens TCP port 4001, as well as any other nonessential UDP and TCP port—from any address on the outside public network! Malicious hosts might try to leverage the unhindered access.

As an alternative, suppose you used the commands listed in Example 9-17 to tighten security to the server. This time, the outside clients have been identified in the access list, along with the control port (TCP 4001) and every possible dynamic port (UDP 4000–5000) that might be used.

Example 9-17   *Better Approach to Permitting Access for a Dynamic Protocol*

```
ciscoasa(config)# access-list OUTSIDE extended permit tcp 10.10.0.0 255.255.0.0
  host 192.168.1.100 eq 4001
ciscoasa(config)# access-list OUTSIDE extended permit udp 10.10.0.0 255.255.0.0
  host 192.168.1.100 range 4000 5000
ciscoasa(config)# access-group OUTSIDE in interface outside
```

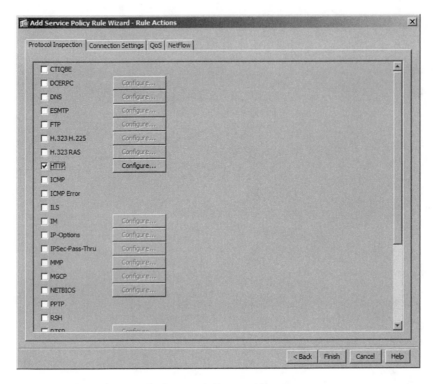

Figure 9-18   *Selecting the Dynamic Protocol Inspector*

An even better approach is to leverage the **established** command to track a known control port and open "pinholes," or temporary rules that allow access on other dynamic ports. As long as the control port is established as expected, the ASA will automatically create rules for subsequent sessions between the same source and destination addresses used in the control session.

You can use the following command to configure an established rule for a dynamic protocol:

```
ciscoasa(config)# established protocol dest_port [src_port] [permitto protocol
  port [-port]] [permitfrom protocol port [-port]]
```

You must identify the protocol (either TCP or UDP) and destination port used for the control connection, although the source port is optional. Next, identify the protocol and destination port or port range that any subsequent connections might use. If you add the **permitfrom** keyword, you can also specify a source protocol and port, if needed. Example 9-18 lists the commands that are necessary to configure a more secure approach to permitting access for a dynamic protocol.

Example 9-18   *Secure Approach to Permitting Access for a Dynamic Protocol*

```
ciscoasa(config)# established tcp 4001 permitto udp 4000-5000
ciscoasa(config)# access-list OUTSIDE extended permit tcp 10.10.0.0 255.255.0.0
  host 192.168.1.100 eq 4001
ciscoasa(config)# access-group OUTSIDE in interface outside
```

Configuring a Policy for Inspecting OSI Layers 5–7

With the ASA MPF structure, you can also configure policies that can be used for inspecting application traffic at OSI Layers 5 through 7. The ASA offers a suite of application inspectors that can provide a variety of security measures. Because applications can be complex and intricate, a security appliance should be able to analyze and limit various aspects of the application traffic to form an overall security policy. An ASA can do just that by leveraging the four key functions listed in Table 9-10 as part of its application inspection and control (AIC) features.

Table 9-10   *Approaches to Application Inspection and Control*

Key Topic

Function	Focus	Strength
Protocol verification	Drops malformed application layer packets	Blocks covertly tunneled data Prevents known and unknown attacks
Protocol minimization	Minimal set of protocol features	Hides unnecessary features and their vulnerabilities Prevents both known and unknown attacks
Payload minimization	Minimal set of protocol payloads	Permits only expected content Prevents both known and unknown attacks
Application layer signatures	Detects malicious content	Prevents mostly known attacks

Before you consider implementing any of the application layer inspection features, you should spend time gathering information about the applications that are used in your network environment. Applications can be complex in nature, so you should understand the impact that any inspection might have on the enterprise and its users.

Sometimes, it is tempting to blindly configure or tune an application inspection without much forethought. Then, once some users or applications begin to have issues communicating, you might be pressured to disable the inspection completely. Doing so might make the users happy, but it might also leave your network vulnerable.

Most environments use the HTTP, FTP, DNS, and Extended Simple Mail Transfer Protocol (ESMTP) application protocols, where the clients and servers are located on opposing sides of an ASA. The application traffic must pass through the firewall, allowing you to leverage the corresponding application protocol inspectors. Because these protocols are the most common and are covered in the FIREWALL v1.0 course, they are covered in detail in this chapter. Other application protocol inspectors that are not covered include DCE RPC, H.323, IM, MGCP, NetBIOS, RTSP, SIP, Skinny, and SNMP.

Configuring HTTP Inspection

HTTP is a protocol that is used between clients and servers. Basically, clients send HTTP requests and servers send HTTP responses. An ASA can inspect the HTTP traffic and apply very granular controls or security policies that you can configure. The HTTP inspector is very versatile and can match against a long list of protocol parameters and regular expressions.

With HTTP inspection, the ASA must sit between the client and server. As you prepare to configure HTTP inspection policies, consider what you want to be protected—the client or the server. For example, if a web server is located on the inside, secure interface of the ASA and the clients are located outside on the public Internet, then you will be protecting the server. If inside clients are connecting to outside web servers, then you will want to protect the clients.

Because the HTTP inspector is so versatile and has so many possible options to configure, you should try to break your HTTP security policies down into the four basic approaches listed previously in Table 9-10. The following list should help you organize the policies into configuration tasks, based on the approaches. An example is provided to help put each approach into context; the configuration of each example is also shown in this chapter.

- **Protocol verification:** Drop any HTTP sessions that do not adhere to the protocol specification. This function has very few user-configurable options; it is usually enabled or disabled (the default).

- **Protocol minimization:** Allow only specific features of the HTTP protocol to be passed on to the protected client or server. When configuring, block everything that is *not* an acceptable action with the "match not" condition; everything else will be permitted.

  For example, suppose you want to minimize the possible HTTP requests that can reach a protected server. Only the GET request should be allowed. In this case, if the request "matches not" GET, then drop it.

- **Payload minimization:** Allow only specific payloads inside HTTP packets to be delivered to the protected client or server. When configuring, block everything that is *not* an acceptable value with the "match not" condition; everything else will be inherently permitted.

  For example, suppose you want to minimize the possible HTTP payloads that can be serviced by a protected server. Only requests involving a URI that begins with /customer should be allowed. In this case, if the URI "matches not" the regular expression /customer, then drop it.

- **Application layer signatures:** Identify and drop known bad HTTP payloads. When configuring, block specific content with the "match" condition. Regular expressions are often used to match content.

  As an example, suppose that GET requests that include an external link to http:// or https:// should be blocked. In this case, you could configure a regular expression to match against http:// or https:// in the HTTP request header arguments and drop those connections.

Although the four security approaches might seem distinct and logical, putting them into practice isn't always straightforward. The ASA HTTP inspector can match against a long list of parameters, but there is no clear distinction as to which parameter belongs to which approach. For example, should the HTTP request method be used to minimize the HTTP protocol, minimize the HTTP payload, or recognize an HTTP signature? There is no clear-cut answer.

Rather than worry about memorizing long lists of HTTP parameters and how they fit into security policy configuration, try to keep things simple. Be sure to know the four security approaches, as Cisco plainly uses them in the FIREWALL course. Also, become familiar with the following two concepts:

- **Minimization:** Identify an HTTP parameter that is needed and approved, and then drop everything else. In effect, you are letting the protected host take care of only a minimal set of acceptable operations, while the ASA filters every other type of operation that might be leveraged for an attack.

- **Application signature:** Identify a specific "bad" HTTP operation or parameter and drop it. In effect, you are creating a blacklist of undesirable things; everything else will be permitted.

Configuring HTTP Inspection Policy Maps Using the CLI

You can use the CLI to configure an HTTP inspection policy map that is applied to the HTTP inspector process. The policy map can use various matching criteria to detect conditions within HTTP connections. In case of a match, the HTTP connections can be dropped, reset, or logged.

You can use the following steps to build and apply an HTTP inspection policy map:

Step 1.   Define the HTTP inspection policy map.

Step 2.   Configure HTTP protocol verification.

Step 3.   Configure a minimization or signature detection, along with an action.

Step 4.   Apply the HTTP inspection policy map.

Step 1: Define the HTTP Inspection Policy Map   Use the following command to define and name the policy map:

```
ciscoasa(config)# policy-map type inspect http http_map_name
```

As an example, suppose you need to define an HTTP inspection policy map called HTTP_MAP_1. You could enter the following command:

```
ciscoasa(config)# policy-map type inspect http HTTP_MAP_1
```

Step 2: Configure HTTP Protocol Verification   You can use the following command sequence to verify that HTTP connections are adhering to the protocol definitions. The ASA can drop, log, or reset violating connections.

```
ciscoasa(config-pmap)# parameters
ciscoasa(config-pmap-p)# protocol-violation [action {drop-connection [log] | log |
  reset}]
```

Continuing from the command entered in Step 1, you could enter the following commands to enable protocol verification and to drop and log violating HTTP connections:

```
ciscoasa(config-pmap)# parameters
ciscoasa(config-pmap-p)# protocol-violation action drop-connection log
ciscoasa(config-pmap-p)# exit
```

Step 3: Configure a Minimization or Signature Detection, Along with an Action   You can define any protocol or payload minimization or HTTP signature by choosing a matching criteria from Table 9-11 and entering the corresponding command. The **match** command will match against exactly the parameters you enter, while the **match not** command will match against anything other than the parameters you enter.

Table 9-11   *Configuration Commands for Matching Against HTTP Content*

Match Criteria	Command Syntax
HTTP method	ciscoasa(config-pmap)# **match [not] request method** *method-name*
	where *method-name* can be one of the following keywords:
	bcopy, bdelete, bmove, bpropfind, bproppatch, connect, copy, delete, edit, get, getattribute, getattributenames, getproperties, head, index, lock, mkcol, mkdir, move, notify, options, poll, post, propfind, proppatch, put, revadd, revlabel, revlog, revnum, save, search, setattribute, startrev, stoprev, subscribe, trace, unedit, unlock, unsubscribe

Table 9-11 *Configuration Commands for Matching Against HTTP Content*

Match Criteria	Command Syntax
HTTP header content or length	ciscoasa(config-pmap)# **match [not] {request	response} header** *field* {{**count gt** *value*}	{**length gt** *value*}	{**regex** {**class** *name*	*regex-name*}}}
	where *field* can be one of the following keywords:
	accept, accept-charset, accept-encoding, accept-language, allow, authorization, cache-control, connection, content-encoding, content-language, content-length, content-location, content-md5, content-range, content-type, cookie, count, date, expect, expires, from, host, if-match, if-modified-since, if-none-match, if-range, if-unmodified-since, last-modified, length, max-forwards, non-ascii, pragma, proxy-authorization, range, referer, regex, te, trailer, transfer-encoding, upgrade, user-agent, via, warning
HTTP request arguments	ciscoasa(config-pmap)# **match [not] request args** {*name*	**class** *regex-class*	**regex** {**class** *name*	*regex-name*}}
	where *name* can be one of the following keywords:
	bcopy, bdelete, bmove, bpropfind, bproppatch, connect, copy, delete, edit, get, getattribute, getattributenames, getproperties, head, index, lock, mkcol, mkdir, move, notify, options, poll, post, propfind, proppatch, put, revadd, revlabel, revlog, revnum, save, search, setattribute, startrev, stoprev, subscribe, trace, unedit, unlock, unsubscribe
HTTP request body content or length	ciscoasa(config-pmap)# **match [not] request body** {{**length gt** *value*}	{**regex** {**class** *name*	*regex-name*}}
HTTP request URI content or length	ciscoasa(config-pmap)# **match [not] request uri** {{**length gt** *value*}	{**regex** {**class** *name*	*regex-name*}}
HTTP response body content or length	ciscoasa(config-pmap)# **match [not] response body** {**active-x**	**java-applet**	**length gt** *value*	**regex** {**class** *name*	*regex_name*}}
HTTP response status line	ciscoasa(config-pmap)# **match [not] response status-line regex** {**class** *name*	*regex_name*}

You can build up a set of inspection policies by configuring multiple match and action pairs in a single HTTP inspection policy map. The matches are not necessarily tried in the order that you enter them; the ASA has a predetermined order that it uses internally. If a **match** command drops or resets an HTTP connection, then no further matches are checked. Otherwise, an HTTP packet can be matched by subsequent **match** commands in the policy map.

Next, use Table 9-12 to choose an action that the ASA should take on the matched HTTP connection. When connections are dropped or reset, you can also add the **log** keyword to generate a logging message to record the action.

Table 9-12 *HTTP Match Action Commands*

Action	Command Syntax
Drop the HTTP connection	ciscoasa(config-pmap-c)# **drop-connection** [log]
Log the HTTP connection	ciscoasa(config-pmap-c)# **log**
Reset the HTTP connection	ciscoasa(config-pmap-c)# **reset** [log]

Suppose you need to add a security policy to minimize the HTTP protocol. Only the HTTP request GET method will be permitted, while other request methods will be dropped. Continuing with the configuration from Step 2, you could use the following commands to define the policy:

```
ciscoasa(config-pmap)# match not request method get
ciscoasa(config-pmap-c)# drop-connection
```

An inspection policy map can be made up of match-action pairs—a single **match** command and a corresponding action in each pair. In some scenarios, you might need to match against multiple conditions for a single action. You can accomplish that by defining an HTTP inspect class map that contains nothing but matching conditions, as follows:

```
ciscoasa(config)# class-map type inspect http [match-all | match-any] cmap_name
ciscoasa(config-cmap)# match [not] {request | response | req-resp} ...
ciscoasa(config-cmap)# match [not] {request | response | req-resp} ...
ciscoasa(config-cmap)# exit
```

To match against any of the **match** commands, as a logical OR operation, define the class map with the **match-any** keyword. To match against *all* of the **match** commands, as a logical AND operation, use the **match-all** keyword instead.

You can then reference the class map in the HTTP inspect policy map with the **class** command, followed by an action, using the following command syntax:

```
ciscoasa(config)# policy-map type inspect http pmap_name
ciscoasa(config-pmap)# class cmap_name
ciscoasa(config-pmap-c)# {drop-connection [log] | log | reset [log]}
ciscoasa(config-pmap-c)# exit
```

As an example, suppose you need to define a class map called MY_HTTP_CLASS that will be used to ultimately drop any HTTP connection that is neither an HTTP GET request nor an HTTP POLL request. Example 9-19 shows the necessary class map and policy map configuration commands.

Example 9-19 *Defining an HTTP Inspect Class Map with Multiple Matching Criteria*

```
ciscoasa(config)# class-map type inspect http match-all MY_HTTP_CLASS
ciscoasa(config-cmap)# match [not] request method get
ciscoasa(config-cmap)# match [not] request method poll
ciscoasa(config-cmap)# exit
ciscoasa(config)# policy-map type inspect http HTTP_MAP_1
ciscoasa(config-pmap)# class MY_HTTP_CLASS
ciscoasa(config-pmap-c)# drop-connection
ciscoasa(config-pmap-c)# exit
```

Some of the **match** commands listed in Table 9-11 have the capability to match against regular expressions found within text fields in HTTP content. Regular expressions, also known as *regex*, can be defined in two ways:

Key
Topic

■ As a single regular expression configured with the following command:

```
ciscoasa(config)# regex regex_name regular_expression
```

■ As a group of regular expressions configured as a class map with the following commands:

```
ciscoasa(config)# class-map type regex match-any regex_cmap_name
ciscoasa(config-cmap)# match regex regex_name
```

The class map consists of one or more **match regex** commands, each referencing a single regular expression configured with the **regex** command.

Within a **regex** command, you can define the actual regular expression as a string of up to 100 characters. You can use regular characters in the *regular_expression* string to match text literally, and you can include special metacharacters to match text in a more abstract way. Table 9-13 lists the metacharacters that you can use, along with their names and functions.

Table 9-13 *Regular Expression Metacharacters*

Metacharacter	Name	Function
.	Dot	Matches any single character.
			Example: b.d matches bad, bbd, bcd, bdd, bed, and so on
( )	Subexpression	Groups the characters inside the parentheses as a single expression for matching with other metacharacters.
		Or	Matches either expression that | separates.
			Example: com|net matches whatever.com or whatever.net
			Example: Ma(r|y) matches Mar or May
?	Question mark	Matches 0 or 1 of the expression just before the ?.
			Example: e?smtp matches smtp (zero e's) or esmtp (1 e)
			Example: (12)? matches 4444, 12444, 1212444, and so on

Table 9-13   *Regular Expression Metacharacters*

Metacharacter	Name	Function
*	Asterisk	Matches 0, 1, or any number of the expression just before the *.
		Example: w* matches cisco.com and www.cisco.com
+	Plus	Matches at least one of the expressions just before the +.
		Example: w+ matches www.cisco.com, but not cisco.com
{n}	Repeat	Matches if the expression just before {n} is repeated exactly n times.
		Example: (test){2} matches testtest but not testtesttest
{n,}	Minimum repeat	Matches if the expression just before {n,} is repeated at least n times.
		Example: (test){2} matches testtest and also testtesttest
[abc]	Character class	Matches any of the characters listed between the square brackets.
		Example: [dfhl]og matches dog, fog, hog, and log, but not frog
[^abc]	Not character class	Matches any character that is not listed between the brackets.
		Example: [^dfhl]og matches cog, but not dog, fog, hog, or log
[a-c]	Character range class	Matches any character in the range from a to c.
		Example: [a-z] matches any lowercase letter, [A-Z] matches any uppercase letter, [0-9] matches any digit
^	Caret	Matches the beginning of a line; any expression following the caret will be matched only if it appears at the beginning of a line.
		Example: ^Dear matches "Dear John" but not "John Dear"
\	Escape	The metacharacter following \ will be treated as a literal character; this is useful when you need to match against something that is normally interpreted as a metacharacter.
		Example: *Test matches *Test*
\r	Carriage return	Matches a carriage return character (ASCII 13 or 0x0d).
\n	Newline	Matches a newline character (ASCII 10 or 0x0a).
\t	Tab	Matches a tab character (ASCII 9 or 0x09).
\f	Form feed	Matches a form feed character (ASCII 12 or 0x0c).

Table 9-13 *Regular Expression Metacharacters*

Metacharacter	Name	Function
\xNN	Escaped hex number	Matches an ASCII character that has the two-digit hex code NN. Example: \x20 matches a space (ASCII 32)
\NNN	Escaped octal number	Matches an ASCII character that has the three-digit octal code NNN. Example: \040 matches a space (ASCII 32)

Suppose you would like to configure an HTTP inspection policy that minimizes the HTTP payload by dropping any connection that does not contain a URI that begins with the string "/customer". You could use the commands listed in Example 9-20 to define a regular expression called Customer-URI and apply it in the HTTP_MAP_1 policy map.

Example 9-20 *Configuring a Regular Expression to Match "/customer"*

```
ciscoasa(config)# regex Customer-URI ^/customer
ciscoasa(config)# policy-map type inspect http HTTP_MAP_1
ciscoasa(config-pmap)# match not request uri regex Customer-URI
ciscoasa(config-pmap-c)# drop-connection
ciscoasa(config-pmap-c)# exit
```

In addition, suppose you need to define a policy that detects HTTP GET requests that include request arguments that contain links to external sites—most likely for malicious purposes. You could define two regular expressions that match against "http://" and "https://", respectively, and then reference them in a regex class map. Example 9-21 lists the configuration commands needed for this approach.

Example 9-21 *Configuring Regular Expressions to Match "http://" or "https://"*

```
ciscoasa(config)# regex Embedded-link1 http://
ciscoasa(config)# regex Embedded-link2 https://
ciscoasa(config)# class-map type regex match-any Embedded-link
ciscoasa(config-cmap)# match regex Embedded-link1
ciscoasa(config-cmap)# match regex Embedded-link2
ciscoasa(config-cmap)# exit
ciscoasa(config)# policy-map type inspect http HTTP_MAP_1
ciscoasa(config-pmap)# match request args regex class Embedded-link
ciscoasa(config-pmap-c)# drop-connection
ciscoasa(config-pmap-c)# exit
```

However, because both strings begin with "http", you could use a single **regex** command instead to match either string. The letter **s** can appear zero or one time in either string, so you could use the **?** metacharacter immediately after the "s" in the regex. Example 9-22 lists the commands needed for this approach.

Example 9-22   *Using a Single Regex to Match "http://" or "https://"*

```
ciscoasa(config)# regex Embedded-link https?://
ciscoasa(config)# policy-map type inspect http HTTP_MAP_1
ciscoasa(config-pmap)# match request args regex Embedded-link
ciscoasa(config-pmap-c)# drop-connection
ciscoasa(config-pmap-c)# exit
```

Regular expressions can be difficult to formulate, especially when metacharacters are used. You can experiment with a regular expression from the regular EXEC level prompt, without having to make any configuration changes first. Use the following command to test a regular expression:

```
ciscoasa# test regex input_text regular_expression
```

Enter some sample input text, as if the ASA is searching through a URI or some other text field. Then enter the regular expression you want to test. If the input text or regular expression contains any spaces, be sure to surround the text string with quotation marks.

The ASA will return the result of the regular expression match. In Example 9-23, the regex **https?://** is tested against the text string https://shadycontent.com/toolz and is successful. Remember that a failed match doesn't necessarily indicate that your regular expression is incorrect or poorly formed—your regular expression needs correcting only if it produces results that don't match your expectations.

Example 9-23   *Testing a Regular Expression Before Configuration*

```
ciscoasa# test regex https://shadycontent.com/toolz https?://
INFO: Regular expression match succeeded.
ciscoasa#
```

Note: In Example 9-23, the **?** metacharacter is used in the regular expression. Because the **test regex** command is used in the EXEC mode, the ASA will try to interpret the question mark as a request for context-based help. If you need to use a question mark in a test, you must enter the **Ctrl-v** escape sequence prior to **?** so that it can be used as a regular text character.

Step 4: Apply the HTTP Inspection Policy Map   After you configure an HTTP inspection policy map, you apply it to an HTTP inspection within a service policy rule using the following command syntax:

```
ciscoasa(config-pmap-c)# inspect http http-map-name
```

Any traffic that is classified or matched by the service policy rule will be sent through the customized inspection. In Example 9-24, IP traffic from any host to servers located in the 10.1.1.0/24 subnet will be subject to HTTP inspection. The shaded line shows how the inspection policy map HTTP_MAP_1 is applied to the HTTP inspector.

Example 9-24   *Applying an HTTP Inspection Policy Map*

```
ciscoasa(config)# access-list SERVERS extended permit ip any 10.1.1.0 255.255.255.0
ciscoasa(config)# class-map c1
ciscoasa(config-cmap)# match access-list SERVERS
ciscoasa(config-cmap)# exit
ciscoasa(config)# policy-map p1
ciscoasa(config-pmap)# class c1
ciscoasa(config-pmap-c)# inspect http HTTP_MAP_1
ciscoasa(config-pmap-c)# exit
ciscoasa(config-pmap)# exit
ciscoasa(config)# service-policy p1 interface outside
```

You can define multiple policies within a regular policy map, each matching a different subset of traffic and each configured to use HTTP inspection with a unique set of HTTP inspection policies. In this case, each **inspect http** command would reference a different HTTP inspection policy map.

Configuring HTTP Inspection Policy Maps Using ASDM

You can also use ASDM to configure an HTTP inspection policy map. ASDM can be a more user-friendly alternative because the large number of parameters and options are presented in an organized fashion. Navigate to **Configuration > Firewall > Objects > Inspect Maps** and select **HTTP**.

As with the CLI configuration, you can accomplish the ASDM configuration with the following steps:

Step 1.   Define the HTTP inspection policy map.

Step 2.   Configure HTTP protocol verification.

Step 3.   Configure a minimization or signature detection, along with an action.

Step 4.   Apply the HTTP inspection policy map.

The sections that follow provide more information about each step of configuring the HTTP inspection policy maps using ASDM.

Step 1: Define the HTTP Inspection Policy Map   Click the **Add** button to add a new inspection policy map. Enter an arbitrary name for the map, as well as an optional description. Figure 9-19 shows a new policy map called HTTP_MAP_1.

The Add HTTP Inspect Map dialog box initially shows a Security Level slider that you can use to quickly set up some basic HTTP inspection parameters. By sliding the pointer up or down, you can choose between the following security levels:

■   **Low:** Enables HTTP protocol verification only

■   **Medium:** Allows only the HTTP GET, HEAD, and POST request methods; enables HTTP protocol verification

■   **High:** Allows only the HTTP GET and HEAD request methods; enables HTTP protocol verification; drops HTTP connections that contain non-ASCII HTTP headers

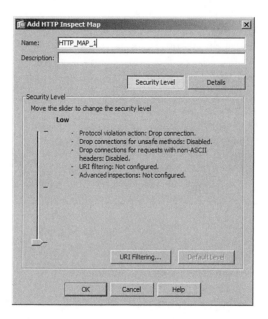

Figure 9-19   *Adding a New HTTP Inspect Map in ASDM*

Step 2: Configure HTTP Protocol Verification   To define detailed HTTP security policies, click the **Details** button. This also changes the bottom portion of the dialog box to display the Parameters tab. You can enable protocol verification by checking the **Check for Protocol Violations** check box, as shown in Figure 9-20. You can choose the action to take on a connection that violates the HTTP protocol, as well as specify any logging for an audit trail.

Don't click the OK button yet, because you need to stay in the same dialog box to define further inspection policies.

Step 3: Configure a Minimization or Signature Detection, Along with an Action   Click the **Inspections** tab to see a list of any HTTP inspection policies that have been configured, as shown in Figure 9-21.

To add a new inspection, click the **Add** button. In the Add HTTP Inspect dialog box, click the **Single Match** radio button to define a single matching condition. Then click **Match** or **No Match** and choose a criterion type from the Criterion drop-down list. The options displayed in the Value section will change depending on the criterion you select. At the bottom of the dialog box, choose the actions that will be taken on the matching HTTP connection. Click the **OK** button to add the new inspection to the HTTP inspection policy map.

As an example, suppose only the HTTP_GET request method is to be permitted; all other request methods should be dropped. As shown in Figure 9-22, click **No Match**, choose the criterion **RequestMethod**, and choose a value of **get**. In other words, if a client sends anything other than a GET request, the connection will be dropped.

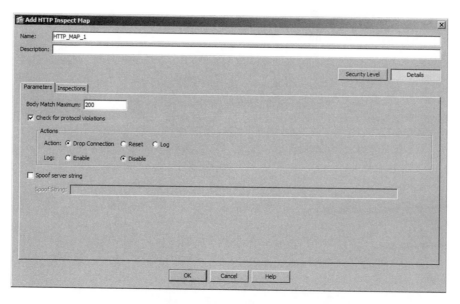

Figure 9-20   *Enabling HTTP Protocol Verification in ASDM*

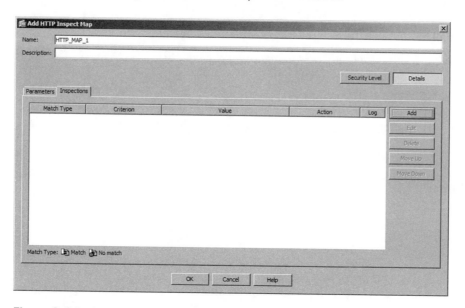

Figure 9-21   *Viewing a List of the Current HTTP Inspection Policies in ASDM*

As an alternative, you might need an HTTP inspection map policy that requires multiple matching conditions. As an example, suppose you would like to drop any connection that is not an HTTP GET request and is not an HTTP POLL request.

Rather than a single match, you would click the **Multiple Matches** radio button in the Add HTTP Inspect dialog box, as shown in Figure 9-23, to define an HTTP inspect class map that will contain the list of matching criteria. ASDM will display a list of preconfigured class maps next to the HTTP Traffic Class field. You can also configure your own class map by clicking the **Manage** button.

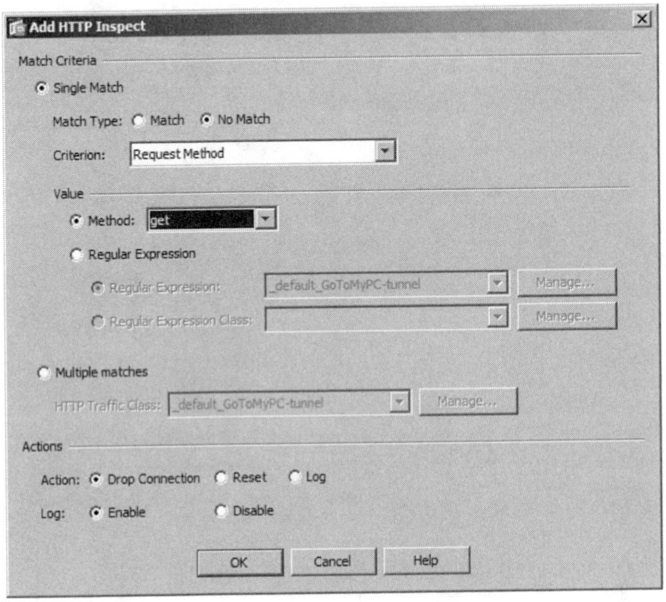

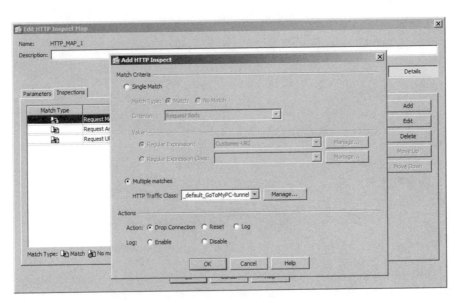

Figure 9-22   *Defining a Protocol Minimization Policy in ASDM*

Figure 9-23   *Using an HTTP Inspect Class Map to Define Multiple Matching Criteria*

ASDM will display a list of all preconfigured HTTP class maps, as shown in Figure 9-24. To create a new class map, click the **Add** button.

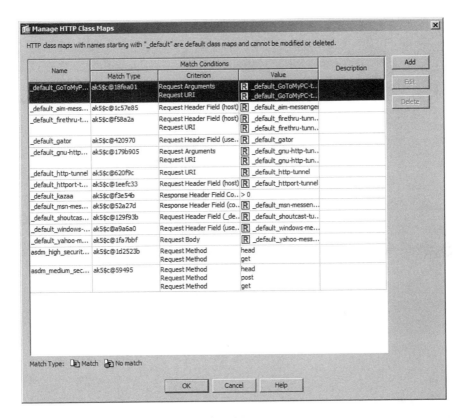

Figure 9-24 *Selecting an HTTP Class Map*

The Add HTTP Traffic Class Map dialog box will appear. Give the new class map a name. In Figure 9-25, the class map has been named MY_HTTP_CLASS. Click the **Add** button to add a matching criterion. Notice that the Match Option in the Add HTTP Traffic Class Map dialog box can be set to Match All or Match Any. For the example scenario, Match All has been selected to match against both of the criterion in the class map.

In the Add HTTP Match Criterion dialog box, you can define the matching criterion and value as before. The first criterion is defined as anything but (No Match) the HTTP request method **get**. Click the **OK** button to add the match criterion to the list in the class map.

Next, click the **Add** button in the Add HTTP Traffic Class Map dialog box to define the second matching criterion. In Figure 9-26, the No Match option for the HTTP request method POLL has been selected. Click **OK** to add the match criterion, and then click **OK** in the Add HTTP Traffic Class Map dialog box to complete the class map configuration.

Click **OK** in the Manage HTTP Class Maps to end the class map configuration. In the Add HTTP Inspect dialog box, as shown in Figure 9-27, choose the new class map (MY_HTTP_CLASS), choose the **Drop Connection** action, and click **OK**.

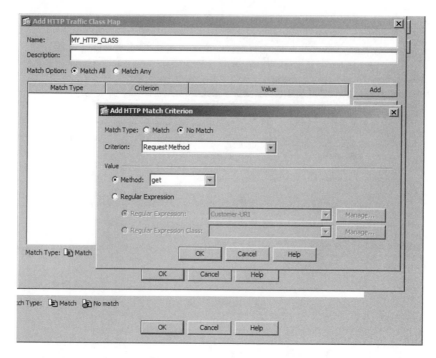

Figure 9-25 *Defining a Matching Criterion in an HTTP Class Map*

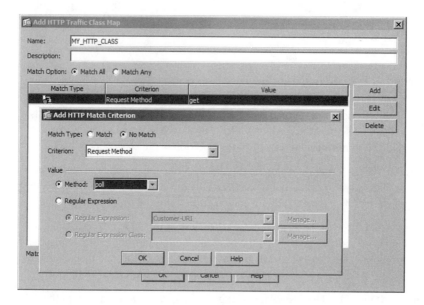

Figure 9-26 *Defining a Second Matching Criterion in an HTTP Class Map*

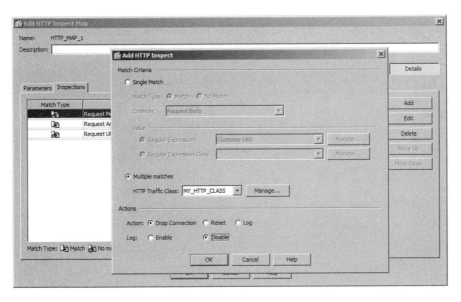

Figure 9-27   *Completing the HTTP Inspect Class Map Configuration*

Some of the matching criteria have the capability to match against regular expressions found within text fields in HTTP content. This can be useful for HTTP payload minimization or HTTP signature detection.

As an example, suppose you need to drop any HTTP connection that does not contain a URI that begins with the string "/customer". In Figure 9-28, a new HTTP inspection has been added. The match criteria is set to a Single Match condition based on the HTTP RequestURI field. Under Value, a regular expression must be used to match against the text string. Because no default regular expression exists for the string "/customer", one must be created. To do this, click the **Manage** button.

The Manage Regular Expressions dialog box will open and list all available regular expressions that can be used for matching. To create a new one, click the **Add** button. Enter a name for the new regular expression, as shown in Figure 9-29, and then click the **Build** button to build and test the expression interactively.

In the Build Regular Expression dialog box, you can specify pieces or snippets of text that will be used to build an entire regular expression string. After you build a snippet, click the **Append Snippet** button to add it to the final regular expression string. In Figure 9-30, the character string "/customer" has been entered.

Tip: You can also click the **Test** button to manually test the regular expression against various text strings that you provide. By testing complex regular expressions, you can be more sure that they will match and give the results you are expecting.

Click the **OK** button to return to the Add Regular Expression dialog box, and then click the **OK** button to add the new regular expression to the list that is available to ASDM. In

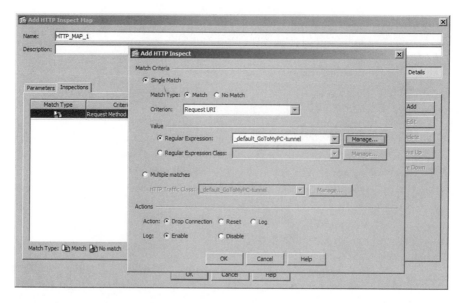

Figure 9-28 *Adding an HTTP Payload Minimization Policy in ASDM*

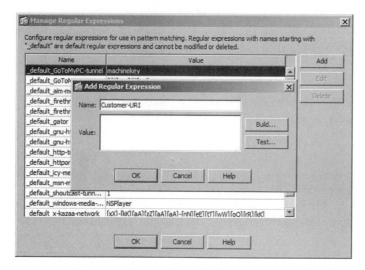

Figure 9-29 *Adding a New Regular Expression in ASDM*

Figure 9-31, the newly defined regular expression named Customer-URI has been added to the bottom of the list. Click the **OK** button to return to the HTTP Inspect Map dialog box.

In the Add HTTP Inspect dialog box, you can click **Regular Expression** and choose the new regular expression from the drop-down list. In Figure 9-32, the Customer-URI regular expression is selected as the match criteria value. Because only connections that do not contain the matching string are to be dropped, the match criteria has been changed to No Match, and the action has been set to Drop Connection. Click **OK** to add the new inspect policy to the HTTP inspect policy map.

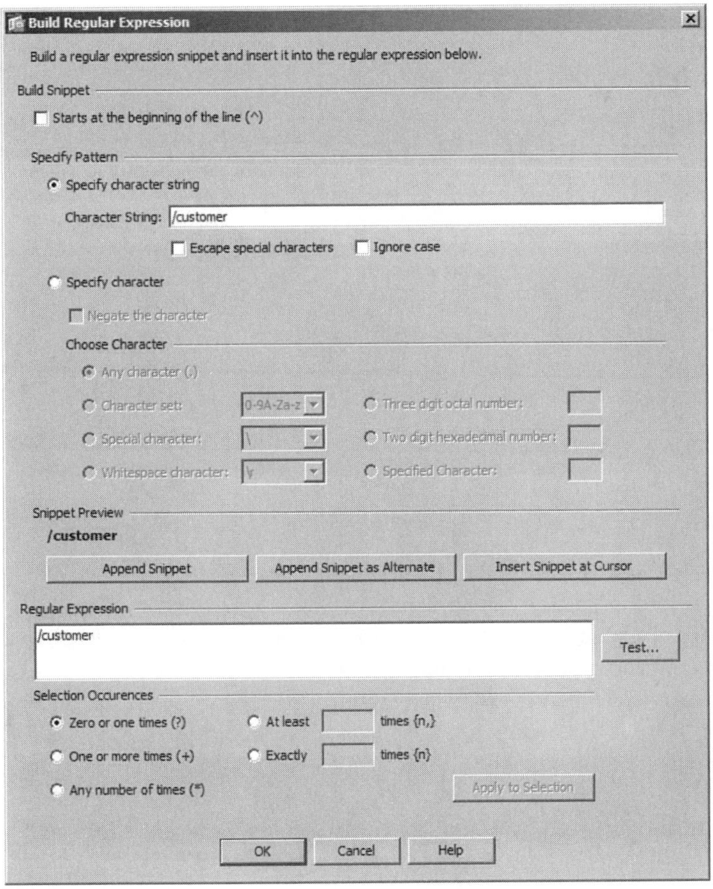

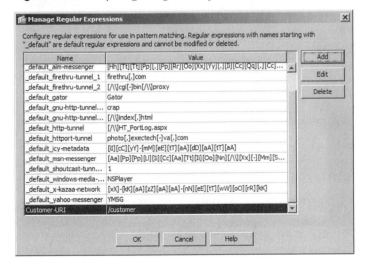

Figure 9-30 *Defining a Regular Expression in ASDM*

Figure 9-31 *New Regular Expression Added to ASDM*

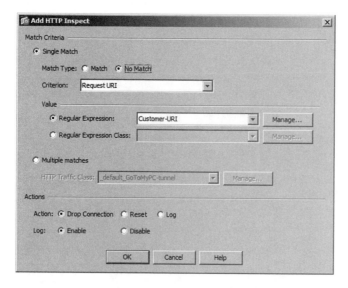

Figure 9-32 *Matching Against a Regular Expression in an HTTP Inspect Policy*

Now suppose you need to define an HTTP inspection policy that detects GET requests that include request arguments that contain external links to other, possibly malicious, locations. You can define a regular expression called Embedded-link that matches against the string "http://" or "https://". In Figure 9-33, the character string "https://" has been entered and appended to the regular expression. Because the letter **s** might or might not appear to match the two target strings, it can appear zero or one time in the HTTP request text. To set up the regular expression, you would select the letter **s**, choose the **Zero or One Times (?)** option, and then click the **Apply to Selection** button.

Because the regular expression is slightly more complex than a simple text string, you should click the **Test** button to verify that it works properly. In Figure 9-34, the regular expression "https?://" is being tested, to make sure that it matches against the string "http://". After you click the Test button, ASDM runs the test and returns the test result Match Succeeded.

Click the **OK** button in the test dialog box, and then click **OK** in the Build Regular Expression dialog box. Finally, complete the Add HTTP Inspect dialog box by specifying the regular expression you want to use for matching. In Figure 9-35, the previously configured Embedded-link regular expression will be used as a matching criteria; connections that match and have the prohibited external link string will be dropped.

Click **OK** to complete the inspection policy configuration. As each policy is completed, it is listed as part of the HTTP inspect map, as shown in Figure 9-36.

Step 4: Apply the HTTP Inspection Policy Map   After you configure an HTTP inspection policy map, you apply it to an HTTP inspection within a service policy rule. Any traffic that is classified or matched by the service policy rule will be sent through the customized inspection.

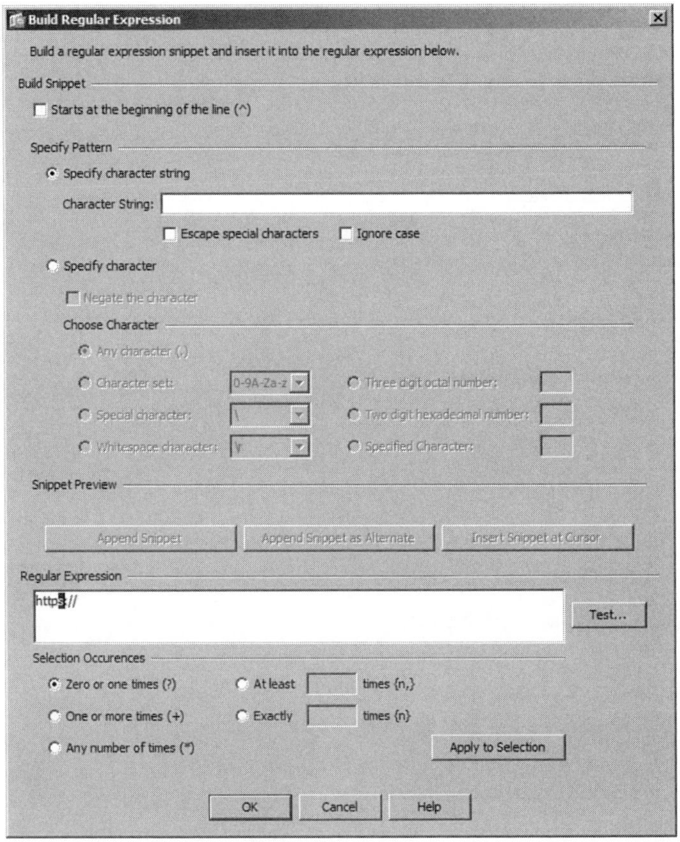

Figure 9-33   *Defining a Regular Expression to Match Either http:// or https://*

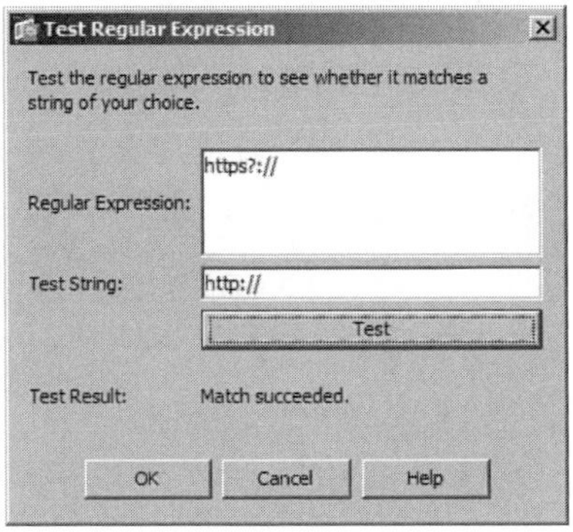

Figure 9-34   *Testing a Regular Expression to Verify the Results*

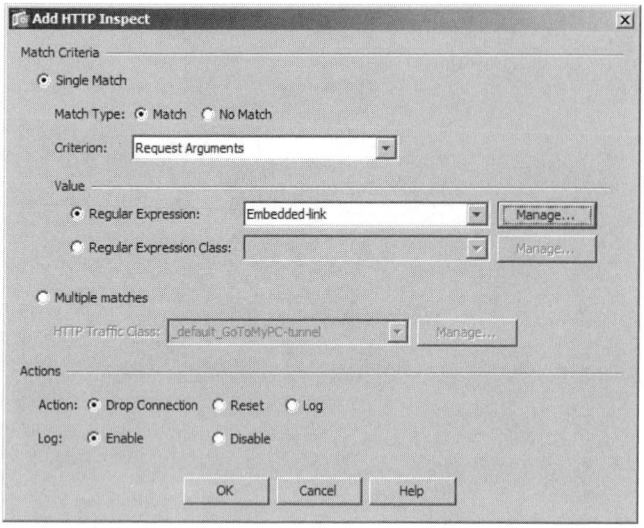

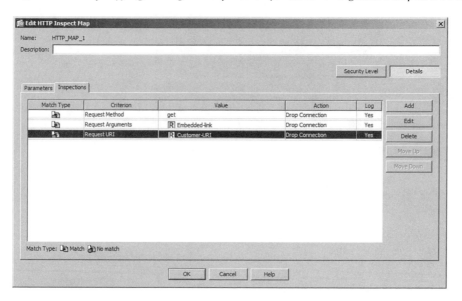

Figure 9-35   *Specifying the Regular Expression for an HTTP Signature Inspection Policy*

Figure 9-36   *Displaying the Inspection Policies Within an HTTP Inspect Map*

First, navigate to **Configuration > Firewall > Service Policy Rules** and select a service policy rule to edit. On the Traffic Classification tab, configure the traffic match criteria. Then click the **Rule Actions** tab. Make sure the HTTP check box is checked on the Protocol Inspection tab. At this point, only the default HTTP inspection will be used. Click the **Configure** button beside HTTP, and then click the **Select an HTTP Inspect Map for Fine Control over Inspection** radio button. Make sure the HTTP inspection policy map name is selected in the list and click **OK**.

In Figure 9-37, the inspection policy map named HTTP_MAP_1 is being applied to HTTP inspection for the service policy rule.

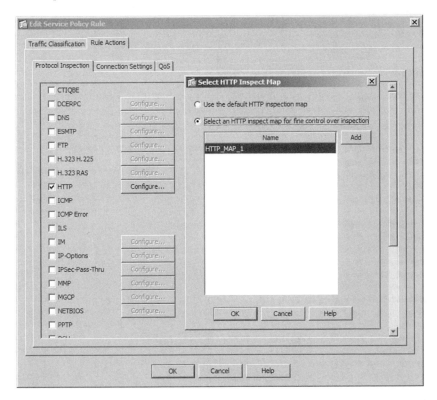

Figure 9-37   *Applying an HTTP Inspection Policy Map to a Service Policy Rule*

Configuring FTP Inspection

The File Transfer Protocol (FTP) is used between clients and servers. Clients can open FTP connections to servers and perform several different file-oriented operations. The ASA offers an FTP application inspector that must sit between the client and server to work properly. The FTP inspector offers the following functions:

- **Protocol verification:** Drop any FTP sessions that do not adhere to the FTP protocol specification and log the URI of all accessed FTP objects. FTP protocol verification is enabled by default and cannot be disabled.

- **Protocol minimization:** Allow only specific FTP commands and functions to be passed on to the protected client or server. For example, any FTP connections that use any request commands other than GET could be dropped.

- **Payload minimization:** Allow only specific FTP payloads to be delivered to the protected server. For example, an ASA can filter FTP connections according to filenames, file types, server names, and usernames.

- **Application layer signatures:** Identify and drop specific FTP payloads.

Configuring FTP Inspection Using the CLI

You can use the CLI to configure an FTP inspection policy map that is applied to the FTP inspector process. The policy map can use various matching criteria to detect conditions within FTP connections. In case of a match, the FTP connections can be reset.

You can use the following steps to build and apply an FTP inspection policy map:

Step 1. Define the FTP inspection policy map.

Step 2. Mask FTP server information.

Step 3. Configure an FTP minimization or detection policy, along with an action.

Step 4. Apply the FTP inspection policy map.

The sections that follow describe what is involved with each step.

Step 1: Define the FTP Inspection Policy Map   Use the following command to define and name the policy map:

```
ciscoasa(config)# policy-map type inspect ftp ftp-map-name
```

As an example, suppose you need to define an FTP inspection policy map called FTP_MAP_1. You could enter the following command:

```
ciscoasa(config)# policy-map type inspect ftp FTP_MAP_1
```

Step 2: Mask FTP Server Information   When a client opens a connection to an FTP server, the server often displays information about itself in a banner message or in its reply when the client sends the FTP SYST command. Malicious hosts might use this information to fingerprint the server's operating system so that known vulnerabilities can be leveraged.

You can configure the ASA to mask the FTP server's banner or its SYST reply with the following commands:

```
ciscoasa(config-pmap)# parameters
ciscoasa(config-pmap-p)# mask-banner
ciscoasa(config-pmap-p)# mask-syst-reply
ciscoasa(config-pmap)# exit
```

Step 3: Configure an FTP Minimization or Detection Policy, Along with an Action   You can define any protocol or payload minimization or FTP signature by selecting a matching criteria from Table 9-14 and entering the corresponding command. The **match** command will match against exactly the parameters you enter, whereas the **match not** command will match against anything other than the parameters you enter.

Table 9-14 *Configuration Commands for Matching Against FTP Content*

Match Criteria	Command Syntax
FTP command	ciscoasa(config-pmap)# **match [not] request-command** *cmd1* [*cmd2...*] where *cmdn* can be one of the following keywords: **appe, cdup, dele, get, help, mkd, put, rmd, rnfr, rnto, site, stou**
Filename	ciscoasa(config-pmap)# **match [not] filename regex** {*regex-name* | **class** *regex-class-map*}
File type	ciscoasa(config-pmap)# **match [not] filetype regex** {*regex-name* | **class** *regex-class-map*}
Server name	ciscoasa(config-pmap)# **match [not] server regex** {*regex-name* | **class** *regex-class-map*}
Username	ciscoasa(config-pmap)# **match [not] username regex** {*regex-name* | **class** *regex-class-map*}

You can build up a set of inspection policies by configuring multiple match and action pairs in a single FTP inspection policy map. If a **match** command drops or resets an FTP connection, then no further matches are checked; otherwise, an FTP packet can be matched by subsequent **match** commands in the policy map.

By default, no action will be taken. You can use the following command to cause the matching FTP connection to be reset by sending a TCP RST:

```
ciscoasa(config-pmap-c)# reset
```

As an example, suppose you need to add a security policy to minimize the FTP protocol such that only GET, PUT, and HELP request commands will be permitted. As well, connections that involve filenames ending with ".exe" will be reset. You can use the following command:

```
ciscoasa(config)# regex FTP_BADNAMES \.exe
ciscoasa(config)# policy-map type inspect ftp FTP_MAP_1
ciscoasa(config-pmap)# match not request-command get put help
ciscoasa(config-pmap-c)# reset
ciscoasa(config-pmap)# match filename regex FTP_BADNAMES
```

Step 4: Apply the FTP Inspection Policy Map   After you have configured an FTP inspection policy map, you apply it to an FTP inspection within a service policy rule using the following command syntax:

```
ciscoasa(config-pmap-c)# inspect ftp ftp-map-name
```

Any traffic that is classified or matched by the service policy rule will be sent through the customized inspection.

Configuring FTP Inspection Using ASDM

You can also use ASDM to configure an FTP inspection policy map. Navigate to **Configuration > Firewall > Objects > Inspect Maps** and select **FTP**.

As with the CLI configuration, you can accomplish the ASDM configuration with the following steps:

Step 1.   Define the FTP inspection policy map.

Step 2.   Configure a minimization or signature detection, along with an action.

Step 3.   Apply the FTP inspection policy map.

The sections that follow describe what is involved with each step.

Step 1: Define the FTP Inspection Policy Map   Click the **Add** button to add a new inspection policy map. Enter an arbitrary name for the map, as well as an optional description. Figure 9-38 shows a new policy map called FTP_MAP_1.

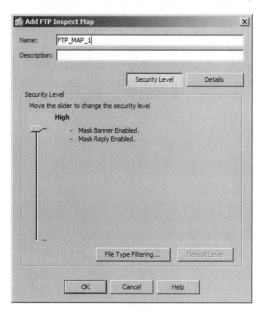

Figure 9-38   *Adding a New FTP Inspect Map in ASDM*

The Add FTP Inspect Map dialog box initially shows a Security Level slider that you can use to quickly set up some basic FTP inspection parameters. By sliding the pointer up or down, you can choose between the following security levels:

■   **Low:** URI logging is enabled.

■   **High:** URI logging is enabled; mask the FTP server banner and server replies to the FTP SYST command.

FTP protocol verification is always enabled, regardless of the slider setting. You can click the **File Type Filtering** button to define inspection rules that filter on FTP filenames.

Step 2: Configure a Minimization or Signature Detection, Along with an Action

Click the **Inspections** tab to see a list of any FTP inspection policies that have been configured. To add a new inspection, click the **Add** button.

Configuration begins in the Parameters tab, as shown in Figure 9-39. You can enable server information masking by checking the **Mask Greeting Banner from the Server** and the **Mask Reply to SYST Command** check boxes.

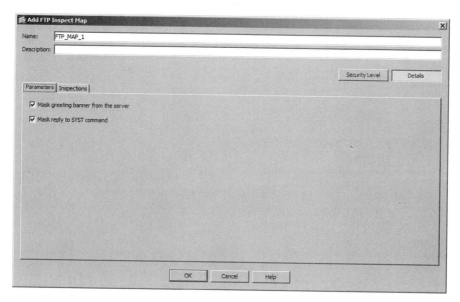

Figure 9-39 *Configuring FTP Server Information Masking*

Next, you can click the **Inspections** tab to list any configured FTP security policies. Click the **Add** button to add a new policy.

In the Add HTTP Inspect dialog box, click the **Single Match** radio button to define a single matching condition. Then click **Match** or **No Match** and choose a criterion type from the Criterion drop-down list. The options displayed in the Value section will change depending on the criterion you select. At the bottom of the dialog box, choose the actions that will be taken on the matching FTP connection. Click the **OK** button to add the new inspection to the FTP inspection policy map.

As an example, suppose that only the FTP GET, PUT, and HELP request commands are to be permitted; all other request methods should have their FTP connections reset. As shown in Figure 9-40, click **No Match** and choose the criterion **Request Command**. The check boxes next to values GET, HELP, and PUT are checked. In other words, if a client sends any FTP command other than these three, the connection will be reset. For FTP inspection, notice that the reset action is mandatory and cannot be disabled.

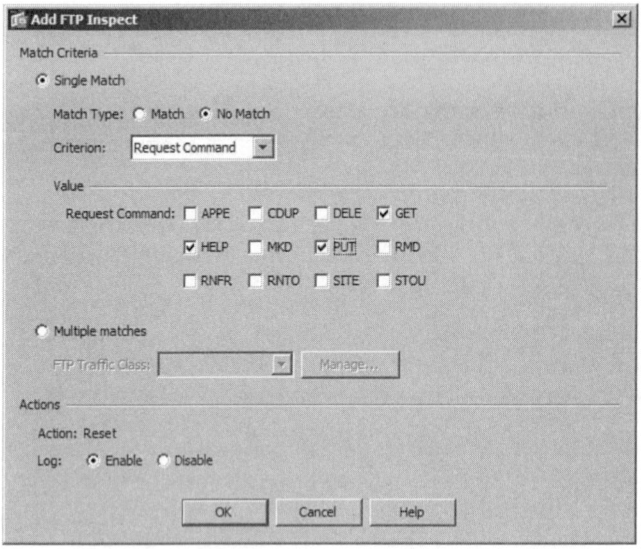

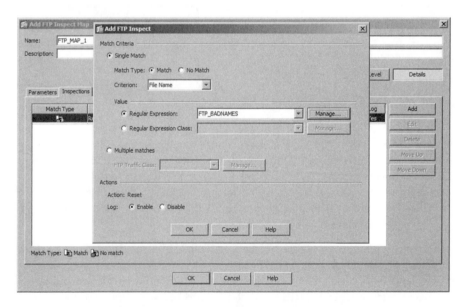

Figure 9-40 *Defining an FTP Request Command Policy*

As a second example, suppose that any FTP connections that involve filenames ending in .exe should be reset. In Figure 9-41, a regular expression called FTP_BADNAMES has been configured and applied to a new policy that uses a single match on the FTP File Name criterion.

Figure 9-41 *Defining a Policy to Match Against FTP Filenames*

Step 3: Apply the FTP Inspection Policy Map After you have configured an FTP inspection policy map, you apply it to an FTP inspection within a service policy rule. Any traffic that is classified or matched by the service policy rule will be sent through the customized inspection.

First, navigate to **Configuration > Firewall > Service Policy Rules** and select a service policy rule to edit. On the Traffic Classification tab, configure the traffic match criteria. Then click the **Rule Actions** tab. Make sure **FTP** is checked on the Protocol Inspection tab.

At this point, only the default FTP inspection will be used. Click the **Configure** button beside FTP, and then click the **Select an FTP Inspect Map for Fine Control over Inspection** radio button. Make sure the FTP inspection policy map name is selected in the list and click **OK**.

In Figure 9-42, the inspection policy map named FTP_MAP_1 is being applied to FTP inspection for the service policy rule.

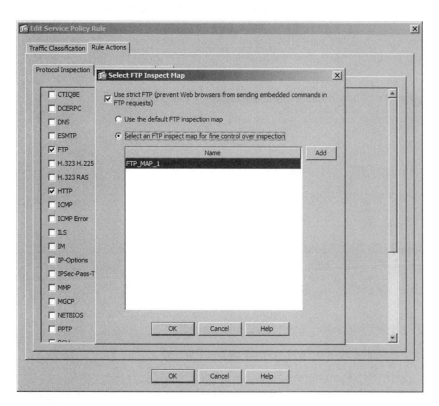

Figure 9-42 *Applying an FTP Inspection Policy Map to a Service Policy Rule*

Configuring DNS Inspection

An ASA can inspect the Domain Name Service (DNS) protocol that is used between clients and servers, as long as the clients and servers are located on opposite sides of the ASA. The DNS inspector offers the following functions:

■ Application of NAT rules to the contents of DNS replies

■ DNS protocol verification

■ Randomization of DNS ID values to protect against DNS spoofing attacks

■ DNS Guard, which closes a DNS UDP connection as soon as the first DNS reply is received

■ Granular inspection and matching of DNS requests and replies

You can use the CLI to configure a DNS inspection policy map that is applied to the DNS inspector process. The policy map can use various matching criteria to detect conditions within DNS transactions. In case of a match, individual DNS packets can be dropped, the whole DNS connection can be dropped, and control over the TSIG parameter can be enforced. By leveraging a DNS inspection policy map, you can mitigate DNS threats such as reconnaissance with nslookup, DoS, cache poisoning, and so on.

Creating and Applying a DNS Inspection Policy Map Using the CLI

You can use the following steps to build and apply a DNS inspection policy map:

Step 1.   Define the DNS inspection policy map.

Step 2.   Inspect DNS parameters.

Step 3.   Define a DNS inspection rule and an action.

Step 4.   Apply the DNS inspection policy map.

Step 1: Define the DNS Inspection Policy Map   Use the following command to define and name the policy map:

```
ciscoasa(config)# policy-map type inspect dns dns-map-name
```

As an example, suppose you need to define a DNS inspection policy map called DNS_MAP_1. You could enter the following command:

```
ciscoasa(config)# policy-map type inspect dns DNS_MAP_1
```

Step 2: Inspect DNS Parameters   You can configure several different DNS inspection functions that control DNS connections and their content. Begin by using the following command to enter the policy map parameter configuration mode:

```
ciscoasa(config-pmap)# parameters
```

Next, choose and enter one or more commands from Table 9-15.

Table 9-15   *DNS Parameter Inspection Commands*

Action	Command Syntax
Enable protocol verification	ciscoasa(config-pmap-p)# **protocol-enforcement**
Enable DNS Guard	ciscoasa(config-pmap-p)# **dns-guard**
Randomize the DNS ID	ciscoasa(config-pmap-p)# **id-randomization**
Log DNS ID all or excessive mismatches	ciscoasa(config-pmap-p)# **id-mismatch action log**
	ciscoasa(config-pmap-p)# **id-mismatch count** *number* **duration** *seconds* **action log**
Rewrite DNS replies according to NAT rules	ciscoasa(config-pmap-p)# **nat-rewrite**
Control DNS message length	ciscoasa(config-pmap-p)# **message-length maximum** {*length* | {{**client** | **server**} *length* [**auto**]}}
Enforce TSIG	ciscoasa(config-pmap-p)# **tsig enforced action** {**drop** | **log**}

As an example, DNS protocol verification and DNS Guard are enabled, along with DNS ID randomization and NAT rewrite. The commands listed in Example 9-25 are used.

Example 9-25   *Enabling DNS Parameter Inspection*

```
ciscoasa(config-pmap)# parameters
ciscoasa(config-pmap-p)# protocol-enforcement
ciscoasa(config-pmap-p)# dns-guard
ciscoasa(config-pmap-p)# id-randomization
ciscoasa(config-pmap-p)# nat-rewrite
ciscoasa(config-pmap-p)# exit
```

Step 3: Define a DNS Inspection Rule and an Action   Choose and enter one or more commands from Table 9-16, followed by an action from Table 9-17.

Table 9-16   *Commands for DNS Inspection Matching Conditions*

Match Criteria	Command Syntax
DNS resource record class	ciscoasa(config-pmap)# **match** [**not**] **dns-class** {**eq** {*class* | **IN**} | {**range** *low high*}}
DNS resource record type	ciscoasa(config-pmap)# **match** [**not**] **dns-type** {**eq** {*type* | **A** | **AXFR** | **CNAME** | **IXFR** | **NS** | **SOA** | **TSIG**} | {**range** *low high*}}
Domain name	ciscoasa(config-pmap)# **match** [**not**] **domain-name regex** {*name* | **class** *regex-class*}
Header flag	ciscoasa(config-pmap)# **match** [**not**] **header-flag** [**eq**] {*hex-flag* | {[**AA**] [**QR**] [**RA**] [**RD**] [**TC**]}}

Table 9-16   *Commands for DNS Inspection Matching Conditions*

Match Criteria	Command Syntax
DNS question	ciscoasa(config-pmap)# **match [not] question**
Resource record	ciscoasa(config-pmap)# **match [not] resource-record {additional | answer | authority}**

Table 9-17   *Commands for a DNS Inspection Action*

Action	Command Syntax
Drop the DNS packet	ciscoasa(config-pmap-c)# **drop [log]**
Drop the DNS connection	ciscoasa(config-pmap-c)# **drop-connection [log]**
Enforce TSIG	ciscoasa(config-pmap-c)# **enforce-tsig {log | drop [log]}**

Step 4: Apply the DNS Inspection Policy Map   After you configure a DNS inspection policy map, you apply it to a DNS inspection within a service policy rule using the following command syntax:

```
ciscoasa(config-pmap-c)# inspect dns dns-map-name
```

Any traffic that is classified or matched by the service policy rule will be sent through the customized inspection.

Be aware that an ASA has a default DNS inspection configuration, as listed in Example 9-26. A DNS inspection policy map called preset_dns_map is used to limit DNS messages to 512 bytes in length. This inspection policy map is applied to the DNS inspector in the global_policy policy map for all types of traffic matched by default, and is applied as a global service policy to all ASA interfaces.

Example 9-26   *Default DNS Inspection Policy Map Configuration*

```
ciscoasa(config)# policy-map type inspect dns preset_dns_map
ciscoasa(config-pmap)# parameters
ciscoasa(config-pmap-p)# message-length maximum 512
ciscoasa(config-pmap-p)# exit
ciscoasa(config-pmap)# exit
ciscoasa(config)# policy-map global_policy
ciscoasa(config-pmap)# class inspection_default
ciscoasa(config-pmap-c)# inspect dns preset_dns_map
ciscoasa(config-pmap-p)# exit
ciscoasa(config-pmap)# exit
ciscoasa(config)# service-policy global_policy global
```

Creating and Applying a DNS Inspection Policy Map Using ASDM

You can also use ASDM to configure a DNS inspection policy map. Navigate to
Configuration > Firewall > Objects > Inspect Maps and select **DNS**.

As with the CLI configuration, you can accomplish the ASDM configuration with the following steps:

Step 1.   Define the DNS inspection policy map.

Step 2.   Configure DNS protocol conformance.

Step 3.   Configure DNS filtering.

Step 4.   Configure DNS ID mismatch rate detection.

Step 5.   Configure detailed DNS inspection policies.

Step 6.   Apply the DNS inspection policy map.

Step 1: Define the DNS Inspection Policy Map   Click the **Add** button to add a new
inspection policy map. Enter an arbitrary name for the map, as well as an optional
description. Figure 9-43 shows a new policy map called DNS_MAP_1.

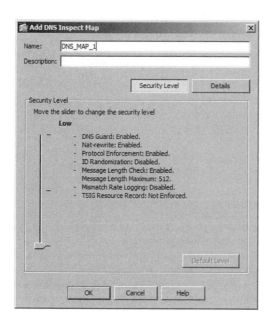

Figure 9-43   *Adding a New DNS Inspect Map in ASDM*

The Add DNS Inspect Map dialog box initially shows a Security Level slider that you can
use to quickly set up some basic DNS inspection parameters. By sliding the pointer up or
down, you can choose between the following security levels:

■   **Low:** Protocol enforcement is enabled, DNS Guard is enabled, NAT rewrite is enabled, and DNS message length is limited to 512 characters.

- **Medium:** Adds DNS ID randomization and DNS ID mismatch rate logging to the Low settings.

- **High:** Adds TSIG resource record enforcement to the Medium settings.

Step 2: Configure DNS Protocol Conformance   Click the **Protocol Conformance** tab in the Add DNS Inspect Map dialog box. As shown in Figure 9-44, you can configure the DNS Guard, NAT rewrite, protocol enforcement, DNS ID randomization, and Transaction Signature (TSIG) enforcement functions.

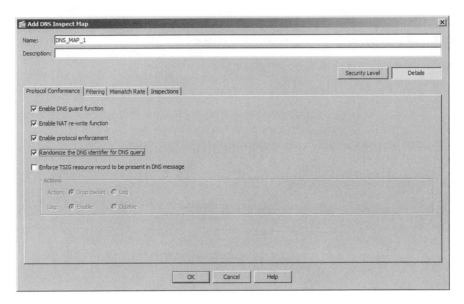

Figure 9-44   *Configuring DNS Protocol Conformance*

Step 3: Configure DNS Filtering   Click the **Filtering** tab in the Add DNS Inspect Map dialog box, as shown in Figure 9-45. You can configure message length filters that control the size of DNS messages sent globally, to servers, or to clients.

Step 4: Configure DNS ID Mismatch Rate Detection   Click the **Mismatch Rate** tab in the Add DNS Inspect Map dialog box, as shown in Figure 9-46. From there, you can enable the ID mismatch function and set thresholds for the number of mismatches detected during a time interval.

Step 5: Configure Detailed DNS Inspection Policies   Click the **Inspections** tab in the Add DNS Inspect Map dialog box to see and configure individual DNS inspection policies. You can add a new inspection policy by clicking the **Add** button. In the Add DNS Inspect dialog box, shown in Figure 9-47, you can choose a match type, match criterion, values to match against, and the actions to take.

Step 6: Apply the DNS Inspection Policy Map   After you configure a DNS inspection policy map, you apply it to a DNS inspection within a service policy rule. Any traffic that is classified or matched by the service policy rule will be sent through the customized inspection.

First, navigate to **Configuration > Firewall > Service Policy Rules** and select a service policy rule to edit. On the Traffic Classification tab, configure the traffic match criteria. Then click the **Rule Actions** tab. Make sure **DNS** is checked on the Protocol Inspection tab.

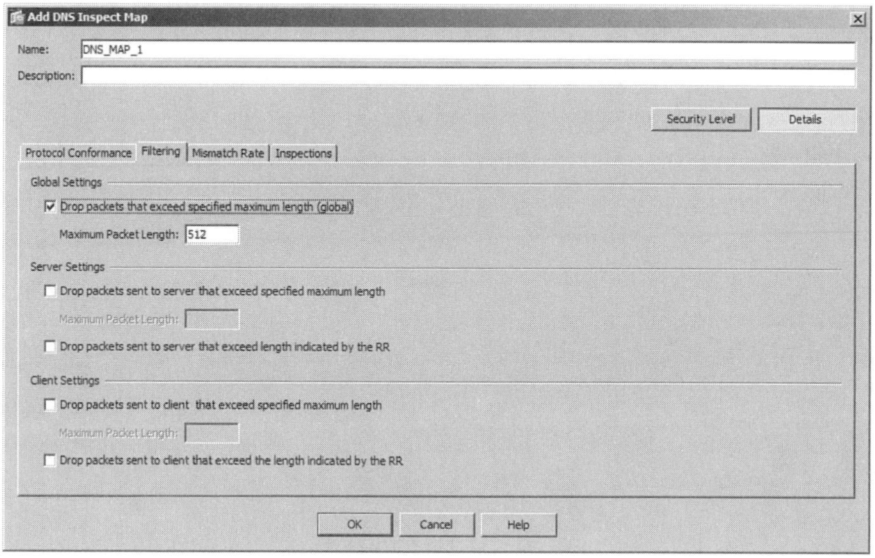

Figure 9-45   *Configuring DNS Filtering*

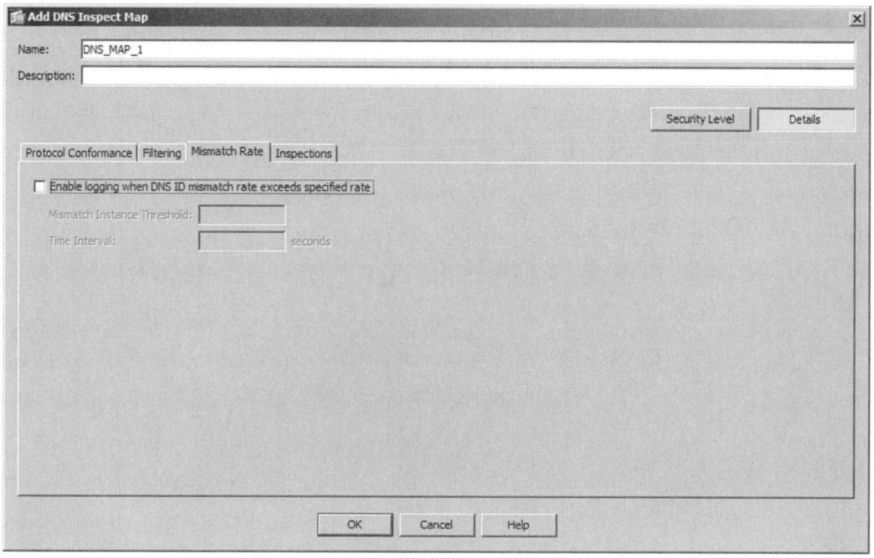

Figure 9-46   *Configuring DNS ID Mismatch Rate Detection*

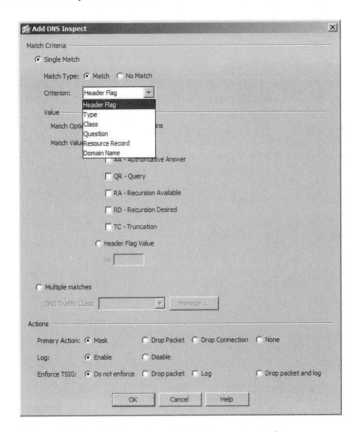

Figure 9-47 *Configuring a DNS Inspection Policy*

Click the **Configure** button beside DNS, and then click the **Select a DNS Inspect Map for Fine Control over Inspection** radio button. Make sure the DNS inspection policy map name is selected in the list and click **OK**. In Figure 9-48, the inspection policy map named DNS_MAP_1 is being applied to DNS inspection for the service policy rule.

Configuring ESMTP Inspection

An ASA can inspect the Extended Simple Mail Transfer Protocol (ESMTP) that is described in RFCs 5321 and 5322. ESMTP is used to transfer email between clients and servers and between servers and other servers. You can configure the ESMTP inspector to perform the following functions:

■ ESMTP protocol verification

■ Control over unauthorized mail relay servers

■ Client and server filtering based on domain names

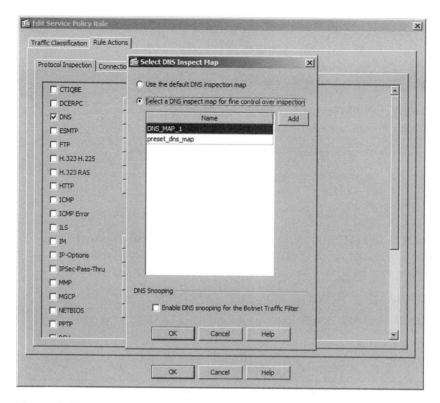

Figure 9-48   *Applying a DNS Inspection Policy Map to a Service Policy Rule*

- Malicious character filtering
- Granular inspection and matching of ESMTP commands and content

Configuring an ESMTP Inspection with the CLI

You can use the CLI to configure an ESMTP inspection policy map that is applied to the ESMTP inspector process. The policy map can use various matching criteria to detect conditions within ESMTP connections. In case of a match, the ASA can log, drop, or reset the ESMTP connections.

You can use the following steps to build and apply an ESMTP inspection policy map:

Step 1.   Define the ESMTP inspection policy map.

Step 2.   Inspect ESMTP parameters.

Step 3.   Define an ESMTP inspection rule and an action.

Step 4.   Apply the ESMTP inspection policy map.

The sections that follow cover the specific tasks involved with each step.

Step 1: Define the ESMTP Inspection Policy Map   Use the following command to define and name the policy map:

```
ciscoasa(config)# policy-map type inspect esmtp esmtp-map-name
```

As an example, if you needed to define an ESMTP inspection policy map called ESMTP_MAP_1, you could enter the following command:

```
ciscoasa(config)# policy-map type inspect estmp ESMTP_MAP_1
```

Step 2: Inspect ESMTP Parameters   You can configure several different ESMTP inspection functions that control ESMTP connections and their content. Begin by using the following command to enter the policy map parameter configuration mode:

```
ciscoasa(config-pmap)# parameters
```

Then choose and enter one or more commands from Table 9-18.

Table 9-18   *Commands for Inspecting ESMTP Parameters*

Action	Command Syntax
Allow TLS ESMTP connections	ciscoasa(config-pmap-p)# **allow-tls** [action log]
Detect mail relays	ciscoasa(config-pmap-p)# **mail-relay** *domain-name* **action** {log | **drop-connection** [log] }
Mask ESMTP server banners	ciscoasa(config-pmap-p)# **mask-banner**
Detect special characters in addresses	ciscoasa(config-pmap-p)# **special-character** {log | **drop-connection** [log]}

Step 3: Define an ESMTP Inspection Rule and an Action   Choose and enter one or more commands from Table 9-19, followed by an action from Table 9-20.

Table 9-19   *Commands for ESMTP Inspection Matching Conditions*

Match Criteria	Command Syntax
Mail message body length	ciscoasa(config-pmap)# **match** [not] **body** [line] **length gt** *value*
Number of recipients	ciscoasa(config-pmap)# **match** [not] **cmd** {RCPT **count gt** *number* | **line length gt** *number*}

Table 9-19 *Commands for ESMTP Inspection Matching Conditions*

Match Criteria	Command Syntax
ESMTP method	ciscoasa(config-pmap)# **match** [not] **cmd verb** *cmd1* [*cmd2* ...] where *cmd1* is one of the following keywords: **AUTH, DATA, EHLO, ETRN, HELO, HELP, MAIL, NOOP, QUIT, RCPT, RSET, SAML, SOML, VRFY**
EHLO reply parameter	ciscoasa(config-pmap)# **match** [not] **ehlo-reply-parameter** *param* where *param* is one of the following keywords: **8bitmime, binarymime, checkpoint, dsn, ecode, etrn, others, pipelining, size, vrfy**
Mail header size	ciscoasa(config-pmap)# **match** [not] **header** {[**line**] **length gt** *number* | **to-fields count gt** *number*}
Invalid recipient address count	ciscoasa(config-pmap)# **match** [not] **invalid-recipients count gt** *number*
MIME header	ciscoasa(config-pmap)# **match** [not] **mime** {**encoding** *type* | **filename length gt** *number* | **filetype regex** {*regex-name* | **class** *regex-class*} where *type* is one of the following keywords: **7bit, 8bit, base64, binary, others, quoted-printable**
Sender address	ciscoasa(config-pmap)# **match** [not] **sender-address** {**length gt** *number* | **regex** {*regex-name* | **class** *regex-class*}}

Table 9-20 *Commands for an ESMTP Inspection Action*

Action	Command Syntax
Log the ESMTP event	ciscoasa(config-pmap-c)# **log**
Drop the ESMTP connection	ciscoasa(config-pmap-c)# **drop-connection** [log]
Reset the ESMTP connection	ciscoasa(config-pmap-c)# **reset** [log]

Step 4: Apply the ESMTP Inspection Policy Map   After you have configured an ESMTP inspection policy map, you apply it to an ESMTP inspection within a service policy rule using the following command syntax:

```
ciscoasa(config-pmap-c)# inspect esmtp esmtp-map-name
```

Any traffic that is classified or matched by the service policy rule will be sent through the customized inspection.

Configuring an ESMTP Inspection with ASDM

You can also use ASDM to configure an ESMTP inspection policy map. Navigate to **Configuration > Firewall > Objects > Inspect Maps** and select **ESMTP**.

As with the CLI configuration, you can accomplish the ASDM configuration with the following steps:

Step 1.   Define the ESMTP inspection policy map.

Step 2.   Configure ESMTP inspection parameters.

Step 3.   Configure ESMTP filtering.

Step 4.   Configure detailed ESMTP inspection policies.

Step 5.   Apply the ESMTP inspection policy map.

The sections that follow cover the specific tasks involved with each step.

Step 1: Define the ESMTP Inspection Policy Map   Click the **Add** button to add a new inspection policy map. Enter an arbitrary name for the map, as well as an optional description. Figure 9-49 shows a new policy map called ESMTP_MAP_1.

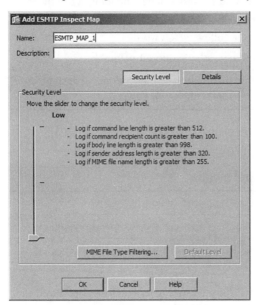

Figure 9-49   *Adding a New ESMTP Inspect Map in ASDM*

The Add ESMTP Inspect Map dialog box initially shows a Security Level slider that you can use to quickly set up some basic ESMTP inspection parameters. By default, ASDM sets the following message content thresholds that are used by the Security Level slider:

■   **Command line length:** 512 characters

■   **Command recipient count:** 100 recipients

- **Body line length:** 998 characters

- **Sender address:** 320 characters

- **MIME filename:** 255 characters

By sliding the pointer up or down, you can choose between the following security levels:

- **Low:** Content that exceeds a threshold is permitted but logged.

- **Medium:** Content that exceeds a threshold is dropped; the ESMTP server banner is masked.

- **High:** Content that exceeds a threshold is both dropped and logged; the ESMTP server banner is masked.

Step 2: Configure ESMTP Inspection Parameters   Click the **Parameters** tab in the Add ESMTP Inspect Map dialog box. As shown in Figure 9-50, you can enable server banner masking and you can bypass inspection for ESMTP connections that are encrypted with TLS.

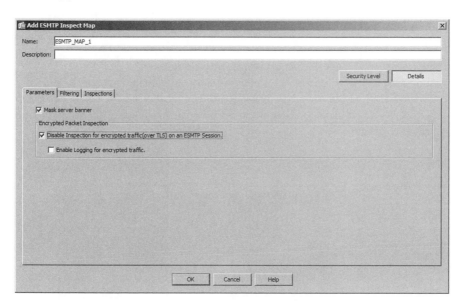

Figure 9-50   *Configuring ESMTP Inspection Parameters*

Step 3: Configure ESMTP Filtering   Click the **Filtering** tab in the Add ESMTP Inspect Map dialog box, as shown in Figure 9-51. You can configure mail relay filtering by domain name, as well as filtering for special characters that are known to be used in recipient addresses for malicious purposes.

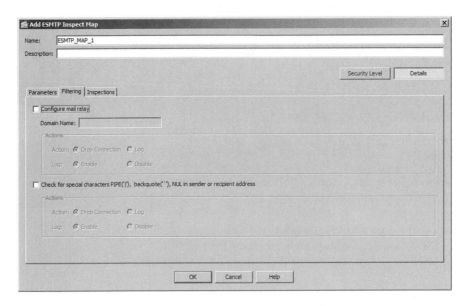

Figure 9-51 *Configuring ESMTP Filtering*

Step 4: Configure Detailed ESMTP Inspection Policies Click the **Inspections** tab in the Add ESMTP Inspect Map dialog box to see and configure individual ESMTP inspection policies. You can add a new inspection policy by clicking the **Add** button. In the Add ESMTP Inspect dialog box, shown in Figure 9-52, you can choose a match type, match criterion, values to match against, and the actions to take.

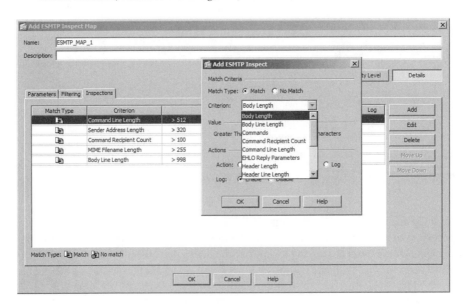

Figure 9-52 *Configuring an ESMTP Inspection Policy*

Step 5: Apply the ESMTP Inspection Policy Map   After you configure an ESMTP inspection policy map, you apply it to an ESMTP inspection within a service policy rule. Any traffic that is classified or matched by the service policy rule will be sent through the customized inspection.

First, navigate to **Configuration > Firewall > Service Policy Rules** and select a service policy rule to edit. On the Traffic Classification tab, configure the traffic match criteria. Then click the **Rule Actions** tab. Make sure **ESMTP** is checked on the Protocol Inspection tab.

Click the **Configure** button beside ESMTP, and then click the **Select an ESMTP Inspect Map for Fine Control over Inspection** radio button. Make sure the ESMTP inspection policy map name is selected in the list and click **OK**. In Figure 9-53, the inspection policy map named ESMTP_MAP_1 is being applied to ESMTP inspection for the service policy rule.

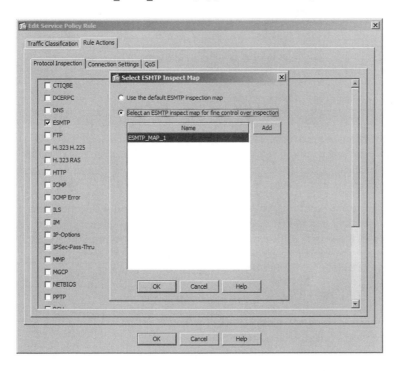

Figure 9-53   *Applying an ESMTP Inspection Policy Map to a Service Policy Rule*

Configuring a Policy for ASA Management Traffic

The MPF is commonly used to configure policies that inspect and control transit traffic, or traffic that is passing through the ASA from one interface to another. You can also configure a management traffic policy to control traffic that is destined for the ASA itself. For example, you might want to match against HTTP over SSL traffic so that you can limit the number of ASDM connections users can attempt to start. Other types of management traffic include SNMP, syslog, TFTP, SSH, and Telnet.

By classifying management traffic as a special case, you can configure specific policies to help prevent denial-of-service attacks on the firewall itself. Otherwise, once you enable the ASA's HTTP server to offer the ASDM management interface, malicious users might also use the HTTP service and perhaps cripple the ASA's CPU.

You can define a management traffic policy by first configuring a special "management" class map type to match specific traffic that terminates on the ASA itself. The command syntax is similar to a normal class map configuration command, except that the **type management** keywords must be added, as follows:

```
ciscoasa(config)# class-map type management mgmt_cmap_name
```

Next, use the **match** command to specify how the management traffic is to be matched or classified. Only two match criteria are possible, as listed in Table 9-21, although the commands can be repeated to match as many different kinds of management traffic as needed.

Table 9-21   *Match Commands Used in a Management Traffic Class Map*

Matching Condition	Command Syntax
Match against an access list	ciscoasa(config-cmap)# **match access-list** *acl_name*
Match one or a range of port numbers	ciscoasa(config-cmap)# **match port** {tcp | udp} {eq *port_number* | **range** *low high*}

After you have configured the management class map, you can reference it with a **class** command within a policy map, as you would a normal Layer 3–4 class map. The only difference is that management traffic terminating on the ASA itself will be classified and handled as a unique policy, separate from any other regular traffic policy.

As an example, suppose you would like to limit the number of inbound connections that potential ASDM users can open from the outside network. The goal is to limit the embryonic connections to TCP port 443 to five, preventing malicious users from trying to exhaust the ASA's memory by opening too many bogus connections. The commands listed in Example 9-27 could be used to configure the management traffic policy.

Example 9-27   *Configuring a Management Class Map and Policy Map*

```
ciscoasa(config)# class-map type management MGMT-CLASS
ciscoasa(config-cmap)# match port tcp eq 443
ciscoasa(config-cmap)# exit
ciscoasa(config)# policy-map p1
ciscoasa(config-pmap)# class MGMT-CLASS
ciscoasa(config-pmap-c)# set connection embryonic-conn-max 5
ciscoasa(config-pmap-c)# exit
ciscoasa(config-pmap)# exit
ciscoasa(config)# service-policy p1 interface outside
```

You can also use ASDM to create security policies that can limit management traffic destined for an ASA. First, navigate to **Configuration > Firewall > Service Policy Rules**. Click beside the **Add** button to expand the options, and then choose **Add Management Service Policy Rule**. Select the interface and service policy where the new management policy will be applied. In Figure 9-54, an existing service policy called p1 will be used on the outside interface.

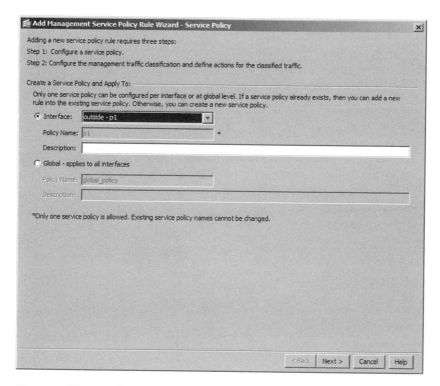

Figure 9-54   *Configuring a New Service Policy to Limit ASA Management Traffic*

Click the **Next** button to define the traffic matching criteria. In Figure 9-55, the management traffic class has been named MGMT-CLASS and will match against a fixed TCP or UDP port number.

In Figure 9-56, TCP port 443 (https) has been chosen. The goal is to limit the number of secure browser connections that can be initiated to the ASA, enabling it to keep control over its own resources.

Next, define the connection and embryonic connection limits that the ASA will impose. These values are 0 by default, permitting an unlimited number. In Figure 9-57, the connection limit has been left at 0, while the embryonic limit has been set to 5. Click the **Finish** button to complete the service policy configuration.

Detecting and Filtering Botnet Traffic

In a botnet attack, individual hosts on the private, protected side of an ASA become infected with malware. Each of the infected hosts tries to contact a botnet control server located somewhere on the public Internet, as shown in Figure 9-58, to receive further instructions. The control server is then able to remotely control many infected hosts and align them in a coordinated attack against other resources.

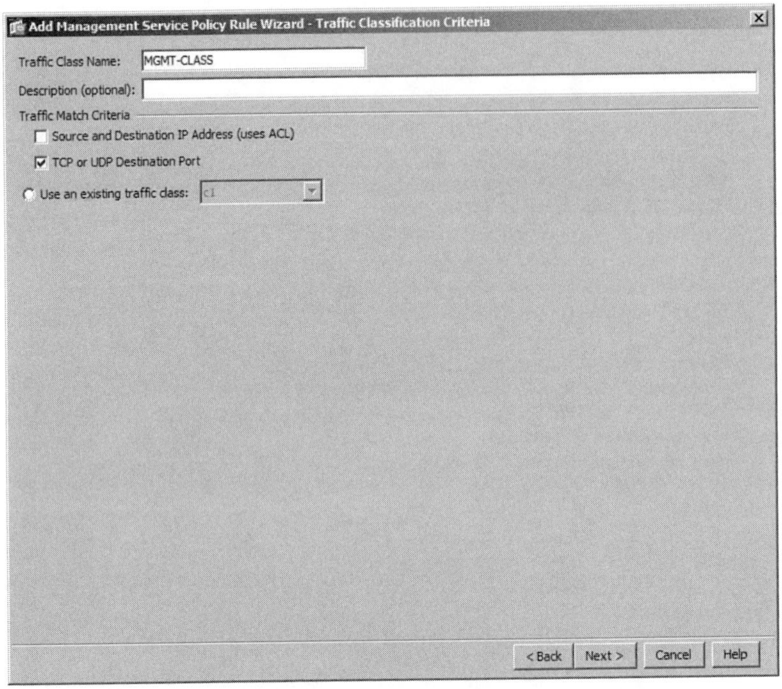

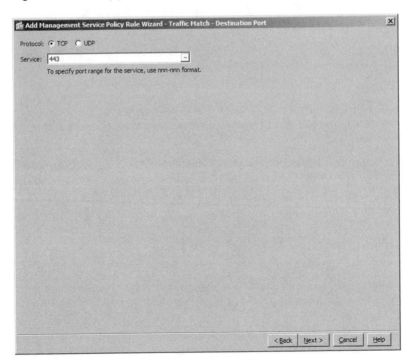

Figure 9-55   *Configuring a Management Class Map*

Figure 9-56   *Specifying Management Traffic to Limit*

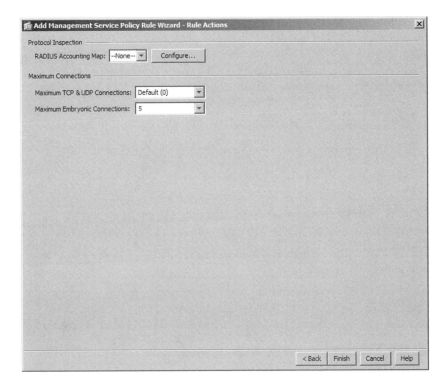

Figure 9-57 *Setting Limits on Management Traffic Connections*

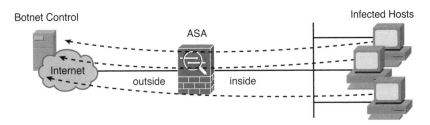

Figure 9-58 *Botnet Activity Between Infected Hosts and a Control Server*

Because the infected hosts are located on a secure side of the ASA, they are likely to be free to open outbound connections just like any other protected host. You can leverage the Cisco ASA Botnet Traffic Filter feature to detect botnet activity and prevent infected hosts from contacting their control servers.

When the Botnet Traffic Filter is enabled, an ASA maintains two reputation databases:

■ A dynamic SensorBase database that is downloaded periodically from Cisco, which contains information about known botnet control servers

■ A static database that you can populate, which can contain a "whitelist" of known good IP addresses and domain names or a "blacklist" of known bad servers

The ASA will monitor DNS queries that involve known bad machines listed in the databases. When a match is found, the ASA adds the name and IP address into a special DNS reverse lookup cache. As it builds new connections, the ASA will compare DNS replies and the source and destination addresses against its databases. If a connection to a known bad machine is found, a logging message is generated and the ASA can drop the connection.

The Botnet Traffic Filter feature is dependent upon four things:

- A Botnet Traffic Filter license purchased from Cisco and installed on the ASA

- A DNS server, which the ASA uses to look up names and addresses in the static database

- Botnet Traffic Filter DNS snooping, which enables the ASA to intercept DNS queries from infected hosts and match against hostnames it finds in the databases

- Live connectivity to the Internet, so that the Botnet Traffic Filter feature can communicate with Cisco

Before you begin configuring Botnet Traffic Filtering, verify that the feature license has been enabled. You can use the **show version** command to see a list of ASA features and their license status. Make sure Botnet Traffic Filter is listed as Enabled, as in Example 9-28.

Example 9-28   *Verifying the Botnet Traffic Filter License Status*

```
ciscoasa# show version
Cisco Adaptive Security Appliance Software Version 8.2(3)
Device Manager Version 6.3(4)
Compiled on Fri 06-Aug-10 07:51 by builders
System image file is "disk0:/asa823-k8.bin"
Config file at boot was "startup-config"
ciscoasa up 12 days 13 hours
[output truncated for clarity]
AnyConnect Essentials          : Disabled
Advanced Endpoint Assessment   : Disabled
UC Phone Proxy Sessions        : 2
Total UC Proxy Sessions        : 2
Botnet Traffic Filter          : Enabled
```

Configuring Botnet Traffic Filtering with ASDM

You can use ASDM to enable and configure Botnet Traffic Filtering. Navigate to **Configuration > Firewall**, expand **Botnet Traffic Filter,** and use the following steps:

Step 1.   Configure the dynamic database.

Step 2.   Configure the static database.

Step 3.   Enable DNS snooping.

Step 4.   Enable the Botnet Traffic Filter.

The sections that follow provide information about the specific tasks involved with each step.

Step 1: Configure the Dynamic Database

Select **Botnet Database** to display the database configuration options, as shown in Figure 9-59. Next, check the **Enable Botnet Updater Client** and **Use Botnet Data Dynamically from Updater Server** check boxes to download and use the dynamic database obtained from Cisco. The database is automatically downloaded and updated periodically at one-hour intervals, but it cannot be saved to the startup configuration. You can manually fetch the database or purge it from the ASA's running memory, if needed, by clicking the respective buttons. Click the **Apply** button to apply your configuration changes.

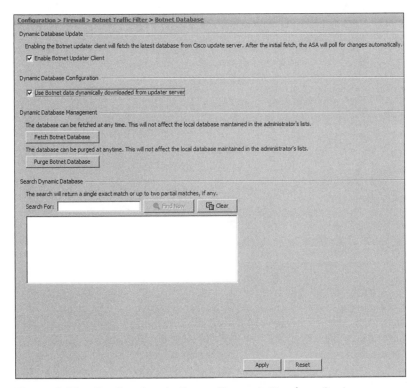

Figure 9-59   *Configuring the Botnet Dynamic Database Options*

Step 2: Configure the Static Database

Select **Black and White Lists** under Botnet Traffic Filter to display configuration options for the blacklist and whitelist in the static database. In Figure 9-60, the name www.mostlynice.com has been added to the whitelist. To add the name www.badnews4u.com to the blacklist, click the **Add** button next to Black List, and then enter the hostname and click **OK**. Once you have finished editing the lists, click the **Apply** button.

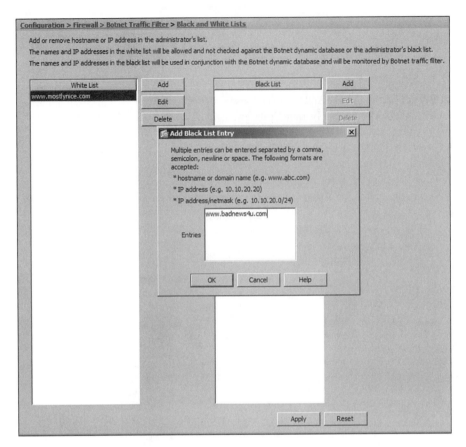

Figure 9-60 *Configuring the Static Blacklist and Whitelist Databases*

Step 3: Enable DNS Snooping

Configuring DNS snooping is much easier in ASDM than it is from the CLI. Select **DNS Snooping** under Botnet Traffic Filter to display the DNS snooping configuration options, as shown in Figure 9-61. To enable DNS snooping globally, just check the box under the heading DNS Snooping Enabled and click the **Apply** button.

Step 4: Enable the Botnet Traffic Filter

Select **Traffic Settings** under Botnet Traffic Filter to display the Traffic Settings options window. In the upper portion of the window, check the box next to each interface where Botnet Traffic Filtering should be enabled. In Figure 9-62, only the outside interface is selected because it is the only one facing the public Internet. As an option, you can click the **Manage ACL** button to create and apply an access list to match a subset of traffic for filtering.

By default, the Blacklisted Traffic Actions section in the bottom portion of the window is empty. This means that any botnet-related traffic will only be logged. If you want to have that traffic dropped instead, you need to add an action by clicking the **Add** button. In

Figure 9-62, an action has been added for the outside interface to drop traffic. The Threat Level has been left to the default, which will match any blacklisted site marked with a threat level of Moderate to Very High. Click the **OK** button to add the action, and then click the **Apply** button to apply your changes.

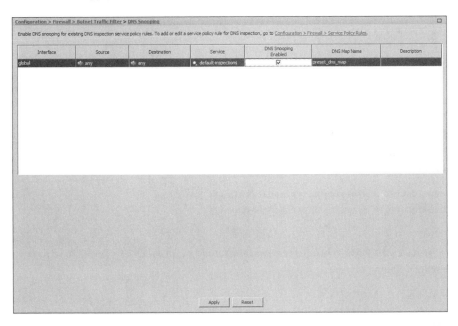

Figure 9-61   *Enabling DNS Snooping for Botnet Traffic Filtering*

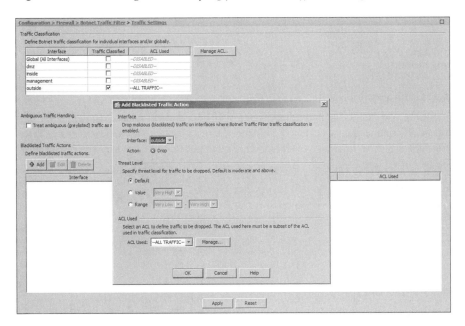

Figure 9-62   *Configuring Botnet Traffic Filter Settings and Actions*

Configuring Botnet Traffic Filtering with the CLI

You can also configure Botnet Traffic Filtering with the CLI by using the following steps:

Step 1.   Configure the dynamic database.

Step 2.   Configure the static database.

Step 3.   Enable DNS snooping.

Step 4.   Enable the Botnet Traffic Filter.

The sections that follow provide information about the specific tasks involved with each step.

Step 1: Configure the Dynamic Database

With the following commands, you can enable database downloading and the use of the database, respectively:

```
ciscoasa(config)# dynamic-filter updater-client enable
ciscoasa(config)# dynamic-filter use-database
```

> **Note:**   The ASA uses DNS to resolve the name of the database server. If you do not have DNS domain lookup configured properly, the ASA will return the following message:
>
> ```
> ciscoasa(config)# dynamic-filter updater-client enable
> WARNING: Can't resolve update-manifests.ironport.com, make sure dns nameserver is
>   configured
> ciscoasa(config)#
> ```

The ASA updates its database once per hour, by default. The local database is stored in running memory.

Step 2: Configure the Static Database

As an option, you can define individual names or IP addresses in a static database. With the following commands, you can add a host to the blacklist or to the whitelist. Any connections discovered to or from a blacklisted host will be dropped, while a whitelisted host will be permitted and logged:

```
ciscoasa(config)# dynamic-filter {blacklist | whitelist}
ciscoasa(config-llist)# name hostname
```

-OR-

```
ciscoasa(config-llist)# address ip-address
```

Step 3: Enable DNS Snooping

As an option, you can enable DNS snooping so that the ASA can match against host names found in the database. DNS snooping is configured in the global_policy policy map, as an additional option to the DNS inspector. You can use the following commands to add DNS snooping to the default DNS inspector configuration:

```
ciscoasa(config)# policy-map global_policy
ciscoasa(config-pmap)# class inspection_default
ciscoasa(config-pmap-c)# inspect dns preset_dns_map dynamic-filter-snoop
```

Step 4: Enable the Botnet Traffic Filter

You can use the **dynamic-filter enable** command to enable botnet monitoring using the dynamic database. Monitoring will log botnet activity, but will not drop any connections. You can identify a specific interface or an access list that will be used to match a subset of traffic; if neither is entered with the following command, then Botnet filter monitoring will be enabled globally:

```
ciscoasa(config)# dynamic-filter enable [interface name] [classify-list access-
  list]
```

To drop connections involved in botnet activity, you use the **dynamic-filter drop blacklist** command:

```
ciscoasa(config)# dynamic-filter drop blacklist [interface name] [action-classify-
  list subset_access_list] [threat-level {eq level | range min max}]
```

You can identify a specific interface or an access list that will be used to match a subset of traffic.

Cisco rates each entry in the dynamic database with one of the following threat levels: very low, low, moderate, high, very high. By default, the Botnet Traffic Filter will drop connections that are involved with hosts from a moderate to a very-high threat level. You can specify a single threat level or a range of threat levels, though it's best to use the default. Entries that are found in the static blacklist automatically receive a threat level of very high.

Note: You should always enable Botnet Traffic Filtering on all interfaces that face the public Internet.

As an example, suppose you would like to begin using Botnet Traffic Filtering, along with DNS snooping. Connections to any blacklisted sites with threat levels moderate to very high should be dropped. In addition to the dynamic database from Cisco, you have discovered that host www.badnews4u.com is a known bad site. Host www.mostlynice.com is a suspect site, but connections to it should be permitted and logged. You could use the commands listed in Example 9-29 to accomplish your goal.

Example 9-29   *Configuring Botnet Traffic Filtering*

```
ciscoasa(config)# dynamic-filter updater-client enable
ciscoasa(config)# dynamic-filter use-database
ciscoasa(config)# dynamic-filter blacklist
ciscoasa(config-llist)# name www.badnews4u.com
ciscoasa(config)# dynamic-filter whitelist
ciscoasa(config-llist)# name www.mostlynice.com
ciscoasa(config-llist)# exit
ciscoasa(config)# policy-map global_policy
ciscoasa(config-pmap)# class inspection_default
ciscoasa(config-pmap-c)# inspect dns preset_dns_map dynamic-filter-snoop
ciscoasa(config-pmap-c)# exit
ciscoasa(config-pmap)# exit
ciscoasa(config)# dynamic-filter drop blacklist interface outside
```

You can use the commands listed in Table 9-22 to verify Botnet Traffic Filtering operation.

Table 9-22   *Commands to Verify Botnet Traffic Filtering Operation*

Function	Command Syntax
Dynamic database status	ciscoasa# **show dynamic-filter updater-client**
Connections filtered	ciscoasa# **show dynamic-filter statistics**
List infected hosts	ciscoasa# **show dynamic-filter report infected-hosts**
Top-n botnet activity	ciscoasa# **show dynamic-filter top [infected-hosts	malware-ports	malware-sites]**

Using Threat Detection

Some malicious activity might occur without any prior background information. For example, a host might use a discovery or attack scheme that is an entirely new approach. An ASA might not have signatures or blacklist information that can be used to match the attack.

Threat detection is a feature that can be leveraged to discover suspicious activity passing through an ASA. By monitoring the rate at which security policies are triggered, the ASA can detect abnormal conditions that might indicate an attack in progress.

The threat detection feature can be described by the following three levels:

- **Basic threat detection:** Monitors the average and burst rate of dropped packets and security events over an interval; generates a logging message when a threshold is exceeded

- **Advanced threat detection:** Gathers statistics for both allowed and denied packets for objects such as hosts, protocols, ports, and access lists; generates a logging message when the TCP Intercept rate exceeds a threshold

■ **Scanning threat detection:** Maintains a database of suspicious activity for each host; can detect a host that is scanning for vulnerable targets based on the average and burst rates of scanning events; generates logging messages and can automatically shun attacking hosts

You can configure threat detection in phases, adding more progressive levels as needed. Be aware that advanced and scanning threat detection can tax the ASA resources because they monitor and gather extensive and granular information.

Configuring Threat Detection in ASDM

You can configure all forms of threat detection from one window in ASDM. Begin by going to **Configuration > Firewall > Threat Detection**. Use the following steps as you move through the configuration:

Step 1.   Configure basic threat detection.

Step 2.   Configure advanced threat detection.

Step 3.   Configure scanning threat detection.

Step 1: Configure Basic Threat Detection

Begin by checking the **Enable Basic Treat Detection** check box at the top of the window, as shown in Figure 9-63. All the default rate intervals and thresholds will already be in place. ASDM does not offer a way to adjust the parameters.

Step 2: Configure Advanced Threat Detection

You can configure advanced threat detection to gather statistics about suspicious activity going either to or from individual objects. Based on the statistics, you can determine which protocols or ports are being used for an attack, which access list rules are being triggered, and if a host is attacking or being attacked.

You can enable advanced threat detection by clicking one of the radio buttons under Threat Detection Statistics. In Figure 9-64, Enable All Statistics has been chosen so that protocol, port, access-list, and host statistics will be collected. Under Rate Intervals, only the least frequent value (1 hour) for Host, Port, and Protocol, has been chosen, to lighten the load on ASA resources.

Advanced threat detection can also gather statistics about TCP Intercept activity and reports when thresholds are exceeded. The TCP Intercepts are counted over the duration of a rate interval monitoring window, which is 30 minutes by default. If the number of attacks, or TCP Intercept events, rises above an average rate threshold (default 200 per second) or above a burst threshold (default 400 per second), a logging message is generated. The default values are shown in Figure 9-64, although you can adjust the values at the bottom of the window.

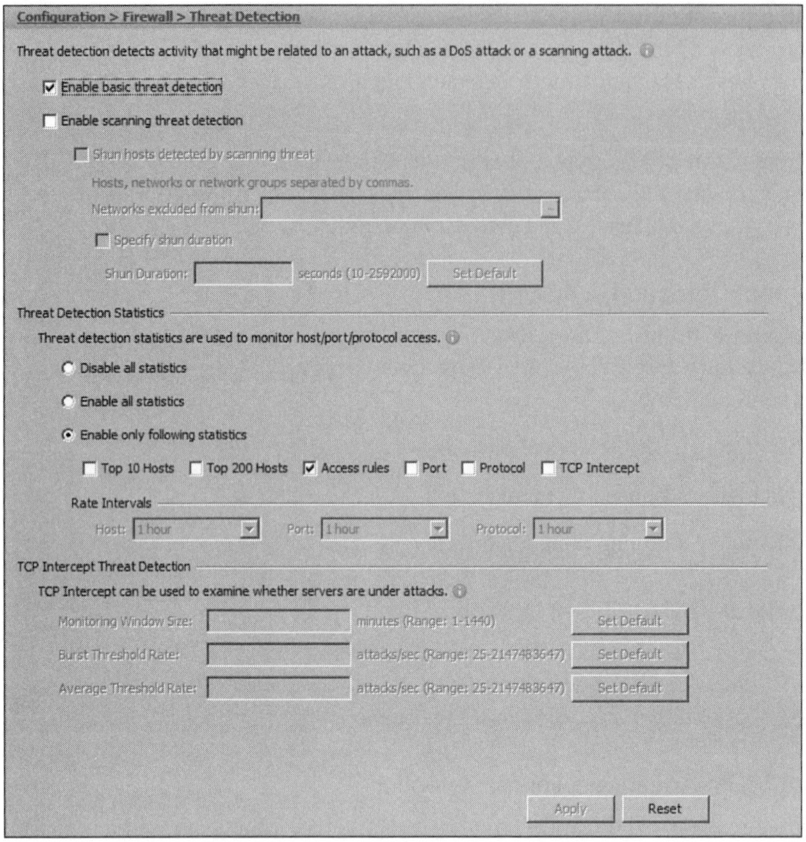

Figure 9-63   *Enabling Basic Threat Detection in ASDM*

Step 3: Configure Scanning Threat Detection

You can enable scanning threat detection by checking the **Enable Scanning Threat Detection** check box at the top of the Threat Detection configuration window. Under that is a check box to enable automatic shunning. You can also identify any IP addresses that should be excluded from shuns and set the shun duration.

In Figure 9-65, scanning threat detection has been enabled. Shuns have also been enabled, but hosts in the 192.168.101.0/24 network will be excluded. The default shun duration of 3600 seconds (1 hour) will be used.

Be sure to click the **Apply** button to apply all of the threat detection configuration changes you have made.

Configuring Threat Detection with the CLI

Use the following steps to configure threat detection with the CLI:

Step 1.   Configure basic threat detection.

Step 2.   Configure advanced threat detection.

Step 3.   Configure scanning threat detection.

Step 1: Configure Basic Threat Detection

Begin by enabling basic threat detection with the following command:

```
ciscoasa(config)# threat-detection basic-threat
```

Each type of detected event has three thresholds that can be set:

- **Rate interval:** The period of time that statistics are averaged

- **Average threshold:** The number of detected events per second that must be exceeded

- **Burst threshold:** The number of detected events per second exceeded over a shorter burst window; the larger of either 10 seconds or 1/30 of the rate interval

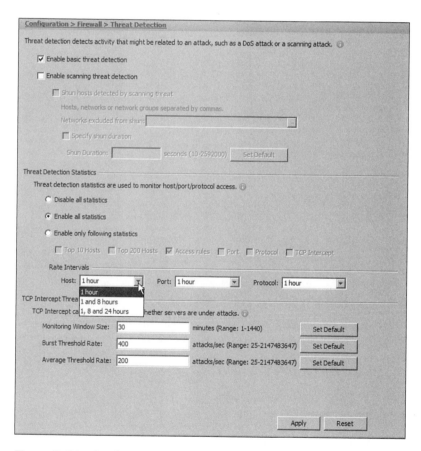

Figure 9-64 *Configuring Advanced Threat Detection in ASDM*

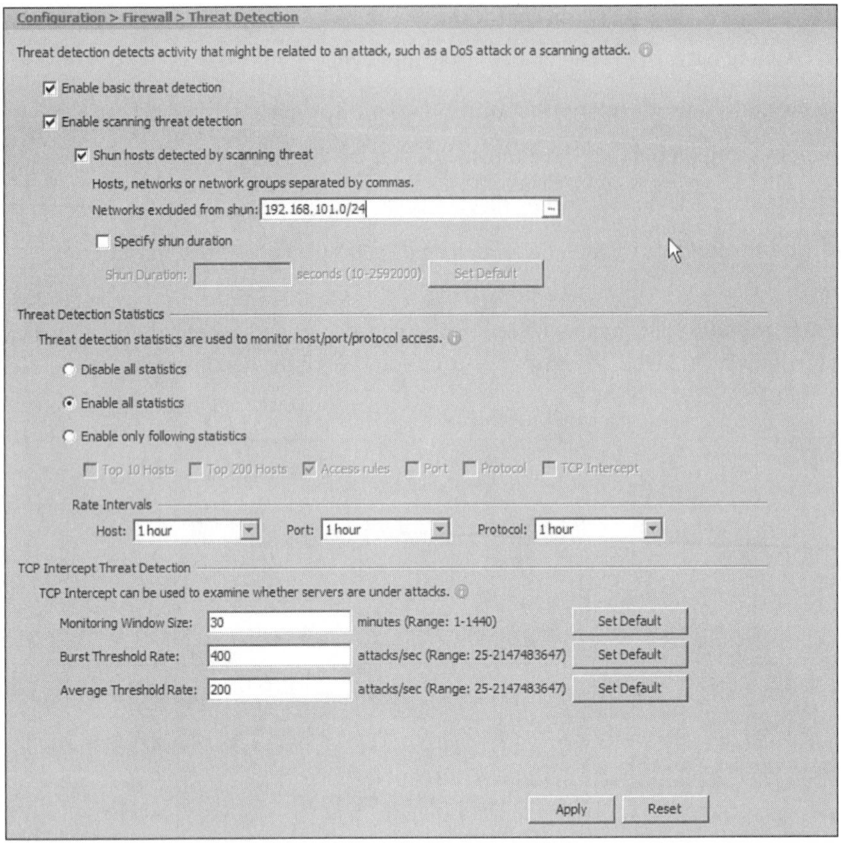

Figure 9-65 *Configuring Scanning Threat Detection in ASDM*

Next, as an option, you can set up the rate interval and thresholds for each type of detected event with the following configuration command:

```
ciscoasa(config)# threat-detection rate [acl-drop | bad-packet-drop | conn-limit-drop
   | dos-drop | fw-drop | icmp-drop | inspect-drop | interface-drop | scanning-threat
   | syn-attack] rate-interval rate_interval average-rate average_threshold_rate
   burst-rate burst_threshold_rate
```

In fact, you can repeat this command up to three times to define multiple rate intervals and thresholds for each event type. By default, each event type has two **threat-detection rate** commands preconfigured. The default configuration should fit most scenarios, but you can tune the parameters to meet your specific needs.

You can get a feel for the events, the event type keywords, and the default rates and thresholds by looking over Table 9-23. You should become familiar with the types of events and the general command syntax, without becoming overwhelmed with the volume of information.

Table 9-23   *Default Basic Threat Detection Rate Intervals and Thresholds*

Event	Configured Commands
ACL denial (**acl-drop**)	threat-detection rate acl-drop rate-interval 600 average-rate 400 burst-rate 800
	threat-detection rate acl-drop rate-interval 3600 average-rate 320 burst-rate 640
Bad packet formats (**bad-packet-drop**)	threat-detection rate bad-packet-drop rate-interval 600 average-rate 100 burst-rate 400
	threat-detection rate bad-packet-drop rate-interval 3600 average-rate 80 burst-rate 320
Exceeded connection limits (**conn-limit-drop**)	threat-detection rate conn-limit-drop rate-interval 600 average-rate 100 burst-rate 400
	threat-detection rate conn-limit-drop rate-interval 3600 average-rate 80 burst-rate 320
DoS attack detection (**dos-drop**)	threat-detection rate dos-drop rate-interval 600 average-rate 100 burst-rate 400
	threat-detection rate dos-drop rate-interval 3600 average-rate 80 burst-rate 320
Basic failed firewall checks (**fw-drop**)	threat-detection rate fw-drop rate-interval 600 average-rate 400 burst-rate 1600
	threat-detection rate fw-drop rate-interval 3600 average-rate 320 burst-rate 1280
Suspicious ICMP packets (**icmp-drop**)	threat-detection rate icmp-drop rate-interval 600 average-rate 100 burst-rate 400
	threat-detection rate icmp-drop rate-interval 3600 average-rate 80 burst-rate 320
Failed application inspections (**inspect-drop**)	threat-detection rate inspect-drop rate-interval 600 average-rate 400 burst-rate 1600
	threat-detection rate inspect-drop rate-interval 3600 average-rate 320 burst-rate 1280
Interface overload conditions (**interface-drop**)	threat-detection rate interface-drop rate-interval 600 average-rate 2000 burst-rate 8000
	threat-detection rate interface-drop rate-interval 3600 average-rate 1600 burst-rate 6400
Scanning attacks detected (**scanning-threat**)	threat-detection rate scanning-threat rate-interval 600 average-rate 5 burst-rate 10
	threat-detection rate scanning-threat rate-interval 3600 average-rate 4 burst-rate 8

Table 9-23 *Default Basic Threat Detection Rate Intervals and Thresholds*

Event	Configured Commands
Incomplete TCP or UDP sessions (**syn-attack**)	threat-detection rate syn-attack rate-interval 600 average-rate 100 burst-rate 200
	threat-detection rate syn-attack rate-interval 3600 average-rate 80 burst-rate 160

Basic threat detection will generate a logging message when an event type threshold is exceeded, so that you can learn about the activity and have an audit trail. In case the average rate and burst rate thresholds are both exceeded for a single event type, then only one logging message will be produced.

Example 9-30 lists the commands that can be used to enable basic threat detection and to change the ACL denial threshold for a 600-second rate interval to have an average rate of 300 drops per second and a burst rate of 600 drops per second.

Example 9-30 *Enabling Basic Threat Detection*

```
ciscoasa(config)# threat-detection basic-threat
ciscoasa(config)# threat-detection rate acl-drop rate-interval 600 average-rate 300
  burst-rate 600
```

Step 2: Configure Advanced Threat Detection

With advanced threat detection, the ASA can gather statistics about suspicious activity going either to or from individual objects. Based on the statistics, you can determine which protocols or ports are being used for an attack, which access list rules are being triggered, and whether a host is attacking or being attacked.

You can choose one or more object types from Table 9-24 and enter the configuration commands listed. As an alternative, you can enter the **threat-detection statistics** command with no further arguments to enable statistics gathering for all event types.

Table 9-24 *Advanced Threat Detection Object Types and Configuration Commands*

Object Type	Command Syntax
Protocols in use	ciscoasa(config)# **threat-detection statistics protocol**
Ports in use	ciscoasa(config)# **threat-detection statistics port**
Access list denies	ciscoasa(config)# **threat-detection statistics access-list**
Hosts involved in scanning activity	ciscoasa(config)# **threat-detection statistics host [number-of-rate {1	2	3}]**

As an alternative, you can enable all types of advanced threat detection statistics gathering by using the **threat-detection statistics** command with no additional arguments.

When the **host** keyword is used, statistics are gathered for three different rate interval configurations (1 hour, 8 hour, and 24 hour) by default. You can add the **number-of-rate** keyword to specify the shortest number of rate intervals to use. Because host statistics gathering is CPU and memory intensive, you should try to minimize its use. If your ASA is under a heavy traffic load, consider enabling host statistics only temporarily.

Advanced threat detection can also gather statistics about TCP Intercept activity and reports when thresholds are exceeded. The TCP Intercepts are counted over the duration of a rate interval monitoring window, which is 30 minutes by default. If the number of attacks, or TCP Intercept events, rises above an average rate threshold (default 200 per second) or above a burst threshold (default 400 per second), a logging message is generated.

You can configure TCP Intercept threat detection by using the following command:

```
ciscoasa(config)# threat-detection statistics tcp-intercept [rate-interval
  rate_interval] [average-rate average_threshold_rate] [burst-rate
  burst_threshold_rate]
```

As an example, suppose you need to enable advanced threat detection to begin collecting statistics about suspicious activity. All possible types of statistics should be collected, but the host statistics should be reduced to one rate interval to conserve ASA memory. TCP Intercept statistics should also be collected using the default threshold values:

```
ciscoasa(config)# threat-detection statistics
ciscoasa(config)# threat-detection statistics host number-of-rate 1
ciscoasa(config)# threat-detection statistics tcp-intercept
```

Step 3: Configure Scanning Threat Detection

Scanning threat detection gathers statistics about individual hosts and their activity. The ASA can determine when a host is actively performing a network scan or sweep. If a scanning threat rate threshold is exceeded, the ASA can generate a logging message and can take aggressive action by shunning the attacker.

You can enable scanning threat detection with the following command:

```
ciscoasa(config)# threat-detection scanning-threat
```

You can also configure a rate interval, an average event rate, and a burst rate with the following command:

```
ciscoasa(config)# threat-detection rate scanning-threat rate-interval
  rate_interval average-rate average_threshold_rate burst-rate
  burst_threshold_rate
```

This command can be repeated to define up to three sets of values. By default, scanning threat detection is configured with the following two commands:

```
ciscoasa(config)# threat-detection rate scanning-threat rate-interval 600
  average-rate 5 burst-rate 10
ciscoasa(config)# threat-detection rate scanning-threat rate-interval 3600
  average-rate 4 burst-rate 8
```

By default, scanning threat detection will generate logging messages when scanning activity is detected. You can configure the ASA to take action by automatically shunning an attacking host with the following command:

```
ciscoasa(config)# threat-detection scanning-threat shun [except {ip-address ip-addr
  mask | object-group network_obj_group_id} | duration seconds]
```

By default, shuns are created with a duration of 3600 seconds (1 hour). If there are IP addresses that you want to exclude, so that shuns are never created for them, you can specify an address and mask or a network object group.

The following commands can be used to enable scanning threat detection and automatic shunning, with the exception of any host in the 192.168.101.0/24 subnet:

```
ciscoasa(config)# threat-detection scanning-threat
ciscoasa(config)# threat-detection scanning-threat shun except ip-address
  192.168.101.0 255.255.255.0
```

You can verify threat detection operation with the **show** commands listed in Table 9-25.

Table 9-25   *Commands Used to Verify Threat Detection Operation*

Function	Command Syntax
Verify basic threat detection	ciscoasa# **show threat-detection rate** [*type*]
Verify advanced threat detection and Top-N statistics	ciscoasa# **show threat-detection statistics** [*type*	**top**]
Verify scanning threat detection attackers and targets	ciscoasa# **show threat-detection scanning-threat** [**attacker**	**target**]
Verify scanning threat detection shuns	ciscoasa# **show threat-detection shun**

Exam Preparation Tasks

As mentioned in the section, "How to Use This Book," in the Introduction, you have a couple of choices for exam preparation: the exercises here, Chapter 17, "Final Preparation," and the exam simulation questions on the CD-ROM.

Review All Key Topics

Review the most important topics in this chapter, noted with the Key Topic icon in the outer margin of the page. Table 9-26 lists a reference of these key topics and the page numbers on which each is found.

Table 9-26   *Key Topics for Chapter 9*

Key Topic Element	Description	Page Number
List	Describes the MPF components	479
List	Lists the functions of the MPF building blocks	483
Paragraph	Describes the steps needed to configure a Layer 3–4 security policy	484
Table 9-2	Lists basic class map matching functions	485
Table 9-3	Lists basic policy map actions	487
Table 9-5	Lists TCP connection timeout limits	496
Table 9-6	Lists connection volume limits	498
Paragraph	Describes the TCP Intercept feature	498
Table 9-7	Lists possible TCP normalizer actions	500
Table 9-9	Lists dynamic protocol inspectors	509
Paragraph	Describes application inspection on a nonstandard port	511
Paragraph	Describes application inspection for a dynamic protocol	516
Table 9-10	Lists application inspection and control functions	517
Paragraph	Describes regular expressions and their configuration	523
Paragraph	Describes the Botnet Traffic Filter	563
List	Describes the three levels of threat detection	570

Define Key Terms

Define the following key terms from this chapter and check your answers in the glossary:

Modular Policy Framework (MPF), service policy, policy map, class map, application inspection engine, embryonic connection, dead connection detection (DCD), TCP normalizer, deep packet inspection (DPI), protocol verification, protocol minimization, payload minimization, application layer signature, regular expression (regex), botnet attack, SensorBase, whitelist, blacklist, threat detection

Command Reference to Check Your Memory

The FIREWALL exam focuses on practical, hands-on skills that are used by a networking professional. Therefore, you should be able to identify the commands needed to configure and test an ASA feature. Review the examples and command syntax tables that are provided throughout this chapter to make sure you can identify the basic keywords that are needed.

This chapter covers the following topics:

- **User-Based (Cut-Through) Proxy Overview:** This section defines this feature and provides an overview of the process on the Cisco ASA.

- **AAA on the ASA:** This section reviews the various roles that AAA can accommodate for the ASA.

- **User-Based Proxy Preconfiguration Steps and Deployment Guidelines:** This section provides expert guidance for deploying the cut-through proxy feature in enterprise environments.

- **Direct HTTP Authentication with the Cisco ASA:** This section explains why this option might be required in an enterprise environment, and details the required configuration.

- **Direct Telnet Authentication:** This section describes the option of direct Telnet authentication and its configuration.

- **Configuration Steps of User-Based Proxy:** This section provides an overview of the steps required to configure user-based proxy.

- **Configuring User Authentication:** This section details the configuration of the user authentication.

- **Configuring Authentication Prompts and Timeouts:** This section describes how to customize the authentication process using custom prompts and custom timeout values.

- **Configuring User Authorization:** This section details the configuration of user authorization.

- **Configuring User Session Accounting:** This section describes the configuration of user session accounting.

CHAPTER 10

Using Proxy Services to Control Access

- **Troubleshooting Cut-Through Proxy Operations:** This section provides a structured approach for troubleshooting issues with cut-through proxy operations and demonstrates the power of syslog with this feature.

- **Using Proxy for IP Telephony and Unified TelePresence:** This section details the various Cisco Unified Communications proxy services that are possible on the Cisco ASA.

The Cisco Adaptive Security Appliance (ASA) now offers many options for proxy services. Thanks to robust support for authentication, authorization, and accounting (AAA) services, what is termed user-based, or cut-through proxy services are possible. This method of proxy allows the ASA to identify the user and then enact particular polices for the user on the network beyond the ASA.

With the popularity of Cisco Unified Communications, the ASA also provides a critical set of Unified Communications–related proxy services, which includes Phone Proxy, TLS Proxy, Mobility Proxy, and Presence Federation Proxy.

"Do I Know This Already?" Quiz

The "Do I Know This Already?" quiz allows you to assess whether you should read this entire chapter thoroughly or jump to the "Exam Preparation Tasks" section. If you are in doubt about your answers to these questions or your own assessment of your knowledge of the topics, read the entire chapter. Table 10-1 lists the major headings in this chapter and their corresponding "Do I Know This Already?" quiz questions. You can find the answers in Appendix A, "Answers to the 'Do I Know This Already?' Quizzes."

Table 10-1 *"Do I Know This Already?" Section-to-Question Mapping*

Foundation Topics Section	Question
User-Based (Cut-Through) Proxy Overview	1
AAA on the ASA	2
User-Based Proxy Preconfiguration Steps	3
User-Based Proxy Deployment Guidelines	4
Direct HTTP Authentication with the Cisco ASA	5

Table 10-1   *"Do I Know This Already?" Section-to-Question Mapping*

Foundation Topics Section	Question
Direct Telnet Authentication	6
Configuration Steps of User-Based Proxy	7
Configuring User Authentication	8
Troubleshooting Cut-Through Proxy Operations	9

Caution: The goal of self-assessment is to gauge your mastery of the topics in this chapter. If you do not know the answer to a question or are only partially sure of the answer, you should mark that question wrong for purposes of the self-assessment. Giving yourself credit for an answer you correctly guess skews your self-assessment results and might provide you with a false sense of security.

1. Which protocol cannot be used to trigger the user-based proxy capability on the ASA?

    a. HTTP

    b. TFTP

    c. HTTPS

    d. FTP

    e. TELNET

2. Which of these is not a typical use of AAA on the Cisco ASA?

    a. To control administrative access

    b. To enable remote-access VPNs

    c. To enable IPS capabilities on the ASA

    d. To control user sessions across the device

3. Which of these is not typically considered prior to configuring user-based proxy?

    a. The Modular Policy Framework Global Policy configuration

    b. Information about the AAA infrastructure

    c. The user-specific policies

    d. Which traffic passing through the device you want to integrate with AAA

4. Which of the following are valid deployment guidelines for user-based proxy services? (Choose all that apply.)

    a. Avoid in cases where IP addresses are shared.

    b. Consider an external AAA server for scalability.

    c. Remove any interface ACLs in place on the inside interface.

    d. Engage in these policies only over trusted networks.

5. Which method of authentication presents to the user a web page from the ASA to input credentials?

    a.   Virtual HTTP

    b.   HTTP redirection

    c.   AAA Local

    d.   AAA External

6. In which situation would you recommend the direct Telnet authentication method?

    a.   You are using local AAA services.

    b.   You are using an external AAA service.

    c.   You are using traffic for which the ASA does not have an authentication proxy.

    d.   Traffic through the ASA is unusually high in volume.

7. Which of the following is not optional when configuring user-based proxy?

    a.   Configure accounting rules.

    b.   Change authentication prompts and timeouts.

    c.   Configure authentication rules on the ASA.

    d.   Configure authorization.

8. Which ASA verification command displays a Most Seen column?

    a.   show aaa users

    b.   show aaa

    c.   show users

    d.   show uauth

9. You need to test your AAA configuration on your Cisco ASA. You want to confirm that a particular server is configured correctly with the correct protocol. You also want to verify that a particular user account and password entry will successfully authenticate. What command should you use?

    a.   show aaa test

    b.   test aaa-server

    c.   test user

    d.   show aaa user test

Foundation Topics

You might be in an environment where you want to configure different network access policies based on the identity of the user who is attempting to communicate through your Cisco ASA. This capability is termed user-based policies. Cisco also calls this cut-through proxy in some of its documentation. This text will use both terms interchangeably. What is a proxy in this context? It is a device that has the capability to terminate and then reoriginate a connection between some client device in the network and a device acting as a server. This chapter provides all the details of this cut-through proxy configuration, including important information you should consider before and after deploying this Cisco ASA functionality.

This chapter also provides details regarding Cisco Unified Communications proxy features. These features enable the Cisco ASA to terminate encrypted communications, apply a security policy of the organization, and then forward the information along in a re-encrypted form. This not only ensures that no prying eyes can see the original information, but also ensures that your organization can enforce its prescribed access and threat defense policies.

User-Based (Cut-Through) Proxy Overview

User-based or cut-through proxy capabilities are possible on the Cisco ASA thanks to the tight integration with authentication, authorization, and accounting (AAA) services. If you properly configure this feature, when a user attempts to transit your Cisco ASA and access a resource, the ASA will check the user's identity against a local or remote user database. This is the authentication aspect of the process. Next, user-specific policies can be applied (authorization). Finally, information about user-specific traffic can be sent to a server set up to collect this information (accounting). Although this process sounds lengthy, most of these mechanics take place only once, after which the traffic of the user is "cut through" efficiently.

User Authentication

Here is a more detailed look at the mandatory user authentication process used in cut-through proxy:

- A user of your network attempts to access a resource that requires authentication. The ASA provides a username/password prompt. You configure exactly which resources you want to trigger this authentication behavior.

- This authentication process needs to occur only once per source IP address for all the authentication rules that you configure on the Cisco ASA. This is where the cut-through part of the name originates. The credentials of the user are cached on the Cisco ASA so that subsequent authentication requests do not have to transpire. You can control the timeout behavior of this process.

- Initial authentication can be triggered only by one of the following protocols: HTTP, HTTPS, FTP, or TELNET.

User Authentication and Access Control

Notice that this user authentication described in the preceding list is an additional layer of access control that the Cisco ASA can provide. For example, you know that interface access rules (access control lists [ACL]) form the basis for access control with the Cisco ASA. In fact, you need to carefully consider this in your design. As you plan for user authentication, realize that interface access rules must also permit the sessions that will require user authentication.

The section, "Configuring User Authorization," covers per-user authorization. This powerful capability allows you to change the default Cisco ASA behavior and have it dynamically download interface access rules on a per-user basis. This could obviously override your need to explicitly permit sessions under the typical interface access rules policy.

Implementation Examples

Perhaps there are ten users in your network that you need to permit to use FTP and HTTPS. There users are located off of the outside interface of your Cisco ASA. The FTP and HTTPS services that they need are located in the inside interface portion of the network. Deploying user-based policies, you can configure the Cisco ASA and the internal AAA server to authenticate these ten users and permit their access. Other end users in your organization can attempt this access through the ASA, but will be denied by the Cisco ASA and the AAA server.

Perhaps this is all working perfectly when it is decided that you do not want one of these ten users to be able to access the FTP services in the inside network. Now, you can add authorization into the mix. The Cisco ASA informs the AAA server that this user is specifically attempting FTP, and the AAA server can fail to authorize such access. As you can see, these per-user policy capabilities add flexibility to the overall Cisco ASA design.

AAA on the ASA

Authentication, authorization, and accounting (AAA) services are used for a variety of purposes on the Cisco ASA. The main three are the following:

- **Administrative access:** Controlling who can access the ASA from an administrative perspective is a key function of AAA services. Often called console access, this is usually the first (and only) job that many administrators think about when they think AAA.

- **Cut-through proxy:** Obviously, the focus of this chapter and the controlling of user sessions that transpire "across" the Cisco ASA.

- **Remote-access VPNs:** AAA also plays a key role when the Cisco ASA participates in the creation of remote-access virtual private networks (VPN) for remote devices to gain secure and managed connectivity to a remote location.

AAA Deployment Options

A key decision that you face when planning to implement cut-through proxy is exactly how you are going to implement the AAA server. You can rely on the Cisco ASA itself to function as the AAA server (using its local authentication database) or you can rely on an external server, such as Cisco Secure Access Control Server (Cisco ACS). There are many versions of the Cisco ACS product, including software-based versions that run on Windows and UNIX platforms.

You should consider using the Cisco ASA local authentication database under the following conditions:

■   You require only a single device (the Cisco ASA itself) to provide authentication of network users.

■   You have a manageable number of user accounts.

■   You require user authentication only in your network environment. You do not need the additional power given to you by authorization and accounting services. (If you also require authorization and accounting, you must have an external server that supports the RADIUS or TACACS+ security protocol.)

■   The use of user accounts with static passwords is acceptable under your organization's security policy.

You should consider using an external AAA server when any of the following conditions is met:

■   Your environment features several devices and several existing user credential databases that you want to participate in cut-through proxy.

■   You want to require stronger passwords than simple, static strings. An example of enforcing stronger password is the use of one-time passwords.

■   You want to take advantage of authorization and accounting services in addition to authentication.

User-Based Proxy Preconfiguration Steps and Deployment Guidelines

Like many of the advanced features of the Cisco ASA, user-based proxy requires important planning before it can be successfully implemented. This section examines the information you should collect prior to deployment and the key criteria you should consider before implementation.

User-Based Proxy Preconfiguration Steps

Before you attempt to deploy user-based proxy configuration on the Cisco ASA, complete the following steps. How long it will take to complete these steps depends on the complexity of your deployment:

Step 1.   Determine which traffic flowing through your Cisco ASA you want to control with AAA settings. Specifically, determine which traffic you need to authenticate and then, additionally, which traffic you need to authorize and provide accounting services for. Gathering this data is absolutely critical so that you can create the appropriate AAA rules on the Cisco ASA.

Step 2. Gather all the appropriate information regarding your AAA infrastructure. You need the names and IP addresses of servers, and details regarding the exact AAA services that are configured and available.

Step 3. Document all information regarding user-specific policies that you want to implement. This information is critical so that you can configure the Cisco ASA to enact the appropriate per-user authorization rules you want.

User-Based Proxy Deployment Guidelines

There are several important deployment guidelines that you need to consider prior to implementing cut-through proxy on the Cisco ASA.

The first deployment guideline is to consider using an external AAA server. The main reason to consider using an external AAA server is scalability. Should your implementation need to grow dramatically in the future, an external server ensures that you can minimize the number of changes necessary to accommodate the larger environment. Another important reason is that the external server allows much more manageability in the AAA implementation. For example, specific management applications and methodologies exist for Cisco ACS that can help you gain control over the network infrastructure and its access. Finally, an external AAA server provides a valuable central store of accounting information regarding user activities. For companies that are interested in storing this information, this external server is absolutely critical.

Another key deployment guideline is that the cut-through proxy feature should not be used over untrusted networks. Because the Cisco ASA tracks authenticated users by their IP address, a man-in-the-middle or spoofing attack could compromise resource access. In fact, the exchange of credential information from your end users and the Cisco ASA is carried out in clear text. This exchange should take place only over a trusted network.

The final deployment guideline is to avoid user-based proxy in any environment where users share IP address information. A classic example of such an environment is one that uses Port Address Translation (PAT, a form of Network Address Translation [NAT]). When two users share the same IP address (as in PAT), the Cisco ASA will authenticate the first user, and then allow subsequent users access based on that IP address. Typically, allowing this type of access is not desired, of course, so be careful implementing cut-through proxy in such environments.

Direct HTTP Authentication with the Cisco ASA

In some environments, sending an internal user's credentials to a remote web server is not desirable. In such an environment, you can configure direct HTTP authentication with the Cisco ASA. This is recommended if your internal users' credentials would be passed over an untrusted network to the remote web server. This is often the case in deployments where the Cisco ASA protects your internal network from the public Internet. Another case in which you might need to configure direct HTTP authentication with the Cisco ASA is where the remote web server requires different username and password credentials using a separate authentication process.

Key Topic

The Cisco ASA provides two solutions for direct HTTP authentication:

■   HTTP redirection

■   Virtual HTTP

HTTP Redirection

With the HTTP redirection method, the Cisco ASA actively listens for HTTP requests on TCP port 80. When the Cisco ASA detects such requests, it redirects internal users to a local web page that is a form for the user to input their appropriate credentials. If the user is authenticated properly with these credentials, the user is then directed to access the external web server. If the external web server requires its own separate authentication process and credentials, it can challenge the user directly at that time. This method nicely accommodates an external web server that has its own authentication scheme. Of the two solutions, HTTP redirection is the newer of the methods and does not require an allocated IP address.

Note: There is an option to redirect the HTTPS sessions of users to an internal web page served by HTTPS. The use of this method is not recommended because it may result in certificate warnings being sent to the end user. These warnings could be interpreted as an attempted man-in-the-middle attack.

Virtual HTTP

Using the virtual HTTP method, the users authenticate against the Cisco ASA using an IP address of the virtual HTTP server inside the Cisco ASA. No web page for credentials is required. Once the user is authenticated, their credentials are not sent further into the outside network in order to access the external web server. Notice that this method works well when you want to prohibit the sending of credentials into an untrusted network.

Direct Telnet Authentication

Key
Topic

You might have a situation where you do not permit through your Cisco ASA the protocols that can trigger cut-through proxy. As a reminder, the protocols that can trigger this behavior are HTTP, HTTPS, FTP, and Telnet. Or you might have a situation where you want authentication to be triggered by a protocol that does not fall into the subset of protocols that function with cut-through proxy. In this case, internal users can be authenticated using the virtual Telnet feature. The user establishes a Telnet session to a virtual Telnet IP address you assign on the Cisco ASA. At this point, the user is challenged for a username and password that can be presented against the AAA services.

An example of an environment in which direct Telnet authentication might be useful is one in which you have internal users that must authenticate before accessing a POP3 mail server located beyond the Cisco ASA. This presents a particular challenge because POP3 is not compatible with the cut-through proxy feature. Users in this case simply authenticate against the virtual Telnet address of the ASA and then are passed beyond it to access the mail server.

Note: You should use great care to not send sensitive information if using the virtual Telnet feature across an untrusted network. Remember, Telnet is a clear-text protocol.

Configuration Steps of User-Based Proxy

The following are the configuration steps for the user-based proxy feature. Note that you do not necessarily have to perform all of these steps in every implementation. This chapter provides more information on each of these steps:

Step 1. Configure the Cisco ASA to communicate with one or more external AAA servers or, alternatively, configure AAA on the Cisco ASA itself.

Step 2. Configure the appropriate authentication rules on the ASA.

Step 3. (Optional) Change the authentication prompts and timeouts.

Step 4. (Optional) Configure authorization.

Step 5. (Optional) Configure the accounting rules.

Configuring User Authentication

If you are using external AAA servers, you need to configure an AAA group that contains your authentication servers and the security protocol (TACACS+ or RADIUS) that is in use. **Key Topic**

Note: You can reuse an existing AAA group setting that you have on your Cisco ASA for other AAA functions.

Configuring an AAA Group

To create your AAA group in the Cisco ASDM, navigate to **Configuration > Device Management > Users/AAA > AAA Server Groups** and click the **Add** button in the AAA Server Groups pane. This opens the Add AAA Server Group dialog box, as shown in Figure 10-1. Enter a name for the AAA server group and, from the Protocol drop-down list, choose the appropriate security protocol used in your environment. Options include the following:

- RADIUS

- TACACS+

- Microsoft NT Domain

- Security Dynamics International (SDI)

- Kerberos

- Lightweight Directory Access Protocol (LDAP)

- HTTP Form (used for SSL VPN users only)

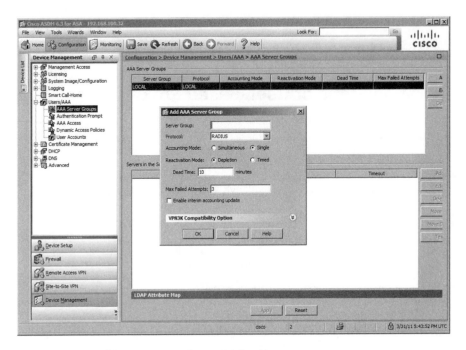

Figure 10-1 *Add AAA Server Group Dialog Box*

Next, choose one of the Accounting Mode radio buttons to specify the accounting mode to be used with the server group. Choosing the Simultaneous button causes the Cisco ASA to send accounting data to all servers in the group, whereas choosing the Single button causes accounting data to be sent only to one server.

Next, choose one of the Reactivation Mode radio buttons to specify when failed servers in the group will be reactivated. Choosing the Depletion button causes a failed server to reactivate only after all the servers in the group are inactive. Choose the Timed button to cause a failed server to reactivate after 30 seconds of downtime.

In the Dead Time field, specify the number of minutes you want to elapse between the failure of the last server in the group and the re-enabling of all the servers. Note that this setting is relevant only if you chose the Depletion option. In the Max Failed Attempts field, enter the number of failed connection attempts allowed before a server in the group is declared inactive.

After you complete this dialog box, click **OK > Apply > Save**.

Configuring an AAA Server

After you create your AAA server group, adding individual servers to the group is simple. Select the server group to which you want to add a server, and then click the **Add** button in the Servers in the Selected Group area of the AAA Server Groups panel. In the Add AAA Server dialog box, shown in Figure 10-2, choose the interface name and enter the IP address of the server. The Interface Name field specifies the Cisco ASA interface from

which the AAA server can be contacted. Use the Timeout field to specify how long the
Cisco ASA waits before attempting to contact another server in the group.

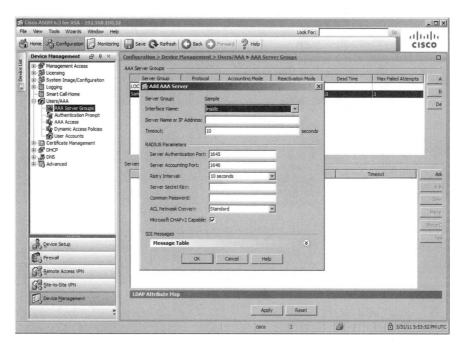

Figure 10-2   *Add AAA Server Dialog Box*

In the Server Authentication Port field of the RADIUS Parameters area, specify the server
port used for authentication. The default is 1645. The latest RADIUS RFC, 2865, states
that port 1812 should be used.

In the Server Accounting Port field, specify the appropriate port. The default is 1646. You
might consider changing this to the latest RFC recommendation of 1813, per the latest
RFC, 2866.

Choose a retry interval from the Retry Interval drop-down list. This specifies the number
of seconds that the ASA should wait after sending a query to the server before it reat-
tempts the communication.

Finally, enter a 64-character secret key in the Server Secret Key field. This value must
match the value configured on your RADIUS server.

After you complete this dialog box, click **OK > Apply > Save**.

Configuring the Authentication Rules

To configure the authentication rules, navigate to **Configuration > Firewall > AAA
Rules > Add > Add Authentication Rule**. In the Add Authentication Rule dialog box, shown
in Figure 10-3, from the Interface drop-down list, specify the interface to which you are

Key
Topic

adding the rule. Verify that the Authenticate radio button (the default) is selected. From the AAA Server Group drop-down list, choose a server group or the local user database.

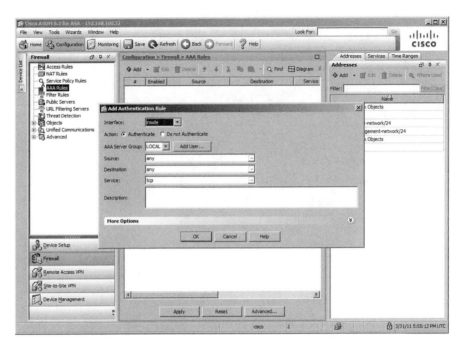

Figure 10-3   *Add Authentication Rule Dialog Box*

In the Source field, enter the IP address of traffic that should be authenticated. You can select IP addresses already defined in the Cisco ASA by clicking the ellipsis button.

In the Destination field, enter the IP address of traffic that should be authenticated. Once again, you can choose IP addresses already defined by clicking the ellipsis button.

Use the Service field to specify the destination service. You can make entries such as **tcp/80** or **tcp/http,tcp/ftp**.

You can give the rule an optional description in plain English by using the Description field.

After you complete this dialog box, click **OK > Apply > Save**.

Example 10-1 demonstrates how this can be accomplished via the command-line interface (CLI) on the ASA.

Example 10-1   *Configuring User Authentication at the CLI*

```
FIREWALL(config)# aaa-server MYGROUP protocol radius
FIREWALL(config-aaa-server-group)# exit
FIREWALL(config)# aaa-server MYGROUP (inside) host 10.0.0.10
FIREWALL(config-aaa-server-host)# key MYKEY
FIREWALL(config-aaa-server-host)# exit
```

```
FIREWALL(config)# object-group service MYSERVICES tcp
FIREWALL(config-service)# port-object eq http
FIREWALL(config-service)# port-object eq ftp
FIREWALL(config-service)# exit
FIREWALL(config)# access-list ACL_IN extended permit tcp any host 192.168.1.101
  object-group MYSERVICES
FIREWALL(config)# aaa authentication match ACL_IN outside MYGROUP
```

Verifying User Authentication

Verifying user-based proxy on the Cisco ASA is easy. Just initiate traffic of the appropriate type across the ASA and, when prompted, enter valid username and password credentials. Once you have done so, you can use the **show uauth** CLI command. This command allows you to easily inspect the following:

- Users currently authenticated by the Cisco ASA

- The IP address of an authenticated user

- The absolute and inactivity timers associated with each authenticated user

Should you need to clear the cached authentication information, use the **clear uauth** command. Note that this command causes users to reauthenticate, but it will not affect the current and established sessions of the authenticated users.

Another CLI command of value for verification is **show aaa-server**. This command enables you to display the following:

- The server group

- The protocol used

- The IP address of the active server in the group

- The status of the server

- Statistics on authentication requests and responses

Configuring HTTP Redirection

To configure the HTTP redirection method, described earlier in the chapter, navigate to **Configuration > Firewall > AAA Rules** and click **Advanced** in the AAA Rules pane. This opens the AAA Rules Advanced Options dialog box, shown in Figure 10-4. Click **Add**, and then click the **HTTP** radio button. You will create another rule associated to HTTP. The key to this configuration is to check the **Redirect Network Users for Authentication Requests** check box.

After you complete this dialog box, click **OK > OK > Apply > Save**.

You can accomplish these results at the command line with the following statement:

```
FIREWALL(config)# aaa authentication listener http outside port http redirect
```

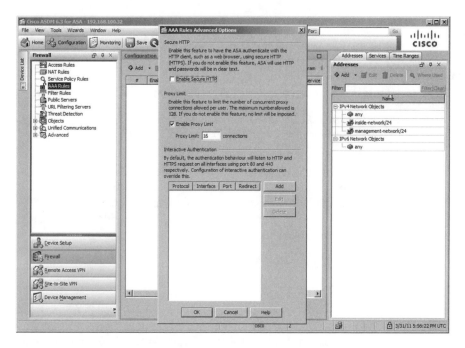

Figure 10-4 *AAA Rules Advanced Options Dialog Box*

Configuring the Virtual HTTP Server

To configure the virtual HTTP method to direct HTTP authentication, described earlier in this chapter, navigate to **Configuration > Firewall > Advanced > Virtual Access**. In the Virtual Access pane, shown in Figure 10-5, check the **Enable HTTP Server** check box and enter an IP address. Click **Apply > Save**.

You can accomplish these results at the command line with the following statement:

```
FIREWALL(config)# virtual http 172.16.1.101
```

Configuring Direct Telnet

The configuration of the direct Telnet authentication option, described earlier in this chapter, is also simple. Navigate to **Configuration > Firewall > Advanced > Virtual Access.** In the Virtual Access pane (refer to Figure 10-5), check the **Enable Telnet Server** check box and provide the appropriate IP address. Click **Apply > Save**.

You can accomplish these results at the command line with the following statement:

```
FIREWALL(config)# virtual telnet 172.16.1.102
```

Configuring Authentication Prompts and Timeouts

You might want to specify a unique authentication prompt that your users will see when they are asked to authenticate by the Cisco ASA. You can also create specific messages that users see when they successfully or unsuccessfully authenticate. This provides a better end-user experience than is provided through the default username and password prompts that display. Without your customization, users see the following:

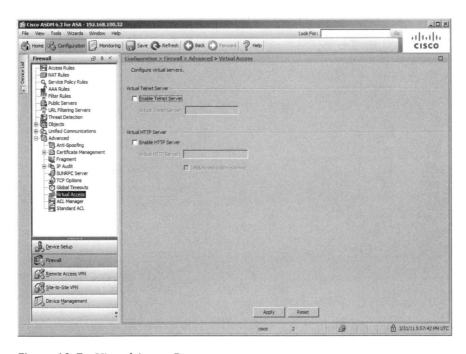

Figure 10-5   *Virtual Access Pane*

- **When authenticating via FTP:** Users see a default "FTP authentication" prompt.

- **When authenticating via HTTP:** Users see a default "HTTP authentication" prompt.

- **When authenticating via Telnet:** Users see no challenge text; instead, they see simple username and password prompts.

Configuring Authentication Prompts

To configure your own customized authentication prompts, navigate to **Configuration > Device Management > Users/AAA > Authentication Prompt**. The Authentication Prompt pane, shown in Figure 10-6, provides customization fields for Prompt, User Accepted, and User Rejected. After you enter your customized messages, click **Apply > Save**.

You can also configure these custom prompts from the command line with the following commands:

```
FIREWALL(config)# auth-prompt prompt
FIREWALL(config)# auth-prompt reject
FIREWALL(config)# auth-prompt accept
```

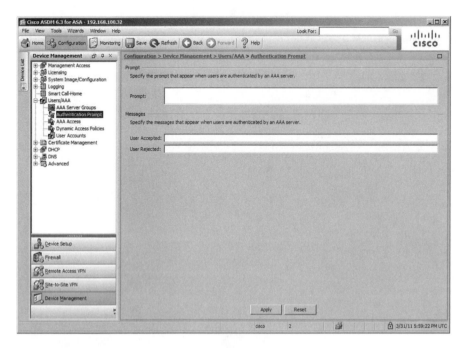

Figure 10-6   *Authentication Prompt Pane*

Configuring Authentication Timeouts

Authentication timeouts are critical because they set the time limits after which a user will be required to reauthenticate. Two types of timeouts are used with cut-through proxy:

■ **Inactivity timeout value:** Controls timing out based on idle time (no user traffic is being forwarded by the Cisco ASA).

■ **Absolute timeout value:** Ignores activity and begins just after the user is authenticated by the device. Obviously, the absolute timer should be set to a longer duration than the inactivity timer.

To set these values, navigate to **Configuration > Firewall > Advanced > Global Timeouts**. In the Global Timeouts pane, shown in Figure 10-7, check the **Authentication Absolute** and **Authentication Inactivity** check boxes and enter their respective values in the fields to the right. When you are finished, click **Apply > Save**.

The corresponding commands at the CLI are as follows:

```
FIREWALL(config)# timeout uauth inactivity
FIREWALL(config)# timeout uauth absolute
```

Configuring User Authorization

As previously described, you can permit all authenticated users to access the same resources using the same services through your Cisco ASA. You must ensure that your interface access rules permit the traffic of your authentication policy and no further configuration is required. If you want some users to access different resources from other users, however, you need to also implement user-based authorization. For example, perhaps you have an internal web and FTP server. You want some users to be able to access this device using both HTTP or FTP, but some other users should have only HTTP access. This is a classic scenario for user-based authorization.

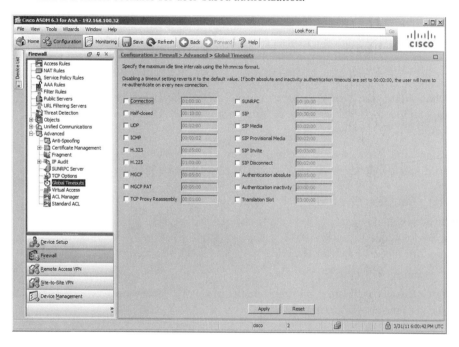

Figure 10-7   *Global Timeouts Pane*

The two user-based authorization methods possible with the Cisco ASA are as follows:

- **Download per-user ACLs from a RADIUS AAA server during the authentication process:** This is the process that Cisco strongly recommends.

- **User authorization based on a TACACS+ AAA server:** The AAA server is configured with rules that are consulted on demand for every attempted user connection. As a result of configuration complexity and potential issues with overhead, this method is discouraged by Cisco and is not covered further in this text.

Per-User Override

An important aspect of the downloadable per-user ACL feature is that it enables you to configure what is called per-user override. The per-user override feature allows the downloaded ACL to override an existing ACL on the interface for the particular user. Cisco recommends that you use this feature because it makes enacting specific policies for specific users in the network easier.

Without per-user override, both the interface ACL and the downloaded ACL are checked for permit statements for the packet to pass. With the per-user override, the interface ACL must still be configured to permit the authentication "trigger" packet.

Configuring Downloadable ACLs

To configure the downloadable ACL authorization feature, you must complete the following tasks:

- Configure the appropriate downloadable ACLs on the Cisco ACS server.

- Assign the downloadable ACLs to a specific user or group.

- Optionally, configure the per-user override feature on the Cisco ASA interface ACLs where the user will be authenticated.

To configure downloadable ACLs on the Cisco ACS server, access the Cisco ACS GUI and choose **Interface Configuration > Advanced Options > User-Level Downloadable ACLs > Submit**. Under Shared Profile Components, choose **Downloadable IP ACLs** and click **Add**.

To assign an ACL to a user account, in the Cisco ACS GUI, choose **User Setup > Add/Edit > Downloadable ACLs > Assign IP ACL > Submit**.

Configuring Per-User Override

Finally, you will most likely want to configure per-user override on ACLs on the Cisco ASA. To do this, in the Cisco ADSM, navigate to **Configuration > Firewall > Access Rules > Advanced > Per User Override**. After you enable this feature by checking the check box, click **OK** and then click **Apply**.

At the CLI, this configuration is a simple matter of using the **per-user-override** keyword at the end of the **access-group** command.

Verification

To verify the authentication of your users and their specific authorization information, use the **show uauth** command, as demonstrated in Example 10-2.

Example 10-2   *Verifying User Authorization Information*

```
FIREWALL# show uauth
                              Current        Most Seen
Authenticated Users           1              1
Authen In Progress            0              1
user 'johns' at 172.16.171.33, authenticated
access-list #ACSACL#-FIREWALLjohns-4bc6b693_
absolute timeout: 2:30:00
inactivity timeout: 0:30:00
```

From this output, you can see that a user named johns is authenticated. Notice that an ACL for this user has been downloaded to the security appliance. The name of the access list is shown in three parts. First, an identifier string of **#ACSACL#-**, and then the actual name of the ACL, as defined on the RADIUS server. In this case, the name is **FIREWALLjohns**. Then, a unique rule version identification code is shown. In this case, the code is **4bc6b693**.

Configuring User Session Accounting

As you will recall from earlier in this chapter, an important reason to use an external AAA server is to support accounting services for user sessions. Understand that if you use accounting services without authentication, you can track information based only on the source IP address. With the authentication required by user-based proxy services, accounting information gains value because it is based on network username.

Configuring User Session Accounting

To configure session accounting, in the Cisco ASDM, navigate to **Configuration > Firewall > AAA Rules > Add > Add Accounting Rule**. In the Add Accounting Rule dialog box, as shown in Figure 10-8, choose the correct interface and click the **Account** radio button. Choose the appropriate AAA server group and then complete the dialog box with the rule defining the traffic for which you want accounting. Click **OK > Apply > Save**.

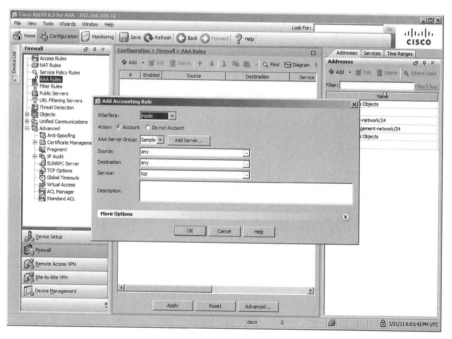

Figure 10-8   *Add Accounting Rule Dialog Box*

Configuring user session accounting is as simple as configuring an ACL to define the target traffic and then configuring an accounting rule using the **aaa accounting match** command. For example:

```
FIREWALL(config)# access-list FIREWALL_ACL extended permit tcp any host
   172.16.0.100
FIREWALL(config)# aaa accounting match FIREWALL_ACL outside FIREWALLAUTH
```

In this example, accounting information on all TCP traffic from any host to the device at **172.16.0.100** over the outside interface is sent to the AAA device in the **FIREWALLAUTH** group.

Verification

To best verify accounting operations, visit the destination AAA server and examine the accounting information that is received there. For example, access the Cisco ACS GUI and choose **Reports and Activity > RADIUS Accounting > RADIUS Accounting Active**. This report should show the latest accounting records received from the properly configured Cisco ASA. Other reports that might be useful include the Passed Authentications and the Failed Attempts reports.

Troubleshooting Cut-Through Proxy Operations

Understand that troubleshooting user-based controls demonstrated in this chapter involves not just the Cisco ASA, but the AAA server in use as well. Key commands and components to keep at hand on the Cisco ASA include the following:

- **show uauth**

- **show aaa-server**

- **test aaa-server**

- System messages

For the AAA server, rely on the various reports and service indicators that are available.

A Structured Approach

It is important to consider a structured approach when troubleshooting cut-through proxy operations. For example, first verify if your users are prompted for authentication in the correct manner. If this is not occurring, ensure that the traffic to be authenticated is permitted through the Cisco ASA as it should be. Obviously, also carefully verify your cut-through proxy configuration, as demonstrated in this chapter.

If your users are prompted for authentication correctly, but there is still an issue, move to the AAA server troubleshooting. Ensure that this server is accessible from the Cisco ASA. Be sure that the shared secret on the AAA device and the Cisco ASA match, and verify that the Cisco ASA has been properly defined on the AAA server.

If all this checks out, it's time to ensure that the correct user account exists on the AAA device and that this user account has the correct credentials defined.

System Messages

As previously mentioned, another extremely valuable source of troubleshooting information is the system messages created on the Cisco ASA. The device consistently logs messages related to the cut-through proxy operations. The system message indicating successful authentication is

```
%ASA-6-109005: Authentication succeeded for user 'johns' from 172.16.1.100/1322
    to 172.16.0.12/80 on interface outside
```

The system message indicating a failure of authentication using the local database is

```
%ASA-6-109006: Authentication failed for user 'johns' from 172.16.1.100/1322 to
    172.16.0.12/80 on interface outside
```

If an issue arises that causes your AAA server to not be accessible, look for the following system message:

```
%ASA-6-113014: AAA authentication server not accessible : server = 172.16.0.101
    : user = johns
```

Using Proxy for IP Telephony and Unified TelePresence

For the FIREWALL exam, although you do not need to know the various configurations for the proxy services available on the Cisco ASA for Cisco Unified IP Telephony and TelePresence, you should be aware of the general concepts. The ASA device's Cisco Unified Communications Proxy feature set includes the following specific capabilities:

- **Phone Proxy:** The Phone Proxy capability permits the ASA to terminate Cisco SRTP/TLS–encrypted IP Phone connections that permit secure remote access. This capability allows the elimination of expensive, dedicated VPN hardware equipment at headquarters, while ensuring that remote users simply need their Cisco IP Phone (and do not need any special VPN tunnels or hardware). This capability within the ASA replaces the Cisco Unified Phone Proxy and opens up these capabilities for Cisco IP Softphones as well.

- **TLS Proxy:** The TLS Proxy capability enables the ASA to intercept and decrypt encrypted information from Unified Communications endpoints en route to the Cisco Unified Communications Manager (CUCM). Once the information is decrypted, the ASA can ensure that the necessary threat protections and access controls are applied. The ASA then has the ability to re-encrypt the information and send it on its way to the CUCM server.

- **Mobility Proxy:** The ASA can also act as a proxy for the TLS signaling used between Cisco Unified Mobile Communicator (UMC) and the Cisco Unified Mobility Advantage (UMA) server. This set of solutions enables companies to take full advantage of mobile handsets.

- **Presence Federation Proxy:** The Cisco Unified Presence solution collects information about the users in the Unified Communications network and their capabilities. For example, it can tell you at what times users are available on Cisco IP Phones and whether they support video. Thanks to the ASA, TLS communications between Unified Presence servers can be terminated and the appropriate security policies can be applied.

Exam Preparation Tasks

As mentioned in the section, "How to Use This Book," in the Introduction, you have a couple of choices for exam preparation: the exercises here, Chapter 17, "Final Preparation," and the exam simulation questions on the CD-ROM.

Review All Key Topics

Review the most important topics in this chapter, noted with the Key Topics icon in the outer margin of the page. Table 10-2 lists a reference of these key topics and the page numbers on which each is found.

Table 10-2 *Key Topics for Chapter 10*

Key Topic Element	Description	Page Number
List	Describes the user authentication process	586
Section	Details direct HTTP authentication	589
Section	Details direct Telnet authentication	590
Section	Covers the configuration of user authentication	591
Section	Covers the configuration of authentication prompts and timeouts	593
Section	Covers the configuration of user authorization	596

Define Key Terms

Define the following key terms from this chapter and check your answers in the glossary:

cut-through proxy, HTTP redirection, virtual HTTP, Phone Proxy, TLS Proxy, Mobility Proxy, Presence Federation Proxy

Command Reference to Check Your Memory

This section includes the most important configuration and EXEC commands covered in this chapter. It might not be necessary to memorize the complete syntax of every command, but you should be able to remember the basic keywords that are needed.

To test your memory of the commands, cover the right side of Tables 10-3 through 10-5 with a piece of paper, read the description on the left side, and then see how much of the command you can remember.

The FIREWALL exam focuses on practical, hands-on skills that are used by a networking professional. Therefore, you should be able to identify the commands needed to configure and test an ASA feature.

Table 10-3 *Commands Related to User Authentication*

Task	Command Syntax
Create a server group	ciscoasa(config)# **aaa-server** server-tag **protocol** server-protocol
Create a server in the group	ciscoasa(config)# **aaa-server** server-tag [(interface-name)] **host** {server-ip | name} [key] [**timeout seconds**]
Specify a server key	ciscoasa(config-aaa-server-host)# **key** key
Enable authentication for connections through the ASA	ciscoasa(config)# **aaa authentication match** acl_name interface_name {server_tag | **LOCAL**}
Enable HTTP listening ports to authenticate network users	ciscoasa(config)# **aaa authentication listener http[s]** interface_name [**port portnum**] [**redirect**]
Display one or all currently authenticated users	ciscoasa# **show uauth** [username]

Table 10-4 *Commands Related to Authentication Prompts and Timeouts*

Task	Command Syntax
Specify or change the AAA challenge text for through-the-ASA user sessions	ciscoasa(config)# **auth-prompt prompt** [**prompt** | **accept** | **reject**] **string**
Set the global time durations for cut-through proxy	ciscoasa(config)# **timeout uauth floating-conn** hh:mm:ss [**absolute** | **inactivity**]

Table 10-5 *Commands Related to User Authorization and Accounting*

Task	Command Syntax
Allow per-user override for downloadable ACLs	ciscoasa(config)# **access-group** access-list {**in** | **out**} **interface** interface_name [**per-user-override** | **control-plane**]
Configure the accounting rules on the ASA	ciscoasa(config)# **aaa accounting match** acl_name interface_name server_tag

This chapter covers the following topics:

- **Handling Fragmented Traffic:** This section explains how a Cisco ASA can virtually reassemble all the fragments of a packet to inspect the contents.

- **Prioritizing Traffic:** This section explains how traffic is handled as it is passed out an ASA interface and how time-critical traffic can be prioritized for premium service.

- **Controlling Traffic Bandwidth:** This section covers traffic policing and traffic shaping, two methods you can configure to rate limit traffic passing through an interface.

CHAPTER 11

Handling Traffic

A Cisco ASA is normally busy inspecting traffic and applying security policies. It also has features that you can leverage to control how it handles packets as they pass through. Even if the packets from different traffic flows all pass the same inspection policies, the ASA can handle them differently to affect how they are forwarded. This chapter covers these features in detail.

"Do I Know This Already?" Quiz

The "Do I Know This Already?" quiz allows you to assess whether you should read this entire chapter thoroughly or jump to the "Exam Preparation Tasks" section. If you are in doubt about your answers to these questions or your own assessment of your knowledge of the topics, read the entire chapter. Table 11-1 lists the major headings in this chapter and their corresponding "Do I Know This Already?" quiz questions. You can find the answers in Appendix A, "Answers to the 'Do I Know This Already?' Quizzes."

Table 11-1 *"Do I Know This Already?" Section-to-Question Mapping*

Foundation Topics Section	Questions
Handling Fragmented Traffic	1–2
Prioritizing Traffic	3–6
Controlling Traffic Bandwidth	7–10

Caution: The goal of self-assessment is to gauge your mastery of the topics in this chapter. If you do not know the answer to a question or are only partially sure of the answer, you should mark this question wrong for purposes of the self-assessment. Giving yourself credit for an answer you correctly guess skews your self-assessment results and might provide you with a false sense of security.

1. Suppose an ASA receives a series of packet fragments from a source host on the outside, destined for a host on the inside. Which one of the following answers correctly describes a possible outcome?

    a. The ASA recognizes the packets as fragments and automatically drops them.

    b. Each fragment is inspected individually and forwarded as appropriate.

    c. The ASA virtually reassembles the fragments into their original complete packets, which are then inspected. If they pass inspection, then the whole packets are forwarded to their destination.

    d. The ASA virtually reassembles the fragments into their original complete packets, which are then inspected. If the whole packets pass inspection, the original fragments are forwarded to the destination.

2. By default, how many fragments can an ASA buffer for virtual reassembly of a single packet?

    a. 1

    b. 2

    c. 16

    d. 24

    e. 1024

3. Which two of the following best describe priority queuing on an ASA?

    a. The ASA platform does not support priority queuing.

    b. Each interface can support one LLQ.

    c. Each interface can support two priority queues.

    d. An interface priority queue must be enabled before it can be used.

4. Which one of the following commands should be used to enable an LLQ on an ASA interface?

    a.
```
ciscoasa(config)# interface ethernet0/0
ciscoasa(config-if)# priority-queue
```

    b.
```
ciscoasa(config)# priority-queue outside
```

    c.
```
ciscoasa(config)# llq enable
```

    d.
```
ciscoasa(config)# interface ethernet0/0
ciscoasa(config-if)# priority
```

5. Which one of the following happens to incoming packets that are classified for priority queuing if the interface priority queue is currently full?

    a. The incoming packets are dropped.

    b. The incoming packets are moved into the best-effort queue instead.

    c. The incoming packets are buffered until the priority queue empties.

    d. Nothing; the priority queue can never fill.

6. Suppose you need to configure an ASA to send packets containing streaming video into a priority queue. You have just configured a class map to match the video packets with the **match** command. Which one of the following correctly describes the next step you should take?

    a. Enter the **priority** command in the class map configuration.

    b. Enter the **policy-map** command, followed by the **priority** command.

    c. Enter the **policy-map** command, followed by the **class** command, followed by the **priority** command.

    d. Enter the **service-policy** command, followed by the **priority** command.

7. Which one of the following traffic handling features can hold specific traffic flows within a bandwidth limit?

    a. Virtual packet reassembly

    b. Priority queuing

    c. Traffic policing

    d. Traffic shaping

8. By default, which one of the following actions will a traffic policer take for packets that don't conform to the bandwidth threshold limit?

    a. Drop the packets.

    b. Transmit the packets.

    c. Delay the packets.

    d. Inspect the packets.

9. Which one of the following is a valid MPF configuration to implement traffic shaping?

    a.
```
class-map test-class
     match any
policy-map test
     class test-class
     shape average 10000000
```

    b.
```
class-map test-class
     match access-list test-acl
policy-map test
     class test-class
     shape average 10000000
```

    c.
```
policy-map test
     class class-default
     shape average 10000000
```

    d.
```
policy-map test
     shape average 10000000
```

10. Which of the following combinations of traffic handling features can be configured simultaneously on the same ASA interface?

    a. Interface priority queuing and traffic shaping.

    b. Interface priority queuing and traffic policing.

    c. Traffic policing and traffic shaping.

    d. None of these answers are correct.

Foundation Topics

Packets coming into an ASA may be fragmented or whole. The same security policies that inspect whole packets aren't as effective when inspecting fragments. An ASA can be configured to intercept packet fragments and virtually reassemble them so that they can be inspected normally.

An ASA can also be configured to identify certain traffic types so that they can be handled in a more efficient manner than is normally done. This allows time- or mission-critical packets to be forwarded ahead of other packets after inspection.

You can also configure an ASA to control the amount of bandwidth used by certain types of traffic. Traffic policing and shaping are two methods to hold traffic bandwidth within predefined limits.

In this chapter, you learn how to configure the traffic handling features.

Handling Fragmented Traffic

When an ASA sends or receives a packet, you might think that the whole packet moves along as a single unit of data. This is true as long as the ASA interface is configured to handle units of data that are at least as large as the packet. This same principle applies to any device that is connected to a network, including hosts, routers, and switches. The maximum size is called the maximum transmission unit (MTU) and is configured on a per-interface basis. MTU configuration is covered in the "Configuring the Interface MTU" section of Chapter 3, "Configuring ASA Interfaces."

By default, any Ethernet interface has its MTU set to 1500 bytes, which is the normal maximum and expected value for Ethernet frames. If a packet is larger than the MTU, it must be fragmented before being transmitted. The resulting fragments are then sent individually; once they arrive at the destination, the fragments are reassembled into the original complete packet.

You can verify the interface MTU settings with the **show running-config mtu** command. If you find that the default MTU value of 1500 needs to be adjusted, you can set the interface MTU from 64 to 65,535 bytes. Be aware that 9216 bytes is a common practical limit known as a "giant" packet. In ASDM, navigate to **Configuration > Device Setup > Interfaces > Edit > Advanced** and enter the new MTU value. In the CLI, you can use the following configuration command:

```
ciscoasa(config)# mtu interface bytes
```

Cisco ASAs can participate in MTU discovery along an end-to-end IP routing path. This process follows RFC 1191, where the source and destination are expected to use an MTU value equal to the smallest allowed MTU along the complete path.

What happens when an ASA receives packets that have already been fragmented? Rather than passing the fragments along toward their destination, an ASA will inspect the fragments to make sure that they aren't part of some malicious activity. To do this, the ASA must store each fragment in a cache and virtually reassemble the fragments so that it can inspect the complete original packet and verify the order and integrity of each fragment. If the reassembled packet passes inspection, then the ASA discards the packet and forwards all of the original fragments toward the destination—as if nothing had happened to them.

Naturally, an ASA has to limit the resources it uses for the virtual packet reassembly process. Otherwise, someone could send an endless stream of fragmented packets and exhaust the ASA's memory. Virtual packet reassembly is limited in the following ways by default:

■   A maximum of 200 unique packets that can be reassembled, per interface

■   A maximum of 24 fragments for a single packet

■   A maximum time of 5 seconds for all fragments of a packet to arrive

Key
Topic

You can also configure virtual packet reassembly from Cisco Adaptive Security Device Manager (ASDM). Select **Configuration > Firewall > Advanced > Fragment**. Select an interface from the list and then click the **Edit** button to change any of the virtual reassembly parameters, as shown in Figure 11-1. You can also click the **Show Fragment** button to display the reassembly counters for each interface.

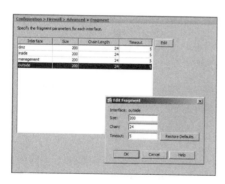

Figure 11-1   *Tuning Virtual Fragment Reassembly in ASDM*

You can make similar virtual packet reassembly adjustments from the CLI with the commands listed in Table 11-2.

Table 11-2   *Commands Used to Configure Virtual Packet Reassembly Limits*

Function	Command Syntax
Limit the number of packets awaiting reassembly.	ciscoasa(config)# **fragment size** *packets* [*interface*]
Limit the number of fragments per packet.	ciscoasa(config)# **fragment chain** *fragments* [*interface*]
Limit the time for all parts of a packet to arrive.	ciscoasa(config)# **fragment timeout** *seconds* [*interface*]

You can monitor an ASA's fragmentation activity with the **show fragment** EXEC command. In Example 11-1, the outside interface has the default fragment settings (database size 200 packets, chain limit 24 fragments, and timeout limit 5 seconds).

Example 11-1   *Displaying Virtual Reassembly Activity*

```
ciscoasa# show fragment outside
Interface: outside
    Size: 200, Chain: 24, Timeout: 5, Reassembly: virtual
    Queue: 2, Assemble: 2562, Fail: 972, Overflow: 713
ciscoasa#
```

The output shows that the ASA has reassembled 2562 packets, and two packets are awaiting reassembly. The output also shows that the reassembly process has failed 972 times. This is because the timeout limit expired while the process was waiting for all fragments to arrive. The process has also had overflow conditions, indicating that for 712 different packets, more than 24 fragments arrived and overflowed the packet buffer.

Prioritizing Traffic

Sometimes, an ASA can inspect and prepare to send packets faster than they can be transmitted on an interface. Each ASA interface has an output queue or buffer that stores outbound packets temporarily until they can be transmitted.

This simple queue structure makes for simple interface operation. The first packet put into the queue is the first one that is taken out and transmitted. There is no differentiation between types of traffic or there are no quality of service (QoS) requirements. Regardless of the packet contents, packets leave the queue in the same order they went into it.

Packets that are placed into the queue are sent in a best-effort fashion This means that the ASA will make its best effort to send the next packet it finds in the interface queue. In fact, this queue is known as a best-effort queue (BEQ), as shown in Figure 11-2. An HTTP packet was the first to arrive in the queue, followed by an RTP packet, and then an SMTP packet.

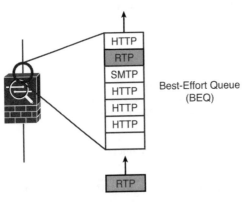

Figure 11-2   *Best-Effort Queue Operation on an ASA Interface*

A BEQ usually works fine for common types of traffic; however, it presents a problem for time-critical data that might pass through an ASA. For example, any type of streaming audio or video must be forwarded in a predictable manner so that packets aren't delayed too much before they reach their destination. Those packets also need to be forwarded at a fairly regular rate; too much variation in packet-to-packet delay (jitter) results in poor-quality audio or video at the destination.

In Figure 11-2, suppose the RTP packets contain pieces of a real-time audio stream. The first RTP packet is near the head end of the queue, almost ready to be transmitted. The next RTP packet is just arriving and will be placed at the tail end of the queue.

Ideally, the RTP packets should be transmitted as closely together as possible to preserve the real-time nature of the contents. When streaming data is mixed with other types of high-volume data passing through a firewall, however, the nonstreaming data can starve the streaming data flow. This can happen simply because the streaming packets get lost in a sea of other packets competing for transmission time.

To help deliver time-critical traffic more efficiently, an ASA can also maintain one priority or low-latency queue (LLQ) on each of its interfaces. Packets are placed in this queue only when they match specific criteria. Any packets in the LLQ are transmitted ahead of any packets in the BEQ, providing priority service. Figure 11-3 demonstrates this concept, where only the RTP packets are being classified and then sent into the LLQ. The ASA always services the LLQ first, so any RTP packets found there are immediately transmitted ahead of anything found in the BEQ.

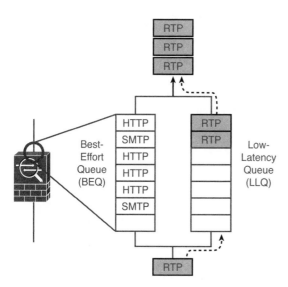

Figure 11-3 *Low-Latency Queue Operation on an ASA Interface*

If either the BEQ or LLQ fills during a time of interface congestion, any other packets destined for the queue are simply dropped. In addition, there is no crossover or fallback between queues. For example, if the LLQ is full, subsequent priority packets are not placed in the BEQ; they are dropped instead.

Both the BEQ and the LLQ are queues maintained in software. In addition, an ASA uses a hardware queue called the *transmit ring* to buffer packets that will be copied directly to the physical interface hardware for transmission. Packets are pulled from the LLQ first, and then the BEQ, and then they are placed in the hardware queue of the egress interface.

You can configure priority queuing through ASDM. Select **Configuration > Device Management > Advanced > Priority Queue**. By default, only a BEQ is enabled and used on each interface. You must specifically enable an LLQ by clicking the **Add** button and selecting the interface name, as shown in Figure 11-4. You can also tune the queue limit and the transmission ring limit, if needed.

Figure 11-4   *Enabling and Tuning an Interface Priority Queue*

As soon as the priority queue is enabled for the first time, the queue depth limit is set to a calculated default value. The limit is the number of 256-byte packets that can be transmitted on the interface over a 500-ms period. Naturally, the default value varies according to the interface speed, but it always has a maximum value of 2048 packets.

The queue limit value in *packets* (1 to 2048) varies according to the amount of ASA memory and the interface speed. In addition, packets can vary in size, but the queue is always measured in generic packets, which can be up to the interface MTU (default 1500 bytes) bytes long.

Similarly, as soon as the interface priority queue is enabled for the first time, the transmit ring limit is set to a calculated default value. The limit is the number of 1500-byte packets that can be transmitted on the interface in a 10-ms period. The packets limit has a minimum of 3 and a maximum that varies according to the interface and available memory.

Next, define a service policy rule by selecting **Configuration > Firewall > Service Policy Rules**, as described in Chapter 9, "Inspecting Traffic." You can either add a new rule or edit an existing one. When you get to the Rule Actions dialog box, be sure to check the **Enable Priority for This Flow** check box, as shown in Figure 11-5.

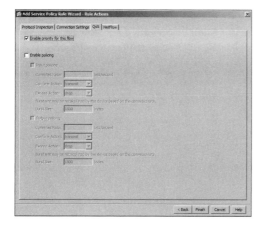

Figure 11-5 *Defining Priority Queuing as an MPF Action in ASDM*

You can configure priority queuing with the CLI by using the following sequence of steps:

Step 1.   **Enable the priority queue on an interface:**

```
ciscoasa(config)# priority-queue interface
```

Step 2.   **Tune the interface queues:**

Use the commands listed in Table 11-3 to set the depth of both the BEQ and LLQ and to set the transmit ring queue depth in *packets*.

Table 11-3 *Commands Used to Tune Interface Queues*

Hardware Queue Parameter	Command Syntax
Set the BEQ and LLQ depth.	Ciscoasa(config-priority-queue)# **queue-limit** *packets*
Set the transmit queue size.	Ciscoasa(config-priority-queue)# **tx-ring-limit** *packets*

To see the current interface queue values, you can use the **show priority-queue config** command, as shown in Example 11-2.

Example 11-2 *Displaying the Current Interface Queue Sizes*

```
ciscoasa# show priority-queue config
Priority-Queue Config interface outside
                current      default       range
queue-limit     2048         2048          0 - 2048
tx-ring-limit   512          512           3 - 512


Priority-Queue Config interface inside
                current      default       range
queue-limit     0            2048          0 - 2048
tx-ring-limit   -1           512           3 - 512
```

Notice that the outside interface is shown with current values of 2048 and 512, which are the same as the default values. However, the inside interface has values 0 and –1. The difference is that the LLQ on the outside interface has been enabled with the **priority-queue outside** command. The inside interface is still using its default BEQ because its LLQ has not been enabled. As a result, the inside priority queue has a **queue-limit**, or depth, of zero packets; the –1 value for **tx-ring-limit** indicates that it is currently disabled.

Step 3.   **Configure the MPF to use the LLQ:** By default, all packets are sent to the best-effort queue, regardless of whether a priority queue has been configured and enabled. To send packets to the priority queue, you must use the Modular Policy Framework (MPF) to configure a service policy that matches specific traffic with a class map and then assigns that traffic to the priority queue. MPF configuration is covered in Chapter 9.

Use Example 11-3 as a guideline for your MPF configuration. Use the **priority** command as the action to send the matched traffic into an LLQ. Actually, the packets are marked to be destined for only a generic priority queue. When the ASA is ready to forward them, they will be placed into the priority queue on the appropriate interface.

Example 11-3   *MPF Structure for Sending Matched Packets into an LLQ*

```
ciscoasa(config)# class-map class_map_name
ciscoasa(config-cmap)# match condition
ciscoasa(config-cmap)# exit

ciscoasa(config)# policy-map policy_map_name
ciscoasa(config-pmap)# class class_map_name
ciscoasa(config-pmap-c)# priority
ciscoasa(config-pmap-c)# exit
ciscoasa(config-pmap)# exit

ciscoasa(config)# service-policy policy_map_name interface interface
```

Controlling Traffic Bandwidth

Priority queuing can give premium service to specific types of traffic without any real regard for the bandwidth being used. If packets sent into a priority queue are always forwarded ahead of any other traffic, the priority queue shouldn't be affected by other traffic flows that might use up significant bandwidth.

Aside from the priority queue, all traffic flows passing through an ASA have to compete for the available bandwidth on an interface. By default, there are no limits on bandwidth usage. This configuration might be fine in many scenarios, where traffic flows are serviced on a "best effort" basis. However, suppose one user initiates a peer-to-peer file sharing connection that transfers a huge amount of data as fast as possible. This one traffic flow might starve out other important or mission-critical flows until it completes. In that case, you might want to have a way to keep runaway bandwidth usage in check.

You can leverage two ASA features to control or limit the amount of bandwidth used by specific traffic flows:

■   Traffic policing

■   Traffic shaping

With either method, the ASA measures the bandwidth used by traffic that is classified by a service policy and then attempts to hold the traffic within a configured rate limit. However, each method accomplishes the bandwidth control in a different manner.

With traffic policing, the packets are forwarded normally as long as the bandwidth threshold is not exceeded. However, packets that do exceed the bandwidth threshold are simply dropped. Figure 11-6 illustrates this process, where the dashed line represents the original traffic flow and the solid line shows the resulting policed traffic.

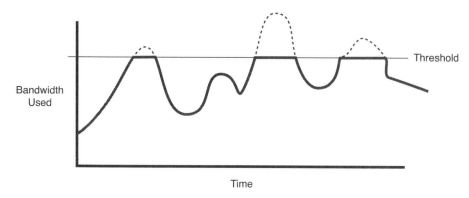

Figure 11-6   *Effects of Traffic Policing*

Notice how the traffic pattern is not changed by the policer, as the traffic rate still rises and falls; only the peaks that would have risen above the threshold are missing because those packets have been dropped. This process doesn't introduce any latency or jitter to the original traffic flow as long as the traffic conforms or stays below the police threshold limit. It can lead to TCP retransmissions if TCP packets are among those dropped, however.

In contrast, traffic shaping takes a more preemptive approach. Traffic is buffered before it is forwarded so that the traffic rate can be shaped or held within the threshold limit. The idea is to pull packets from the buffer at a rate that is less than the threshold so that no packets are dropped. Figure 11-7 illustrates this process; again, the dashed line shows the original traffic and the solid line shows the resulting shaped traffic.

Notice how traffic shaping has smoothed out any rises and falls of the original traffic rate. Although this process smoothes out the traffic flow and holds it within the threshold, it also introduces a variable delay or jitter as the packets are buffered and then forwarded at varying times. Because packets are not normally dropped during shaping, TCP retransmissions are minimized.

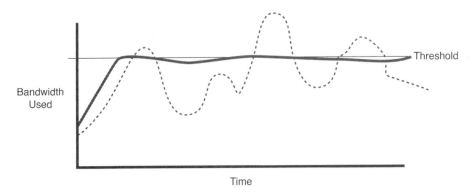

Figure 11-7   *Effects of Traffic Shaping*

Traffic shaping can be performed only on outbound traffic on an interface. In addition, traffic shaping operates on the bulk traffic passing through an interface rather than on specific traffic matched by a class map. This property makes traffic shaping handy when a high-speed ASA interface is connected to a lower-speed device, such as a broadband Internet service. In that case, the traffic shaping threshold can be configured to match the lower-speed bandwidth.

Configuring a Traffic Policer

To use ASDM to configure traffic policing, begin by navigating to **Configuration > Firewall > Service Policy Rules** and adding a new service policy rule or editing an existing one. Define a matching condition that will classify the traffic that will be policed. Next, click the **QoS** tab in the Rule Action dialog box, as shown in Figure 11-8.

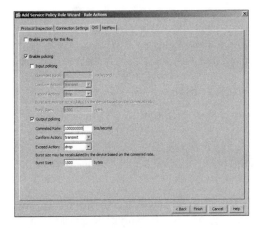

Figure 11-8   *Configuring a Traffic Policer in ASDM*

Check the **Enable Policing** check box, and then choose either **Input Policing** or **Output Policing**. Packets that are matched and policed are held to a strict bandwidth policy. You can enter the bandwidth limit threshold as the **Committed Rate**, given in bits per second, as 8000 (8 kbps) to 2,000,000,000 (2 Gbps). As long as the bandwidth is not exceeding the committed rate, the ASA takes the **Conform Action** and either drops the conforming packets or transmits them (the default).

You can also specify an "instantaneous" amount of burst traffic that is allowed when the conform rate is exceeded. This is given as the **Burst Size,** from 1000 (1 KB) to 512,000,000 (512 MB), with a default of 1500 bytes. If the committed rate is exceeded by more than the burst size, the traffic is considered nonconforming, and the **Exceed Action** is taken. The ASA can either **drop** (the default) or **transmit** the nonconforming packets.

It might seem odd that the conform rate is specified in bits per second while the burst is given in bytes, but that is how the policer operates. A 10-ms clock interval is used to measure policed traffic. The byte counts of matching packets are added to a "bucket" whose "high-water mark" is set to the amount of traffic that can be transmitted in one clock tick. In addition, the bucket is emptied at every interval of the policer clock (10 ms).

As long as the committed rate is not exceeded, the bucket should never fill. If a burst size is configured, it is added to the bucket's high-water mark. Therefore, in one clock tick (10 ms), the amount of matching traffic can exceed the conforming amount by the burst size in bytes.

As an example, suppose you need to configure a policer to limit outbound HTTP traffic to an aggregate rate of 100 Mbps. Conforming traffic should be forwarded normally, but traffic that exceeds the conform rate should be dropped. The HTTP servers are located on the inside of the ASA, and all relevant clients are located outside. Figure 11-8 shows the values you could use to configure the service policy.

Finally, click the **Finish** button to complete the service policy rule. The new rule and the policer action will be shown in the summary list, as shown in Figure 11-9.

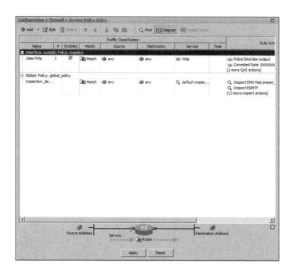

Figure 11-9   *Verifying the Traffic Policer Policy Rule Action*

If you choose to use the CLI instead, you can configure traffic policing by defining a service policy using the MPF. Be sure to match the traffic that will be policed by defining a class map. Reference the class map in a policy map and define the policy action to be one of the commands listed in Table 11-4. The *conform_rate* in the CLI command is identical to the committed rate in ASDM.

Table 11-4 *Command Syntax for Traffic Policing or Shaping*

Function	Command Syntax
Policing	ciscoasa(config-pmap-c)# **police** {**output**	**input**} *conform_rate* [*burst_bytes*] [**conform-action** {**drop**	**transmit**}] [**exceed-action** {**drop**	**transmit**}]
Shaping	ciscoasa(config-pmap-c)# **shape average** *rate* [*burst-size*]

Chapter 9 covers MPF configuration in greater detail. Use Example 11-4 as a guideline for your MPF configuration. Use the **police** command as the action to send the matched traffic into a traffic policer.

Example 11-4 *MPF Structure for Traffic Policing*

```
ciscoasa(config)# class-map class_map_name
ciscoasa(config-cmap)# match condition
ciscoasa(config-cmap)# exit

ciscoasa(config)# policy-map policy_map_name
ciscoasa(config-pmap)# class class_map_name
ciscoasa(config-pmap-c)# police ...
ciscoasa(config-pmap-c)# exit
ciscoasa(config-pmap)# exit

ciscoasa(config)# service-policy policy_map_name interface interface
```

Example 11-5 lists the commands you can use to configure a service policy to implement the scenario used in Figure 11-8.

Example 11-5 *Configuring a Traffic Policer to Control Outbound HTTP Traffic*

```
ciscoasa(config)# access-list outbound_http extended permit tcp any eq http any
ciscoasa(config)# class-map class_http
ciscoasa(config-cmap)# match access-list outbound_http
ciscoasa(config-cmap)# exit
!
ciscoasa(config)# policy-map mypolicy
ciscoasa(config-pmap)# class class_http
ciscoasa(config-pmap-c)# police output 100000000 conform-action transmit exceed-
  action drop
ciscoasa(config-pmap-c)# exit
```

```
ciscoasa(config-pmap)# exit
!
ciscoasa(config)# service-policy mypolicy interface outside
```

You can verify traffic policer operation by entering the **show service-policy police** command, as demonstrated in Example 11-6. From the command output, you can see that the bandwidth threshold ("cir," or committed information rate) is 100 Mbps and the burst size is 50,000 bytes. The command output also shows current estimates of the bits per second for traffic that conformed or exceeded the threshold.

Example 11-6   *Displaying Information About Traffic Policing*

```
ciscoasa# show service-policy police
Interface outside:
  Service-policy: outside-policy
    Class-map: class-http
      Output police Interface outside:
        cir 100000000 bps, bc 50000 bytes
        conformed 1431 packets, 351327 bytes; actions:  transmit
        exceeded 339 packets, 53871 bytes; actions:  drop
        conformed 50002 bps, exceed 42556 bps
ciscoasa#
```

Configuring Traffic Shaping

To configure traffic shaping in ASDM, begin by adding a new service policy rule or editing an existing one. Traffic shaping doesn't shape specific matched traffic; it shapes the default traffic that isn't matched or classified by any other traffic class. Therefore, you have to use the class-default class map to match the traffic. This is done by selecting the **Use Class-Default As the Traffic Class** option in the Traffic Classification Criteria dialog box, as shown in Figure 11-10.

Next, click the **QoS** tab in the Rule Actions dialog box and check **Enable Traffic Shaping** as the policy action, as shown in Figure 11-11. (If you chose any matching criteria other than class-default, the Enable Traffic Shaping option will not be shown.)

Traffic shaping buffers packets and attempts to hold the interface bandwidth close to an average rate. You can set the **Average Rate** parameter in bits per second, from 64,000 to 154,400,000, in multiples of 8000 bps.

You can also specify a burst size in bits, which determines the amount of traffic that can be sent in excess of the average rate. The burst size is automatically calculated by default, based on the average rate you configure, but is shown blank in ASDM. The default size is based on how much traffic can be sent in a 4-ms time period at the average rate. Normally, the default value is optimal, so you should not have to specify a burst size. If you do decide to set it explicitly, the *burst-size* parameter can range from 2048 to 154,400,000 bits.

Can you configure both priority queuing and traffic shaping, so that some traffic will be handled ahead of the rest of the traffic that will be shaped? In a nutshell, no—an ASA does not support both features configured on the same interface. However, the ASDM traffic shaping configuration does support a "hierarchical priority queuing" if you check the **Enforce Priority to Selected Shaped Traffic** check box under the Average Rate and Burst Size parameters.

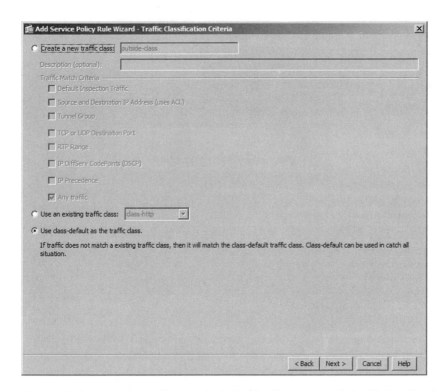

Figure 11-10 *Using the Class-Default Traffic Class to Match Traffic for Shaping*

Once the option is selected, you can click the **Configure** button to define a matching criteria in a subsequent dialog box, as shown in Figure 11-12. This criteria will be used to match traffic being sent into the traffic shaper. The matched traffic will be given priority service within the traffic shaping process, but the packets are not sent into an interface priority queue.

You can also use the CLI to configure traffic shaping. Use Example 11-7 as a guideline for your MPF configuration. Use the **shape** command as the action to send the matched traffic into a traffic shaper. Traffic shaping can be applied only to the bulk amount of traffic passing through an interface. Therefore, the matching condition you enter into the policy map configuration is important. The only permissible command is **class class-default**, followed by the **shape** command action.

Example 11-7 *MPF Structure for Traffic Shaping*

```
ciscoasa(config)# class-map class_map_name
ciscoasa(config-cmap)# match condition
ciscoasa(config-cmap)# exit
```

```
ciscoasa(config)# policy-map policy_map_name
ciscoasa(config-pmap)# class class-default
ciscoasa(config-pmap-c)# shape ...
ciscoasa(config-pmap-c)# exit
ciscoasa(config-pmap)# exit


ciscoasa(config)# service-policy policy_map_name interface interface
```

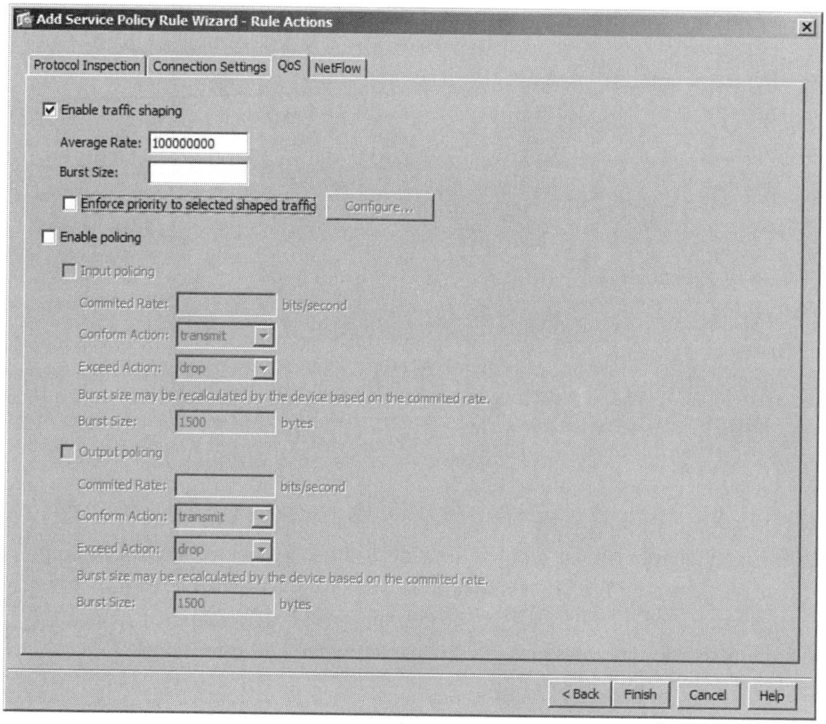

Figure 11-11 *Configuring Traffic Shaping in ASDM*

In Example 11-8, traffic shaping is configured for an average rate of 100 Mbps. Notice that no class map has been defined. Instead, the policy map uses the **class-default** class map to match against all traffic. This scenario matches the one configured in ASDM in Figure 11-11.

Example 11-8 *Configuring Traffic Shaping*

```
ciscoasa(config)# policy-map outside-policy
ciscoasa(config-pmap)# class class-default
ciscoasa(config-pmap-c)# shape average 100000000
ciscoasa(config-pmap-c)# exit
ciscoasa(config-pmap)# exit
!
ciscoasa(config)# service-policy outside-policy interface outside
```

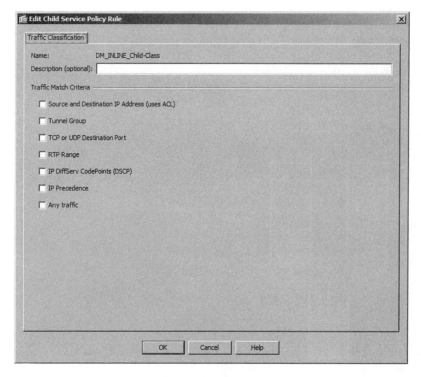

Figure 11-12   *Configuring a Matching Criteria for Priority Handling in the Traffic Shaper*

You can verify traffic shaper operation by entering the **show service-policy shape** command, as shown in Example 11-9. The command output shows that the bandwidth average threshold is 100 Mbps and the burst size is 400,000 bits. The traffic shaper is using a buffer queue that can hold 1666 packets waiting to be shaped and forwarded.

Example 11-9   *Displaying Information About Traffic Shaping*

```
ciscoasa# show service-policy shape
Interface outside:
  Service-policy: outside-policy
    Class-map: class-default

      shape (average) cir 100000000, bc 400000
      Queueing
      queue limit 1666 packets
      (queue depth/total drops/no-buffer drops) 0/0/0
      (pkts output/bytes output) 0/0
ciscoasa#
```

Exam Preparation Tasks

As mentioned in the section, "How to Use This Book," in the Introduction, you have a couple of choices for exam preparation: the exercises here, Chapter 17, "Final Preparation," and the exam simulation questions on the CD-ROM.

Review All Key Topics

Review the most important topics in this chapter, noted with the Key Topic icon in the outer margin of the page. Table 11-5 lists a reference of these key topics and the page numbers on which each is found.

Table 11-5   *Key Topics for Chapter 11*

Key Topic Element	Description	Page Number
List	Explains virtual packet reassembly	611
Paragraph	Explains the best-effort queue (BEQ)	612
Paragraph	Explains the low-latency queue (LLQ)	613
Paragraph	Explains traffic policing	617
Paragraph	Explains traffic shaping	617

Key
Topic

Define Key Terms

Define the following key terms from this chapter and check your answers in the glossary:

virtual reassembly, maximum transmission unit (MTU), best-effort queue (BEQ), low-latency queue (LLQ), traffic policing, traffic shaping

Command Reference to Check Your Memory

This section includes the most important configuration and EXEC commands covered in this chapter. It might not be necessary to memorize the complete syntax of every command, but you should be able to remember the basic keywords that are needed.

To test your memory of the commands, cover the right side of Tables 11-6 through 11-8 with a piece of paper, read the description on the left side, and then see how much of the command you can remember.

The FIREWALL exam focuses on practical, hands-on skills that are used by a networking professional. Therefore, you should be able to identify the commands needed to configure and test an ASA feature.

Table 11-6 *Commands Related to ASA Fragment Handling*

Task	Command Syntax
Set the interface MTU	ciscoasa(config)# **mtu** *interface bytes*
Limit the number of packets awaiting re-assembly	ciscoasa(config)# **fragment size** *packets* [*interface*]
Limit the number of fragments per packet	ciscoasa(config)# **fragment chain** *fragments* [*interface*]
Limit the time for all parts of a packet to arrive	ciscoasa(config)# **fragment timeout** *seconds* [*interface*]
Display fragmentation activity	ciscoasa# **show fragment**

Table 11-7 *Commands Related to Priority Handling*

Task	Command Syntax
Enable the LLQ on an interface	ciscoasa(config)# **priority-queue** *interface*
Set the BEQ and LLQ depth	ciscoasa(config-priority-queue)# **queue-limit** *packets*
Set the transmit queue size	ciscoasa(config-priority-queue)# **tx-ring-limit** *packets*
Send packets to the LLQ	ciscoasa(config-pmap-c)# **priority**
Display interface queue sizes	ciscoasa# **show priority-queue config**

Table 11-8 *Commands Related to Controlling Traffic Bandwidth*

Task	Command Syntax
Police traffic	ciscoasa(config-pmap-c)# **police** {**output**	**input**} *conform_rate* [*burst_bytes*] [**conform-action** {**drop**	**transmit**}] [**exceed-action** {**drop**	**transmit**}]
Shape traffic	ciscoasa(config-pmap-c)# **shape average** *rate* [*burst-size*]
Display traffic policing activity	ciscoasa# **show service-policy police**
Display traffic shaping activity	ciscoasa# **show service-policy shape**

This chapter covers the following topics:

- **Firewall Mode Overview:** This section provides an overview of the two firewall modes that an ASA can use.

- **Configuring Transparent Firewall Mode:** This section covers the configuration steps necessary to use transparent firewall mode.

- **Controlling Traffic in Transparent Firewall Mode:** This section explains how to use access lists to control the movement of traffic when an ASA is configured for transparent firewall mode.

- **Using ARP Inspection:** This section covers the feature that can be used to inspect ARP replies to prevent ARP spoofing attacks.

- **Disabling MAC Address Learning:** This section discusses how to disable MAC address learning to prevent MAC address spoofing attacks that can confuse or overwhelm an ASA in transparent firewall mode.

CHAPTER 12

Using Transparent Firewall Mode

The Cisco Adaptive Security Appliance (ASA) can operate in one of two firewall modes. This chapter explains the concepts behind routed firewall mode, operating at Layer 3, and transparent mode, operating at Layer 2. In addition, this chapter covers how to configure and use transparent mode and how to prevent some attacks on it.

"Do I Know This Already?" Quiz

The "Do I Know This Already?" quiz allows you to assess whether you should read this entire chapter thoroughly or jump to the "Exam Preparation Tasks" section. If you are in doubt about your answers to these questions or your own assessment of your knowledge of the topics, read the entire chapter. Table 12-1 lists the major headings in this chapter and their corresponding "Do I Know This Already?" quiz questions. You can find the answers in Appendix A, "Answers to the 'Do I Know This Already?' Quizzes."

Table 12-1 *"Do I Know This Already?" Section-to-Question Mapping*

Foundation Topics Section	Questions
Firewall Mode Overview	1–3
Configuring Transparent Firewall Mode	4–5
Controlling Traffic in Transparent Firewall Mode	6–7
Using ARP Inspection	8–9
Disabling MAC Address Learning	10

Caution: The goal of self-assessment is to gauge your mastery of the topics in this chapter. If you do not know the answer to a question or are only partially sure of the answer, you should mark that question as wrong for purposes of the self-assessment. Giving yourself credit for an answer you correctly guess skews your self-assessment results and might provide you with a false sense of security.

1. When an ASA begins to operate in transparent firewall mode, what information does it use to forward packets?

   a. Source IP addresses.

   b. Destination IP addresses.

   c. Source MAC addresses.

   d. Destination MAC addresses.

   e. All of the answers are correct.

2. When an ASA is operating in transparent firewall mode, how many interfaces can be active in a bridge group?

   a. 1

   b. 2

   c. 3

   d. As many as the license key supports

   e. As many as are installed

3. Which of the following are valid applications for an ASA operating in transparent firewall mode? (Choose all that apply.)

   a. When only IP packets need to be inspected

   b. When non-IP packets need to be inspected

   c. A network where IP addressing cannot be reworked to support a firewall

   d. A network that can be segmented into new IP subnets on each side of a firewall

4. When the **firewall transparent** command is entered, what happens first?

   a. The ASA reboots.

   b. The ASA begins bridging traffic with the current configuration.

   c. All interface IP addresses are cleared.

   d. The running configuration is cleared.

5. How many IP addresses can you configure on an ASA and its interfaces in a bridge group when transparent firewall mode is active?

   a. 1

   b. 2

   c. 3

   d. One per interface

6. Which of the following are correct statements about the default behavior of transparent firewall mode as it controls packet movement? (Choose all that apply.)

   a. ARP packets are forwarded.

   b. Broadcast packets are not forwarded.

   c. Multicast packets are forwarded.

   d. Non-IP packets are not forwarded.

7. Which one of the following commands should be used to permit Spanning Tree Protocol packets to pass through an ASA in transparent firewall mode? Assume that the access list will be applied to the ASA interfaces.

a. access-list STP extended permit stp any any

b. access-list STP ethertype permit bpdu

c. access-list STP broadcast permit bpdu any

d. access-list STP extended permit bpdu

8. Which of the following are valid reasons to use ARP inspection? (Choose all that apply.)

a. To prevent ARP packets from being exchanged with the outside network

b. To prevent spoofed ARP packets in a man-in-the-middle attack

c. To make sure that ARP packets are adhering to the ARP protocol standard

d. To prevent a denial-of-service attack on the ASA's MAC address table

9. Once ARP inspection is enabled, which one of the following describes the additional information that is needed for ARP to function properly across an ASA in transparent firewall mode?

a. Nothing; ARP inspection is self-sufficient.

b. The IP addresses of any ARP servers in the network.

c. Static ARP entries for all trusted hosts.

d. An access list to permit ARP packets on all ASA interfaces.

10. By default, what information does an ASA learn and maintain in its MAC address table?

a. Source MAC address, ingress interface

b. Destination MAC address, ingress interface

c. Source MAC address, egress interface

d. Destination MAC address, egress interface

Foundation Topics

Beneath all the security features and processes an ASA offers, it must forward traffic from one interface to another. An ASA can operate in either routed firewall mode, similar to a router, or in transparent firewall mode, much like a transparent bridge.

You can configure an ASA for either firewall mode, depending on the security requirements and the network topology. This chapter discusses the two modes in detail and how you can leverage them appropriately in practice.

Firewall Mode Overview

By default, an ASA operates by performing all of its operations at OSI Layer 3 using IP packets and IP addresses. All the traffic inspection and forwarding decisions are based on Layer 3 (IP address) parameters, although the ASA can look at higher layers within the IP packets being examined. The ASA itself maintains IP addresses on its own interfaces and acts as a router or gateway to the networks that connect to it. This is known as the *routed* firewall mode.

As with a router, each ASA interface must be connected to a different IP subnet and be assigned an IP address on that subnet. This arrangement is shown in Figure 12-1, where the inside interface sits on IP subnet 192.168.200.0/24 and the outside interface sits on 192.168.100.0/24. Management traffic can be permitted on either interface, or the ASA can have a dedicated management interface on yet another subnet.

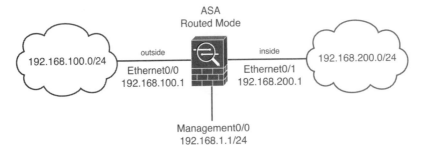

Figure 12-1   *Example of an ASA in Routed Firewall Mode*

In routed firewall mode, an ASA bases its packet forwarding decisions on the destination IP address. It can use static routes or participate in dynamic IP routing with other neighboring routers.

When an ASA in routed firewall mode is installed or inserted into a network for the first time, the network must become segmented across the ASA's interfaces. For example, where a single IP subnet used to be, the inside and outside interfaces now form the boundary of two separate subnets.

This can make the installation difficult, as some readdressing must take place. The easiest approach is to keep the original IP addressing on the ASA's inside interface, where the majority of protected hosts reside. The outside interface can take on an address from a new subnet that is shared between the ASA and the next-hop router. In other words, the outside of the ASA usually has fewer directly connected hosts to readdress to a new subnet.

An ASA can also be configured to operate in *transparent* firewall mode, such that it appears to operate as a Layer 2 device, without becoming a router hop or a gateway to its connected networks. This is also known as a Layer 2 firewall or a stealth firewall, because the ASA's interfaces have no assigned IP addresses and cannot be detected or manipulated. Only a single management address is used for traffic sourced by the transparent firewall itself or destined for a management session.

As a Layer 2 device, an ASA in transparent firewall mode can be installed or wedged into an existing network, separating the inside and outside without changing any existing IP addresses. In Figure 12-2, notice how the ASA running in transparent firewall mode has its inside and outside interfaces connected to the same IP subnet. This is commonly called a "bump-in-the-wire" because the ASA doesn't break or segment the IP subnet along a wire but instead more or less becomes part of the wire. This makes a new installation straightforward.

Figure 12-2   *Example of an ASA in Transparent Firewall Mode*

You can think of a transparent mode firewall as a type of transparent bridge, where packets are bridged from one interface to another based only on their MAC addresses. The ASA must maintain a MAC address table of the source address learned in each received packet, along with the interface on which the packet arrived. Once a MAC address has been learned, the ASA is able to forward a packet to that address by knowing the location or the egress interface where that same address has been active before.

What if a MAC address is not found in the table? A transparent bridge would flood the original packet out the other interface automatically, assuming that the MAC address must be out there somewhere. The ASA cannot do that simply because it has to maintain security policies that might limit where a packet should go. Instead, an ASA will attempt to discover a destination MAC address by probing for its existence in one of the following ways:

■ **ARP request:** When the destination IP address is located on a local subnet that is directly connected to the ASA, the ASA will send an ARP request to force the destination to answer with its own MAC address in an ARP reply. Once the reply is received, the ASA has learned the location of the MAC address.

■ **Ping request:** When the destination IP address is located on some distant subnet, the ASA will send an ICMP echo request (ping) to the destination. When the destination host or a router responds, the ASA can learn the location of the next-hop router's MAC address that can be used to reach the destination.

In transparent firewall mode on ASAs running software release 8.4(1) or later, the ASA interfaces can be mapped into one or more logical bridge groups. Each bridge group functions as an independent transparent firewall; traffic passing through one bridge group cannot reach any other bridge group internally. If traffic must be passed from one bridge group to another, an external router must be used. Up to eight bridge groups are supported on a physical ASA platform, with 2–4 interfaces assigned to each. At a minimum, a bridge group must contain two interfaces—usually named the inside and outside.

You can leverage multiple bridge groups to create several independent transparent firewalls, as opposed to using multiple security context mode. Figure 12-3 shows an ASA that has been configured with two bridge groups. Although the bridge groups are isolated from each other, be aware that firewall-management functions, such as syslog and AAA server configurations, are shared across all the bridge groups configured on a single ASA.

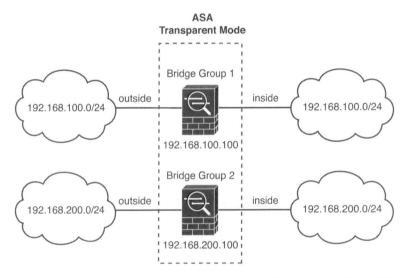

Figure 12-3   *Example of Two Bridge Groups in Transparent Firewall Mode*

Software releases prior to 8.4.1 support one inherent bridge group. Only two interfaces are supported: the inside and the outside. You can assign the inside and outside names to two interfaces arbitrarily. Once those interfaces are configured, the ASA will not permit a third interface to be configured. The only exception is the management-only interface, which you can configure and use to reach the ASA for administration purposes.

In multiple context mode, each context can support one or more bridge groups. Each context must use a set of interfaces that is different than the set used by any other context. In other words, contexts cannot share inside and outside interfaces due to the bridging operation. Security contexts are covered in detail in Chapter 13, "Creating Virtual Firewalls on the ASA."

In transparent firewall mode, all of the interfaces in a bridge group must share the same IP subnet; however, IP packets are still inspected without the Layer 2 limitation. Full extended access lists (IP protocol and port numbers) are used to evaluate traffic policies, and the ASA's application inspection engines are able to interpret IP activity at any layer. As of release 8.0(2), an ASA can integrate Network Address Translation (NAT) with transparent firewall mode.

In routed firewall mode, an ASA can inspect and forward only IP packets. Transparent firewall mode doesn't share that same limitation because it focuses on Layer 2 and MAC addresses and is able to handle non-IP packets as well. Non-IP packets can be permitted by configuring a special interface access list that contains specific EtherType values.

Before you choose either routed or transparent firewall mode, you should be aware of the strengths and weaknesses of each mode. Table 12-2 provides a summary of the mode characteristics.

Table 12-2   *Comparison of the Routed and Transparent Firewall Modes*

Key
Topic

Routed Firewall Mode	Transparent Firewall Mode
Use when only IP packets are to be inspected.	Use when non-IP packets must be forwarded.
Network readdressing is necessary across the ASA.	Network readdressing is not necessary.
All interfaces can be used.	Only 2–4 interfaces can be used per bridge group.
All ASA features are available.	The following features are not available: ■ Dynamic routing protocols ■ Dynamic DNS ■ DHCP Relay ■ Multicast IP routing ■ Quality of service ■ VPN termination for transit traffic

Configuring Transparent Firewall Mode

Before you begin configuring transparent firewall mode, you should verify which mode is currently in use. You can do that with the **show firewall** EXEC command. In Example 12-1, the ASA is running in the default routed (or "router") mode.

Example 12-1   *Verifying the Current Firewall Mode*

```
ciscoasa# show firewall
Firewall mode: Router
ciscoasa#
```

You can enable transparent firewall mode with the following command:

```
ciscoasa(config)# firewall transparent
```

Transparent firewall mode begins immediately and doesn't require a reload; however, because transparent and routed firewall modes use different approaches to network security, the running configuration will be cleared as soon as transparent firewall mode begins. The idea is to enter transparent firewall mode and build an appropriate configuration from scratch.

For that reason, you should save the routed firewall mode running configuration to flash memory or to an external server before enabling transparent firewall mode. That way, you will have a copy of the configuration in case you need to revert to routed firewall mode or refer to some portion of that configuration. Because the configuration is cleared, ASDM does not offer any way to change the firewall mode.

Next, you will need to set aside ASA interfaces and configure them for transparent firewall use. For ASA release 8.4(1) or later, you can configure up to four interfaces as part of a bridge group. With earlier releases, you must use exactly two interfaces—one interface will face the "outside," less secure part of the network, while the other will face the "inside," more secure area.

Configure the interfaces exactly as you would with routed firewall mode, with the exception of any IP addresses, by supplying the following parameters:

- Interface speed and duplex mode

- Interface name

- Security level

- Bridge group number (ASA release 8.4(1) and later)

In ASDM, navigate to **Configuration > Device Setup > Interfaces**, select an interface, and click **Edit**. You can enter the interface parameters as shown in Figure 12-4. Be sure to configure the same bridge group number on all interfaces that will become part of the same bridge group.

If you choose to configure interfaces with the CLI instead, you can use the **nameif**, **security-level**, and **bridge-group** interface configuration commands. As an example, suppose the Ethernet0/0 interface will face the outside, while Ethernet0/1 will face the inside. Both interfaces will be part of bridge group 1. You could use the commands listed in Example 12-2 to configure the two interfaces.

Example 12-2 *Configuring Interfaces in Transparent Firewall Mode*

```
CISCOASA(config)# interface ethernet0/0
CISCOASA(config-if)# nameif outside
CISCOASA(config-if)# security-level 0
CISCOASA(config-if)# bridge-group 1
CISCOASA(config-if)# no shutdown
CISCOASA(config-if)# exit
```

```
CISCOASA(config)# interface ethernet0/1
CISCOASA(config-if)# nameif inside
CISCOASA(config-if)# security-level 100
CISCOASA(config-if)# bridge-group 1
CISCOASA(config-if)# no shutdown
CISCOASA(config-if)# exit
```

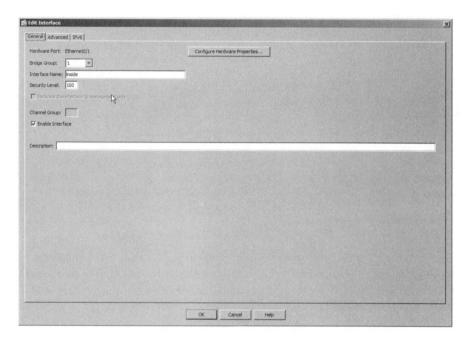

Figure 12-4 *Configuring a Transparent Firewall Interface*

Next, assign a single IP address to each bridge group as a whole. This address will be used for management traffic, such as Telnet, SSH, HTTP, SNMP, syslog, TFTP, FTP, and so on. If you configure the ASA for multiple context mode, you should configure one IP address for each bridge group on each security context, including the admin context. From the interface list in ASDM, select **Add** and choose **Bridge Virtual Interface (BVI)**. Configure the bridge group number and IP address, as shown in Figure 12-5.

From the CLI, you can use the following command to configure an IP address for a bridge group:

```
CISCOASA(config)# interface BVInumber

ciscoasa(config-if)# ip address ip-address subnet-mask
```

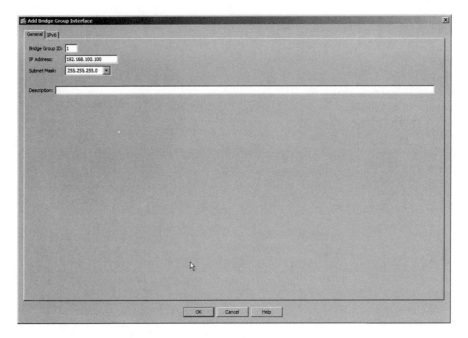

Figure 12-5   *Configuring a BVI with an IP Address*

Before the ASA can communicate with any host that is located outside the local subnet, it will need additional routing information. Dynamic routing protocols are not supported in transparent firewall mode. However, you can configure one or more static routes instead; enter the following command for each one:

```
ciscoasa(config)# route interface network mask gateway [metric]
```

The remote IP network and subnet mask can be found on the named interface using the next-hop gateway router address. You can also specify a distance metric, which is the number of router hops until the gateway is reached. If you omit the metric, it defaults to one hop.

Figure 12-6 shows a scenario where an ASA in transparent firewall mode is configured with bridge group 1 using IP address 192.168.100.100. The ASA must be able to communicate with hosts on the 192.168.200.0/24 and 192.168.201.0/24 networks, which are located behind a router at 192.168.100.5. The ASA also needs a default route that points to a router on the outside interface at 192.168.100.1. The commands listed in Example 12-3 can be used to configure the necessary static routes.

Example 12-3   *Commands Used to Configure Static Routes for Figure 12-6*

```
ciscoasa(config)# route inside 192.168.200.0 255.255.255.0 192.168.100.5
ciscoasa(config)# route inside 192.168.201.0 255.255.255.0 192.168.100.5
ciscoasa(config)# route outside 0.0.0.0 0.0.0.0 192.168.100.1
```

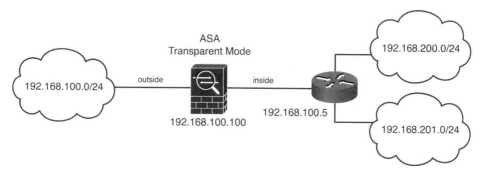

Figure 12-6 *Example Scenario Requiring Static Routes*

You should also configure static routes for any NAT entries that involve IP addresses that are not located on the local network. As well, static routes are necessary for voice traffic inspection when the endpoints are located more than one router hop away.

Controlling Traffic in Transparent Firewall Mode

An ASA can enforce its security policies in transparent firewall mode just as it does in routed firewall mode. For instance, unicast IP packets are permitted to flow from an interface configured with a higher security level to one with a lower security level interface, while explicit access list rules must be used to permit packets to flow from lower to higher security levels. IP packets are also subject to the ASA's traffic inspection engines and MPF configuration.

However, transparent firewall mode differs from routed firewall mode in several ways:

- ARP packets are permitted to pass in both directions without any explicit ACL rules. You can configure ARP inspection, covered in the section, "Using ARP Inspection," to control their movement.

- Broadcast and multicast packets are not permitted by default; explicit ACL rules are required.

- Routed non-IP traffic can be permitted by using EtherType ACLs.

If you plan to allow specific broadcast- or multicast-based protocols to pass through a transparent firewall mode ASA, you will need to configure an ACL that permits the packets. The ACL should be applied to an ASA interface in the inbound direction, to permit the packets to flow into the ASA and be forwarded out the other side. For protocols that are bidirectional, you can configure and apply an ACL inbound on both ASA interfaces.

Because broadcast and multicast traffic are not subject to the normal application inspection processes, you should configure the ACLs to be as specific as possible. Be sure to identify the protocol, any destination port number, and the destination address used in the inbound packets. Broadcast packets can use the all-networks 255.255.255.255 address or a subnet broadcast address as the destination. Multicast packets must be identified by the multicast group address as the destination.

As an example, suppose an ASA in transparent firewall mode separates the two routers shown in Figure 12-7. The routers exchange routing information with Open Shortest Path First (OSPF) protocol, which uses IP protocol 89 with destination addresses 224.0.0.5 and 224.0.0.6. You can use the commands listed in Example 12-4 or their equivalent in ASDM to permit the OSPF packets to pass through the ASA.

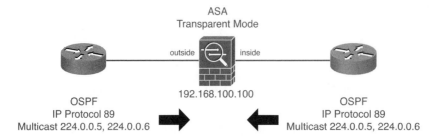

Figure 12-7 *IDS and IPS Operational Differences*

Example 12-4 *Commands to Configure the Access Lists for Figure 12-7*

```
ciscoasa(config)# access-list EXTRA-TRAFFIC extended permit ospf any host 224.0.0.5
ciscoasa(config)# access-list EXTRA-TRAFFIC extended permit ospf any host 224.0.0.6
ciscoasa(config)# access-group EXTRA-TRAFFIC in interface outside
ciscoasa(config)# access-group EXTRA-TRAFFIC in interface inside
```

By default, only IP packets are allowed to pass through an ASA, provided that the packets are permitted by the various inspection processes. If you need to pass non-IP traffic through an ASA, you can create a special EtherType access list that permits only packets with specific EtherType values.

Key Topic

To add a new EtherType rule in ASDM, navigate to **Configuration > Firewall > Ethertype Rules**, then select **Add**. Identify the interface where the access list will be applied, along with the action (Permit or Deny), the EtherType value, and an optional description. You can enter the EtherType value as a hex number or select from a pull-down list of values. You can keep adding more EtherType rules as needed.

As an example, suppose you want to permit IEEE 802.1d Spanning Tree BPDU packets, as well as TRILL packets (EtherType 0x22F3). Figure 12-8 shows the resulting EtherType rule list. Notice that the same two rule entries have been created and applied to the inside and outside interfaces.

In the CLI, use the following command to create an entry in an EtherType ACL. You can repeat the command to define more entries.

```
ciscoasa(config)# access-list acl_id ethertype {permit | deny} {any | bpdu | ipx |
mpls-unicast | mpls-multicast | ethertype}
```

The *ethertype* value can be a 16-bit hex number greater than 0x600, or one of the following keywords:

- **any:** Any non-IP packet

- **bpdu:** Bridge protocol data units used for Spanning Tree Protocol operation

- **ipx:** Novell IPX

- **mpls-unicast:** MPLS unicast

- **mpls-multicast:** MPLS multicast

Example 12-5 lists the commands necessary to permit IEEE 802.1d Spanning Tree BPDU packets, as well as TRILL packets (EtherType 0x22F3). After you have configured the EtherType ACL, you must apply it to both interfaces in the inbound direction using the **access-group** command.

Example 12-5   *Configuring an EtherType Access List for Non-IP Traffic*

```
ciscoasa(config)# access-list MY-ETHERTYPES ethertype permit bpdu
ciscoasa(config)# access-list MY-ETHERTYPES ethertype permit 0x22f3
ciscoasa(config)# access-group MY-ETHERTYPES in interface outside
ciscoasa(config)# access-group MY-ETHERTYPES in interface inside
```

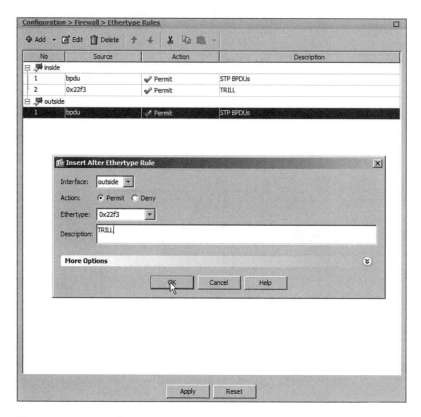

Figure 12-8   *Configuring an EtherType Access List in ASDM*

What if you need to permit some broadcast traffic and some non-IP traffic? You can apply one EtherType access list and one extended IP access list to the same interface.

Using ARP Inspection

Hosts on a network use the Address Resolution Protocol (ARP) to correlate IP addresses with MAC addresses. When a host needs to send a packet, it knows the destination's IP address but not necessarily the destination's MAC address. The host can send an ARP request packet that is broadcast to all nodes on the local network to ask for the MAC address of a given IP address. If a node using that IP address exists, it can send an ARP reply packet to identify itself by its MAC address.

By default, an ASA in transparent firewall mode forwards all ARP packets it receives on one interface out the other interface. This means that protected hosts on the inside ASA interface will exchange ARP packets with unprotected hosts on the outside interface. Normally, that isn't a problem, as long as the unprotected hosts use ARP appropriately.

A malicious host, however, can abuse ARP to leverage a man-in-the-middle attack. Figure 12-9 shows how this is possible. Host 192.168.100.222 on the inside of the ASA is configured to use 192.168.100.1 as its default gateway. That address exists on the outside router. When the inside host needs to communicate with a destination that is outside its local 192.168.100.0/24 subnet, it must send those packets to the gateway, which will relay the packets on toward their destination. The inside host does this by sending the packets to the gateway router's MAC address. If the MAC address isn't already known, the inside host must send an ARP request to ask for the MAC address that goes with IP address 192.168.100.1.

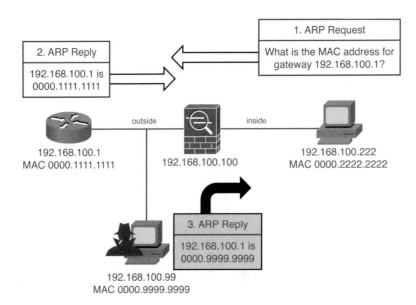

Figure 12-9 *ARP Spoofing Attack with an ASA in Transparent Firewall Mode*

The ASA will forward the ARP request to the outside, where it reaches the router. The router will answer with an ARP reply that contains its own IP and MAC addresses. So far, so good—after the ASA forwards the ARP reply back on its inside interface, the host will learn the router's MAC address.

Now, suppose that a malicious host exists on the unprotected outside part of the network and would like to insert itself in the middle of the inside host's conversations so that it can intercept and examine the traffic. When the ARP request packet is forwarded to the outside, the malicious host also receives it and sends its own spoofed ARP reply. The reply announces that IP address 192.168.100.1 (the gateway router) can be found at MAC address 0000.9999.9999 (the malicious host).

When the inside host receives this ARP reply, it will replace any other ARP entry for 192.168.100.1 with the MAC address of the malicious host. From now on, the inside host will send all of its outbound packets to the malicious host's MAC address, unaware that the packets are now being intercepted, as shown in Figure 12-10.

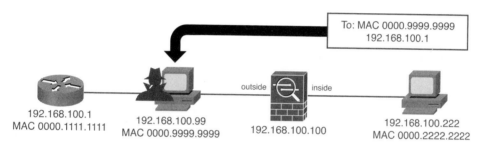

Figure 12-10 *Man-in-the-Middle Attack Using Spoofed ARP Packets*

The malicious host might also decide to send spoofed ARP replies that announce itself as the inside host too. If that happens, it can intercept all packets going to or coming from the inside host. This is known as a man-in-the-middle attack, which can be accomplished with exploit tools that are freely and readily available for downloading.

A transparent firewall can also maintain an ARP table, where MAC and IP addresses are associated as a pair. These are learned from ARP replies that are overheard on an interface. Normally, the ARP table is used only for management traffic to and from the transparent firewall, when the firewall itself needs to send packets to a destination.

To detect and prevent ARP spoofing, you can configure the ASA to support ARP inspection. ARP inspection uses static ARP entries as the basis for its inspection process. The ASA will examine each ARP reply packet it overhears and compare the source IP and MAC addresses, as well as the source interface, to known static entries in its own ARP table.

If the ARP reply matches an existing entry, the ASA forwards it out the other interface. If any of the ARP information conflicts with an existing entry, the ASA will assume the ARP reply contains spoofed addresses and will drop the packet. If an existing ARP entry can't be found, the ASA can be configured to transmit or drop the ARP reply packet.

ARP inspection is only effective in handling ARP packets that need to traverse the ASA. In other words, the ARP requester and responder are located on different ASA interfaces. If both hosts are located on the same interface, the ARP reply can be answered directly without having to pass through the ASA.

To configure ARP inspection, begin by defining static ARP entries for all of the known hosts. Each entry will associate an IP address with a MAC address (dotted triplet nnnn.nnnn.nnnn format). These addresses are expected to be found on the specified ASA interface. Static ARP entries never age out.

In ASDM, navigate to **Configuration > Device Management > Advanced > ARP > ARP Static Table.** Click the **Add** button, and then select the interface and enter an IP and MAC address pair, as shown in Figure 12-11. The Proxy ARP check box is meant for routed firewall mode and does not apply to transparent firewall mode.

Figure 12-11   *Configuring a Static ARP Entry for ARP Inspection*

Next, select **ARP Inspection.** Select an ASA interface, click the **Edit** button, and then check the **Enable ARP Inspection** check box to enable the feature, as shown in Figure 12-12. You can also check the **Flood ARP Packets** check box to enable flooding.

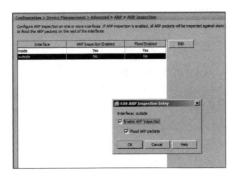

Figure 12-12   *Enabling ARP Inspection in ASDM*

Once ARP Inspection is enabled, the ASA takes one of the following actions as ARP reply packets are received:

■   If the MAC address and the IP address are both found in a single ARP table entry, the ARP reply must be valid and therefore is allowed to pass through the ASA.

■   If either the MAC address or the IP address is found in the ARP table, but not both in a single entry, the ARP reply contains invalid or spoofed information. Therefore, it is dropped and not forwarded through the ASA.

- If neither MAC address nor IP address is found in the ARP table, you can select the action as either **flood** (forward or flood the ARP packet out the other firewall interface so it can reach its destination) or **no-flood** (drop the ARP packet without forwarding it). By default, the **flood** action is assumed.

If you choose to use the CLI instead, you can use the following command to define each static ARP entry. To clear a static ARP entry, repeat the command by beginning with the **no** keyword.

```
ciscoasa(config)# arp interface ip_address mac_address
```

By default, ARP inspection is disabled on all ASA interfaces. You can enable it on an ASA interface by entering the following command:

```
ciscoasa(config)# arp-inspection interface enable [flood|no-flood]
```

As an example, suppose you want to use ARP inspection in the scenario shown in Figure 12-6. The only two valid hosts are the router and the inside host, so you should configure static ARP entries for them. You could use the commands listed in Example 12-6 to prevent ARP spoofing attacks.

Example 12-6   *Configuring ARP Inspection*

```
ciscoasa(config)# arp inside 192.168.100.222 0000.2222.2222
ciscoasa(config)# arp outside 192.168.100.1 0000.1111.1111
ciscoasa(config)# arp-inspection inside enable
ciscoasa(config)# arp-inspection outside enable
```

You can verify the ARP inspection status on each interface with the **show arp-inspection** command. In Example 12-7, ARP inspection is enabled on both ASA interfaces.

Example 12-7   *Verifying ARP Inspection Status*

```
ciscoasa# show arp-inspection
interface              arp-inspection          miss
-------------------------------------------------------
outside                enabled                 flood
inside                 enabled                 flood
ciscoasa#
```

Disabling MAC Address Learning

In transparent firewall mode, an ASA will learn MAC addresses as they are received on either of its interfaces. This process works fine as long as hosts place their actual MAC addresses in the source address field of packets they send. The ASA's MAC address table will be populated with results that can be trusted.

Suppose a malicious host is located on the outside of the ASA, as shown in Figure 12-13. Before the malicious host begins it work, the inside host has sent a packet and the ASA has learned that its source MAC address (0000.2222.2222) is located on the inside interface.

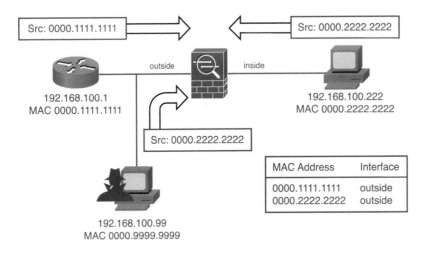

Figure 12-13 *Attack Involving Spoofed MAC Addresses*

Now, the malicious host is free to begin sending its own packets, but with spoofed MAC addresses in the source MAC address field. By sending a packet with source address 0000.2222.2222, the host can force the ASA to learn what is actually the inside host's address on the outside interface. At this point, any packets arriving from the outside and destined for the inside host will simply be dropped because the host's MAC address has been learned on the outside.

The malicious host might not stop with just one spoofed MAC address. It might also send so many packets with spoofed addresses that the ASA's MAC address table is overrun. In effect, this would be a denial-of-service attack on the ASA, rendering it unable to forward any packets correctly.

To prevent MAC address spoofing attacks, you can disable MAC address learning completely. Without the capability to learn dynamically, the ASA must use statically configured MAC address entries instead. MAC address learning is configured on a per-interface basis.

You can use ASDM to configure static MAC address entries. Go to **Configuration > Device Management > Advanced > Bridging** and select **MAC Address Table**. Click the **Add** button to create a new static MAC address table entry, and then specify the interface name and the MAC address. Figure 12-14 shows two static entries that correspond to the scenario depicted in Figure 12-13.

Next, disable MAC address learning by selecting **Bridging > MAC Learning**. You can disable or enable MAC address learning on each interface individually. Select an interface, and then click the **Enable** or **Disable** button. In Figure 12-15, learning has been disabled on the inside interface.

To use the CLI instead, configure a static MAC address entry by specifying the interface and MAC address with the following command:

```
ciscoasa(config)# mac-address-table static interface mac_address
```

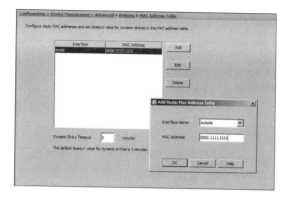

Figure 12-14   *Creating Static MAC Address Table Entries in ASDM*

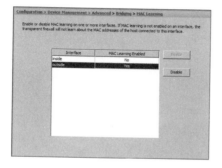

Figure 12-15   *Disabling MAC Address Learning in ASDM*

Then, disable MAC learning on an interface:

```
ciscoasa(config)# mac-learn interface disable
```

Example 12-8 lists the commands necessary to disable MAC address learning and build two static entries for the two legitimate devices, as depicted in Figure 12-13.

Example 12-8   *Disabling MAC Address Learning*

```
ciscoasa(config)# mac-learn inside disable
ciscoasa(config)# mac-learn outside disable
ciscoasa(config)# mac-address-table static outside 0000.1111.1111
ciscoasa(config)# mac-address-table static inside 0000.2222.2222
```

To verify the MAC address learning status and to display the contents of the MAC address table, you can use the **show mac-learn** and **show mac-address-table** commands, respectively.

Exam Preparation Tasks

As mentioned in the section, "How to Use This Book," in the Introduction, you have a couple of choices for exam preparation: the exercises here, Chapter 17, "Final Preparation," and the exam simulation questions on the CD-ROM.

Review All Key Topics

Review the most important topics in this chapter, noted with the Key Topic icon in the outer margin of the page. Table 12-3 lists a reference of these key topics and the page numbers on which each is found.

Table 12-3   *Key Topics for Chapter 12*

Key Topic Element	Description	Page Number
Paragraph	Describes transparent firewall mode	633
List	Explains how an ASA can learn an unknown MAC address	633
Table 12-2	Compares routed and transparent firewall modes	635
List	Describes unique properties of transparent firewall mode	639
Paragraph	Explains EtherType access lists	640
Paragraph	Describes a man-in-the-middle ARP spoofing attack	642
Paragraph	Explains how to disable MAC address learning	646

Define Key Terms

Define the following key terms from this chapter and check your answers in the glossary:

routed firewall mode, transparent firewall mode, bump-in-the-wire, EtherType access list, ARP inspection, MAC address learning

Command Reference to Check Your Memory

This section includes the most important configuration and EXEC commands covered in this chapter. It might not be necessary to memorize the complete syntax of every command, but you should be able to remember the basic keywords that are needed.

To test your memory of the commands, cover the right side of Table 12-4 with a piece of paper, read the description on the left side, and then see how much of the command you can remember.

The FIREWALL exam focuses on practical, hands-on skills that are used by a networking professional. Therefore, you should be able to identify the commands needed to configure and test an ASA feature.

Table 12-4   *Commands Related to ASA Interface Configuration and Verification*

Task	Command Syntax
Verify firewall mode	ciscoasa# **show firewall**
Enable transparent firewall mode	ciscoasa(config)# **firewall transparent**
Add an interface to a bridge group	ciscoasa(config)# **interface** interface ciscoasa(config-if)# **nameif** *name* ciscoasa(config-if)# **security-level** *level* ciscoasa(config-if)# **bridge-group** *number*
Configure an IP address on a bridge group interface	ciscoasa(config)# **interface BVI***number* *ciscoasa(config-if)#* **ip address** *ip_address subnet_mask*
Create an EtherType access list	ciscoasa(config)# **access-list** *acl_id* **ethertype** {**permit** | **deny**} {**any** | **bpdu** | **ipx** | **mpls-unicast** | **mpls-multicast** | *ethertype*}
Create a static ARP entry	ciscoasa(config)# **arp** *interface ip_address mac_address*
Enable ARP inspection	ciscoasa(config)# **arp-inspection** *interface* **enable** [**flood** | **no-flood**]
Verify ARP inspection status	ciscoasa# **show arp-inspection**
Disable MAC address learning	ciscoasa(config)# **mac-learn** *interface* **disable**
Create a static MAC address entry	ciscoasa(config)# **mac-address-table static** *interface mac_address*

This chapter covers the following topics:

- **Cisco ASA Virtualization Overview:** This section presents an overview of the virtual firewall capabilities on the Cisco ASA.

- **Virtual Firewall Deployment Guidelines:** This section describes the information you will need to gather before you deploy virtual firewalls. The section also covers the caveats and limitations of using virtual firewalls on the ASA.

- **Configuration Tasks Overview:** This section provides an overview of the configuration tasks that you must perform to implement virtual firewalls on the Cisco ASA.

- **Configuring Security Contexts:** This section details the actual virtual firewall configuration process systematically.

- **Verifying Security Contexts:** This section details how you can easily verify the virtual firewalls and their configuration.

- **Managing Security Contexts:** This section describes the various management tasks you may need to perform on your virtual firewalls.

- **Configuring Resource Management:** This section describes how to manage the various resources consumed by the virtual firewalls.

- **Verifying Resource Management:** This section describes how to verify the implementation of your resource management.

- **Troubleshooting Security Contexts:** This section covers details required to effectively troubleshoot a Cisco ASA implementation that includes virtual firewalls.

CHAPTER 13

Creating Virtual Firewalls on the ASA

The Cisco Adaptive Security Appliance (ASA) is known for the robustness and flexibility of its features. Supporting that reputation is the capability of the device to be "carved up" into multiple virtual firewalls. Each virtual firewall can serve a specific customer or a specific need within an organization. Virtual firewalls are created in the Cisco ASA using a technology called Security Contexts. This chapter provides you with all the information you need to know about this process for success on the FIREWALL exam and beyond.

"Do I Know This Already?" Quiz

The "Do I Know This Already?" quiz allows you to assess whether you should read this entire chapter thoroughly or jump to the "Exam Preparation Tasks" section. If you are in doubt about your answers to these questions or your own assessment of your knowledge of the topics, read the entire chapter. Table 13-1 lists the major headings in this chapter and their corresponding "Do I Know This Already?" quiz questions. You can find the answers in Appendix A, "Answers to the 'Do I Know This Already?' Quizzes."

Table 13-1 *"Do I Know This Already?" Section-to-Question Mapping*

Foundation Topics Section	Question
Cisco ASA Virtualization Overview	1
Virtual Firewall Deployment Guidelines	2
Configuration Tasks Overview	3
Configuring Security Contexts	4
Verifying Security Contexts	5
Managing Security Contexts	6
Configuring Resource Management	7
Verifying Resource Management	8
Troubleshooting Security Contexts	9

Caution: The goal of self-assessment is to gauge your mastery of the topics in this chapter. If you do not know the answer to a question or are only partially sure of the answer, you should mark that question wrong for purposes of the self-assessment. Giving yourself credit for an answer you correctly guess skews your self-assessment results and might provide you with a false sense of security.

1. Before you can implement virtual firewalls on the Cisco ASA, you must convert the device into which mode?

   a. Virtual firewall mode

   b. Multiple mode

   c. Advanced mode

   d. Virtual mode

2. Which of the following deployment guidelines is not correct?

   a. When you use transparent firewall mode and multiple mode, you cannot use shared interfaces.

   b. When you use shared interfaces, assign a different MAC address to the interface in each context.

   c. Each Security Context can be configured for transparent mode or routed mode.

   d. Consider resource management with your Security Contexts to avoid system failures.

3. Which of these is not a valid configuration procedure with virtual firewalls on the Cisco ASA?

   a. Map each Security Context to an ASA image file.

   b. Configure Security Context resource management.

   c. Create Security Contexts.

   d. Configure each Security Context as a separate security appliance.

4. Which Security Context does the Cisco ASA create automatically during the conversion for virtual firewalls?

   a. Base

   b. Main

   c. System

   d. Admin

5. Which command do you use to view Security Context information, including allo-cated interfaces, the configuration file URL, and the number of Security Contexts that you have configured?

   a.   show virtual-firewall

   b.   show context

   c.   show partitions

   d.   show versions

6. Which command do you use to switch from one Security Context to another in the CLI?

   a.   revert

   b.   moveto

   c.   changeto

   d.   enter-context

7. By default, each Security Context belongs to which resource class?

   a.   Main

   b.   Admin

   c.   Default

   d.   System

8. Which command displays the resource allocation for each resource across all classes?

   a.   show usage

   b.   show resource usage

   c.   show resource classes

   d.   show resource allocation

9. Which is not a common command to use when troubleshooting virtual firewalls?

   a.   show context

   b.   show interface

   c.   show resource usage

   d.   show virtual devices

Foundation Topics

Perhaps you are an Internet service provider and would like to set up multiple firewalls for different customers that use your services. Alternatively, perhaps you are a network engineer for a large enterprise that wants multiple firewalls for different areas of the enterprise network. A powerful option that the Cisco ASA provides is the use of *virtual firewalls* inside a single Cisco ASA. This configuration is a possibility thanks to what are called *Security Contexts*, which can be created once the ASA is switched to *multiple mode*. This chapter provides you with all the information you will need to plan for and implement the use of virtual firewalls inside your Cisco ASA. You will also be able to properly verify and troubleshoot such a configuration.

Cisco ASA Virtualization Overview

Cisco ASA virtualization refers to the capability to create multiple virtual firewalls inside a single Cisco ASA. This can be useful if you have dramatically different security policies and rules that you want to enforce for different customers or different departments within your organization. Through the Cisco ASA virtualization process, you define *Security Contexts* on the device. You create a separate Security Context to represent each new virtual firewall that you want to create. Before you can create these additional Security Contexts, you must convert the ASA to multiple mode. Once you have done this and have defined your contexts, you can assign interfaces, administrators, and security policies to each context just as though it is an independent firewall device.

The multiple virtual firewalls inside the Cisco ASA have the capability to run most of the features found on the Cisco ASA itself. There are some notable exceptions. The following features are not supported in multiple mode with the different virtual firewalls:

- IP Security (IPsec) VPNs and other IPsec services
- Secure Sockets Layer (SSL) VPNs
- Dynamic routing protocols
- Phone Proxy
- Threat detection
- Multicast IP routing

You might wonder about a key interface on the Cisco ASA in multiple mode. For example, you have an important interface that connects to the Internet. This physical interface can actually be shared across different Security Contexts for use by the different virtual firewalls with different security policies.

A High-Level Examination of a Virtual Firewall's Configuration

As described in the previous section, in pure Cisco terms, a virtual firewall is called a Security Context. You might think of this Security Context as its own firewall within the Cisco ASA. You can define your own security policy for this virtual firewall. It can possess it own interfaces or even share interfaces with other virtual firewalls (with the exception of transparent mode virtual firewalls). It can even feature its own administrative user accounts. In fact, for those responsible for the device, it will appear to be a fully functional standalone device, and they can even be completely unaware of the fact that it is truly a firewall within another firewall.

As you might expect, to have a Cisco ASA engage in this rather remarkable capability, you must convert the operational mode of the device. Thus, an important first step in the configuration is converting the device to what is termed "multiple mode."

Once the device is in the correct mode to support virtualization, the job of the administrator is to create the required Security Contexts and assign the required resources. The administrator can also configure important resource limits for the various contexts to ensure the overall Cisco ASA does not have its performance degraded due to resource oversubscription. Finally, the Cisco ASA administrator must configure each context with the required IP addressing and access controls appropriate for each virtual device.

The System Configuration, System Context, and Other Security Contexts

As the previous section described, when you want to partition your single ASA into multiple virtual devices, you do so by creating additional Security Contexts. Each Security Context then becomes akin to a separate ASA, with its own security policy, its own interfaces, and even its own administrators if needed. Obviously, the different Security Contexts that you define as the Cisco ASA administrator are critical for defining the different virtual firewalls. But even more critical is what Cisco terms the *system configuration*. This critical system configuration defines basic security settings for the Cisco ASA itself and is the entity that stores information about all the other Security Contexts. The system configuration also maintains the settings of the physical interfaces inside the Cisco ASA. As when running your ASA in a single mode of operation, the system configuration resides as the startup configuration in flash memory.

The system administrator adds and manages contexts by configuring each context location and other such parameters. All of this is done in the system configuration. The system configuration does not include any interfaces for the System Contexts. This means that if the System Context needs to access network resources (such as Cisco ASDM), the System Context uses the networking resources assigned to a special Security Context called the *admin context*. The admin context is just like any other context, except that when a user logs in to this context, they have administrative rights over all the Security Contexts set up on the system.

The individual Security Context configurations that you create and edit can be stored on the local disk (flash memory). They can also be downloaded from external servers, such as TFTP or HTTPS servers.

Packet Classification

Creating a Security Context on the Cisco ASA does not automatically assign interfaces to the context. Note that an exception to this rule is the admin context. All interfaces that were enabled in single mode are available to this important context.

A context can use physical or subinterfaces of the Cisco ASA. In transparent mode, only two interfaces can be used for user traffic, and one additional management interface is supported.

As previously described, in routed mode, an interface can be shared between contexts. Obviously, this might be required when there is a single interface that provides Internet connectivity for multiple virtual firewalls. The Cisco ASA uses a "classifier algorithm" to determine the destination Security Context for an inbound packet on the shared interface. The following criteria are used in this process:

- **Unique interfaces:** This is the method always used in transparent firewall mode because interfaces cannot be shared between contexts in this mode.

- **Unique MAC addresses:** The classifier uses the packet destination MAC address and compares it to the interface MAC address for each context sharing the interface. Obviously, you should set a unique MAC address for each context; the Cisco ASA even provides automation of this process should you elect for it.

- **Network Address Translation (NAT):** If there are not unique MAC addresses configured, the classifier uses the NAT configuration to determine the subnets serviced by each context. The destination IP address is matched to either a global IP address in a static configuration or to an address in the xlate table in the result of a dynamic configuration.

Note: If you are using a shared interface, and you fail to configure unique MAC addresses, and you are not using NAT, the classifier is forced to drop packets. Cisco recommends that unique MAC addresses be used to solve this issue. Obviously, this is the only option if you are not using NAT.

Virtual Firewall Deployment Guidelines

Like many other aspects of the Cisco ASA implementation, you will want to plan carefully before implementing your virtual firewalls. Be sure to determine the following:

- **The number of Security Contexts you require:** You will use this information to create and name the Security Contexts you require. Note that the number of Security Contexts that you can create depends on the type of license you have purchased with your ASA.

- **The configuration storage for each context:** The options are Flash memory or external servers.

- **The network topology information for your deployment:** You need to carefully plan which interfaces will be associated with which Security Contexts. You also need to plan for the IP addressing and routing to use inside each Security Context.

- **The security policy used inside each of the Security Contexts:** This information could be quite elaborate and involved, depending on the complexity of the network and the associated security policies.

Deployment Choices

You may be forced to use single mode with your Cisco ASA implementation if you require features that are available only in single mode. Multiple physical ASA devices are the solution in this case.

When you are deciding whether to use virtual firewalls, consider the following conditions that typically necessitate their usage:

- You have distinct security policies that need to be assigned to different customers or different departments within your enterprise network.

- You are an Internet service provider (ISP) that needs to separate traffic from different customers.

- You are interested in providing robust redundancy in your firewall environment. The use of multiple Security Contexts enables the use of active/active failover. This method of failover is detailed in Chapter 14, "Deploying High Availability Features."

You also need to plan for your use of shared interfaces. Remember, if your Security Contexts are in transparent mode, they cannot use shared interfaces at all. If your Security Contexts are in routed mode, they can use shared interfaces if they connect to the same network. For interfaces that connect to different networks, you cannot implement the shared interfaces feature.

Deployment Guidelines

There are plenty of other important deployment guidelines you should consider before implementing a multiple mode Cisco ASA with multiple Security Contexts. Here are some of the most critical for you to consider and memorize for the FIREWALL exam:

- The transparent mode option cannot be set on a per-Security Context basis. If you need a transparent mode Security Context, all of your other virtual firewalls must also use transparent mode.

- When creating a transparent mode device, make that change first, and then create your Security Contexts. If you create your Security Contexts first and then initiate the cutover to transparent mode, the Security Contexts will be removed.

- Only two interfaces are supported in a Security Context running in transparent mode.

- Shared interfaces cannot be used when the Security Contexts are running in transparent mode.

- When using shared interfaces, ensure that you assign a unique MAC address to the interface in each context.

- Always consider the use of context resource management to ensure that a single context cannot deplete all resources available on the Cisco ASA. (Resource management is covered in depth later in this chapter.)

Limitations

Here are some of the most important limitations you should know regarding virtual firewalls on the Cisco ASA:

- Key features that are not supported on a Cisco ASA in multiple mode are dynamic routing protocols, IPsec and SSL VPNs, multicast IP routing, threat detection, and Phone Proxy.

- The Cisco ASA 5505 does not support multiple mode.

- The number of Security Contexts you can create depends on the software license you possess and the Cisco ASA hardware model you are using.

Configuration Tasks Overview

When you are preparing to implement complex configurations on the Cisco ASA, it is valuable to examine a high-level overview of the configuration process. Here is an overview for the configuration of virtual firewalls on the Cisco ASA. This chapter covers these steps in detail.

Step 1.   Enable multiple mode on the Cisco ASA.

Step 2.   Create a Security Context.

Step 3.   Allocate interfaces to the context.

Step 4.   Specify the startup configuration location for the context.

Step 5.   Configure the Security Context resource management.

Step 6.   Configure each Security Context as a separate security appliance.

Configuring Security Contexts

Before you dive in and start reconfiguring your Cisco ASA for virtual firewalls, you should make sure that you understand the major changes that are about to take place in your Cisco ASA configuration. As you know, an important first step in this configuration process is to change the Cisco ASA from single mode to multiple mode. When this change occurs, the following changes take place within the device:

- The Cisco ASA automatically creates a Security Context named admin. (The following section, "The Admin Context," elaborates more on this important Security Context.)

- The running configuration of the device is converted to a system configuration for the admin Security Context. The file is stored as admin.cfg.

- The original running configuration is saved as old_running.cfg.

- Interfaces that were enabled in single mode are added to the admin Security Context.

- Disabled interfaces at the time of conversion are not assigned to any Security Context.

As mentioned previously, a new Security Context is not operational until you specify the location for the context startup configuration. You specify this location as a URL. Options include the following:

- **Disk0/flash:** Stored in flash memory

- **Disk1:** Stored on a CompactFlash memory card

- **Tftp:** Stored on an external TFTP server

- **Ftp:** Stored on an external FTP server

- **http(s):** Stored on a web server or SSL web server

Note: The admin context must be stored on internal flash (Disk0/flash:).

The Admin Context

The system configuration relies on the admin context to access interfaces that can pass traffic. Common uses of this special context are to retrieve configurations for other contexts and to send system-level syslog messages. When you want to create new contexts or change the system configuration in any way, you log in to the admin context. Note that you can change the name of this context from the default of admin.

Configuring Multiple Mode

The switch to multiple mode is one of those unique configurations on the Cisco ASA that can be accomplished only by using the command-line interface (CLI). Use the **mode** command in global configuration mode. There is a **noconfirm** keyword option that makes the change without a confirmation request. This option is useful for automating the process with a script.

Here is an example of using the command:

```
ciscoasa(config)# mode multiple noconfirm
```

Note: This change requires a reboot of the Cisco ASA.

Creating a Security Context

Security Contexts can be created using the ASDM or the CLI. To use the ASDM, first ensure you are in the system execution space by double-clicking the **System** option in the Device List pane, shown in Figure 13-1.

Next, navigate to **Configuration > Context Management > Security Contexts,** and click **Add** to open the Add Context dialog box, as shown in Figure 13-2.

Enter a name in the Security Context field. Click the **Add** button in the Interface Allocation area to add the appropriate interfaces to the Security Context. Finally, specify where the configuration file should be stored for the context.

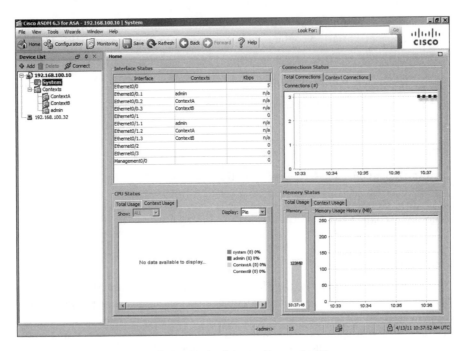

Figure 13-1   *Ensuring You Are in the System Execution Space*

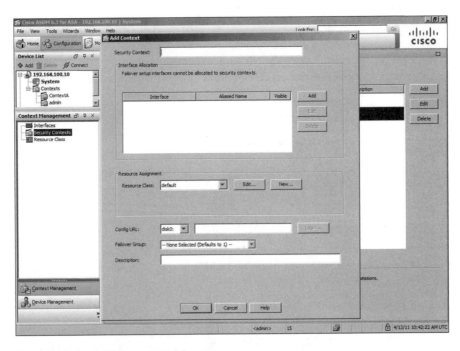

Figure 13-2   *Add Context Dialog Box*

In the CLI, use the **context** command to create a context and the **allocate-interface** command to provision the correct interfaces. Use the **config-url** command to specify the configuration file location.

Verifying Security Contexts

When you are in the system execution space at the CLI, you can easily view a list of Security Contexts on the system. The name of each Security Context is displayed along with the allocated interfaces and the configuration URL. As demonstrated in Example 13-1, the command to display all of this information is simply **show context**. Note that an asterisk (*) to the left of the context name indicates the current admin context. Remember, by default, this is the context named admin.

Example 13-1 show context *Command Output*

```
CiscoASA# show context
Context Name          Interfaces                    URL
*admin                GigabitEthernet0/1.100        disk0:/admin.cfg
                      GigabitEthernet0/1.101
contexta              GigabitEthernet0/1.200        disk0:/contexta.cfg
                      GigabitEthernet0/1.201
contextb              GigabitEthernet0/1.300        disk0:/contextb.cfg
                  GigabitEthernet0/1.301
Total active Security Contexts: 3
```

Managing Security Contexts

Managing a Security Context is a matter of entering the context environment. In the ASDM, this is a simple matter of double-clicking the context name in the Device List pane. You will notice that the ASDM allows you to configure for the virtual firewall almost all the options that you can configure for the original firewall itself. The only features that are missing are those that are not supported for multiple mode, as mentioned earlier in the chapter.

Key Topic

To change between contexts using the CLI, use the **changeto** command in privileged mode. For example:

```
ciscoasa# changeto MYCONTEXT
```

or

```
ciscoasa# changeto system
```

You can easily edit or delete a Security Context using the ASDM. Navigate to **Configuration > Context Management > Security Contexts,** and then click the **Edit** or **Delete** button. Realize that deleting a context does not automatically remove its configuration files.

Packet Classification Configuration

Remember, when your Security Contexts are in routed mode and are sharing interfaces across contexts, the Cisco ASA requires some method for determining to which context it should send a packet. The ASA always checks for the following to do this:

■ A unique interface

■ A unique MAC address

■ A global IP address in a NAT configuration

Remember, as stated earlier, using unique MAC addresses is always recommended if you are in multiple mode with Security Contexts. You can change MAC addresses manually, or you can call upon the Cisco ASA to generate a unique MAC address for you. To do the latter, navigate to **Configuration > Context Management > Security Contexts** and check the **Enable auto-generation of MAC addresses for context interfaces that share a system interface** check box, as shown in Figure 13-3.

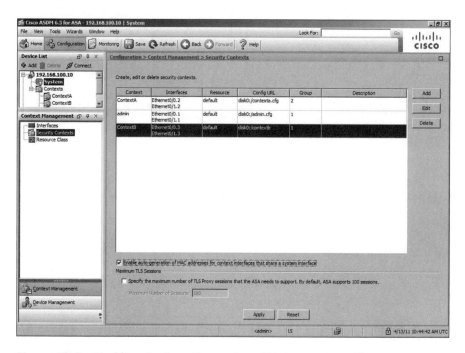

Figure 13-3 *Enabling the Auto-Generation of Unique MAC Addresses*

To change the MAC address at the CLI, use the **mac-address** command. You can use the optional **auto** keyword to configure the dynamic assignment.

Changing the Admin Context

To change the context that is the admin context, use the **admin-context** command in privileged mode and simply specify the name of the new admin context, as demonstrated here:

```
ciscoASA(config)# admin-context administrator
```

Editing and Removing Contexts

To edit or remove a Security Context, in the ASDM, choose **Configuration > Context Management > Security Contexts.** Choose a context, and click the **Edit** or **Delete** button as needed.

Note: Deleting a context does not automatically remove its configuration file from its storage location. This must be deleted manually if desired.

Configuring Resource Management

Although technically, configuring resource management on your multiple mode Cisco ASA is optional, you should consider it. The reason is that, by default, a particular Security Context has unlimited access to the resources of the Cisco ASA. By engaging the powerful resource management capabilities, you can impose limits on the use of specific hardware resources per Security Context. This is obviously an important aspect of virtual firewall implementation and can guard against malicious or accidental issues. Realize that a single context that is depleting a large number of resources of the Cisco ASA can have an impact on all the Security Contexts on the device.

You can configure resource limits for the following:

■ Cisco ASDM sessions

■ Connections (two options, count and rate, are available)

■ Hosts that can connect

■ SSH sessions

■ Telnet sessions

■ Address translations

■ Rate of application inspections per second

■ Rate of system log messages per second

■ Number of MAC addresses allowed in the MAC address table

The Default Class

Resource management for a multiple mode Cisco ASA requires the creation and configuration of resource classes. You create and define resource classes and then assign Security Contexts to these classes. By default, there is a resource class created on the Cisco ASA called the default class. This class has predefined limits, and every Security Context you have created belongs to this class. Initially, when you create a new resource class, it will inherit the settings of the default class.

Creating a New Resource Class

To create a resource class in the ASDM, first ensure that you are in the system configuration mode by double-clicking **System** in the Device List pane. Once you have confirmed you are in the correct area, choose **Configuration > Context Management > Resource Class**, and then click **Add** to open the Add Resource Class dialog box, shown in Figure 13-4.

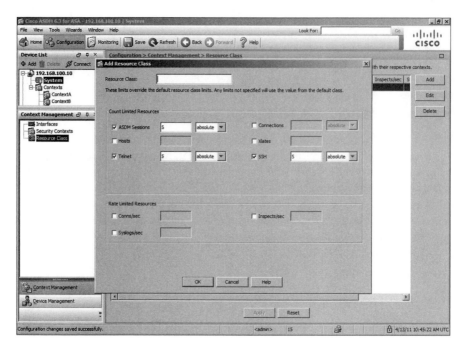

Figure 13-4 *Add Resource Class Dialog Box*

You can name the class and then configure resource limits for the various parameters. The Cisco ASA organizes the resources that you can control by Count Limited and Rate Limited.

To assign a context to a resource class, navigate to **Configuration > Context Management > Security Contexts** and click **Edit**. Use the Resource Class drop-down list to assign the resource class.

Caution: Do not assign more than 100 percent of your resources across Security Contexts. It is up to you to plan and implement the available resources. The configuration software will allow you to overallocate resources, resulting in poor performance and access to fewer resources than intended.

To configure a resource class at the CLI, simply use the **class** command. Use the **limit-resource** command to set resource limits. Finally, use the **member** command in context configuration mode to assign the resource class. Example 13-2 demonstrates how to configure a resource class.

Example 13-2   *Configuring a Resource Class*

```
hostname(config)# class gold
hostname(config-class)# limit-resource mac-addresses 10000
hostname(config-class)# limit-resource conns 15%
hostname(config-class)# limit-resource rate conns 1000
hostname(config-class)# limit-resource rate inspects 500
hostname(config-class)# limit-resource hosts 9000
hostname(config-class)# limit-resource asdm 5
hostname(config-class)# limit-resource ssh 5
hostname(config-class)# limit-resource rate syslogs 5000
hostname(config-class)# limit-resource telnet 5
hostname(config-class)# limit-resource xlates 36000
! And then later to make the context a member of the class:
hostname(config-ctx)# member gold
```

Verifying Resource Management

As demonstrated in Example 13-3, entering the **show resource allocation** command at the CLI displays the resource allocation for each resource across all classes and class members. Notice that the output shows the total allocation for each resource both as an absolute value and as a percentage of the available system resources.

Example 13-3   show resource allocation *Command Output*

```
hostname# show resource allocation
Resource            Total        % of Avail
  Conns [rate]       35000          N/A
  Inspects [rate]    35000          N/A
  Syslogs [rate]     10500          N/A
  Conns             305000         30.50%
  Hosts              78842          N/A
  SSH                   35         35.00%
  Telnet                35         35.00%
  Xlates             91749          N/A
  All              unlimited
```

The **show resource usage** command displays the resource usage for each context, enabling you to see a resource, the current resource usage, and the peak resource usage.

Troubleshooting Security Contexts

Troubleshooting Cisco ASA devices in multiple mode poses extra challenges that do not exist in single mode systems. Troubleshooting efforts will often be split between time in the system execution space and time in individual Security Contexts. In the system configuration area, you'll often rely on the **show context, show interface,** and **show resource usage** commands. While in a particular context, you often simply need to use **show interface.**

A common set of steps to use when troubleshooting Security Context issues is as follows:

Step 1.   Verify interface status in the system execution space; use the **no shutdown** command as necessary.

Step 2.   Verify interface status in a context environment. Use the **no shutdown** command as necessary.

Step 3.   In the case of shared interfaces, ensure that packets can be classified properly into specific Security Contexts. Perhaps you need to create unique MAC addresses or properly configure NAT.

Step 4.   Verify resource usage.

Step 5.   Troubleshoot within a Security Context as if you were troubleshooting a standalone security appliance. Refer to the "Troubleshooting" sections in other chapters for guidance.

Note: The Cisco ASA logs system messages when a context cannot pass traffic due to a resource limit. You should monitor for these messages carefully.

Exam Preparation Tasks

As mentioned in the section, "How to Use This Book," in the Introduction, you have a couple of choices for exam preparation: the exercises here, Chapter 17, "Final Preparation," and the exam simulation questions on the CD-ROM.

Review All Key Topics

Review the most important topics in this chapter, noted with the Key Topic icon in the outer margin of the page. Table 13-2 lists a reference of these key topics and the page numbers on which each is found.

Table 13-2   *Key Topics for Chapter 13*

Key
Topic

Key Topic Element	Description	Page Number
Section	Describes the different types of Security Contexts in the Cisco ASA	655
List	Describes the various deployment guidelines for virtual firewalls	657
List	Describes the configuration of virtual firewalls on the Cisco ASA	658
Section	Details the configuration of Security Contexts	658
Section	Covers the management of Security Contexts	661
Section	Covers the topic of resource management	663

Define Key Terms

Define the following key terms from this chapter, and check your answers in the glossary:

single mode, multiple mode, Security Context, admin context, shared interface, resource class, default class, virtual firewall

Command Reference to Check Your Memory

This section includes the most important configuration and EXEC commands covered in this chapter. It might not be necessary to memorize the complete syntax of every command, but you should be able to remember the basic keywords that are needed.

To test your memory of the commands, cover the right side of Tables 13-3 through 13-5 with a piece of paper, read the description on the left side, and then see how much of the command you can remember.

The FIREWALL exam focuses on practical, hands-on skills that are used by a networking professional. Therefore, you should be able to identify the commands needed to configure and test an ASA feature.

Table 13-3 *Commands Related to Configuring and Verifying Security Contexts*

Task	Command Syntax
Change to multiple mode	ciscoasa(config)# **mode** {**single** | **multiple**} [**noconfirm**]
Create a context	ciscoasa(config)# **context** *name*
Allocate interfaces	ciscoasa(config-ctx)# **allocate-interface** *physical_interface.subinterface*[-*physical_ interface.subinterface*] [**map_name**[-*map_name*]] [**visible** | **invisible**]
Specify the configuration location	ciscoasa(config-ctx)# config-url url
Verify the contexts	ciscoasa# **show** *context*

Table 13-4 *Commands Related to Managing Security Contexts*

Task	Command Syntax
Enter a Security Context	ciscoasa# **changeto** {*system* | *context name*}
Assign a MAC address to an interface or subinterface	ciscoasa(config)# **mac-address auto prefix** *prefix*
Specify the admin context	ciscoasa(config)# **admin-context** *name*

Table 13-5 *Commands Related to Resource Management*

Task	Command Syntax
Create a resource class	ciscoasa(config)# **class** *name*
Place a limit on a resource in a resource class	ciscoasa(config-class)# **limit-resource** {**all 0** | [**rate**] *resource_name* **number**[%]}
Make a context a member of a resource class	ciscoasa(config-ctx)# **member** *class_name*
Display resource allocations	ciscoasa# **show resource allocation** [**detail**]
Display resource usage	ciscoasa# **show resource usage** [**context** *context_name* | **top** *n* | **all** | **summary** | **system** | **detail**] [**resource** {[*rate*] *resource_name* | **all**}] [**counter** *counter_name*[*count_threshold*]]

This chapter covers the following topics:

- **ASA Failover Overview:** This section provides an overview of high availability or failover operation between two compatible Cisco ASA devices.

- **Configuring Active-Standby Failover Mode:** This section explains the configuration steps that are needed for two ASAs to operate as an active-standby failover pair.

- **Configuring Active-Active Failover Mode:** This section covers the configuration steps that are needed when two ASA are to operate as an active-active failover pair.

- **Tuning Failover Operation:** This section discusses the ways you can fine-tune threshold conditions that trigger an ASA pair to failover. A method to handle asymmetrically routed packets is also explained, along with the commands needed to manually control failover roles.

- **Verifying Failover Operation:** This section describes the command output you can use to observe and verify failover operation in an ASA failover pair.

- **Leveraging Failover for a Zero Downtime Upgrade:** This section explains the sequence of steps needed to upgrade the operating system on a live failover pair of ASAs, without causing network downtime in the process.

CHAPTER 14

Deploying High Availability Features

When a single Cisco Adaptive Security Appliance (ASA) is configured with security features and policies, it can offer reliable protection—as long as it continues to run properly, has a continuous source of power, and has consistent network connectivity. Power and connectivity are resources that are provided outside the ASA, but the ASA itself might experience a hardware or software failure, making it a single point of failure.

You can configure two ASAs as a failover pair, allowing them to operate in tandem. The result is greater reliability because one or both ASAs are always available for use. This chapter covers the configuration and operation of a high availability pair.

"Do I Know This Already?" Quiz

The "Do I Know This Already?" quiz allows you to assess whether you should read this entire chapter thoroughly or jump to the "Exam Preparation Tasks" section. If you are in doubt about your answers to these questions or your own assessment of your knowledge of the topics, read the entire chapter. Table 14-1 lists the major headings in this chapter and their corresponding "Do I Know This Already?" quiz questions. You can find the answers in Appendix A, "Answers to the 'Do I Know This Already?' Quizzes."

Table 14-1 *"Do I Know This Already?" Section-to-Question Mapping*

Foundation Topics Section	Questions
ASA Failover Overview	1–7
Configuring Active-Standby Failover Mode	8–9
Configuring Active-Active Failover Mode	10
Tuning Failover Operation	11–12
Verifying Failover Operation	13
Leveraging Failover for a Zero Downtime Upgrade	14

Caution: The goal of self-assessment is to gauge your mastery of the topics in this chapter. If you do not know the answer to a question or are only partially sure of the answer, you should mark that question as wrong for purposes of the self-assessment. Giving yourself credit for an answer you correctly guess skews your self-assessment results and might provide you with a false sense of security.

1. Which one of the following best describes the high availability attributes of active-standby failover mode?

   a. Interface redundancy

   b. Device redundancy with load balancing

   c. Context redundancy

   d. Device redundancy with no load balancing

2. What is the maximum number of ASAs that can be configured together for failover operation?

   a. 1

   b. 2

   c. It depends on the license purchased.

   d. An unlimited number

3. When an ASA is configured to operate in multiple context mode, which one of the following failover methods can be used?

   a. No failover mode

   b. Single failover mode

   c. Active-standby mode

   d. Active-active mode

4. Suppose two ASAs are configured as a failover pair. Which one of the following best describes what happens to an interface on the standby unit when a failover occurs and it takes on the active role?

   a. The interface IP address changes to match the previous active unit's address, but the MAC address stays the same.

   b. The interface IP address and MAC address both change to match that of the previous active unit.

   c. The interface MAC address changes to match the previous active unit's address, but the IP address stays the same.

   d. Nothing; both the interface IP and MAC addresses stay the same.

5. In active-active failover mode, security contexts can be assigned to how many failover groups?

    a. 1

    b. 2

    c. One per context

    d. An unlimited number

6. Which one of the following links is used to replicate ASA configuration commands?

    a. LAN failover link

    b. Standby link

    c. Stateful failover link

    d. Cluster link

7. Which of the following is not something that is synchronized between failover peers? (Choose all that apply.)

    a. Address translation entries

    b. ARP table entries

    c. TCP connections

    d. Running configuration changes

    e. Operating system image files

8. The following configuration commands have been entered on an ASA, yet the failover process doesn't seem to be working. What command could be added to make failover work?

```
ciscoasa(config)# failover lan unit primary
ciscoasa(config)# failover lan interface LANfo Ethernet0/2
ciscoasa(config)# failover interface ip LANfo 192.168.200.1 255.255.255.0
  standby 192.168.200.2
ciscoasa(config)# failover key B1gs3cr3tk3y
ciscoasa(config)# failover link stateful Ethernet0/3
ciscoasa(config)# failover interface ip stateful 192.168.201.1 255.255.255.0
  standby 192.168.201.2
ciscoasa(config)# failover replication http
```

    a. failover active

    b. failover link stateful ethernet0/4

    c. no failover standby

    d. failover

9. When stateful failover is configured, which one of the following actions should be taken to synchronize HTTP connection state information?

   a. Nothing; HTTP connections are always synchronized.

   b. Enter the **failover http** command.

   c. Enter the **failover replication http** command.

   d. Enter the **failover link http** command.

10. Under which of the following conditions can an ASA preempt its failover peer to take over the active role?

    a. Never; the failover role cannot change until the next failure occurs.

    b. The **preempt global** configuration command has been entered.

    c. The **preempt failover** group configuration command has been entered.

    d. Failover peers can always preempt to take over the active role.

11. By default, how long does it take for a dead ASA peer to be detected to trigger a failover?

    a. 1 second

    b. 5 seconds

    c. 15 seconds

    d. 30 seconds

12. By default, how many ASA interfaces must fail before a failover is triggered?

    a. 1

    b. 2

    c. None; failover occurs only if an ASA unit fails.

    d. All interfaces

13. Which one of the following commands should be used to determine the current failover status?

    a. **show failover**

    b. **show failover status**

    c. **show active**

    d. **show standby**

14. A new ASA software image has been released. Which one of the following describes the best upgrade process you should use to upgrade a failover pair in your network?

    a. Download the new image to both units, and then reload them both at the same time.

    b. Download the new image to both units; power cycle one unit, and then power cycle the other unit.

    c. Download the new image to both units; reload the standby unit first, and then reload the active unit.

    d. Download the new image to both units; reload the standby unit first, toggle the active and standby roles, and then reload the new standby unit.

Foundation Topics

With its rich, versatile feature set, a single ASA can provide robust protection for a network. If that ASA experiences a failure of some sort, it might not be able to inspect and pass traffic until it is repaired. As a remedy, this chapter covers the methods you can use to configure two ASAs as a failover pair, providing redundancy and high availability.

ASA Failover Overview

Two ASAs can be configured to operate as a high availability or "failover" pair. The idea is to leverage two separate devices so that one of them is always available in case the other one fails. Naturally, there is a possibility that both ASAs might fail within the same timeframe, but your goal as a network professional should be to minimize that chance. For example, you might want to install each ASA in a different building to give them physical separation, in case power fails in one building for an extended time.

Cisco ASAs support two forms of failover:

- **Active-standby:** One ASA takes on the active role, handling all the normal security functions. The other ASA stays in standby mode, ready to take over the active role in the event of a failure. The active-standby failover mode provides device redundancy.

- **Active-active:** When the ASAs are running multiple security contexts, the contexts can be organized into groups. One ASA is active for one group of contexts, and the other ASA is active for another group. In effect, both ASAs are actively involved in providing security functions, but not in the same security context simultaneously. The active-active failover mode provides both device redundancy and load balancing across contexts.

Failover Roles

To coexist as a failover or redundant pair, two ASAs must be an identical model and must coordinate their failover roles. In active-standby failover, one ASA must function as the active unit, handling all traffic inspection at any given time. The other ASA must always sit idle, waiting to take over the active role. Figure 14-1 illustrates this arrangement. The topmost ASA is active, while the bottommost ASA is in standby mode.

Notice that the ASA pair must share identical sets of interfaces. For example, each unit has an inside and an outside interface, and the similar interfaces must be connected together. This is for two reasons:

- The standby unit must be ready to take over handling traffic at any time, so its interfaces must be connected and ready to use.

- The two ASAs monitor each other's health by communicating over each of their interfaces.

If a failure is detected on the active unit, the two ASAs effectively swap roles, as shown in Figure 14-2. The lower ASA was previously in the standby mode, but has moved into the active role.

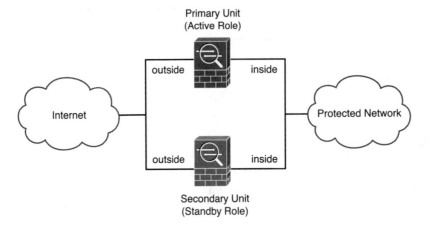

Figure 14-1   *Active-Standby Failover Mode*

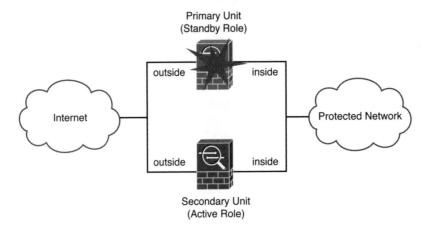

Figure 14-2   *Failure Detected in Active-Standby Failover Mode*

Once a failure is detected, the ASAs swap roles until the next failure. If an ASA moves into the standby role, it is not permitted to preempt its peer and take over the active role again—unless the active ASA has a failure of its own. This creates a stable mechanism where the ASAs toggle roles only when failures occur.

Each ASA maintains a unique MAC address and a unique IP address on each of its interfaces. In addition to swapping the active and standby roles, the ASAs must also swap MAC and IP addresses so that the active unit always uses consistent and predictable values—regardless of which physical unit is active at any time. Figure 14-3 illustrates this process. The address swap occurs on every ASA interface except the LAN failover, which always remains unchanged.

The MAC and IP addresses used for the active role are taken from the burned-in MAC addresses or the values that might be configured on only one of the two ASAs. Therefore, one of the two units must be configured as the *primary* unit. The other ASA becomes the *secondary* unit, which supplies the addressing values for the standby role. The primary and secondary designations only determine the active and standby addresses—not the active and standby roles.

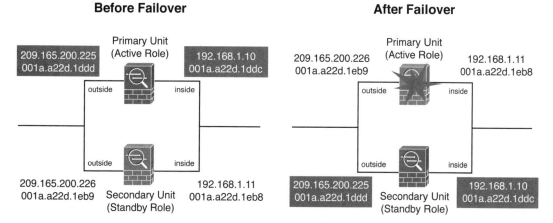

Figure 14-3   *Address Swapping During Failover*

When two ASAs are configured to operate in active-active failover mode, they still alternate their roles so that one unit is active and one is in standby; however, the active-standby combination is carried out on a per-failover group basis, with each ASA running failover groups containing multiple security contexts. If the active-standby roles are alternated across different security contexts, both units can actively inspect traffic at the same time—hence the term *active-active failover*, where neither unit is required to sit completely idle.

Figure 14-4 illustrates the active-active concept, in which each ASA is configured to run three separate security contexts: ContextA, ContextB, and ContextC. Each context in the primary ASA can take on either the active or standby role, while the corresponding context in the secondary ASA takes on the alternate role. In the figure, the primary ASA has the active role for ContextA and ContextC; the secondary ASA is active for ContextB.

Notice how the failover roles of each context can be collected into two logical failover groups, corresponding to the physical ASA unit, as listed in Table 14-2. At any given time, one ASA will have the active role for all contexts that are assigned to its failover group, while the other ASA will be active for all contexts assigned to the other failover group.

Key Topic

Table 14-2   *Failover Group Roles in Active-Active Failover Mode*

Failover Group	Primary ASA	Secondary ASA
1	Active role	Standby role
2	Standby role	Active role

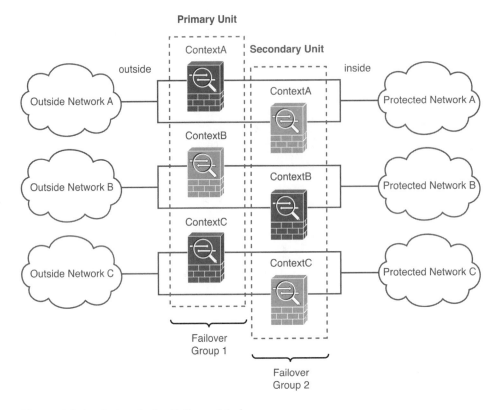

Figure 14-4 *Active-Active Failover Mode*

During a failure in active-active failover mode, the two ASAs effectively swap roles, but only on a failover group basis. In Figure 14-5, the entire primary ASA has failed, rendering both of its contexts in failover group 1 useless. The secondary ASA then takes on the active role for failover group 1 (ContextA and ContextC), although it was already active for failover group 2 (ContextB).

In either active-standby or active-active mode, a failover pair of ASAs must have a special-purpose link set aside for failover communication between them. The LAN-based failover link, as shown in Figure 14-6, is used to check on the health of a failover peer ASA and to pass configuration updates and commands between peers.

Note: The LAN failover interface should be connected to a switch that is separate from other ASA interfaces so that the ASAs can detect a switch failure that affects regular ASA interfaces without affecting the LAN failover interface and the failover process itself. To add even more resilience, you can configure the LAN failover interface using a pair of redundant interfaces, each connected to a different switch.

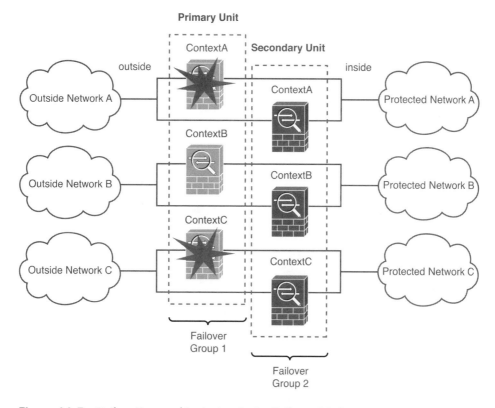

Figure 14-5   *Failure Detected in Active-Active Failover Mode*

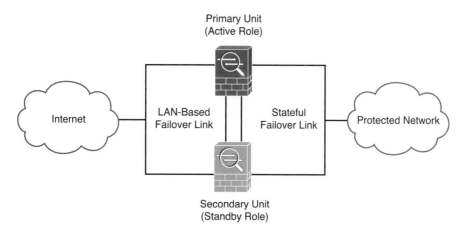

Figure 14-6   *Links Used for Failover Communication*

The ASA configurations are always maintained on the active unit. As you make changes to the running configuration, the commands are automatically synchronized from the active unit to the standby unit. You can force the running configuration synchronization by entering the **write standby** command on the active unit.

The startup configuration, however, is not automatically synchronized. The **copy running-config startup-config** command saves the running configuration to flash memory on the active unit and then to the flash on the standby unit.

Each ASA maintains its own flash file system, but files are not replicated between the units as a part of failover. This means that each ASA maintains its own operating system and ASDM images. To upgrade a software image, you must upgrade each of the failover peers independently. The "hitless upgrade" or "zero downtime upgrade" feature allows failover operation to continue, even while the two ASAs are running different, but compatible, software releases. The upgrade process is covered in more detail in the section, "Leveraging Failover for a Zero Downtime Upgrade."

By default, an ASA failover pair operates in a *stateless failover* mode. The active unit stays busy building and tearing down address translations and connections, but does not inform the standby unit at all. If the active unit fails, none of the active UDP or TCP connections will be preserved because the standby unit doesn't have anything in its connection state tables. Therefore, hosts will have to reinitiate any connections that they were using at the time.

To make the failover operation more seamless, you can configure an ASA pair to use *stateful failover* instead. A second special-purpose stateful failover link must be used to pass connection state information between failover peers, so that the standby unit can keep its translation and connection tables in sync with the active unit. Figure 14-6 shows this link. If the active unit fails, the standby unit will be fully equipped to pick up all existing stateful inspections so that no connections will be lost.

Stateful failover synchronizes many types of information between the active and standby units. Table 14-3 lists the types of state information that are replicated and the types that are not. You should leverage stateful failover whenever possible, to make the failover process as seamless as possible.

Table 14-3 *State Information Synchronization Between Stateful Failover Peers*

State Information Replicated	State Information Not Replicated
NAT table entries	User authentication Cut-through Proxy
ARP table entries	DHCP server address leases
MAC address table entries	Phone proxy information
UDP connections	Security Services Module activity
TCP connections	
H.323 and SIP signaling sessions	
MGCP connections	
HTTP connections (if explicitly enabled)	

Table 14-3 *State Information Synchronization Between Stateful Failover Peers*

State Information Replicated	State Information Not Replicated
Dynamic routing table entries*	—

*Beginning with software image release 8.4, ASAs are able to participate in dynamic routing protocols and to synchronize dynamic routing table entries between peers.

When stateful failover is used, you can dedicate one interface to LAN failover and another to stateful failover, or you can use a single interface to share both LAN failover and stateful failover information. The stateful failover data stream is usually much larger than the LAN failover data stream because of the large number of connections that come and go as traffic passes through the ASA pair. However, you should never use a regular data interface to carry stateful failover information, to prevent high volumes of data from crowding out critical failover updates. You should set aside the fastest interface that is available for stateful failover.

Be aware that even with stateful failover enabled, HTTP connection state information is not replicated between the active and standby units by default. You can remedy that by enabling HTTP connection synchronization to force the active unit to update the standby unit as HTTP and HTTPS connections are built and torn down.

Detecting an ASA Failure

Two ASAs must be configured with their primary and secondary failover identities, so that the active unit can determine which MAC and IP addresses to use. But what determines which unit takes on the active role? Each ASA must go through an election process when it boots.

By listening on the LAN failover interface, an ASA can determine which state its failover peer is in and can decide which role to use for itself. The failover peers can also compare their "health" rating by seeing if all interfaces are up and if the Security Services Module (SSM) is installed and functional.

The election process takes place as follows:

Key Topic

- If a peer is detected, is trying to negotiate its own role, and is equally healthy as the booting ASA, the primary unit will become active and the secondary unit will become standby.

- If a peer is detected, is trying to negotiate its own role, but is not equally healthy, the healthier of the two ASAs will become active.

- If a peer is detected and it already has the active role, the booting ASA will become standby.

- If no peer is detected at all, the booting ASA will become active.

- If the booting ASA becomes active, but later detects its peer that is also active, it will begin negotiating roles with its peer to elect only one active role.

Once failover is enabled and active, the two ASA peers continuously communicate and monitor each other. Hello packets are sent at regular intervals over the LAN failover interface and every interface that is configured to be monitored. By listening for hello packets from a peer device, an ASA can determine the health of its peer.

An ASA monitors the health of its peer according to the following rules:

- As long as hellos are received over the LAN failover interface, the peer must be alive and no failover occurs.

- If hellos are not received over the LAN failover interface, but hellos are received on other monitored interfaces, the peer must be alive and no failover occurs. Only the LAN failover interface is declared to be "failed" and should be repaired as soon as possible.

- If no hellos are received on any interface for a hold time interval, the peer is declared to be "failed" and failover occurs.

By default, hello packets are sent over the LAN failover interface every 1 second. The default hold timer is 15 seconds. You can shorten the failover unit poll (hello) and hold timers so that a failure is detected sooner, if desired. The failover timers are covered in more detail in the section, "Tuning Failover Operation."

Each interface of one ASA must connect to the same network as the corresponding interface of the peer ASA. Hello packets are also sent on all interfaces that are configured to be monitored for failover, so that an ASA can determine the health of each interface on its peer.

The poll and hold times used by the interface-based hello monitoring are different from those used by the unit-based hello monitoring on the LAN failover interface. By default, interface hellos are sent and polled every 5 seconds, with an interface hold timer of five times the interface poll time.

If hello packets are not seen on a monitored interface within half of the hold time, that interface is moved into a "testing" mode to determine if a failure has occurred. The peer ASA is notified of the test via the LAN failover interface.

Interfaces in the "testing" mode are moved through the following sequence of tests:

Key Topic

1. **Interface status:** The interface is failed if the link status is down.

2. **Network activity:** If no packets are received over a 5-second interval, the next testing phase begins; otherwise, the interface can still be used.

3. **ARP:** The interface stimulates received traffic by sending ARP requests for the ten newest entries in the ASA's ARP table. If no traffic is received in 5 seconds, the next testing phase begins.

4. **Broadcast ping:** Traffic is stimulated by sending an ICMP echo request to the broadcast address on the interface. If no replies are received over a 5-second interval, the interface is marked in a "failed" state; however, if the same interface on the peer ASA also fails the test, then the interface is marked in an "unknown" state because an actual failure cannot be determined.

At the conclusion of the tests, the two ASAs attempt to compare their status. If the active unit has more failed interfaces than a configured threshold, a failover occurs.

Once a monitored interface is marked as "failed," it will become operational again as soon as any traffic is received on it.

Configuring Active-Standby Failover Mode

You can use ASDM to configure and enable failover. ASDM offers a wizard that will step through the configuration and push failover commands to the secondary unit automatically. Otherwise, you can configure failover parameters under separate ASDM tabs on the primary and secondary units manually. Both strategies are covered in the sections that follow.

As a configuration example, the failover scenario shown in Figure 14-7 is to be implemented. The inside and outside MAC addresses should be configured to the values shown in the figure. By default, all interfaces will be monitored for failover; because the Management0/0 interface is not used in this scenario, it should not be monitored.

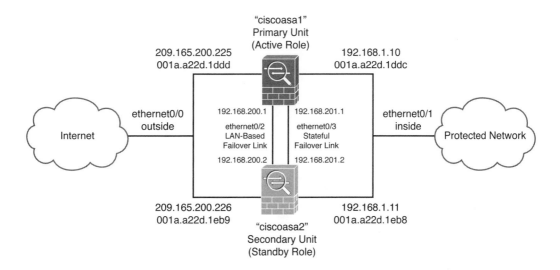

Figure 14-7   *Network Diagram for the Example Active-Standby Failover Scenario*

Configuring Active-Standby Failover with the ASDM Wizard

To use the wizard, start ASDM on the primary failover unit. Navigate to **Configuration > Device Management > High Availability**, and then select **HA/Scalability Wizard**. In the window shown in Figure 14-8, click the **Launch High Availability and Scalability Wizard** button.

Next, click the **Configure Active/Standby Failover** radio button, as shown in Figure 14-9, and then click **Next**.

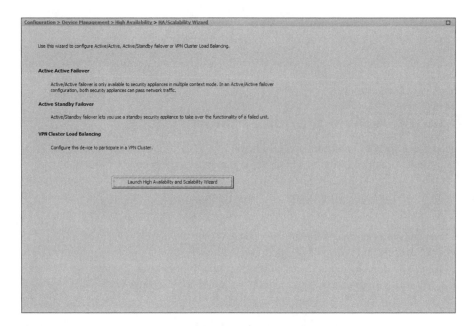

Figure 14-8 *Accessing the High Availability Wizard to Configure Failover*

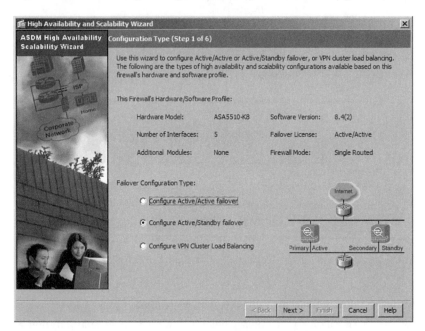

Figure 14-9 *Beginning Active-Standby Failover Configuration*

The wizard will begin by asking for the failover peer's IP address. Enter the address of one of the secondary unit's interfaces. In Figure 14-10, the address of the secondary inside interface has been entered. When you click the **Next** button, ASDM will go through a series of seven steps to communicate with the secondary unit and to make sure the two units are compatible for failover. The steps begin with question marks, as shown in the figure, and progress to green check marks after the failover tests are successful.

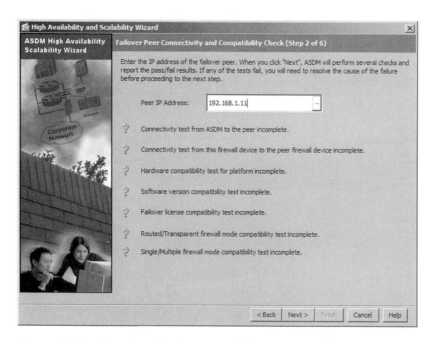

Figure 14-10   *Testing Failover Compatibility in the ASDM Wizard*

Before these tests can succeed, you must configure the secondary unit with enough information to be live on the network and to respond to the tests. At a minimum, the secondary unit must have at least one interface configured with an IP address, and the unit must allow remote access on that interface. ASDM will prompt for a username and password so that it can log in to the secondary unit remotely and parse through its configuration.

Next, the wizard will ask you to enter information about the LAN failover link and the stateful failover link. You will need to identify the interfaces and assign IP addresses to the active and standby units. These steps are shown in Figures 14-11 and 14-12. Be sure to choose the appropriate stateful failover link arrangement, whether the link will be shared with LAN failover or be a separate link.

As a final step, the wizard will display a list of regular data interfaces on the ASA, as shown in Figure 14-13. You need to configure the active and standby IP addresses for each. To change an address, double-click in the address field and enter a new value. In the rightmost column, select each interface that should be monitored for failover.

Once you click the **Next** button, the wizard will display all the failover parameters it will send to the secondary ASA. After you review the list, click the **Finish** button. ASDM will send the commands and wait about 30 seconds for the two units to recognize their failover peer relationship and synchronize their configurations and interface states.

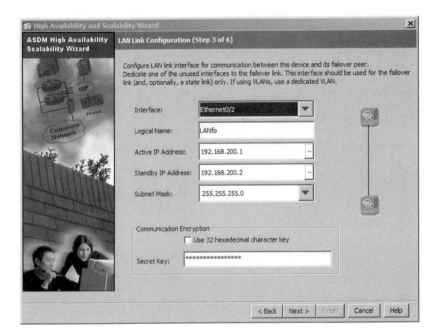

Figure 14-11 *Configuring the LAN Failover Link in the ASDM Wizard*

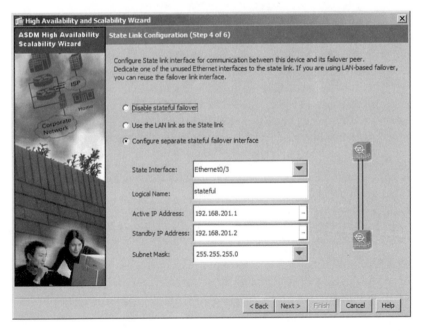

Figure 14-12 *Configuring the Stateful Failover Link in the ASDM Wizard*

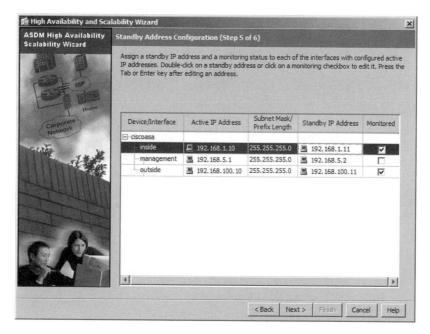

Figure 14-13   *Configuring ASA Interfaces for Failover in the ASDM Wizard*

Configuring Active-Standby Failover Manually in ASDM

To configure each aspect of active-standby failover, start ASDM on the primary failover unit. Navigate to **Configuration > Device Management > High Availability,** and then select **Failover.** You can enable failover and enter information about the LAN failover and stateful failover links on the Setup tab, as shown in Figure 14-14.

Click the **Interfaces** tab to configure active and standby IP addresses on each data interface, as shown in Figure 14-15. You can also select which interfaces will be monitored for failover.

If you decide to configure predetermined MAC addresses on some normal data interfaces, you can do that under the **MAC Addresses** tab. Click the **Add** button to select an interface. As shown in Figure 14-16, choose an interface from the drop-down list and enter both an active and a standby MAC address.

You can make adjustments to the failover timers and health monitoring thresholds on the **Criteria** tab. These configuration changes are discussed in detail in the section, "Tuning Failover Operation."

Finally, you will need to start ASDM on the secondary ASA and complete the failover configuration there.

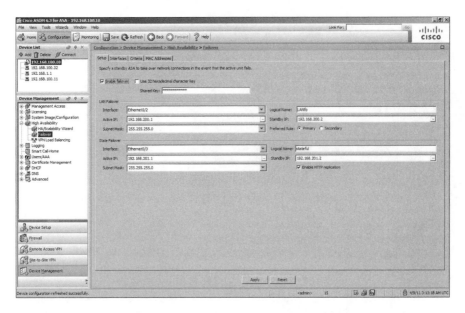

Figure 14-14   *Configuring the LAN Failover and Stateful Failover Interfaces*

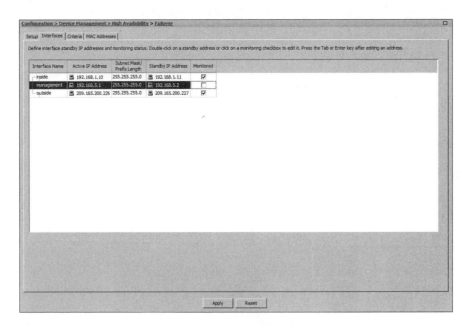

Figure 14-15   *Configuring Failover Operation on Data Interfaces*

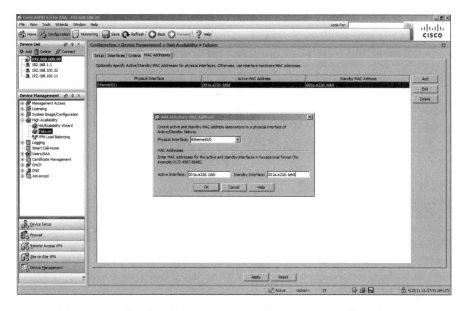

Figure 14-16 *Configuring Failover MAC Addresses on Data Interfaces*

Configuring Active-Standby Failover with the CLI

You can use the CLI to configure active-standby failover mode according to the following steps:

Step 1.   Configure the primary failover unit.

Step 2.   Configure failover on the secondary device.

Step 1: Configure the Primary Failover Unit

Begin by connecting to the primary unit and identifying it as such with the following command:

```
ciscoasa(config)# failover lan unit primary
```

Identify the LAN failover interface by its logical and physical names with the **failover lan interface** command. Then specify the IP address that will be used on the active and standby units with the **failover interface ip** command. You should also configure LAN failover encryption by giving an encryption key string with the **failover key** command. The key string is an arbitrary text string of up to 63 characters or a string of exactly 32 hex digits.

The commands needed to configure the LAN failover interface and to enable failover are as follows:

```
ciscoasa(config)# failover lan interface int_name [physical_int]
ciscoasa(config)# failover interface ip int_name ip_address mask  standby
  ip_address
ciscoasa(config)# failover key {key-string | hex key}
ciscoasa(config)# failover
```

Next, select a stateful failover interface with the **failover link** command. Assign an IP address for the active and standby units with the **failover interface ip** command. Enter the **failover replication http** command if you want stateful failover of HTTP connections.

```
ciscoasa(config)# failover link int_name [physical_int]
ciscoasa(config)# failover interface ip int_name ip_address mask  standby
  ip_address
ciscoasa(config)# failover replication http
```

For each interface that will carry normal data, you will need to configure the active and standby unit IP addresses. You can do this with the **ip address** interface configuration command, followed by the **standby** keyword, as follows:

```
ciscoasa(config-if)# ip address active_addr subnet_mask standby standby_addr
```

Normally, the active and standby units use their own burned-in MAC addresses for a regular data interface and inform each other through failover messages. The active MAC address can stay consistent, regardless of which unit has the active role. However, in the rare "corner" case where the standby unit is booted alone, it will use its own burned-in address instead.

You can prevent this from happening by using the following global configuration command to set the active and standby unit MAC addresses to unique, predetermined values. You should use arbitrary unique values or the burned-in MAC addresses from the primary and secondary units, as shown in the **show interface** command output:

```
ciscoasa(config)# failover mac address int_name active_mac standby_mac
```

By default, every ASA interface will be monitored to detect a failure that might trigger a failover. If you want to exclude an interface from being monitored, enter the following command:

```
ciscoasa(config)# no monitor-interface int_name
```

Interface and health monitoring are covered in detail in the section, "Tuning Failover Operation."

At this point, the primary unit is configured for failover and is waiting to detect a secondary failover unit. Because it has been configured first, the primary unit will take on the active failover role.

Step 2: Configure Failover on the Secondary Device

Connect to the secondary ASA and identify it as the secondary failover unit. Configure the LAN failover interface with the following commands:

```
ciscoasa(config)# failover lan unit secondary
ciscoasa(config)# failover lan interface int_name [physical_int]
ciscoasa(config)# failover interface ip int_name ip_address mask  standby
  ip_address
ciscoasa(config)# failover key {key-string │ hex key}
ciscoasa(config)# failover
```

The final **failover** command enables the failover function. Once the primary and secondary units recognize each other, the secondary unit should take on the standby role. The LAN failover interface will be used to replicate configuration commands from the active to the standby unit—including most of the failover commands you have already entered. From this point on, you should enter all configuration changes only on the ASA that has the active role.

Refer to Figure 14-7 for a network diagram of a configuration example. The configuration commands listed in Example 14-1 are entered on the primary ASA, while the commands listed in Example 14-2 are entered on the secondary ASA.

Example 14-1 *Configuring Failover on the Primary ASA*

```
ciscoasa(config)# failover lan unit primary
ciscoasa(config)# failover lan interface LANfo Ethernet0/2
ciscoasa(config)# failover interface ip LANfo 192.168.200.1 255.255.255.0 standby
  192.168.200.2
ciscoasa(config)# failover key B1gs3cr3tk3y
ciscoasa(config)# failover
!
ciscoasa(config)# failover link stateful Ethernet0/3
ciscoasa(config)# failover interface ip stateful 192.168.201.1 255.255.255.0
  standby 192.168.201.2
ciscoasa(config)# failover replication http
!
ciscoasa(config)# interface Ethernet0/0
ciscoasa(config-if)# nameif outside
ciscoasa(config-if)# security-level 0
ciscoasa(config-if)# ip address 209.165.200.226 255.255.255.0 standby
  209.165.200.227
ciscoasa(config-if)# exit
!
ciscoasa(config)# interface Ethernet0/1
ciscoasa(config-if)# nameif inside
ciscoasa(config-if)# security-level 100
ciscoasa(config-if)# ip address 192.168.1.10 255.255.255.0 standby 192.168.1.11
ciscoasa(config-if)# exit
ciscoasa(config)# failover mac address inside 001a.a22d.1ddd 001a.a22d.1eb9
ciscoasa(config)# failover mac address outside 001a.a22d.1ddc 001a.a22d.1eb8
ciscoasa(config)# no monitor-interface management0/0
```

Example 14-2 *Configuring Failover on the Secondary ASA*

```
ciscoasa(config)# failover lan unit secondary
ciscoasa(config)# failover lan interface LANfo Ethernet0/2
ciscoasa(config)# failover interface ip LANfo 192.168.200.1 255.255.255.0 standby
  192.168.200.2
```

```
ciscoasa(config)# failover key B1gs3cr3tk3y
ciscoasa(config)# failover
```

Configuring Active-Active Failover Mode

Configuring active-active failover is similar to configuring active-standby mode. The two failover units need the same LAN failover and stateful failover link configurations, and the same active and standby addresses on each interface. However, each ASA must be assigned its primary or secondary role in each of the two failover groups. As well, each security context must be assigned to a failover group.

As an example, the failover scenario shown in Figure 14-17 is to be implemented. Three security contexts are used. Failover group 1 should contain the admin and ContextB contexts, with the primary ASA normally having the active role. Failover group 2 should contain only ContextA, normally active on the secondary ASA.

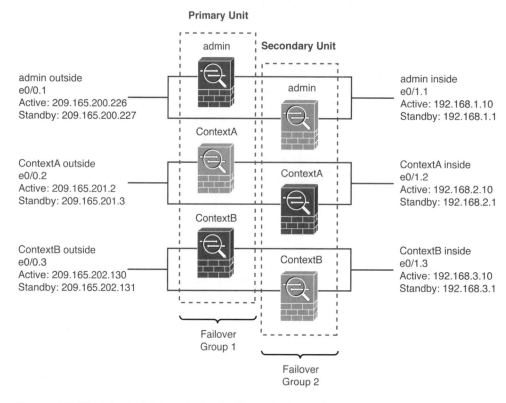

Figure 14-17 *Network Diagram for the Example Scenario*

Configuring Active-Active Failover in ASDM

You can use ASDM to configure active-active failover. As with active-standby failover, you can use the ASDM High Availability and Scalability Wizard to configure both the primary and secondary ASAs from the primary unit. To do that, double-click the **System** context in the device list. Then navigate to **Configuration > Device Management > High Availability** and select **HA/Scalability Wizard**.

Otherwise, you can configure active-active failover on the primary and secondary units manually. On the primary unit, double-click the **System** context in the device list, and then navigate to **Configuration > Device Management > High Availability** and select **Failover**.

On the Setup tab, shown in Figure 14-18, you can configure the LAN failover and stateful failover links, as well as enable failover.

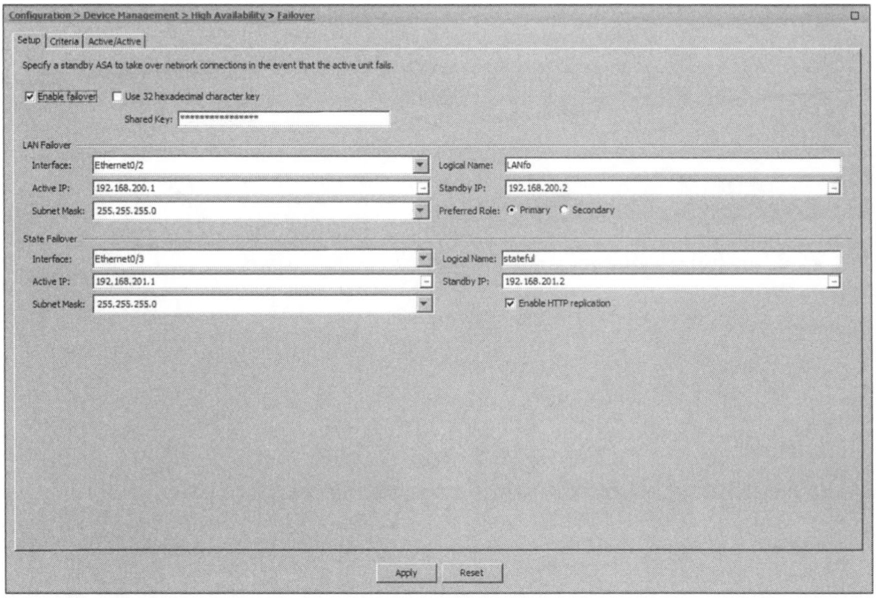

Figure 14-18   *Configuring Failover Links for Active-Active Failover Mode*

Under the Criteria tab, as shown in Figure 14-19, you can configure failover timers and health monitoring parameters. These are discussed in the section, "Tuning Failover Operation."

Next, click the **Active/Active** tab to configure the ASA for its primary or secondary role in each failover group. Select a failover group from the list and click the **Edit** button to make changes. In Figure 14-20, the primary ASA has been configured to have the primary (normally active) role for failover group 1 and the secondary (normally standby) role for failover group 2.

Next, you will need to assign each security context to one of the two failover groups. By default, all contexts belong to failover group 1. Navigate to **Configuration > Context Management** and select **Security Contexts**. Each context that is configured on the ASA will be displayed in a list. To assign the failover group, select a context, click the **Edit** button, and then select a failover group, as shown in Figure 14-21.

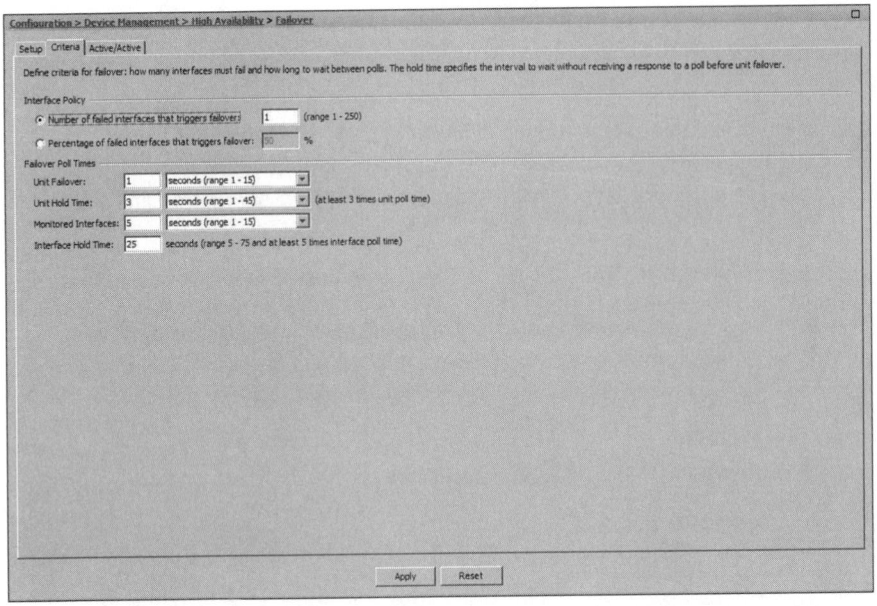

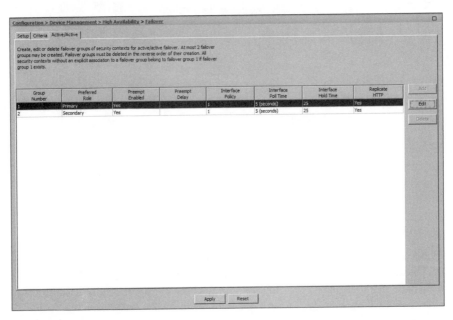

Figure 14-19 *Configuring Failover Criteria in Active-Active Mode*

Figure 14-20 *Configuring Failover Group Roles for Active-Active Failover Mode*

Now that the primary ASA is configured for active-active failover operation, you must visit each context to configure the active and standby IP addresses on each interface. You can also configure interface monitoring. In the device list, double-click a context name, navigate to **Configuration > Device Management**, and select **Failover**. Figure 14-22 shows the interfaces in the admin context. You can double-click in any of the address fields to edit or change the IP address values.

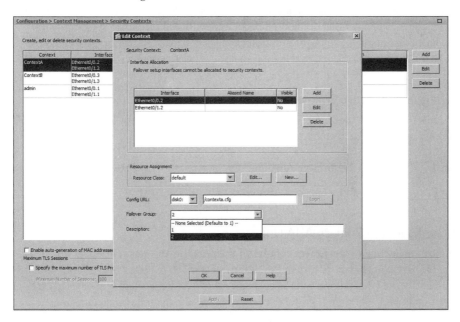

Figure 14-21   *Assigning Security Contexts to Active-Active Failover Groups*

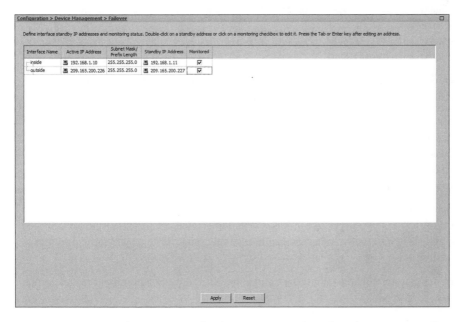

Figure 14-22   *Configuring the Admin Context Interfaces for Active-Active Failover Mode*

Finally, don't forget to open an ASDM session with the secondary ASA and configure active-active failover in its system execution space. Once the LAN failover and stateful failover links are configured and failover is enabled, the primary unit will synchronize the system, admin, and any other context configuration with the secondary unit automatically. From that point on, any configuration changes you make should be entered on the ASA that currently has the active role for a specific security context.

Configuring Active-Active Failover with the CLI

You can use the CLI to configure active-active failover mode. Use the following steps to configure one ASA, and then move to the other ASA and repeat the steps there:

Step 1.   Configure the primary ASA unit.

Step 2.   Configure the secondary ASA unit.

Step 1: Configure the Primary ASA Unit

Begin by connecting to the system context of the primary ASA unit. Designate the ASA as the primary unit so that its system execution context can manage configuration replication. Identify the LAN failover interface, specify the IP addresses that will be used on the failover units, and configure LAN failover encryption with the following commands:

```
ciscoasa(config)# failover lan unit primary
ciscoasa(config)# failover lan interface int_name [physical_int]
ciscoasa(config)# failover interface ip int_name ip_address mask  standby
  ip_address
ciscoasa(config)# failover key {key-string  |  hex key}
ciscoasa(config)# failover
```

Next, configure the failover unit role in each failover group. Use the following commands to assign the role in one failover group, and then repeat the commands to assign the role in the other failover group:

```
ciscoasa(config)# failover group {1  |  2}
ciscoasa(config-fover-group)# {primary  |  secondary}
ciscoasa(config-fover-group)# [no] preempt
ciscoasa(config-fover-group)# exit
```

By default, the primary and secondary ASAs trade active and standby roles only after a failure. When a previously active unit is restored to service, it isn't allowed to preempt its peer and resume the active role. You can change that behavior by entering the **preempt** command.

Next, select a stateful failover interface and assign IP addresses with the following commands:

```
ciscoasa(config)# failover link int_name [physical_int]
ciscoasa(config)# failover interface ip int_name ip_address mask  standby
  ip_address
```

If needed, interface MAC addresses and HTTP state replication must be configured in each failover group with the following commands:

```
ciscoasa(config)# failover group {1 | 2}
ciscoasa(config)# failover mac address int_name active_mac standby_mac
ciscoasa(config-fover-group)# replication http
ciscoasa(config-fover-group)# exit
```

You must assign each security context to one of the two failover groups, effectively distributing the load across the two ASA units. Use the following commands to assign a context to a failover group:

```
ciscoasa(config)# context context-name
ciscoasa(config-ctx)# join-failover-group {1 | 2}
ciscoasa(config-ctx)# exit
```

Next, use the **changeto context** command to move into each security context. For each interface that will carry normal data, you will need to configure the active and standby unit IP addresses. You can do this with the **ip address** interface configuration command, followed by the **standby** keyword, as follows:

```
ciscoasa/context(config-if)# ip address active_addr subnet_mask standby
  standby_addr
```

By default, every physical ASA interface will be monitored to detect a failure that might trigger a failover. You can use the following command to enable monitoring or add the **no** keyword to prevent monitoring:

```
ciscoasa/context(config)# [no] monitor-interface int_name
```

Interface and health monitoring are covered in detail in the section, "Tuning Failover Operation."

At this point, the first ASA is configured for failover and is waiting to detect a failover peer unit.

Step 2: Configure the Secondary ASA Unit

Connect to the system context of the secondary ASA unit. Designate it as the secondary unit, and configure its failover role in each failover group. Use the following commands:

```
ciscoasa(config)# failover lan unit secondary
ciscoasa(config)# failover lan interface int_name [physical_int]
ciscoasa(config)# failover interface ip int_name ip_address mask  standby
  ip_address
ciscoasa(config)# failover key {key-string | hex key}
```

Next, configure the failover unit role in each failover group. Use the following commands to assign the role in one failover group, and then repeat the commands to assign the role in the other failover group. Make sure the roles assigned to the primary ASA are opposite those assigned to the secondary ASA:

```
ciscoasa(config)# failover group {1 | 2}
ciscoasa(config-fover-group)# {primary | secondary}
```

```
ciscoasa(config-fover-group)# [no] preempt
ciscoasa(config-fover-group)# exit
ciscoasa(config)# failover
```

The final **failover** command enables the failover function. Once the ASA units recognize each other, they will negotiate their roles in each failover group. The LAN failover interface will be used to replicate configuration commands from the active to the standby unit—including most of the failover commands you have already entered. From this point on, you should enter all configuration changes only on the ASA that has the active role for a specific security context.

See Figure 14-23 for a network diagram of an example scenario. The configuration commands listed in Examples 14-3 through 14-6 are entered on the primary ASA, while the commands listed in Example 14-7 are entered on the secondary ASA.

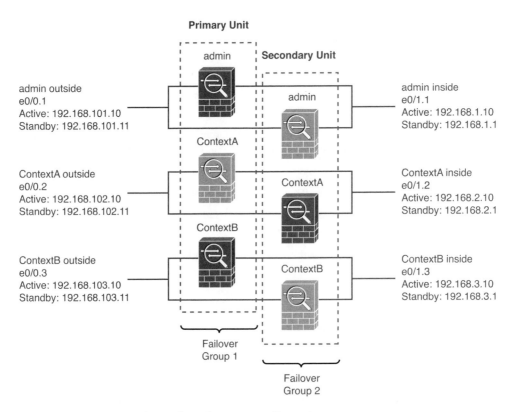

Figure 14-23   *Network Topology for ASA Configurations*

Example 14-3   *Configuring Failover on the Primary ASA*

```
ciscoasa(config)# failover lan unit primary
ciscoasa(config)# failover lan interface LANfo Ethernet0/2
ciscoasa(config)# failover interface ip LANfo 192.168.200.1 255.255.255.0 standby
  192.168.200.2
ciscoasa(config)# failover key B1gs3cr3tk3y
ciscoasa(config)# failover
!
ciscoasa(config)# failover group 1
ciscoasa(config-fover-group)# primary
ciscoasa(config-fover-group)#  preempt
ciscoasa(config-fover-group)# replication http
ciscoasa(config-fover-group)# exit
ciscoasa(config)# failover group 2
ciscoasa(config-fover-group)# secondary
ciscoasa(config-fover-group)# preempt
ciscoasa(config-fover-group)# replication http
ciscoasa(config-fover-group)# exit
!
ciscoasa(config)# failover link stateful Ethernet0/3
ciscoasa(config)# failover interface ip stateful 192.168.201.1 255.255.255.0
  standby 192.168.201.2
!
ciscoasa(config)# context admin
ciscoasa(config-ctx)# allocate-interface Ethernet0/0.1
ciscoasa(config-ctx)# allocate-interface Ethernet0/1.1
ciscoasa(config-ctx)# config-url disk0:/admin.cfg
ciscoasa(config-ctx)# join-failover-group 1
ciscoasa(config-ctx)# exit
!
ciscoasa(config)# context ContextA
ciscoasa(config-ctx)# allocate-interface Ethernet0/0.2
ciscoasa(config-ctx)#  allocate-interface Ethernet0/1.2
ciscoasa(config-ctx)# config-url disk0:/contexta.cfg
ciscoasa(config-ctx)# join-failover-group 2
ciscoasa(config-ctx)# exit
!
ciscoasa(config)# context ContextB
ciscoasa(config-ctx)# allocate-interface Ethernet0/0.3
ciscoasa(config-ctx)# allocate-interface Ethernet0/1.3
ciscoasa(config-ctx)# config-url disk0:/contextb.cfg
ciscoasa(config-ctx)# join-failover-group 1
ciscoasa(config-ctx)# exit
ciscoasa(config)# exit
```

Example 14-4   *Configuring the Primary ASA "admin" Context Interfaces for Failover*

```
ciscoasa/admin(config)# interface Ethernet0/0.1
ciscoasa/admin(config-if)# nameif outside
ciscoasa/admin(config-if)# security-level 0
ciscoasa/admin(config-if)# ip address 209.165.200.226 255.255.255.224 standby
  209.165.200.227
!
ciscoasa/admin(config-if)# interface Ethernet0/1.1
ciscoasa/admin(config-if)# nameif inside
ciscoasa/admin(config-if)# security-level 100
ciscoasa/admin(config-if)# ip address 192.168.1.10 255.255.255.0 standby
  192.168.1.11
ciscoasa/admin(config-if)# exit
!
ciscoasa/admin(config)# monitor-interface inside
ciscoasa/admin(config)# monitor-interface outside
```

Example 14-5   *Configuring the Primary ASA "ContextA" Interfaces for Failover*

```
ciscoasa/ContextA(config)# interface Ethernet0/0.1
ciscoasa/ContextA (config-if)# nameif outside
ciscoasa/ContextA (config-if)# security-level 0
ciscoasa/ContextA (config-if)# ip address 209.165.201.2 255.255.255.224 standby
  209.165.201.3
!
ciscoasa/ContextA(config-if)# interface Ethernet0/1.1
ciscoasa/ContextA(config-if)# nameif inside
ciscoasa/ContextA(config-if)# security-level 100
ciscoasa/ContextA(config-if)# ip address 192.168.2.10 255.255.255.0 standby
  192.168.2.11
ciscoasa/ContextA(config-if)# exit
!
ciscoasa/ContextA(config)# monitor-interface inside
ciscoasa/ContextA(config)# monitor-interface outside
```

Example 14-6   *Configuring the Primary ASA "ContextB" Interfaces for Failover*

```
ciscoasa/ContextB(config)# interface Ethernet0/0.1
ciscoasa/ContextB(config-if)# nameif outside
ciscoasa/ContextB(config-if)# security-level 0
ciscoasa/ContextB(config-if)# ip address 209.165.202.130 255.255.255.224 standby
  209.165.202.131
!
ciscoasa/ContextB(config-if)# interface Ethernet0/1.1
ciscoasa/ContextB(config-if)# nameif inside
ciscoasa/ContextB(config-if)# security-level 100
```

```
ciscoasa/ContextB(config-if)# ip address 192.168.3.10 255.255.255.0 standby
  192.168.3.11
ciscoasa/ContextB(config-if)# exit
!
ciscoasa/ContextB(config)# monitor-interface inside
ciscoasa/ContextB(config)# monitor-interface outside
```

Example 14-7 *Configuring Failover on the Secondary ASA*

```
ciscoasa(config)# failover lan unit secondary
ciscoasa(config)# failover lan interface LANfo Ethernet0/2
ciscoasa(config)# failover interface ip LANfo 192.168.200.1 255.255.255.0 standby
  192.168.200.2
ciscoasa(config)# failover key B1gs3cr3tk3y
!
ciscoasa(config)# failover group 1
ciscoasa(config-fover-group)# secondary
ciscoasa(config-fover-group)#  preempt
ciscoasa(config-fover-group)# replication http
ciscoasa(config-fover-group)# exit
ciscoasa(config)# failover group 2
ciscoasa(config-fover-group)# primary
ciscoasa(config-fover-group)# preempt
ciscoasa(config-fover-group)# replication http
ciscoasa(config-fover-group)# exit
ciscoasa(config)# failover
```

Tuning Failover Operation

When two ASA peers are configured to operate in failover mode, they use two mechanisms to determine each other's health:

- Failover timers
- Interface failure threshold

These failover mechanisms, along with other configurable options, are discussed in the following sections.

Configuring Failover Timers

By default, failover hello messages are sent between the peers at a poll time interval of 1 second. If hello messages are not received from a peer within a default hold time period of 15 seconds, that peer is declared to have failed.

In active-standby mode, you can tune the failover timers by entering the following command on the active unit. For active-active failover, the command must be entered in the system execution space.

```
ciscoasa(config)# failover polltime [unit] [msec] polltime [holdtime [msec]
  holdtime]
```

You can set the poll time from 1 to 15 seconds, or from 200 to 999 milliseconds if you add the **msec** keyword. The **unit** keyword is not necessary; it exists only to make the command easier for administrators to interpret.

You can set the hold time by adding the **holdtime** keyword. The *holdtime* value must always be set to a minimum of three times the poll time or hello interval, so that a peer will wait for three missing hellos before declaring a failure. You can set the hold time from 1 to 45 seconds, or from 800 to 999 milliseconds if you add the **msec** keyword.

The most aggressive peer monitoring policy has a unit interval of 200 milliseconds and a minimum hold time of 800 milliseconds. This allows a standby unit to detect a failure with the active unit and take over its role within 800 milliseconds, or under 1 second. However, be careful if you decide to tighten up the unit and hold time intervals for a more aggressive failure detection policy. Delayed or lost hellos on a congested LAN failover interface could be misinterpreted as a failure.

If your LAN failover traffic is carried over switches that separate the two ASA units, make sure the switches are configured to use the most efficient spanning-tree and link-negotiation features possible. Specifically, be sure to enable the Spanning Tree PortFast feature on switch interfaces that connect to the ASAs.

Failover peers also send hello messages to each other over each interface that they have in common. By default, the interface poll time is 5 seconds with a hold time of 25 seconds. You can configure interface polling with the following command in active-standby mode:

```
ciscoasa(config)# failover polltime interface [msec] polltime [holdtime holdtime]
```

In active-active failover mode, the interface timers must be configured within a failover group in the system execution space. The command syntax is slightly different, as follows:

```
ciscoasa(config)# failover group {1 | 2}
ciscoasa(config-fover-group)# polltime interface [msec] polltime [holdtime
  holdtime]
```

In ASDM, you can adjust the failover timers under the Criteria tab, as shown in the lower portion of Figure 14-24.

Configuring Failover Health Monitoring

By default, if an ASA tests and finds that at least one of its monitored interfaces has failed, it declares itself failed. In that case, if the ASA was in active mode, the other unit takes over the active role.

In active-standby mode, you can set the interface failure threshold with the following command:

```
ciscoasa(config)# failover interface-policy number[%]
```

Enter a specific number of failed interfaces as *number* or as a percentage of the total number of interfaces by adding the percent sign.

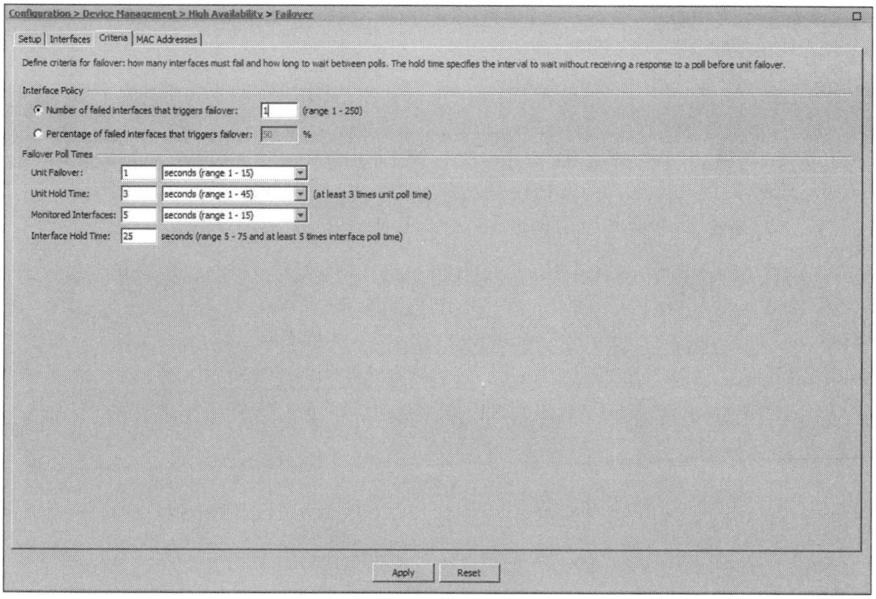

Figure 14-24 *Configuring Failover Timer and Health Criteria*

For active-active mode, you can use a similar command syntax in a failover group configuration in the system execution space. Use the following commands:

```
ciscoasa(config)# failover group {1 | 2}
ciscoasa(config-fover-group)# interface-policy number[%]
```

In ASDM, you can adjust the failover timers under the Criteria tab, as shown in the upper portion of Figure 14-23.

Detecting Asymmetric Routing

When two ASAs are configured as an active-active failover pair, traffic normally flows through one unit or the other for any given security context. After all, one unit is always active for a context while the other unit has the standby role. In some scenarios, however, two contexts might be configured to connect to the same network—effectively providing two active firewalls that can share or load balance the traffic load. The two contexts might be connected to different Internet service providers, yet connect to the same broad Internet on the outside, public network.

Although such scenarios are possible, they can be difficult to configure correctly. For example, outbound traffic can be handled by either of the two active contexts, but return traffic must come back through the same context that handled the connection originally. Otherwise, one context will build state information about the connection, while the other context will have no knowledge of it and will drop the return traffic.

This means that the upstream routers that connect the two contexts must be able to forward the return traffic to the appropriate ASA, to keep all packets belonging to the same traffic flow passing through the same firewall. This might require policy-based routing or a load-balancing function on the routers.

Sometimes, packets might exit one ASA, but the return traffic arrives on the other ASA. This is called asymmetric routing (ASR) and is shown in Figure 14-25. The ASA pair cannot prevent this from happening, but it can attempt to correct the mistake and keep related traffic flows that share the same source and destination address pairs together.

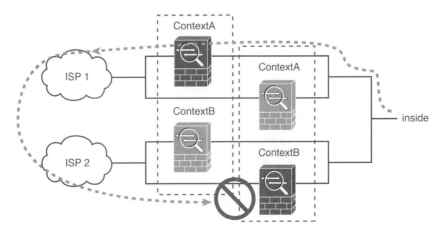

Figure 14-25 *Asymmetric Routing*

On ASA interfaces where asymmetric routing might be likely, you can configure the context interfaces into an ASR group. If a packet arrives on a grouped interface, the ASA will check for existing connection state information. If none is found, the ASA will check for other interfaces in the ASR group—even if they are located on the other active-active failover peer. If nothing is still found, the packet is dropped.

However, if connection state information is found on another interface in the group, the ASA will rewrite the Layer 2 header information and will resend the packet so that it is redirected to the correct interface, where it can be processed successfully. Packets will continue to be redirected as long as the traffic flow continues.

ASR groups require three features as prerequisites:

■ Active-active failover

■ Stateful failover between peers

■ HTTP connection replication using the **replication http** command

To configure an ASR group, you must visit a specific context and configure the appropriate interface there. Interfaces in the same ASR group should be configured with the same group number, using the following commands:

```
ciscoasa/context(config)# interface phys_interface
ciscoasa/context(config-if)# asr-group number
```

In Examples 14-8 and 14-9, the outside interfaces in contexts ContextA and ContextB are assigned to the same ASR group, respectively.

Example 14-8   *Configuring the ContextA Outside Interface for ASR Group 1*

```
ciscoasa/ContextA(config)# interface ethernet0/0
ciscoasa/ContextA(config-if)# nameif outside
ciscoasa/ContextA(config-if)# security-level 0
ciscoasa/ContextA(config-if)# ip address 209.165.201.2 255.255.255.0 standby
  209.165.201.3
ciscoasa/ContextA(config-if)# asr-group 1
```

Example 14-9   *Configuring the ContextB Outside Interface for ASR Group 1*

```
ciscoasa/ContextB(config)# interface ethernet0/0
ciscoasa/ContextB(config-if)# nameif outside
ciscoasa/ContextB(config-if)# security-level 0
ciscoasa/ContextB(config-if)# ip address 209.165.202.130 255.255.255.0 standby
  209.165.202.131
ciscoasa/ContextB(config-if)# asr-group 1
```

Administering Failover

Sometimes, you might be connected to the active failover unit and find that you need to do something on the other failover unit. Rather than opening a new connection to the other unit, you can execute a command remotely on a failover peer.

Use the following command to send a command string to the appropriate failover unit and execute it there:

```
ciscoasa# failover exec {active | standby | mate} command_string
```

You can use the **active** keyword to execute the command string on the currently active unit, the **passive** keyword to execute on the currently passive unit, or the **mate** keyword to execute the command on the mate or peer unit, regardless of its current role.

As an example, suppose you are currently connected to the active unit. You can easily use the **show version | include Serial** command to display the unit's serial number. You can use the **failover exec** command to run the same command on the failover peer remotely to get its serial number, as shown in Example 14-10.

Example 14-10   *Remotely Executing the* **show version** *Command on a Failover Peer*

```
ciscoasa# show version | include Serial
Serial Number: JMX1114L158
ciscoasa# failover exec mate show version | include Serial
Serial Number: JMX1114L14Z
ciscoasa#
```

Failover peers normally change their roles automatically, as failures are detected. In some cases, you might need to manually intervene to force a role change, so that you can take a unit out of service, upgrade the software, and so on. Use the **failover active** command to force the active role, or add the **no** keyword to force the standby role, as follows:

```
ciscoasa# [no] failover active
```

Verifying Failover Operation

Once you configure an ASA pair for failover operation, you can use the **show failover** command to verify the current status. The command output shows useful information like the failover timer values, operating system versions, the timestamp of the last failover event, the current peer roles, and the status of all monitored interfaces. Example 14-11 shows example output on an active-standby failover pair.

Example 14-11 *Sample Output of the* **show failover** *Command in Active-Standby Mode*

```
ciscoasa# show failover
Failover On
Failover unit Primary
Failover LAN Interface: LANfo Ethernet0/2 (up)
Unit Poll frequency 1 seconds, holdtime 3 seconds
Interface Poll frequency 5 seconds, holdtime 25 seconds
Interface Policy 1
Monitored Interfaces 2 of 110 maximum
failover replication http
Version: Ours 8.2(3), Mate 8.2(3)
Last Failover at: 03:25:39 UTC Apr 9 2011
        This host: Primary - Active
                Active time: 145986 (sec)
                slot 0: ASA5510 hw/sw rev (2.0/8.2(3)) status (Up Sys)
                  Interface outside (209.165.200.226): Normal
                  Interface inside (192.168.1.10): Normal
                  Interface management (192.168.5.1): Normal (Not-Monitored)
                slot 1: empty
        Other host: Secondary - Standby Ready
                Active time: 0 (sec)
                slot 0: ASA5510 hw/sw rev (2.0/8.2(3)) status (Up Sys)
                  Interface outside (209.165.200.227): Normal
                  Interface inside (192.168.1.11): Normal
                  Interface management (192.168.5.2): Normal (Not-Monitored)
                slot 1: empty

Stateful Failover Logical Update Statistics
        Link : stateful Ethernet0/3 (up)
        Stateful Obj    xmit        xerr        rcv         rerr
        General         2262311522 0            117471377  0
```

```
         sys cmd          13406589   0          13406554   0
         up time          0          0          0          0
         RPC services     18924      0          26         0
         TCP conn         1953115393 0          91774144   0
         UDP conn         200649501  0          12117485   0
         ARP tbl          95121115   0          173168     0
         Xlate_Timeout    0          0          0          0
         IPv6 ND tbl      0          0          0          0
         VPN IKE upd      0          0          0          0
         VPN IPSEC upd    0          0          0          0
         VPN CTCP upd     0          0          0          0
         VPN SDI upd      0          0          0          0
         VPN DHCP upd     0          0          0          0
         SIP Session      0          0          0          0


         Logical Update Queue Information
                          Cur    Max    Total
         Recv Q:          0      8      110944928
         Xmit Q:          0      23     108546628
ciscoasa#
```

Example 14-12 shows example output from the **show failover** command for an active-active failover pair. The output is similar to that of active-standby mode, but contains useful information about the current failover role for each failover group.

Example 14-12   *Sample Output of the* show failover *Command in Active-Active Mode*

```
ciscoasa# show failover
Failover On
Failover unit Primary
Failover LAN Interface: LANfo Ethernet0/2 (up)
Unit Poll frequency 1 seconds, holdtime 3 seconds
Interface Poll frequency 5 seconds, holdtime 25 seconds
Interface Policy 1
Monitored Interfaces 0 of 110 maximum
failover replication http
Version: Ours 8.2(3), Mate 8.2(3)
Group 1 last failover at: 02:00:24 UTC Apr 11 2011
Group 2 last failover at: 02:16:40 UTC Apr 11 2011

  This host:    Primary
  Group 1       State:        Active
                Active time:  48024 (sec)
  Group 2       State:        Standby Ready
                Active time:  626 (sec)
[output truncated for clarity]
```

```
Other host:     Secondary
  Group 1       State:          Standby Ready
                Active time:    0 (sec)
  Group 2       State:          Active
                Active time:    47401 (sec)
[output truncated for clarity]
```

Finally, you can use the **show failover history** command to display a running record of failover activity. This output can be useful if you need to see how a failover event unfolded or evidence of a chain of failure events. Example 14-13 lists some sample output.

Example 14-13 *Sample Output from the* show failover history *Command*

```
ciscoasa# show failover history
==========================================================================
Group     From State            To State              Reason
==========================================================================
02:00:24 UTC Apr 11 2011
   2      Active Config Applied  Active                No Active unit found

02:10:32 UTC Apr 11 2011
   2      Active                 Standby Ready         Other unit wants me Standby

02:16:21 UTC Apr 11 2011
   2      Standby Ready          Just Active           Set by the config command

02:16:21 UTC Apr 11 2011
   2      Just Active            Active Drain          Set by the config command

02:16:21 UTC Apr 11 2011
   2      Active Drain           Active Applying Config Set by the config command
```

Leveraging Failover for a Zero Downtime Upgrade

Upgrading the operating system on a single standalone ASA is straightforward:

Step 1.   Download a new image to the firewall.

Step 2.   Save the running configuration.

Step 3.   Reload the ASA.

Obviously, this should all be done during a scheduled maintenance time in your network, because the reload will interrupt network connectivity for a relatively long time.

A failover pair of ASAs can provide high availability even during a software upgrade by providing a "hitless upgrade" or "zero downtime upgrade." The ASAs can be upgraded one at a time, and the failover function will maintain seamless operation even while the two units are running different releases of the software image. However, a zero downtime upgrade is possible only in the following scenarios:

- Upgrade from one maintenance release to another, such as from 8.3(1) to 8.3(4)

- Upgrade from one minor release to the next minor release increment, such as from 8.2(1) to 8.3(1)

- Upgrade from the last minor release of one major release to the first minor release of the next major release, such as from 8.4(7) to 9.0(1)

You can perform a zero downtime upgrade on a failover pair that is in either the active-standby or active-active mode. Although there are six steps to remember, they are all performed from the primary or active unit.

In a nutshell, the idea is to juggle the active and standby roles so that the standby unit is always the one being upgraded. Whichever unit has the active role at any time will always have the newer, upgraded image, and will continue to forward traffic and maintain all the state information. You should carefully follow these steps for a zero downtime upgrade:

Step 1.   Download a new software image to both ASA devices.

Step 2.   Use the **boot system** command to specify the new image file, and then save the running configuration.

Step 3.   From the active unit, force the standby unit to reload by entering the **failover reload-standby** command, and then wait for it to finish booting completely.

Step 4.   Force the active unit into the standby role by entering the **no failover active** command.

Step 5.   Reload the former active unit by entering the **reload** command.

Step 6.   Restore the former active unit to the active role by entering the **failover active** command.

Key
Topic

Exam Preparation Tasks

As mentioned in the section, "How to Use This Book," in the Introduction, you have a couple of choices for exam preparation: the exercises here, Chapter 17, "Final Preparation," and the exam simulation questions on the CD-ROM.

Review All Key Topics

Review the most important topics in this chapter, noted with the Key Topic icon in the outer margin of the page. Table 14-4 lists a reference of these key topics and the page numbers on which each is found.

Key
Topic

Table 14-4   *Key Topics for Chapter 14*

Key Topic Element	Description	Page Number
List	Describes the two failover modes	675
Paragraph	Describes role swapping in active-active failover groups	677
Table 14-3	Lists stateful failover synchronization	680
List	Explains the failover election process	681
List	Describes the interface testing sequence	682
Paragraph	Discusses aggressive failover timer configurations	702
Paragraph	Describes the asymmetric routing feature	704
List	Describes the steps necessary for a zero downtime upgrade	709

Define Key Terms

Define the following key terms from this chapter and check your answers in the glossary:

active-standby failover, active-active failover, LAN failover interface, stateless failover, stateful failover, failover group, asymmetric routing, zero downtime upgrade

Command Reference to Check Your Memory

This section includes the most important configuration and EXEC commands covered in this chapter. It might not be necessary to memorize the complete syntax of every command, but you should be able to remember the basic keywords that are needed.

To test your memory of the commands, cover the right side of Tables 14-5 through 14-7 with a piece of paper, read the description on the left side, and then see how much of the command you can remember.

The FIREWALL exam focuses on practical, hands-on skills that are used by a networking professional. Therefore, you should be able to identify the commands needed to configure and test an ASA feature.

Table 14-5   *Commands Used for Active-Standby Failover Mode*

Task	Command Syntax
Identify the failover unit	ciscoasa(config)# **failover lan unit** {**primary** | **secondary**}
Configure the LAN failover link	ciscoasa(config)# **failover lan interface** *int_name* [*physical_int*]
	ciscoasa(config)# **failover interface ip** *int_name ip_address mask* **standby** *ip_address*
	ciscoasa(config)# **failover key** {*key-string* | **hex** *key*}
Enable failover operation	ciscoasa(config)# **failover**
Configure the stateful failover link	ciscoasa(config)# **failover link** *int_name* [*physical_int*]
	ciscoasa(config)# **failover interface ip** *int_name ip_address mask* **standby** *ip_address*
	ciscoasa(config)# **failover replication http**
Configure interface failover parameters	ciscoasa(config-if)# **ip address** *active_addr subnet_mask* **standby** *standby_addr*
	ciscoasa(config)# **failover mac address** *int_name active_mac standby_mac*
	ciscoasa(config)# **no monitor-interface** *int_name*

Table 14-6   *Commands Used for Active-Active Failover Mode*

Task	Command Syntax
Identify the failover device	ciscoasa(config)# **failover lan unit** {**primary** | **secondary**}
Configure the LAN failover link	ciscoasa(config)# **failover lan interface** *int_name* [*physical_int*]
	ciscoasa(config)# **failover interface ip** *int_name ip_address mask* **standby** *ip_address*
	ciscoasa(config)# **failover key** {*key-string* | **hex** *key*}
Enable failover operation	ciscoasa(config)# **failover**
Configure the failover group roles	ciscoasa(config)# **failover group** {**1** | **2**}
	ciscoasa(config-fover-group)# {**primary** | **secondary**}
	ciscoasa(config-fover-group)# [**no**] **preempt**
	ciscoasa(config-fover-group)# **exit**

Table 14-6   *Commands Used for Active-Active Failover Mode*

Task	Command Syntax
Configure the stateful failover link	ciscoasa(config)# **failover link** *int_name* [*physical_int*] ciscoasa(config)# **failover interface ip** *int_name* *ip_address mask* **standby** *ip_address*
Configure unique MAC addresses and HTTP state replication	ciscoasa(config)# **failover group** {1 | 2} ciscoasa(config)# **failover mac address** *int_name* *active_mac standby_mac* ciscoasa(config-fover-group)# **replication http** ciscoasa(config-fover-group)# **exit**
Assign contexts to a failover group	ciscoasa(config)# **context** *context-name* ciscoasa(config-ctx)# **join-failover-group** {1 | 2} ciscoasa(config-ctx)# **exit**
Configure a context interface for failover	ciscoasa/*context*(config-if)# **ip address** *active_addr subnet_mask* **standby** *standby_addr* ciscoasa/*context*(config)# [**no**] **monitor-interface** *int_name*

Table 14-7   *Commands Used to Tune Failover Operation*

Task	Command Syntax
Set the failover unit timers	ciscoasa(config)# **failover polltime** [**unit**] [**msec**] *polltime* [**holdtime** [**msec**] *holdtime*]
Set the interface timers in active-standby mode	ciscoasa(config)# **failover polltime interface** [**msec**] *polltime* [**holdtime** *holdtime*]
Set the interface timers in active-active mode	ciscoasa(config)# **failover group** {1 | 2} ciscoasa(config-fover-group)# **polltime interface** [**msec**] *polltime* [**holdtime** *holdtime*]
Set the health monitoring threshold in active-standby mode	ciscoasa(config)# **failover interface-policy** *number*[**%**]

Table 14-7   *Commands Used to Tune Failover Operation*

Task	Command Syntax
Set the health monitoring threshold in active-active mode	ciscoasa(config)# **failover group** {**1**	**2**} ciscoasa(config-fover-group)# **interface-policy** *number*[%]
Assign context interfaces to an ASR group	ciscoasa/context(config)# **interface** *phys_interface* ciscoasa/context(config-if)# **asr-group** *number*
Remotely execute a command	ciscoasa# **failover exec** {**active**	**standby**	**mate**} *command_string*
Manually change the failover role	ciscoasa# [**no**] **failover active**
Display failover status information	ciscoasa# **show failover**
Display a history of failover events	ciscoasa# **show failover history**
Display stateful failover routing information	ciscoasa# **show route failover**

This chapter covers the following topics:

- **Cisco ASA Security Services Modules Overview:** This section provides an overview of the various Security Services Modules (SSM) and Security Services Cards (SSC) available for the Cisco ASA.

- **Installing the ASA AIP-SSM and AIP-SSC:** This section describes the installation of the AIP-SSM and AIP-SSC.

- **Integrating the ASA CSC-SSM:** This section details how to install and integrate the CSC-SSM.

CHAPTER 15

Integrating ASA Service Modules

The Cisco Adaptive Security Appliance (ASA) can be extended even further to secure an organization. These additional capabilities are possible thanks to modules and cards that can be added to the modular chassis of the Cisco ASAs. To equip the device with intrusion prevention services, the ASA features support for the Advanced Inspection and Prevention Security Services Module (AIP-SSM) and the AIP Security Services Card (AIP-SSC). For content security and filtering services, the ASA can integrate with the Content Security and Control SSM (CSC-SSM).

"Do I Know This Already?" Quiz

The "Do I Know This Already?" quiz allows you to assess whether you should read this entire chapter thoroughly or jump to the "Exam Preparation Tasks" section. If you are in doubt about your answers to these questions or your own assessment of your knowledge of the topics, read the entire chapter. Table 15-1 lists the major headings in this chapter and their corresponding "Do I Know This Already?" quiz questions. You can find the answers in Appendix A, "Answers to the 'Do I Know This Already?' Quizzes."

Table 15-1 *"Do I Know This Already?" Section-to-Question Mapping*

Foundation Topics Section	Question
Cisco ASA Security Services Modules Overview	1
Module Components	2
General Deployment Guidelines	3
Cisco Content Security and Control SSM Licensing	4
Inline Operation	5
Promiscuous Operation	6
Supported Cisco IPS Software Features	7
Installing the ASA AIP-SSM and AIP-SSC	8
Integrating the ASA CSC-SSM	9

> **Caution:** The goal of self-assessment is to gauge your mastery of the topics in this chapter. If you do not know the answer to a question or are only partially sure of the answer, you should mark that question as wrong for purposes of the self-assessment. Giving yourself credit for an answer you correctly guess skews your self-assessment results and might provide you with a false sense of security.

1. Which is not a form of traffic that you can control with the Cisco CSC-SSM?

    a. HTTP

    b. IPsec

    c. SMTP

    d. FTP

2. Which device does not feature an out-of-band management port?

    a. SSM-40

    b. SSM-20

    c. SSC-5

    d. SSM-10

3. Which management software package might you use with your CSC-SSM?

    a. Trend Micro Control Manager

    b. Cisco Security MARS

    c. Cisco IME

    d. Cisco SDM

4. Which type of license for the SSM-10 allows 50 users?

    a. Standard license

    b. Optional license

    c. Extended license

    d. Base license

5. Which mode of operation for the AIP-SSM ensures that the device inspects traffic while the module participates in the actual path of data?

    a. IPS-mode

    b. Inline

    c. In-band

    d. Promiscuous

6. Which mode of operation is often used with IDS implementations?

   a. Inline

   b. In-band

   c. Promiscuous

   d. Detect-mode

7. Which of the following is a Cisco IPS Software feature supported on all of the AIP-SSMs and AIP-SSCs?

   a. Virtualization

   b. Anomaly detection

   c. Risk Rating System

   d. External management interface

8. What does a flashing green LED on your AIP-SSM indicate?

   a. The module is broken.

   b. The module is passing traffic.

   c. The module is healthy.

   d. The module is booting.

9. Which interface on the CSC-SSM is most commonly used to access the module's CLI from the CLI of the Cisco ASA?

   a. Internal data channel

   b. Out-of-band management channel

   c. Internal IOS channel

   d. Internal control channel

Foundation Topics

This chapter explores the various options for additional security services on the Cisco ASA, specifically intrusion prevention and content security services. The various Security Services Modules (SSM) and Security Services Cards (SSC) that make these additional services possible are explored in detail. The primary function of the Cisco ASA Advanced Inspection and Prevention SSM (AIP-SSM) is to protect the network from attacks and misuse. The primary function of the Cisco ASA Content Security and Control SSM (CSC-SSM) is to protect your network clients from malicious content.

Cisco ASA Security Services Modules Overview

There are many different options for adding sophisticated and efficient intrusion prevention and content security services on the Cisco ASA thanks to a wide variety of modules and cards. For intrusion prevention and, in some cases, content security services, the following modules are available:

- SSC-5
- SSM-10
- SSM-20
- SSM-40
- IPS SSP-10
- IPS SSP-20
- IPS SSP-40
- IPS SSP-60

Note: SSP stands for Security Services Processor.

For modules that support content security and control, services that are secured include secure HTTP, POP3, SMTP, and FTP traffic. The modules that can perform content security and control are the SSM-10 and SSM-20.

Module Components

One of the most exciting aspects of the modules is that they are able to offload much of the CPU- and memory-intensive features of intrusion prevention and content security onto devices that are connected to the ASA. These connected modules possess their own hardware that can be dedicated to the important security jobs. Each module boasts the following:

- A dedicated CPU for intrusion prevention or content security

- Dedicated RAM for the security services

- Dedicated flash memory and a separate file system for the software image

- Out-of-band port for management (SSMs only)

Note: The amount of dedicated resources and the specific hardware characteristics will vary from module to module.

Admittedly, the Cisco IPS SSP line of modules, while exciting, is not without its limitations. For example,

- The IPS SSP devices require the installation of the Firewall/VPN SSP.

- All traffic must flow through the firewall/VPN SSP, which must be installed in the bottom slot of your Cisco ASA. After traffic passes through this device, it can be redirected to the Cisco IPS SSP installed in the top slot.

- Cisco IPS SSP interfaces are down during resets of the module.

- Cisco IPS SSPs cannot be hot swapped. To replace the module, you must issue the **hw-module shutdown** command.

General Deployment Guidelines

Although you will need to master specific details about each SSC and SSM for the FIRE-WALL exam, there are some general deployment guidelines that you should understand. For example, you should connect to the management port of an SSM from a management network. This will allow you to configure the module using the Cisco Adaptive Security Device Manager (ASDM) or the Cisco IPS Device Manager (IDM) Software. In the case of the Cisco CSC-SSM, connecting to this management interface from the management network allows you to use the Cisco ASDM or the Trend Micro InterScan GUI.

You should also consider integrating your SSMs with management and reporting tools. You can add the CSC-SSM to the Trend Micro Control Manager. This permits you to manage multiple Trend Micro devices and monitor various activities such as security violations and virus events. You can integrate the AIP-SSM with the Cisco IPS Manager Express (IME) or with the Cisco Security Monitoring, Analysis, and Response System (MARS).

Overview of the Cisco ASA Content Security and Control SSM

This powerful module runs the popular and powerful Trend Micro InterScan for CSC-SSM software. The CSC-SSM provides protection against malware through its antivirus, antispyware, and antispam features. It performs content control by engaging in URL blocking and filtering, antiphishing, HTTP and FTP file blocking, and email content filtering. The CSC-SSM also features a management interface that is simple to use, and a system of automatic updates to ensure proper operation and the best rate of true positives.

Cisco Content Security and Control SSM Licensing

Key Topic

The SSM-10 and SSM-20 modules are options for Cisco CSC-SSM functionality. The key difference between the two modules is scalability. For example, the Base license for the SSM-10 allows 50 users, whereas the Base license for the SSM-20 allows 500 users.

There are two types of licenses for the Cisco CSC-SSM: the Base license and optional licenses. The optional licenses come in several varieties and can be used to add more features to the module or to upgrade the number of users supported. For example, the SSM-20 can use an optional upgrade license to raise the number of supported users from 500 users to 1000 users. This license is often called a Plus license.

With a Base license, users can take advantage of antivirus, antispyware, and file blocking capabilities. With a feature upgrade license, users can take advantage of antispam, e-mail content control, URL filtering, URL blocking, and antiphishing capabilities.

Overview of the Cisco ASA Advanced Inspection and Prevention SSM and SSC

These powerful modules and cards can offload the processing and memory requirements for either Intrusion Detection Systems (IDS) or Intrusion Prevention Systems (IPS). Intrusion Detection can notify an administrator that an attack against the network is taking place, whereas Intrusion Prevention can actually stop the attack. The Cisco Intrusion Prevention System (IPS) Software used in the modules and cards permits the intrusion detection or prevention to use signature-, anomaly-, and reputation-based prevention algorithms. This makes for an extremely robust and more foolproof implementation.

With the signature-based approach, network traffic is compared to a database of well-known attacks. With the anomaly-based approach, network traffic is compared to a statistical profile of normal baseline usage. Finally, with the reputation-based approach, the source of network traffic is compared to a reputation database that determines the reputation of the source of traffic. Reputation analysis is facilitated by a global correlation feature that Cisco uses. This allows the Cisco IPS device to participate in a centralized threat database called SensorBase.

Inline Operation

Key Topic

Typically, you configure the AIP-SSM or AIP-SSC in inline mode of operation. This means that the original packets that a source on the network is sending travel through the IPS device. In this configuration, the module or card is in the data forwarding path, allowing intrusion prevention to take place in the system. If a malicious packet is detected, the system can drop the packet before it is permitted to reach the intended target. After the drop, the system can alert management through various alarm configurations. Figure 15-1 illustrates this inline placement.

Figure 15-1 *Inline Mode*

Promiscuous Operation

The promiscuous mode of operation copies the packets moving through the ASA and sends them to the module or card for analysis. Under this deployment, the original packets still flow through the ASA and reach their target. This mode is used for intrusion detection as opposed to intrusion prevention. Figure 15-2 illustrates this configuration.

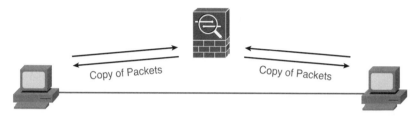

Figure 15-2   *Promiscuous Mode*

Supported Cisco IPS Software Features

The AIP-SSC-5 can support the following Cisco IPS Software features:

■   Passive operating system fingerprinting

■   Risk Rating System

■   Enhanced password recovery

The AIP-SSMs support the aforementioned features and more, including

■   Sensor virtualization

■   Cisco Global Correlation support

■   Custom signature support

■   Anomaly detection

■   External management interface

Installing the ASA AIP-SSM and AIP-SSC

This section details the steps you take to implement the various modules and cards.

Installing the Cisco ASA AIP-SSC or AIP-SSM involves completing the following steps:

Step 1.   Power down the Cisco ASA.

Step 2.   Remove the slot cover.

Step 3.   Insert the Cisco AIP-SSC or the AIP-SSM into the appropriate slot.

Step 4.   Attach the screws.

Step 5.   Power up the Cisco ASA.

Step 6.   Check the LEDs on the card for status information. The LED on the card will flash green when the card is booting and then turn solid green when the system passes its diagnostics. An amber color for the status LED indicates that there is a problem with the device's initialization process.

The Cisco AIP-SSM and AIP-SSC Ethernet Connections

The AIP-SSM features the following Ethernet connections:

■ **Internal control channel:** This Fast Ethernet interface is used to access the module CLI via the ASA CLI.

■ **Internal data channel:** This Gigabit Ethernet interface is used to redirect packets that need to be inspected by the module.

■ **Out-of-band management channel:** This Gigabit Ethernet interface is used for management access and for downloading the appropriate ASA AIP-SSM software.

The AIP-SSC features the following Ethernet connections:

■ **Internal control channel:** This Fast Ethernet interface is used for management access and downloading the AIP-SSC software.

■ **Internal data channel:** This Fast Ethernet interface is used to redirect packets that are to be inspected by the module.

Failure Management Modes

When you are deploying your AIP-SSM or your AIP-SSCs, you will need to decide on your failure mode. These modes are available in the inline and promiscuous modes of operation. In the Fail Open mode, if the card or module fails, traffic is permitted to flow through the Cisco ASA as normal. In the Fail Closed mode, traffic will no longer flow if that traffic is to be inspected by the module or card.

Managing Basic Features

To manage the modules and cards, you need to perform the following steps:

Step 1.   On the AIP-SSC only, configure a VLAN management interface.

Step 2.   Upload the Cisco IPS software to the module.

Step 3.   Administer the module.

Example 15-1 demonstrates configuring the management interface for the AIP-SSC.

Example 15-1   *Configuring the Management Interface for the AIP-SSC*

```
ASA# show run
interface vlan 1
  no allow-ssc-mgmt
!
interface vlan 5
  allow-ssc-mgmt
  ip address 192.168.1.100 255.255.255.0
```

```
  nameif inside
!
interface Ethernet 0/5
  switchport access vlan 5
  no shutdown
```

To upload the software to the module (Step 2), use the **hw-module 1 recover configure** command followed by the **hw-module 1 recover boot** command.

You can use the following commands to administer the module:

■ **hw-module module 1 password-reset:** Resets the module password to "cisco"

■ **hw-module module 1 reload:** Reloads the module software

■ **hw-module module 1 reset:** Performs a hardware reset and then reloads the module

■ **hw-module module 1 shutdown:** Shuts down the module

■ **show module 1:** Allows you to verify the module; use the **details** keyword to get even more information

Initializing the AIP-SSM and AIP-SSC

To initialize the modules or cards, you need to complete the following steps:

Step 1.   Open a CLI session to the module.

Step 2.   Configure the basic module settings with the interactive setup dialog.

Step 3.   Access the Cisco IDM to configure the Cisco IPS Software on the module.

To open the session, use the **session 1** command. The default username and password are "cisco" and "cisco." You will be prompted to change the password after your first login using the default username and password.

To run the interactive setup wizard for the initial configuration of the module or card, use the **setup** command.

Configuring the AIP-SSM and AIP-SSC

Configuration of the AIP-SSM or AIP-SSC involves three steps:

Step 1.   Create a new IPS service policy rule.

Step 2.   Identify traffic to redirect using a class map.

Step 3.   Apply IPS redirection to the identified traffic using a policy map.

This can be accomplished either in the GUI application for the module or at the command line, as follows:

```
policy-map OUTSIDE_POLICY
  class class-default
```

```
      ips inline fail-open
    !
    service-policy OUTSIDE_POLICY interface outside
```

Integrating the ASA CSC-SSM

Key Topic

This section details how to install, manage, initialize, and operate the Content Security and Control SSM with the Cisco ASA. Just like the AIP-SSM and AIP-SSC, the ASA CSC-SSM must be configured for Fail Open or Fail Closed operation.

Installing the CSC-SSM

To install the CSC-SSM, follow these steps:

Step 1. Power down the Cisco ASA.

Step 2. Remove the slot cover.

Step 3. Insert the CSC-SSM into the appropriate slot.

Step 4. Attach the screws.

Step 5. Power on the Cisco ASA.

Step 6. Check the LEDs for status.

Ethernet Connections

The CSC-SSM has the following Ethernet connections:

- **Internal control channel:** This Fast Ethernet interface is used to access the module CLI from the ASA CLI.

- **Internal data channel:** This Gigabit Ethernet interface is used to internally redirect packets that should be scanned by the module.

- **Out-of-band management channel:** This Gigabit Ethernet interface is used for management access and for downloading the CSC-SSM software and updates.

Managing the Basic Features

To upload the software to the module, use the **hw-module 1 recover configure** command followed by the **hw-module 1 recover boot** command.

You can use the following commands to administer the module:

- **hw-module module 1 password-reset:** Resets the module password to "cisco"

- **hw-module module 1 reload:** Reloads the module software

- **hw-module module 1 reset:** Performs a hardware reset and then reloads the module

- **hw-module module 1 shutdown:** Shuts down the module

- **show module 1:** Enables you to verify the module; use the **details** keyword to get even more information

Initializing the Cisco CSC-SSM

To initialize the device, follow these steps:

Step 1.   Open a CLI session to the module.

Step 2.   Configure basic settings with the Setup Wizard.

Step 3.   (Optional) Configure basic module settings using the Cisco ASDM.

Step 4.   Access the Trend Micro InterScan GUI.

To open the session, use the **session 1** command. The default username and password are "cisco" and "cisco." You will be prompted to change the password after your first login using the default username and password.

To run the interactive Setup Wizard for the initial configuration of the module or card, use the **setup** command.

After changing the password, the Trend Micro InterScan for Cisco CSC-SSM Setup Wizard. starts. Follow the onscreen prompts to complete the wizard and initialize the device.

To access the Trend Micro InterScan GUI, point your web browser to https://<*module_IP_address*>:8443.

Configuring the CSC-SSM

Configuration of the ASA CSC-SSM involves a three-step process:

Step 1.   Create a new service policy rule.

Step 2.   Identify traffic to redirect (class map).

Step 3.   Apply a CSC-SSM action to the identified traffic (policy map).

Exam Preparation Tasks

As mentioned in the section, "How to Use This Book," in the Introduction, you have a couple of choices for exam preparation: the exercises here, Chapter 17, "Final Preparation," and the exam simulation questions on the CD-ROM.

Review All Key Topics

Review the most important topics in this chapter, noted with the Key Topic icon in the outer margin of the page. Table 15-2 lists a reference of these key topics and the page numbers on which each is found.

Table 15-2   *Key Topics for Chapter 15*

Key Topic Element	Description	Page Number
Section	Provides an overview of the different modules and cards	718
Section	Describes the various options for licensing and what the options control	720
Section	Describes the inline mode of operation	720
Section	Explains how to install the AIP-SSM	721
Section	Explains how to install the CSC-SSM	724

Define Key Terms

Define the following key terms from this chapter and check your answers in the glossary:

AIP-SSM, CSC-SSM, Trend Micro InterScan GUI, Base license, optional licenses, intrusion detection, intrusion prevention, inline operation, promiscuous operation, Fail Open, Fail Closed

Command Reference to Check Your Memory

This section includes the most important configuration and EXEC commands covered in this chapter. It might not be necessary to memorize the complete syntax of every command, but you should be able to remember the basic keywords that are needed.

To test your memory of the commands, cover the right side of Table 15-3 with a piece of paper, read the description on the left side, and then see how much of the command you can remember.

The FIREWALL exam focuses on practical, hands-on skills that are used by a networking professional. Therefore, you should be able to identify the commands needed to configure and test an ASA feature.

Table 15-3   *Commands Related to Installing and Integrating SSMs*

Task	Command Syntax
Configure the management interface	ciscoasa(config-if)# **allow-ssc-mgmt**
Load a recovery image for the SSM from a TFTP server; initiate the image	ciscoasa# **hw-module module 1 recover {boot | stop | configure [**url *tfp_url* | **ip** *port_ip_address* | **gateway** *gateway_ip_address* | **vlan** *vlan_id*]}
Reset the password	ciscoasa# **hw-module 1 password-reset**
Reload the software	ciscoasa# **hw-module 1 reload**
Perform a hardware reset	ciscoasa# **hw-module 1 reset**
Perform a shutdown	ciscoasa# **hw-module 1 shutdown**
Verify the module	ciscoasa# **show module 1 [detail]**

This chapter covers the following topics:

- **Testing Network Connectivity:** This section covers the **ping** and **traceroute** commands, which you can use to test connectivity and reachability.

- **Using Packet Tracer:** This section covers a method to trace virtual packets through a Cisco ASA to verify which actions will be taken by a variety of security features.

- **Using Packet Capture:** This section explains how you can capture actual packets as they pass through ASA interfaces.

CHAPTER 16

Traffic Analysis Tools

Sometimes, you might want to verify connectivity from an ASA to some other device or how an ASA and its security features will behave when certain packets arrive. You might also want to know what sort of traffic has passed through an ASA to reach a certain host or why packets are not being forwarded through the ASA. The ASA offers the following traffic analysis tools that you can use:

- **Ping:** A test is sent from an ASA interface toward a destination, as a test to see whether the destination is reachable and will send a reply.

- **Traceroute:** A packet is sent from an ASA interface toward a destination, in an effort to discover each router hop along the path.

- **Packet Tracer:** A simulated packet is sent through the ASA security features, as a test to see whether the packet will be forwarded or not.

- **Packet Capture:** Packets passing through an interface and matching given conditions are captured in a buffer and can be displayed later.

Most likely, these tools will be covered in the CCNP FIREWALL exam, so you should be familiar with their functions and use.

"Do I Know This Already?" Quiz

The "Do I Know This Already?" quiz allows you to assess whether you should read this entire chapter thoroughly or jump to the "Exam Preparation Tasks" section. If you are in doubt about your answers to these questions or your own assessment of your knowledge of the topics, read the entire chapter. Table 16-1 lists the major headings in this chapter and their corresponding "Do I Know This Already?" quiz questions. You can find the answers in Appendix A, "Answers to the 'Do I Know This Already?' Quizzes."

Table 16-1 *"Do I Know This Already?" Section-to-Question Mapping*

Foundation Topics Section	Questions
Testing Network Connectivity	1–2
Using Packet Tracer	3–7
Using Packet Capture	8–12

1. Which ASA command can be used as a test to verify that a host is reachable via ICMP and TCP from an ASA interface? (Choose one.)

    a.   ping

    b.   traceroute

    c.   test

    d.   icmp permit

    e.   tcp permit

2. By default, what protocol does an ASA use in its traceroute probe packets? (Choose one answer.)

    a.   ICMP echo request

    b.   ICMP echo reply

    c.   UDP port 65535

    d.   UDP port 33434

    e.   UDP port 171

3. Which one of the following is the most correct statement about the Packet Tracer ASA feature?

    a.   Packet Tracer displays packets that are received on an ASA interface.

    b.   Packet Tracer uses traceroute packets to trace a path through the network.

    c.   Packet Tracer uses a virtual packet to trace the path through the ASA functions.

    d.   Packet Tracer injects real packets into the protected network.

4. Which one of the following describes the type of traffic that can be tested with Packet Tracer?

    a.   An HTTP connection between two hosts

    b.   Only ICMP echo (ping) packets

    c.   A stream of RTP packets

    d.   A single virtual packet

5. Which of the following represent ASA functions that can be tested with Packet Tracer? (Choose all that apply.)

   a. Routing table lookup

   b. Network address translation entries

   c. Host connection limits

   d. Access list results

   e. All of these answers are correct.

6. Which of the following packet parameters can be configured with Packet Tracer? (Choose all that apply.)

   a. Number of packets to send

   b. Protocol

   c. Source IP address and port number

   d. Destination IP address and port number

   e. QoS information (IP ToS and DSCP)

7. How does an ASA determine which interface to use when a virtual packet is injected as part of a Packet Tracer test?

   a. It uses the source IP address found in the virtual packet.

   b. It performs a reverse path forwarding (RPF) lookup.

   c. You must specify the ingress interface.

   d. The virtual packet is injected into all configured and connected interfaces.

8. Suppose the following command is entered to perform a packet capture:

```
ciscoasa# capture data
```

Which of the following answers correctly describes the data that will be captured?

   a. All packets moving through all active interfaces.

   b. No packets; an access list has not yet been defined.

   c. No packets; an interface has not been specified.

   d. Only packets entering an interface.

9. Suppose the following commands have been entered on an ASA:

```
ciscoasa(config)# access-list MYACL extended permit ip any host 192.168.3.4
ciscoasa# capture MYDATA access-list MYACL interface outside
```

Which of the following correctly describes the resulting actions?

   a. Only packets destined for inside host 192.168.3.4 will be captured on the outside interface.

   b. Only packets destined for outside host 192.168.3.4 will be captured on the outside interface.

   c. Only packets destined for host 192.168.3.4 will be captured and forwarded; the implicit "deny" statement in the access list will drop all other packets, preventing them from being forwarded.

   d. No packets will be captured because the access list has not been applied to the ASA interface.

10. By default, how many bytes of data can a capture buffer contain?

   a. An unlimited number

   b. 128 KB

   c. 512 KB

   d. 1 MB

11. Suppose a capture session named MYCAPTURE has been configured to capture packets on the outside interface. Which one of the following commands should you use to stop the running capture so that you can view the buffer contents?

   a. `ciscoasa# clear capture MYCAPTURE`

   b. `ciscoasa# no capture MYCAPTURE`

   c. `ciscoasa# capture MYCAPTURE pause`

   d. `ciscoasa# no capture MYCAPTURE interface outside`

12. Which of the following answers best describes the purpose of the following command:

`ciscoasa# capture outside type asp-drop shunned`

   a. You want to capture and shun packets on the outside interface.

   b. You want to capture packets that have been shunned, regardless of the interface.

   c. You want to capture packets that have been shunned only on the outside interface.

   d. You want to capture packets in a capture buffer in the asp-drop format.

Foundation Topics

After you have configured an ASA to become part of a network, you might need to do some simple testing to verify that it can reach other devices successfully. Once you have configured it to protect a network with security policies, it isn't always easy to verify that the policies have been configured correctly. For example, you might read through the modular policy framework (MPF) and access list configurations and mentally work through the operations. If the configuration is complex, you might miss something. You might also depend on users to report connections getting dropped or applications not working.

You might also need to gain some visibility into the traffic that is coming into or going out of an ASA interface. Without a dedicated external network analyzer or "sniffer," how can you view and verify packets that arrive or leave the ASA?

This chapter discusses each of these topics in detail and presents ASA features that you can use to validate how traffic will be handled and view traffic in motion.

Testing Network Connectivity

When you have connected and configured ASA interfaces and the necessary IP routing information, you might want to verify that the ASA can reach other parts of the network. You can use the **ping** command to send test packets from the ASA toward a destination to make sure that the destination is reachable. The destination might be something as simple as the next-hop router, which would verify that the ASA can reach devices on its local subnet. You might also test destinations further away, to see if the intervening network path is up and functioning.

To start a ping test, use the following command syntax:

ciscoasa# **ping** [*if_name*] *destination* [**data** *pattern*] [**repeat** *count*] [**size** *bytes*] [**timeout** *seconds*] [**validate**]

At the least, you can specify only the destination IP address or hostname. If you do not specify an interface name, the ASA will use a route lookup to determine which of its interfaces will source the ping packets. Example 16-1 shows the results of two ping commands with minimal arguments. The first command is successful, where an exclamation mark denotes each successful reply. The second command is not; each ping packet was not returned from the destination, as denoted by question marks.

Example 16-1 *Using the* **ping** *Command to Test Reachability*

```
ciscoasa# ping 209.165.200.225
Type escape sequence to abort.
Sending 5, 100-byte ICMP Echos to 209.165.200.225, timeout is 2 seconds:
!!!!!
Success rate is 100 percent (5/5), round-trip min/avg/max = 1/1/1 ms
ciscoasa#
```

```
ciscoasa# ping 209.165.200.228
Type escape sequence to abort.
Sending 5, 100-byte ICMP Echos to 209.165.200.228, timeout is 2 seconds:
?????
Success rate is 0 percent (0/5)
ciscoasa#
```

You can also use the **data** keyword to specify a 16-bit hexadecimal data pattern to be sent in the ICMP packet payload, the **repeat** keyword to specify the number of ICMP packets to send (default 5), the **size** keyword to specify the packet size (default 64 bytes), the **timeout** keyword to set the number of seconds to wait for each ICMP packet to be returned (default 2 seconds), and the **validate** keyword to validate each reply packet that is received.

If you use the **ping** command without any other arguments, the ASA will prompt for each one, as shown in Example 16-2. Default values are shown within square brackets. You can type the Enter key to accept a default.

Example 16-2   *Using the* **ping** *Command Alone to Prompt for Arguments*

```
ciscoasa# ping
Interface: outside
Target IP address: 209.165.200.225
Repeat count: [5]
Datagram size: [100]
Timeout in seconds: [2]
Extended commands [n]: y
Verbose? [no]:
Validate reply data? [no]:
Data pattern [0xabcd]:
Sweep range of sizes [n]:
Type escape sequence to abort.
Sending 5, 100-byte ICMP Echos to 209.165.200.225, timeout is 2 seconds:
!!!!!
Success rate is 100 percent (5/5), round-trip min/avg/max = 1/1/1 ms
ciscoasa#
```

By default, an ASA will permit any inbound ICMP packets to terminate on and be answered by any of its interfaces. For example, a host on a public network could successfully ping the ASA's outside interface to determine that the ASA is alive or that it exists. You can use the **icmp** command to control what ICMP traffic is allowed to reach an ASA interface. You can specify the source IP address and mask, an optional ICMP Type field, and the ASA interface name where ICMP packets are received, as follows:

```
ciscoasa(config)# icmp {permit | deny} ip_address mask [icmp_type] if_name
```

The *icmp_type* field can be one of the following keywords or numeric values: **echo-reply** (0), **unreachable** (3), **echo** (8), **time-exceeded** (11).

Suppose you want to prevent hosts from being able to ping the ASA itself on its outside interface. You could use the following command to keep the ASA from responding to pings:

ciscoasa(config)# **icmp deny any outside**

Even though it might be tempting to deny all inbound ICMP traffic, you might also be blocking some ICMP packet types that are necessary for networking functions. For example, ICMP unreachable (type 3) packets are used by the Path MTU Discovery function to determine what MTU size can be used along a network path for a VPN connection. You could permit ICMP unreachables and deny all other types with the following commands:

ciscoasa(config)# **icmp permit any unreachable outside**

ciscoasa(config)# **icmp deny any outside**

Beginning with ASA release 8.4(1), you can leverage the **ping tcp** command to test TCP reachability. The ASA will attempt to open a new TCP connection by sending a TCP SYN to the destination host. If the destination is reachable and agreeable, it will reply with a SYN. At that point, the ASA will send a TCP RST to reset the connection and repeat the process if further repeats are necessary.

Use the following command syntax:

ciscoasa# **ping tcp** [*if_name*] *destination* [*port*]] [**repeat** *count*] [**source** *address port*] [**timeout** *seconds*]

You can specify the source ASA interface, the destination, the destination TCP port, the repeat count, a source address and TCP port, and a timeout value. In Example 16-3, the ASA is testing TCP reachability to destination 209.165.201.199 at TCP port 25.

Example 16-3   *Using the* **ping tcp** *Command to Test TCP Reachability*

```
ciscoasa# ping tcp outside 209.165.201.199 25
Type escape sequence to abort.
No source specified. Pinging from identity interface.
Sending 5 TCP SYN requests to 209.165.201.199 port 25
from 209.165.200.227, timeout is 2 seconds:
!!!!!
Success rate is 100 percent (5/5), round-trip min/avg/max = 1/1/1 ms
ciscoasa#
```

Ping tests can show whether a destination is reachable or not, but they don't provide any information about the path that the test packets took to reach the destination. You can use the **traceroute** command to test the path from the ASA to the destination, on a hop-by-hop basis.

736 CCNP Security FIREWALL 642-618 Official Cert Guide

Traceroute sends a sequence of probe packets toward the destination. The first probe has its time-to-live (TTL) set to one; at the first router hop, the TTL is decremented and expires, so that router returns an ICMP time-exceeded packet to the ASA. The ASA increments the TTL value in each successive probe packet so that routers located at increments along the path will make themselves known too. In this way, the ASA is able to trace the path toward the destination one hop at a time.

The **traceroute** command has the following syntax:

```
ciscoasa# traceroute destination [port number] [numeric] [probe probe_num] [source
    source] [timeout seconds] [ttl ttl_min ttl_max] [use-icmp]
```

By default, probe packets are sent using UDP port 33434. You can use the **port** keyword to use a different UDP port instead, or you can use the **use-icmp** keyword to send ICMP echo request packets. You can also specify a source, and the timeout period that the ASA will wait for each probe to be answered. As each probe is answered, the ASA will attempt to resolve the name of the router through a DNS lookup, unless you specify the **numeric** keyword to display IP addresses only.

By default, the ASA will begin with a TTL value of one and will keep incrementing indefinitely. You can use the **ttl** keyword to specify the minimum and maximum TTL limits. The ASA will send three probes at each TTL increment by default. You can use the **probe** keyword to change the number of probes.

Example 16-4 shows a traceroute to destination 72.247.200.170. Two router hops have been discovered; beyond that point, the probe packets have been dropped. Undiscovered router hops are displayed with an asterisk.

Example 16-4 *Using the* traceroute *Command to Discover a Network Path*

```
ciscoasa# traceroute 72.247.200.170 numeric
Type escape sequence to abort.
Tracing the route to 72.247.200.170
 1   209.165.200.225 0 msec 0 msec 0 msec
 2   192.168.254.6 0 msec 0 msec 0 msec
 3   *  *  *
 4   *  *     [Ctrl-c typed here]
ciscoasa#
```

Note: You can interrupt lengthy ping or traceroute processes on an ASA by entering an escape sequence of Ctrl-c.

Using Packet Tracer

After you have configured a variety of security features on an ASA, you might have a difficult time verifying that packets can move successfully from one interface to another. You might also want to verify that a specific security feature will block certain types of traffic.

You can use the Packet Tracer feature to verify many of the ASA security mechanisms, in the order that they are encountered as a packet moves from one ASA interface to another. A typical series of security features tested might look like the following:

- **Flow lookup:** Checks for existing xlate and conn entries

- **UN-NAT:** Checks for address translation entries

- **Access list lookup:** Checks for any applicable ACL entries

- **IP options lookup:** Checks handling of IP options in the ingress packet

- **NAT:** Checks the Reverse Path Forwarding (RPF) information

- **NAT:** Checks for host connection limits

- **IP options lookup:** Checks handling of IP options in egress packet

- **Flow creation:** Creates new xlate and conn entries, if needed

- **Route lookup:** Checks for a route to the destination address

The exact list of security features tested depends on the current ASA configuration. First, Packet Tracer takes a look at the running configuration to build the list of features, and then it carries out its tests on each feature. Packet Tracer doesn't include tests from any of the ASA's application inspection engines because only a single packet is used for the end-to-end test.

Packet Tracer uses a virtual or synthetic packet that is injected into the data stream on an ingress interface. The virtual packet is passed through each of the ASA functions, as if a real packet were being handled. This means that you will even see actual syslog information being generated on the ASA as the trace progresses. The ASA will remove the virtual packet once it is queued in the egress interface buffer for transmission so that it never appears on the network.

You can define many parameters about the virtual packet so that it will represent a typical real packet that might be encountered on the network.

You can use Packet Tracer from Cisco Adaptive Security Device Manager (ASDM) by selecting **Tools > Packet Tracer**. A new Packet Tracer window will appear, containing a string of symbols representing each ASA function that will be tested. Enter the following information to define the test packet:

- Choose the ingress interface, where the packet will enter the firewall; at the upper-left corner of the window, select an interface name from the drop-down menu.

- Select the Packet Type, either TCP, UDP, ICMP, or IP, from the list across the top of the window.

- Enter the Source IP Address and Source Port.

- Enter the Destination IP Address and Destination Port.

Click the **Start** button. Packet Tracer will animate a packet as it moves from function to function. When the trace is complete, the results will be shown in the bottom half of the window. Be aware that the animation causes the step-by-step progression to appear rather slowly. You can speed up the trace by unchecking the **Show Animation** check box.

As an example, suppose you have configured an ASA to permit HTTPS traffic from the public Internet to reach inside host 192.168.1.199, but all other traffic should be denied. Figure 16-1 shows the results of an HTTPS test packet that has passed each test, designated by green check marks in the Action column next to each successful phase.

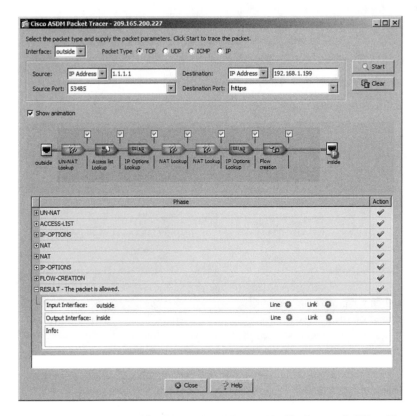

Figure 16-1   *Using Packet Tracer in ASDM to Verify Successful Handling of a Packet*

Figure 16-1 also shows that you can expand RESULT to see the ingress and egress interfaces, indicating that the packet is able to enter and exit the ASA. The outcome of each phase is shown in a collapsed list. You can click the plus sign next to any phase to see more detailed information about the test.

If the trace is not successful and the packet is dropped, you will see a red X symbol next to the phase that failed or denied the packet. As an example, Figure 16-2 shows the results of a Packet Tracer test using an HTTP packet. The access list has denied and dropped the HTTP packet, so a red X is shown next to the ACCESS-LIST test phase, as well as above the inside interface icon in the animation.

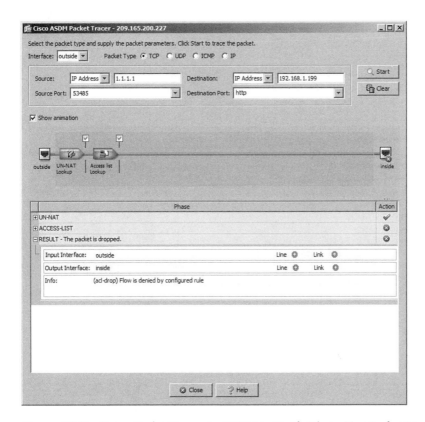

Figure 16-2   *Using Packet Tracer in ASDM to Verify That a Test Packet Has Been Dropped*

You can also use Packet Tracer from the command-line interface (CLI) by entering the following command:

```
ciscoasa# packet-tracer input src_interface protocol src_addr src_port dest_addr
   dest_port [detailed] [xml]
```

You can add the **detailed** keyword to display more detailed information about packets that are dropped. By adding the **xml** keyword, the ASA will provide the Packet Tracer output in XML format.

Example 16-5 shows the command used to test with an HTTPS packet, while Example 16-6 shows the results of an HTTP packet test. Each phase of the Packet Tracer output represents one security feature or mechanism that is being tested. These examples show the same packet tests used in the ASDM Packet Tracer shown in Figures 16-1 and 16-2, respectively.

Example 16-5 *Using Packet Tracer to Test ASA Rules for an Inbound HTTPS Packet*

```
ciscoasa# packet-tracer input outside tcp 1.1.1.1 53485 192.168.1.199 https
Phase: 1
Type: UN-NAT
Subtype: static
Result: ALLOW
Config:
static (inside,outside) 192.168.1.199 192.168.1.199 netmask 255.255.255.255
  match ip inside host 192.168.1.199 outside any
    static translation to 192.168.1.199
    translate_hits = 0, untranslate_hits = 5
Additional Information:
NAT divert to egress interface inside
Untranslate 192.168.1.199/0 to 192.168.1.199/0 using netmask 255.255.255.255


Phase: 2
Type: ACCESS-LIST
Subtype: log
Result: ALLOW
Config:
access-group OUTSIDE in interface outside
access-list OUTSIDE extended permit tcp any host 192.168.1.199 eq https
Additional Information:


Phase: 3
Type: IP-OPTIONS
Subtype:
Result: ALLOW
Config:
Additional Information:


Phase: 4
Type: NAT
Subtype: rpf-check
Result: ALLOW
Config:
static (inside,outside) 192.168.1.199 192.168.1.199 netmask 255.255.255.255
  match ip inside host 192.168.1.199 outside any
    static translation to 192.168.1.199
    translate_hits = 0, untranslate_hits = 5
Additional Information:


Phase: 5
Type: NAT
Subtype: host-limits
```

```
Result: ALLOW
Config:
static (inside,outside) 192.168.1.199 192.168.1.199 netmask 255.255.255.255
  match ip inside host 192.168.1.199 outside any
    static translation to 192.168.1.199
    translate_hits = 0, untranslate_hits = 5
Additional Information:

Phase: 6
Type: IP-OPTIONS
Subtype:
Result: ALLOW
Config:
Additional Information:

Phase: 7
Type: FLOW-CREATION
Subtype:
Result: ALLOW
Config:
Additional Information:
New flow created with id 48, packet dispatched to next module

Result:
input-interface: outside
input-status: up
input-line-status: up
output-interface: inside
output-status: up
output-line-status: up
Action: allow

ciscoasa#
```

Example 16-6 *Using Packet Tracer to Test ASA Rules for an Inbound HTTP Packet*

```
ciscoasa# packet-tracer input outside tcp 1.1.1.1 53485 192.168.1.199 http
Phase: 1
Type: UN-NAT
Subtype: static
Result: ALLOW
Config:
static (inside,outside) 192.168.1.199 192.168.1.199 netmask 255.255.255.255
  match ip inside host 192.168.1.199 outside any
```

```
         static translation to 192.168.1.199
         translate_hits = 0, untranslate_hits = 9
Additional Information:
NAT divert to egress interface inside
Untranslate 192.168.1.199/0 to 192.168.1.199/0 using netmask 255.255.255.255

Phase: 2
Type: ACCESS-LIST
Subtype:
Result: DROP
Config:
Implicit Rule
Additional Information:

Result:
input-interface: outside
input-status: up
input-line-status: up
output-interface: inside
output-status: up
output-line-status: up
Action: drop
Drop-reason: (acl-drop) Flow is denied by configured rule

ciscoasa#
```

Using Packet Capture

To gain visibility into the traffic that is entering or exiting an ASA, you could use an external network protocol analyzer or packet sniffer—provided that it is connected to a network switch that can mirror traffic to it. A more convenient approach is to use the packet capture feature that is integrated into the ASA.

You can use the packet capture feature to collect a copy of packets as they enter and exit ASA interfaces. You can define one or more capture sessions on an ASA, each operating independently. Captured packets are stored in a memory buffer and can be viewed much like a protocol analyzer or sniffer trace. You can also copy the buffer contents onto an external device for viewing and analysis.

Using the Packet Capture Wizard in ASDM

You can also set up a packet capture in ASDM by using the Packet Capture Wizard. The wizard configures capture sessions that are identical to the **capture** command in the CLI, except that a GUI front end is used instead.

The Packet Capture Wizard sets up two separate capture sessions: one on an ingress interface and one on an egress interface. Each session captures traffic in both directions, collecting packets as they enter and exit the ASA.

To use the ASDM Packet Capture Wizard, choose **Wizards > Packet Capture Wizard**. A window describing the five steps of the wizard will appear, as shown in Figure 16-3. Click the **Next** button.

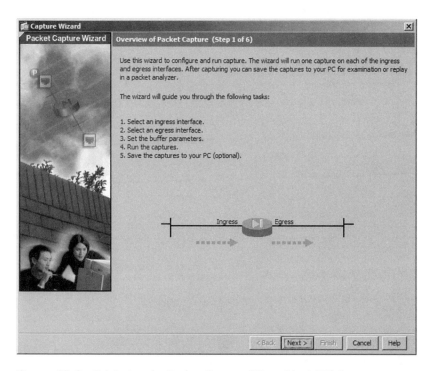

Figure 16-3 *Initiating the Packet Capture Wizard in ASDM*

Enter the ingress interface traffic information, as shown in Figure 16-4. This includes the ingress interface (inside in the example), source and destination addresses and subnet masks, and the protocol. In the example, all IP traffic will be captured. Click the **Next** button.

Enter the egress interface traffic information, as shown in Figure 16-5. This includes the egress interface (outside in the example) and the source and destination addresses and subnet masks. In the example, all IP traffic will be captured. Click the **Next** button.

Enter the capture buffer parameters, as shown in Figure 16-6. The maximum packet size (1522 in the example) and capture buffer size (524,288 bytes in the example) are given here. Check the **Use Circular Buffer** check box if you want the capture to use a circular buffer. By default, the capture will stop when the buffer is full. By default, you will manually tell the Packet Capture Wizard when to collect the capture buffer contents. Otherwise, you can check the **Get Capture Every 10 Seconds** check box to automatically fetch the buffers at regular intervals. Click the **Next** button to continue.

A summary window will display, as shown in Figure 16-7. The summary shows all the CLI commands that ASDM will add to the ASA configuration to build the two packet capture sessions. Click the **Next** button to continue.

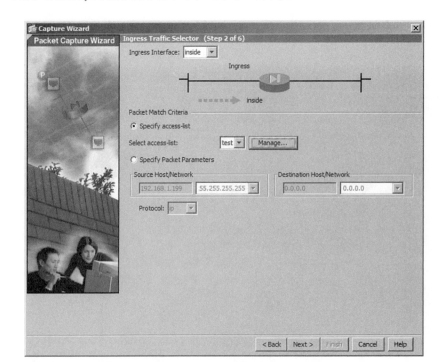

Figure 16-4   *Configuring the Ingress Interface Capture Session*

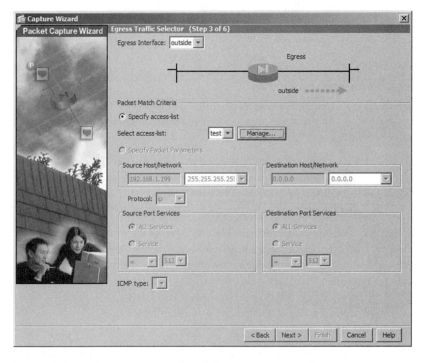

Figure 16-5   *Configuring the Egress Interface Capture Session*

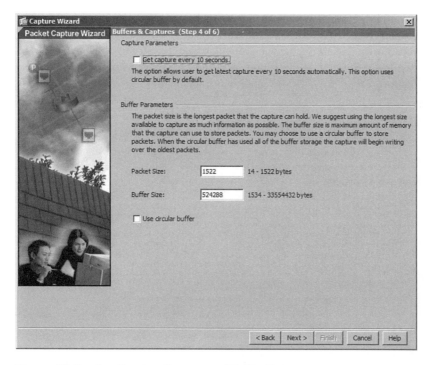

Figure 16-6 *Configuring Capture and Buffer Parameters*

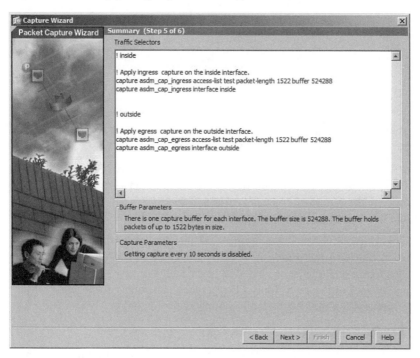

Figure 16-7 *Reviewing the Capture Session Commands*

Start the captures by clicking the **Start** button. If you have configured the capture to fetch the buffer contents every 10 seconds, packet headers will be shown in the Run Captures window automatically. Otherwise, the window will remain mostly empty while the capture is running; to see the capture buffer contents, click the **Get Capture Buffer** button, as shown in Figure 16-8.

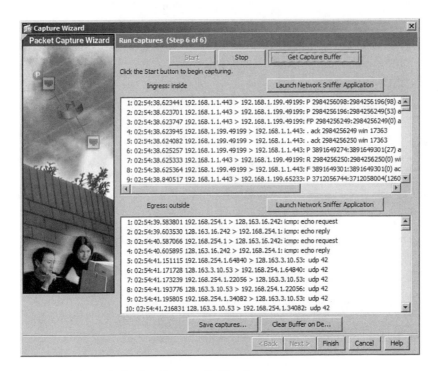

Figure 16-8 *Displaying Capture Buffer Contents*

The capture buffer for the ingress interface capture session is shown in the topmost box, while the egress interface session is shown in the bottom box.

You can save the capture buffers on your local PC by clicking the **Save Captures** button. Select **ASCII** to save the capture in plaintext, or **PCAP** to save it in a standard format that a network analyzer like Wireshark or OmniPeek can decode. Click **Save Ingress Capture** or **Save Egress Capture** to begin saving the capture buffer to a file on your local machine.

You can also load the capture directly into a network analyzer application by clicking the **Launch Network Sniffer Application** button. You should have a PCAP-compliant network analyzer application installed on your local machine. If you have problems getting ASDM to find the application, go to **Tools > Preferences**, and choose the location of the application's startup file in the Network Sniffer Application box.

Capturing Packets from the CLI

While ASDM presents a streamlined approach to configuring a packet capture, you can use the CLI instead for more versatile control.

Key
Topic

Begin by defining an access list that will be used to identify the traffic to be captured. You can set up a capture session that doesn't use an access list at all, but it will capture all traffic passing through. The access list is used to flag packets for capture—not to permit or deny them from passing through the interface. Therefore, only the **permit** keyword is useful here. An implicit deny statement is at the end of the access list, which causes all other traffic to pass without being captured.

If you need to specify IP addresses or port numbers, you should use values that are relevant to any NAT or PAT configured on the ASA. For example, a capture session can monitor inbound traffic on an interface before NAT is performed, and it can monitor outbound traffic after NAT is performed.

Next, use the following command to define a capture session:

```
ciscoasa# capture session_name [interface {int_name | asa_dataplane | cplane}
  [parameters]
```

By default, all packets moving through all ASA interfaces are captured. You should try to narrow the scope of the captured packets as much as possible so that only packets of interest are captured. You can specify the ASA interface name where the capture should take place.

If you need to capture packets that are passing internally between the ASA and an integrated security module, you can use the **asa_dataplane** keyword to capture data packets or the **cplane** keyword to capture control plane packets, respectively.

You can specify additional parameters, as listed in Table 16-2, to make the capture session more specific.

Table 16-2   *Capture Session Parameters for the* **capture session_name** *Command*

Parameter	Description
access-list *acl*	Use an access list to identify packets to capture
buffer *bytes*	Size of the capture buffer; defaults to 512K bytes
circular-buffer	Capture continuously in a circular packet buffer; default is to stop once the buffer fills
ethernet-type {**802.1Q**	*type*	**arp**	**ip**	**ip6**	**ipx**	**ppoed**	**ppoes**	**rarp**	**vlan**}	Capture a specific EtherType; default is **ip**
headers-only	Capture L2/L3/L4 packet headers only, without any payload; default is complete packet
match *5-tuple-1* [**match** *5-tuple-2*] [**match** *5-tuple-3*]	Capture packets matching the 5-tuple consisting of: *protocol source src-port destination dest-port*
packet-length *length*	Capture a maximum number of bytes per packet; default is 1518 bytes

Table 16-2   *Capture Session Parameters for the* **capture session_name** *Command*

Parameter	Description
real-time	Display packets as they are captured, rather than collecting them into a memory buffer
type {raw-data | tls-proxy}	Set the capture type; default is **raw-data**, or regular packets as they move in and out of interfaces

As an example, suppose you want to capture all packets that involve HTTPS connections with inside host 192.168.1.199, as they are seen on the outside ASA interface. Example 16-7 shows the configuration commands that can be used to define the capture access list and to define the capture session. Notice that the access list has two parts: one line permits HTTPS packets destined toward the server, and another line permits HTTPS packets coming from the server. In this way, the ASA will capture bidirectional traffic at the outside interface.

Example 16-7   *Commands Used to Configure a Capture Session*

```
ciscoasa(config)# access-list CAPTURE1 extended permit tcp any host 192.168.1.199
  eq https
ciscoasa(config)# access-list CAPTURE1 extended permit tcp host 192.168.1.199 eq
  https any
ciscoasa(config)# exit
ciscoasa# capture example access-list CAPTURE1 interface outside
```

In some situations, you might want to define several capture sessions. For example, you might want to use one capture session to capture packets on the outside interface, and use another capture session to capture packets on the inside interface. You can also assign multiple capture sessions to the same interface, each capturing a different subnet of traffic. Each capture session is independent and captures its own data in a separate capture buffer.

After you have defined a capture session, you need to monitor it for activity and retrieve the captured data. If you have defined several capture sessions, you might have trouble remembering which one is performing a certain function. You can list the current capture sessions with the **show capture** command. In Example 16-8, the ASA has three capture sessions defined: two bound to the outside interface and one bound to the inside interface.

Example 16-8   *Displaying Capture Sessions*

```
ciscoasa# show capture
capture example type raw-data access-list CAPTURE1 interface outside  [Capturing -
  229170 bytes]
capture cap-out type raw-data access-list CAPTURE2 interface outside [Capturing -
  8721 bytes]
capture cap-in type raw-data interface inside [Buffer Full - 524080 bytes]
ciscoasa#
```

You can display the contents of a capture session buffer at any time, even if the capture is still active. To view the buffer contents from the CLI, you can use the following command:

```
ciscoasa# show capture session_name [access-list acl_name] {detail |dump |decode}
   [packet-number packet] [count count]
```

A summary of each packet saved in the capture buffer named *session_name* is displayed, even though the capture session is still active. You can add the **access-list** keyword to use an ACL (defined ahead of time) as a display filter. Only packets that are permitted by the display filter access list are displayed.

By default, the **decode** keyword is assumed, displaying packets in an abbreviated form. Example 16-9 lists some of the packet contents from the capture session defined in Example 16-7.

Example 16-9   *Displaying the Contents of a Packet Capture Session*

```
ciscoasa# show capture example
1003 packets captured
   1: 17:55:51.562150 192.168.1.199.443 > 10.4.1.2.35074: R
1521662497:1521662497(0) ack 2531877694 win 6422
   2: 17:55:52.047665 10.4.1.2.35114 > 192.168.1.199.443: F
3066883736:3066883736(0) ack 1904075855 win 64051
   3: 17:55:52.048520 10.4.1.2.35563 > 192.168.1.199.443: S
2049110290:2049110290(0) win 64512 <mss 1350,nop,nop,sackOK>
   4: 17:55:52.051678 192.168.1.199.443 > 10.4.1.2.35114: . ack 3066883737 win 5123
   5: 17:55:52.051846 192.168.1.199.443 > 10.4.1.2.35563: S 142125136:142125136(0)
ack 2049110291 win 3900 <mss 1300,sackOK,eol>
   6: 17:55:52.052029 192.168.1.199.443 > 10.4.1.2.35114: F
1904075855:1904075855(0) ack 3066883737 win 5123
```

If the capture buffer is large, you can display only a subset of captured packets. Add the **packet-number** keyword to specify the first packet number to display, and the **count** keyword to specify the number of packets to display.

The **show capture** command can display packet contents in several formats, depending on which keyword is given. Table 16-3 lists the possible keywords, output formats, and corresponding examples in Figure 16-9.

Key Topic

Table 16-3   show capture *Keywords and Output Formats*

Keyword	Packet Contents Displayed	Shown in Figure 16-9
decode	Headers in an abbreviated format; the default	Top
detail	Headers along with the source and destination MAC addresses and various IP and TCP fields	Middle
dump	Headers and payload contents	Bottom

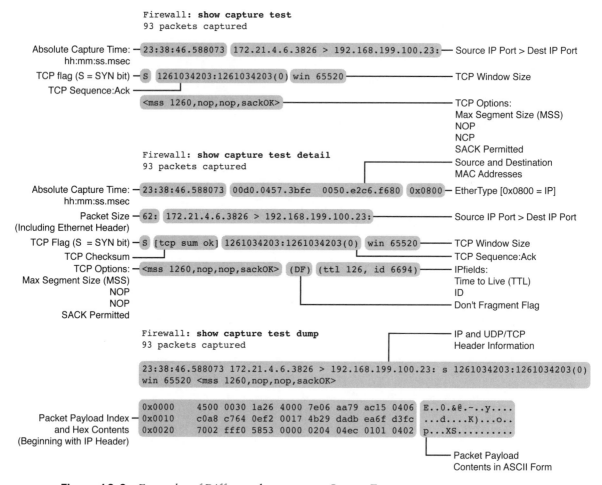

Figure 16-9   *Examples of Different* **show capture** *Output Formats*

Controlling a Capture Session

After a capture session is defined and activated, you might need to stop it as soon as some interesting data is captured. You might also want to clear the buffer so that new data can be captured in an empty buffer. When you are finished with a capture session, you need to delete it.

You can use the commands listed in Table 16-4 to control an existing capture session.

Table 16-4   *Commands to Control a Data Capture Session*

Command	Description
ciscoasa# **clear capture** *capture_name*	Empties the capture buffer and retains the session
ciscoasa# **no capture** *capture_name* **interface** *int_name*	Stops the capture, detaches it from the interface, and retains the capture session and buffer
ciscoasa# **no capture** *capture_name* **access-list** *acl_name*	Stops the capture, detaches the access list from it, and retains the capture session and buffer
ciscoasa# **no capture** *capture_name*	Deletes a capture session and the capture buffer

Copying Capture Buffer Contents

Sometimes you might find that viewing the contents of a capture buffer from a command-line interface becomes too cumbersome or confusing. This can happen when the capture buffer becomes very large—too large to navigate with CLI commands or display filters.

At other times, the capture buffer might contain useful information that deserves further review. For example, you might have a PC-based tool that can import captured data for viewing and analysis. You also might want to archive the capture buffer for future use.

You can copy a capture session to a TFTP server with the following command:

```
ciscoasa# copy capture:session-name tftp://server/path [pcap]
```

The entire buffer from the capture session named *session-name* is copied to the TFTP server at IP address *server* into the file and directory defined by *path*, which is relative to the TFTP server's root directory. The resulting capture file contains the same text that is seen with the **show capture** command. You can also add the **pcap** keyword to save the capture buffer in the PCAP format, which can be imported into many network analysis tools.

With the following command, the capture session named bigtest is copied to the TFTP server at 192.168.254.10 as file bigtest in the TFTP root directory:

```
ciscoasa# copy capture:bigtest tftp://192.168.254.10/bigtest
```

You can also use a web browser to display a capture buffer as if you had used the **show capture** command. You also can download the capture buffer in PCAP format and save it as a file—all without leaving your web browser and without needing a TFTP server running on your PC.

First, enable the HTTP server on the ASA with the **http server enable** command. By doing this, HTTPS (TCP port 443) will be enabled by default. Be sure to allow your web browser's IP address to access the ASA by entering the **http** *ip-address* command. Next, open a web browser to the following URL:

https://*asa_address*/**capture**/*session_name*[/**pcap**]

Figure 16-10 shows a capture session named test being viewed in a web browser. As soon as the capture buffer text is displayed in the web browser, you can save it as a file through your browser application.

Figure 16-10 *Using a Web Browser to Display the Contents of a Capture Buffer*

You can also use the web browser to download the capture buffer as a file in PCAP format. To do this, add the **/pcap** keyword to the end of the URL. This time, the browser automatically fetches the capture file rather than displaying the capture text. As soon as you have the capture file downloaded in PCAP format, you can use a network analysis tool to examine and interpret the contents.

Capturing Dropped Packets

Suppose you use a packet capture and expect to see certain packets. However, for some reason, the packets don't appear in the capture buffer. Perhaps the missing packets are being dropped for some reason, but the normal raw data packet capture doesn't provide any helpful information.

The ASA offers a novel packet capture feature that can capture packets that are dropped internally, anywhere along the accelerated security path (ASP). This allows you to see which packets were dropped and the reason why. Because the ASP drop capture collects packets that are dropped by internal security features, the capture cannot be applied to any specific ASA interface.

You can use the following command syntax to define an ASP drop capture session:

```
ciscoasa# capture session_name type asp-drop drop-code [parameters]
```

Specify one of the *drop-code* reason keywords listed in Table 16-5, as well as any other capture session parameters needed to narrow the packet capture.

Table 16-5   drop-code *Keywords for the* capture type asp-drop *Command*

drop-code Keyword	Description
acl-drop	Flow is denied by the access rule
all	All packet drop reasons
async-lock-queue-limit	Async lock queue limit is exceeded
bad-crypto	Bad crypto return in packet
bad-ipsec-natt	Bad IPsec NAT-T packet
bad-ipsec-prot	IPsec isn't AH or ESP
bad-ipsec-udp	Bad IPsec UDP packet
bad-tcp-cksum	Bad TCP checksum
bad-tcp-flags	Bad TCP flags
channel-closed	Data path channel is closed
conn-limit	Connection limit is reached
connection-lock	Unable to obtain a connection lock
cp-event-queue-error	CP event queue error
cp-syslog-event-queue-error	CP syslog event queue error
ctm-error	Crypto Transform Manager (CTM) returned an error
dispatch-block-alloc	Core local block allocation failure
dispatch-decode-err	Dispatch decode error
dns-guard-app-id-not-matched	DNS Guard application ID didn't match
dns-guard-out-of-app-id	DNS Guard out of application ID
dst-l2_lookup-fail	Destination MAC L2 lookup failed
flow-being-freed	Flow is being freed
flow-expired	Expired flow
fo-standby	Dropped by the standby failover unit
fragment-reassembly-failed	Fragment reassembly failed

Table 16-5 drop-code *Keywords for the* **capture type asp-drop** *Command*

drop-code Keyword	Description
host-limit	Host limit
host-move-pkt	FP host move packet
ifc-classify	Virtual firewall classification failed
inspect-dns-app-id-not-matched	DNS Inspect application ID didn't match
inspect-dns-invalid-domain-label	DNS Inspect invalid domain label
inspect-dns-invalid-pak	DNS Inspect invalid packet
inspect-dns-out-of-app-id	DNS Inspect out of application ID
inspect-dns-pak-too-long	DNS Inspect packet was too long
inspect-icmp-error-different-embedded-conn	ICMP error inspection different inspection connection
inspect-icmp-error-no-existing-conn	ICMP error inspect had no existing connection
inspect-icmp-out-of-app-id	ICMP Inspect out of application ID
inspect-icmp-seq-num-not-matched	ICMP inspect sequence number not matched
inspect-icmpv6-error-invalid-pak	ICMPv6 Error Inspect invalid packet
inspect-icmpv6-error-no-existing-conn	ICMPv6 Error Inspect had no existing connection
inspect-rtcp-invalid-length	Inspect Real-Time Transport Control Protocol (RTCP) invalid packet length
inspect-rtcp-invalid-payload-type	Inspect RTCP invalid payload type
inspect-rtcp-invalid-version	Inspect RTCP invalid version
inspect-rtp-invalid-length	Inspect Real-time Transport Protocol (RTP) invalid packet length
inspect-rtp-invalid-payload-type	Inspect RTP invalid payload type
inspect-rtp-invald-version	Inspect RTP invalid version
inspect-rtp-max-outofseq-paks-probation	Inspect RTP maximum number of out-of-sequence packets
inspect-rtp-sequence-num-out of-range	Inspect RTP sequence number is out of range
inspect-rtp-ssrc-mismatch	Inspect RTP SSRC mismatch

Table 16-5   drop-code *Keywords for the* capture type asp-drop *Command*

drop-code Keyword	Description
inspect-srtp-client-port-not-present	Inspect Secure RTP (SRTP) client port not populated
inspect-srtp-decrypt-failed	Inspect SRTP decryption failed
inspect-srtp-encrypt-failed	Inspect SRTP encryption failed
inspect-srtp-generage-authtag-failed	Inspect SRTP generate authentication tag failed
inspect-srtp-no-media-session	Inspect SRTP media session not found
inspect-srtp-no-output-flow	Inspect SRTP find output flow failed
inspect-srtp-no-remote-phone-proxy-ip	Inspect SRTP remote phone proxy IP not found
inspect-srtp-one-part-no-key	Inspect SRTP keys not available for one party
inspect-srtp-setup-srtp-failed	Inspect SRTP failed to set up SRTP with Cisco Telepresence Manager (CTM)
inspect-srtp-validate-authtag-failed	Inspect SRTP validate authentication tag failed
intercept-unexpected	Unexpected packet was intercepted
interface-down	Interface is down
invalid-app-length	Invalid application length
invalid-encap	Invalid encapsulation
invalid-ethertype	Invalid EtherType
invalid-ip-header	Invalid IP header
invalid-ip-length	Invalid IP length
invalid-ip-option	IP option configured drop
invalid-tcp-hdr-length	Invalid TCP length
invalid-udp-length	Invalid UDP length
ip-fragment	IP fragment unsupported
ips-fail	IPS config removed for flow
ips-fail-close	IPS card is down
ips-no-ipv6	Executing IPS Software does not support IPv6
ips-request	IPS module requested packet drop
ipsec-clearpkt-notun	IPsec clear packet with no tunnel

Table 16-5   drop-code *Keywords for the* **capture type asp-drop** *Command*

drop-code Keyword	Description
ipsec-ipv6	IPsec via IPv6
ipsec-lock-error	IPsec locking error
ipsec-need-sa	IPsec SA not negotiated yet
ipsec-spoof	IPsec spoof detected
ipsec-tun-down	IPsec tunnel is down
ipsecudp-keepalive	IPsec/UDP keepalive message
ipv6_sp-security-failed	IPv6 slowpath security checks failed
l2_acl	Fast Path (FP) L2 rule drop
l2_same-lan-port	L2 source/destination same LAN port
loopback-buffer-full	Loopback buffer is full
lu-invalid-pkt	Invalid failover logical update (LU) packet
mp-pf-queue-full	PF module queue full
mp-svc-addr-renew-response	Service module received address renew response data frame
mp-svc-bad-framing	Service module received badly framed data
mp-svc-bad-length	Service module received bad data length
mp-svc-compress-error	Service module compression error
mp-svc-decompress-error	Service module decompression error
mp-svc-delete-in-progress	Service module received data while connection was being deleted
mp-svc-flow-control	Service module is in flow control
mp-svc-invalid-mac	Service module found invalid L2 data in the frame
mp-svc-invalid-mac-len	Service module found invalid L2 data length in the frame
mp-svc-no-channel	Service module does not have a channel for reinjection
mp-svc-no-fragment	Service module is unable to fragment a packet
mp-svc-no-mac	Service module is unable to find L2 data for frame
mp-svc-no-prepend	Service module does not have enough space to insert header
mp-svc-no-session	Service module does not have a session
mp-svc-unknown-type	Service module received unknown data frame

Table 16-5   drop-code *Keywords for the* capture type asp-drop *Command*

drop-code Keyword	Description
natt-keepalive	NAT-T keepalive message
no-adjacency	No valid adjacency
no-mcast-entry	Fast Path (FP) has no multicast entry
no-mcast-intrf	Fast Path (FP) has no multicast output interface
no-route	No route to host
non-ip-pkt-in-routed-mode	Non-IP packet received in routed mode
np-socket-closed	Dropped pending packets in a closed socket
np-sp-invalid-spi	Invalid SPI
punt-no-mem	Punt no memory
punt-queue-limit	Punt queue limit exceeded
punt-rate-limit	Punt rate limit exceeded
queue-removed	Queued packet dropped
rate-exceeded	QoS rate exceeded
rm-conn-limit	Resource management (RM) connection limit reached
rm-conn-rate-limit	RM connection rate limit reached
rpf-violated	Reverse-path verify failed
security-failed	Early security checks failed
send-ctm-error	Send to Crypto Transform Manager (CTM) returned an error
shunned	Packet is shunned
sp-security-failed	Slowpath security checks failed
ssm-app-fail	Service module is down
ssm-app-request	Service module requested drop
ssm-asdp-invalid	Invalid ASDP packet received from SSM card
ssm-dpp-invalid	Invalid packet received from SSM card
tcp-3whs-failed	TCP failed three-way handshake
tcp-ack-syn-diff	TCP ACK in SYNACK invalid
tcp-acked	TCP duplicate and has been ACKed
tcp-bad-option-list	TCP option list invalid
tcp-buffer-full	TCP packet buffer full

Table 16-5   drop-code *Keywords for the* **capture type asp-drop** *Command*

drop-code Keyword	Description
tcp-buffer-timeout	TCP out-of-order packet buffer timeout
tcp-conn-limit	TCP connection limit reached
tcp-data-past-fin	TCP data send after FIN
tcp-discarded-ooo	TCP packet out of order
tcp-dual-open	TCP dual open denied
tcp-dup-in-queue	TCP duplicate of packet in out-of-order queue
tcp-fo-drop	TCP replicated flow packet drop
tcp-global-buffer-full	TCP global out-of-order packet buffer full
tcp-invalid-ack	TCP invalid ACK
tcp-mss-exceeded	TCP maximum segment size (MSS) was too large
tcp-not-syn	First TCP packet not SYN
tcp-paws-fail	TCP packet failed Protect Against Wrapped Sequence numbers (PAWS) test
tcp-reserved-set	TCP reserved flags set
tcp-rst-syn-in-win	TCP RST/SYN in window
tcp-rstfin-ooo	TCP RST/FIN out of order
tcp-seq-past-win	TCP packet SEQ past window
tcp-seq-syn-diff	TCP SEQ in SYN/SYN-ACK invalid
tcp-syn-data	TCP SYN with data
tcp-syn-ooo	TCP SYN on established connection
tcp-synack-data	TCP SYN-ACK with data
tcp-synack-ooo	TCP SYN-ACK on established connection
tcp_xmit_Partial	TCP retransmission partial
tcpnorm-rexmit-bad	TCP bad retransmission
tcpnorm-wim-variation	TCP unexpected window size variation
telnet-not-permitted	Telnet not permitted on last secure interface
tfw-no-mgmt-ip-config	No management IP address configured for transparent firewall
unable-to-add-flow	Flow hash full
unable-to-create-flow	Out of flow cache memory

Table 16-5   drop-code *Keywords for the* capture type asp-drop *Command*

drop-code Keyword	Description
unexpected-packet	Unexpected packet
unsupport-ipv6-hdr	Unsupported IPv6 header
unsupported-ip-version	Unsupported IP version
vpn-handle-error	VPN handle error
vpn-handle-mismatch	VPN handle mismatch error
wccp-redirect-no-route	WCCP redirect packet no route
wccp-return-no-route	WCCP returned packet no route

In Example 16-10, a capture session has been created to collect all packets that have been dropped by any interface access list. Notice that the capture buffer lists the packet headers, but gives no specific information about which ACL dropped them.

Example 16-10   *Capturing Dropped Packets Due to an Interface ACL*

```
ciscoasa# capture ACL-DROPS type asp-drop acl-drop
ciscoasa# show capture ACL-DROPS
578 packets captured
 1: 11:18:10.787984 209.63.99.134 > 192.168.1.30: icmp: net 66.213.244.62 unreachable
 2: 11:18:13.910811 209.63.99.134 > 192.168.1.30: icmp: net 66.213.244.62 unreachable
 3: 11:18:14.514835 96.17.157.62.3478 > 192.168.1.30.1032:  udp 66
 4: 11:18:29.092829 10.100.22.134.68 > 255.255.255.255.67:  udp 300
 5: 11:18:51.725762 66.220.147.33.80 > 192.168.1.30.19679: .
 1457242373:1457242870(497) ack 428983025 win 4607
 6: 11:19:03.121713 10.100.22.32.68 > 255.255.255.255.67:  udp 300
 7: 11:19:17.184270 10.100.20.201.32768 > 255.255.255.255.9900:  udp 504
 8: 11:19:37.721138 209.63.99.134 > 192.168.1.30: icmp: net 66.213.244.62 unreachable
```

Example 16-11 shows a different capture session that collects packets that are dropped because the first packet in a TCP connection is not a SYN. In this case, each initial packet had the FIN bit set.

Example 16-11   *Capturing Dropped Packets Due to Unexpected TCP SYN*

```
ciscoasa# capture TCP-SYN type asp-drop tcp-not-syn
ciscoasa# show capture TCP-SYN
6 packets captured
  1: 11:08:14.674830 10.100.21.246.2400 > 74.125.113.103.80: F 2121766286:21217
     66286(0) ack 1104027538 win 64365
  2: 11:08:14.675151 10.100.21.246.2400 > 74.125.113.103.80: F 2121766286:21217
     66286(0) ack 1104027538 win 64365
  3: 11:08:14.784368 10.100.21.246.2320 > 74.125.113.103.80: F 1229347491:12293
     47491(0) ack 2129350502 win 64365
```

```
    4:  11:08:14.784947 10.100.21.246.2321 > 74.125.113.103.80: F 1791113785:17911
        13785(0) ack 1674072656 win 64365
    5:  11:08:17.534182 10.100.21.246.2401 > 74.125.113.103.80: F 92431968:9243196
        8(0) ack 1601214786 win 64365
    6:  11:08:19.159064 10.100.21.246.2400 > 74.125.113.103.80: F 2121766286:21217
        66286(0) ack 1104027538 win 64365
6 packets shown
ciscoasa#
```

Combining Packet Tracer and Packet Capture

An ASA can gather Packet Tracer information about packets as they are captured, providing the best of both tools in one location. The capture session is configured normally, with the addition of the **trace** keyword. By default, Packet Tracer information will be collected for the first 50 packets that are captured and require inspection. You can add the **trace-count** keyword to specify the number of packets to trace, using the following command syntax:

ciscoasa# **capture** *session-name* **trace** [**trace-count** *packets*] [*parameters*]

You can display the capture buffer contents, along with the Packet Tracer results, by adding the **trace** keyword to the **show capture** command, as follows:

ciscoasa# **show capture** *session-name* **trace**

Example 16-12 shows the commands used to create a packet capture with packet tracing for 100 packets, as well as the results collected in the capture buffer.

Example 16-12   *Adding Packet Tracer Information to a Packet Capture*

```
ciscoasa# capture CAP-TRACE access-list HOSTS trace trace-count 100 interface outside
ciscoasa# show capture CAP-TRACE trace
1244 packets captured
    1:  11:29:27.530261 192.168.103.30.21738 > 65.55.5.233.80: .
        368454744:368455956(1212) ack 792630732 win 64512


Result:
Action: allow


    2:  11:29:27.530459 192.168.103.30.21738 > 65.55.5.233.80: P
        368455956:368456428(472) ack 792630732 win 64512


Result:
Action: allow


    3:  11:29:27.584411 192.168.16.212.80 > 192.168.103.30.21849: S
        864712665:864712665(0) ack 3416467652 win 3900 <mss 1300,sackOK,eol>


Phase: 1
Type: FLOW-LOOKUP
```

```
Subtype:
Result: ALLOW
Config:
Additional Information:
Found flow with id 2032063, using existing flow


Phase: 2
Type: ROUTE-LOOKUP
Subtype: output and adjacency
Result: ALLOW
Config:
Additional Information:
found next-hop 10.100.20.1 using egress ifc inside
adjacency Active
next-hop mac address 0000.0c07.ac00 hits 287316


Result:
Action: allow


   4: 11:29:27.585006 192.168.103.30.21849 > 192.168.16.212.80: . ack 864712666
      win 64512


Result:
Action: allow
```

Summary

By becoming familiar with the Packet Tracer and packet capture features, you can leverage these advanced tools to gain additional visibility into traffic movement within an ASA. Packet Tracer can provide insight into some "what if" scenarios to validate how a simulated packet will be handled. Packet capture can provide evidence of the actual packets that have passed into, passed out of, or been dropped by an ASA.

Exam Preparation Tasks

As mentioned in the section, "How to Use This Book," in the Introduction, you have a couple of choices for exam preparation: the exercises here, Chapter 17, "Final Preparation," and the exam simulation questions on the CD-ROM.

Review All Key Topics

Review the most important topics in this chapter, noted with the Key Topic icon in the outer margin of the page. Table 16-6 lists a reference of these key topics and the page numbers on which each is found.

Key
Topic

Table 16-6   *Key Topics for Chapter 16*

Key Topic Element	Description	Page Number
Paragraph	Describes the Packet Tracer operation	737
Paragraph	Explains how to use Packet Tracer in ASDM	737
Paragraph	Describes how to define a capture session in the CLI	746
Table 16-3	Lists commands to control a capture session	750
Paragraph	Discusses the ASP drop capture	752

Command Reference to Check Your Memory

This section includes the most important configuration and EXEC commands covered in this chapter. It might not be necessary to memorize the complete syntax of every command, but you should be able to remember the basic keywords that are needed.

To test your memory of the commands, cover the right side of Table 16-7 with a piece of paper, read the description on the left side, and then see how much of the command you can remember.

The FIREWALL exam focuses on practical, hands-on skills that are used by a networking professional. Therefore, you should be able to identify the commands needed to configure and test an ASA feature.

Table 16-7 *Commands Related to Traffic Analysis*

Task	Command Syntax
Test ICMP reachability	ciscoasa# **ping** [*if_name*] *destination* [**data** *pattern*] [**repeat** *count*] [**size** *bytes*] [**timeout** *seconds*] [**validate**]
Filter incoming ICMP traffic terminating on an ASA interface	ciscoasa(config)# **icmp** {**permit** | **deny**} *ip_address mask* [*icmp_type*] *if_name*
Test TCP reachability	ciscoasa#**ping tcp**[*if_name*] *destination*[*port*]] [**repeat** *count*] [**source** *address port*] [**timeout** *seconds*]
Discover router hops along a path to a destination	ciscoasa# **traceroute** *destination* [**port** *number*] [**numeric**] [**probe** *probe_num*] [**source** *source*] [**timeout** *seconds*] [**ttl** *ttl_min ttl_max*] [**use-icmp**]
Perform a Packet Tracer test	ciscoasa# **packet-tracer input** *src_interface protocol src_addr src_port dest_addr dest_port* [**detailed**] [**xml**]
Define a capture session	ciscoasa# **capture** *session_name* [interface {*int_name* | **asa_dataplane** | **cplane**} [*parameters*]
Define an ASP drop capture session	ciscoasa# **capture** *session_name* **type asp-drop** *drop-code* [*parameters*]
Display the contents of a capture session buffer	ciscoasa# **show capture** *session_name* [**access-list** *acl_name*] {**detail** | **dump** | **decode**} [**packet-number** *packet*] [**count** *count*]
Copy a capture session buffer to a TFTP server	ciscoasa# **copy capture:***session-name* **tftp:**//*server*/*path* [**pcap**]
URL used to display a capture session buffer in a web browser	**https://***asa_address*/**capture**/*session_name*[/**pcap**]

CHAPTER 17

Final Preparation

The first 16 chapters of this book cover the technologies, protocols, commands, and design concepts and considerations required to pass the 642-618 FIREWALL v2.0 exam. Although these chapters supply detailed information, most people need more preparation than simply reading the first 16 chapters of this book. This chapter details a set of tools and a study plan to help you complete your preparation for the exam.

This short chapter has two main sections. The first section lists the exam preparation tools that are useful at this point in the study process. The second section lists a suggested study plan now that you have completed all the earlier chapters in this book.

Tools for Final Preparation

This section lists some information about the available tools and how to access the tools.

Pearson Cert Practice Test Engine and Questions on the CD

The CD in the back of this book includes the Pearson Cert Practice Test engine—software that displays and grades a set of exam-realistic multiple-choice questions. Using the Pearson Cert Practice Test engine, you can either study by going through the questions in Study mode or take a simulated (timed) FIREWALL exam.

The installation process requires two major steps. This book's CD has a recent copy of the Pearson Cert Practice Test engine. The practice exam—the database of FIREWALL exam questions—is not on the CD.

Note: The cardboard CD case in the back of this book includes the CD and a piece of paper. The paper lists the activation key for the practice exam associated with this book. *Do not lose the activation key*. On the opposite side of the paper from the activation code is a unique, one-time-use coupon code for the purchase of the *CCNP Security FIREWALL Official Cert Guide*, Premium Edition.

Install the Software from the CD

The software installation process is quite routine compared with other software installation processes. The following steps outline the installation process:

Step 1.   Insert the CD into your PC.

Step 2.   The software that automatically runs is the Cisco Press software to access and use all CD-based features, including the exam engine and viewing the CD-only appendixes. From the main menu, click the **Install the Exam Engine** option.

Step 3.   Respond to the prompts as with any typical software installation process.

The installation process gives you the option to activate your exam with the activation code supplied on the paper in the CD sleeve. This process requires that you establish a Pearson website login. You need this login to activate the exam, so register when prompted. If you already have a Pearson website login, there is no need to register again. Just use your existing login.

Activate and Download the Practice Exam

After the exam engine is installed, activate the exam associated with this book (if you did not do so during the installation process), as follows:

Step 1.   Start the Pearson Cert Practice Test (PCPT) software from the Windows Start menu or from your desktop shortcut icon.

Step 2.   To activate and download the exam associated with this book, from the **My Products** or **Tools** tab, click the **Activate** button.

Step 3.   At the next screen, enter the activation key from the paper inside the cardboard CD holder in the back of the book. After you enter this, click the **Activate** button.

Step 4.   The activation process downloads the practice exam. Click **Next** and then click **Finish**.

After the activation process is completed, the My Products tab should list your new exam. If you do not see the exam, make sure that you have selected the **My Products** tab on the menu. At this point, the software and practice exam are ready to use. Simply select the exam and click the **Use** button.

To update a particular exam that you have already activated and downloaded, simply select the **Tools** tab and click the **Update Products** button. Updating your exams ensures that you have the latest changes and updates to the exam data.

If you want to check for updates to the PCPT exam engine software, simply select the **Tools** tab and click the **Update Application** button. This ensures that you are running the latest version of the software engine.

Activating Other Exams

The exam software installation process, and the registration process, has to happen only once. Then, for each new exam, only a few steps are required. For example, if you buy another new Cisco Press Official Cert Guide or Pearson IT Certification Cert Guide, extract the activation code from the CD sleeve in the back of that book. (You don't even need the CD at this point.) From there, just start the exam engine (if it is not still up and running) and perform Steps 2 through 4 of the previous list.

Premium Edition

In addition to the free practice exam provided on the CD-ROM, you can purchase additional exams with expanded functionality directly from Pearson IT Certification. The Premium Edition of this title contains an additional two full practice exams and an eBook (in both PDF and ePub format). In addition, the Premium Edition title also has remediation for each question to the specific part of the eBook that relates to that question.

Because you have purchased the print version of this title, you can purchase the Premium Edition at a deep discount. A coupon code in the CD sleeve contains a one-time-use code and instructions for where you can purchase the Premium Edition.

To view the Premium Edition product page, go to http://www.pearsonitcertification.com/title/9780132979436.

Cisco Learning Network

Cisco provides a wide variety of CCNP Security preparation tools at a Cisco website called the Cisco Learning Network. This site includes a large variety of exam preparation tools, including sample questions, forums on each Cisco exam, learning video games, and information about each exam.

To reach the Cisco Learning Network, go to www.cisco.com/go/learnnetspace, or just search for "Cisco Learning Network." You need to use the login that you created at www.cisco.com. If you don't have such a login, you can register for free. To register, simply go to www.cisco.com, click **Register** at the top of the page, and supply the requested information.

Chapter-Ending Review Tools

Chapters 1–16 have several features in the "Exam Preparation Tasks" section at the end of each chapter. Many of you have probably reviewed each chapter using these tools. You may have used some or all of these tools. It can also be helpful to use these tools again as you make your final preparations for the exam.

Suggested Plan for Final Review/Study

This section lists a suggested study plan from the point at which you finish reading Chapter 16 until you take the 642-618 FIREWALL v2.0 exam. Certainly, you can ignore this plan, use it as is, or just take suggestions from it.

The plan uses three steps:

Step 1.   **Review the key topics and the Do I Know This Already? (DIKTA) questions:** You can use the table that lists the key topics in each chapter, or just flip the pages looking for key topics. Also, reviewing the DIKTA questions from the beginning of the chapter can be helpful for review.

Step 2.   **Review command references:** Go through the command reference tables at the end of each chapter, where all the commands presented in the chapter are collected in a concise format. These tables can help you remember command syntax and the basic steps needed to configure a feature.

Step 3.   **Use the Pearson Cert Practice Test engine to practice:** The Pearson Cert Practice Test engine on the CD can be used to study using a bank of unique exam-realistic multiple-choice questions available only with this book.

Using the Exam Engine

The Pearson Cert Practice Test engine on the CD includes a database of questions created specifically for this book. The Pearson Cert Practice Test engine can be used in either Study mode or Practice Exam mode, as follows:

■   **Study mode:** Study mode is most useful when you want to use the questions for learning and practicing. In Study mode, you can select options such as whether you want to randomize the order of the questions, automatically view answers to the questions as you go, test on specific topics, refer to specific sections of the text that resides on the CD, and so on.

■   **Practice Exam mode:** This mode presents questions in a timed environment, providing you with a more exam-realistic experience. It also restricts your ability to see your score as you progress through the exam, view answers to questions as you are taking the exam, and refer to sections of the text. These timed exams not only allow you to study for the actual 642-618 FIREWALL v2.0 exam, but they also help you simulate the time pressure that can occur on the actual exam.

When doing your final preparation, you can use Study mode, Practice Exam mode, or both. However, after you see each question a couple of times, you will likely start to remember the questions, and the usefulness of the exam database may be reduced. So, consider the following options when using the exam engine:

■   Use this question database for review. Use Study mode, and study the questions by major book part, just as with the other final review steps listed in this chapter. Plan on getting another exam (possibly from the Premium Edition) if you want to take additional simulated exams.

- Save the question database, not using it for review during your review of each book part. Save it until the end so that you will not have seen the questions before. Then, use Practice Exam mode to simulate the exam.

Choosing the correct mode from the exam engine's user interface is obvious. The following steps show how to move to the screen from which to select Study or Practice Exam mode:

Step 1.   Click the **My Products** tab if you are not already in that screen.

Step 2.   Select the exam you want to use from the list of available exams.

Step 3.   Click the **Use** button.

By taking these actions, the engine should display a window from which you can choose **Study** mode or **Practice Exam** mode. When in Study mode, you can further choose the book chapters, limiting the questions to those explained in the specified chapters of the book.

Summary

The tools and suggestions listed in this chapter have been designed with one goal in mind: to help you develop the skills required to pass the 642-618 FIREWALL v2.0 exam. This book has been developed from the beginning to not just tell you the facts, but also to help you learn how to apply the facts. No matter what your experience level leading up to when you take the exam, it is our hope that the broad range of preparation tools, and even the structure of this book, will help you pass the exam with ease.

Answers to the "Do I Know This Already?" Quizzes

Chapter 1

1. B, D, and E
2. B
3. C
4. C
5. D
6. B
7. E
8. D
9. C
10. E
11. C, D, E, and F
12. B

Chapter 2

1. A, B, D, E, and F
2. D
3. C
4. D
5. C
6. E
7. B. The original startup-configuration will be used because the running configuration has not yet been saved. If the running configuration had been saved, "CONFIG_FILE variable" would be shown as "disk0:/new-startup.cfg."

8. B
9. C
10. B and D
11. D
12. B

Chapter 3

1. C and D
2. B
3. D
4. C
5. C
6. B and D
7. A
8. A, C, and D
9. C
10. B
11. B
12. B and F. Answer E might also be true, but you cannot confirm that a security level has been configured from the command output given. Because an interface name has not been configured with the **nameif** command, neither the interface name nor the security level is shown in the output.

Chapter 4

1. B
2. D
3. A
4. B and C
5. A
6. B and C
7. C
8. C
9. A and D
10. A
11. A
12. C

Chapter 5

1. B and D
2. A
3. A, B, C, and E
4. B
5. D
6. C
7. D
8. A, B, C, and D
9. C
10. C

Chapter 6

1. B and D
2. A
3. B
4. D
5. A and C
6. B
7. A
8. B and C
9. A

10. C
11. B and C
12. C
13. D
14. B

Chapter 7

1. B
2. C
3. B
4. E
5. C
6. D
7. B
8. D
9. D
10. A
11. B
12. C
13. A
14. E
15. C
16. A
17. A, C, E, and F
18. E
19. A
20. C
21. B
22. C

Chapter 8

1. B and D
2. A, B, C, and E
3. A, C, and D
4. D
5. D

6. B
7. B
8. B
9. C
10. B
11. C
12. C
13. D
14. A, B, and D
15. A, D, E, and G
16. D
17. D
18. B

Chapter 9

1. C
2. B
3. A
4. A
5. A
6. C
7. C
8. B
9. D
10. D
11. A
12. C
13. B
14. B
15. C
16. B and D
17. A
18. A, B, and C
19. D
20. C
21. D

Chapter 10

1. B
2. C
3. A
4. A, B, and D
5. B
6. C
7. C
8. D
9. B

Chapter 11

1. D
2. D
3. B and D
4. B
5. A
6. C
7. C
8. B
9. C
10. B

Chapter 12

1. D
2. B
3. B and C
4. D
5. A
6. A, B, and D
7. B
8. B and D
9. C
10. A

Chapter 13

1. B
2. C
3. A
4. D
5. B
6. C
7. C
8. D
9. D

Chapter 14

1. D
2. B
3. D
4. B
5. B
6. A
7. E
8. D
9. C
10. C
11. C
12. A
13. A
14. D

Chapter 15

1. B
2. C
3. A
4. D
5. B
6. C
7. C
8. D
9. D

Chapter 16

1. A
2. D
3. C
4. D
5. E
6. B, C, and D
7. C
8. A
9. A
10. C
11. D
12. B

Over time, reader feedback allows Cisco Press to gauge which topics give our readers the most problems when taking the exams. To assist readers with those topics, the authors may create new materials that clarify and expand upon those troublesome exam topics. As mentioned in the "Introduction," the additional content about the exam will be posted as a PDF document on this book's companion website, at www.informit.com/title/9781587142710.

This appendix provides you with updated information if Cisco makes minor modifications to the exam upon which this book is based. When Cisco releases an entirely new exam, the changes are usually too extensive to provide in a simple updated appendix. In those cases, you need to consult the new edition of the book for the updated content.

This appendix fills the void that occurs with any print book. In particular, this appendix does the following:

- Mentions technical items that might not have been mentioned elsewhere in the book

- Covers new topics if Cisco adds new content to the exam over time

- Provides a way to get up-to-the-minute current information about content for the exam

CCNP Security 642-618 FIREWALL Exam Updates: Version 1.0

Always Get the Latest at the Companion Website

You are reading the version of this appendix that was available when your book was printed. However, given that the main purpose of this appendix is to be a living, changing document, it is important that you look for the latest version online at the book's companion website. To do so, follow these steps:

Step 1. Browse to www.ciscopress.com/title/9781587142710.

Step 2. Select the Updates option under the More Information box.

Step 3. Download the latest "Appendix B" document.

Note: The downloaded document has a version number. When comparing the version of this print Appendix B (Version 1.0) with the latest online version of this appendix, you should do the following:

- **Same version:** Ignore the PDF that you downloaded from the companion website.

- **Website has a later version:** Ignore this Appendix B in your book and read only the latest version that you downloaded from the companion website.

If no appendix is posted on the book's website, that simply means that there have been no updates to post, and Version 1.0 is still the latest version.

Technical Content

The current version of this appendix does not contain any additional technical coverage.

Glossary of Key Terms

A

active-active failover   A high availability mode where both ASAs in a failover pair can stay active and inspect traffic. Each ASA must be active for a different group of security contexts.

active-standby failover   A high availability mode where one ASA functions as the active unit, providing all traffic inspection, while the other ASA stays idle and waits to take over the active role.

admin context   A special Security Context used for overall device management in multiple mode.

administrative distance   An arbitrary index from 0 to 255 that reflects the trustworthiness of a routing information source.

AIP-SSM   Cisco Advanced Intrusion and Prevention Security Services Module, designed to help protect the network from attacks and misuse.

application inspection and control (AIC) filtering   Security policies that are based on information inside the application layer protocols.

application inspection engine   An ASA feature that is used to inspect traffic related to a specific application or protocol.

application layer access control   Security policies based on information found in the Layers 5 through 7 packet headers and packet content.

application layer gateway (ALG)   Also referred to as a proxy, a device that acts as a gateway or intermediary between clients and servers.

application layer signature   Detection of known bad content or payloads in packets used by a specific application.

ARP inspection   An ASA feature that prevents ARP spoofing attacks. The ASA inspects ARP reply packets and compares the source IP address, source MAC address, and source interface against known static entries in the configuration.

asymmetric routing   A condition where packets from a single traffic flow are forwarded through one ASA of an active-active failover pair, but the return traffic arrives on the alternate ASA. Because one ASA is not aware of any connection state that the other ASA has built, packets are subject to loss.

auto NAT   Also referred to as object NAT, auto NAT contains translation rules defined as part of the network object definition itself. This allows each object definition to contain a single translation only.

B

Base license   The basic license for an SSM on the Cisco ASA.

best-effort queue (BEQ)   A buffer that holds packets waiting for transmission, but services them in the order that they were received.

bidirectional NAT   Applying both inside NAT and outside NAT to the same traffic flow (almost always due to overlapping IP addresses on a network requiring communication).

blacklist   A static list of known bad servers that are involved in botnet activity.

botnet attack   Malicious activity that infects individual hosts in a protected network, allowing them to be remotely controlled to align them in a coordinated attack against other resources.

bump-in-the-wire   A transparent mode firewall that is positioned between two network segments but does not break or alter the IP subnet on either side.

C

class map   Defines which traffic will be matched in a security policy.

CSC-SSM   Cisco Content Security and Control Security Services Module, designed to help protect users of the network from encountering malicious content such as viruses and spyware.

cut-through proxy   The ability to configure different network access policies based on the identity of a user that is attempting to communicate through a Cisco ASA.

D

dead connection detection (DCD)   A mechanism used to probe for defunct idle connections, indicating that a host is dead or unresponsive.

deep packet inspection (DPI)   Examination beyond simple UDP or TCP header inspection, to look further into the UDP or TCP packet payloads to understand their contents.

default class   The resource class assigned to all Security Contexts on the Cisco ASA by default. Newly created resource classes inherit the limits defined in the default class.

demilitarized zone (DMZ)   An area of the network that is positioned between the trusted, internal network and the untrusted Internet.

DHCP relay   An ASA feature that relays DHCP requests received on one interface to a DHCP server found on another interface.

DHCP server   An ASA feature that provides IP addresses and parameters dynamically to requesting clients.

DNS Rewrite   An ASA feature that resolves issues in a network where internal clients make DNS queries to an external DNS server, when looking for an internal server.

dynamic inside NAT   A translation feature that creates a temporary translation entry (slot) in the translation table when a host on a more secure interface sends traffic through the ASA to a less secure interface.

dynamic NAT   Temporary translation where an original host is assigned an address from an available pool, and that address is returned to the pool after a configurable idle time.

dynamic outside NAT   A translation mechanism that is applied to packets that ingress an interface with a lower security level than that of the interface they egress (inbound traffic).

E

egress interface   Interface where the packet will exit the ASA.

EIGRP   Enhanced Interior Gateway Routing Protocol, a Cisco proprietary dynamic routing protocol that uses a complex routing metric and exchanges routing information to neighboring Layer 3 devices.

embryonic connection   A TCP connection that has been initiated, but not completely opened with a three-way handshake.

EtherChannel   A logical link built up of two or more physical interfaces between an ASA and a switch.

EtherType access list   A special access list that can be used in transparent firewall mode to filter packets based on hexadecimal EtherType values.

F

Fail Closed   The configuration of IPS or IDS that states traffic should be dropped if there is a failure of the inspection device.

Fail Open   The configuration of IPS or IDS that states traffic should be passed through if there is a failure of the inspection device.

failover group   A logical grouping of security contexts that is used by an active-active failover pair of ASAs. Each failover group is active on one ASA and standby on the other ASA.

firewall   A device that enforces an access control policy between two or more security domains.

G–H

global configuration mode   The CLI mode that allows commands to be entered to configure features that affect the ASA as a whole. Global configuration mode is reached only from the privileged-EXEC mode.

hardware name   The interface hardware type, module, and port number that uniquely identifies a physical interface, as in Ethernet0/0 or GigabitEthernet3/0.

HTTP redirection   Method by which the Cisco ASA actively listens for HTTP requests on TCP port 80 and, upon detecting those requests, redirects internal users to a local web page that is a form for users to input their appropriate credentials.

I–K

ingress interface   Interface where the original packet enters the ASA.

inline operation   The configuration of IPS in which traffic is passing through the inspecting device.

inside NAT   The address translation performed if the packets arriving at the ASA from a host subject to translation ingress an interface with a security level higher than that of the interface they egress.

interface name   An arbitrary logical name used to reference an ASA interface from a security perspective, as in "inside" or "outside."

intrusion detection   The process of inspecting network traffic and alerting an administrator about malicious traffic.

intrusion prevention   The process of identifying malicious traffic attempting to enter the network and dropping that traffic.

L

LACP (Link Aggregation Control Protocol)   A standards-based protocol that is used to negotiate an EtherChannel between an ASA and a switch.

LAN failover interface   A link that is used between two ASAs in a failover pair. Each ASA uses the link to check on the health of its failover peer.

low-latency queue (LLQ)   A buffer that holds packets that are time sensitive and are to be transmitted ahead of other packets in the BEQ. The LLQ is also called the priority queue.

M

MAC address learning   The default process that an ASA uses to learn the location of source MAC addresses from packets as they are received. When MAC addresses are spoofed by malicious hosts, MAC address learning can be disabled and replaced by static entries.

manual NAT   Allows an administrator to define translation rules to be compared to traffic flows before the other NAT rules. These rules are usually very specific. For example, you can add entries using manual NAT if a host requires multiple translation rules, which depend on the input or output interfaces or the destination address. Also, manual NAT—after auto NAT—allows for translation rules that could conflict with the entries in higher priority NAT rules. These entries are configured the same way as other manual NAT rules (but are generally less specific).

maximum transmission unit (MTU)   The maximum size packet that can be transmitted on an interface without fragmentation.

member interface   A physical interface that has been configured to be a member of a redundant interface pair.

Mobility Proxy   Enables the ASA to act as a proxy for the TLS signaling used between Cisco Unified Mobile Communicator (UMC) and the Cisco Unified Mobility Advantage (UMA) server.

Modular Policy Framework (MPF)   A modular, hierarchical scheme used to configure ASA security policies.

MTU   Maximum transmission unit, which indicates the maximum Ethernet frame size that can be sent over a physical interface.

multiple mode   The mode of operation that permits the creation of virtual firewalls.

N

NAT   Network Address Translation, a mechanism used to translate private (local) IP addresses to public (global), routable addresses when a host on a private network needs to communicate with hosts outside of that private network.

NAT control   A feature that configures the ASA to enforce NAT usage.

NAT exemption   A method to perform no translation in situations where NAT control is enabled.

NAT Table   The NAT Table contains three sections. NAT rules are searched from top to bottom in the NAT Table, and the first rule that matches the packet being analyzed is always applied, regardless of whether it is a static or dynamic rule, a translation exemption, or whether the source is on a higher or lower security interface than the destination.

network behavior analysis (NBA) system   A system that examines network traffic over time to build statistical models of normal, baseline activity.

network intrusion prevention system (NIPS)   A security strategy that examines and analyzes network traffic and compares it to a database of known malicious activity.

network layer access control   Security functions that use decisions based on information found in the Layers 2 through 4 headers.

network object   A network object defines a single IP address, range of addresses, network, or FQDN. The host, range, or subnet that is defined by a network object is used to identify the real, nontranslated, IP address in a NAT configuration. A network object can also be used to define any available translation addresses.

O

optional licenses   Licenses on the Cisco ASA that allow the devices to scale to more users or add additional features.

OSPF   Open Shortest Path First, a standards-based link-state routing protocol that can partition a network into a hierarchy of distinct numbered areas.

outside NAT   The address translation performed if packets arriving from a host subject to translation ingress an interface with a lower security level than that of the interface they egress.

P-Q

PAT   Port Address Translation, a method of translating IP addresses, translating source port numbers in TCP or UDP packets, thus allowing many-to-one translation of source IP addresses. This allows numerous internal hosts to share a single public IP address when communicating with external networks.

payload minimization   The process of limiting the payload of packets such that they contain only expected content.

permissive access control   Allow all traffic to pass through a firewall unless it is explicitly blocked.

Phone Proxy   Permits the ASA to terminate Cisco SRTP/TLS encrypted IP Phone connections that permit secure remote access.

physical interface   An ASA interface that has physical hardware and connects to a network through physical cabling.

policy map   Defines the actions that are to be taken on matched traffic in a security policy.

Presence Federation Proxy   Permits the ASA to terminate TLS communications between Unified Presence servers and apply and the appropriate security policies.

privileged-EXEC mode   The highest-level CLI mode, which offers full access to all ASA commands and information.

promiscuous operation   The configuration of IDS in which traffic is copied to the device that is doing the inspection.

protocol minimization   The process of limiting the protocol features to the absolute minimum needed for an application or service to function.

protocol verification   The process of verifying that packets conform to a protocol standard or definition.

proxy ARP   A technique in which one host, usually a router, answers ARP requests intended for another machine. By "faking" its identity, the router accepts responsibility for routing packets to the "real" destination. Proxy ARP can help machines on a subnet reach remote subnets without the need to configure routing or a default gateway.

R

redundant interface   A logical interface that comprises two physical interfaces configured in a redundant pair. Only one of the two interfaces takes on the active role at any given time.

regular expression (regex)   A string of characters and special metacharacters that defines the content that should be matched in a text field.

resource class   An object for setting resource limits on virtual firewalls.

restrictive access control   Allows no traffic to pass through the firewall unless it is explicitly allowed.

RIPv2   Routing Information Protocol Version 2, a dynamic distance vector routing protocol used to exchange routing information with other Layer 3 devices.

ROMMON (ROM monitor) mode   The CLI mode available as an ASA is booting, only by escaping the normal booting sequence when a countdown option is presented. Only a limited set of commands is available.

routed firewall mode   The ASA operating mode by which packets are forwarded based on IP address and routing information.

running configuration   The set of configuration commands the firewall uses while it is running. The running configuration is stored in RAM.

S

security context   A virtual instance of a firewall. One physical firewall hardware platform can run multiple security contexts, each acting as an independent firewall.

security domain   A trusted portion of a network.

security level   An arbitrary number between 0 and 100 that denotes the relative protection or security that will be applied to an interface. A higher number indicates more trust or more security.

SensorBase   A dynamic database of known botnet servers, as provided by Cisco.

service policy   An entire set of security policies that is applied to one or all ASA interfaces.

shared interface   An interface used by multiple Security Contexts when in multiple mode.

single mode   The operational mode of a Cisco ASA when not capable of virtual firewalls.

SLA monitor   A process that monitors the reachability of a target device to implement a conditional static route.

specific configuration modes   CLI modes where specific ASA features can be configured. These modes are reachable only from global configuration mode.

startup configuration   The set of configuration commands that the firewall applies when it starts up. The startup configuration is permanent and is stored in nonvolatile flash memory.

stateful failover   A failover mode where the active ASA inspects traffic and passes connection state and many other types of information to the standby ASA so that it can take over immediately if active unit fails.

stateful packet filtering (SPF)   Decisions to forward or block a packet are based on a dynamic state table for each active connection.

stateless failover   A failover mode where the active ASA inspects traffic but never informs the standby ASA of any of its activities. If the active unit fails, the standby unit will have to rebuild all of its connection state information.

stateless packet filtering   Decisions to forward or block a packet are made on each packet independently, with no concept of a connection state.

static inside NAT   A translation mechanism that creates a permanent, fixed translations between a local address on the inside network and a global address on the outside network.

static NAT   Fixed translation, where an original address is permanently mapped to the translated IP address.

static outside NAT   A translation mechanism that creates a permanent, fixed translation between a global address on the outside network and a local address on the inside network.

static route   A route that is manually configured and does not change.

T

TCP normalizer   An inspection feature that examines information in the TCP header of packets and can normalize or alter the values so that they conform to configured limits.

threat detection   An ASA feature that can discover suspicious activity passing through an ASA by monitoring traffic statistics and detecting abnormal conditions that might indicate an attack in progress.

TLS Proxy   Permits the ASA to intercept and decrypt encrypted information from Unified Communication endpoints en route to the Cisco Unified Communications Manager (CUCM).

traffic policing   A method of measuring the bandwidth of traffic and limiting it to a predefined threshold or limit. Packets above the limit are usually dropped.

traffic shaping   A method of measuring the bandwidth of traffic and buffering it so that it is sent at or below an average rate. Because the limit is seldom exceeded, packets are not normally dropped.

transparent firewall mode   The ASA operating mode by which packets are forwarded based on Layer 2 MAC address information.

Trend Micro InterScan GUI   Management software for the CSC-SSM on a Cisco ASA.

twice NAT   Technically, all manual NAT rules are twice NAT rules. However, the term is more commonly used only for a manual NAT rule, which actually performs translation on both source and destination address and/or port parameters.

U–V

user EXEC mode   The default CLI mode, which offers a limited set of commands.

unidirectional manual static NAT   A manual NAT rule that applies only to traffic sourced from a defined network object. Traffic destined to the object won't use the NAT rule. Normally, manual NAT rules apply bidirectionally.

virtual HTTP   Method that enables users to authenticate against a Cisco ASA using an IP address of the virtual HTTP server inside the Cisco ASA.

virtual reassembly   The process by which fragmented packets are buffered and reassembled in memory so that the ASA can inspect them.

VLAN interface   A logical ASA interface that connects to a virtual LAN, either internally or externally through a VLAN trunk link.

VLAN trunk link   A physical interface that is configured as an IEEE 802.1Q trunk. Packets from multiple VLANs can be carried over a trunk by adding a VLAN tag to each. At the far end of the trunk link, the VLAN tags are removed and the packets are sent into the respective VLAN.

W–Z

whitelist   A static list of known good or trusted servers.

xlate table   Maintained by a Cisco ASA device for each host that makes connection. Any active connection defines a host's xlate entry. An xlate entry is created only when the relevant traffic passes through the firewall. The xlate table can also be formed dynamically as any new connection is established.

zero downtime upgrade   The software image upgrade process on a pair of ASAs operating in stateful failover mode. The operating system images can be upgraded on each ASA individually, without interrupting network connectivity.

Index

D

E

F

V-Z

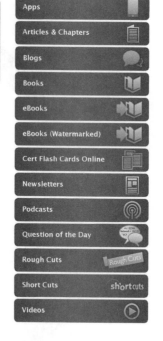

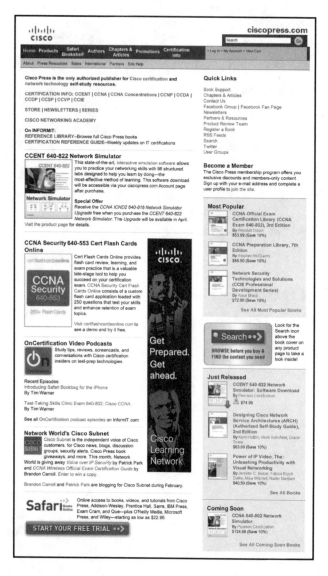

FREE
Online Edition

Your purchase of *CCNP Security FIREWALL 642-618 Official Cert Guide* includes access to a free online edition for 45 days through the **Safari Books Online** subscription service. Nearly every Cisco Press book is available online through **Safari Books Online**, along with thousands of books and videos from publishers such as Addison-Wesley Professional, Exam Cram, IBM Press, O'Reilly Media, Prentice Hall, Que, Sams, and VMware Press.

Safari Books Online is a digital library providing searchable, on-demand access to thousands of technology, digital media, and professional development books and videos from leading publishers. With one monthly or yearly subscription price, you get unlimited access to learning tools and information on topics including mobile app and software development, tips and tricks on using your favorite gadgets, networking, project management, graphic design, and much more.

Activate your FREE Online Edition at
informit.com/safarifree

STEP 1:   Enter the coupon code: XKRPXAA.

STEP 2:   New Safari users, complete the brief registration form.
Safari subscribers, just log in.

If you have difficulty registering on Safari or accessing the online edition,
please e-mail customer-service@safaribooksonline.com